HACKERS TOEFL READING 200% 활용법

KB101077

토플 보카 외우기

이용방법 고우해커스(goHackers.com) 접속 ▶
상단 메뉴 [TOEFL → 토플보카외우기] 클릭하여 이용하기

토플 스피킹/라이팅 첨삭 게시판

이용방법 고우해커스(goHackers.com) 접속 ▶
상단 메뉴 [TOEFL → 스피킹게시판/라이팅게시판] 클릭하여 이용하기

토플 공부전략 강의

이용방법 고우해커스(goHackers.com) 접속 ▶
상단 메뉴 [TOEFL → 토플공부전략] 클릭하여 이용하기

토플 자료 및 유학 정보

이용방법 유학 커뮤니티 고우해커스(goHackers.com)에 접속하여
다양한 토플 자료 및 유학 정보 이용하기

고우해커스 바로 가기 ▶

빈출어휘 암기&지문녹음 MP3

이용방법 해커스인강(HackersIngang.com) 접속 ▶
상단 메뉴 [토플 → MP3/자료 → 무료 MP3/자료] 클릭하여 이용하기

MP3/자료 바로 가기 ▶

iBT 리딩 실전모의고사

이용방법 해커스인강(HackersIngang.com) 접속 ▶
상단 메뉴 [토플 → MP3/자료 → 무료 MP3/자료] 클릭 ▶
본 교재의 실전모의고사 프로그램 이용하기

MP3/자료 바로 가기 ▶

|H|A|C|K|E|R|S|
TOEFL
READING

해커스 어학연구소

무료 토플자료 · 유학정보 제공
goHackers.com

PREFACE

최신 토플 경향을 반영한
Hackers TOEFL Reading (iBT)을 내면서

해커스 토플은 토플 시험 준비와 함께 여러분의 영어 실력 향상에 도움이 되고자 하는 마음에서 시작되었습니다. 해커스 토플을 처음 출간하던 때와 달리, 이제는 많은 토플 책들을 서점에서 볼 수 있지만, 그럼에도 해커스 토플이 여전히 독보적인 베스트셀러의 자리를 지킬 수 있는 것은 늘 처음과 같은 마음으로 더 좋은 책을 만들기 위해 고민하고, 최신 경향을 반영하기 위해 끊임없이 노력하기 때문입니다.

이러한 노력의 결실로, 새롭게 변경된 토플 시험에서도 학습자들이 영어 실력을 향상하고 토플 고득점을 달성하는 데 도움을 주고자 **최신 토플 경향을 반영한** 『Hackers TOEFL Reading (iBT)』을 출간하게 되었습니다.

해커스 토플 리딩은 실전에 강합니다!
『Hackers TOEFL Reading (iBT)』은 iBT 토플 리딩의 최신 경향을 반영한 방대한 양의 실전 문제를 수록하였으며, 실전과 동일한 난이도와 구성의 iBT TOEFL 리딩 실전모의고사를 온라인으로 제공하여 보다 철저히 실전에 대비할 수 있도록 하였습니다.

고득점도 문제 없습니다!
『Hackers TOEFL Reading (iBT)』은 토플 리딩 고득점 달성에 꼭 필요한 문제 유형별 학습 전략을 제시하여, 혼자서 공부하는 학습자라도 효과적으로 학습할 수 있도록 하였습니다.

『Hackers TOEFL Reading (iBT)』이 여러분의 토플 목표 점수 달성에 확실한 해결책이 되고 영어 실력 향상, 나아가 여러분의 꿈을 향한 길에 믿음직한 동반자가 되기를 소망합니다.

David Cho

CONTENTS

TOPIC LIST	6
고득점 공략, 『해커스 토플 리딩』으로 가능한 이유!	8
『해커스 토플 리딩』 미리보기	10
iBT TOEFL 소개 및 시험장 Tips	12
iBT TOEFL Reading 소개	14
iBT TOEFL Reading 전략	16
iBT TOEFL Reading 화면 구성	18
NOTE-TAKING	20
수준별 맞춤 학습 방법	22
학습 성향별 맞춤 공부 방법	24
해커스 학습플랜	26
실전모의고사 프로그램 활용법	28
Diagnostic Test	31

PART 01 Identifying Details

Chapter 01   Sentence Simplification   42

Chapter 02   Fact & Negative Fact   76

Chapter 03   Vocabulary   110

Chapter 04   Reference   144

PART 02 Making Inference

Chapter 05   Rhetorical Purpose   178

Chapter 06   Inference   212

PART 03 Recognizing Organization

Chapter 07   Insertion   248

Chapter 08   Summary   280

Chapter 09   Category Chart   318

Actual Test 1   360

Actual Test 2   368

정답 · 해석 · 정답단서 [책 속의 책]   377

실전모의고사(온라인) 2회분
해커스인강(HackersIngang.com) 접속 → [MP3/자료] 클릭 → [무료 MP3/자료] 클릭하여 이용

TOPIC LIST

다음의 TOPIC LIST는 교재에 수록된 지문을 주제별로 구분하여 목록으로 구성한 것이다.

교재에 수록된 모든 지문은 실제 iBT 토플 Reading 시험의 주제별 출제 경향을 충실히 반영하여 구성되었다. 따라서 교재를 처음부터 끝까지 학습하면서 많이 출제되는 주제가 무엇인지, 자신이 취약한 주제가 무엇인지 파악할 수 있다. 특히 취약하다고 생각되는 주제만 골라 다시 한번 풀어보고, 해당 주제의 단어를 외워서 취약점을 보완한다.

Humanities	Anthropology	DT [2] Ch 03 HP 07 10 14 Ch 05 HP 03 15 Ch 07 HP 09 Ch 09 HP 03, HT [2]	Ch 01 HP 07 15 Ch 04 HP 07 12 13 18, HT [4] Ch 06 HP 04 14 Ch 08 HT [1]
	Archaeology	Ch 01 HP 05, HT [2]	
	Architecture	Ch 01 HT [4]	Ch 02 HT [2]
	Art	Ch 01 HP 01 Ch 03 HT [2] Ch 05 HT [3] Ch 07 HP 12 13 17 Ch 09 HP 05 09	Ch 02 HP 02 06 07 12 16 Ch 04 HP 19 Ch 06 HP 01 05 12 15 Ch 08 HP 01 실전 1 [1] [2]
	Film	Ch 01 HP 11 Ch 07 HT [2]	Ch 03 HP 17 Ch 08 HP 03 09
	History	Ch 01 HP 02 13 14 17 Ch 03 HP 16 Ch 05 HP 01 07 09 Ch 07 HP 16 Ch 09 HP 08, HT [4]	Ch 02 HP 01 11, HT [4] Ch 04 HP 10 Ch 06 HP 02 07 08 10 11, HT [1] Ch 08 HP 04 05 11, HT [4] AT 1 [2]
	Literature	Ch 06 HT [4]	
	Music	Ch 02 HP 04 Ch 08 HP 12	Ch 03 HP 08 Ch 09 HP 06 12
	Theater	Ch 01 HP 09 Ch 07 HP 05	Ch 02 HT [3]

Social Science	Economics	**Ch 02** HT [1] **Ch 05** HT [1]	**Ch 03** HP 21
	Engineering	**Ch 07** HT [3]	**Ch 08** HP 07
	Sociology	**Ch 01** HP 06 12 **Ch 05** HP 06 **Ch 09** HP 11	**Ch 03** HP 04 **Ch 06** HP 16, HT [3]
	Psychology	**Ch 02** HP 14 **Ch 04** HT [1]	**Ch 03** HP 15 **Ch 05** HP 14

Natural Science	Astronomy	**Ch 02** HP 10 **Ch 05** HP 10, HT [2] **Ch 08** HP 02	**Ch 03** HP 06 19 22 **Ch 07** HP 11 **AT 2** [2]
	Biology	**DT** [1] **Ch 02** HP 08 15 **Ch 04** HP 02 03 04 06 09 14 15 17 **Ch 06** HP 06 09 13, HT [2] **Ch 08** HP 08 10, HT [3] **AT 2** [1]	**Ch 01** HP 16, HT [1] **Ch 03** HP 09 11 13, HT [3] [4] **Ch 05** HP 05 08 12 **Ch 07** HP 01 04 06 08, HT [1] **Ch 09** HP 01 04, HT [3] **실전 2** [2]
	Chemistry	**Ch 08** HP 06	**Ch 07** HP 07
	Earth Science	**Ch 01** HP 03 **Ch 03** HP 01 03 18 20, HT [1] **Ch 05** HP 02 11 13 **Ch 07** HP 10 14, HT [4] **AT 1** [1]	**Ch 02** HP 09 13 **Ch 04** HP 08, HT [3] **Ch 06** HP 03 **Ch 09** HP 02 10, HT [1] **실전 2** [1]
	Environmental Science	**Ch 01** HP 04, HT [3] **Ch 03** HP 05 **Ch 07** HP 02 15	**Ch 02** HP 05 **Ch 04** HP 16 **Ch 08** HT [2]
	Physics	**Ch 02** HP 03 **Ch 09** HP 07	**Ch 03** HP 12
	Physiology	**Ch 01** HP 08 10 **Ch 04** HP 01 05 11, HT [2] **Ch 07** HP 03	**Ch 03** HP 02 **Ch 05** HP 04, HT [4]

DT: Diagnostic Test   **HP:** Hackers Practice   **HT:** Hackers Test   **AT:** Actual Test   **실전:** 실전모의고사 프로그램

고득점 공략, 『해커스 토플 리딩』으로 가능한 이유!

01 최신 출제 경향을 반영한 전 분야의 지문 수록

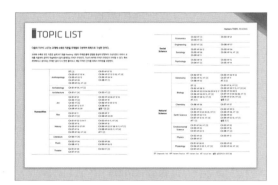

이 책은 iBT 토플 리딩의 **최신 출제경향을 철저히 분석하여 모든 지문과 문제에 반영**하였다. 실제 시험에 등장하는 다양한 주제의 지문들을 학습하며 토플시험에 필요한 배경지식 또한 충분히 쌓을 수 있다.

02 고득점을 위한 완벽한 전략 제시

문제 해결을 위한 유형별 핵심전략을 챕터별 **Hackers Strategy**에 상세하게 수록하였다. 문제 해결 순서에 따른 3가지 전략을 학습하고, **Hackers Strategy Application**에서 이를 적용하는 훈련을 함으로써 학습효과를 극대화할 수 있다.

03 단계별 학습으로 기본부터 실전까지 완벽 대비

Hackers Strategy에서는 유형별 문제 풀이 전략을 단계별로 설명하여 각 문제 유형을 효과적으로 공략할 수 있는 방법을 제시하였고, 연습 문제인 **Hackers Practice**와 실전 형태의 **Hackers Test**를 통해 문제 풀이 훈련을 할 수 있도록 하였다. 마지막으로 실전 난이도의 지문과 문제로 구성된 **Actual Test**를 풀어봄으로써 시험에 보다 완벽하게 대비할 수 있게 하였다.

04 효과적인 학습을 위한 학습플랜 및 무료 학습자료 제공

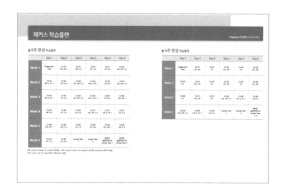

학습자가 자신에게 맞는 학습 계획을 세울 수 있도록 **6주와 4주 완성 학습플랜**을 제시하였다. **해커스인강**(HackersIngang.com)에서 무료로 제공하는 실전모의고사 프로그램을 통해 실제 시험과 같은 환경에서 실전에 대비할 수 있도록 하였고, '토플 빈출어휘 정리 노트' MP3를 통해 효율적인 단어학습이 가능하도록 하였다. **고우해커스**(goHackers.com)에서는 토플에 관한 다양한 정보가 공유되며, 본 교재에 대해서도 자유롭게 토론할 수 있다.

『해커스 토플 리딩』 미리보기

1. Diagnostic Test

iBT 토플 리딩 시험의 전반적인 유형 및 난이도 등을 이해하고, 현재 자신의 실력을 진단하여 더욱 **효과적인 학습을 계획할 수 있도록** 책의 앞부분에 실제 시험의 구성과 경향을 반영한 **Diagnostic Test**를 제공한다.

2. Hackers Strategy

철저히 분석된 iBT TOEFL 리딩 시험의 실제 경향에 근거하여, 리딩 시험에서 고득점이 가능한 **문제 유형별 핵심 전략을 예제와 함께 제시**하였다. 또한, 각 전략을 연습할 수 있는 **Hackers Strategy Application**을 통해 효과적인 문제풀이 훈련을 할 수 있다.

3. Hackers Practice

실전 리딩 문제를 체계적으로 학습할 수 있도록, 각 문제 유형에 맞추어 제작된 다양한 형태의 연습 문제들을 **Hackers Practice**에서 제공한다. 한 가지 문제 유형에 대해 **단계별로 짜임새 있는 연습 문제들을 제공**함으로써 학습자들이 자연스럽게 문제 유형에 익숙해질 수 있도록 하였다.

4. Hackers Test

Hackers Test에서는 실전과 같은 난이도 및 형태의 문제들을 지문별 문제 풀이 제한 시간과 함께 제공한다. 실전 수준의 문제들을 집중적으로 풀어봄으로써, 각 문제 유형에 대한 실전 감각을 기를 수 있도록 하였다.

5. Actual Test (책 + 온라인)

책을 모두 학습한 후 토플 리딩 영역에 대한 종합적인 이해도와 실력을 측정할 수 있는 **Actual Test**가 제공된다. iBT 토플 리딩 시험과 같은 구성 및 난이도의 테스트를 풀어봄으로써, 실제 시험을 치르기 전에 자신의 실력을 점검해 볼 수 있도록 하였다.

6. 정답·해석·정답단서

교재에 수록된 모든 **지문의 정확한 해석 및 정답의 단서를 제공**하여, 학습자가 지문을 보다 쉽게 이해하고 정답과 오답의 근거를 스스로 파악할 수 있도록 하였다.

iBT TOEFL 소개 및 시험장 Tips

■ iBT TOEFL이란?

iBT(Internet-based test) TOEFL(Test of English as a Foreign Language)은 종합적인 영어 실력을 평가하는 시험으로 읽기, 듣기, 말하기, 쓰기 능력을 평가하는 유형의 문제 외에도, 듣기-말하기, 읽기-듣기-말하기, 읽기-듣기-쓰기와 같이 각 능력을 연계한 통합형 문제가 출제된다. iBT TOEFL은 Reading, Listening, Speaking, Writing 영역의 순서로 진행되며, 4개의 시험 영역 모두 노트테이킹을 허용하므로 문제를 풀 때 노트테이킹한 내용을 참고할 수 있다.

■ iBT TOEFL 구성

시험 영역	출제 지문 및 문항 수	시험 시간	점수 범위	특징
Reading	· 2개 지문 출제 지문당 길이: 약 700단어 지문당 10문항 출제	36분	0~30점	· 지문 길이가 길고, 다양한 구조의 지문이 출제됨 · 사지선다 형태, 지문 클릭(지문에 문장 삽입하기) 형태, 또는 정보를 분류하여 요약표나 정보 분류표에 넣는 형태 등이 출제됨
Listening	· 2개 대화 출제 대화당 길이: 약 3분 대화당 5문항 출제 · 3개 강의 출제 강의당 길이: 3~5분 강의당 6문항 출제	41분	0~30점	· 대화 및 강의의 길이가 길고, 실제 상황에 가까움 · 사지선다 형태, 다시 듣고 푸는 형태, 정보를 분류해 표 안에 넣거나 순서대로 배열하는 형태 등이 출제됨
Speaking	· 독립형 1문항 출제 · 통합형 3문항 출제	17분 준비: 15~30초 답변: 45~60초	0~30점	· 독립형 문제 (1번) – 특정 주제에 대해 의견 말하기 · 통합형 문제 (2~4번) – 읽고 들은 내용에 기초하여 말하기
Writing	· 통합형 1문항 출제 · 토론형 1문항 출제	35분	0~30점	· 통합형 문제 – 읽고 들은 내용에 기초하여 글쓰기 · 토론형 문제 – 토론 주제에 대해 글쓰기
		2시간 내외	총점 120점	

■ iBT TOEFL 접수 및 성적 확인

실시일	ETS Test Center 시험은 1년에 60회 이상 실시되며, 홈에디션 시험은 일주일에 약 4~5일 실시됨
시험 장소	ETS Test Center에서 치르거나, 집에서 홈에디션 시험으로 응시 가능 (홈에디션 시험 응시 가능한 장비 및 환경 요건은 ETS 토플 웹사이트에서 확인 가능)
접수 방법	ETS 토플 웹사이트 또는 전화상으로 접수
시험 비용	(2024년 현재 기준이며, 가격 변동 있을 수 있음) · 시험 접수 비용 US $220 · 시험일 변경 비용 US $60 · 추가 접수 비용 US $40 　(응시일로부터 2~7일 전에 등록할 경우)　· 추가 리포팅 비용 US $25 (대학당) · 취소한 성적 복원 비용 US $20 · Speaking/Writing 재채점 비용 US $80 (영역당)
시험 당일 주의사항	· 공인된 신분증 원본 반드시 지참하며, 자세한 신분증 규정은 ETS 토플 웹사이트에서 확인 가능 · 홈에디션 시험에 응시할 경우, 사전에 ProctorU 프로그램 설치하여 정상 작동 여부 확인 · 홈에디션 시험에 응시할 경우, 휴대폰 또는 손거울, 화이트보드 또는 투명 시트와 지워지는 마카 지참 　(일반 종이와 필기구, 헤드폰 및 이어폰은 사용 불가)
성적 및 리포팅	· 시험 응시 후 바로 Reading/Listening 영역 비공식 점수 확인 가능 · 시험 응시일로부터 약 4~8일 후에 온라인으로 성적 확인 가능 · 시험 접수 시, 자동으로 성적 리포팅 받을 기관 선택 가능 · MyBest Scores 제도 시행 (최근 2년간의 시험 성적 중 영역별 최고 점수 합산하여 유효 성적으로 인정)

■ 시험장 Tips

1. **입실 절차** 고사장에 도착한 순서대로 번호표를 받아 입실하고, 입실 순서대로 시험을 시작한다.

2. **신분 확인** 신분증 확인 후 성적표에 인쇄될 사진을 찍은 다음, 감독관의 안내에 따라 시험을 볼 자리에 앉는다.

3. **필기도구** 연필과 종이는 감독관이 나누어주므로 따로 챙겨갈 필요가 없다. 부족한 경우 조용히 손을 들고 요청하면 된다.

4. **헤드폰 음량 및 마이크 음량 조절** 헤드폰 음량은 Listening, Speaking, Writing 영역 시작 전이나 시험 중간에 화면의 음량 버튼을 이용하여 조절할 수 있다. 적절한 크기로 하되 주위에 방해가 되지 않는 크기로 설정한다. 마이크 음량은 시험 시작 직후와 Speaking 영역을 시작하기 전에 조절할 수 있다. 평소 말하는 톤으로 음량을 조절한다.

5. **주의 집중** 응시자들의 시험 시작 시간이 달라 고사장이 산만할 수 있으나, 집중하도록 노력한다. 특히 Listening이나 Writing 영역 시험을 보고 있을 때 다른 응시자의 Speaking 답변 소리가 들리더라도 자신의 시험에 집중한다.

iBT TOEFL Reading 소개

iBT TOEFL Reading 영역에서는 대학 교재 수준의 지문에 대한 학생들의 이해도를 평가한다. 다양한 분야의 지문이 등장하지만, 문제에 답하기 위해 해당 지문에 관한 특별한 전문 지식이 필요하지는 않으며 문제를 푸는 데 필요한 모든 정보는 지문에서 찾을 수 있다. 그러나 짧은 시간 내에 긴 지문을 읽고 많은 문제를 풀어야 하므로 지문을 빨리 읽고 정확하게 이해하며 정리하는 능력이 요구된다.

■ iBT TOEFL Reading 구성

1. 지문 구성

시험은 총 2개의 지문으로 구성되며, 지문당 10문항이 출제된다. 지문당 길이는 약 700단어이다.

2. 문제 형식

크게 사지선다, 지문 클릭(지문에 문장 삽입하기), 또는 주요 정보를 분류하여 요약표(Summary)나 정보 분류표(Category Chart)에 넣기 등 3가지 형식의 문제가 출제된다.

■ iBT TOEFL Reading 특이사항

1. Note-taking

시험을 치르는 동안 Note-taking이 가능하다.

2. 지문의 제목

지문의 상단에 해당 지문의 제목이 제시된다.

3. Glossary 기능

전문 용어나 해당 토픽 내에서 특별한 의미를 가지고 있는 어휘의 뜻을 보여주는 Glossary 기능이 있다. 지문에 파란색으로 밑줄이 그어져 있고 이 단어를 클릭하면 해당 어휘의 definition(정의)이 화면에 나타난다.

4. Review 기능

현재 풀고 있는 모든 문제의 답 체크 여부(Answered, Not Answered, Not Viewed)를 한눈에 확인할 수 있는 Review 기능이 있다.

■ iBT TOEFL Reading 문제 유형 소개

문제 형태	해당 문제 유형	유형 소개	배점	지문당 문항 수
Identifying Details 지문 내용에 대한 기본적인 이해를 요하는 문제	Sentence Simplification	주어진 문장의 핵심 정보를 가장 정확하고 간결하게 바꾸어 쓴 것을 선택하는 문제 유형	1점	0~1개
	Fact & Negative Fact	지문의 세부 정보를 찾아 지문과 일치(Fact) 또는 불일치(Negative Fact)하는 내용을 선택하는 문제 유형	1점	2~5개
	Vocabulary	주어진 표현과 가장 유사한 의미의 어휘를 찾는 문제 유형	1점	1~2개
	Reference	지시어가 가리키는 대상을 찾는 문제 유형	1점	0~1개
Making Inference 지문 내용의 기저에 놓인 실 질적인 의미를 파악하는 문제	Rhetorical Purpose	작가의 수사적 의도를 가장 잘 나타내고 있는 것을 선택하는 문제 유형	1점	0~3개
	Inference	지문에 명백하게 드러나 있지는 않지만 제시된 정보로 추론이 가능한 것을 선택하는 문제 유형	1점	0~2개
Recognizing Organization 지문 전체 또는 일부 내용을 종합해서 풀어야 하는 문제	Insertion	지문에 지정되어 있는 4개의 [■] 중에서 주어진 문장을 삽입하기 가장 적절한 곳을 찾는 문제 유형	1점	1개
	Summary	6개의 보기 중, 지문의 주요 내용을 언급하고 있는 3개를 골라 지문 요약을 완성시키는 문제 유형	2점 (부분 점수 있음)	0~1개
	Category Chart	지문에서 비교·대조되고 있는 정보들을 각 범주에 맞게 분류하는 문제 유형	3~4점 (부분 점수 있음)	Summary 문제가 출제되지 않는 경우에 한해 1개 출제

iBT TOEFL Reading 전략

■ 시험 보기 전

01 토플 빈출 토픽에 대한 배경지식을 쌓자!

배경지식을 많이 알고 있을수록 글의 내용을 이해하는 것이 수월하므로 시험에 자주 출제되는 토픽과 관련된 내용을 많이 알아둔다.

02 Paraphrase & 요약 연습을 하자!

시험에 출제되는 거의 모든 문제와 답은 paraphrase되어 있으므로 한 단어부터 시작해 한 문장, 한 단락 전체를 paraphrase하는 연습을 해본다. 또한, 글을 읽고 해당 내용의 중심 정보만을 추려 요약(summary)하는 연습을 해 보는 것도 좋다.

03 글의 구조 파악을 통해 전략적으로 지문에 접근하자!

각 단락의 앞부분만을 빠르게 훑는 skimming으로 큰 주제를 빠르게 파악하고, scanning을 통해 지문의 keyword 를 찾는 연습을 하는 것은 지문 독해에 있어 매우 중요하다. 또한, 문장 및 문단 간의 관계를 확인하는 구조 파악 훈련 은 글 전체의 흐름을 이해하는 데 많은 도움이 된다.

04 토플 영어와 친해지자!

· 어휘력을 기른다!
어휘력이 풍부해야 글을 읽는 데 막힘이 없으므로 평소에 많은 어휘를 외워두도록 한다. 이외에도 글에 사용된 어휘 중 모르는 것은 주위 문맥을 이용하여 그 뜻을 추측해 보는 연습을 병행한다.

· 영문으로 된 글을 자주 읽는다!
독해력은 많이 읽을수록 향상되므로 다양한 분야의 글을 읽되, 학술적인 글을 특히 많이 읽도록 한다.

■ 시험 볼 때

01 특정 지문에 너무 많은 시간을 소요하지 말자!

시간 내에 모든 지문을 읽고 문제를 풀기 위해서는, 특정 지문에 너무 많은 시간을 소요하지 않도록 화면 상단의 시간 카운트를 잘 활용하여 각 지문에 적절한 시간을 분배해야 한다.

02 문제에 따라 시간을 전략적으로 투자하자!

시간이 모자랄 경우에는, 다른 유형에 비해 상대적으로 수월한 Vocabulary 문제나 Reference 문제를 먼저 푼 후, 다른 문제를 푸는 것이 유리하다. 또한, 각 지문의 마지막에 출제되는 Summary 문제와 Category Chart 문제의 경우, 다른 유형보다 배점이 높으므로 이 두 유형에 좀 더 많은 시간을 투자해야 높은 점수를 받을 수 있다.

03 Note-taking을 활용하자!

지문을 읽을 때, 각 단락의 중요 정보를 Note-taking해 놓으면 핵심 내용을 파악하는 데 도움이 되고, 특히 Summary 문제를 풀 때 효과적이다.

04 Review 기능을 활용하자!

Review 버튼을 누르면 현재 풀고 있는 모든 문제의 답 체크 여부가 나오므로 어떤 문제를 안 풀고 넘어갔는지를 바로 확인할 수 있다.

iBT TOEFL Reading 화면 구성

1. Reading Direction 화면

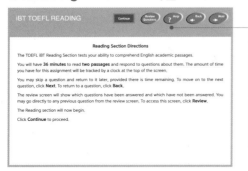

리딩 영역 시험 진행 방식에 대한 전반적인 디렉션이 주어지고, **Tool Bar** 이용에 관한 간단한 설명이 이어진다.

시험 도중에 Help 버튼을 누르면 시험 진행 과정과 관련된 정보를 볼 수 있다. 이때 시험 시간은 계속해서 카운트 된다.

2. 지문과 문제 화면

처음에는 지문만 화면에 등장하며, 스크롤을 내려 지문 전체를 한 번 읽은 후 **Next 버튼**을 눌러야 문제로 넘어갈 수 있다. 문제 간에 이동하려면 **Next 버튼**과 **Back 버튼**을 사용한다. 또한, 지문에 파란색으로 밑줄이 그어져 있는 단어를 클릭하면 우측 하단에 **Glossary**로 해당 단어의 의미가 나타난다.

Hide Time 버튼을 누르면 시간 카운트가 창에서 사라지고 Show Time 버튼이 나타나며, Show Time 버튼을 누르면 시간 카운트가 Hide Time 버튼과 함께 창에 다시 나타난다.

3. Summary 문제 화면

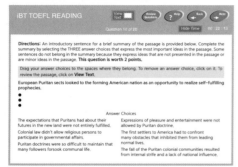

Summary 문제가 나오면 지문이 사라지고 문제만 화면에 나온다. 상단의 **View Text 버튼**을 누르면 지문이 나오고, **View Question 버튼**을 누르면 문제로 돌아간다. 답을 선택할 때는 Answer Choices 아래 있는 보기를 정답 자리에 끌어오고, 답을 바꿀 때는 선택한 보기를 한 번 더 클릭하면 정답 자리에서 사라진다.

4. Category Chart 문제 화면

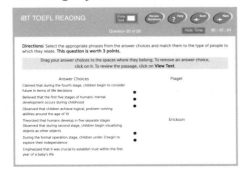

Category Chart 문제가 나올 때 역시 화면에서 지문이 사라지고, 문제가 화면 전체에 나타난다. Summary 문제와 동일하게, 지문을 보기 위해서는 █ View Text를, 문제를 보기 위해서는 █ View Question을 클릭해야 하며, 답을 선택할 때는 Answer Choices 아래 있는 보기를 정답 자리에 끌어오면 된다.

5. Review 화면

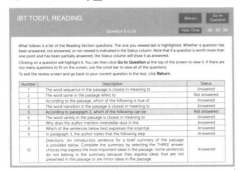

문제 화면에서 █ Review Questions 버튼을 누르면 현재 풀고 있는 문제 목록이 나타나며 각 문제별 답을 체크했는지 여부가 다음과 같은 3가지 형태로 나타난다.

· 문제의 답을 클릭하고 넘어갔을 경우 — Answered
· 문제의 답을 클릭하지 않고 넘어갔을 경우 — Not Answered
· 문제를 아직 보지 않았을 경우 — Not Viewed

목록에 있는 각 문제를 클릭한 상태에서 █ Go to Question 버튼을 누르면 해당 문제로 바로 이동하며, █ Return 버튼을 누르면 직전의 화면으로 이동한다.

6. 시험이 끝났을 때 나오는 화면

시험이 끝나고 나오는 디렉션 화면에서 █ Continue 버튼을 누르면 다음 영역으로 넘어가고, 리딩 영역으로 **다시 되돌아갈 수 없다.** 따라서 다음 영역으로 넘어가기 전에 █ Review 버튼을 활용하여 리딩 영역의 모든 문제에 답했는지를 반드시 확인해야 한다.

NOTE-TAKING

iBT 토플 리딩에서는 시험을 보는 동안 Note-taking이 허용된다. Note-taking을 효과적으로 이용하기 위해서는 지문의 모든 내용을 정리하는 것보다는 단락의 중심 내용이나 핵심 내용만을 간략하게 정리하는 요령이 필요하다.

■ Note-taking 방법

1. 각 단락의 중심 정보를 적는다.
   글 전체에 하나의 주제가 있는 것처럼 각 단락 역시 하나의 중심 정보로 구성된다. 따라서 각 단락별로 중심 정보를 간단히 정리한다.

2. 기호 및 약어를 이용한다.
   Note-taking을 할 때 본인이 알아볼 수 있는 기호 및 약어를 이용하면 시간을 줄일 수 있다.

· 기호 및 약어 표

=	equals, to be	∴	therefore, so
+	and, plus	∵	because
&	and	←	from
>	more than	→	become, result, change to
<	less than	@	at
↑	increase	#	number (of)
↓	decrease	/	per, each
~	approximately, about	X	not, no
b.f.	before	imprt.	important
bldg	building	max.	maximum
c.	century	min.	minimum
edu.	education	ppl.	people
e.g.	for example	tech.	technology
etc.	and so on	vs.	versus
fr.	from	w/	with
info.	information	w/o	without

Note-taking Example

지문

The Puritans from Europe, mostly England, came to America in the 17th century in search of religious freedom and to avoid the prosecution they were experiencing across the continent. Influenced by the teachings of John Calvin, these people had given up attempts to reform the Church of England and laid their sights on turning America into a land of prosperous Puritan faith.

When the first Puritans left their native lands for opportunity in the far West, they envisioned that America would be a place where they could establish their communities with little or no resistance and spread their religious beliefs to other Christians. They envisaged communitarian societies in which all property was communally owned. Leaders of the Massachusetts Bay Colony perpetuated the westward movement of Puritan settlements in order to ensure the spread of their way of life. Although each of the communities differed slightly in their interpretation of the Puritan way of life, they were held together by a belief that the Bible was literal instruction about how to properly live.

However, the reality of early American Puritan life did not match up with ideals. The communities found considerable difficulties dealing with the combination of typical frontier life, plagued by physical and economic hardship, and maintaining their exclusive and rigidly structured society. Puritan belief in a strict adherence to Biblical instruction meant that any kind of deviance from a strictly devout lifestyle was punishable. People were to abstain from such activities as laughing, gambling, singing, and any other kind of enjoyable endeavor. To keep such high standards of moral behavior, the Puritans had to isolate themselves from the rest of the society.

Possible Notes

- P1. Puritans: Europe to America 17th c.
- P2. establish communities & spread religious beliefs
  – commun. society, W mvmt, Bible = literal instruction
- P3. reality ≠ ideals – diffic., phys. & economic hardship
  – deviance → punishable, isolate fr. rest of society

* 위 예시는 앞 지문의 내용을 Note-taking한 것으로, 단락별 중심 정보가 약어와 기호를 사용하여 간략하게 정리되어 있다.

수준별 맞춤 학습 방법

p.31의 Diagnostic Test 결과에 따라, 본인의 점수대에 맞는 학습 방법을 찾아 학습하면 효과적이다.

Level 1

맞은 개수 0~10개 (실제 시험 예상 점수: 0~14점대)

추천 플랜 6주 완성 학습플랜(p.26)
학습 방법 기본적인 독해 실력을 키우자!

1. 학습플랜에 따라 챕터별로 각 페이지의 전략을 꼼꼼하게 읽고 정리한다.
2. Hackers Practice와 Hackers Test를 풀고 나서 시간이 걸리더라도 각 지문의 주제와 중심 정보를 파악하는 훈련을 한다.
3. 독해력 향상을 위한 기본적인 문법들을 익히도록 노력하고, '토플 빈출어휘 정리 노트'를 적극 활용하여 어휘 실력도 꾸준히 쌓는다.

Level 2

맞은 개수 11~14개 (실제 시험 예상 점수: 15~21점대)

추천 플랜 6주 완성 학습플랜(p.26)
학습 방법 세부 정보를 확인하는 데 주력하자!

1. Note-taking을 하며 중심 정보와 세부 정보를 구분하여 정리하는 연습을 한다.
2. Hackers Strategy와 Hackers Practice를 풀며 각 문제 유형을 익히는 데 중점을 두고, Hackers Test를 통해 학습 성과를 평가한다.
3. 꾸준히 단어를 암기하는 것 외에, 지문에 모르는 단어가 나왔을 경우 문맥을 이용해 단어의 뜻을 유추해 내는 연습을 한다.

Level 3

맞은 개수 15~18개 (실제 시험 예상 점수: 22~27점대)

추천 플랜　**4주 완성 학습플랜(p.27)**
학습 방법　**실전에 대비하자!**

1. 짧은 시간 안에 많은 글을 읽는 훈련을 통해 빠른 독해를 연습한다.
2. Hackers Practice와 Hackers Test의 지문에 쓰인 표현을 paraphrase하는 연습을 통해 문제풀이 능력을 향상시킨다.
3. 난도가 높은 Summary 문제와 Category Chart 문제에 대비하여 지문의 전체 내용을 요약하는 연습과 정보를 구체적 기준에 따라 분류, 정리하는 연습을 한다.

Level 4

맞은 개수 19~20개 (실제 시험 예상 점수: 28~30점대)

추천 플랜　**4주 완성 학습플랜(p.27)**
학습 방법　**만점을 준비하자!**

1. 단어 하나의 쓰임과 예시 하나에도 출제자의 의도가 있다는 것을 염두에 두고 글을 읽는다.
2. 글을 읽은 후에는 단순히 내용을 이해하는 것에 그치지 않고, 읽은 내용을 바탕으로 결론을 도출해보는 연습을 한다.
3. Hackers Practice에서는 틀린 문제만 다시 확인하고 넘어가고 Hackers Test에 중점을 두어 학습한다.

학습 성향별 맞춤 공부 방법

* 해커스 학습플랜은 pp.26~27에 수록되어 있습니다.

 개별학습 혼자서 공부할 때 가장 집중이 잘 된다!

1. 나만의 학습플랜을 세운다!
p.31의 Diagnostic Test를 통하여 자신의 현재 실력을 확인하고, 해커스 학습플랜을 참고하여 본인에게 맞는 학습 계획을 세운다.

2. 매일매일 정해진 학습 분량을 공부한다!
학습플랜에 따라 매일의 정해진 분량을 반드시 마치도록 하고, 만약 그러지 못했을 경우에는 계속 진도를 나가되 일주일이 지나기 전에 해당 주의 학습 분량을 모두 끝낸다.

3. 시간을 정하여 풀고 오답 분석을 한다!
문제를 풀 때는 항상 시간을 정해놓고 푸는 것을 원칙으로 하며, 문제를 다 푼 후에는 지문 정독과 함께 본인이 선택한 정답과 오답을 분석한다.

* 고우해커스(goHackers.com)의 [해커스 Books > 토플 리딩 Q&A]에서 궁금한 사항을 질문할 수 있습니다.

 스터디학습 다른 사람과 함께 공부할 때 더 열심히 한다!

1. 개별 예습으로 스터디를 준비한다!
각 문제 유형별 Hackers Strategy를 숙지하고 Hackers Practice와 Hackers Test를 미리 풀어본다.

2. 토론 학습으로 완벽하게 이해한다!
미리 예습해 온 문제를 함께 토론하면서 답을 수렴해 나간다. 서로의 답을 공개하고 왜 그것을 답으로 선택하게 되었는지 토론한 후, 책의 정답을 확인한다.

3. 개별 복습으로 마무리 한다!
스터디가 끝난 후, 각 챕터 마지막에 수록된 토플 빈출어휘 정리 노트의 단어를 확인하고, 해커스인강(HackersIngang.com)에서 무료로 다운로드 받을 수 있는 '토플 빈출어휘 정리 노트' MP3를 활용하여 개별 복습한다.

동영상학습 원하는 시간, 원하는 장소에서 강의를 듣고 싶다!

1. 동영상 강의 학습플랜을 세운다!
해커스인강(HackersIngang.com)에서 『샘플강의보기』를 통해 강의 구성을 미리 파악하고, 『스터디플랜』에 따라 자신의 학습 계획을 세운다.

2. 이해될 때까지 반복해서 듣는다!
학습플랜에 따라 오늘 공부해야 할 강의를 집중해서 듣고, 잘 이해가 되지 않는 부분은 완전히 이해될 때까지 반복해서 시청한다.

3. 『선생님께 질문하기』를 적극 활용한다!
강의를 듣다가 모르는 부분이 있거나 질문할 것이 생기면 『선생님께 질문하기』를 이용하여 확실히 이해하도록 한다.

 학원학습 선생님의 강의를 직접 들을 때 가장 효과적이다!

1. 100% 출석을 목표로 한다!
자신의 스케줄에 맞는 수업을 등록하고, 개강일부터 종강일까지 100% 출석을 목표로 빠짐없이 수업에 참여한다.

2. 예습과 복습을 철저히 한다!
수업 전에 미리 그날 배울 내용을 훑어본다. 수업이 끝난 후에는 자신이 취약한 부분을 확인하고 복습한다.

3. 적극적으로 질문한다!
수업 시간에 잘 이해되지 않은 부분은 쉬는 시간이나 해커스어학원(Hackers.ac)의 『반별게시판』을 이용해 선생님께 질문함으로써 확실히 짚고 넘어간다.

해커스 학습플랜

■ 6주 완성 학습플랜

	Day 1	Day 2	Day 3	Day 4	Day 5	Day 6
Week 1	Diagnostic Test	Ch 01 HS, HP 1	Ch 01 HP 2~3	Ch 01 HT 1~2	Ch 01 HT 3~4	Ch 02 HS, HP 1~2
Week 2	Ch 02 HP 3, HT 1	Ch 02 HT 2~4	Ch 03 HS, HP 1~2	Ch 03 HP 3, HT 1	Ch 03 HT 2~4	Ch 04 HS, HP 1~2
Week 3	Ch 04 HP 3, HT 1	Ch 04 HT 2~4	Ch 05 HS, HP 1~2	Ch 05 HP 3, HT 1	Ch 05 HT 2~4	Ch 06 HS, HP 1
Week 4	Ch 06 HP 2~3	Ch 06 HT 1~2	Ch 06 HT 3~4	Ch 07 HS, HP 1~2	Ch 07 HP 3, HT 1	Ch 07 HT 2~4
Week 5	Ch 08 HS, HP 1	Ch 08 HP 2~3	Ch 08 HT 1~2	Ch 08 HT 3~4	Ch 09 HS, HP 1	Ch 09 HP 2~3
Week 6	Ch 09 HT 1~2	Ch 09 HT 3~4	Actual Test 1	Actual Test 2	온라인 실전모의고사 Actual Test 1	온라인 실전모의고사 Actual Test 2

HS: Hackers Strategy (각 chapter의 앞부분)   **HP:** Hackers Practice (각 chapter는 3단계의 practice로 이루어져 있음)

HT: Hackers Test (각 chapter에는 4개의 test가 있음)

■ 4주 완성 학습플랜

	Day 1	Day 2	Day 3	Day 4	Day 5	Day 6
Week 1	Diagnostic Test	Ch 01 HS, HP	Ch 01 HT	Ch 02 HS, HP	Ch 02 HT	Ch 03 HS, HP
Week 2	Ch 03 HT	Ch 04 HS, HP	Ch 04 HT	Ch 05 HS, HP	Ch 05 HT	Ch 06 HS, HP
Week 3	Ch 06 HT	Ch 07 HS, HP	Ch 07 HT	Ch 08 HS, HP 1~2	Ch 08 HP 3, HT 1	Ch 08 HT 2~4
Week 4	Ch 09 HS, HP 1~2	Ch 09 HP 3, HT 1	Ch 09 HT 2~4	Actual Test 1	Actual Test 2	온라인 실전모의고사 Actual Test 1, 2

실전모의고사 프로그램 활용법

해커스인강(HackersIngang.com)에서는 실제 토플 시험과 유사한 환경에서 리딩 시험을 풀어볼 수 있도록 해커스 어학연구소에서 자체 제작한 실전모의고사 프로그램을 제공한다. 이 프로그램에 수록되어 있는 2회분의 Actual Test는 iBT TOEFL 리딩과 동일한 난이도 및 시험 진행 방식을 갖추고 있어 자신의 실력을 점검해 보는 것은 물론, 실제 시험 환경에 익숙해지는 데에도 큰 도움이 될 것이다.

*온라인 실전모의고사 프로그램 이용 경로
해커스인강(HackersIngang.com) 접속 ▶ [MP3/자료] 클릭 ▶ [무료 MP3/자료] 클릭하여 이용

■ TEST 보기

프로그램을 실행한 후, 초기 화면에서 Actual Test 1, 2 중 하나를 클릭하면 실제 시험과 유사한 화면 구성과 진행 방식으로 문제를 풀어볼 수 있다. 문제를 푸는 도중 좌측 상단의 Exit 버튼을 누르면 언제든 시험을 중단할 수 있다.

실제 시험과 동일한 진행 방식으로 문제를 풀어볼 수 있다.

실제 시험과 유사한 화면 구성으로 실전 적응력을 높일 수 있다.

■ 채점 결과 및 각 문항의 정답 · 해석 · 정답단서 확인하기

1회분의 Test를 마치면 자동으로 채점이 되어 결과가 화면에 나타난다. '해석 보기' 버튼을 클릭하면 정답, 해석, 정답단서를 확인할 수 있다.

Test에서 풀었던 문제의 정·오답 여부를 확인할 수 있다.

문제 유형별로 맞은 개수가 그래프로 표시되어 자신이 취약한 유형을 확인할 수 있다.

'해석 보기' 버튼을 클릭하면 '지문·해석·정답단서', '문제·정답'을 확인할 수 있으며, 모든 지문문제와 해석을 출력할 수 있다.

goHackers.com

Hackers **TOEFL** READING

DIAGNOSTIC
TEST

실제 TOEFL 리딩 시험과 유사한 Diagnostic Test를 통해 본인의 실력을 평가해 봅니다.
그리고 본인에게 맞는 학습방법(p.22)을 확인한 후, 본 교재를 효율적으로 학습합니다.

DIAGNOSTIC TEST

01　**Bluegills**

1　Anglers will recognize the bluegill as one of the most popular gaming fish in North America and it is frequently found in freshwater lakes and ponds. This relatively small fish which rarely reaches length over 6-9 inches(15-23cm) has also been the subject of intense study by many wildlife biologists for its unusual mating habits. While similar to other fish in that the male cares for the offspring, the alpha males which are larger than the females and other males can never be sure that it is truly their own fry which they are raising since there are others which try to circumvent the mating rituals and fertilize the eggs by deception.

2　➡ Comprising roughly 80 percent of the breeding population, large parental males, distinguished by their size, copper colored bars across the top of their heads behind the eyes, and silvery blue breasts that may turn yellow or orange during the spawning season, commonly manage bluegill reproduction. They do not reach sexual maturity until their third or fourth year and this delay allows them to direct their consumed food resources to developing a large body mass, which is advantageous for successfully defending their territory and fighting off predators. Because these fish are colony spawners, adult parental males will excavate plate-sized nests in groups of 20 or 30, called "beddings," by sweeping their tail fins across the sandy floor to make depressions. Then, in the shallow water, the male circles the nest and makes grunting noises to attract one or more females. The male guards the newly deposited and fertilized eggs and continues to do so even after the hatch and the emergence of the fry until they are old enough to survive on their own.

3　➡ A small proportion — about 20 percent — of bluegill males do not wait until they are large enough to defend territory before entering the reproductive process. Cuckolds, or sneakers, divert most of their energy towards their gonads that produce milt, a secretion from their testes containing spermatozoa; as a result, they have invested in a procreative strategy requiring them to take advantage of nearby nests. Cuckolds are too meek to successfully attract a female fish on their own. They seek out a large parental male, hide in the weeds adjacent to the parental male's breeding grounds, and wait for a school of female fish to pass over. Once a female chooses a partner, she will tilt her body and release roughly 30 eggs in a motion referred to as a "dip." Normally, the resident parental male would shower these eggs with his own milt, but before he has a chance to reach all of them, the diminutive cuckold will leave his safety zone and dart into the dangerous nest area to squirt his own milt toward the eggs, quickly returning to his point of origin without being caught. With this tactic, he hopes to fertilize as many of the eggs as possible before they settle into the hole, and will use his undersized body to advance with utmost agility. If fortunate enough to complete the task without encountering any significant harm, the cuckold will go on to stalk other parental male nests over the same season.

4 ➡ ■ The rapid dashing technique is limited to only two seasons since his physical maturation, while delayed, cannot be halted resulting in a larger body with less agility and so as to increase the likelihood of passing his genes onto the next generation, he develops a new method of mimicry to achieve his goal. ■ An adult cuckold bluegill is still not as beefy as a parental male and can easily be mistaken for a female of the species. ■ As he ages, the cuckold will acquire similar markings, which completely disguise him from parental males and allow him to easily slip into schools of female fish unnoticed. ■ In this fashion, he will travel around the warm waters until a nearby female decides to spurt her eggs downward toward an established nest. The cuckold swoops down, maneuvers fairly close to the fallen eggs, and ejects his milt. If a good selection is fertilized with cuckold spermatozoa, then the fish has accomplished his reproductive duties.

1 The word "their" in the passage refers to

(A) anglers
(B) biologists
(C) alpha males
(D) females

2 The word "deception" in the passage is closest in meaning to

(A) jeopardy
(B) acquisition
(C) velocity
(D) trickery

3 In paragraph 2, the author mentions grunting noises in order to

(A) emphasize the effort required to create the depressions
(B) describe a nursery song which parental males sing for their fry
(C) give an example of measures to shield the nest from predators
(D) show a way in which parental males draw the opposite sex

Paragraph 2 is marked with an arrow [➡].

4 Which of the following is true of spawning in paragraph 2?

(A) The largest males are the ones which are most attractive to the females.
(B) Males arrange nests in advance before they lure females into their nests.
(C) Females show no preference when choosing a place to lay their eggs.
(D) The ability of the male to circle the nest shows its fitness in raising fry.

5 In paragraph 3, the author implies that cuckolds

(A) begin attempting to fertilize eggs at a younger age than parental males
(B) first try to build a nest before trying to sneak into others
(C) are limited to a single strategy during their entire lifetime
(D) have much more effective means to entice females than parental males

Paragraph 3 is marked with an arrow [➡].

6 The word "agility" in the passage is closest in meaning to

(A) nimbleness
(B) carelessness
(C) maturity
(D) multiplicity

7 Which of the sentences below best expresses the essential information in the highlighted sentence in the passage? *Incorrect* choices change the meaning in important ways or leave out essential information.

(A) The cuckold causes damage to the nests of the parental males he pursues during the mating season.
(B) The cuckold after being successful will continue to stalk the same nest over many seasons.
(C) The cuckold will attempt to employ the same strategy at other sites if successful at one location.
(D) The cuckold is very fortunate if it is able to accomplish one task before succumbing to injury.

8 According to paragraph 4, which of the following is true of cuckolds?

(A) They eventually grow large enough to allure females on their own.
(B) They are always unsuccessful due to their increasing size and decreasing speed.
(C) They have to travel further to pass down their genes from generation to generation.
(D) They must alter the method by which they sneak into the parental male's nest.

Paragraph 4 is marked with an arrow [➡].

9 Look at the four squares [■] that indicate where the following sentence could be added to the passage.

Usually, females have lighter colored scales, a prominent black spot on the hind edges of their gill covers, and a second dark spot at the base of the rear section of their dorsal fins.

Where would the sentence best fit?

Click on a square [■] to add the sentence to the passage.

Directions: An introductory sentence for a brief summary of the passage is provided below. Complete the summary by selecting the THREE answer choices that express the most important ideas in the passage. Some sentences do not belong in the summary because they express ideas that are not presented in the passage or are minor ideas in the passage. **This question is worth 2 points.**

Drag your answer choices to the spaces where they belong. To remove an answer choice, click on it. To review the passage, click on **View Text**.

Bluegill males are not homogeneous but can be categorized by their mating strategies.

-
-
-

Answer Choices

(A) Female bluegills make a series of dips into the nests of the parental males.

(B) Some bluegills dash rapidly into the nest of reproducing pairs, depositing their milt.

(C) The swift dashing technique is not as successful as the mimicking later employed by the sneakers.

(D) Parental males use their matured body to defend a nest for mating and protecting their offspring.

(E) Parental males are not certain that the eggs and hatchlings they secure are their own because of the cuckolds.

(F) Some males adapt to look like the females of the species as they age.

Incan and Mayan Civilizations

1   The arrival of the Spanish conquistadors in the New World permanently and drastically reshaped the culture and the lives of the indigenous populations, leading to the disappearance of two of the greatest civilizations in the Americas, the Inca and the Maya, shortly after the Europeans discovered them. They left remarkable cities, with few records about the vanished inhabitants, forcing archaeologists to try to piece together what remains in an attempt to learn more about these lost civilizations.

2   ➡ The majority of the information that has been collected came from the ruins of their cities, which have withstood the passage of time since they worked primarily with stone. Yet, while both used the same material, they integrated their cities very differently into the surrounding environment. For the Inca, their skill enabled them to accomplish this almost seamlessly by sculpting nearby objects and incorporating terraces into their cities for use as farms or gardens. In comparison, Mayan urban planning appears almost haphazard. While lacking the extensive road system and organized layout of the Incans, Mayan cities tended to grow more organically from a central plaza that contained the most important buildings, such as the royal palaces, temples, and ball-courts, and since they had developed a mortar from crushed limestone, they didn't need to spend the same amount of time hewing stones that would perfectly complement each other.

3   ➡ This loose confederation of buildings was somewhat indicative of Mayan governance. Each city, with its surrounding area, was headed by its own supreme hereditary ruler who was the focal point, and as a result, the Mayan empire was not a unified nation, but was comprised of disparate city-states that were bound by a similar culture. The Incas, however, had one ruler, known as the Sapa Inca, or, unique Inca, who had to be the direct descendant of the original Inca tribe and had absolute power over the entire region, which was broken up into four regions, with each controlled by a governor who in turn oversaw local officials. The hierarchal provinces were also unique in that there were separate chains of command for the religious and military branches of government that effectively acted as a system of checks and balances. The Sapa Inca was able to exert his influence over the region, since there was a highly-developed road network that enabled messengers' swift passage to the far-flung reaches of the kingdom.

4   Despite not having this courier network, the Maya had one immeasurable advantage, which many researchers believe to be the reason why the Mayan Empire lasted for over a thousand years, whereas the Incas lasted for less than two hundred. The Mayans had developed a formal writing system, which, while often compared to Egyptian hieroglyphics, was more phonetically based and enabled them to transmit and store vast amounts of information. ■ While over 1,000 different glyphs have been discovered, it seems that no more than 500 were used at any one time and that 200 of those had a phonetic interpretation, as opposed to the others which were logographic. ■ While much of the language that has been reconstructed has come from works inscribed in stone or pottery, the Mayans also were known to use the bark of trees to form codices, called primitive books, which unfortunately all were nearly destroyed by Spanish priests. ■ There has been some recent work by linguists who claim that the Incan quipus, strings of colored knotted cords, could have been used to convey messages, but this view is not widely accepted since all evidence seems to suggest that messengers were used to relay all of the information, and proponents have

yet to develop any means to translate them. ■

5   In spite of their similar locations and overlapping time frames, the Mayans and Incans established vastly different cultures, both of which were marked by some of the most spectacular buildings in pre-Columbian America. Unfortunately, their destruction at the hands of the Spanish resulted in the loss of more than just their relics, but the loss of two great civilizations.

11   The word "withstood" in the passage is closest in meaning to

    (A) forged
    (B) deepened
    (C) resisted
    (D) appraised

12   According to paragraph 2, the reason parts of the Incan and Mayan cities survived was

    (A) the preservation work done by modern archaeologists
    (B) a high degree of skill with which the structures were built
    (C) their impressive level of integration with their surroundings
    (D) the durability of the material which they were constructed from

    Paragraph 2 is marked with an arrow [➡].

13   Which of the following can be inferred about the building practices of the Incans in paragraph 2?

    (A) They carved stone blocks that would match each other.
    (B) They were more concerned with the function than the appearance.
    (C) They showed a great deal of variety from city to city.
    (D) They only worked with material that was locally available.

14   What does the author mean by "This loose confederation of buildings was somewhat indicative of Mayan governance" in paragraph 3?

    (A) The permanence of the structures was also reflected in the society.
    (B) The manner Mayans governed affected the style in the building construction.
    (C) The Mayan government played a significant role in the construction of buildings.
    (D) The manner of building planning was similar to the organization of the government.

    Paragraph 3 is marked with an arrow [➡].

15 The word "disparate" in the passage is closest in meaning to

(A) united
(B) different
(C) intimate
(D) compatible

16 Which of the sentences below best expresses the essential information in the highlighted sentence in the passage? *Incorrect* choices change the meaning in important ways or leave out essential information.

(A) In an effort to tighten his reign, the Incan King devised a complicated system of roads to allow quick travel.
(B) Because of the road system by which messages could traverse the realm, the Incan King could maintain control.
(C) The Incan King created the advanced collection of roads to assure that couriers could travel throughout the domain.
(D) Messengers that utilized the road network could carry the commands of the Incan King to a distance.

17 It can be inferred from the passage that a writing system

(A) usually develops from a pictorial based system
(B) needs to be phonetically based to be effective
(C) is essential to establish a government system
(D) helps to ensure the long-term stability of a culture

18 Which of the following is NOT mentioned as a medium used for writing by the Mayans?

(A) Outer layers of trees
(B) Pieces of dried clay
(C) Sections of rope
(D) Fragments of stone

19 Look at the four squares [■] that indicate where the following sentence could be added to the passage.

Current research has been using computers to analyze the knots to search for patterns.

Where would the sentence best fit?

Click on a square [■] to add the sentence to the passage.

20 **Directions**: Select the appropriate phrases from the answer choices and match them to the type of civilization they represent. **This question is worth 4 points.**

Drag your answer choices to the spaces where they belong. To remove an answer choice, click on it. To review the passage, click on **View Text**.

Answer Choices	The Incan
(A) Went through several internal wars over the right of succession	•
(B) Created towns that began to spread from the central square	•
(C) Devised an advanced system of thoroughfares on all sides	•
(D) Had an autocratic monarch who held absolute authority over the country	•
(E) Created a concrete-like material from pulverized rocks which is put between bricks	**The Mayan**
(F) Existed for less than two centuries	•
(G) Had a complex system of transmitting information using symbols	•
(H) Could fend off the Spanish conquerors for the first few centuries	•
(I) Included terraces in the hills for the purpose of cultivating the soil	

정답 및 해석 p.378

*채점 후 p.22를 보고 본인의 맞은 개수에 해당하는 학습 방법을 참고하세요.
*진단고사 무료 해설 강의가 해커스 동영상강의 포털 해커스인강(HackersIngang.com)에서 제공됩니다.

goHackers.com

Hackers TOEFL READING

PART 01

Identifying Details

Chapter 01 Sentence Simplification

Chapter 02 Fact & Negative Fact

Chapter 03 Vocabulary

Chapter 04 Reference

Chapter 01
Sentence Simplification

OVERVIEW

Sentence Simplification 문제는 하나의 문장(sentence)을 가장 잘 simplify한 것을 선택하는 유형이다. 여기서 simplification이란 한 문장에서 부가적인 정보는 빼고 핵심 정보만을 뽑아 간결하게 바꾸어 쓰기(paraphrase) 한 것을 말한다.

따라서 Sentence Simplification 문제를 제대로 풀기 위해서는 주어진 문장의 핵심 정보가 무엇인지를 정확하게 파악하고 그 핵심 정보를 paraphrase하는 연습이 필요하다. Sentence Simplification 문제는 물론이고 토플 리딩 문제에 나오는 거의 모든 보기는 지문에 나온 표현을 그대로 쓰지 않고 바꾸어 쓰기 때문에 paraphrase를 정확하게 이해하고 연습해야 한다.

Sentence Simplification 문제는 보통 한 지문당 0~1개의 문제가 출제된다.

TYPES OF QUESTIONS

지문에 한 문장이 음영 처리되어 있으며, 선택지에는 4개의 문장이 보기로 주어진다.
Sentence Simplification 문제의 전형적인 질문 유형은 아래와 같다.

- Which of the sentences below best expresses the essential information in the highlighted sentence in the passage? *Incorrect* answer choices change the meaning in important ways or leave out essential information.

HACKERS **STRATEGY**

CH 01
CH 02
CH 03
CH 04
CH 05
CH 06
CH 07
CH 08
CH 09

Hackers TOEFL Reading

전략 1 음영 처리된 문장의 핵심 정보를 파악한다.

Sentence Simplification 문제를 풀기 위해서는 가장 먼저 지문에 주어진 음영 처리된 문장에서 핵심 정보만을 뽑아내야 한다.

● 부가 정보 제거한 후 핵심 정보 파악하기

한 문장의 핵심 정보는 수식을 위한 관계절, 동격, 예시와 같은 부가 정보를 제거하고 남는 부분에 해당한다.

Ex The underlying subject matter in early intricate shamanistic ceremonies, ① the invocations for blessings, ② which developed into theater, was the cycle of life, ③ encompassing birth and death, sexual and emotional desires, physical needs, and material forces.

➡ ①은 shamanistic ceremonies와 동격이므로 생략
②는 shamanistic ceremonies를 수식하는 관계절이므로 생략
③은 cycle of life에 해당하는 예시이므로 생략
단, 이런 예시의 경우 general한 용어로 간략화하여 encompassing various aspects of it(=life)으로 바꿀 수 있음.

핵심 정보 문장
The underlying subject matter in early intricate shamanistic ceremonies was the cycle of life.

● 지시어가 가리키는 지시 대상 확인하기

음영 처리된 문장에 지시어가 있는 경우, 주변 문장을 읽어 지시어가 가리키는 것이 무엇인지 확인한 후, 핵심 정보를 파악한다.

Ex Nematode's tolerance for temperature is remarkable. In hot springs, nematodes live at temperatures as high or higher than any other metazoa. Although ① they have adapted mechanisms to survive extremities of climate, their activity is stimulated by the return of more moderate conditions, ② such as periods after rain in desert soils or after a relatively warm interval in soils of polar regions.

➡ ①의 지시어 they가 가리키는 대상은 앞 문장의 nematodes임을 알 수 있다.
②는 more moderate conditions에 해당하는 예시이므로 생략

핵심 정보 문장
Although nematodes have adapted mechanisms to survive extremities of climate, their activity is stimulated by the return of more moderate conditions.

해석 p.382

전략 2 핵심 정보를 가장 잘 paraphrase한 보기를 고른다.

핵심 정보 문장이 파악되었으면 이제 주어진 4개의 보기 중에서 그 핵심 정보를 가장 잘 paraphrase한 보기를 고른다. Paraphrase는 원문의 의미는 그대로 살리되 문장 구조를 바꾸거나 비슷한 단어 혹은 구를 사용하여 '바꾸어 쓰기' 한 것을 말한다.

Ex

핵심 정보 문장	Paraphrase한 문장
The **underlying subject matter** in **early intricate shamanistic ceremonies** was **the cycle of life**.	**Ancient shamanistic rituals dealt with life**.

➡ Paraphrase한 문장에는 핵심 정보 문장의 주어인 underlying subject matter가 동사 dealt with로 표현되었고, early intricate shamanistic ceremonies가 Ancient shamanistic rituals로 바뀌어 쓰였으며, the cycle of life가 life로 축약 표현되어 있다.

● **문장 구조 paraphrase**

비슷한 의미를 갖지만 문장의 구조를 변화시키는 다른 연결어(접속사, 전치사)를 사용하거나, 원인/결과의 진술 순서 역전 혹은 문장 성분 간의 위치변화 등 문장의 앞뒤가 바뀌어 paraphrase된다.

Ex

원문	Paraphrase한 문장
It is unlikely that the amount of seaweed consumed in the west will ever be more than a fraction of that used by the Japanese, **although** there has been an upsurge of interest in seaweed as food.	**Despite** the increased interest in seaweed as diet in the west, the Japanese probably eat much more seaweed than Western people.

➡ 연결어 although와 비슷한 의미를 가진 Despite를 사용하여 원문의 의미는 그대로 전달하면서 문장 구조가 바뀌어 표현되었다.

● **단어나 구 paraphrase**

원문에 쓰인 단어나 구와 유사한 의미의 단어나 구를 사용하여 paraphrase된다. 이 과정에서 paraphrase 되는 단어나 구의 문장 성분 혹은 품사가 원문과 비교하여 바뀔 수 있다.

Ex

원문	Paraphrase한 문장
Drying, smoking, and salting could preserve meat **for a short time**, but the **availability** of **fresh meat** was **very limited**.	There was **little chance to obtain unprocessed meat** although meat conserved by drying, smoking, and salting was **temporarily** available.

➡ For a short time이 temporarily로, availability가 to obtain으로, fresh meat이 unprocessed meat으로, very limited가 little chance로 바뀌어 쓰여 있다.

CH 01

CH 02

CH 03

CH 04

CH 05

CH 06

CH 07

CH 08

CH 09

Hackers TOEFL Reading

전략 3 보기 중 오답을 확인한다.

최종적으로 나머지 보기들을 검토하여 오답임을 확인한다. Sentence Simplification 문제의 오답은 주로 음영된 문장의 핵심 정보를 빠뜨렸거나 의미를 현저하게 바꾸어버린 경우에 해당한다.

Ex Acid rain **contains** such acidic **compounds** as sulfuric acid and nitric acid, which are produced by the combination of atmospheric water with oxides released when hydrocarbons are burned and is widely considered **responsible** for **damaging organisms** such as forests and aquatic life.

Q: Which of the sentences below best expresses the essential information in the highlighted sentence in the passage? *Incorrect* answer choices change the meaning in important ways or leave out essential information.

A: Acid rain **includes** an acidic **mixture** and is largely **blamed** for **harming living things**. (○)

➡ 음영된 문장에서 산성 화합물과 유기체의 예를 드는 부가 정보를 제거하면 남는 핵심 정보는 '산성비가 산성 화합물을 함유하고 있고 유기체 파괴를 초래하는 것으로 여겨진다'이다. 정답 문장에서는 contains가 includes로, compounds가 mixture로, responsible이 blamed로, damaging이 harming으로, organisms가 living things로 각각 paraphrase되어 있다.

핵심 정보를 빠뜨린 오답

The harmful effects of acid rain are the result of acids generated by the blend of atmospheric water with oxides. (×)

이 보기 문장은 산성비가 유기체를 파괴한다는 음영된 문장의 핵심 정보를 빠뜨리고 있다.

원문의 의미를 현저하게 바꾸어버린 오답

Sulfuric and nitric acid causes acid rain to combine water with oxides and to interfere with the areas where organisms prefer to live. (×)

이 보기 문장은 '황산과 질산이 산성비가 물을 산화물과 결합하도록 하여 유기체가 서식하는 지역을 해친다'라는 내용을 담고 있어 원문의 의미를 현저하게 바꾸어버렸다.

HACKERS STRATEGY **APPLICATION**

The concept of natural, open space in architecture soon spread from residential houses to skyscrapers, commercial enterprises, bridges, and gas stations, among others, all displaying an inherent belief that the essential focus of the structure should be derived from its purpose, implying artistic expression is tantamount to communication of meaning and quality. Wright argued that a bank should look like a bank, not a Greek temple, and thus the design and construction materials should be relative to its function. Nature offers the best example of wholesome integration of purpose and design, so he referred to this new ideology as "organic architecture," one that is not only a radical departure from tradition, but understands an intricate relationships between structure, time and site, integrating all three into one meaningful whole where harmony exists between those that reside in the dwelling and its physical environment.

Which of the sentences below best expresses the essential information in the highlighted sentence in the passage? *Incorrect* answer choices change the meaning in important ways or leave out essential information.

(A) The notion that aesthetic representation is equivalent to communication of meaning and quality was inherent in the various types of buildings.

(B) A variety of different structures adopted the idea of natural, open space and reflected the view that their purpose should be the main point in constructing buildings.

(C) Architecture has been compared to art since both focus on trying to communicate quality which in architecture is achieved through different types of structures.

(D) Skyscrapers and commercial enterprises focused on expanding space inside the buildings and decorating their exterior.

해석 p.382

CH 01

CH 02

CH 03

CH 04

CH 05

CH 06

CH 07

CH 08

CH 09

Hackers TOEFL Reading

| 전략 1 적용 | 음영된 문장에서 부가 정보는 제거하고 핵심 정보만 남긴다. |

The concept of natural, open space in architecture soon spread ① **from residential houses to skyscrapers, commercial enterprises, bridges, and gas stations, among others**, all displaying an inherent belief that the essential focus of the structure should be derived from its purpose, ② ~~implying artistic expression is tantamount to communication of meaning and quality~~.

위의 음영된 문장에서 부가 정보인 ①을 over a variety of different structures로 간략화하고 ②를 생략하면 아래의 핵심 정보 문장만 남는다.

The concept of natural, open space in architecture soon spread over a variety of different structures, all displaying an inherent belief that the essential focus of the structure should be derived from its purpose.

| 전략 2 적용 | 핵심 정보를 가장 잘 paraphrase한 문장은 (B)이다. |

핵심 정보 문장	Paraphrase한 문장
The concept of natural, open space in architecture soon spread over **a variety of different structures**, all **displaying an inherent belief** that the essential focus of the structure should be derived from its purpose.	**A variety of different structures** adopted **the idea of natural, open space** and **reflected the view** that their purpose should be the main point in constructing buildings.

위 핵심 정보 문장의 목적어와 주어가 보기 (B)에서 주어와 목적어로 바뀌어 쓰여 있고, displaying an inherent belief ~가 reflected the view ~로 바뀌어 쓰여 있다.

| 전략 3 적용 | (A) 핵심 정보를 빠뜨린 오답
음영된 문장의 핵심 정보에 해당하는 '건축물의 초점은 목적에서 찾아야 한다'라는 내용을 빠뜨리고 있다.

(C) 원문의 의미를 현저하게 바꾸어버린 오답
'건축은 예술에 견주어진다'라는 것은 음영된 문장의 의미를 현저하게 바꾸어버린 것이다.

(D) 원문의 의미를 현저하게 바꾸어버린 오답
'고층건물과 상업용 건물이 공간 확장과 건물 외부 장식에 초점을 맞추었다'라는 내용은 음영된 문장의 의미를 현저하게 바꾸어버린 것이다. |

| 정답 | (B) |

Choose the correctly simplified sentence for each given sentence.

1 Although these days quilts are considered to be precious works of art, throughout history they represented little more than a ⬚frugal⬚ means of reutilizing the clothing that people no longer cared to keep.

(A) Quilts were once ways to cheaply reuse unwanted clothes, but now they are regarded as valuable art pieces.

(B) While quilts were traditionally valued for their artistic merit, they were primarily used for economical purposes.

2 Despite the fact that British governors in America encountered opposition that ⬚mostly⬚ centered on matters of taxation, a handful reported to London that mandates of any sort would lead to insurrection by the colonies.

(A) The resistance governors faced concerning taxes was revealed when the colonies told London they would rather revolt than obey commands.

(B) Some British governors claimed that any orders would result in rebellion, though the colonies largely opposed them because of taxes.

3 The arid climate of the Great Basin-Mojave Desert region is primarily caused by the Sierra Nevada, which prevents water vapor from reaching the desert by ⬚capturing⬚ storm fronts upon arrival from the Pacific.

(A) Since precipitation from the Pacific never arrives at the Sierra Nevada, the Great Basin-Mojave Desert stays arid.

(B) Because the Sierra Nevada keeps moisture from getting to the Great Basin-Mojave Desert, the area is very dry.

VOCABULARY	The word ⬚⬚ in the passage is closest in meaning to			
1 frugal	(A) peremptory	(B) salubrious	(C) cautious	(D) thrifty
2 mostly	(A) desperately	(B) promptly	(C) mainly	(D) hardly
3 capturing	(A) seizing	(B) evading	(C) amplifying	(D) evaporating

4 Artificial reefs can cause problems if poorly designed and mounted because insufficiently weighted materials such as car bodies, tires, old vessels, and concrete rubble which end up miles away from the reef site by strong windstorms can damage ⬚sedentary⬚ organisms of nearby natural reef sites.

(A) A danger that carelessly planned artificial reefs pose is the possibility that the materials involved in constructing them may disturb the inhabitants in nearby natural reefs.

(B) One problem with artificial reefs is that they are easily damaged if the debris used to build them has been weighted incorrectly thus leaving the possibility of being loosened by winds.

5 The original fossil of Pakicetus was comprised of nothing more than a shattered mandible and a small quantity of teeth, but careful scrutiny of the molars suggested that it is reasonable to ⬚assume⬚ that the creature was omnivorous even though the specimen was far from complete.

(A) Presuming that Pakicetus had an omnivorous diet simply from a mandible and a handful of teeth is a rational conclusion, though it cannot be proven.

(B) Although the first Pakicetus fossil was partial, it is safe to conclude from an examination of the molars that the animal was an omnivore.

6 While there is a vocal minority of libertarians who eschew any sort of government interference in an individual's fiscal matters, such as limiting the accumulation of private property, the vast preponderance of them find the slightest authoritative restriction on their freedom of expression, like curtailing free speech or the passage of obscenity laws, even less ⬚appealing⬚.

(A) Most libertarians agree that the government should not engage in the limitation of civil rights, but they rarely concur on its role in intervening in people's monetary issues.

(B) A small number of libertarians strongly reject all government involvement in personal finance, whereas most of them more adamantly oppose reducing their right to express themselves.

VOCABULARY	The word ⬚ in the passage is closest in meaning to			
4 sedentary	(A) tranquil	(B) stationary	(C) serial	(D) various
5 assume	(A) suppose	(B) undertake	(C) pretend	(D) wilt
6 appealing	(A) apparent	(B) desirable	(C) timely	(D) mundane

CH 01
CH 02
CH 03
CH 04
CH 05
CH 06
CH 07
CH 08
CH 09

Hackers TOEFL Reading

Choose all correctly simplified sentences for each given sentence.

7   The Taos' tribal customs remained largely unchanged due in part to a $\boxed{\text{strict}}$ taboo on marriage outside of the pueblo that maintained racial purity, cultural integrity as well as a strong sense of the community even though the Taos people had $\boxed{\text{friendly}}$ relationships with other tribes.

(A) Although the Taos pueblo enjoyed amiable relations with other tribes, it kept its customs intact through prohibition of marriage outside the immediate tribe.

(B) The tribal rituals of the Taos remained invariable largely because the Taos were able to sustain positive, friendly relations with their non-Taos neighbors.

(C) Despite the fact that the Taos were on friendly terms with non-Taos Indians, their tribal customs were affected after a ban on marriage outside the community was imposed.

(D) While remaining friendly with outsiders, the Taos were able to preserve their tribal customs by banning marriage outside the tribe.

8   Studies reveal that in a range of animal species, calorie restriction not only reduces the metabolic rate, but is also a $\boxed{\text{key}}$ component in curbing oxidative stress at the cellular level, which has $\boxed{\text{substantial}}$ implications for staving off disease and extending longevity.

(A) Studies suggest that calorie and metabolic rate reduction are necessary for many animals to limit oxidative stress.

(B) According to research, the animals that can best prevent disease and prolong longevity are those that control caloric intake.

(C) Reducing calories has been shown to moderate metabolism and lower oxidative stress, which help a variety of animals avoid disease and live longer.

(D) Research shows that restricting calories regulates cellular oxidative stress in many animals, leading to healthier and longer lives, as well as slowing metabolism.

VOCABULARY   The word [   ] in the passage is closest in meaning to

7	strict	(A) groundless	(B) lubricious	(C) repulsive	(D) rigid
	friendly	(A) myopic	(B) ragged	(C) favorable	(D) reserved
8	key	(A) leading	(B) rudimentary	(C) bustling	(D) natural
	substantial	(A) standard	(B) significant	(C) prolific	(D) affluent

9 In the Aristotelian tradition, dramatic performances evoked the purging of fear and pity from the soul either by portraying the downfall of better than average humans (i.e. heroes, kings, gods) from an elevated position to bad fortune, or representing average people who were raised to better standards when circumstances shifted from unfavorable to indulgent or advantageous.

(A) People who saw Aristotelian dramas in which the mighty fell or the low were elevated felt that their souls were cleansed.

(B) The depiction of the downfall of the power holders and the elevation of ordinary people in Aristotelian dramas was the way of removing fear and pity from viewers.

(C) Aristotelian tradition led to the relief of fear and pity from the people who saw the performances that featured the events in the lives of both the rich and the poor.

(D) Aristotelian dramas rid the soul of fear and pity, focusing on either the decline of the powerful or the rise of the normal.

10 Although two cerebral hemispheres in humans demonstrate intricate communication with each other across the corpus callosum, a large collection of neural fibers that unites both areas of the brain, the partnership between them is not equitable and most experiments show that one usually dominates the other, as illustrated by handedness, the manifestation of higher motor functions using either the left or right hand.

(A) Experiments on the human brain have shown that the corpus callosum is responsible for transmitting information from one hemisphere to the other.

(B) The unequal transmission of information between the two hemispheres of the human brain results from the malfunction of the corpus callosum.

(C) People's preference for their left or right hands demonstrates that if both halves of the brain exchange information, the connection between the two is evident.

(D) Despite the interaction between the two hemispheres of the human brain via the corpus callosum, one half generally has power over the other.

CH 01
CH 02
CH 03
CH 04
CH 05
CH 06
CH 07
CH 08
CH 09

Hackers TOEFL Reading

| VOCABULARY | The word ☐ in the passage is closest in meaning to |

9	portraying	(A) entailing	(B) spawning	(C) depicting	(D) enlisting
	circumstances	(A) substratums	(B) situations	(C) maneuvers	(D) crests
10	dominates	(A) compels	(B) echoes	(C) mitigates	(D) controls
	manifestation	(A) demonstration	(B) mastery	(C) presentiment	(D) onset

11   Of course there had previously been some forms of mass consumption, such as vaudeville, plays, and lectures, which had all been presented to large groups of spectators, but the projection of film and the ⌈ensuing⌉ craze and popularity with which the public received it encouraged large capital investments and the production of new titles to satiate the public ⌈demand⌉.

(A) Films became so popular that they overwhelmed the ability of previous forms of amusing performances to entertain spectators.

(B) Whereas types of mass consumption were present earlier, the projection of film and the public enthusiasm inspired funding and the creation of more titles to meet the demand.

(C) Although forms of mass consumption were in existence before, the film projection and its popularity interested a great deal of capital in making movies.

(D) Since movies in general required so much investment to produce new titles, there wasn't enough to satisfy the public demand for them.

12   Herbert C. Hoover is best remembered for his ⌈perceived⌉ inaction in responding to the Great Depression, as compared to the almost frenetic interventionism of his popular successor, Franklin D. Roosevelt, but this is ⌈lamentable⌉ because although Hoover was somewhat of a failure as President, outside of those four years of his life he was a very successful humanitarian.

(A) While the general public has a high opinion of Roosevelt because of his prompt action responding to the Great Depression, it tends to belittle Hoover's political achievements.

(B) Hoover remains in people's memory as a failed President because of his insufficient response to the Great Depression, but actually he was a generous benefactor before and after his White House years.

(C) Even though he is most remembered for failing to react promptly to the Great Depression, Hoover was an accomplished philanthropist prior to and following his Presidency.

(D) Hoover had no choice but to watch Roosevelt intervene aggressively in the Great Depression because he was too politically weak to object to Roosevelt's action.

VOCABULARY	The word	☐	in the passage is closest in meaning to		
11 ensuing	(A) retreating	(B) unconvincing	(C) following	(D) foreboding
demand	(A) requirement	(B) projection	(C) embellishment	(D) inclination
12 perceived	(A) disillusioned	(B) corrupted	(C) activated	(D) discerned
lamentable	(A) malleable	(B) estimable	(C) reachable	(D) deplorable

Read each passage and answer the corresponding questions for each.

13 When lithography was accidentally invented by a German playwright, lithographs included a single color: black. [1]Before long, however, multicolor lithographs were accomplished by creating a print of an image in black outline and then making color additions by hand, often using watercolors, somewhat akin to the method a child employs to fill in the pages of a coloring book. But true *chromolithography* — the use of a range of colors in the printing process itself to duplicate images — did not transpire until the early 19th century. [2]Anticipating chromolithography's potential profitability in the commercial market for inexpensive reproductions of paintings, sold at far below the price of an original, entrepreneurs such as Louis Prang of Boston capitalized on the technology by offering prints that the masses could afford. Prang successfully branded chromolithographs by saying they represented the democratization of art, a world hitherto unavailable to the common man.

1 Which of the sentences below best expresses the essential information in the highlighted sentence in the passage? *Incorrect* choices change the meaning in important ways or leave out essential information.

(A) Lithographs of more than one color were soon achieved through hand-coloring a picture printed in black outline.

(B) Just as a child adds color to a coloring book, lithographers filled in images by hand using a variety of colors.

(C) The printing of multicolor lithographs involved manually fitting the printer with more than one color.

(D) The accomplishment of making lithographs of more than one color eliminated the need for an image in black outline.

2 Which of the sentences below best expresses the essential information in the highlighted sentence in the passage? *Incorrect* choices change the meaning in important ways or leave out essential information.

(A) Because most people could not afford an original painting, they chose to buy prints from chromolithographers instead.

(B) The new technology made it possible for entrepreneurs to charge significant sums of money for their mass-produced copies.

(C) Enterprising individuals predicted how lucrative chromolithography could be and profited through the production of affordable prints.

(D) Many businesspeople turned to chromolithography only after it became commercially profitable to pursue.

VOCABULARY	The word		in the passage is closest in meaning to		
13 accidentally	(A) instinctively	(B) incidentally	(C) additionally	(D) tightly
range	(A) bond	(B) subject	(C) extent	(D) friction
duplicate	(A) reproduce	(B) exaggerate	(C) annul	(D) substantiate

CH 01
CH 02
CH 03
CH 04
CH 05
CH 06
CH 07
CH 08
CH 09
Hackers TOEFL Reading

14   Among the earliest commercially produced typewriters was the Hansen Writing Ball, a practical writing tool invented by Rasmus Malling-Hansen in 1865 to allow more expeditious written communication. [1]Due to the fact that the ingenious contraption allocated specific alphabetic letters to individual fingers, it could generate as much as 300 percent more syllables per second than conventional writing, which was typically done by dipping a pen in ink and putting it on paper. Hansen designed the machine around a half sphere boasting showy brass keys, giving it the appearance of a pincushion, and he frequently made improvements to the initial design. [2]In addition to tactically rearranging the keys, which totaled fifty-six, to maximize productivity, with the propensity of vowels placed on the left side of the machine and most of the consonants on the right, Hansen affixed an electromagnetic battery, an innovation that moved the paper along and made his device the world's first electric typewriter.

1 Which of the sentences below best expresses the essential information in the highlighted sentence in the passage? *Incorrect* choices change the meaning in important ways or leave out essential information.

(A) Because the machine could limit the alphabet needed to communicate, it reduced the writing burden by 300 percent.

(B) In order to make conventional writing faster, the contraption reduced the number of syllables by approximately 300 percent.

(C) Given that the apparatus resulted in 300 percent more efficiency, traditional writing was used less and less.

(D) Per second, the apparatus generated a 300 percent increase in writing productivity because letters were assigned to particular fingers.

2 Which of the sentences below best expresses the essential information in the highlighted sentence in the passage? *Incorrect* choices change the meaning in important ways or leave out essential information.

(A) The addition of an electromagnetic battery allowed Hansen to move paper and generate maximum efficiency through the rearrangement of keys.

(B) Hansen strategically altered the keys for maximum efficiency and added an electromagnetic battery that changed the paper's position and set his device apart.

(C) By affixing an electromagnetic battery to his device, Hansen established the first electric typewriter, but this impeded his goal of maximum efficiency.

(D) Hansen's addition of an electric battery required him to increase the number of keys to 56, and this helped him maximize the device's efficiency.

VOCABULARY   The word ☐ in the passage is closest in meaning to

14	practical	(A) pliable	(B) primeval	(C) pertinent	(D) pragmatic
	boasting	(A) bombarding	(B) displaying	(C) battering	(D) broadening
	frequently	(A) chronically	(B) rigorously	(C) precisely	(D) radically

15   The Sun Dance ceremony was held by several Plains Indian tribes, but is usually attributed to the Hopi Indians of the southwestern United States. It was an `occasion` when all members of the community and some invited guests would gather to reaffirm their `underlying` belief systems about the role of the universe and the supernatural in their lives. [1]In complex versions of this spring festival, selected tribal members made a commitment to perform, and spent part of the winter season preparing colorful costumes, beaded headdresses, and drums in preparation for the dance. Once the festivities began, the chosen few would don their apparel, form a camp circle, and erect a pole in the center to symbolize spiritual power and mystical energy. Dancing `commenced` around this pole, continuing intermittently for days until the actors fell into frenzy, sometimes performing self-torture to end the rite, or simply collapsing from exhaustion. [2]Because the Sun Dance inspired all members of the tribe to work together and was a way to reach the incredible power of the spirit world, it was a method of maintaining social cohesion as well as ensuring a balance between earthly desires and the divine.

1   Which of the sentences below best expresses the essential information in the highlighted sentence in the passage? *Incorrect* choices change the meaning in important ways or leave out essential information.

(A) Although many different items were needed for the spring festival, only a few people participated in making them.

(B) A chosen portion of the tribe would spend the previous season preparing for the performance after pledging to dance at the spring festival.

(C) Only those deemed worthy were allowed to dance at the spring festival and to spend the winter getting ready.

(D) Tribal members would promise several months in advance to have time to arrange for the more elaborate festivals.

2   Which of the sentences below best expresses the essential information in the highlighted sentence in the passage? *Incorrect* choices change the meaning in important ways or leave out essential information.

(A) Due to the total tribal participation and connection to the divinity, the Sun Dance had both social and spiritual significance for the tribe.

(B) The religious element of the Sun Dance meant that most tribal members rejected their earthly concerns during the festival.

(C) The various members of the tribe had to be cohesive to make the Sun Dance successful and balanced to harmonize with the spirit world.

(D) The goal of the Sun Dance was to foster good inter-tribal relationships and to reflect their spiritual beliefs through dancing.

VOCABULARY   The word [   ] in the passage is closest in meaning to

15 occasion	(A) oversight	(B) affair	(C) adage	(D) intent
underlying	(A) placid	(B) austere	(C) outstanding	(D) intrinsic
commenced	(A) launched	(B) loomed	(C) muttered	(D) thrusted

CH 01
CH 02
CH 03
CH 04
CH 05
CH 06
CH 07
CH 08
CH 09
Hackers TOEFL Reading

16 The problem that many paleontologists and evolutionary biologists have with phenetic classifications is that they do not always accurately depict evolutionary relationships. In other words, the categories often group organisms that are not necessarily closely related, just similar in their overall grade of evolution. This has the effect of excluding some organisms that have inherited a conspicuous evolutionary novelty and lumping together other organisms based on more primitive traits. For example, birds are now known to be the direct evolutionary descendants of small, predatory dinosaurs. [1]The skeletal similarities between Mesozoic birds and Coelurosaurian dinosaurs are remarkable, yet birds are not classified as reptiles because they have feathers. Feathers are the evolutionary novelties that distinguish birds from reptiles. Therefore, because dinosaurs lack feathers, they are grouped with crocodiles as reptiles, even though they are much more distantly related to crocodiles than they are to birds. Another example is the so called "mammal-like reptiles," a group of extinct animals that are defined on their lack of several key features possessed by modern mammals. [2]These animals are classified as reptiles because they appear to be at a reptilian grade of evolution — sprawling stance, lack of inner ear bones — even though they have only a distant evolutionary relationship to reptiles.

1 Which of the sentences below best expresses the essential information in the highlighted sentence in the passage? *Incorrect* choices change the meaning in important ways or leave out essential information.

(A) Although Coelurosaurian dinosaurs and Mesozoic birds have many things in common, they are not evolutionarily related.

(B) The possession of feathers has prevented Mesozoic birds from being categorized as reptiles.

(C) Since birds are feathered, they are not put into the same category as dinosaur despite their similarities.

(D) Mesozoic birds are extraordinary because they have a skeletal structure similar to a Coelurosaurian dinosaur.

2 Which of the sentences below best expresses the essential information in the highlighted sentence in the passage? *Incorrect* choices change the meaning in important ways or leave out essential information.

(A) Although they are not closely related to reptiles in evolution, "mammal-like reptiles" are termed reptiles due to some reptilian traits.

(B) Due to the absence of some mammalian features, "mammal-like reptiles" are classified as reptiles to demonstration.

(C) The classification of "mammal-like reptiles" as reptiles is based on general characteristics rather than a close evolutionary relationship.

(D) The sprawling stance and the lack of inner ear bones are two of the distinguishing characteristics of a reptile.

VOCABULARY The word [ ] in the passage is closest in meaning to

16 overall	(A) sectional	(B) terminal	(C) total	(D) dubious
conspicuous	(A) catastrophic	(B) salient	(C) headstrong	(D) trifling
possessed	(A) owned	(B) enhanced	(C) engrossed	(D) hyped

17   The history of mining in Nevada, nicknamed the "Silver State", is so intertwined with the history of the state that at certain points the two cannot be separated . In fact, were it not for mining, Nevada would probably not have achieved statehood until decades later than it did. As it was, the Silver State bought its way into the Union with silver mined in the famous Comstock Lode. In the middle 1800s, the area that would become Nevada was mostly a highway for those heading to search for gold in California. In 1859, however, the discovery of massive silver deposits quickly made Virginia City the most famous of all western mining camps. The rapid influx of prospectors and settlers resulted in the organization of the Nevada Territory just two years later. In the east, the American Civil War was brewing. [1]Lincoln, realizing the area's great mineral wealth could help the Union, and needing another Northern state to support his proposed anti-slavery amendment to the Constitution, encouraged the territory to seek admission to the Union. Even though Nevada boasted only about one-fifth of the 127,381 people required for statehood, Congress accepted the proposed state constitution and admitted Nevada as the 36th state in 1864. Nevada's motto, "Battle Born," reflects its role in this stormy period of history. [2]Since then, mining's impact on Nevada's economy has remained immense, both in the influx of money it has brought in boom times and in the noticeable economic downturns when mineral demand wanes.

1   Which of the sentences below best expresses the essential information in the highlighted sentence in the passage? *Incorrect* choices change the meaning in important ways or leave out essential information.

(A) Lincoln wanted the Nevada Territory to join the Union because its great wealth would be an asset to the anti-slavery movement.

(B) On account of economic and political circumstances, Lincoln advocated Nevada's application to become part of the Union.

(C) Using its great wealth and promising to support Lincoln, the Nevada Territory was able to become a member of the Union.

(D) The Nevada Territory was inspired to apply for statehood because it would render aid for anti-slavery amendment to the Union.

2   Which of the sentences below best expresses the essential information in the highlighted sentence in the passage? *Incorrect* choices change the meaning in important ways or leave out essential information.

(A) The decreasing demand for minerals has led to Nevada spending a great deal of money to support the mining industry.

(B) The boom and bust of the Nevada mining industry has had a huge influence on the region's economy.

(C) The Nevada economy has been boosted by the inpouring of funds from the mining industry.

(D) The ups and downs of the Nevada's economy have caused considerable changes in mineral demands.

VOCABULARY	The word ☐ in the passage is closest in meaning to			
17 separated	(A) snared	(B) abominated	(C) substantiated	(D) split
quickly	(A) timidly	(B) inordinately	(C) swiftly	(D) intimately
influx	(A) coalition	(B) inundation	(C) entreaty	(D) interference

정답 및 해석 p.383

CH 01
CH 02
CH 03
CH 04
CH 05
CH 06
CH 07
CH 08
CH 09
Hackers TOEFL Reading

HACKERS **TEST**

⏱ 제한 시간: 12분

01   Electric Fish

1   Visual, auditory, and chemical correspondence is available to organisms in all environments. Electrical communication, however, is limited to water, as air is too effective an insulator to pass signals from sender to receiver. [1]While many fish are able to detect small currents, electric fish are unique in that they are able to navigate and communicate by generating, receiving, and processing electric signals via highly specialized electric organs. Electric eels, the most well known of these, belong to a class known as "strongly electric" that is capable of giving off discharges of up to 150 volts. Others, such as the black ghost knife, are classified as "weakly electric," because their maximum emissions are generally less than a single volt. Apart from the strong volleys used by the former for predation, each sort uses its electric organs in similar ways.

2   [3]The electric organs are composed of cells called electrocytes, which resemble muscle cells in the sense that they exist at the end of axons, as a muscle cell would, although they have no contracting ability. Having a distinctly disc-like form, these are aligned like cells in a battery. Up to 200,000 coordinate in series, each capable of producing a small voltage via biochemical activity. When discharged simultaneously, the currents amalgamate into a potential difference that is the sum of each voltage. To stun or kill, strongly electric fish can modulate this to exude large blasts. Otherwise, both classes utilize electrocytes to create a weak perpetual field around their bodies.

3   This works in tandem with a series of electro receptors spread across the fish's body surface. Each acts like a miniature voltmeter that monitors the voltage across the skin, which in turn conveys sensory information to the brain that creates a "picture" of objects in the surrounding waters. This process is called electrolocation. When nearby objects in the water perturb the fish's field, it alters the pattern of current flow. [5]If the object is less conductive than the water, such as a rock, electric current will be deflected around the object, but if it is more conductive, such as a minnow, electric current will be routed through, because it represents a path of lower resistance. This allows the fish to detect changes in its field — information that it uses to gauge differences between prey, obstacles, enemies, and allies.

4   Electrical data can also be used by the fish to communicate with each other with the object of reproducing by means of electric organ discharge(EOD), which can be encoded with some information. Each electric fish's EOD is released within a unique range of frequencies. When a male receives a feminine EOD, it causes deliberate changes to its EOD frequency in order to display its reproductive prowess and encourage the female to select it as a mate. Since its eligibility for being selected is usually determined by its frequency range, males which are able to send out electrical impulses on the most

extreme frequencies have better opportunities to attract females and spawn. In schools where mating possibilities are limited, fights may erupt between two males for the same female. One will alter its EOD to mimic that of the other, effectively jamming its opponent's signal, and then engage in a battle that will continue until one of them is worn out and ceases emitting its EOD in surrender. However, when natural frequencies match without aggressive intent, the fish will reflexively shift them to avoid conflict. [6]When one detects another that has nearly the same frequency, it can alter its oscillation to be slightly higher; subsequently, the other will modulate its own to be marginally lower. This function, known as the Jamming Avoidance Response, or JAR, ensures peaceful cohesion within the immediate population.

1 Which of the sentences below best expresses the essential information in the highlighted sentence in the passage? *Incorrect* choices change the meaning in important ways or leave out essential information.

(A) The ability to communicate and navigate using electric currents is a common attribute in a variety of different types of fish.

(B) Although other fish can sense electricity, electric fish are special because they utilize this ability for different purposes.

(C) The possession of distinctive electric organs allows electric fish to use electricity for a variety of functions unavailable to other fish.

(D) Electric fish use their specialized electric organs to generate currents of electricity that are too small for other fish to detect.

2 The phrase "Apart from" in the passage is closest in meaning to

(A) In substitute for
(B) Unlike
(C) Besides
(D) Far from

CH 01
CH 02
CH 03
CH 04
CH 05
CH 06
CH 07
CH 08
CH 09
Hackers TOEFL Reading

3 Which of the sentences below best expresses the essential information in the highlighted sentence in the passage? *Incorrect* choices change the meaning in important ways or leave out essential information.

(A) Except for the lack of contraction facility, the electrocytes that form the electric organs are comparable to muscle cells.

(B) Although electrocytes making up the electric organs are unable to contract, they are similar to muscle cell in their location.

(C) The electric organs known as electrocytes are analogous to muscle cells because they are found on the end of axons.

(D) Electrocytes are a form of contracting muscle cell that are commonly found on the tips of axons in electric fish.

4 The word "aligned" in the passage is closest in meaning to

(A) inflated
(B) alleged
(C) jeered
(D) ordered

5 Which of the sentences below best expresses the essential information in the highlighted sentence in the passage? *Incorrect* choices change the meaning in important ways or leave out essential information.

(A) Electric currents are deflected around less conductive objects like rocks, but pass through more conductive objects like minnows.

(B) The manner in which objects in the water react to the electric current is dependent on how well they conduct electricity.

(C) The greater the conductivity of an object, the less resistance it will offer to the electrical current in the water.

(D) The electric current will behave differently depending on the conductivity of the object it encounters relative to the water.

6 Which of the sentences below best expresses the essential information in the highlighted sentence in the passage? *Incorrect* choices change the meaning in important ways or leave out essential information.

(A) Electric fish will change their oscillation when faced with another that uses a similar signal.

(B) Electric fish with similar frequencies must alter their oscillation in order to detect each other.

(C) If two electric fish with similar frequencies meet, the lower oscillation will be increased.

(D) Electric fish frequently adjust their frequency to have a higher oscillation than other fish.

7 **Directions**: An introductory sentence for a brief summary of the passage is provided below. Complete the summary by selecting the THREE answer choices that express the most important ideas in the passage. Some sentences do not belong in the summary because they express ideas that are not presented in the passage or are minor ideas in the passage. **This question is worth 2 points.**

Drag your answer choices to the spaces where they belong. To remove an answer choice, click on it. To review the passage, click on **View Text**.

Electric fish are a unique type of an animal capable of using electricity as one of their senses.

-
-
-

Answer Choices

(A) Strongly electric fish emit a broad spectrum of voltages in response to assaults from a variety of invaders.

(B) The field around electric fish's body enables them to recognize the objects in their surrounding environment.

(C) Electric fish use their electric organ discharges for the purpose of mating communication.

(D) Electric fish have the capacity for generating electric charges through long arrays of cells in their body.

(E) Electric fish which have almost the same frequency change their frequencies in Jamming Avoidance Response.

(F) A multitude of emissions by electric fish require them to adopt limited frequencies for communications.

정답 및 해석 p.388

CH 01

CH 02

CH 03

CH 04

CH 05

CH 06

CH 07

CH 08

CH 09

Hackers TOEFL Reading

1　The Fremont people were named by Noel Morss of Harvard's Peabody Museum after the Fremont River in Utah, where they settled between 400 and 1300 A.D. Most archaeologists believe that the first people to settle the region were hunter-gatherers from the Colorado Plateau, who immigrated to the area between 2,500 and 1,500 years ago. From about 2,000 years ago, maize and other plants began to be cultivated in what is now central Utah. [1]These early Fremont did not build settled villages and continued their nomadic ways, spreading the knowledge of farming and pottery building all around the area, but 700 years later, less itinerant lifestyles emerged, with a number of farming communities developing, which consisted of semi-subterranean timber and mud pit houses with above ground granaries. They also developed farming techniques as sophisticated as their contemporaries, using water diversion techniques such as irrigation.

2　It was their construction of irrigation canals and houses, virtually indistinguishable in form and technology from the Anasazi, a well-studied group which had lived south of Utah, that initially led to the belief that they were an offshoot, or had previously separated from the Anasazi. While less socially organized, with many more disparate groups than their counterparts, the Fremont were much more adaptable, with pockets occupying actually every niche and landscape in the region. As more remnants of their culture were excavated, Morss was able to prove that the Fremont were a separate group. [3]One difficulty he encountered was trying to demonstrate that the scattered multiple small communities constituted a cohesive culture and that they had affinities that extended beyond just their location.

3　Despite not fitting as neatly in archaeological schemes as other ancient civilizations, distinct actions and patterns tie the disparate groups together. The first is the Fremont one-rod and bundle basketry style that often employed cattails or bulrushes and was easily distinguishable from the coiled style of the Anasazi precursors, the Basketmakers. The Fremont also constructed moccasins from the hock of a bison or the forelegs of deer or sheep. These had the dewclaws of animals sewn into the heels as hobnails, which gave extra traction in slippery conditions. [4]Although leather usually does not preserve well, a few samples have been found due to the arid conditions in Utah and are easily discriminated from the yucca sandals made by those who moved into the regions later. Thin-walled gray pottery shards have been found at every site, which unfortunately, because of their fragility, are not complete specimens. Most notably, they had a distinctive artistic style, which they often carved on walls, depicting trapezoidal human figures bedecked with necklaces which can be seen in every settlement regardless of the location or the materials used in construction.

4　From 1250 A.D., the Fremont inexplicably began to disappear in the haphazard manner in which they appeared, leaving scant details to explain the abruptness of their departure. [6]Like the Anasazi, the exact reasons for their disappearance are unknown, but there was no single cause, but rather a group of factors, which in combination brought about the change. The most commonly cited reason is that the changes in the climate, including decreased precipitation, may have forced the Fremont to become more dependent upon wild game. Another factor may have been the migration of other peoples into the region, which may have either displaced the Fremont via competition for resources or absorbed them into their cultures. Owing to the length of time and the paucity of relics left behind, perhaps the cause of their demise may never be known, but it is clear that these resourceful and creative people had a deep understanding of the land they inhabited.

Glossary
hock tarsal joint of the hind leg of hoofed mammals

CH 01
CH 02
CH 03
CH 04
CH 05
CH 06
CH 07
CH 08
CH 09

Hackers TOEFL Reading

1 Which of the sentences below best expresses the essential information in the highlighted sentence in the passage? *Incorrect* choices change the meaning in important ways or leave out essential information.

(A) As the Fremont accumulated knowledge of farming and pottery, they gradually settled into secure communities.

(B) Because of the need to exchange information with others in the area, the settlement of the Fremont was delayed.

(C) Although the Fremont initially wandered from place to place, they eventually established many agrarian societies.

(D) Once the Fremont gained methods required to build permanent structures, they gave up their nomadic lifestyles.

2 The word "remnants" in the passage is closest in meaning to

(A) aspects
(B) clues
(C) beliefs
(D) remains

3 Which of the sentences below best expresses the essential information in the highlighted sentence in the passage? *Incorrect* choices change the meaning in important ways or leave out essential information.

(A) The Fremont were the only culture to use multiple sites, making it difficult for Morss to verify they were really one.

(B) The fact that numerous different groups at a distance had a similar culture was an obstacle to Morss' work.

(C) Morss attempted to tie the disparate groups together by their similarities with no consideration of their respective location.

(D) Without a central place for meeting, Morss was unable to prove that the diverse camps all belonged to one culture.

4 Which of the sentences below best expresses the essential information in the highlighted sentence in the passage? *Incorrect* choices change the meaning in important ways or leave out essential information.

(A) The leather shoes of the Fremont were kept in good condition by the weather even though their quality was lower than the yucca sandals found later in Utah.

(B) Yucca sandals have been better preserved than those of the Fremont although the weather conditions for the preservation of leather greatly improved over time.

(C) Due to the dry weather in Utah, some of the moccasins created by the Fremont are still available.

(D) Despite their perishable nature, the climate in Utah made it possible for Fremont leather shoes, distinct from those made of yucca, to survive.

5 The word "depicting" in the passage is closest in meaning to

(A) dismissing
(B) portraying
(C) supporting
(D) revealing

6 Which of the sentences below best expresses the essential information in the highlighted sentence in the passage? *Incorrect* choices change the meaning in important ways or leave out essential information.

(A) The collapse of the Anasazi gave rise to many changes that led to the disappearance of the Fremont.

(B) The vanishment of the Fremont was the result of many combined factors that are obscure.

(C) The extinction of the Anasazi and the Fremont is somehow related, although the cause is not known.

(D) The destruction of the Fremont happened in the same manner in which the Anasazi disappeared.

7 The word "demise" in the passage is closest in meaning to

    (A) overtone
    (B) affiliation
    (C) bevy
    (D) fall

8 **Directions**: An introductory sentence for a brief summary of the passage is provided below. Complete the summary by selecting the THREE answer choices that express the most important ideas in the passage. Some sentences do not belong in the summary because they express ideas that are not presented in the passage or are minor ideas in the passage. **This question is worth 2 points.**

> Drag your answer choices to the spaces where they belong. To remove an answer choice, click on it. To review the passage, click on **View Text**.

The Fremont in Utah were a distinct group which developed independent of other cultures.

- ●
- ●
- ●

Answer Choices

(A) While a number of communities were widely distributed, they all had lots of cultural traits in common.

(B) They had some relations with the Anasazi as can be seen in their constructions and farming.

(C) They set up many villages and adapted to a wide variety of environments.

(D) They exhausted all the game in the area with excessive hunting and had to abandon their cities.

(E) They are best known for their carvings which showed unusually shaped people.

(F) Not enough information has remained to accurately account for why their civilization ended.

정답 및 해석 p.389

CH 01
CH 02
CH 03
CH 04
CH 05
CH 06
CH 07
CH 08
CH 09
Hackers TOEFL Reading

1   Increasing demographic pressure and environmental concerns have been the impetus for renewed research into feasible alternative energies which can power society into the 21st century. Unlike conventional fossil fuels, water is an abundant, clean, renewable source of power that many believe holds great promise. ²Although large-scale, turbine-driven hydroelectric dams are a staple of industrialized societies, their social and ecological fallout has resulted in detractors effectively blocking the construction of new ones in some countries, and delaying them in others. However, their turbine-driven technologies offer tantalizing possibilities for environmentally conscious aspirants interested in modifying them harmlessly.

2   Currently, there are approximately 40,000 big hydroelectric dams worldwide that supply 20 percent of global power needs. These accumulate water in a reservoir that gets channeled downward into a substation, the force of which rotates turbines that generate electricity. ³As the amount of extractable energy is directly proportional to the distance between reservoir and substation, it is therefore prudent to build towering dams that hold tremendous amounts of water. This means that enormous swaths of acreage must be submerged. Over the past century, this has necessitated the forcible relocation of millions of people from their ancestral lands and cultural attachments, a diaspora that no amount of compensation may ever replace. Additionally, man-made saturation wipes out all land flora resulting in the simultaneous decomposition of massive amounts of biomass. This mass extinction also precipitates the release of toxic levels of mercury previously kept inert in rocks into the water, bringing about a lethal result to many fish species. As these problems are inevitable with the wholesale flooding of inhabitable lands, environmental researchers have turned their attention toward ocean-based methods of turbine rotation, predominantly via its tides and waves.

3   The prevalent tidal harnessing innovation is the Ebb Generator, which erects a dam, known as a barrage, across an estuary, with sluice gates fitted with turbines that allow the basin to fill on the incoming high tides and to exit on the outgoing one, producing energy each way. The largest such system, the La Rance plant in France, is capable of generating 240 megawatts daily and accounts for 10 percent of France's annual hydroelectric power production, although its environmental ramifications are a cause for concern. ⁶Because estuaries often have a high volume of sediments moving through them to the sea, the introduction of a barrage reduces their dispersal and accumulates concentrations of pollutants within the basin, leading to increased bacteria growth. Further, when barrage gates are closed, fish attempt to pass through turbines. Even the most fish-friendly turbine design has a mortality-per-pass rate of approximately 15 percent, a devastating figure for local species that traverse nearby on a daily basis.

4   Eliminating these altogether by working instead with the power of waves has therefore drawn attention from speculative environmentalists, who also tout the fact that waves can be exploited in more locations, with coastal regions such as the UK possibly able to churn out as much as 5 percent of its power requirements from this source. ⁷Current wave

energy systems place objects on the water's surface and yield power by rising and falling with the motion of the surf as an oscillating action within their internal mechanism pivots a turbine that can send electricity through an undersea cable to a power station on the shore. More commonly, they feature a column that looks like a chimney which stands on the seabed and admits waves through an opening near its base. In the latter, as breakers rise and fall, so does the water inside the column. When the water level rises, air is forced up and out through a turbine, which spins and drives the generator. As it falls again, air is sucked back in from the atmosphere to fill the resulting vacuum and once again the generator is activated. The development of prototypes using these methods has been stunted by their high cost and the need of wave technologies to be protected from the pounding surf and saltwater corrosion. Proponents argue that if society truly values the environmental benefits of such benevolent undertakings, huge initial investments are certainly worthwhile, even if they portend only vague returns at some undefined point in the future.

1 The word "impetus" in the passage is closest in meaning to

(A) result
(B) stimulus
(C) scent
(D) verge

2 Which of the sentences below best expresses the essential information in the highlighted sentence in the passage? *Incorrect* choices change the meaning in important ways or leave out essential information.

(A) The diverse problems associated with dams keep new ones from being built despite reliance on dams in industrialized societies.

(B) Social and ecological concerns have hampered the construction of new hydroelectric dams in a lot of countries.

(C) Large-scale dams are vital in industrialized countries, but their construction has been delayed in other countries.

(D) Industrialized societies have reduced their dependence on hydroelectric dams because of the social and ecological ramifications.

3 Which of the sentences below best expresses the essential information in the highlighted sentence in the passage? *Incorrect* choices change the meaning in important ways or leave out essential information.

(A) Large dams are needed because of the relationship between available energy and their holding capacity for water.

(B) The distance of reservoirs and substations is a point to be considered in a ground plan for a hydropower plant.

(C) Since efficiency tends to be affected by the scale of the dam, it is wise to build dams retaining large amounts of water.

(D) The construction of lofty dams is efficient since when water falls a greater distance, more power is generated.

CH 01
CH 02
CH 03
CH 04
CH 05
CH 06
CH 07
CH 08
CH 09

Hackers TOEFL Reading

4 The word "simultaneous" in the passage is closest in meaning to

(A) improvident
(B) ancient
(C) synchronous
(D) vigorous

5 The word "wholesale" in the passage is closest in meaning to

(A) unwonted
(B) worldly
(C) indiscriminate
(D) voluble

6 Which of the sentences below best expresses the essential information in the highlighted sentence in the passage? *Incorrect* choices change the meaning in important ways or leave out essential information.

(A) A barrage stimulates bacteria development by increasing contaminants that prevent soil deposits in tidal river areas from spreading out the ocean.

(B) When the volume of sediments in the estuaries grows, the amount of contaminants increases, resulting in the proliferation of bacteria.

(C) Increased bacteria levels resulting from the buildup of pollutants are often found in estuaries with dams, as these stunt the dispersion of sediments.

(D) Due to their high level of bacteria-causing pollutants, estuaries with a great deal of sediments are usually not suitable locations for a barrage.

7 Which of the sentences below best expresses the essential information in the highlighted sentence in the passage? *Incorrect* choices change the meaning in important ways or leave out essential information.

(A) Oscillation of the objects on the water surface produces power to rotate a turbine connected to a power station, which in turn transforms it into electricity.

(B) Electricity is generated in wave systems with the movement of buoyant objects by the fluctuation of the waves, being sent to the shore station via a cable.

(C) Wave energy systems make use of turbines that receive their power by way of an undersea cable attached to a generating station.

(D) Wave energy is generated by the movement of a turbine in a device that is placed close to the shore and is affected by the motion of waves.

8 The word "stunted" in the passage is closest in meaning to

(A) hampered
(B) incited
(C) jostled
(D) manipulated

9 **Directions**: An introductory sentence for a brief summary of the passage is provided below. Complete the summary by selecting the THREE answer choices that express the most important ideas in the passage. Some sentences do not belong in the summary because they express ideas that are not presented in the passage or are minor ideas in the passage. **This question is worth 2 points.**

> Drag your answer choices to the spaces where they belong. To remove an answer choice, click on it. To review the passage, click on **View Text**.

Water has long been used to generate electricity and newer hydroelectric systems are being tested.

- ●
- ●
- ●

Answer Choices

(A) Waves are substantially usable source of power with their motion of rising and falling.

(B) The system which uses the force of tidal currents to turn turbines as they come in and out is in operation.

(C) Because of the high cost of maintenance, few wave energy models have been performed in the open sea.

(D) When the lands near dams are flooded, the entire ecosystem is destroyed due to increased levels of mercury.

(E) The system most commonly used now is the Ebb Generator which has a minimal impact on the environment.

(F) Traditional hydroelectric systems stored water in dams and then directed it toward a lower substation.

정답 및 해설 p.391

CH 01
CH 02
CH 03
CH 04
CH 05
CH 06
CH 07
CH 08
CH 09

Hackers TOEFL Reading

1   In the early 19ᵗʰ century, America consisted of eighteen states, thirteen of which lay to the east of the Appalachian Mountains along the coast, while on the other side were several territories surrounding the Great Lakes that were rich in timber, minerals, and fertile farmland. ¹For coastal settlers, the ocean provided convenient access to sources of supplies and markets for their products, but for those west of the mountains, wagon haulage over onerous tracts was their only means of connection to the Atlantic.

2   When New York Governor DeWitt Clinton proposed linking the upper Hudson River (a tributary of the Atlantic) with the eastern shore of Lake Erie via the Mohawk River valley by way of a canal that could pass through a gap in the mountains, he was met with opposition from skeptics who were unconvinced that the economic burden required to build the complicated engineering undertaking would proportionally benefit the region. ²Besides, because the strip of land between Lake Erie and the Mohawk River rises up almost 600 feet(183 meters), and canal technology of the time could only manage a change of up to 12 feet(3.5 meters), safe passage would require the implementation of 84 separate canal locks, engineered contraptions that enable a boat to pass a section of the canal at one water level to another section at a different water level, but do not allow water to flood from the higher elevation into the lower. In addition, the construction would need to erect 18 aqueducts, one more than 800 feet long, to redirect stream flowage and a 900-foot dam to restructure the course of the river.

3   In 1817 Clinton convinced the state legislature to authorize the expenditure of $7 million for what was to become the Erie Canal, the most successful public works project of the era that generated an enormous series of social and economic changes and made New York the primary port city in the United States. Upon opening eight years later, the canal had an immediate impact on the local area and beyond. Clinton's prophecy of a trade explosion became a reality as freight rates from Buffalo to New York — $10 per ton, compared with $100 per ton by road — attracted a massive amount of business. Because flatboats could haul as much as 50 tons of freight from point to point in less than six days, the quantity and variety of merchandise being brought to market skyrocketed, while at the same time prices dropped dramatically, with the consequences being felt all across America. For instance, by 1827, wheat from central New York State could be bought for less in Savannah, Georgia, than that grown in Georgia's own interior. ⁵Nationwide demand for products from the state became so high that within a decade, New York had become the busiest port in America, with thousands of boats coming in and out daily, moving tonnages greater than those of Boston, Baltimore, and New Orleans combined.

4   New York City's population surged while Rochester, Buffalo, and a plethora of other industrial boom towns emerged along the canal route. The production and consumption of goods in each of these places rose as the populations did, increasing canal traffic. An increasing number of boats also headed west to the Great Lakes region, taking with them a wave of New England emigrants and European immigrants lured by the expanses of prolific and inexpensive land in the area. Within three decades of the canal's opening, the Midwest

had become the breadbasket of America, as wheat production expanded exponentially, from 14 thousand bushels to eight million bushels. [7]While canal traffic historically flowed to the west, the current changed once the Great Lakes region established itself as the heart of national agriculture, and by the middle of the 19th century, the majority of trade along the canal headed east with the tonnage of staples more than doubling.

5   From New York, huge amounts of commodities were shipped to Europe, the West Indies, and down along the domestic coast. The demand for the export and import of commodities grew substantially and spurred barge manufacturers to develop faster boats capable of taking on larger hauls, a change that forced the state to re-examine the Erie Canal in 1918. Original locks were too narrow to support the passage of wider flatboats, and more importantly, businesses were insisting that smaller rivers which were previously unutilized be dredged for access to shorten the transportation time. The New York Barge Canal, a new system incorporating parts of the Erie Canal, was completed soon after and remained in operation until the mid-1950s when massive road infrastructures and the introduction of long-haul trucks took over the continental shipping burden.

1   Which of the sentences below best expresses the essential information in the highlighted sentence in the passage? *Incorrect* choices change the meaning in important ways or leave out essential information.

(A) Dwellers near the seashore were favored with the Atlantic Ocean as compared with others in the west who needed the additional transportation to get to the seaside.

(B) People on the eastern seaboard used the sea to trade goods whereas the inhabitants in the west of the Appalachian Mountains relied on wagons to reach the Atlantic.

(C) Those inhabiting the regions close to the coast had a significant advantage over people who lived further inland since they could ship via the ocean.

(D) Since those living on the western side of the Appalachian Mountains did not have access to ocean routes, they employed wagons for transport of the products.

2   Which of the sentences below best expresses the essential information in the highlighted sentence in the passage? *Incorrect* choices change the meaning in important ways or leave out essential information.

(A) The construction of the canal depended upon the use of a lot of canal locks which raised the water level in one section to match the level in another.

(B) In order to allow the safe passage of ships through the canal, engineers were forced to develop new technology that would prevent the canal locks from being flooded.

(C) Due to the great difference in the height of the two bodies of water and the technological limitations to deal with it, numerous canal locks would be needed.

(D) The topographical conditions of the proposed canal location pushed the boundaries of existing canal technology and presented significant engineering challenges.

CH 01
CH 02
CH 03
CH 04
CH 05
CH 06
CH 07
CH 08
CH 09
Hackers TOEFL Reading

3 The word "primary" in the passage is closest in meaning to

(A) preeminent
(B) excellent
(C) imminent
(D) negligent

4 The word "consequences" in the passage is closest in meaning to

(A) dimensions
(B) estimations
(C) confrontations
(D) ramifications

5 Which of the sentences below best expresses the essential information in the highlighted sentence in the passage? *Incorrect* choices change the meaning in important ways or leave out essential information.

(A) As products from New York became the most popular, a large number of boats shipped its products all over the country.

(B) The economic impact of the Erie Canal was so huge that New York became the outstanding port city in America.

(C) The vast quantities of ships that moved through the New York port enabled it to meet the nation's demand for new products.

(D) New York grew to have the greatest volume of river traffic in America because of increased needs for its goods.

6 The word "prolific" in the passage is closest in meaning to

(A) barren
(B) abundant
(C) arable
(D) distant

7 Which of the sentences below best expresses the essential information in the highlighted sentence in the passage? *Incorrect* choices change the meaning in important ways or leave out essential information.

(A) The agricultural importance of the Great Lakes region in the mid 1800s brought about a drastic increment in the amount of canal traffic heading east.

(B) The need to convey agricultural products from the Great Lakes region led to the doubling of the tonnage of goods being shipped on the canal.

(C) Whereas the flow of canal traffic was traditionally from the east to the west, the trend was reversed with the increase in farm production of the Great Lakes area.

(D) The majority of canal traffic was composed of eastward bound trade once the land around the Great Lakes became an important agricultural area.

8 The word "spurred" in the passage is closest in meaning to

(A) allowed
(B) enabled
(C) stimulated
(D) invited

9 **Directions**: An introductory sentence for a brief summary of the passage is provided below. Complete the summary by selecting the THREE answer choices that express the most important ideas in the passage. Some sentences do not belong in the summary because they express ideas that are not presented in the passage or are minor ideas in the passage. **This question is worth 2 points.**

> Drag your answer choices to the spaces where they belong. To remove an answer choice, click on it. To review the passage, click on **View Text**.

The construction of the Erie Canal played a significant role in economic growth for the whole country.

-
-
-

Answer Choices

(A) The rise and growth of New York as a commercial center was a direct result of its shipping status.

(B) People living in the areas around the Great Lakes received their supplies from the states near the Atlantic coast.

(C) Many areas along the canal underwent an increase in population and trade.

(D) The construction of the canal was initially obstructed because of the unimaginable costs and technological constraints.

(E) The amount of goods sent to the Great Lakes decreased rapidly as the territories became self-sufficient.

(F) Clinton urged New York city to expand public money for the canal project.

정답 및 해석 p.393

토플 빈출어휘 정리 노트

Chapter 01에 수록된 어휘들을 빈출도 순으로 정리했습니다. 음성파일을 들으며 꼭 암기하세요.

토플 최빈출어휘 [★★★]

☐ be considered to ~으로 여겨지다

☐ capture [kǽptʃər] 붙잡다 (=seize)

☐ assume [əsúːm] 가정하다 (=suppose)

☐ substantial [səbstǽnʃəl] 상당한 (=significant)

☐ key [kiː] 필수적인 (=essential)

☐ portray [pɔːrtréi] 묘사하다 (=depict)

☐ circumstance [sə́ːrkəmstæns] 상황 (=situation)

☐ demonstrate [démənstrèit] 보여주다 (=exhibit)

☐ intricate [íntrikət] 복잡한 (=complex)

☐ dominate [dámənèit] 압도하다 (=control)

☐ manifestation [mæ̀nəfestéiʃən] 표명 (=demonstration)

☐ ensue [insúː] 결과로서 일어나다 (=follow)

☐ encourage [inkə́ːridʒ] 촉진시키다 (=promote)

☐ duplicate [djúːplikeit] 복제하다 (=reproduce)

☐ retain [ritéin] 유지하다 (=preserve)

☐ application [æ̀pləkéiʃən] 적용

☐ boast [boust] 자랑하다 (=display)

☐ be attributed to 기인하다

☐ erect [irékt] 세우다 (=build)

☐ intermittently [ìntərmítntli] 간헐적으로 (=from time to time)

☐ overall [óuvərɔ̀ːl] 전반적인 (=total)

☐ conspicuous [kənspíkjuəs] 괄목할만한 (=salient)

☐ noticeable [nóutisəbl] 현저한 (=marked)

☐ apart from 제외하고 (=besides)

☐ contract [kəntrǽkt] 수축하다

☐ cease [siːs] 멈추다 (=stop)

☐ remnant [rémnənt] 잔재 (=remain)

☐ excavate [ékskəvèit] 발굴하다 (=dig out)

☐ depict [dipíkt] 나타내다 (=portray)

☐ haphazard [hæphǽzərd] 우연의 (=random)

☐ relic [rélik] 유물 (=remains)

☐ demise [dimáiz] 소멸 (=fall)

☐ impetus [ímpətəs] 자극 (=stimulus)

☐ tantalizing [tǽntəlàiziŋ] 매력적인 (=tempting)

☐ tremendous [triméndəs] 엄청난 (=huge)

☐ saturation [sæ̀tʃəréiʃən] 포화

☐ simultaneous [sàiməltéiniəs] 동시적인 (=synchronous)

☐ wholesale [hóulsèil] 상대를 가리지 않는 (=indiscriminate)

☐ mortality [mɔːrtǽləti] 사망률

☐ stunted [stʌ́ntid] 발전이 더디어진 (=hampered)

☐ enormous [inɔ́ːrməs] 엄청난 (=extremely large)

☐ primary [práimeri] 가장 중요한

☐ consequence [kánsəkwèns] 결과 (=ramification)

☐ prolific [prəlífik] 풍부한 (=abundant)

☐ spur [spəːr] 촉진하다 (=stimulate)

토플 빈출어휘 [★★]

☐ reutilize [riːjúːtəlàiz] 재사용하다

☐ frugal [frúːgəl] 절약하는 (=thrifty)

☐ mostly [móustli] 대부분 (=mainly)

☐ convenient [kənvíːnjənt] 편리한 (=handy)

☐ insufficiently [ìnsəfíʃəntli] 불충분하게

☐ sedentary [sédntèri] 정착성의 (=stationary)

☐ appealing [əpíːliŋ] 매력적인 (=desirable)

☐ strict [strikt] 엄격한 (=rigid)

☐ friendly [fréndli] 친밀한 (=favorable)

☐ implication [ìmplikéiʃən] 영향

☐ longevity [lɑːndʒévəti] 수명

☐ represent [rèprizént] 나타내다

☐ demand [dimǽnd] 수요 (=requirement)

☐ perceive [pərsíːv] 인지하다 (=discern)

☐ respond [rispánd] 대응하다

☐ compare [kəmpɛ́ər] 비교하다

☐ invent [invént] 발명하다 (=devise)

☐ accidentally [æ̀ksədéntəli] 우연히 (=incidentally)

☐ profitability [prɑ́ːfitəbiləti] 수익성

☐ range [reindʒ] 범위 (=extent)

☐ practical [prǽktikəl] 실용적인 (=pragmatic)

☐ allocate [ǽləkeit] 배치시키다

*해커스 동영상강의 포털 해커스인강(HackersIngang.com)에서 '토플 빈출어휘 정리 노트' 음성파일을 무료로 다운로드할 수 있습니다.

☐ underlying [ʌ́ndərlàiiŋ] 근본적인 (=intrinsic)

☐ symbolize [símbəlàiz] 상징하다

☐ commence [kəméns] 시작하다 (=launch)

☐ incredible [inkrédəbl] 엄청난 (=astonishing)

☐ exclude [iksklú:d] 제외하다

☐ lack [læk] 없음

☐ separate [sépərèit] 떼어놓다 (=split)

☐ quickly [kwíkli] 빠르게 (=swiftly)

☐ territory [térətɔ̀:ri] 지역 (=realm)

☐ detect [ditékt] 감지하다

☐ emission [imíʃən] 방출

☐ align [əláin] 정렬하다 (=order)

☐ surrender [səréndər] 항복

☐ irrigation [ìrəgéiʃən] 관개

☐ fragility [frədʒíləti] 부서지기 쉬움

☐ scant [skænt] 빈약한 (=thin)

☐ creative [kriéitiv] 창의적인 (=ingenious)

☐ compensation [kàmpənséiʃən] 보상

☐ wipe out 몰살하다

☐ ramification [ræ̀məfikéiʃən] 영향

☐ proportionally [prəpɔ́:rʃənli] 비례하여

☐ convince [kənvíns] 설득시키다

☐ immediate [imí:diət] 즉각적인 (=instantaneous)

토플 기출어휘 [★]

☐ governor [gʌ́vərnər] 총독

☐ artificial [ɑ̀:rtəfíʃəl] 인공의

☐ indulgent [indʌ́ldʒənt] 견딜만한

☐ downfall [dáunfɔ̀:l] 몰락

☐ advantageous [æ̀dvəntéidʒəs] 유리한

☐ experiment [ikspérəmənt] 실험

☐ lamentable [lǽməntəbl] 유감스러운 (=deplorable)

☐ expeditious [èkspədíʃəs] 효율적인

☐ frequently [frí:kwəntli] 자주 (=chronically)

☐ ensure [inʃúər] 보장하다

☐ occasion [əkéiʒən] 의식

☐ rite [rait] 의식

☐ cohesion [kouhí:ʒən] 결속

☐ classification [klæ̀səfikéiʃən] 분류

☐ novelty [návəlti] 참신

☐ extinct [ikstíŋkt] 멸종된

☐ possess [pəzés] 지니다 (=own)

☐ intertwine [íntərtwàin] 밀접하게 연관시키다

☐ influx [ínflʌks] 유입 (=inundation)

☐ downturn [dáuntə̀:rn] 침체

☐ visual [víʒuəl] 시각의

☐ auditory [ɔ́:dətɔ̀:ri] 청각의

☐ marginally [má:rdʒinli] 약간

☐ nomadic [noumǽdik] 유목의

☐ itinerant [aitínərənt] 이동하는

☐ offshoot [ɔ́:fʃù:t] 분파

☐ disparate [díspərət] 이종의

☐ precursor [pri:kɔ́:rsər] 선조

☐ discriminate [diskrímənèit] 구별하다

☐ inexplicably [inéksplikəbli] 불가사의하게

☐ precipitation [prisìpətéiʃən] 강우량

☐ displace [displéis] 쫓아내다

☐ demographic [dèməgrǽfik] 인구학의

☐ fallout [fɔ́:làut] 부작용

☐ attachment [ətǽtʃmənt] 애착

☐ decomposition [di:kàmpəzíʃən] 변질

☐ corrosion [kəróuʒən] 부식

☐ benevolent [bənévələnt] 선의의

☐ portend [pɔːrténd] 미리 알다

☐ onerous [ónərəs] 성가신

☐ undertaking [ʌ̀ndərtéikiŋ] 사업

☐ aqueduct [ǽkwədʌ̀kt] 수로

☐ prophecy [práfəsi] 예언

☐ plethora [pléθərə] 과다

☐ exponentially [èksponénʃəli] 기하급수적으로

CH 01
CH 02
CH 03
CH 04
CH 05
CH 06
CH 07
CH 08
CH 09

Hackers TOEFL Reading

Chapter 02
Fact & Negative Fact

OVERVIEW

Fact & Negative Fact 문제는 지문에 명시적으로 주어진 세부 정보를 묻는 질문에 대해 가장 정확하게 답을 한 것을 선택하는 유형이다. Fact 문제는 지문의 내용과 일치하는 것을, Negative Fact 문제는 지문의 내용과 일치하지 않거나 지문에 언급되지 않은 것을 답으로 선택한다. 이때 자신의 배경 지식에 근거하지 않고 지문을 통해 알 수 있는 사실에만 근거해서 보기가 사실인지 아닌지를 판단해야 한다.

Fact & Negative Fact 문제를 해결하기 위해서는, 먼저 긴 지문에서 문제 해결에 필요한 정보를 제대로 찾아내는 scanning 기술이 필요하다. 또한, 찾은 정보가 보기에 제대로 paraphrase되어 있는지 여부를 확인하는 연습이 필요하다.

Fact & Negative Fact 문제는 보통 한 지문당 2~5개가 출제된다.

TYPES OF QUESTIONS

단락 번호가 문제에 함께 제시되며 화면에 해당 단락이 [➡] 표시로 나타나고 4개의 보기가 주어진다. 종종 단락이 제시되지 않고 전체 지문의 내용을 종합적으로 판단해서 세부 정보의 사실 여부를 파악해야 하는 문제도 출제된다.

Fact & Negative Fact 문제의 전형적인 질문 유형은 아래와 같다.

Fact
- According to paragraph #[the passage], which of the following is true of ____?
- According to paragraph #[the passage], what/how/why ____?
- In paragraph #, the author states that
- Paragraph # suggests/mentions/supports which of the following ____?
- Select the **TWO** answer choices that are ____. To receive credit, you must select **TWO** answers.

Negative Fact
- All of the following are mentioned in paragraph # EXCEPT
- According to the passage, which of the following is NOT true of ____?

HACKERS **STRATEGY**

CH 01
CH 02
CH 03
CH 04
CH 05
CH 06
CH 07
CH 08
CH 09
Hackers TOEFL Reading

전략 1   문제의 keyword가 지문의 어디에 나왔는지 scanning을 통해 찾는다.

Fact & Negative Fact 문제를 풀 때는 먼저 문제에서 묻고 있는 핵심이 무엇인지를 파악한 후, 그 문제 해결의 clue가 되는 keyword가 언급된 부분을 지문에서 빠르게 찾아내야 한다.

● **Scanning하여 정보 확인하기**

지문을 빠르게 훑어보며 문제의 keyword가 언급된 부분을 찾은 뒤 해당 정보를 확인한다.

Ex **Mule deer** are active primarily in mornings, evenings and moonlit nights. This **inactivity during the heat of the day** is **a behavioral adaptation to the desert environment that conserves water and keeps the body temperature** within livable limits. Characteristically, mule deer bed down in a cool, secluded place. The mature buck seems to prefer rocky ridges for bedding grounds, while the doe and fawn are more likely to bed down in the open.

Q: According to the passage, **mule deer** are **inactive in the middle of the day in order to**

➡ 먼저 문제의 keyword인 mule deer, inactive in the middle of the day를 지문에서 찾는다. 이때 in the middle of the day는 지문의 during the heat of the day를 paraphrase한 것이다. 그리고 문제에서 묻고 있는 정보는 in order to에서 알 수 있듯이 mule deer가 in the middle of the day에 inactive한 이유이므로 a behavioral adaptation ~ the body temperature라는 것을 알 수 있다.

TIP 1. 토플은 대부분 지문에 언급된 순서대로 문제가 나오기 때문에 앞 문제의 clue 다음 부분부터 scanning을 하면 된다.

2. Scanning할 때 고유명사나 숫자를 이용하면 clue를 훨씬 쉽게 찾을 수 있다.
   Which of the following is mentioned as a characteristic of a postcard before 1898?
   핵심어 characteristic of a postcard와 함께 숫자 1898이 언급된 부분을 찾는다.

해석 p.396

지문에서 확인한 정보를 제대로 paraphrase한 보기를 고른다.

지문에서 정보를 확인한 후에는 그 정보를 제대로 표현하고 있는 보기를 고르면 된다. 다만 보기에는 그 정보가 그대로 나오지 않고 paraphrase되어 나오기 때문에 제대로 paraphrase되어 있는지 확인해야 한다.

Ex The ozone depletion process begins when CFCs and other ozone-depleting substances(ODS) leak from equipment. Winds efficiently mix the troposphere and evenly distribute the gases. Since **CFCs are extremely stable**, they do **not even dissolve in rain**. After a period of several years, ODS molecules reach the stratosphere and are broken apart by strong UV(ultraviolet) light.

Q: According to the passage, **CFCs** are **not soluble in water because**

A: they are fixed to a very great degree

➡ 먼저 문제의 keyword인 CFCs, not soluble in water를 지문에서 찾는다. 이때 not soluble in water는 지문의 not even dissolve in rain이 paraphrase된 것이다. 문제에서 묻고 있는 정보는 because에서 알 수 있듯이 not soluble in water인 이유이므로 CFCs are extremely stable이라는 것을 알 수 있다.

지문의 정보를 제대로 paraphrase한 보기 찾기

확인한 정보	Paraphrase한 보기
CFCs are extremely stable	they are fixed to a very great degree

지문의 **extremely stable**이 보기에서는 **fixed to a very great degree**로 바뀌어 쓰여 있다.

Ex If **aquatic life**, which is susceptible to DDT, **is exposed to the chemical, its population would be dramatically reduced**. The entire food chain would be altered, and omnivores and carnivores that consume microorganisms and their predators would in turn suffer from lack of resources.

Q: According to the passage, **when DDT is given**, DDT-sensitive **aquatic life**

A: will become much smaller in number

➡ 먼저 문제의 keyword인 DDT is given, aquatic life를 지문에서 찾는다. 이때 DDT is given은 지문의 is exposed to the chemical이 paraphrase된 것이다. 문제에서 묻고 있는 정보는 when에서 알 수 있듯이 DDT is given일 때의 상황인 것이므로 its population would be dramatically reduced라는 것을 알 수 있다.

지문의 정보를 제대로 paraphrase한 보기 찾기

확인한 정보	Paraphrase한 보기
its population would be dramatically reduced	will become much smaller in number

지문의 **its population would be dramatically reduced**가 보기에서는 **will become much smaller in number**로 바뀌어 쓰여 있다.

전략 3 보기 중 오답을 확인한다.

최종적으로 나머지 보기들을 검토하여 오답임을 확인한다. Fact의 오답은 주로 지문의 내용과 상반되거나 지문에 언급되지 않은 경우에 해당한다. 단, 이러한 오답이 Negative Fact 문제에서는 반대로 정답이 된다.

Ex The population growth rate began to slow in the late 1980s and has continually decreased since then. Although the population growth rate is declining, the population in the world still increases by between 1.3–1.9 percent per year, according to statistics claimed by the United Nations. A number of factors have contributed to the increase in population in the world, dating all the way back to ancient times when the first agricultural communities arose, creating a capability of sustaining higher numbers of people.

The next major force came in the 18th century when the Industrial Revolution pushed up living standards, resulting in a drop in the famines and epidemics that had plagued humanity from the 14th to 17th centuries, especially in Europe. The trend continued after World War II, as the populations in developing countries showed rise. Such nations lacked the birth control awareness required to maintain a balanced birth rate. Despite high death rates and rather short life expectancies in comparison with **developed countries**, babies were being produced faster than people who were dying. **Those high populations were supported economically with food and medical aid from developed nations wanting to lay their stakes for future prospects.**

Q: According to paragraph 2, which of the following is true of **developed countries**?

A: They took a positive attitude toward the high population growth in developing countries. (○)

➡ 문제의 keyword인 developed countries가 언급된 부분을 찾아, 그 부분의 정보를 제대로 표현하고 있는 보기를 고른다. 정답 보기에서는 지문의 high populations were supported ~ prospects가 took a positive attitude로 paraphrase되어 있다.

지문의 내용과 상반된 오답

Right after World War II, the number of people who passed away was larger than that of people who were born in developing countries. (×)

지문의 babies were being produced faster than people who were dying의 내용과 상반된 오답이다.

지문에 언급되지 않은 오답

European countries from the 14th to 17th centuries had taken all possible measures to counteract starvation and epidemics. (×)

지문의 the Industrial Revolution pushed up living standards, resulting in a drop in the famines and epidemics that had plagued humanity from the 14th to 17th centuries, especially in Europe에 언급되지 않은 오답이다.

HACKERS STRATEGY **APPLICATION**

Fact Question

About one billion years ago, a fracture in the earth running from what is now Oklahoma to Lake Superior generated volcanic activity that almost split North America. Over a period of 20 million years, lava intermittently flowed from the fracture. This geomorphic age created mountains covering the regions now known as northern Wisconsin and Minnesota, and the Laurentian mountains were formed in eastern Canada. Over time these mountains eroded while occasional volcanic activity continued. Molten magma below the highlands of what is now Lake Superior spewed out to its sides, causing the highlands to sink and form a mammoth rock basin that would one day hold Lake Superior. Eventually the fracture stabilized and, over time, the rock tilted down from north to south.

1. According to the passage, the formation of Laurentian mountains is the result of the period

   (A) when volcanoes erupted due to a crevice within North America
   (B) when North America was nearly split by a severe earthquake
   (C) when colossal rock beds across North America clustered together
   (D) when the highlands across North America subsided greatly

Negative Fact Question

Jane Addams, a member of a well-to-do, cultured family, was so distressed about the misery of the poor that she left home to spend her life in the slums of Chicago. In 1889 she established a "settlement house" there, called Hull House, where she initiated many humanitarian projects. Among these were hot-lunch service for factory workers, day-care centers for little children, and free classes for young people and adults. Immigrants came to Hull House to get advice and help, as well as to learn. Addams also was active in fighting against the use of child labor and worked for woman's suffrage. Not everyone appreciated the work of Jane Addams, though. Indeed some disapproved of what they considered her meddling in other people's affairs. Nevertheless, she exerted great influence on the development of social work in the United States and also in other parts of the world. She promoted the idea of responsibility for the welfare of the underprivileged, and her programs were widely adopted. Settlement houses modeled on Hull House were founded in many poor neighborhoods to help children and adults to make their lives more meaningful. In recognition of her contributions to society, Jane Addams was awarded the Nobel Peace Prize in 1931.

2. According to the passage, which of the following is NOT true of Jane Addams?

   (A) She won a Nobel Prize for Peace in acknowledgment of her devotion to society.
   (B) She was held in great respect by every single person.
   (C) She extended education to people without compensation.
   (D) She was engrossed in improving the quality of children and women's life.

해석 p.396

CH 01

CH 02

CH 03

CH 04

CH 05

CH 06

CH 07

CH 08

CH 09

Hackers TOEFL Reading

1 전략 1 적용 문제의 keyword인 formation of Laurentian mountains와 result of the period를 지문에서 찾는다. 이때 문제의 formation은 지문의 formed가 paraphrase된 것이다.

정보 확인하기

a fracture ~ generated volcanic activity, This geomorphic age created ~

전략 2 적용

확인한 정보	Paraphrase한 보기
a fracture ~ generated volcanic activity	when volcanoes erupted due to a crevice within North America

위 지문에서 확인한 정보의 a fracture가 보기에서는 a crevice로, generated volcanic activity가 volcanoes erupted로 paraphrase되어 있다.

전략 3 적용 (B) 지진에 관한 내용은 지문에 언급되지 않았다.

(C) 암반이 밀집되어 있었다는 내용은 지문에 언급되지 않았다.

(D) 산악 지대가 가라앉은 것은 산맥이 형성된 후의 일이므로 지문의 내용과 상반된다.

정답 (A)

2 전략 1 적용 문제의 keyword는 Jane Addams인데 지문 전체적으로 Jane Addams가 언급되어 있으므로 보기에서 문제 해결의 단서를 찾아 관련 내용이 지문의 어디에 언급되어 있는지 찾는다.

(A) 단서 Nobel Prize for Peace → 지문 마지막 문장에 Nobel Peace Prize 언급됨

(B) 단서 respect by → 지문 7번째 줄에 appreciated 언급됨

(C) 단서 education → 지문 4번째 줄에 free classes 언급됨

(D) 단서 children and women → 지문 6번째 줄에 child, woman 언급됨

전략 2 적용

확인한 정보	Paraphrase한 보기
(A) ~ her contributions to society, Jane Addams was awarded the Nobel Peace Prize	(A) won a Nobel Prize for Peace in acknowledgment of her devotion to society
(C) free classes for ~	(C) extended education to people without compensation
(D) ~ active in fighting against the use of child labor and worked for woman's suffrage	(D) engrossed in improving the quality of children and women's life

전략 3 적용 (B)는 지문의 7번째 줄의 Not everyone appreciated the work of Jane Addams, though와 상반된 내용이다.

정답 (B)

Read each passage and answer the corresponding question for each.

1 When the Patent Act was passed in 1790, it included a provision requiring that miniature working models must be produced for every new invention. These patent models — unique artifacts of U.S. patent history — were then displayed publicly in the Patent Office. In 1836, the second Patent Act established guidelines for their construction: "The model, not more than 12 inches square, should be neatly made and the name of the inventor should be printed or engraved upon, or affixed to it, in a durable manner." Unfortunately, two separate Patent Office fires destroyed the majority of these models, as well as all records of early U.S. patent history. In 1880, the model requirement was declared impractical and their construction ended.

● Find the sentence that describes the reason why many early patent models do not exist today.

Answer _____

2 Batik is an Indonesian method of textile dyeing that uses wax resistance to create a variety of intricate patterns. The process starts by creating a pattern of dots and lines of wax on the textile using a spouted tool called a canting or a copper stamp referred to as a cap. Next, the material is completely immersed in a dye. The parts of the cloth coated in wax resist the dye. After that, the textile is put into boiling water to remove the wax, and the process can be repeated. This makes it possible for artisans to selectively add different colors and patterns. The more complicated and colorful a piece of batik is, the higher number of times it has undergone the wax-resistance process.

● Find the sentence that indicates the action that allows for the addition of various colors and designs.

Answer _____

VOCABULARY The word ☐ in the passage is closest in meaning to

1	unique	(A) cogent	(B) virtuous	(C) distinct	(D) fetching
	durable	(A) lethal	(B) long-lasting	(C) prevalent	(D) abundant
2	immersed	(A) precluded	(B) intensified	(C) submerged	(D) conciliated

3   Fiber optics technology owes its inception to research conducted in the early twentieth century when physicists discovered and proved that images could be transmitted through bundles of optical fibers. For decades, early studies were typically ignored by scientists until subsequent work was undertaken and discussed in a 1960 article, in which the term *fiber optics* first appeared. Fiber optics relies on *total internal reflection*, which is the complete reflection of light in a dense medium, such as a bundle of fibers, whereby it encounters the medium at a steep angle and propagates through the core. Optical fibers eventually became utilized in applications in telecommunication, computer networking, and remote sensing, and flexible fiber-optic cables helped usher in the information revolution.

● Find the sentence that explains how fiber optics are used in pragmatic ways.

Answer _____

4   Many musicians saw the cultural revolution of the 1960s as an opportunity to interject radical change in their own music. For instance, Miles Davis helped create jazz fusion, a genre that mixed elements from jazz and rock to create a blend of sounds never previously heard or recorded. Yet what he and his peers viewed as progress proved to be controversial. Some critics lauded this synthesis of sounds as an unprecedented musical innovation. However, others, particularly jazz purists, claimed that Davis had gone too far and even abandoned his musical roots in classical jazz for a commercially inspired replacement. While both assessments have their adherents, and jazz fusion subsequently became virtually commercially obsolete, most commentators agree that Miles Davis was one of the greatest jazz artists of all time.

● Find the sentence that suggests a negative view of jazz fusion.

Answer _____

CH 01
CH 02
CH 03
CH 04
CH 05
CH 06
CH 07
CH 08
CH 09
Hackers TOEFL Reading

VOCABULARY   The word [ ] in the passage is closest in meaning to

3	typically	(A) exceedingly	(B) extensively	(C) potentially	(D) ordinarily
	flexible	(A) malleable	(B) discernable	(C) legible	(D) portable
4	innovation	(A) creation	(B) enactment	(C) allegiance	(D) envision
	assessments	(A) attires	(B) evaluations	(C) surmises	(D) blockades

5   When the notion that plants play a crucial role in carbon sequestration first surfaced, environmentalists began to pay close attention to the removal of botanical biomass. They urged governments to not only acknowledge the invaluable role plants have in maintaining healthy ecosystems suitable for life but also to pursue regulations to perpetually protect lands covered by vegetation. Ultimately, however, scientists realized they had to convince political leaders that removing carbon from the atmosphere was economically beneficial. A Harvard University study used a standard social cost measurement of just over $40 per metric ton for carbon damage. It determined that the lands governed by the National Park Service remove approximately 17.5 million metric tons, which amounts to an annual economic savings of around $707 million in averted carbon costs.

- Find the sentence that indicates that sequestering atmospheric carbon generates a favorable economic impact.

Answer _____

6   The first jeweled egg created by Peter Carl Fabergé was made for Russian Tsar Alexander III as an anniversary present to his wife, the Empress Maria. Ultimately, Maria was so pleased with the gift that the Tsar appointed Fabergé to be an official goldsmith to the crown, and he started making one of the dainty pieces every year for the royal family. These eggs became known as the Imperial Eggs, and the designs progressively became more elaborate. Fabergé intended that each egg hold a surprise, such as a royal coach, a rose, or even an elephant. Naturally, each surprise was also made of precious metals and gemstones. However, interest in Fabergé's eggs did not lie solely with the royal family. He also made eggs for private clientele who were quite eager to copy the members of Russia's Imperial court and own one of the popular art objects.

- Find the sentence that claims Fabergé's eggs found their way into the hands of non-royals.

Answer _____

VOCABULARY	The word [ ] in the passage is closest in meaning to

5	surfaced	(A) arose	(B) fraternized	(C) vaporized	(D) feigned
	invaluable	(A) implausible	(B) imaginable	(C) inestimable	(D) impregnable
6	dainty	(A) devoid	(B) exquisite	(C) pious	(D) nauseating
	eager	(A) arduous	(B) nimble	(C) innominate	(D) anxious

If the statement for each passage is correct, mark T, otherwise mark F.

7 During Medieval times, it was fashionable to add illustrations and embellishments to manuscripts. This process was known as illumination, and it both added colorful artistry to books and provided visual aids relevant to the subject matter of the manuscript. A significant technique used in illuminating books was gilding, whereby gold leaf or powder was affixed to the pages to achieve a shimmering effect. Once the gold was applied, it was burnished, and this polishing-through-rubbing process caused the material to shine brilliantly. According to the Italian artist Cennino, the tooth of a dog mounted on a wooden handle was frequently used for this purpose. Artists, usually monks, also added vivid colors that they derived by combining egg whites with ground minerals or dyes from plants, resulting in a form of tempera paint. Illumination became so popular that consumer expectations made it virtually mandatory for all commercially viable printed works.

_____ (A) Illumination was used to help readers understand difficult subject matter.
_____ (B) The technique of burnishing was invented by an Italian artist named Cennino.
_____ (C) Artists incorporated several different natural materials to create the colorful paint they used.
_____ (D) Illuminated works were initially in vogue and became economically unfeasible over time.

8 Porpoises and other marine mammals are better equipped than humans physiologically to dive to considerable depths in the ocean. The blood of these animals has approximately 30 percent higher capacity for oxygen transport and storage than has human blood. They also possess increased stores of respiratory pigment in their muscles which may contribute significantly to their oxygen reserve. The respiratory center in the brain, which regulates breathing movements in all mammals, is driven by carbon dioxide in the surrounding blood. In porpoises and other diving mammals, this center is far less sensitive to carbon dioxide in fluids than in other mammals. Consequently, they can tolerate considerably higher concentrations of carbon dioxide. Moreover, all diving animals, from birds to reptiles to mammals, experience a drastic slowing of the heart rate when diving. In seals, whose normal surface heart rate may be seventy to eighty times a minute, the heart slows to six and ten beats a minute upon diving.

_____ (A) Porpoises and other marine mammals have roughly 30 percent more oxygen than humans.
_____ (B) Heightened levels of respiratory pigment retained in muscles may help porpoises save oxygen.
_____ (C) Due to decreased responsiveness of their respiratory center to carbon dioxide, porpoises can withstand higher levels of it.
_____ (D) When porpoises venture into lower waters, their heart rate slows down.

| VOCABULARY | The word ____ in the passage is closest in meaning to |

		(A)	(B)	(C)	(D)
7	significant	(A) incidental	(B) communicable	(C) important	(D) lethal
8	regulates	(A) fabricates	(B) monitors	(C) peels	(D) purloins
	drastic	(A) void	(B) cardinal	(C) nascent	(D) radical

CH 01
CH 02
CH 03
CH 04
CH 05
CH 06
CH 07
CH 08
CH 09
Hackers TOEFL Reading

9　A windsock is a cloth tube that is shaped like a cone. It is usually attached to a vertical pole, in locations such as airports, and is used for determining both the direction and speed of wind. When the object is exposed to wind, it becomes fully or partially inflated, depending on the strength of a gale. When this happens, the windsock's tip will point, indicating the direction the wind is currently blowing. The speed of wind can be figured out by looking at the sock's angle relative to the pole on which it is hanging. In low winds a windsock will not fully inflate and tends to droop, while strong gales will fill it and force it to fly horizontally. Usually, windsocks are made of a bright orange, nylon material, but some are striped in orange and white so that a more specific wind speed estimate can be determined. Each stripe represents three knots, and velocity is calculated by looking at where the windsock droops.

_____ (A) Windsocks will point to the direction a gale is coming from.

_____ (B) Wind speed is calculated by viewing the angle of a windsock on a pole.

_____ (C) A partly deflated windsock indicates that the strength of a current wind is low.

_____ (D) The bright orange color of windsocks was chosen for its high visibility.

10　The planet Uranus is surrounded by active clouds of gases, and researchers long debated whether the clouds were made up of ammonia (NH_3) or hydrogen sulfide (H_2S). However, they had no way to corroborate either hypothesis; even after a mission to Uranus by the NASA space probe Voyager 2 in 1986, the clouds' chemical composition still could not be confirmed. But through the use of new spectroscopic technology — specifically, the Near-Infrared Field Spectrometer (NIFS) — a team of astronomers was able to gather data that finally solved the mystery. Researchers making observations with the Gemini North telescope in Hawaii took measurements of reflected sunlight from immediately above Uranus's main visible cloud layer, and then inferred the chemical composition by calculating light absorption rates. They determined that the upper atmosphere of Uranus contains high levels of hydrogen sulfide, a compound that has a noxious odor that is reminiscent of that of rotten eggs. The presence of this compound sets Uranus apart from the inner gas planets Saturn and Jupiter, each of which has an atmosphere that is dominated by the presence of ammonia.

_____ (A) The primary purpose of NASA's Voyager 2 mission was to confirm the clouds' chemistry.

_____ (B) Scientists used a telescope to determine the primary gases contained in the upper atmosphere of Uranus.

_____ (C) Hydrogen sulfide levels vary according to their location in the atmosphere.

_____ (D) The high level of ammonia surrounding Saturn and Jupiter distinguishes them from Uranus.

VOCABULARY　The word [　　] in the passage is closest in meaning to

9	exposed	(A) lauded	(B) subjected	(C) concocted	(D) hampered
	indicating	(A) signaling	(B) silhouetting	(C) reversing	(D) rectifying
10	active	(A) animated	(B) infectious	(C) congenital	(D) illiberal
	noxious	(A) elusive	(B) sturdy	(C) detrimental	(D) fickle

11   A replica of the original Statue of Liberty was erected in Paris and inaugurated on July 4, 1889. This quarter-scale copy of the sculpture given by France to America in 1885 was donated to the city by US citizens living in France. It was meant to $\boxed{\text{commemorate}}$ the centennial celebration of the French Revolution. At the base of the figure is a plaque containing the dates of American independence and France's Bastille Day. The statue is situated on a small, artificial island in the Seine River and originally faced east toward the Eiffel Tower, but was moved in 1937 for the World's Fair. Since then, it has looked west in the direction of the original statue in New York. Unlike its 300-foot counterpart in the US, the one in France is just over 70 feet in height, which makes $\boxed{\text{transit}}$ less challenging. In 1998, the statue was taken from Paris to Japan and displayed on a manmade island in Tokyo Bay. It was there for a full year as part of a cultural exchange program between the two nations but has remained in Paris ever since.

_____ (A) A copy of the New York statue was gifted to France from American expatriates living there at the time.

_____ (B) In order to make the Parisian statue face the Eiffel Tower, it was moved during the World's Fair in 1937.

_____ (C) The imitation in Europe is smaller and easier to move than the American version.

_____ (D) While on display in Japan as part of a cultural exchange program, the statue attracted numerous visitors.

12   Contrary to popular opinion, the word "totem" does not denote the ornate wooden poles of the native peoples of northwestern North America; it actually refers to spirit beings. These totems served as means to express the identities of tribes, clans, or families, much like the crests that were used in Europe. Sculptors used a single log to carve each of the totem poles, and traditionally they employed locally collected stones, bones, and shells to craft them. From the 1700s, however, metal implements acquired from European colonists were commonly employed. Before any carving commenced, the logs were debarked and totem creatures were sketched onto the wood using charcoal. Each pole consisted of multiple totems that were carved one on top of the other, with the most important totem to the community, tribe, or family carved at the bottom. Each totem depicted stories that were recounted during celebrations or tribal festivals, throughout which audiences would sit and view the totem poles, which were generally placed $\boxed{\text{upright}}$ in front of tribal lodges, while tribal leaders or elders told historical narratives that explained the totems.

_____ (A) Many people wrongly think the word "totem" refers to objects made of wood.

_____ (B) The natives customarily used indigenous tools prior to obtaining others from settlers.

_____ (C) Totems carved at the bottom of poles had more significance to tribe members.

_____ (D) During festivals, the entire tribe would gather around lodges to hear stories.

VOCABULARY	The word ☐ in the passage is closest in meaning to			
11 commemorate	(A) enfeeble	(B) venerate	(C) thrash	(D) observe
transit	(A) jolt	(B) conveyance	(C) lease	(D) contraband
12 upright	(A) economical	(B) essential	(C) antiseptic	(D) erect

CH 01
CH 02
CH 03
CH 04
CH 05
CH 06
CH 07
CH 08
CH 09
Hackers TOEFL Reading

Read each passage and answer the corresponding questions for each.

13 Sand dunes are closely associated with areas of high $\boxed{\text{aridity}}$, and their formation depends on a steady supply of wind, loose sediment, and some form of obstacle that causes sediment to settle and accumulate. Dune enlargement is accomplished by several interrelated types of erosion: in saltation, medium-sized particles are catapulted into the air and transported horizontally, typically covering a distance of around four times their altitude while "bouncing" along the way. As they violently collide with the surface, they encounter larger particles that are too massive to be moved by wind, dislodge them, and roll them along the ground in a process known as creep. Additionally, bits of sand advance by way of suspension, whereby they are lofted high into the air and form massive dust storms that can completely obscure the distinction between the sky, the horizon, and the earth. Each of these modes of transport contributes to persistent $\boxed{\text{accretion}}$ as the prevailing wind continually propels sediment up the windward side of the dune until the leeward side collapses. The fact that this subsidence often creates a slope of between 30° and 34° supports the $\boxed{\text{assertion}}$ that there is an ideal angle, called the angle of repose, which makes the perpetual expansion of the dune feasible.

1 According to the passage, sediment comes to rest and amasses because of

(A) the lack of a slope
(B) the presence of an impediment
(C) the cessation of wind
(D) the absence of erosive force

2 According to the passage, the claim for the existence of an optimal angle for dune expansion is reinforced by

(A) the reality that dunes typically occur only when certain environmental conditions are met

(B) studies that revealed leeward and windward sides of dunes have different compositions

(C) data that suggests dunes form specifically in areas with consistent prevailing winds

(D) the tendency of the slumping face of dunes to result in a fairly predictable slope

---

VOCABULARY The word $\boxed{}$ in the passage is closest in meaning to

13 aridity	(A) acidity	(B) dryness	(C) abnormity	(D) tentativeness
accretion	(A) demeanor	(B) constituent	(C) accumulation	(D) acme
assertion	(A) claim	(B) continence	(C) treason	(D) turbulence

14 Research conducted by psychologists Margo Gardner and Laurence Steinberg at Temple University clearly demonstrated the power of peer pressure in teenagers. The researchers assessed three groups in the study: teenagers up to 14 years of age, teenagers up to 19 years of age, and adults. For the experiment, participants were tasked with a computer driving simulation. As the simulation progressed, they were faced with a series of yellow lights and had to decide whether or not to drive through them. Doing so earned them points, but at the risk of having an accident with a hidden vehicle. The more risks taken, the greater number of points participants could accumulate, but they would lose points for accidents. The psychologists had each participant perform the simulation twice. The first time, drivers conducted the simulation in a room on their own to see how they would react unobserved. In this case, each group took a comparable number of risks. However, for the second simulation, the researchers placed pairs of individuals from the same age group in rooms together so that they completed the simulation within view of a peer. In those instances, the outcome was markedly different. Members of the 14-and-under group took double the number of risks when paired together than they had on their own, while the group with teens up to age 19 took 50 percent more risks than they had previously. In contrast, the adults showed little change in risk-taking behavior. The study showed that the power of peer conformity amongst young teens is much stronger than for any other age bracket. It furthermore offered evidence that the influence peer pressure has on decision-making lessens with age. Adults feel far less of a need to blindly follow the behavior that they witness in their peers.

1 According to the passage, researchers had participants do the first simulation

- (A) to determine responses to risk-taking when alone
- (B) to figure out how to separate participants into groups
- (C) to study the influence of having others in the room
- (D) to demonstrate how the simulation's point system worked

2 According to the passage, when younger teens were viewed during the simulation

- (A) they were influenced less than the older teenagers
- (B) they had results comparable to other age brackets
- (C) they took twice as many chances as before
- (D) they were 50 percent more likely to take risks

VOCABULARY The word ☐ in the passage is closest in meaning to

14 progressed	(A) visualized	(B) continued	(C) precluded	(D) assessed
conformity	(A) acclamation	(B) respite	(C) pretense	(D) compliance
blindly	(A) courageously	(B) abruptly	(C) recklessly	(D) equivocally

CH 01
CH 02
CH 03
CH 04
CH 05
CH 06
CH 07
CH 08
CH 09

Hackers TOEFL Reading

15 A worker bee flies from flower to flower in search of nectar and pollen. As it lands on a blossom, it automatically picks up pollen. This transfer is aided by bristles on the bee's legs and body, which latch onto the grains of pollen. The pollen is then relocated to other blossoms by the bee, resulting in pollination. In this regard, the humble bee is a vital creature to farmers. Once the worker bee has collected enough nectar and pollen, it returns to its hive. The interior of the hive consists of honeycombs, which are masses of densely arranged hexagonal cells made of beeswax. Bees regurgitate nectar into the cells, where salivary enzymes initiate chemical decomposition of sugars, and subsequent evaporation converts the liquid to honey. Honey is stored as a source of nourishment in the upper part of the hives, while the cells several rows below are reserved for pollen storage. Underneath those are two additional levels of cells used to house the eggs, larvae, and pupae. The first of these layers house the fertilized eggs, which become worker bees, and the second is reserved for unfertilized eggs, which result in drones. The queen bee has her own cell that is generally situated at the lower portion of the honeycomb, though usually not at the very bottom. This overall arrangement rarely varies in natural hives, which typically are anchored to the sides of hollowed trees, caves, or cavities in rocks, keeping them relatively safe from disturbance.

1 According to the passage, the enzymes in the saliva of bees

(A) facilitate the digestion of nectar and pollen
(B) contribute to the structural integrity of the honeycomb
(C) start the process of breaking down sugars
(D) expedite the evaporation of moisture in the honey

2 According to the passage, fertilization of honeybee eggs

(A) is more abundant in nature than in artificial hives
(B) is accomplished by drones and worker bees
(C) occurs near the base of the honeycomb
(D) determines the type of bee they become

VOCABULARY	The word ⬜ in the passage is closest in meaning to			
15 aided	(A) disinterred	(B) furthered	(C) lashed	(D) scaled
humble	(A) heedful	(B) gluttonous	(C) common	(D) salutary
anchored	(A) secured	(B) codified	(C) eschewed	(D) inflamed

16 Obelisks — tall, four-sided, monoliths with pyramid-shaped tops — originated in ancient Egypt, where they were typically arranged in pairs and situated in front of the tombs of pharaohs. Egyptian obelisks were quarried from red granite and sculpted into a single stone that in some cases weighed hundreds of tons. Due to the tremendous challenge of constructing an obelisk and the primitive tools available to the stonemasons, precisely how the ancients may have created these stupendous pillars has long fascinated Egyptologists.

Hoping to solve this conundrum, Denys Stocks, an ancient-tool expert, sought to experimentally emulate archaic technological limitations by trying to cut granite with a saw made of copper. Initially, he attempted to slice through the solid rock using only the copper saw but found that the soft metal quickly degraded, making this method impractical. However, he discovered that adding sand to the groove made it possible to generate perfect linear cuts when the two were used concurrently. This is because the sand crystals are as hard as granite and essentially do the cutting for the saw. His experiments successfully showed that solid granite can be quarried with rudimentary materials and means, though exactly how the Egyptians achieved this remains a mystery.

Production of obelisks by the Egyptians lasted from 2300 to 1300 BC, but the legacy of the obelisk prevailed. Virtually every conqueror or foreign ruler of Egypt took an obelisk as a souvenir, and many great world leaders subsequently commissioned the erection of obelisks or are memorialized by them. Two notable examples occur in America and respectively commemorate the first president of the United States, George Washington, and the only president of the Confederate States, Jefferson Davis. The former, located in Washington, D.C., towers 555 feet above the capital and is the tallest obelisk on Earth, while the latter, situated in an unassuming town in rural Kentucky, holds the distinction of being the world's highest non-reinforced concrete structure.

1 According to the passage, which of the following is true of the experiments carried out by Denys Stocks?

  (A) They proved that granite could be shaped with basic methods and tools.
  (B) They revealed the sculpting process used by the ancient Egyptians.
  (C) They showed that solid rock cannot be quarried with only sand and copper.
  (D) They demonstrated how laborious carving obelisks was in ancient times.

2 According to the passage, the obelisks in America are noteworthy because

  (A) they are the only monoliths in the US dedicated to presidents.
  (B) they each rank at the top of a category related to height.
  (C) they were transported to the United States from Egypt.
  (D) they both are constructed in a material that is not natural stone.

VOCABULARY The word ⬚ in the passage is closest in meaning to

16	emulate	(A) dissect	(B) irritate	(C) proscribe	(D) follow
	concurrently	(A) concomitantly	(B) singularly	(C) casually	(D) utterly
	lasted	(A) persisted	(B) capitulated	(C) deferred	(D) faded

정답 및 해석 p.397

CH 01
CH 02
CH 03
CH 04
CH 05
CH 06
CH 07
CH 08
CH 09
Hackers TOEFL Reading

HACKERS **TEST**

| 01 | The Automobile Boom |

1 ➡ During the early 1900s, companies rushed to implement large-volume output technology, including a rapid changeover to a new manufacturing process designed to produce massive quantities of identical high-quality goods at a low cost per unit. As such, the stages of assembly were standardized, utilizing precision-made, interchangeable parts and factories were carefully reorganized to allow the flow of raw materials through a set of sequential steps. These innovations caused great advancement in the American automobile industry in particular, most notably by carmaker Henry Ford. His business strategies with underlying mass production philosophy prompted an automobile boom, elevating the entire country into an economic upswing.

2 [3]Originally, Ford's company was staffed with professional engineers who were trained in every aspect of building internal combustion engines and designing the framework for the vehicles, and thus, the office was based on stationary production points wherein assistants would carry necessary parts for each car. Ford's implementation of an assembly line, however, broke the manufacturing up into a lot of small steps; employees stood side-by-side, concentrating on their individual task, as the materials rolled along a conveyor belt. The amount of training needed to carry out only one job, as opposed to many, was minimal, and the company was able to replace highly skilled employees with men who were unskilled or semi-skilled and therefore inexpensive to employ. In addition to saving him money on payroll, the transition also reduced the manufacturing time by assigning easily perfected repetitive chores. Together, these two changes resulted in a startling increase in productivity without compromising quality.

3 On the whole, the new manufacturing methods dramatically modified the organization of the workplace, altering the concept of the American factory environment. Whereas the previous industrial model ensured that engineers had interesting, whole projects to work on, as well as continued education, an assembly line demanded a minute division of labor, each person performing a single monotonous task. Laborers quickly became bored of their jobs and lost interest, threatening to bring down the value of their end products. Ford, realizing that his new factory necessitated a strict monitoring of employees to assure that expected outputs were maintained, established a hierarchical system of supervisors to maintain productivity at peak output levels, and encouraged the many professionals who had initially lost their engineering jobs to join the higher ranks of the now rigid and controlled company structure.

4 The triumph of the Ford plant had a revolutionary effect on the collective industry as well as inspiring newer peripheral industries to develop in order to accommodate increased automobile production. After all, assembly lines required raw materials for input, so steel

92 | 토플 인강 · 단어암기 MP3 HackersIngang.com

mills, glass factories, and metal foundries sprang up in clusters close to huge manufacturing plants. [7]At the same time, machine tool and die makers who provided all the precision parts and mechanical devices for the factory infrastructure flourished as technology continued to improve, the offshoots of which reared a range of new and exciting careers, particularly of interest to the large groups of young men returning from military duty around this time, and kept unemployment rates down while boosting overall spending. In the end, this booming economy together with better automation allowed Ford to drop his selling price from about $850 in 1908 to less than $300 in 1925, at which time sales figures skyrocketed as average customers could now afford to purchase a vehicle, feeding back into the overall health of companies that were involved with car making.

5 The mounting popularity of personal transportation ultimately had repercussions on the cities and countryside as they rapidly changed to make room for the astounding increase in cars. Dirt roads were replaced with paved streets and freeways while urban developers hurried to design gutters, curbs, traffic signs, and other infrastructure that was previously unnecessary. [9]Leisure time now circled around car ownership, bringing forth entertainment venues such as the drive-in theater or touring on newly constructed highways with accompanying gas stations, rest stops, billboards, and even motels to lodge weary travelers along the way. The entire cultural landscape was altered to focus on driving and the needs of the automobile consumer, the impact of which has had major reverberations on the economic survival of the country.

1 The word "rapid" in the passage is closest in meaning to

(A) fast
(B) strategic
(C) broad
(D) clever

2 Which of the following is true of the automobile industry in America in paragraph 1?

(A) Advanced business strategies resulted in a need for fewer factories.
(B) A large increase in quality was achieved with a reduction in costs.
(C) An automobile boom originated from the process of mass production.
(D) The increased inflow of raw materials lowered the cost of automobiles.

Paragraph 1 is marked with an arrow [➡].

CH 01 CH 02 CH 03 CH 04 CH 05 CH 06 CH 07 CH 08 CH 09 Hackers TOEFL Reading

3 Which of the sentences below best expresses the essential information in the highlighted sentence in the passage? *Incorrect* choices change the meaning in important ways or leave out essential information.

(A) The initial factory was laid out with each car being constructed in a designated area by workers drilled in all facets of the task.

(B) Because of the static production facility, Ford hired people with necessary skills to complete all aspects of the car construction.

(C) The manufacturing process required that all the vehicles be assembled by the same workers, who would transport the parts to numerous stations.

(D) Ford's first company was dependent on individual workers who were capable of completing the whole manufacturing process.

4 According to the passage, the introduction of an assembly line brought about all of the following EXCEPT

(A) a reduction in the time needed to produce goods
(B) a period of working hours that was shortened
(C) a manufacturing process with many small stages
(D) a decrease in the personnel expenses

5 The word "monotonous" in the passage is closest in meaning to

(A) base
(B) reflective
(C) tedious
(D) brief

6 Which of the following can NOT be answered based on the information presented in the passage?

(A) What was a feature of the workplace prior to the assembly line?
(B) What was the outcome of the implementation of a minute division of labor?
(C) How did Ford keep track of worker productivity in the factory?
(D) How did supervisors respond to incompetent and unproductive workers?

7 Which of the sentences below best expresses the essential information in the highlighted sentence in the passage? *Incorrect* choices change the meaning in important ways or leave out essential information.

(A) Young men returning from military duty gained employment in technological fields, including machine tool and die making.

(B) The new careers generated by the automobile industry led to an increase in spending by the general population.

(C) The automation process gave rise to a number of new industries that contributed significantly to the economy.

(D) Industries which supported the automobile plant infrastructure thrived, providing a steady source of jobs.

8 The word "figures" in the passage is closest in meaning to

(A) costs
(B) prices
(C) numbers
(D) claims

9 Which of the sentences below best expresses the essential information in the highlighted sentence in the passage? *Incorrect* choices change the meaning in important ways or leave out essential information.

(A) The dramatic expansion of the transportation network ensured that the new entertainment facilities had easy access to drivers.

(B) Many new businesses cropped up in order to accommodate the new population whose recreation activities revolved around their cars.

(C) The increase in the number of privately-owned vehicles resulted in the expansion of the tertiary sector of the economy.

(D) The increasing focus on cars led to the development of many new and profitable service industries along the highways.

10 **Directions**: An introductory sentence for a brief summary of the passage is provided below. Complete the summary by selecting the THREE answer choices that express the most important ideas in the passage. Some sentences do not belong in the summary because they express ideas that are not presented in the passage or are minor ideas in the passage. **This question is worth 2 points.**

> Drag your answer choices to the spaces where they belong. To remove an answer choice, click on it. To review the passage, click on **View Text**.

The automobile boom in America uplifted the economy substantially.

-
-
-

Answer Choices

(A) Ford used professional engineers to ensure the high quality of his products.

(B) Mass production methods significantly decreased the cost of new automobiles in the mid 1920s.

(C) Ford's use of the assembly line greatly improved productivity in the workplace.

(D) The increased use of private automobiles caused related business sectors to be developed.

(E) The need for superintendence led to the institution of a hierarchy in factories.

(F) The application of the assembly line had a major effect on the layout and structure of factories.

정답 및 해석 p.403

CH 01

CH 02

CH 03

CH 04

CH 05

CH 06

CH 07

CH 08

CH 09

Hackers TOEFL Reading

1   Rapid industrialization in the late 1800s centralized businesses into urban centers suddenly dense with teeming masses of rural migrants attracted by the economic boom of the time. Although real estate prices skyrocketed, demand outpaced supply — a conundrum solved by maximizing limited spaces with the unprecedented concept of vertically-designed buildings, thus granting developers the luxury of squeezing huge amounts of income out of relatively small pieces of land.

2 ➡ In the beginning, the construction of tall buildings was limited to certain heights because most of the technologies needed to accommodate taller ones simply did not exist. First, early elevator systems were clumsy, so the idea of running up and down dozens of flights of stairs on a daily basis seemed like lunacy. Next, water pressure potency at the time could only pump water to heights of about 50 feet, making high-rise plumbing facilities a pipe dream. Finally, limited awareness about the importance of structural support beams meant that most early models were entirely supported by a thick base of solid brick, load-bearing walls. In a four or five story erection, this required ground floors to be comprised of disproportionately thick walls with minimal usable space.

3 ➡ This changed with the advent of a low-cost system to mass-produce steel — dubbed the "Bessemer process" after its British developer — that gave architects the freedom to design taller structures with thinner walls buttressed by lightweight support skeletons, making brick bases and cast iron materials wholly redundant. In 1883, the 10-story Home Insurance Building in Chicago — widely considered America's first authentic skyscraper — premiered Bessemer's ingenuity with a frame consisting of vertical steel columns and horizontal beams that provided far more structural integrity than the conventional slab base, yet at only one-third the weight. Functionally, this internal scaffolding meant that exterior walls no longer had to provide intrinsic abutment, allowing for the aesthetically-pleasing addition of windows. As a testament to the brilliance of this design, the fundamentals of its steel cage entrails are still widely used.

4 ➡ Once steel became cheaper to produce, it was used in combination with another building material — concrete — to bring about even taller skyscrapers. Architects and engineers had long favored concrete because it had high resistance to fire and was capable of shutting off sound, but, since it would easily crack, it was used only to build warehouses, factories, or other low-rise buildings. However, with the latest discovery, engineers could reinforce concrete by incorporating steel bars into the mixture. In 1903, the construction of the Ingalls Building used this compound, and it proved to be an ideal compromise between steel's tendency to melt at high temperatures and concrete's to snap (rather than bend) under severe pressure. Solid concrete smothered an internal network of twisted steel bars to raise a massive edifice fifteen stories high, leading local media to speculate that it would collapse as soon as its outer construction supports were taken out; to their disappointment, the building remained intact. It was designated a National Historical Civil Engineering Landmark in 1974, and still stands to this very day.

CH 01
CH 02
CH 03
CH 04
CH 05
CH 06
CH 07
CH 08
CH 09
Hackers TOEFL Reading

5 ➡ Though considered a huge success at the time, even this architectural feat was somewhat diminished by the fact that fifteen stories are not of much use without some kind of transportation system to traverse from floor to floor. Thus, perfection of a reliable elevator system became something of a Holy Grail among architecture enthusiasts. Steam and hydraulic systems had been in use since 1850, but were known to be slow, loud, and hard to control. Then in 1903, the Otis Elevator Company developed a high-speed, gearless electrical contraption that was based on a relatively simple design similar to a pulley lowering a bucket on a rope into a well. It utilized an electric device with a grooved wheel, over which a cable was looped, with one end attached to the elevator and the other to a counterweight. Once it was proven feasible in the 49-story Tower Building in New York City, buildings of any height became possible.

6 Today, the astonishing evolution in skyscraper building is still progressing. Currently, the Taipei 101 in Taiwan, reaching an amazing 1,670 feet, is the world's tallest, although its title as the "world's tallest" will certainly not last, given that architects and engineers continue to experiment with new building techniques and styles.

1 The word "unprecedented" in the passage is closest in meaning to

(A) symbolic
(B) obsolete
(C) conventional
(D) novel

2 According to paragraph 2, which of the following was NOT a technological limitation for the construction of tall buildings?

(A) Too much support on lower levels limited the accessible areas.
(B) There was a great need for a number of flights of stairs.
(C) Devices that could carry people up and down were inefficient.
(D) Pumps were unable to supply higher floors with plumbing.

Paragraph 2 is marked with an arrow [➡].

3 The word "redundant" in the passage is closest in meaning to

(A) fruitful
(B) superfluous
(C) august
(D) inconceivable

4 The word "authentic" in the passage is closest in meaning to

(A) genuine
(B) splendid
(C) synthetic
(D) exclusive

5 According to paragraph 3, which of the following is true of the Home Insurance Building in Chicago?

(A) Its internal structure made it no taller than ten stories.
(B) The beams built into structure carried the majority of its weight.
(C) The inner walls were designed to sustain the building's frame.
(D) It was constructed with lightweight steel frame.

Paragraph 3 is marked with an arrow [➡].

6 Which of the sentences below best expresses the essential information in the highlighted sentence in the passage? *Incorrect* choices change the meaning in important ways or leave out essential information.

(A) Although construction workers made efforts to use concrete in erecting buildings, it enjoyed only limited success as a building material.

(B) As concrete would often crack, it was not a suitable material for the construction of important industrial buildings, in spite of its many advantages.

(C) Although concrete was popular for its fireproof qualities and the ability to muffle sound, it was not widely used because of its brittleness.

(D) Despite its tendency to snap, concrete was an obvious choice for a variety of low-rise buildings because it could withstand fire and shut out sound.

7 The phrase "intact" in the passage is closest in meaning to

(A) level
(B) undamaged
(C) defective
(D) upright

8 According to paragraph 4, all of the following are true of the combination of concrete and steel EXCEPT

(A) The building constructed with this method still exists today.
(B) The method complemented the drawbacks of each steel and concrete.
(C) Journalists were skeptical about the building using this method.
(D) Architects longed to erect a building by this method for long.

Paragraph 4 is marked with an arrow [➡].

9 According to paragraph 5, which of the following is true of the Otis elevator?

(A) It was a plain device with gears.
(B) It was modeled on a pulley.
(C) It was controlled with electricity.
(D) It required a heavy counterweight.

Paragraph 5 is marked with an arrow [➡].

10 **Directions**: An introductory sentence for a brief summary of the passage is provided below. Complete the summary by selecting the THREE answer choices that express the most important ideas in the passage. Some sentences do not belong in the summary because they express ideas that are not presented in the passage or are minor ideas in the passage. **This question is worth 2 points.**

> Drag your answer choices to the spaces where they belong. To remove an answer choice, click on it. To review the passage, click on **View Text**.

As technology advanced, construction began to focus upwards.

-
-
-

Answer Choices

(A) The need for taller buildings grew out of the centralization of the people in urban areas.

(B) The Ingalls Building was the first to use the reinforced concrete for its construction.

(C) Reinforcing concrete with steel gave architects a good opportunity to raise tall buildings.

(D) Once efficient and dependable elevators were developed, they removed obstacles for making buildings higher.

(E) The tallest building is now in Taiwan but will most likely be supplanted by newer one in the foreseeable future.

(F) Steel frameworks provided much greater support than other types of foundations.

정답 및 해석 p.405

CH 01
CH 02
CH 03
CH 04
CH 05
CH 06
CH 07
CH 08
CH 09

Hackers TOEFL Reading

1　Born in the Chicago suburb of Fullersburg, Illinois, Marie Louise Fuller began her theatrical career as a child actress when she made her debut in Chicago at the age of four. For 25 years hence, she toured the American countryside with various stock companies, performing burlesque and vaudeville as well as taking part in the famous Buffalo Bill's Wild West Show. Although she was at one time criticized for her lack of technique because she possessed no formal training in choreography, she honed her skill through experimentation and by observing other modern dance pioneers of the era. By 1888, her grandiose "natural movement" performances had earned her modest success in New York and London, where she shared the stage with several well-known actors and actresses who encouraged her to adopt the pseudonym Loie Fuller that would later become a household name.

2　➡ What brought her fame was her way of manipulating voluminous folds of silk while having beams of colored light play upon them. While preparing to star in the melodrama called "Quack, M.D." in which she would portray a woman under hypnosis, she began experimenting with technical effects that would light her skirt, giving it the appearance of voluminosity and ethereal splendor by enhancing the theater's lighting. Rumored to be inspired by Chinese paper lanterns, she came up with the idea of placing strips of colored silk over the aperture of each lighting fixture, including spotlights and floodlights, in the path of light to create a wash of pigmented glow across the stage. In order to direct the beams in certain directions, mirrors, which could reflect the rays in desired directions, were strategically placed in the wings, bouncing multicolored lights off the performer's attire.

3　Spurred by this new technological wizardry, Fuller, who frequently sewed her own costumes, started to test the effects of reflective materials on clothing. She eventually incorporated strips of translucent silk with reflective properties into her long flowing skirts, producing an effect that made her look like an apparition or ghost. This moved critics to dub her the most innovative dancer of her day. She was emboldened by the positive reviews and searched for new ways to manipulate the combination of color and costume in order to evoke a particular mood, aim focus at a certain character, or alter the perception of time and location of the performance. One way to elicit a response was to piece phosphorescent material into her clothes that would exploit any light that struck its surface, bending the rays into dynamic hues.

4　Realizing her mechanical novelties were a breakthrough, Fuller filed and was awarded several US patents for her inventions, while continuing to work on new designs. She even approached her friend, the chemist and radiation pioneer Marie Curie, for advice on how to incorporate radium into the theater, but Curie quickly turned her down, warning that the element was far too chancy for general use. Undaunted, she continued her own experiments with chemical salts, one that resulted in an explosion in her homemade laboratory. She was unharmed, but swiftly turned her attention to choreographing a new dance that would highlight the advancements that she had made in the field of stage lighting and costuming.

5 Gradually, Fuller's innovative techniques evolved into a performance she called "The Serpentine Dance," and in February 1892, at the revue "Uncle Celestin" in New York, she presented her free dance routine to considerable acclaim. The show traveled to Paris, receiving a warm reception that persuaded her to remain in France to become a regular entertainer at the Folies Bergere, the premiere international venue for experimental performances. Here, Fuller, the first modern dancer to perform in Europe, headlined numerous shows, most significantly "Fire Dance," in which she danced on glass illuminated from below. At a time when the Art Nouveau movement was all the rage, she burst upon the scene as its living embodiment and garnered the respect of many French artists such as Henri de Toulouse-Lautrec, who painted many of her promotional posters, and Auguste Rodin, who later used Fuller as a model for his sculptures. Scientists also flocked to Paris to witness firsthand the avant-garde lighting designs. By 1908, when she opened her own natural movement school, the European community, and, to some extent, her American compatriots, had accepted free dance, in which her inventions and talent coalesced as a serious art form.

Glossary
stock companies a theatrical company that performs plays from a repertoire

1 According to the passage, which of the following statements regarding the early career of Loie Fuller is true?

(A) Fuller was inspired by the progressive approach utilized in the Wild West Show.

(B) Fuller received tribute for her natural style of dance and her technical proficiency.

(C) Fuller played her first important theatrical role in a production in New York City.

(D) Fuller compensated for deficiencies in her education by studying innovative dancers.

2 The word "manipulating" in the passage is closest in meaning to

(A) controlling
(B) inspecting
(C) layering
(D) detaching

3 The word "splendor" in the passage is closest in meaning to

(A) magnificence
(B) transparency
(C) vacancy
(D) benevolence

4 According to paragraph 2, the color of the stage lights

(A) was similar to the color of lights from Chinese paper lanterns
(B) could be changed into other colors by covering them with fabric
(C) was altered depending on the direction of the path of light
(D) could be partially caused by the mirrors used to reflect them

Paragraph 2 is marked with an arrow [➡].

5 Which of the sentences below best expresses the essential information in the highlighted sentence in the passage? *Incorrect* choices change the meaning in important ways or leave out essential information.

(A) After looking for ways to get affirmative reviews, Fuller decided to work on the light and costumes to evoke changes in the audience.

(B) Encouraged by favorable feedback, Fuller looked for more techniques to control the impression made by her performances.

(C) Fuller was promoted to experiment with stage lighting and attire to strengthen the quality of her dance routine.

(D) After getting good responses, Fuller sought new methods of mixing color and clothing to achieve certain effects on the audience.

6 According to the passage, Fuller abandoned her laboratory experiments to choreograph a new dance because

(A) she was cautioned that radioactive materials were too hazardous
(B) she was able to further develop her stagecraft innovations while dancing
(C) she caused a detonation during her experiments with chemical salts
(D) she had already been granted several patents for her discoveries

7 The word "chancy" in the passage is closest in meaning to

(A) undaunted
(B) risky
(C) rash
(D) extant

8 According to the passage, the spirit of Art Nouveau

(A) was widespread in the 18th century
(B) was embraced by American artists
(C) was represented in Fuller's dance
(D) was an intrinsic part of modern dance

9 **Directions**: An introductory sentence for a brief summary of the passage is provided below. Complete the summary by selecting the THREE answer choices that express the most important ideas in the passage. Some sentences do not belong in the summary because they express ideas that are not presented in the passage or are minor ideas in the passage. **This question is worth 2 points.**

> Drag your answer choices to the spaces where they belong. To remove an answer choice, click on it. To review the passage, click on **View Text**.

Loie Fuller started from unremarkable beginnings to become a world-renowned dancer.

-
-
-

Answer Choices

(A) Loie Fuller's first starring role was in a melodrama entitled, "Quack, M.D." in which she acted as a patient.

(B) Although Loie Fuller won recognition from the general public and critics, she was disregarded by her contemporary artists.

(C) With her revolutionary techniques, Loie Fuller introduced a free dance style that created a sensation.

(D) Loie Fuller tried to have desired effect which was accomplished by creating various hues from reflective fabrics.

(E) Fuller started her own dance school in Paris, following the tradition of natural movement.

(F) Loie Fuller was well remembered for her experiments in which colored light was reflected off her clothes.

정답 및 해석 p.407

CH 01
CH 02
CH 03
CH 04
CH 05
CH 06
CH 07
CH 08
CH 09

Hackers TOEFL Reading

⏱ 제한 시간: 16분

1 ➡ In AD 645, the imperial government of Japan instituted the Taika Reforms, which centralized control of Japan under the emperor. As part of the reforms, the government established a set of regulations regarding land ownership called *ritsuryō*. These guidelines were influenced by Confucianism and based on the Chinese legalist tradition, which had also been used as a centralization tool in China. Under ritsuryō, land was strictly allocated according to an enforced registration system. Those who registered were awarded land according to their sex, age, and social position. In return for the allocated land, families were taxed and males were expected to serve in the military.

2 For much of the Nara period(710 to 794), the allocation system worked. Private landholdings were generally limited to major temples and the imperial aristocracy. As such, virtually all property was technically owned by the emperor. By the beginning of the Heian period(794 to 1185), however, the bureaucratic ritsuryō system eventually deteriorated.

3 ➡ Several factors led to the erosion of the land allotment system. Many farmers could barely produce enough crops to cover taxes and feed their families. Productivity was particularly impacted during extended dry periods, and droughts were a continual concern. Not all farmers were fortunate enough to be allocated prime, fertile land near rivers, and those with insufficient irrigation technology found it difficult to generate a sufficient harvest in drought years, so they frequently moved to unoccupied areas in hidden mountain valleys where they could covertly cultivate pockets of land near streams while escaping detection. Other cultivators simply gave up farming for more secure occupations, such as fishing or textile production. In one province alone, official records indicate that nearly 70 percent of the allocated land was not being cultivated. To make matters worse, epidemics continually ravaged the country, and infectious diseases, such as smallpox and influenza, devastated local populations. The end results of these problems were increasing abandonment of cultivable land and diminished tax revenues for the government. It was simply impossible for the government to keep track of thousands of individual deserters.

4 ➡ In order to cope with this dilemma, the government made some concessions regarding land policy, and officials began to take a lax attitude toward land acquisition and development by private parties. There were various ways to acquire private land. Wealthy nobility, such as local officials and warlords, could afford to purchase land outright, and some families came to control vast estates, the rights to which were perpetual and hereditary. Owners of small plots of land would often voluntarily donate their property to large temples or wealthy families in return for protection and support, because powerful landowners had the necessary resources to hire warriors as well as provide agricultural technology. People could also assume rights to land by reclamation. The government allowed new wilderness areas and wasteland that had never been farmed to be acquired as long as it was cultivated. Likewise, land that had been long deserted was considered alienable and was given to people willing to cultivate it. The government sometimes

offered inducements, such as tax exemptions, on reclaimed land.

5 These differing attitudes among the ruling elite resulted in the proliferation of *shōen*. Shōen were private estates that had been granted full or partial tax-exempt status via legal changes or formal negotiation with the central government. Whether temples or wealthy families, shōen owners had the right to establish full dominion over all residents of the estate, as well as to collect rents and a portion of all produce within the property boundaries of the estate. The owners, who often lived far from the property, frequently relied upon managers to oversee the land. Successful managers easily found labor in peasants eager to escape the tax requirements for the use of allocated fields. Although cultivators under the domain of the estates did not have to pay taxes to the central government, their rents and fees often exceeded what they would have been responsible for under the allocation system.

6 ➡ The lasting effect of the central government's liberalization of land policy was that peasants ultimately came under the control of powerful landlords. Under the ritsuryō system, distribution of land had been relatively equitable, but privatization put an exclusive group of individuals and families in control of not only huge parcels of land but also the inhabitants therein. This dual control — over the people and the land — enabled the possibility of a lord-vassal relationship that would be exploited by local warlords and gave rise to the samurai, who would seize political control of Japan in the twelfth century.

CH 01
CH 02
CH 03
CH 04
CH 05
CH 06
CH 07
CH 08
CH 09

Hackers TOEFL Reading

1 According to paragraph 1, which of the following is true of the *ritsuryō* system?

(A) It raised awareness of Chinese legal traditions in Japan.
(B) It spurred a resurgence of nationalism in China.
(C) It required beneficiaries of land to register with authorities.
(D) It compelled landowners to transfer land to the government.

Paragraph 1 is marked with an arrow [➡].

2 Which of the sentences below best expresses the essential information in the highlighted sentence in the passage? *Incorrect* choices change the meaning in important ways or leave out essential information.

(A) Farmers who could not produce enough food during dry periods began to encroach upon other farmers' allocated land, which led to disputes over water use.

(B) Because some farmers lacked ideal farmland and the technology to be productive during droughts, they often farmed around streams in reclusive mountain lowlands.

(C) Some farmers fortunately benefited from fertile lands with plenty of water, but many who did not often failed to produce a bountiful harvest during droughts.

(D) In search of water, many farmers descended the mountains and began cultivating land near streams that only they knew existed.

3 According to paragraph 3, which of the following can NOT be answered?

(A) What was a determinant in the loss of productivity?
(B) What was the fiscal result of the abandonment of land?
(C) Why did some farmers retire from cultivating the land?
(D) Why did the government raise taxes on cultivable land?

Paragraph 3 is marked with an arrow [➡].

4 The word "perpetual" in the passage is closest in meaning to

(A) peremptory
(B) retractable
(C) permanent
(D) ephemeral

5 According to paragraph 4, some people voluntarily conceded their own land

(A) in return for a position in the government
(B) to avoid paying inheritance taxes
(C) in exchange for guardianship
(D) to preserve threatened wilderness areas

Paragraph 4 is marked with an arrow [➡].

6 The word "deserted" in the passage is closest in meaning to

(A) bequeathed
(B) divided
(C) retained
(D) abandoned

7 The word "proliferation" in the passage is closest in meaning to

(A) increase
(B) absence
(C) creation
(D) promotion

8 According to paragraph 6, which of the following resulted from the government's more flexible land policy?

(A) Landholders joined with local warlords to overthrow the central government.
(B) Increasing conflict developed between landlords and renters.
(C) Extensive landholdings fell into the hands of a privileged few.
(D) Landlords were required to distribute a portion of land to their vassals.

Paragraph 6 is marked with an arrow [➡].

9 **Directions**: An introductory sentence for a brief summary of the passage is provided below. Complete the summary by selecting the THREE answer choices that express the most important ideas in the passage. Some sentences do not belong in the summary because they express ideas that are not presented in the passage or are minor ideas in the passage. **This question is worth 2 points.**

> Drag your answer choices to the spaces where they belong. To remove an answer choice, click on it. To review the passage, click on **View Text**.

Around the ninth century, land privatization gradually began to replace the allocation system that had been in place for over a century.

-
-
-

Answer Choices

(A) The land allotment system was based on Chinese precedent, but it was not as successful in Japan as it had been in China.

(B) The government found it increasingly challenging to monitor land use, and the land allotment system began to unravel.

(C) Tenancy on private estates provided cultivators with a substantial tax savings that ultimately improved their financial situation.

(D) Farmers who were allotted fertile land offered jobs to those who were forced to abandon their less desirable plots.

(E) Officials responded to changing circumstances by relaxing their rules on land use, thus paving the way for privatization.

(F) Expansion of private landholdings led to the creation of large private estates over which owners had complete jurisdiction in matters of tenancy.

정답 및 해석 p.408

토플 빈출어휘 정리 노트

Chapter 02에 수록된 어휘들을 빈출도 순으로 정리했습니다. 음성파일을 들으며 꼭 암기하세요.

토플 최빈출어휘 [★★★]

- [ ] unique[ju:ní:k] 독특한 (=distinct)
- [ ] durable[djúərəbl] 영구적인 (=long-lasting)
- [ ] immerse[imə́:rs] 담그다 (=submerge)
- [ ] transmit[trænsmít] 전달하다 (=convey)
- [ ] flexible[fléksəbl] 유연한 (=malleable)
- [ ] undertake[ʌ̀ndərtéik] 착수하다
- [ ] typically[típikəli] 대개 (=ordinarily)
- [ ] appreciate[əprí:ʃièit] 감상하다
- [ ] assessment[əsésmənt] 평가 (=evaluation)
- [ ] extensive[iksténsiv] 광범위한 (=widespread)
- [ ] interject[ìntərdʒékt] 개입시키다
- [ ] dainty[déinti] 정교한 (=exquisite)
- [ ] obsolete[ὰ:bsəlí:t] 한물간
- [ ] eager[í:gər] 갈망하는 (=anxious)
- [ ] significant[signífikənt] 중요한 (=important)
- [ ] engrave[ingréiv] 조각하다
- [ ] advent[ǽdvent] 출현 (=arrival)
- [ ] approximately[əpráksəmətli] 대략 (=about)
- [ ] capacity[kəpǽsəti] 능력 (=ability)
- [ ] regulate[régjulèit] 조절하다 (=monitor)
- [ ] aridity[ərídəti] 건조 (=dryness)
- [ ] designated[dézignèitid] 지정된
- [ ] subject[sʌ́bdʒikt] 주제
- [ ] physiologically[fìziəládʒikəli] 생리학적으로
- [ ] vital[váitl] 필수적인 (=essential)
- [ ] accumulate[əkjú:mjəleit] 축적하다
- [ ] rapid[rǽpid] 급격한 (=fast)
- [ ] notably[nóutəbli] 특히 (=especially)
- [ ] monotonous[mənátənəs] 지루한 (=tedious)
- [ ] figure[fígjər] 전체의 양 (=number)
- [ ] unprecedented[ʌ̀nprésədèntid] 새로운 (=novel)
- [ ] redundant[ridʌ́ndənt] 불필요한 (=superfluous)
- [ ] authentic[ə:θéntik] 진정한 (=genuine)
- [ ] ingenuity[ìndʒənjú:əti] 독창력 (=creativeness)

- [ ] reinforce[rì:infɔ́:rs] 강화하다 (=intensify)
- [ ] intact[intǽkt] 손상되지 않은 (=undamaged)
- [ ] feat[fi:t] 업적 (=accomplishment)
- [ ] manipulate[mənípjulèit] 능숙히 다루다 (=control)
- [ ] splendor[spléndər] 장엄함 (=magnificence)
- [ ] exploit[éksplɔit] 이용하다 (=make use of)
- [ ] breakthrough[bréikθrù:] 획기적인 발견 (=innovation)
- [ ] patent[pǽtnt] 특허
- [ ] chancy[tʃǽnsi] 위험한 (=risky)
- [ ] perpetual[pərpétʃuəl] 영속적인 (=permanent)
- [ ] inducement[indjú:smənt] 유인책 (=incentive)

토플 빈출어휘 [★★]

- [ ] artifact[á:rtəfæ̀kt] 유물
- [ ] establish[istǽbliʃ] 제정하다
- [ ] declare[diklέər] 공표하다
- [ ] steep[sti:p] 가파른
- [ ] medium[mí:diəm] 매체
- [ ] absorption[æbsɔ́:rpʃən] 흡수
- [ ] reflection[riflékʃən] 반사
- [ ] propagate[prá:pəgeit] 퍼지다
- [ ] innovation[ìnəvéiʃən] 혁신 (=creation)
- [ ] laud[lɔ:d] 칭찬하다
- [ ] vegetation[vèdʒətéiʃən] 초목
- [ ] invaluable[invǽljuəbl] 매우 귀중한 (=inestimable)
- [ ] surface[sə́:rfis] 떠오르다 (=arise)
- [ ] ecosystem[í:kousistəm] 생태계
- [ ] manufacture[mæ̀njufǽktʃər] 만들다
- [ ] appoint[əpɔ́int] 임명하다
- [ ] considerable[kənsídərəbl] 상당한 (=substantial)
- [ ] tolerate[tálərèit] 견디다
- [ ] drastic[drǽstik] 급격한 (=radical)
- [ ] indicate[índikèit] 알려주다 (=signal)
- [ ] exposed[ikspóuzd] 위험을 당하기 쉬운 (=subjected)
- [ ] active[ǽktiv] 활동적인 (=animated)

*해커스 동영상강의 포털 해커스인강(HackersIngang.com)에서 '토플 빈출어휘 정리 노트' 음성파일을 무료로 다운로드할 수 있습니다.

☐ transit [trǽnsit] 운반 (=conveyance)

☐ upright [ʌ̀práit] 수직의 (=erect)

☐ erosion [iróuʒən] 부식

☐ sediment [sédəmənt] 퇴적물

☐ conformity [kənfɔ́:rməti] 순응성 (=compliance)

☐ markedly [má:rkidli] 뚜렷하게

☐ mass [mæs] 덩어리

☐ humble [hʌ́mbl] 보잘것없는 (=common)

☐ last [læst] 계속하다 (=persist)

☐ sequential [sikwénʃəl] 일련의

☐ elevate [éləvèit] 고양시키다

☐ necessitate [nəsésətèit] 필요로 하다 (=call for)

☐ hierarchical [hàiərá:rkikəl] 위계의

☐ accommodate [əkámədèit] 수용하다

☐ astounding [əstáundiŋ] 놀라운 (=astonishing)

☐ weary [wíəri] 지친 (=exhausted)

☐ outpace [àutpéis] 앞지르다

☐ collapse [kəlǽps] 무너지다

☐ era [írə] 시대

☐ inspire [inspáiər] 영감을 주다

☐ acclaim [əkléim] 호평

☐ hereditary [hərédətèri] 세습적인

☐ exceed [iksí:d] 초과하다

토플 기출어휘 [★]

☐ affix [əfíks] 붙이다

☐ publicly [pʌ́blikli] 공개적으로

☐ impractical [imprǽktikəl] 실효 없는

☐ vertical [vá:rtikl] 수직의

☐ velocity [vəlá:səti] 속도

☐ corroborate [kərá:bəreit] 입증하다

☐ noxious [nákʃəs] 유독성의 (=detrimental)

☐ commemorate [kəmémərèit] 기념하다 (=observe)

☐ horizontally [hɔ̀r:əzántli] 수평으로

☐ replica [réplikə] 복제품

☐ inaugurate [inɔ́:gjəreit] 개관하다

☐ accretion [əkríːʃən] 증대 (=accumulation)

☐ assertion [əsə́:rʃən] 주장 (=claim)

☐ progress [prəgrés] 진행하다 (=continue)

☐ blindly [bláindli] 맹목적으로 (=recklessly)

☐ anchored [ǽŋkərd] 고정된 (=secured)

☐ aid [eid] 촉진하다 (=further)

☐ denote [dinóut] 의미하다

☐ emulate [émjulèit] 모방하다 (=follow)

☐ stupendous [stu:péndəs] 거대한

☐ prevail [privéil] 널리 퍼져 있다

☐ concurrently [kənkə́:rəntli] 동시에 (=concomitantly)

☐ upswing [ʌ́pswiŋ] 상승

☐ combustion [kəmbʌ́stʃən] 연소

☐ peripheral [pərífərəl] 주변의

☐ spring up 나타나다

☐ boost [bu:st] 증진시키다

☐ skyrocket [skáiràkit] 급등하다

☐ teeming [tí:miŋ] 많은

☐ dub [dʌb] 호칭을 붙이다

☐ premiere [primíər] 최초로 선보이다

☐ compromise [kámprəmàiz] 절충안

☐ traverse [trǽvə:rs] 가로지르다

☐ hone [houn] 연마하다

☐ hypnosis [hipnóusis] 최면술

☐ attire [ətáiər] 의상

☐ translucent [trænslú:snt] 반투명의

☐ venue [vénju:] 장소

☐ coalesce [kòuəlés] 뭉치다

☐ covertly [kóuvərtli] 몰래

☐ ravage [rǽvidʒ] 초토화하다 (=destroy)

☐ reclamation [rèkləméiʃən] 개간

☐ alienable [éiljənəbl] 양도할 수 있는

☐ equitable [ékwətəbl] 공평한

☐ parcel [pá:rsəl] 구획

Chapter 03
Vocabulary

OVERVIEW

Vocabulary 문제는 주어진 어휘의 동의어 또는 완벽한 동의어는 아니지만 문맥상 유사한 의미를 가진 어휘를 선택하는 유형이다. 각 어휘는 한 개 이상의 서로 다른 의미를 가질 수 있는데, 그중 문맥 속에서 사용된 의미를 파악한 후 보기 중에서 그와 가장 유사한 의미를 가진 어휘를 골라야 한다.

따라서 Vocabulary 문제를 해결하기 위해서는 평소 단어의 여러 가지 의미를 익혀두고 문맥에 맞는 의미를 정확하게 파악하는 연습이 필요하다. 또한, 평소에 다양한 지문을 접하면서 충분한 어휘를 익히고, 이때 각 어휘뿐만 아니라 그 어휘의 동의어군을 함께 외워두는 것이 문제풀이에 많은 도움이 된다.

Vocabulary 문제는 보통 한 지문당 1~2개가 출제된다.

TYPES OF QUESTIONS

지문에 어휘 또는 구가 음영 처리되어 있으며 4개의 보기가 주어진다.
Vocabulary 문제의 전형적인 질문 유형은 아래와 같다.

• The word "   " in the passage is closest in meaning to
• The phrase "   " in the passage is closest in meaning to

HACKERS **STRATEGY**

CH 01
CH 02
CH 03
CH 04
CH 05
CH 06
CH 07
CH 08
CH 09

Hackers TOEFL Reading

전략 1 사전적 의미를 바탕으로 어휘 또는 구가 문맥 내에서 어떤 의미로 쓰였는지 파악한다.

Ex Only through communication can one animal influence the behavior of another. Compared with the enormous communicative potential of human speech, however, nonhuman communication is severely restricted.

➡ enormous는 '막대한, 거대한'이라는 사전적 의미를 가지고 있다. 문맥에서 however를 통해 인간의 발화가 갖는 커뮤니케이션 잠재력이 enormous한 것에 비해, 인간이 아닌 생물의 커뮤니케이션은 지극히 restricted하다고 대조하고 있으므로, enormous가 restricted와 반대되는 의미를 나타내기 위해 사용되었음을 알 수 있다. 즉, enormous가 '막대한'이라는 의미로 쓰였음을 확인할 수 있다.

Ex As stars form and evolve within the nebulae over time, they release high-energy radiation that causes the surrounding gas to glow brightly, creating stunning and colorful displays. The ionized gas can take on a variety of shapes and sizes, with some emission nebulae forming long, filamentary structures, while others take on a more irregular or blob-like appearance.

➡ over time은 '시간이 지남에 따라'라는 사전적 의미를 가지고 있다. 문맥에서 별들이 시간이 지남에 따라 성운 내에서 형성되고 진화함으로써 높은 에너지 방출을 일으킨다고 언급하였으므로, over time이 시간의 흐름에 따라 벌어지는 일을 언급하기 위해 사용되었다는 것을 알 수 있다. 즉, over time이 '시간이 지남에 따라'라는 의미로 쓰였음을 확인할 수 있다.

TIP 1 문제로 제시된 어휘 또는 구가 여러 의미를 가질 경우, 문맥 내에서 어떤 의미로 쓰였는지 파악한다.

In the 1950s the United States accounted for 25 percent of the world's total exports. Recently, however, countries such as China and India have emerged as the leading sources for the world's merchandise and services.
지문의 accounted for는 ① (부분·비율을) 차지하다, ② 설명하다 등의 의미를 가진다. 지문에서 미국이 전 세계 총 수출량의 25퍼센트를 accounted for한다고 했으므로, 문맥 내에서는 '(부분·비율을) 차지하다'라는 의미로 사용되었음을 알 수 있다.

TIP 2 어휘 또는 구의 사전적 의미를 전혀 모를 경우 아래의 단서들을 활용할 수 있다.

1. 관계절이나 부사절, 혹은 comma(,), dash(—), or 등과 같은 부연 설명 표현을 통해 어휘의 의미를 유추할 수 있다.
   Doctors use **jargons**, which are special language used by particular group, or profession, so that patients do not understand what they need not know.
   Jargons에 대한 부가 설명을 하고 있는 which 관계절을 통해 jargons가 '특정한 사람들이 사용하는 특별한 언어'를 의미한다는 것을 알 수 있다.

2. 문장의 앞뒤 논리 구조(대조, 인과 등)를 통해 어휘의 의미를 유추할 수 있다.
   The fort appeared **deserted**, but inside it was full of government soldiers and officers.
   But이라는 대조 표현을 통해 deserted가 '가득 찬'이라는 의미를 가진 full과 상반되는 '황량한'이라는 의미를 가지고 있음을 알 수 있다.

해석 p.411

문맥에서 쓰인 의미와 가장 유사한 의미를 담고 있는 것으로 예상되는 보기를 고른다.

Ex As human settlements increased in size, by reason of the technological advances in irrigation and cultivation, the need for improving the circulation of goods and people became ever more acute. Pre-neolithic men leading a nomadic existence in their never-ending search for food moved largely by foot and carried their essential goods with the help of their family.

Q: The word "acute" in the passage is closest in meaning to

  (A) radical

  (B) critical

  (C) possible

  (D) reasonable

➡ acute는 '중대한, (질병이) 급성의, 예민한' 등의 여러 가지 사전적 의미를 가지고 있다. 위 지문에서 인간의 정착 규모가 증가하면서 재화 및 인력 순환을 개선시킬 필요성이 그 어느 때보다 acute해졌다고 하였으므로, acute는 지문에서 '중대한'의 의미로 사용되었다는 것을 알 수 있다. 따라서 '중요한, 결정적인'이라는 의미를 가진 (B) critical을 정답으로 고를 수 있다.
(A) 급진적인 (B) 중요한 (C) 가능한 (D) 이성적인

Ex The allocation of energy must maintain an equilibrium that ensures all organisms are capable of surviving within their particular physical environment while reserving enough strength to defend against predators, obtain adequate food, procreate, and grow into a given body design. Most of the time, the proportion of energy designated for the particular function is genetically determined, not consciously assigned, and all members of the species display relatively similar physiological states.

Q: The word "reserving" in the passage is closest in meaning to

  (A) saving

  (B) searching

  (C) uniting

  (D) dominating

➡ reserve는 '비축하다, 예약하다, 유보하다' 등의 여러 가지 사전적 의미를 가지고 있다. 위 지문에서 유기체는 포식자로부터 자신을 방어하고, 충분한 식량을 획득하고, 생산하는 등의 목적을 위해 충분한 힘을 reserve해야 한다고 하였으므로, reserve는 '비축하다'의 의미로 사용되었다는 것을 알 수 있다. 따라서 이와 가장 유사한 의미인 '저장하다'라는 의미를 가진 (A) saving을 정답으로 고를 수 있다.
(A) 저장하다 (B) 찾다 (C) 통합하다 (D) 지배하다

전략 3   예상 답을 음영 처리된 어휘의 자리에 대입하여 문맥이 자연스러운지 확인한다.

예상 답을 음영 처리된 어휘의 자리에 대입하여 문맥 속에서 문제로 제시된 어휘와 같은 의미로 사용되는지 확인한다.

Ex The location on which the Inuit people lived was extremely inhospitable and the population relied heavily on traditional hunting and gathering techniques for survival. In order to acquire sufficient supplies, they dwelt in temporary settlements, moving to a bountiful source, depleting it, and moving to the next.

Q: The word "depleting" in the passage is closest in meaning to

     (A) sparing

     (B) accumulating

     (C) exhausting

     (D) stealing

➡ 문제의 **depleting**은 '고갈시키는'의 사전적 의미를 가지고 있다. 따라서 이와 유사한 '소모시키는'이라는 의미를 가진 (C) exhausting을 후보로 고를 수 있다.
(A) 아끼는 (B) 축적하는 (C) 소모시키는 (D) 훔치는

문맥이 자연스러운지 확인

답으로 예상되는 (C) exhausting을 지문의 depleting 자리에 대입하면 'Inuit족은 임시 거주지에 살았고 풍부한 자원을 찾아 이동하여 그 자원을 소모시키고 다른 곳으로 이동했다'라고 해석되어 문맥이 자연스러우므로 정답으로 선택할 수 있다.

CH 01
CH 02
CH 03
CH 04
CH 05
CH 06
CH 07
CH 08
CH 09

Hackers TOEFL Reading

HACKERS STRATEGY **APPLICATION**

Regardless of their environment, all chimpanzee communities are patriarchal, or dominated by males, although adult females can outnumber adult males by two or three times. Like community memberships, the hierarchy among male chimpanzees is highly flexible, with males associating with each other, joining and leaving subgroups at will. While the male hierarchy is more or less linear, it is dominated by one alpha male. He may assume power through acts of aggression, strength or intelligence, often by using "dominance displays." Such a display might include charging a group of males while making loud noises. Alternatively, one male chimpanzee might attack the reigning alpha male head-on, challenging his position in front of the others. This is precisely how a low-ranking chimpanzee is able to take over the alpha male position.

1. The word "flexible" in the passage is closest in meaning to

(A) prudent
(B) obstinate
(C) sheer
(D) variable

Smart dust consists of a large amount of millimeter-scale microelectromechanical devices referred to individually as motes. Motes are as tiny as dust particles, and composed of a bi-directional wireless transceiver which has remote sensors. Thousands of motes can be spread throughout buildings or into the atmosphere to collect and monitor data. What makes smart dust noteworthy is that it has a networking capability: a single mote can only provide a very small piece of information, but hundreds of motes communicating with each other can produce a very detailed picture of what is happening somewhere. Smart dust devices, therefore, have applications in everything from military to meteorological to medical fields.

2. The word "composed" in the passage is closest in meaning to

(A) completed
(B) contrived
(C) comprised
(D) consumed

해석 p.411

CH 01

CH 02

CH 03

CH 04

CH 05

CH 06

CH 07

CH 08

CH 09

Hackers TOEFL Reading

1 | 전략 1 적용 | 문제로 제시된 flexible은 '잘 구부러지는, 융통성 있는'이라는 사전적 의미를 가진다. flexible 뒤에 'with males associating with each other, joining and leaving subgroups at will', 즉 '수컷들이 서로 어울리며 마음대로 소집단에 들어오거나 나간다'라는 내용으로 보아 flexible이 '융통성 있는'이라는 의미로 사용되었다는 것을 알 수 있다.

| 전략 2 적용 | 보기 중 '가변적인'이라는 의미를 가지는 variable을 지문 속 flexible(융통성 있는)과 가장 유사한 의미를 가진 후보로 고를 수 있다.
(A) 신중한 (B) 완고한 (C) 완전한 (D) 가변적인

| 전략 3 적용 | 답으로 예상되는 (D) variable을 지문의 flexible 자리에 대입하면 '수컷 침팬지들의 서열은 매우 가변적이다'라고 해석되어 문맥이 자연스러운 것을 확인할 수 있다.

| 정답 | (D)

2 | 전략 1 적용 | 문제로 제시된 composed는 '~로 구성된, 침착한'이라는 사전적 의미를 가진다. 문맥에서 Smart dust가 mote라고 불리는 마이크로 전자기계 장치로 'composed' 되어 있다는 이야기가 나오므로, '~로 구성된'의 뜻으로 쓰였음을 알 수 있다.

| 전략 2 적용 | 보기 중 '~로 이루어진'이라는 의미를 가지는 comprised를 지문 속 composed(~로 구성된)와 가장 유사한 의미를 가진 후보로 고를 수 있다.
(A) 완성된 (B) 인위적인 (C) ~로 이루어진 (D) 소비된

| 전략 3 적용 | 답으로 예상되는 (C) comprised를 지문의 composed 자리에 대입하면 'smart dust가 mote라고 불리는 마이크로 전자기계 장치로 이루어졌다'라고 해석되어 문맥이 자연스러운 것을 확인할 수 있다.

| 정답 | (C)

Write the word that is closest in meaning to the highlighted word in each passage and then choose a group of synonyms for it. The correct answer can be any part of speech.

1 The traditional and very inefficient oscillating sprinkler, which sprays water high in the air, lavishes water to winds and evaporation, and sprinklers which produce mists or fine sprays similarly waste large volumes of water to evaporation.

1 _____

2 A group of synonyms for "lavishes" is

(A) sacrifices, gives up, concedes
(B) squanders, expends, throws away
(C) infects, pollutes, contaminates
(D) loses, misplaces, yields

2 While the body's largest organ, the skin, protects the outer surface of the body from penetration and damage by microorganisms, the immune system uses specialized cells such as leukocytes to thwart devastation by infectious invaders inside the body.

1 _____

2 A group of synonyms for "devastation" is

(A) result, outcome, consequence
(B) barrier, obstacle, obstruction
(C) injury, destruction, hurt
(D) speck, blot, splotch

3 The initial carbon dioxide in the atmosphere of the young Earth was emitted by volcanic activity; this was essential for a warm and stable climate conducive to life. Volcanic activity now exudes about 130 to 230 teragrams of carbon dioxide each year.

1 _____

2 A group of synonyms for "exudes" is

(A) makes use of, exploits, applies
(B) prevails over, overrides, eclipses
(C) gives off, radiates, sends out
(D) does away with, eliminates, removes

VOCABULARY	The word	in the passage is closest in meaning to		
1 traditional	(A) folk	(B) conventional	(C) fixed	(D) established
2 outer	(A) poignant	(B) proficient	(C) acrid	(D) exterior
3 emitted	(A) awarded	(B) immersed	(C) discharged	(D) abandoned

4   The Supreme Court and Congress restrict the amount of power the US president can wield over government, but parliamentary systems typically allow prime ministers to execute greater authority than their American counterparts.

1 _____

2 A group of synonyms for "wield" is

(A) exercise, exert, use
(B) expect, anticipate, predict
(C) convoke, summon, call
(D) create, form, invent

5   The cost of oil fluctuates due to factors such as the regulatory context of oil extraction in supplying countries, but importers are limited in their ability to combat price volatility.

1 _____

2 A group of synonyms for "fluctuates" is

(A) deviates, straggles, wanders
(B) keeps still, remains stationary, stays put
(C) subsides, abates, dies down
(D) varies, changes, sways

6   Most stars are of nearly constant luminosity. The Sun is a good example of one which goes through relatively little change in brightness (usually about 0.1 percent over an 11 year solar cycle). Many stars, however, undergo significant variations in luminosity, and these are known as variable stars.

1 _____

2 A group of synonyms for "luminosity" is

(A) bulk, size, volume
(B) radiance, brilliance, glitter
(C) tranquility, serenity, calmness
(D) movement, motion, gesture

VOCABULARY   The word [   ] in the passage is closest in meaning to

4	counterparts	(A) equivalents	(B) supplements	(C) opponents	(D) colleagues
5	limited	(A) restricted	(B) redeemed	(C) implored	(D) maimed
6	undergo	(A) endure	(B) experience	(C) enjoin	(D) manage

CH 01
CH 02
CH 03
CH 04
CH 05
CH 06
CH 07
CH 08
CH 09
Hackers TOEFL Reading

7 Prior to the arrival of the horse on the plains, the tipi had to be of sufficient size to be carried from place to place by the women and dogs. With the coming of the horse, however, this changed dramatically. One result was that lodge poles, which used to be only five to six feet high, now extended to an average of fifteen feet. By using three horses the dwelling could now be moved quite comfortably.

1 _____

2 A group of synonyms for "carried" is

   (A) ditched, renounced, forsaken
   (B) conveyed, transferred, transported
   (C) disjointed, dismantled, disintegrated
   (D) fortified, strengthened, reinforced

8 The Dalcroze Method, a combination of body movement and musical theory, encourages students to adopt a natural feel for musical expression by using the human body as a musical instrument. As a whole, it consists of three equally important fundamentals: solfege, improvisation, and eurhythmics, which together amount to what Jacque-Dalcroze considered a complete musical training. Ideally, an amalgamation of these principles results in a creative and artistic individual.

1 _____

2 A group of synonyms for "principles" is

   (A) phases, stages, periods
   (B) standards, foundations, criteria
   (C) impacts, effects, influences
   (D) knacks, aptitudes, talents

9 Although the division of labor is fairly clear-cut based on age, research has shown that in a worker bee population with an unbalanced age structure resulting from some catastrophic event, individual worker bees adapt and assume duties that are not normal for their age. When they are forced to modify their behavior in this fashion, they perform less effectively than when they follow a normal sequence of development.

1 _____

2 A group of synonyms for "modify" is

   (A) acknowledge, observe, recognize
   (B) revise, adjust, alter
   (C) subjugate, smother, subdue
   (D) withstand, confront, defy

VOCABULARY	The word	☐	in the passage is closest in meaning to		
7	dramatically	(A) chiefly	(B) strikingly	(C) profusely	(D) shortly
8	combination	(A) decease	(B) stimulus	(C) clout	(D) hybrid
9	fashion	(A) vogue	(B) manner	(C) satire	(D) creed

Choose the word that best completes the blank in each sentence.

10 A population delineated as being at _____ is one with a death rate that is the same as the birth rate and thus does not alter.

(A) fluidity
(B) medium
(C) weight
(D) equilibrium

11 Although bees and wasps are not closely related biologically, they share some anatomical characteristics, such as the anterior antennae they use as 'feelers' and the venomous stingers that extend from the _____ of their abdomens when they perceive that a threat is imminent.

(A) prior
(B) posterior
(C) superior
(D) inferior

12 Atoms and molecules are electrically neutral in that the number of negatively charged electrons is an exact _____ to the number of positively charged protons.

(A) copy
(B) match
(C) pair
(D) inverse

13 A notorious meat-eating dinosaur known as *Tyrannosaurus rex* underwent a massive growth spurt, eventually reaching some 5,000 kilograms, but the dinosaur became too _____ to move quickly and had to scare away more effective predators in order to steal their meals.

(A) bright
(B) hefty
(C) scanty
(D) petite

CH 01
CH 02
CH 03
CH 04
CH 05
CH 06
CH 07
CH 08
CH 09
Hackers TOEFL Reading

VOCABULARY The word ☐ in the passage is closest in meaning to

10 delineated	(A) suggested	(B) insinuated	(C) described	(D) constructed
11 extend	(A) drag	(B) protrude	(C) approach	(D) stretch
12 exact	(A) intense	(B) accurate	(C) amiable	(D) forceful
13 notorious	(A) vulgar	(B) devout	(C) infamous	(D) fearful

14 Arabica and Robusta coffee beans are clearly _____ in shape: Arabica beans are flat and oblong with a crooked furrow, while Robusta beans are convex and round with a straight center furrow.

(A) adaptable
(B) erratic
(C) sustainable
(D) distinguishable

15 Whether automatic or _____, the behavioral changes that inevitably accompany the physical and physiological alterations in adolescents are of great interest to psychologists.

(A) faint
(B) deliberate
(C) involuntary
(D) incessant

16 The ideals of four presidents on Mount Rushmore laid a foundation for America as _____ as the rock from which their figures are carved.

(A) imposing
(B) solid
(C) rigorous
(D) unpredictable

17 Kinetoscopes typically showed _____ films, but sometimes, as in the case of a famous boxing match, they would display successive rounds of the fight.

(A) elemental
(B) concise
(C) discrete
(D) surreal

VOCABULARY   The word [   ] in the passage is closest in meaning to

14 clearly	(A) definitely	(B) normally	(C) purely	(D) largely
15 accompany	(A) indict	(B) compile	(C) companion	(D) affront
16 carved	(A) dissipated	(B) incised	(C) deemed	(D) capsized
17 display	(A) exhibit	(B) adjourn	(C) pound	(D) recollect

Read each passage and answer the corresponding questions for each.

18 The aurora borealis is a beautiful exhibition of lights that can be seen over the northern pole of Earth. It will appear in the northern part of the sky and have a ribbon-like shape that changes and shimmers over time. It will have hues that range from very pale white to green to blue and sometimes purple. Usually it is most visible in more northern latitudes, such as Canada and Alaska, although if it is bright enough and large enough, it can be discernible as far south as Florida. There is a similar phenomenon called the aurora australis in the southern hemisphere that behaves the same way.

1 The word "exhibition" in the passage is closest in meaning to

(A) medley
(B) display
(C) series
(D) flow

2 The word "visible" in the passage is closest in meaning to

(A) instrumental
(B) latent
(C) evident
(D) spectacular

3 The word "discernible" in the passage is closest in meaning to

(A) acute
(B) perceptible
(C) bountiful
(D) vagarious

CH 01
CH 02
CH 03
CH 04
CH 05
CH 06
CH 07
CH 08
CH 09
Hackers TOEFL Reading

VOCABULARY	The word ☐ in the passage is closest in meaning to			
18 appear	(A) retire	(B) cease	(C) assemble	(D) emerge
phenomenon	(A) testimony	(B) predicament	(C) occurrence	(D) promptitude
behaves	(A) handles	(B) acts	(C) consorts	(D) surpasses

19 Investigations by stargazers hoping to unlock the secrets of the universe began in ancient times. But until the advent of modern science and the development of its complex technology, mathematics, and rigorous hypotheses, those studying celestial bodies struggled to solve this mystery. One of the most prevalent questions astronomers wrestled with was how the solar system and the rest of the physical phenomena beyond it came into existence to begin with. The answer, according to nearly all contemporary astronomical thought, is that the onset of the universe resulted from a single and massive explosive event, commencing at a point of infinite density, known as the singularity, and resulting in an intensely hot sea of protons, neutrons, photons, and other sub-atomic particles shooting off in all directions. It was from this original "primordial soup" that all stars, planets, and life in the cosmos subsequently formed.

1 The word "prevalent" in the passage is closest in meaning to

(A) frivolous
(B) dominant
(C) succinct
(D) constant

2 The word "onset" in the passage is closest in meaning to

(A) concluding
(B) midpoint
(C) beginning
(D) fallout

3 The word "subsequently" in the passage is closest in meaning to

(A) later
(B) longer
(C) simultaneously
(D) sparsely

20 Glaciation begins with falling snow, and because individual snowflakes typically have a hexagonal structure with arms that branch freely, minute air bubbles become trapped between the snowflakes as they accumulate. If enough snow falls, it becomes subject to compaction under its own weight due to gravity. The granular intermediate form between snow and ice is called *firn*, and with continued compression, it can transform into dense, rock-like glacial ice. At the surface of the glacier, the ice is brittle, but near the bottom, it is so strong and hard that it grinds the underlying bedrock and creates striations. As the glacier flows, it picks up sediment and carries it downstream so that eventually, when it melts, the sediment is deposited, often leaving fertile land in its wake. The surface left behind after glaciers recede can be dramatically altered, such as in characteristic glaciated valleys, which are often shaped like troughs with steep, near-vertical cliffs where the glaciers chiseled away the mountainsides. In areas adjacent to the sea, the valleys sometimes become submerged with seawater following the glacier's retreat, resulting in long, narrow coastal inlets known as *fjords* — a term aptly derived from Norwegian as Norway's coast is dominated by the presence of nearly 1,200 of these geological features, which collectively account for 29,000 out of 31,500 kilometers of the country's shoreline.

1 The phrase "subject to" in the passage is closest in meaning to

(A) witnessed for
(B) practiced on
(C) dodged into
(D) susceptible to

2 The word "brittle" in the passage is closest in meaning to

(A) firm
(B) fragile
(C) fatal
(D) furious

3 The phrase "adjacent to" in the passage is closest in meaning to

(A) overlooking
(B) adjoining
(C) facing
(D) reaching

VOCABULARY The word ⬚ in the passage is closest in meaning to

20 minute	(A) slender	(B) clumsy	(C) diminutive	(D) general
dense	(A) compact	(B) profound	(C) mammoth	(D) deep
fertile	(A) prosaic	(B) valiant	(C) contingent	(D) teeming

CH 01
CH 02
CH 03
CH 04
CH 05
CH 06
CH 07
CH 08
CH 09

Hackers TOEFL Reading

21　During his presidency, Andrew Jackson continuously attacked the national bank and its supporters. He argued that the ability of the Bank of the United States to regulate the amount of money in circulation served to inhibit local financial institutions from extending credit. Therefore, Jackson swiftly responded to Congress's endorsement of the bank's re-charter in 1832 by vetoing it, effectively initiating the dismantling of the federal banking system. One of the effects this had was renewing the practice of locally printing money, and banks did it on a vast scale. The total amount of currency skyrocketed from $59 million in 1832 to $140 million in 1836. Liberal lending practices, speculation in real estate, and failure to sufficiently back the currency with gold and silver in reserves combined with rapid inflation to devastate the economy and usher in one of America's worst economic depressions. Those who had favored a strong central bank explicitly blamed Jackson for the economic shocks that led to the market's rapid downturn.

1　The word "inhibit" in the passage is closest in meaning to

   (A) restrain
   (B) stimulate
   (C) prolong
   (D) foresee

2　The word "endorsement" in the passage is closest in meaning to

   (A) support
   (B) refusal
   (C) discipline
   (D) criticism

3　The word "vast" in the passage is closest in meaning to

   (A) diminutive
   (B) average
   (C) huge
   (D) selective

VOCABULARY　The word ☐ in the passage is closest in meaning to

21	continuously	(A) certainly	(B) collectively	(C) continually	(D) charitably
	renewing	(A) resuming	(B) recruiting	(C) resolving	(D) replenishing
	favored	(A) shunned	(B) advocated	(C) swerved	(D) presaged

22 Over the last 15 years or so a new approach has emerged to make direct quantifications of the internal structure and dynamics of the Sun and, ultimately, other stars as well. The discovery of propagating sound waves in the Sun in the 1960s and their explanation in the 1970s led to the development of an exciting new technique called helioseismology. This approach is actually a form of acoustical spectroscopy applied to solar seismic waves. Helioseismology investigates waves that are strewn throughout the Sun to measure, for the first time, the invisible internal structure and dynamics of a star. There are millions of distinct, resonating sound waves seen by the Doppler shifting of light emitted at the Sun's surface. The periods of these waves depend on their propagation speeds and the depths of their resonant cavities, and the large number of resonant modes, with different cavities, allows the construction of extremely narrow probes of the temperature, chemical composition, and motions from just below the surface down to the very core of the Sun.

1 The word "quantifications" in the passage is closest in meaning to

(A) configurations
(B) imitations
(C) amendments
(D) measurements

2 The word "strewn" in the passage is closest in meaning to

(A) scattered
(B) woven
(C) broken
(D) suspended

3 The word "composition" in the passage is closest in meaning to

(A) template
(B) makeup
(C) accessory
(D) layer

VOCABULARY   The word ☐ in the passage is closest in meaning to

22	investigates	(A) typifies	(B) examines	(C) induces	(D) shrinks
	resonating	(A) swiveling	(B) alluring	(C) slumbering	(D) resounding
	probes	(A) inquiries	(B) upsurges	(C) vestiges	(D) successions

정답 및 해석 p.412

HACKERS TEST

1   The term tundra, evolved from the Finnish word "tundar," meaning treeless plain, describes a region of physical geography where the growth of trees is suppressed by freezing temperatures. Low-lying vegetation such as lichens, mosses, herbs, and shrubs, which tend to appear brownish-green in color and exhibit slower than average species succession, characterizes the common flora found on the terrain.

2   ➡ The ecosystem of a tundra can be classified into two broad categories, based on its location of the plain: in the Polar Regions, the Arctic tundra features rolling or level ground encircling the north pole and extending south to the edge of the equatorial timberline; the alpine tundra begins at any latitude where the altitude is high enough to cripple normal tree growth.

3   At alpine tundra elevations, subalpine forests of spruce and firs transition into Krummholz and then, if soil is well-developed, into open meadows on gentle slopes, or, in areas with dramatic erosion, into windswept slopes where cushion plants thrive. A significant amount of annual precipitation fosters short vegetation, as does the inclination of the mountainsides, providing good drainage for spring meltwater and heavy summer rains. This, combined with moderate temperatures ranging from −20°C in the winter to around 20°C in the warmer season, even allows some shrubs to grow, especially along streams or where snow accumulates in deep drifts as on the lee side of ridges or in shallow valleys. Where severe conditions prevail, plants are still fortunate enough to have a long growing season, 180 days on the average, and despite the danger of nighttime frost, lichen and moss manage to subsist.

4   Vegetation situated nearby burrows also succeeds due to an additional boost from nitrogen and other nutrients leached into the soil from animal manure. Some fauna, like ground squirrels and marmots, remain quite close to these dens for most of the year, collecting food in the summer and early autumn and retreating during the winter to hibernate. Others, like rabbits, continue to live among the snow during the winter, foraging for what they consume, or living off stored fat reserves as long as they can. Mountain sheep, wildcats, and many birds, only partially adapted to the cold environment, enter a vertical migration pattern, descend down onto warmer slopes throughout the winter, and seek food and more comfortable weather.

5   Animals in the Arctic tundra, with the exception of birds, cannot escape the wintry conditions because the expansive region, covering roughly one-tenth of the total surface of the Earth, is too big for migration to easily occur. Instead, they have adapted to handle long stretches of extremely cold weather by breeding and raising young quickly in the

summer months, taking on white coats to camouflage from predators during periods when the area is blanketed in snow, or developing a layer of fat to both store energy and retain heat. Caribou and reindeer cope with the low temperatures from about −35°C to 5°C by preventing great heat dispersal through their massive body surface areas. They support their bulky frames by consuming large amounts of short patchy plants, mostly lichens, mosses, and small herbs that poke up through the nearly frozen top layer of the ground and cluster together in groups to tolerate the inclement weather. Overall, vegetation is stifled by a short growing season, only 50 to 60 days, little precipitation, and several weeks of daytime darkness, and unlike the alpine tundra, biological diversity is quite low. Shrubs and taller herbs, even if they can weather the poorly drained nutrient-deficient soil, are often unable to adjust to fluctuating temperatures and variations in daily sunlight. Of greater importance to the overall environment is the fact that approximately one-third of the planet's soil-bound carbon is stored in the Arctic tundra with the potential to greatly aggravate the effects of global warming if the permafrost, a frozen bog built from layers of freezing precipitation, is subjected to unusually high temperatures.

1 The word "suppressed" in the passage is closest in meaning to

(A) counterbalanced
(B) arrested
(C) befuddled
(D) repaired

2 According to paragraph 2, how are the two types of tundra differentiated?

(A) By the amount of annual rainfall
(B) By the sorts of plants
(C) By the types of ground
(D) By the place in which they occur

Paragraph 2 is marked with an arrow [➡].

3 The word "fosters" in the passage is closest in meaning to

(A) proclaims
(B) regains
(C) promotes
(D) refrains

CH 01
CH 02
CH 03
CH 04
CH 05
CH 06
CH 07
CH 08
CH 09
Hackers TOEFL Reading

4 The word "subsist" in the passage is closest in meaning to

(A) endure
(B) lapse
(C) flee
(D) seethe

5 According to the passage, animals in the alpine tundra aid plant growth by

(A) depositing wastes that contain nutritive elements
(B) removing ice that covers the plants
(C) storing seeds over the winter in their burrows
(D) clearing areas of competing vegetation

6 Which of the sentences below best expresses the essential information in the highlighted sentence in the passage? *Incorrect* choices change the meaning in important ways or leave out essential information.

(A) Due to the harsh conditions of the Arctic tundra, only birds make an attempt to leave the area during the winter.

(B) The weather conditions of the Arctic tundra make it impossible for most animals to follow seasonal migration patterns.

(C) As the Arctic tundra covers such a large portion of the Earth surface, animal migration routes are broad.

(D) The enormous size of the Arctic tundra prohibits almost all animals from leaving the area during the winter.

7 The phrase "cope with" in the passage is closest in meaning to

(A) reckon
(B) enrich
(C) handle
(D) exclude

8 The word "dispersal" in the passage is closest in meaning to

(A) ignition
(B) shudder
(C) distribution
(D) cycle

9 The word "aggravate" in the passage is closest in meaning to

(A) alleviate
(B) worsen
(C) hasten
(D) appease

10 **Directions**: Select the appropriate phrases from the answer choices and match them to the type of geography to which they relate. **This question is worth 3 points.**

> Drag your answer choices to the spaces where they belong. To remove an answer choice, click on it. To review the passage, click on **View Text**.

Answer Choices	Alpine Tundra
(A) Has a great deal of yearly rain that hastens the growth of plants	●
(B) Is in danger of being destroyed by human activity in a short time	●
(C) Functions as a reservoir for gas, which possibly increases earth temperatures	●
(D) Lacks light during the daytime for a period of a few weeks	**Arctic Tundra**
(E) Can be found in any region at a certain altitude	●
(F) Has extensive forests of spruce and firs on mountain ridges	●
(G) Enables vegetation to grow for roughly half a year	

정답 및 해석 p.417

CH 01
CH 02
CH 03
CH 04
CH 05
CH 06
CH 07
CH 08
CH 09
Hackers TOEFL Reading

1   Growing out of a long period of conservative, traditionalistic art, the Baroque period started around 1600 in Rome, Italy, in response to a perceived banality in Renaissance style. The name was adopted from the Portuguese noun "barroco," meaning an irregular pearl, and is used to describe elaborate techniques or thematic extravagances, which are characterizations that envelop the period as well as its fashion. At the height of Baroque popularity, critics of its ostentatious grandeur began using the word Rococo to brand a lighter and more intimate form of decoration that was achieving prominence in and around France. By the mid-18th century, Rococo, in and of itself, had become an artistic movement combining architecture, painting, sculpture, and music. Contemporary art historians often categorize the two genres in comparison to each other, with differences in one defining the distinguishing qualities of the other.

2   Historically, the production of pre-Baroque art was conceived of within the rigid confines of the Roman Catholic Church. This religious body was reorganized during the Protestant Reformation, a political movement that, throughout the 16th century, agitated for public access to Biblical scripts without the mediation of clergy. As a result of the new-found ability for non-clergy to take personal interest in Holy Scripture, ecclesiastical art was stripped of its esoteric church-controlled representation, allowing artists to create such works as paintings, murals, and sculptures that were, for the first time, commissioned by secular offices or private citizens to adorn spaces outside of the church. Overall, the artistic content was not suited for a well-informed and literate clergy familiar with the Bible but rather intended for mass consumption by the illiterate public. For this reason, Baroque art tends to focus on the Saints and the Virgin Mary in particular by illustrating famous stories for a widespread audience.

3   ➡ Due to its prevailing accessibility, by the end of the 17th century, Baroque art was so entrenched in the European identity that King Louis XIV declared it the official style of France, embellishing his Palace of Versailles in the fashion and building magnificent reception rooms, courts, and anterooms. The undertaking prompted anti-monarchists, who had grown tired of the king's overindulgences, to respond by developing their own unique decorative arts, which they called Rococo, taking a conscious turn away from Baroque and utilizing strikingly different motifs.

4   At the outset of the Rococo style, only architectural design was affected; walls, ceilings, moldings, and engravings on residences were ornamented with abstract "s" curves and "c" scrolls combined with naturalistic motifs which were derived from shells and plants, with pastel and ivory white colors appearing most frequently. Mirrors were utilized to create the illusion of space and etherealness, usually framed in ornate mother-of-pearl with inlaid gold and silver. The effervescence stood in stark contrast to the king's heavy, passionate designs, which blended the great, serious drama of the Bible with rich, deep colors and intense shadows. Whereas Baroque illustrated serious religious undercurrents by exaggerating motion in concise detail, Rococo alleviated this tension.

5   As Rococo moved from architecture into visual art, paintings and sculptures began to reflect playfulness and lightness, often portraying carefree aristocratic couples on leisurely outings, or cherubs representative of the myths of love, and integrated a variety of diverse characteristics, including a taste for Oriental designs and asymmetric compositions. Balance, an important aspect of the Baroque style coming about in the age of mathematical and geometrical advancements, was discarded in favor of its antithesis. At the same time, Baroque works such as Bernini's carved marble fountains, undoubtedly the most conspicuous examples of the style, as well as his busts and figures, which were meticulously proportioned, fell out of fashion. Misshapen chandeliers, disfigured shellwork and paintings that depicted some figural elements larger than others, came to exemplify the Rococo genre, recoiling from any works that were overly conscientious or weighty in nature.

6   The refusal of Rococo artists to produce any works that could be deemed as profound has provoked some debate between art historians who attempt to situate the genre into a meaningful discussion about its long-lasting impacts on culture. While some believe that Rococo is merely a brief reaction to Baroque's manifest style, others argue that the nature of Rococo is no less distinct.

1   The word "prominence" in the passage is closest in meaning to

(A) agreement
(B) clemency
(C) prestige
(D) overturn

2   According to the passage, prior to the Protestant Reformation, religious art

(A) was used to teach those who couldn't read the Bible
(B) was requested by the church for decorative purposes
(C) was only to be understood by studying Holy Scripture
(D) was restricted to works produced by the church

3   According to paragraph 3, the anti-monarchists developed Rococo in response to

(A) the then current king's prodigal manner
(B) the need to adorn the Palace of Versailles
(C) the lack of an accepted European identity
(D) Baroque's adoption as the national style

Paragraph 3 is marked with an arrow [➡].

CH 01
CH 02
CH 03
CH 04
CH 05
CH 06
CH 07
CH 08
CH 09

Hackers TOEFL Reading

4 The word "outset" in the passage is closest in meaning to

(A) vagary
(B) outline
(C) regard
(D) start

5 Which of the sentences below best expresses the essential information in the highlighted sentence in the passage? *Incorrect* choices change the meaning in important ways or leave out essential information.

(A) A difference between Baroque and Rococo was how each dealt with religious themes.
(B) The tension which was expressed in Baroque paintings was absent in Rococo works.
(C) Baroque's focus on detail and accuracy was much different from the Rococo style.
(D) Rococo contrasted with Baroque by reducing the solemnity of religious themes.

6 The word "discarded" in the passage is closest in meaning to

(A) fitted
(B) rejected
(C) separated
(D) adopted

7 The word "profound" in the passage is closest in meaning to

(A) superficial
(B) insincere
(C) deep
(D) jubilant

8 The word "provoked" in the passage is closest in meaning to

(A) instigated
(B) grieved
(C) unveiled
(D) whittled

9 The word "manifest" in the passage is closest in meaning to

(A) hidden
(B) uniform
(C) complimentary
(D) patent

10 **Directions**: Select the appropriate phrases from the answer choices and match them to the type of art they represent. **This question is worth 4 points.**

> Drag your answer choices to the spaces where they belong. To remove an answer choice, click on it. To review the passage, click on **View Text**.

Answer Choices	Baroque Art
(A) Was a precursor to the reconstruction of the Roman Catholic Church	•
(B) Made use of glasses to provoke delusion of space and heavenliness	•
(C) Placed great emphasis upon symmetry	•
(D) Was characterized by distorted figures and pieces	•
(E) Highlighted well-known figures to appeal to the masses	
(F) Was planned to be used by a knowledgeable and literate cleric	**Rococo Art**
(G) Amalgamated dark colors and intensely dramatic design	•
(H) Was initially an Italian art devised in reply to mundane Renaissance styles	•
(I) Applied many curved lines with themes taken from nature	•

정답 및 해석 p.419

CH 01
CH 02
CH 03
CH 04
CH 05
CH 06
CH 07
CH 08
CH 09
Hackers TOEFL Reading

1   The world's second largest freshwater lake after Lake Superior, Lake Victoria is home to an astonishing array of tropical fish, the most remarkable of which are the five hundred different species of cichlids, a group of fish ranging in size from three centimeters to one meter. This variety is even more amazing when considering that only sixty species in total inhabit all of Western Europe.

2   Because Lake Victoria completely dried up several times in its history due to the formation of glaciers and severe drought, the incredible range of cichlid diversity in the lake must have developed in a relatively short evolutionary time period. In fact, sediment samples taken from the bottom of the lake indicate that it was desiccated as recent as twelve thousand years ago at the end of the most recent ice age. This means that any endemic cichlids must have died out or taken refuge elsewhere in the region where liquid water remained. The few that survived endured severe conditions and were confined to ever-shrinking streams or pools of water, and these environmental constraints would have deterred rapid speciation. When the climate warmed and regular rains eventually returned to the region, rivers began to rise and gradually refill Lake Victoria, making it possible for fish to colonize the lake once again. These pioneers — perhaps including only a single species of cichlid — were the ancestors of every cichlid species found in Lake Victoria today.

3   ➡ These first fish had the advantage of facing no competition for resources, so they quickly flourished and populated their comparatively stable and unrestricted new environment. At first, most of the pioneers probably congregated in the most favorable areas of the lake. As their numbers grew, however, conspecific internecine conflict inevitably arose and the abundant cichlids had to segregate and form separate populations in various microhabitats. Some entered deep water with rocky or silt bottoms, while others settled in the shallows with ample vegetation. These varying circumstances required expeditious adaptations in behavior, anatomy, and morphology to allow individual populations to exploit a niche more efficiently. Such rapid diversification into new forms is known as *adaptive radiation*.

4   One of the main factors that enabled cichlids to diversify so quickly was their possession of multiple jaws. Unlike most other fish, they have a bony structure in their throat known as a pharyngeal apparatus that functions very much like teeth, whereas the teeth in the mouth serve more like hands. The pharyngeal jaws are quite agile — the upper is able to move up and down and dislocate, while the lower is capable of moving forwards and backwards. Since the pharyngeal set is used for feeding, the teeth in the mouth are free to adapt without interfering with the ability of the fish to ingest sustenance. The teeth of the cichlids found in Lake Victoria have morphed into a variety of different types of feeding implements, such as shovel-like scrapers and tweezer-like pinchers.

5   Yet feeding alone does not put the requisite selective pressure to explain the myriad types of these fish found; an additional driving force for rapid speciation was the cichlids' color-restricted mating rituals. In species in which the males play little or no role in

parenting and attempt multiple matings each season, sexual selection by females can play a powerful evolutionary role. When females have a wide variety of partners to choose from, they are allowed to be more particular about their mates. The males, on the other hand, have to find some way to overcome the enormous competition. In cichlids, it has led to spectacular male courtship exhibitions, using colors designed to entice females into spawning. Since females endemic to Lake Victoria select partners with particular features, it increases the chances that groups preferring alternate characteristics will then sympatrically divide into separate species.

6   Unfortunately, the incredible diversity has been decreasing and now over 250 indigenous types can no longer be found in Lake Victoria. In the 1950s, over the objections of wildlife ecologists, the British colonial government, hoping to give the local fishery a bigger fish to catch, released a non-native species, the Nile perch, into the lake. Commonly referred to as a voracious predator, the perch can grow into a hefty six-foot, two-hundred-pound giant. The thinking at the time was that the large predator would feed on the smaller fishes (i.e. the numerous small cichlids) and lead an immense growth in the fishing industry in the area. It was quick to establish itself and fundamentally changed the lake's ecology by eating, to the point of extinction, at least half of the cichlid species. At present, cichlids constitute less than 1 percent of fish in Lake Victoria.

1   The word "severe" in the passage is closest in meaning to

(A) volatile
(B) barren
(C) harsh
(D) arid

2   The word "deterred" in the passage is closest in meaning to

(A) bemoaned
(B) stopped
(C) ordained
(D) protracted

3   The word "colonize" in the passage is closest in meaning to

(A) settle
(B) desert
(C) join with
(D) conform to

4   According to paragraph 3, why did cichlids segregate into separate populations?

(A) They faced intense opposition from other invasive species.
(B) They were cut off from one another by fluctuating water levels in the lake.
(C) Their growing numbers created destructive competition within the species.
(D) Their initial habitat in the lake was unfavorable to survival.

Paragraph 3 is marked with an arrow [➡].

CH 01
CH 02
CH 03
CH 04
CH 05
CH 06
CH 07
CH 08
CH 09
Hackers TOEFL Reading

5 The phrase "interfering with" in the passage is closest in meaning to

(A) violating
(B) hindering
(C) distorting
(D) sacrificing

6 The word "requisite" in the passage is closest in meaning to

(A) necessary
(B) spoilable
(C) piteous
(D) encouraging

7 The word "entice" in the passage is closest in meaning to

(A) vex
(B) enliven
(C) tempt
(D) revive

8 Which of the sentences below best expresses the essential information in the highlighted sentence in the passage? *Incorrect* choices change the meaning in important ways or leave out essential information.

(A) Due to the specificity of the displays of the males in Lake Victoria, non-native cichlids are unable to mate with the locals.
(B) The mating displays of male cichlids produce alternating responses in the females, resulting in the development of new species of cichlids.
(C) Because female cichlids choose certain traits in their mates, there is a greater chance that distinct species will be formed in one place.
(D) As female cichlids only react to the mating exhibitions of males of their own species, closely related species of cichlids can coexist without interbreeding.

9 The word "immense" in the passage is closest in meaning to

(A) exact
(B) enormous
(C) imprudent
(D) abstruse

10 **Directions**: An introductory sentence for a brief summary of the passage is provided below. Complete the summary by selecting the THREE answer choices that express the most important ideas in the passage. Some sentences do not belong in the summary because they express ideas that are not presented in the passage or are minor ideas in the passage. **This question is worth 2 points.**

> Drag your answer choices to the spaces where they belong. To remove an answer choice, click on it. To review the passage, click on **View Text**.

The Lake Victoria cichlid underwent rapid diversification following the last ice age.

-
-
-

Answer Choices

(A) Once entering the lake, the cichlid began to thrive with the absence of competition and quickly separated into many different species.

(B) One reason for the swift adaptation of the cichlid was the ability of its jaws to chew various types of food.

(C) Since female cichlids are selective in choosing mates, males have had to develop extensive color exhibitions to attract females.

(D) All the cichlid species in the Lake Victoria region twelve thousand years ago had previously been isolated from each other.

(E) The transformation of the cichlid tooth structure caused by the existence of its multiple jaws led to manifold feeding adaptations.

(F) The need to adapt to the rapidly changing environment in Lake Victoria resulted in unique evolutionary patterns in cichlids.

정답 및 해석 p.420

1 ➡ In prehistoric times, lions roamed large expanses of Europe. Like other megafauna at the time, these European lions suffered devastating losses during the last ice age, and by around 10,000 years ago, the lion population of Europe was virtually extinguished. Scientists have traditionally held that a scarce food supply was the sole reason that led to the European lion's decline. But while its quarry were becoming less common, fossil records show that some of its favored prey, such as reindeer and musk oxen, survived even after their large feline predators dwindled. This indicates that the reasons for the creature's deterioration were probably more complex than was previously thought. It is now believed that a combination of climatic and vegetative change, along with food scarcity, led to their disappearance from most of Europe. As the global climate warmed, the vast steppes European lions depended on were gradually replaced by forest, severely limiting the available space for hunting. With less space and prey at their disposal, lions were simply unable to sustain their prehistoric numbers.

2 There were, however, occasional records of lion sightings in southern Europe during historic times, which suggests that there were surviving populations in some locales or an influx of lions from neighboring regions. According to the Greek historian Herodotus, when the Persian commander Xerxes invaded Greece in the 5th century B.C., his transport camels were attacked by lions. Herodotus also pointed out that lions were largely confined to the area between the Achelos and Nestos rivers, which indicates that their geographical distribution was severely limited and status endangered. And from approximately two thousand years ago, there are no records of wild lions in southern Europe. If lions did indeed occupy the area, their tenure was brief, and their demise was no doubt hastened by sport hunting among Greek leaders, such as Alexander the Great, and to a lesser extent, by the Roman demand for lions to fight in their arenas.

3 ➡ In Africa and Asia, lions survived in significant numbers until modern times. Then in the 19th century, there was a rapid decline in African and Asian lion populations. The central causes were the advent of industrial technology and the explosion of the human population. Modern machinery allowed people to harness wilderness areas for human habitation, forestry, and agriculture. In turn, human contact with lions increased, and modern firearms and chemical pesticides made it easier to kill lions in mass quantities and with shocking rapidity. Put simply, the lions had far less room to hunt, and if they entered areas that were occupied by humans, they were commonly shot or poisoned. It is estimated that between 1800 and 2000, the human population grew by 600 percent while the lion population decreased by 95 percent.

4 ➡ The vast majority of the world's lions are now confined to sub-Saharan Africa. There they live in pockets of land scattered across the subcontinent. Of the approximately 30,000 or so lions left in Africa, many are still in danger from poaching by hunters and poisoning by livestock farmers. The situation with lions in Asia is even more perilous. The

sole surviving Asiatic lion population now lives in India's Gir lion sanctuary, which is home to only a few hundred lions. Despite their protected status, these last remaining Asiatic lions are in severe danger of extinction for two reasons. First, they are descendents of only about a dozen lions that happened to be saved by a wealthy Indian prince. Their shared heredity means they have a very narrow gene pool and are highly inbred. It is feared that inbreeding may have left them genetically weak and highly vulnerable to disease. If a contagious illness were to gain a foothold in the population, many of the lions could perish, and their numbers might fall to unrecoverable levels. Second, there remains some occasional conflict with the few residents who still inhabit the park, and whose livelihoods depend on raising livestock. When lions prey on the livestock, it creates disdain for lions among the local people. In order to guarantee the lions' future in the park, it is necessary to continue the ongoing efforts of protecting livestock as well as maintaining sufficient numbers of wild ungulates that the lions depend on for food.

1 According to paragraph 1, the conventional view of scientists was that prehistoric lion populations in Europe diminished because of

(A) competition with other large predators
(B) the overhunting of prehistoric humans
(C) hypothermia and contagious diseases
(D) the shrinking availability of sustenance

Paragraph 1 is marked with an arrow [➡].

2 The word "sole" in the passage is closest in meaning to

(A) likely
(B) primary
(C) only
(D) petty

3 The word "status" in the passage is closest in meaning to

(A) operation
(B) function
(C) elevation
(D) position

4 Which of the sentences below best expresses the essential information in the highlighted sentence in the passage? *Incorrect* choices change the meaning in important ways or leave out essential information.

(A) Whether or not lions occupied the region is unknown in part because the Greek and Roman records refer to only a brief period in history.

(B) Any lion occupation of the region would have been short-lived, and the decline of lions was certainly precipitated by Greek and Roman sport.

(C) Not long after lions occupied the area they were quickly exterminated by Greek leaders or sent to fight in Roman arenas.

(D) Occupation of the region by lions would have been more extensive if their numbers were not decimated by Greeks and Romans.

5 The word "harness" in the passage is closest in meaning to

(A) restrict
(B) maximize
(C) obstruct
(D) utilize

6 Which of the following was NOT mentioned in paragraph 3 as a human threat to lions in modern times?

(A) the use of poisons
(B) development of uninhabited areas
(C) a skyrocketing population
(D) easement of gun restrictions

Paragraph 3 is marked with an arrow [➡].

7 The word "commonly" in the passage is closest in meaning to

(A) supposedly
(B) generally
(C) reportedly
(D) actually

8 According to paragraph 4, which of the following questions can NOT be answered?

(A) What specific region currently contains most of the world's lions?
(B) Who was responsible for saving the ancestors of Gir's lions?
(C) What changes were made in Africa to protect its lions?
(D) Why are India's lions still in danger of extinction?

Paragraph 4 is marked with an arrow [➡].

9 Select the **TWO** answers that are mentioned in paragraph 4 as reasons that Asiatic lions are in peril. To receive credit, you must choose **TWO** answers.

(A) They are descendants from an isolated genetic line.
(B) The regulations designed to protect them are being ignored.
(C) They face antagonism from human occupants of the park.
(D) The diseases prone to affect them are common in the sanctuary.

10 **Directions**: An introductory sentence for a brief summary of the passage is provided below. Complete the summary by selecting the THREE answer choices that express the most important ideas in the passage. Some sentences do not belong in the summary because they express ideas that are not presented in the passage or are minor ideas in the passage. **This question is worth 2 points.**

> Drag your answer choices to the spaces where they belong. To remove an answer choice, click on it. To review the passage, click on **View Text**.

Over the course of time, lions have undergone periods of population decline.

-
-
-

Answer Choices

(A) Although lions once roamed much of Europe, environmental changes nearly wiped them out in prehistoric times, and they disappeared from Europe in Greek and Roman times.

(B) During the 19th and 20th centuries, the human population increased multifold while the world's lion population declined precipitously.

(C) Despite a few historical references regarding lions in Greece, it remains unclear whether lions in fact repopulated southern Europe in ancient times.

(D) The Asiatic lions in India's Gir sanctuary faced almost certain extinction, but conservation efforts have increased their numbers to sustainable levels.

(E) Lions subsisted mainly in Asia and Africa up until the 19th century, when human activity became increasingly deleterious to lions.

(F) Most lions currently reside in sub-Saharan Africa, and the few remaining Asiatic lions are particularly vulnerable due to genetic isolation and hostility from agriculturalists.

정답 및 해석 p.422

토플 빈출어휘 정리 노트

Chapter 03에 수록된 어휘들을 빈출도 순으로 정리했습니다. 음성파일을 들으며 꼭 암기하세요.

토플 최빈출어휘 [★★★]

- lavish [lǽviʃ] 낭비하다 (=waste)
- devastation [dèvəstéiʃən] 손상 (=harm)
- emit [imít] 방출하다 (=discharge)
- exude [igzúːd] 방출하다 (=emit)
- wield [wiːld] 행사하다 (=exercise)
- counterpart [káuntərpàːrt] 상응하는 것 (=equivalent)
- fluctuate [flʌ́ktʃuèit] 불안정하다 (=vary)
- sufficient [səfíʃənt] 충분한 (=adequate)
- modify [mάdəfài] 변경하다 (=adapt)
- fashion [fǽʃən] 방식 (=manner)
- rigorous [rígərəs] 엄격한
- discernible [disə́ːrnəbl] 식별할 수 있는 (=perceptible)
- phenomenon [finάmənən] 현상 (=occurrence)
- prevalent [prévələnt] 우세한 (=dominant)
- subsequently [sʌ́bsikwəntli] 그 후에 (=later)
- subject to 하기 쉬운 (=susceptible to)
- grind [graind] 갈다
- brittle [brítl] 약한 (=fragile)
- dense [dens] 고밀도의 (=compact)
- retreat [ritríːt] 후퇴하다
- ultimately [ʌ́ltəmətli] 궁극적으로
- strew [struː] 흩어지다 (=scatter)
- probe [proub] 조사 (=inquiry)
- suppress [səprés] 억제하다 (=arrest)
- foster [fɔ́ːstər] 촉진하다 (=promote)
- subsist [səbsíst] 존속하다 (=endure)
- dispersal [dispə́ːrsəl] 분산 (=distribution)
- aggravate [ǽgrəvèit] 가중시키다 (=worsen)
- prominence [prάmənəns] 주목 (=prestige)
- embellish [imbéliʃ] 장식하다 (=make attractive)
- ornament [ɔ́ːrnəmənt] 장식하다 (=adorn)
- discard [diskάːrd] 버리다 (=reject)
- meticulously [mətíkjuləsli] 세심하게 (=carefully)
- profound [prəfáund] 심오한

- provoke [prəvóuk] 불러일으키다 (=instigate)
- astonishing [əstάniʃiŋ] 놀라운 (=incredible)
- constraint [kənstréint] 제약 (=restriction)
- deter [ditə́ːr] 방해하다 (=stop)
- colonize [kάlənàiz] 정착하다 (=settle)
- apparatus [æ̀pərǽtəs] 기관
- requisite [rékwəzit] 필수적인 (=necessary)
- entice [intáis] 유혹하다 (=tempt)
- indigenous [indídʒənəs] 고유의 (=native)
- harness [hάːrnis] 이용하다 (=utilize)
- vulnerable [vʌ́lnərəbl] 취약한 (=easily damaged)

토플 빈출어휘 [★★]

- traditional [trədíʃənl] 전통적인 (=conventional)
- initial [iníʃəl] 초기의 (=first)
- limited [límitid] 한정된 (=restricted)
- carry [kǽri] 운반하다 (=move)
- dramatically [drəmǽtikəli] 극적으로 (=strikingly)
- combination [kàmbənéiʃən] 결합 (=hybrid)
- principle [prínsəpl] 원칙 (=fundamental)
- delineate [dilínièit] 묘사하다 (=describe)
- extend [iksténd] 확장하다 (=stretch)
- exact [igzǽkt] 정확한 (=accurate)
- clearly [klíərli] 명확히 (=definitely)
- shift [ʃift] 변화 (=change)
- accompany [əkʌ́mpəni] 동반하다 (=companion)
- carve [kɑːrv] 조각하다 (=incise)
- display [displéi] 보여주다 (=exhibit)
- successive [səksésiv] 연속적인 (=in sequence)
- exhibition [èksəbíʃən] 전시 (=display)
- appear [əpíər] 나타나다 (=emerge)
- visible [vízəbl] 명백한 (=evident)
- onset [άːnsèt] 시초 (=beginning)
- investigation [invèstəgéiʃən] 조사 (=examination)
- infinite [ínfənət] 무한한 (=measureless)

*해커스 동영상강의 포털 해커스인강(HackersIngang.com)에서 '토플 빈출어휘 정리 노트' 음성파일을 무료로 다운로드할 수 있습니다.

☐ minute [máinjuːt] 미세한 (=diminutive)

☐ fertile [fɔ́ːrtl] 비옥한 (=teeming)

☐ favor [féivər] 지지하다 (=advocate)

☐ devastate [dévəsteit] 무너뜨리다

☐ renew [rinjúː] 갱신하다 (=resume)

☐ inhibit [inhíbit] 억제하다 (=restrain)

☐ continuously [kəntínjuəsli] 계속해서 (=continually)

☐ vast [væst] 큰 (=huge)

☐ endorsement [indɔ́ːrsmənt] 지지 (=support)

☐ investigate [invéstəgèit] 연구하다 (=examine)

☐ camouflage [kǽməflàːʒ] 위장하다

☐ cope with 대처하다 (=handle)

☐ extravagance [ikstrǽvəgəns] 무절제함

☐ manifest [mǽnəfest] 명백한 (=patent)

☐ endemic [endémik] 지역 고유의

☐ take refuge in 도피하다

☐ sustenance [sʌ́stənəns] 음식물

☐ immense [iméns] 엄청난 (=enormous)

☐ sole [soul] 단 하나의 (=only)

☐ status [stéitəs] 상태 (=position)

☐ commonly [kámənli] 흔히 (=generally)

☐ perilous [pérələs] 위험한

☐ disdain [disdéin] 경멸 (=scorn)

토플 기출어휘 [★]

☐ oscillate [ásəlèit] 진동하다

☐ organ [ɔ́ːrgən] 기관

☐ stable [stéibl] 안정된

☐ undergo [ʌ̀ndərgóu] 겪다 (=experience)

☐ amalgamation [əmæ̀lgəméiʃən] 융합

☐ fairly [fɛ́ərli] 상당히

☐ catastrophic [kæ̀təstráfik] 대이변의

☐ ideally [aidíːəli] 이론적으로

☐ posterior [pɑstíəriər] 뒷부분의

☐ anterior [æntíəriər] 앞부분의

☐ notorious [noutɔ́ːriəs] 악명 높은 (=infamous)

☐ predator [prédətər] 육식 동물

☐ crooked [krúkid] 구부러진

☐ behave [bihéiv] 작용하다 (=act)

☐ circulation [sɔ̀ːrkjəléiʃən] 유통

☐ existence [igzístəns] 존재 (=presence)

☐ dynamics [dainǽmiks] 역학

☐ narrow [nǽrou] 정밀한

☐ chisel [tʃízl] 깎다

☐ compaction [kəmpǽkʃən] 압축

☐ explicitly [iksplísitli] 노골적으로

☐ speculation [spèkjuléiʃən] 투기

☐ quantification [kwàntəfikéiʃən] 수량화

☐ resonate [rézənèit] 공명하다 (=resound)

☐ composition [kàmpəzíʃən] 구성 (=makeup)

☐ altitude [ǽltətjùːd] 고도

☐ hibernate [háibərnèit] 겨울잠 자다

☐ stifle [stáifl] 억제하다

☐ outset [áutsèt] 시초 (=start)

☐ undercurrent [ʌ́ndərkɔ̀ːrənt] 저의

☐ asymmetric [èisəmétrik] 비대칭의

☐ antithesis [æntíθəsis] 반대

☐ disfigured [disfígjərd] 형상이 일그러진

☐ desiccate [désikèit] 마르게 하다

☐ morphology [mɔːrfálədʒi] 형태

☐ ingest [indʒést] 섭취하다

☐ parenting [pɛ́ərəntiŋ] 돌봄

☐ courtship [kɔ́ːrtʃìp] 구애

☐ sympatrically [simpǽtrikəli] 같은 지역에서

☐ prehistoric [prìːhistɔ́ːrik] 선사 시대의

☐ roam [roum] 돌아다니다

☐ extinguish [ikstíŋgwiʃ] 소멸시키다

☐ sanctuary [sǽŋktʃuèri] 보호구역

☐ resident [rézədənt] 거주자

☐ livelihood [láivlihùd] 생계

CH 01
CH 02
CH 03
CH 04
CH 05
CH 06
CH 07
CH 08
CH 09

Hackers TOEFL Reading

Chapter 04
Reference

OVERVIEW

Reference 문제는 주어진 지시어가 실제로 가리키는 지시 대상이 무엇인지를 선택하는 문제 유형이다. 지시어는 글의 간결성과 응집성(coherence)을 확보하기 위해 똑같은 단어를 반복해서 사용하지 않고 '대신 사용'하는 대명사 등을 일컫는 말이다. 따라서 문장의 의미를 올바르게 이해하기 위해서는 지시어가 가리키는 대상이 무엇인지를 정확하게 파악해야만 한다.

Reference 문제를 풀기 위해서는 지시어로 자주 쓰이는 여러 표현의 쓰임을 익히고 문맥 속에서 그 지시어가 지칭하는 대상을 찾는 연습이 필요하다.

Reference 문제는 보통 한 지문당 0~1개가 출제된다.

TYPES OF QUESTIONS

지문에 어휘 또는 구가 음영 처리되어 있으며 4개의 보기가 주어진다.
Reference 문제의 전형적인 질문 유형은 아래와 같다.

- The word "⬛⬛⬛" in the passage refers to
- The phrase "⬛⬛⬛" in the passage refers to

HACKERS **STRATEGY**

CH 01
CH 02
CH 03
CH 04
CH 05
CH 06
CH 07
CH 08
CH 09

Hackers TOEFL Reading

전략 1 지시어가 가리키는 지시 대상을 지시어 주변에서 찾는다.

지시 대상은 문제에 주어진 지시어보다 앞서 언급되는 것이 일반적이므로 문제로 나온 지시어보다 앞의 문장 또는 문단을 검토하여 지시어가 가리키는 대상을 확인한다.

Ex A human **brain** performs many operations simultaneously. It monitors bodily functions, perceives the environment, and produces speech all at the same time.

➡ 지시어 It이 가리키는 것은 지시어보다 앞서 언급된 brain(A human brain)이다.

간혹 지시어가 지시 대상보다 먼저 나오는 경우가 있는데, 이는 아래 예문과 같이 한 문장 내에서 주절의 주어를 대명사로 취하여 부사구(절) 등이 콤마(,) 앞에 나오는 경우이다.

Ex In their report, **the biotech companies** claim that the improved technology is a solution to a serious drawback of genetically modified crops.

➡ 지시어 their가 가리키는 것은 지시어보다 뒤에 언급되는 주절의 주어 the biotech companies이다.

전략 2 각 지시어의 성격을 파악하면 지시 대상을 좀 더 쉽게 찾을 수 있다.

토플에 자주 나오는 지시어의 쓰임과 특성을 잘 익혀두면 그 각각의 지시 대상을 쉽게 파악할 수 있다.

● **인칭대명사**
자주 출제되는 인칭대명사로는 단수에 쓰이는 it, its와 복수에 쓰이는 they, their, them이 있다.

Ex As the trade **winds** pass over the ocean at a rate of 11–13 miles per hour, they displace some of the warmer surface water in their path, creating a 0.5 meter difference in sea level in the western Pacific.

➡ 복수를 나타내는 인칭대명사 they가 가리키는 것은 winds이다.

● **지시대명사**
자주 출제되는 지시대명사로는 단수에 쓰이는 this, that과 복수에 쓰이는 these, those, 단수와 복수 모두에 쓰이는 the former, the latter가 있다.

Ex During Jackson's second term, his popularity compelled his opponents to unify themselves into what became known as the Whig Party, a collective that proposed a sharply contrasting **ideology** to that of the ruling party.

➡ Ruling party의 that이 Whig Party의 ideology와 contrasting되는 것이므로, that이 가리키는 것은 앞서 언급된 ideology이다.

해석 p.425

Ex There are two types of looms, which are the **ground loom** and the warp-weighted loom. The former first came into use in North Africa.

➡ The former는 '전자'를 의미하므로 두 대상 중 먼저 언급된 ground loom을 가리킨다.

● 지시형용사

주로 this/that + 단수명사, these/those + 복수명사의 형태로 출제되며 지시형용사 뒤에 나오는 명사를 통해 지시 대상을 쉽게 찾을 수 있다.

Ex The world of **the crustaceans** is a world of bizarre shapes and adaptations. These animals are best-known for their hard outer shell.

➡ 지시형용사 + 명사의 형태를 갖춘 These animals가 가리키는 것은 앞서 언급된 the crustaceans이다.

● 부정대명사

자주 출제되는 부정대명사로는 some, others, one, another, none 등이 있으며, 특히 others는 'other + 복수명사'를 줄인 말로 some과 짝을 이루어 쓰이는 표현이다. 또한 one과 another 역시 자주 짝을 이루어 사용된다.

Ex During the cloth-making process, the harnesses raise **some warp yarns** and lower others.

➡ Some warp yarns와 others는 대비되는 것으로 others는 some과 짝을 이루어 사용되고 있으므로 others가 가리키는 것은 warp yarns이다.

Ex For many animals, moving the body from **one place** to another is one of the most important everyday tasks.

➡ Another는 one과 짝을 이루어 사용되는 대명사로 another가 가리키는 것은 place이다.

● 관계대명사

보통 관계대명사가 가리키는 것은 바로 앞의 선행사인 경우가 많다. 자주 출제되는 관계대명사로는 who, which, that이 있다.

Ex Insects become scarce in the winter in northern latitudes, so **insectivorous birds**, which are dependent upon insects for their diet, must move closer to the equator.

➡ 관계대명사 which는 바로 앞의 선행사 insectivorous birds를 가리킨다.

● 지시부사

자주 출제되는 지시부사로는 장소를 나타내는 there와 시간을 나타내는 then이 있다.

Ex Einstein moved to **Berlin** in 1914 with his wife and two sons to continue his research and lecture. Unhappy with life there, his wife Mileva returned to Switzerland.

➡ There은 장소를 나타내는 지시부사로 앞 문장의 Berlin을 가리킨다.

예상 답을 지시어 자리에 대입하여 해석한 후 문맥이 자연스러운지 확인한다.

예상 정답을 고른 후에는 반드시 그 답을 지시어 자리에 직접 대입하여 문장이 자연스럽게 해석되는지를 검토해봐야 한다. 만약 해석했을 때 문맥상 연결이 자연스럽지 않으면 오답이다.

Ex Bryophytes are considered the simplest plants, in part because they are the only nonvascular plants. Since they have no means of transporting water, essential minerals, and dissolved sugar for extensive distances within their bodies, bryophytes are typically quite small. Although **some** possess a cuticle, others do not and instead absorb water directly through the surfaces of their leafy shoots. They generally require a moist environment for active growth and reproduction, although a few bryophytes are tolerant of dry areas.

Q: The word "others" in the passage refers to

    (A) plants

    (B) minerals

    (C) bodies

    (D) bryophytes

➡ 부정대명사 others는 some과 짝을 이루는 대명사로 여기서 some과 others는 원래 some bryophytes와 other bryophytes이다. 즉, others가 가리키는 것은 앞 문장의 주어인 **(D) bryophytes**이다.

문맥이 자연스러운지 확인

Bryophytes를 others 자리에 대입하면 '일부 선태류 식물은 상피를 가지고 있지만, 다른 선태류 식물은 그렇지 않고 대신 잎이 무성한 싹의 표면을 통해 물을 직접 흡수한다'라고 해석되어 문맥이 자연스럽다.

TIP 토플에는 4개 보기가 모두 지시어와 수 일치되어 나오므로, 지시어가 지시 대상과 수 일치되는지 여부를 가지고 문제를 풀 수는 없다는 점을 명심해야 한다.

CH 01
CH 02
CH 03
CH 04
CH 05
CH 06
CH 07
CH 08
CH 09

Hackers TOEFL Reading

HACKERS STRATEGY **APPLICATION**

Broadly defined as the geographical limit to forest survival in a mountain environment, the timberline is an ecotone between the alpine region above and the boreal forest below. Because timberline occurs normally in areas where the average daily summer temperature is quite cool, it can fluctuate in its latitudinal location based on proximity to the Equator, as seen by the Arctic treeline that forms a ring around the Arctic Ocean, and altitude. Therefore, despite mitigating precipitation, the timberline should appear slightly higher in the mountainous equatorial regions. Yet in North America, this transitional zone is relatively low due to cooler atmospheric climate, and presents at about 3,500 meters (11,500 feet) above sea level, making it more accessible for studies by humans. Ongoing research has shown that there are several factors that stimulate the creation of a timberline. Certainly the difference in elevation, affecting the amount of biologically useful thermal energy, is the primary agent for inhibiting tree maturation. Minimum summer temperatures dictate the length of season, or number of days that a plant is able to grow. Topography also plays a role because temperature variations are affected by convex southern-facing ranges with better solar radiation saturation or by descending cold air currents in the northern reaches, for example.

1. The phrase "this transitional zone" in the passage refers to

(A) Equator

(B) ring

(C) altitude

(D) timberline

2. The word "that" in the passage refers to

(A) meters

(B) studies

(C) humans

(D) factors

1

전략 1 적용 Because timberline occurs normally in areas where the average daily summer temperature is quite cool, it can fluctuate in its latitudinal location based on proximity to the (A) **Equator**, as seen by the Arctic treeline that forms a (B) **ring** around the Arctic Ocean, and (C) **altitude**. Therefore, despite mitigating precipitation, the (D) **timberline** should appear slightly higher in the mountainous equatorial regions. Yet in North America, this transitional zone is relatively low due to cooler atmospheric climate, and presents at about 3,500 meters (11,500 feet) above sea level, making it more accessible for studies by humans.

보기로 제시된 어휘들은 모두 지시어와 수 일치가 되어 있고 지시어의 앞에 위치해 있다. 문맥상 this transitional zone이 가리키는 것은 (D) timberline이다.

전략 2 적용 지시형용사 this 뒤에 오는 명사 transitional zone을 통해 이것이 가리키는 지시 대상을 유추해 볼 수 있다.

전략 3 적용 This transitional zone 자리에 timberline을 대입하여 해석하면 문맥이 자연스럽다.

'그러나 북미에서는 더 선선한 대기 때문에 수목한계선이 비교적 낮고, 해발 약 3,500미터에 나타나 인간의 연구를 위한 접근이 더 용이하다.'

정답 (D)

2

전략 1 적용 Yet in North America, this transitional zone is relatively low due to cooler atmospheric climate, and presents at about 3,500 (A) **meters** (11,500 feet) above sea level, making it more accessible for (B) **studies** by (C) **humans**. Ongoing research has shown that there are several (D) **factors** that stimulate the creation of a timberline.

보기로 제시된 어휘들은 모두 that 자리에 넣었을 때 관계대명사 that절의 동사와 수 일치가 되며, 모두 지시어의 앞에 위치해 있다. 문맥상 that이 가리키는 것은 (D) factors이다.

전략 2 적용 관계대명사의 선행사는 주로 바로 앞에 오는 명사이므로 that이 가리키는 지시 대상을 쉽게 짐작할 수 있다.

전략 3 적용 that절의 관계대명사 that에 factors를 대입하여 해석하면 문맥이 자연스럽다.

'진행 중인 연구는 수목한계선의 생성을 자극하는 여러 요인이 있다는 것을 보여준다.'

정답 (D)

CH 01
CH 02
CH 03
CH 04
CH 05
CH 06
CH 07
CH 08
CH 09
Hackers TOEFL Reading

HACKERS **PRACTICE**

Read each passage and choose the word or phrase that the highlighted word or phrase in the passage represents.

1 Even though vitamins vary in their chemical structures and do not produce usable energy directly, they do enable enzymes to release energy from carbohydrates, proteins, and fats. They are coenzymes or integral parts of coenzymes, which means that they function as catalysts in specific metabolic functions within cells.

Answer _____

2 Green, light-emitting cells utilized alongside a darkly toned throat enable cookie cutter sharks to deceive prey, including sperm whales and tuna, by imitating small fish. This allows them to consume a range of creatures that are fooled by the uniquely misleading display.

Answer _____

3 Virtually all bivalved mollusks, including clams, are capable of secreting a calcareous pearl of sorts, but only those species that contain an iridescent nacre, known as mother-of-pearl, can produce pearls that have commercial value. Clamshells do not include nacre; hence, their pearls lack luster and are of relatively little value.

Answer _____

4 Feathers are a diagnostic feature of avian populations, so those who see Archaeopteryx as a bird resort to them as their main evidence since these protrusions are exclusive to ornithological creatures. They argue that detailed inspection shows its clavicles, which most reptiles don't even possess, fused into a wishbone, similar to latter-day fowl.

Answer _____

VOCABULARY	The word ☐ in the passage is closest in meaning to

1 integral	(A) excitable	(B) negligible	(C) indispensable	(D) submissive
2 consume	(A) spend	(B) devour	(C) absorb	(D) waste
3 hence	(A) decisively	(B) eventually	(C) later	(D) consequently
4 exclusive	(A) seductive	(B) decomposed	(C) peculiar	(D) perilous

5   Humans contain between 20,000 and 25,000 genes, which are distinct sequences of nucleotides that form part of the chromosomes that encode cells to perform biological actions. These determine traits such as susceptibility to particular diseases, height potential, and hair color. Genes may be permanently altered by mutations, which can be inherited or caused by environmental factors.

Answer _____

6   Organisms vary from microscopic soft-bodied protists to large creatures with massive skeletons. Organisms are constructed of an enormous variety of substances, all of them under selection for subsistence during life.

Answer _____

Read each passage and choose the word or phrase that the highlighted word or phrase in the passage represents.

7   The people of ancient Mesopotamia were among the first to develop fixed settlements due to an advanced economy that was primarily based on agriculture. In contrast to earlier societies that relied on a hunter-gatherer lifestyle, the Mesopotamian civilization cultivated barley as an essential food source. As farming methods developed, a crop surplus ensued, and the extra harvest was employed as a form of payment for products and services. Gradually, small villages transformed into towns that established trade networks with nearby areas. The culture soon flourished as the staple endowed the region with a reliable economic resource.

Answer _____

CH 01
CH 02
CH 03
CH 04
CH 05
CH 06
CH 07
CH 08
CH 09

Hackers TOEFL Reading

VOCABULARY	The word ☐ in the passage is closest in meaning to			
5 traits	(A) features	(B) issues	(C) impairments	(D) deceptions
6 massive	(A) opulent	(B) huge	(C) dogged	(D) spacious
7 flourished	(A) prospered	(B) flaunted	(C) stung	(D) blotted out

8   Geysers are rare natural features that develop from vents in the earth's surface. These vents can eject jets of water and steam into the air, and the height of the expulsion ranges from 1.5 meters to nearly 100 meters. Geysers form where there is a combination of hot rocks and a groundwater reservoir, as well as fissures in the surface through which they deliver the highly pressurized water and steam. Most geysers discharge infrequently and unpredictably, although a few, such as "Old Faithful" in Yellowstone National Park, are known for regular eruptions. Others, such as "Clepsydra," which is also in Yellowstone, maintain a nearly continuous state of eruption.

Answer   _____

9   In those fish species in which artificial fertilization has been successful, the process sometimes requires injections of various compounds, chiefly mammalian hormones and salmon pituitary extract, into the fish to induce ripening of sperm and eggs. The amount and kinds of materials injected depend on the size and species of fish used. When the eggs are ready to be fertilized, they are stripped from the female fish by pressure applied to the abdomen and are then placed in a small bowl. Sperm is similarly stripped from the males and the two are mixed together to effect fecundation. If done correctly, a large percentage of the eggs are usually inseminated. These are aerated and incubated until they hatch.

Answer   _____

10   The California Gold Rush began in 1848 after a local newspaper reported the discovery of a single gold nugget. At the time, San Francisco was populated by just 1,000 people, but it rapidly swelled to 25,000 residents within two years, with most living in rudely constructed shanties or tents. The gold rush also generated steady immigration from overseas. For example, the number of Chinese in California rose from around 50 in 1849 to more than 150,000 by 1876. At first, they were welcomed as a cheap source of labor, but as the easily extracted gold became scarce, native miners began to turn on the Chinese and other foreigners working beside them, accusing them of having no allegiance to the country and blaming them for stealing America's wealth.

Answer   _____

VOCABULARY	The word [ ] in the passage is closest in meaning to			
8 continuous	(A) congenial	(B) uninterrupted	(C) occasional	(D) innocuous
9 effect	(A) disclose	(B) install	(C) complete	(D) disrupt
10 rudely	(A) coarsely	(B) unusually	(C) customarily	(D) markedly
allegiance	(A) encouragement	(B) flair	(C) underpinning	(D) fidelity

11 Recent work by memory researchers has highlighted the importance of slow-wave sleep, a phase that is commonly associated with dreaming and sleepwalking. They found that it is essential for optimal memory consolidation, a process that transforms memories into representations that can be allocated to long-term storage. In this operation, the brain actively engages an experience and encodes it in a form that can be readily recalled. However, these recollections can become destabilized as time passes and require enhancement, which occurs in the rapid-eye-movement period of sleep, suggesting that longer sleep also generates stronger memories.

Answer _____

12 The Miwok people of northern California did not represent a uniform group as they inhabited a variety of ecosystems with varying climates, which led to distinguishing characteristics. For instance, tribes that lived in warm regions wore very little clothing, while those in colder areas often donned coats and leggings, and in particularly frigid weather or at night, a blanket might serve as a substitute for attire. Yet sometimes cultural uniformity was exemplified through custom, such as in the widespread practice of intentionally binding the head of an infant to a board, which tightly pressed against the rear of the skull and created a flattened surface. The Miwok universally considered this feature to be attractive.

Answer _____

13 In Ancient Greece, the prevailing religious traditions centered around Dionysus, a savior god who was associated with the sowing and reaping of corn, the production of grapes, and intoxication. Patrons held seasonal festivals in his honor, the most important of which was the autumn wine tasting celebration, known as the Dionysus Festival, and this included the recitation of choric poems or hymns. Revelers chanted odes, called dithyrambs, to their illustrious god while a priest would respond in a symbolic interaction between humans and the spirits. Due to its popularity within the higher and lower social classes, by the 6th century B.C., the Corinthian king established a dithyramb competition and invited a select group of poets to compose and perform these pseudo-dramas; for the first time the plays were freed from their roots in religious rituals and transformed into full-fledged works of art. The changing theater environment altered the general public attitude and thus triggered a newfound mass interest that would bring about refinement of the art form.

Answer _____

VOCABULARY	The word ☐ in the passage is closest in meaning to

11 associated	(A) connected	(B) sheared	(C) composed	(D) organized
12 substitute	(A) stock	(B) replacement	(C) basis	(D) compound
intentionally	(A) invariably	(B) sedulously	(C) deliberately	(D) unwittingly
13 attitude	(A) facility	(B) object	(C) concern	(D) stance

Read each passage and answer the corresponding questions for each.

14   Although countless kinds of bacteria are found throughout the sea, they occur in the greatest concentration at the surface and at the bottom, with the mid waters having the lowest. The reason for this is that the distribution of decomposing organic matter, on which the bacteria thrive, is most clustered at these depths. Oceanic bacteria are extremely important insofar as they assist with decomposition of organic matter to water-soluble materials which serve as basic food materials for the sea plants, which in turn form the food basis for marine animals.

1 The word "which" in the passage refers to

(A) bottom
(B) reason
(C) distribution
(D) organic matter

2 The word "they" in the passage refers to

(A) waters
(B) depths
(C) bacteria
(D) materials

15   Considered by most as a purely dietary staple, corn is actually the basis of a number of products utilized widely throughout the United States and many other nations as well. The majority of corn, around 60 percent of total annual production, is processed as feed for farm animals such as cattle and pigs. Only about 3 percent is readied for human consumption in the form of whole ears or cereal, while roughly 8 percent of it is used in chemical sweeteners, or other additives such as corn starch. The rest of the annual output of corn is exported or fermented to make the fuel alcohol ethanol, which pollutes significantly less than its counterpart, gasoline.

1 The word "it" in the passage refers to

(A) corn
(B) feed
(C) consumption
(D) cereal

VOCABULARY   The word ☐ in the passage is closest in meaning to

14 distribution	(A) transportation	(B) circulation	(C) dispersal	(D) supply
extremely	(A) vaguely	(B) prohibitively	(C) respectively	(D) mainly
15 roughly	(A) approximately	(B) dubiously	(C) eagerly	(D) painstakingly

16 The eventual environmental impact of the nuclear waste from electricity-generating reactors is impossible to estimate, but what is clear is that containment presents a serious ecological challenge. Because nuclear byproducts remain highly radioactive for thousands of years, any leakage can require the surrounding area to be abandoned indefinitely. Conventional storage methods typically necessitate a two-part process that utilizes short-term and long-term repositories. Temporarily, spent nuclear fuel can be kept onsite in a pool or specialized cask designed to prevent its escape. However, once the available space fills up, the hazardous material must be moved to an underground facility that uses natural geological isolation in conjunction with engineered barriers to safeguard against any contact with groundwater.

1 The word "its" in the passage refers to

(A) process
(B) fuel
(C) pool
(D) cask

17 Yarrow, *Achillea millefolium*, has been utilized as a medicinal plant for millennia. Its unique astringent properties have been recognized since ancient times, and recently nutritionists have identified it as a source of micronutrients. Yarrow contains organic chemicals called *polyphenols*, which protect plants against harmful bacteria and other pathogens. In low concentrations, these compounds can make mucous membranes impermeable, preventing the penetration of microorganisms. They also act as effective enzyme inhibitors, which can obstruct the reproduction or growth of harmful pathogens. In addition, the fresh leaves of yarrow plants are used by herbalists, who grind them with a mortar and pestle and place poultices directly onto wounds. They can also be used to make an aromatic tea if steeped in hot water for ten to fifteen minutes.

1 The phrase "these compounds" in the passage refers to

(A) micronutrients
(B) *polyphenols*
(C) harmful bacteria
(D) pathogens

2 The word "They" in the passage refers to

(A) fresh leaves
(B) herbalists
(C) poultices
(D) wounds

CH 01
CH 02
CH 03
CH 04
CH 05
CH 06
CH 07
CH 08
CH 09

Hackers TOEFL Reading

VOCABULARY The word ☐ in the passage is closest in meaning to

16 estimate	(A) gauge	(B) conclude	(C) propose	(D) approve
abandoned	(A) discharged	(B) failed	(C) retrieved	(D) vacated
17 properties	(A) prospects	(B) characteristics	(C) outlooks	(D) assets

18 Communication with the spiritual world could take place on an individual level, and this would manifest in vision quests, where a young man (rarely a woman) was sent on a solitary vigil, and by fasting and the recitation of prayer, he would enter into a dream-like trance to visit a supernatural land, the qualities of which repeatedly appeared in art. For the most part, this unusual state evoked a metaphysical reaction wherein the partaker would have a significant interaction with an animal creature, generally considered a guardian spirit that would give advice and teach songs. Once the ritual was completed, he would return to the waking world and attempt to recreate these visions by painting on rock walls, animal hide, or wood. Aesthetic qualities varied based on the talent of each artist, but the illustration of experience was an essential part of the vision quest and stimulated complete integration of the religious and the temporal nature of the tribe.

1 The word "this" in the passage refers to

    (A) communication
    (B) world
    (C) level
    (D) vigil

2 The phrase "this unusual state" in the passage refers to

    (A) fasting
    (B) prayer
    (C) trance
    (D) interaction

VOCABULARY The word ☐ in the passage is closest in meaning to

18 solitary	(A) serene	(B) separated	(C) shabby	(D) sensuous
evoked	(A) strained	(B) transacted	(C) educed	(D) upbraided
integration	(A) consolidation	(B) inflation	(C) manifestation	(D) exploration

19 Cubism, as exemplified by the influential works of Picasso and Cézanne, is considered one of the most significant art movements of the twentieth century. It is considered an ideal representation of a brief period in the early 1900s, when modern art, literature, and architecture developed their fundamentals. In Cubist art, a subject was extracted from its background, deconstructed, and reassembled in an abstract form that emphasized multiple perspectives and angled planes. Divided into multiple phases, Cubism was initially limited to just a few artists in the Paris area that imitated the geometric, simplistic forms espoused in Picasso's 1907 painting, *Les Demoiselles d'Avignon*. New styles appeared in the following years, wherein painters did not properly shape their subjects but instead delved into full abstraction, dislocating these elements from the artwork entirely, and creating a short-lived artistic splinter group. These artists, known as the Orphists, preferred the use of bright colors, sharply going against the monochromatic style of their predecessors. Their combination of abstract structures and vivid colors prompted a general shift toward large geometric shapes and contrasting colors. From 1925, Cubism experienced a decline as artists at the forefront of the movement began to explore novel avenues of expression, including geometric abstraction and Surrealism.

1 The word "that" in the passage refers to

(A) perspectives
(B) planes
(C) phases
(D) artists

2 The phrase "these elements" in the passage refers to

(A) forms
(B) styles
(C) painters
(D) subjects

VOCABULARY The word ⬚ in the passage is closest in meaning to

19		(A)	(B)	(C)	(D)
	ideal	(A) stunted	(B) wizened	(C) microscopic	(D) optimal
	extracted	(A) touted	(B) drawn	(C) berated	(D) torn apart
	properly	(A) suitably	(B) overwhelmingly	(C) fractionally	(D) robustly

정답 및 해석 p.426

CH 01
CH 02
CH 03
CH 04
CH 05
CH 06
CH 07
CH 08
CH 09
Hackers TOEFL Reading

HACKERS TEST

01	**Placebo Effect**

제한 시간: 13분

1 ➡ The etymology of the word *placebo* is derived from the Latin verb for "I shall please," and in the classical sense, a placebo is an imitation medicine that a doctor gives to calm an anxious patient, or to placate a persistent one perhaps demanding pills the physician is unwilling to administer. A placebo contains no pharmacological substances and therefore strictly speaking, it is not categorized as a medicament. However, a patient is led to believe that something more than mere sugar pills is being prescribed to alleviate or even cure a health condition, thus indicating that it has more to do with the power of suggestion coupled with the strength of a patient's belief in an ultimate recovery.

2 Medical practitioners in favor of doling out placebos are certain that more powerful than their actual diagnosis of a patient is the prescription slip containing reassurance to a patient that a particular ailment can be overcome. Studies confirm this conviction by showing that up to 90 percent of patients who seek medical attention are suffering from self-limiting disorders that are well within the range of the body's own power to heal. Both researchers and physicians who vouch for the virtue of placebos concede that there is still a lot that remains unverified about the psychological power invested by the human mind that causes placebos to work, but clearly the patient's beliefs and the physician's attitude both seem to play a key part, including the doctor's ability to gain the patient's full confidence in the dummy drug. These are all vital factors in maximizing the performance of a placebo.

3 According to records on file at the U.S. Food and Drug Administration(FDA), 35 percent of patients who have been allotted placebos throughout drug trials claim long-term relief from symptoms, thereby astonishing researchers with this considerable success rate in the fight against disease. Analyses and interpretation of the results indicate that the simple process of administering a placebo without a patient's prior knowledge has direct and often beneficial results; yet despite what the reports reveal, the majority of medical researchers strongly oppose this practice, suggesting it violates doctor-patient relationships. Medical ethics standards maintain that the notion of trust should be paramount and doctors are expected to convey the truth, but on occasion, some are faced with the dilemma of how to remain wholly truthful to someone undergoing medical supervision while acting in their best interests. A number of researchers have called into question the legitimacy of some doctors' discretionary tactics used in the treatment of particular cases. Misinformation has been reported to work in the opposite direction, as in the example where practitioners are tempted to paint a more optimistic picture in order to convince patients indisposed to undertake a more aggressive treatment like chemotherapy, which in retrospect they may not have chosen to submit to had they had access to information about their rate of cancer and their body's actual condition.

4 Further studies report of some patients learning that they have been given placebos in place of clinically tested and approved drugs, thus breaching the trust established in their physicians in some cases and inducing the reverse "nocebo" effects to occur in others. This exacerbates further a patient's medical state and occasionally accelerates causes leading to death. The actual use of placebos in clinical practice has become increasingly uncommon due to possible malpractice suits, and they are almost exclusively used in research where the subjects are now more likely to be advised in advance of the possible risks and benefits of a treatment. Along with this, doctrines and policies are implemented to ensure that informed consent is observed, thus aligning standards for medical research and practice with the need for further investigation into the so-called placebo effect.

CH 01

CH 02

CH 03

CH 04

CH 05

CH 06

CH 07

CH 08

CH 09

Hackers TOEFL Reading

1 The word "one" in the passage refers to

(A) sense
(B) placebo
(C) doctor
(D) patient

2 According to paragraph 1, for which of the following reason is a placebo not classified as a real drug?

(A) It is not prescribed by a practitioner.
(B) It lacks any medicinal ingredients.
(C) It does not affect a patient's health.
(D) It merely depends on a patient's faith.

Paragraph 1 is marked with an arrow [➡].

3 The word "alleviate" in the passage is closest in meaning to

(A) violate
(B) irritate
(C) relieve
(D) revive

4 The word "it" in the passage refers to

(A) placebo
(B) medicament
(C) health condition
(D) recovery

5 The word "that" in the passage refers to

(A) medical attention
(B) success
(C) psychological power
(D) human mind

6 The phrase "this practice" in the passage refers to

(A) dispensing with placebos
(B) the fight against disease
(C) analyses and interpretation of the results
(D) administering a placebo

7 The word "they" in the passage refers to

(A) researchers
(B) doctors
(C) practitioners
(D) patients

8 The word "others" in the passage refers to

(A) studies
(B) drugs
(C) cases
(D) effects

9 According to the passage, because of the threat of litigation, placebos

(A) are only used by physicians who take a potential risk of malpractice
(B) are required to reduce their anticipated reverse effects on patients
(C) are being thoroughly investigated by doctors on their components
(D) are rarely administered in direct medical treatment of patients

10 **Directions**: An introductory sentence for a brief summary of the passage is provided below. Complete the summary by selecting the THREE answer choices that express the most important ideas in the passage. Some sentences do not belong in the summary because they express ideas that are not presented in the passage or are minor ideas in the passage. **This question is worth 2 points.**

Drag your answer choices to the spaces where they belong. To remove an answer choice, click on it. To review the passage, click on **View Text**.

The use of placebos is a controversial treatment method that appears to be effective in certain situations.

-
-
-

Answer Choices

(A) Whether a placebo is able to effectively treat a disease is dependent on which substances are included.

(B) Despite the desirability of transparency in medical practices, it is difficult for practitioners to share information with patients.

(C) Ethical problems arise when a doctor employs a placebo as a medical cure with keeping a patient ignorant of it.

(D) Success of a placebo stems from the fact that it seems to positively influence the body's capability to heal itself.

(E) A concern over using a placebo is that it causes patients to believe that their medical condition is not so serious.

(F) When patients discover that they have been administered a placebo, adverse reactions occur which are sometimes fatal.

정답 및 해석 p.430

CH 01
CH 02
CH 03
CH 04
CH 05
CH 06
CH 07
CH 08
CH 09
Hackers TOEFL Reading

1　Single cellular organisms are able to directly absorb gasses and dispose of wastes into their environment, but more complex creatures need to have a system to allow interior cells, far removed from direct exposure with the external system, some way to replenish their nutrients. Methods of internal tubing using spicules to straightly expose the interior cells to air are inefficient and limit the size of the organisms, so in order to regulate their internal environments, large animals need other precise networks. They have a closed circulatory system filled with liquid that prevents the body from dehydration, but more importantly they utilize specialized cells to facilitate vital gas exchange and defend themselves from viral and bacterial attacks.

2　The most numerous cells found in the blood are erythrocytes, commonly referred to as red blood cells, whose level remains relatively stable unless an organism is exposed long-term to low oxygen environments, and which are significantly smaller than the other cells in the body. These biconcave disks are actually straw colored and only turn their characteristic red due to the presence of oxygenated hemoglobin. They are produced in the bone marrow by blood-forming stem cells and since they lack nuclei, they are unable to replicate themselves. They are constantly in the process of being made, since these red blood cells generally do not last more than 100 to 120 days. And while some may be stored in the spleen to be released at times of heightened stress, the majority of them are in constant circulation in the vascular systems.

3　➡ While in motion around the body, each red blood cell, packed with millions of hemoglobin molecules, is responsible for transporting oxygen to all the cells within the body and removing carbon dioxide. Its small size and extreme flexibility allows it to access exceptionally small spaces like capillaries (tiny blood vessels) where it releases the oxygen needed for respiration and bonds to the waste, carbon dioxide, which is excreted by the cells, in a process that is then reversed when the erythrocytes return to the lungs.

4　Much larger but less numerous are the leukocytes, or white blood cells, which can keep off foreign invaders and infectious diseases as part of the immune system and be differentiated into many sub-categories. Like red blood cells, these are created from stem cells in the bone marrow, but they have a nucleus that allows them to replicate themselves in a few very limited circumstances. Some leukocytes have a lifespan of only a week, although there are other types which can be longer lived, depending upon the level of bacterial activity in the body. Based on how much of a threat the body faces, leukocyte levels fluctuate widely, with the body keeping reserves in the lymph nodes and thymus.

5　The white blood cells have different mechanisms for defending the body when an invader is detected, and the neutrophil provides a good example of this. Neutrophils have a two-stage method for attacking antigens such as bacteria. The first stage is phagocytosis, in which the neutrophil literally engulfs the invading cell. It achieves this by connecting to the antigen and using part of its cell membrane to create a sort of bubble around it, which neutralizes the bacteria, protecting the rest of the body outside the cell. The other is the release of lysosomal enzymes, which attach to "the bubble." The secretion of lysosomal enzymes causes the bacteria to break down, and the entire process results in the death of the leukocyte and the invader.

6 Once the neutrophils have served their purpose, they are no longer valuable, and since they contain toxic products, they need to be swiftly removed from the body either via the lymph system, which filters and then excretes the used cells, or more directly by emitting a thick yellowish liquid from infected sites and expectorating phlegm from the lungs. In contrast, erythrocytes contain valuable iron. Once an erythrocyte approaches the end of its life cycle, it is taken out of circulation, but not all of the iron is lost. In order to be reused, some of the iron is liberated and stored in the spleen prior to the erythrocyte's destruction. This iron then is directed to newly developing erythrocytes.

1 The word "their" in the passage refers to

(A) gasses
(B) wastes
(C) interior cells
(D) animals

2 The word "some" in the passage refers to

(A) stem cells
(B) nuclei
(C) red blood cells
(D) vascular systems

3 The word "which" in the passage refers to

(A) flexibility
(B) oxygen
(C) respiration
(D) carbon dioxide

4 According to paragraph 3, when the red blood cells are in the lungs

(A) they are safe from exterior attacks
(B) they expel refuse gas and absorb oxygen
(C) they lose their hemoglobin to the nearby tissues
(D) they don't have to compress in size

Paragraph 3 is marked with an arrow [➡].

CH 01
CH 02
CH 03
CH 04
CH 05
CH 06
CH 07
CH 08
CH 09

Hackers TOEFL Reading

5 The word "these" in the passage refers to

(A) leukocytes
(B) invaders
(C) diseases
(D) red blood cells

6 Which of the sentences below best expresses the essential information in the highlighted sentence in the passage? *Incorrect* choices change the meaning in important ways or leave out essential information.

(A) The number of leukocytes varies according to the degree of external intimidation with surpluses kept in some parts of the body.
(B) In order to compensate for decreased leukocyte levels due to infection, the body stores white blood cells in other systems.
(C) Without a method for keeping white blood cells in excess, the levels would change so much and endanger the organism.
(D) The amount of white blood cells is subject to sharp fluctuations depending on the body conditions and reserve levels.

7 The phrase "The other" in the passage refers to

(A) antigen
(B) stage
(C) cell membrane
(D) body

8 The word "swiftly" in the passage is closest in meaning to

(A) wholly
(B) quickly
(C) finally
(D) easily

9 According to the passage, iron is removed from erythrocytes

(A) before it is driven out into the lungs
(B) due to its comparatively short lifespan
(C) by neutrophils before it reaches toxic levels
(D) for the purpose of being used again

10 **Directions**: Select the appropriate phrases from the answer choices and match them to the type of blood cells they represent. **This question is worth 3 points.**

> Drag your answer choices to the spaces where they belong. To remove an answer choice, click on it. To review the passage, click on **View Text**.

Answer Choices	Erythrocytes
(A) Survive for a third of a year at the utmost	•
(B) Contain nuclei which enable them to reproduce on rare occasions	
(C) Can be regenerated automatically when they are injured	•
(D) Turn a different color when hemoglobin combined with oxygen is in existence	•
(E) Check the invasion from outside harmful organisms	**Leukocytes**
(F) Give out venomous substances when they encounter hazard	•
(G) Are in charge of gas interchange between lungs and the other body parts	•

정답 및 해석 p.432

CH 01
CH 02
CH 03
CH 04
CH 05
CH 06
CH 07
CH 08
CH 09

Hackers TOEFL Reading

1   On occasion, the Earth's orbit will shift and pull the planet slightly farther away from the sun than normal, causing colder weather to engulf the terrain and disallowing the usual seasonal melting that generally occurs in the spring season. During the cooler period, precipitation continues to fall, forming aggregates of oddly shaped, interlocking crystals ranging in size from several millimeters to a centimeter, which come together to generate increasingly thicker layers of ice.

2   ➡ The pressure and weight of the overlying layers compress the ice into denser firn which over a period of years will become glacial ice. The pressure also lowers the freezing point of water, producing melt water which flows throughout the glacier and lubricates its movement. Large sheets migrate from a higher elevation to a lower one as available melt water trickles downhill and appear dirty as they pick up gravel and sedimentary particles from the surface while moving. When they fall into the ocean, they become ice shelves forming high ridges over the sea where they pose a substantial threat to ocean traffic since only ten to twelve percent is visible while the remainder lies under the surface. Ice shelves, because of their proximity to human populations and pristine compositions, tend to be the most commonly studied glacial formation. The Amery Ice Shelf floats at the head of Prydz Bay in the Indian Ocean near Antarctica and lies at the foot of the Lambert Glacier. Claimed as Australian territory in 1933 by explorer Douglas Mawson, the region supports rare ice formations in bottle-green hues. Early reports, quickly discarded due to lack of evidence, attributed the unusual green shade of some Amery icebergs to high levels of metallic compounds in the ice, leaving the causation of the color a matter of contention and sparking a series of exploratory studies.

3   One such expedition hypothesized that the color was the result of a visual fallacy created when normal ice, which has a blue tinge due to reflections of the sun striking the ocean waters, is illuminated by a low lying red sun as [6]it sets on the horizon. In an attempt to prove their hypothesis, the glaciologists made numerous spectral analytic observations at established intervals throughout an average summer day and measured the color of the iceberg under various intensities of light, repeating the test again in the spring and fall when the sun appears in alternate places in the sky. Upon completion, they discovered that the level of noticeable green did not fade or become enhanced in fluctuating sunlight, refuting the perception that the shade was an optical illusion.

4   ➡ Recently, a group of glaciologists proposed a new theory by suggesting that the colored areas of the glaciers are, in fact, the exposed underside of floating shelves, visible only after normal ice, melting as the Earth's orbit returns to its usual situation closer to the sun, has capsized, leaving behind a layer of greenish marine ice. It is suggested that when, like other glacial formations, marine ice undergoes densification, [8]it picks up biological material, including the remains of dead krill and water-born vegetation living close to the basal side of the freezing block which is bubble-free. It has been already well-known that red snow is caused by the incorporation of red algae Phyllophora into the snow layers; ergo it is feasible that a similar organism could be the primary factor in the

odd coloration of green ice. One of the most common algae in the ocean surrounding the Amery Ice Shelf is actually the single-celled, ice-dwelling Euglena, a photosynthetic member of the Protista Kingdom that contains a large number of green chlorophyll molecules. Exposed marine ice containing a heavy concentration of Euglena would appear to take on the coloration of the algae, manifesting as green glacial ice.

5   However plausible the notion of the marine organism causation may appear, it is still controversial and remains unproven. A thorough examination of the Amery Ice Shelf and its encompassing geography should be initiated before any final conclusions about the mysterious presence of green ice can be deduced.

Glossary
krill shrimp-like planktonic crustaceans

1   Which of the sentences below best expresses the essential information in the highlighted sentence in the passage? *Incorrect* choices change the meaning in important ways or leave out essential information.

(A) Due to the falling temperatures, the unusual shape of the crystals results in thicker ice.

(B) The snow that falls in cold weather clumps together to form ice layers.

(C) With increased pressure from piles of snow, large aggregates of ice are made.

(D) The accumulated snow stays frozen on the ground if the frigid weather continues.

2   The word "which" in the passage refers to

(A) pressure
(B) weight
(C) ice
(D) firn

3   The word "one" in the passage refers to

(A) freezing point
(B) water
(C) glacier
(D) elevation

CH 01
CH 02
CH 03
CH 04
CH 05
CH 06
CH 07
CH 08
CH 09

Hackers TOEFL Reading

4 According to paragraph 2, ice shelves in the ocean can be an obstacle to ships because

(A) their submerged parts are located close to human settlements
(B) they form ridges over the sea which can crack
(C) the majority of them are below the surface and unseen
(D) chunks of them interfere with the ships' propellers

Paragraph 2 is marked with an arrow [➡].

5 The word "pristine" in the passage is closest in meaning to

(A) unspoiled
(B) gentle
(C) blemished
(D) stale

6 The word "it" in the passage refers to

(A) fallacy
(B) ice
(C) tinge
(D) sun

7 The word "refuting" in the passage is closest in meaning to

(A) disproving
(B) complementing
(C) restating
(D) affirming

8 The word "it" in the passage refers to

(A) group
(B) orbit
(C) marine ice
(D) densification

9 According to paragraph 4, Euglena affects the color of ice in the ocean

(A) as it multiplies in the ice in large quantities
(B) because it diffracts light entering into the ice
(C) when it absorbs green wavelengths under water
(D) since it includes many green colored substances

Paragraph 4 is marked with an arrow [➡].

10 **Directions**: An introductory sentence for a brief summary of the passage is provided below. Complete the summary by selecting the THREE answer choices that express the most important ideas in the passage. Some sentences do not belong in the summary because they express ideas that are not presented in the passage or are minor ideas in the passage. **This question is worth 2 points.**

> Drag your answer choices to the spaces where they belong. To remove an answer choice, click on it. To review the passage, click on **View Text**.

The appearance of green ice in the ocean near Antarctica has led to multiple theories to explain its origin.

-
-
-

Answer Choices

(A) It is probable that the inclusion of certain organisms in the ice is responsible for the change in ice color.

(B) It is true that all glaciers pick up some debris as they condense and contain some type of colored flora.

(C) The hypothesis that the greenish hue comes out when bluish ice is lighted up at sunset was suggested.

(D) Some theorized that embedded metals within the ice would cause it to appear green.

(E) It is likely that the pressure of the top ice layers influences the rate at which the glaciers change their color.

(F) It is claimed that the alteration in the path the Earth makes around the Sun aids in magnifying light for photosynthetic algae.

정답 및 해석 p.434

CH 01
CH 02
CH 03
CH 04
CH 05
CH 06
CH 07
CH 08
CH 09

Hackers TOEFL Reading

1 Ancestral Pueblo Indians inhabited the Four Corners area of the Colorado Plateau for over a millennium. There they cultivated the land around their modest homesteads, made products such as baskets and pottery, and traded amongst themselves and with neighboring peoples. For most of their history, they had lived in sunken, rudimentary huts constructed in excavated pits. These were mainly scattered, single-family dwellings. But after the 10th century, the living patterns of the Pueblo in the Four Corners area evolved dramatically, and the changes transpired in two successive phases.

2 In the 11th and 12th centuries, the Pueblo began to congregate in villages in canyon bottomlands, where they built expansive, multi-family, aboveground dwellings known as pueblos, meaning "town," for which the Spanish named the people to distinguish them from other nomadic tribes. Surrounding the villages was a network of paths or roads that connected ancillary fields and houses with the central confederation. The most notable example of this type of community was at Chaco Canyon, where there were vast compounds of multi-story structures, some five stories tall, with several hundred rooms. As needed, adjacent structures were added horizontally and additional rooms were stacked vertically, somewhat reminiscent of modern apartment complexes. These new, expansive, multistory complexes point to the presence of orderly, stable, and cooperative civilizations.

3 So why did the Pueblo begin to live communally? A primary factor was environmental stress. Dendrologists have demonstrated from analysis of tree rings that there were severe recurring droughts throughout the region. With little rainfall, people were forced into smaller pockets of arable land. These oases were often in the bottom of canyons, where springs and streams flowed even during droughts. Through pollen analysis of lake beds, scientists have also inferred that the region experienced a miniature ice age, whereby temperatures declined and the growing season shortened. Unable to produce enough food in the high plateaus to provide for their families, people began to form cooperative arrangements in the bottomlands.

4 ➡ Working and living together in densely packed communities allowed people to maximize the returns of their labor. A distribution of work emerged, and there was some degree of specialization. Some people irrigated fields, while others harvested wood for building homes and making fires. They also constructed communal storage facilities to stockpile resources. However, population density had its downsides. Intensive agriculture eroded the land, excessive waste generated problems with hygiene and sanitation, and overharvesting of wood depleted nearby forests. Moreover, the adverse climatic conditions did not relent, and this created competition for meager resources and social unrest.

5 ➡ In the 13th century, the Pueblo began to build dwellings on cliff faces, and these marked the height of their architectural achievement. These cliff dwellings were typically constructed on a ledge or around an existing cave, or at the apex of a plateau. The question arises of why, under difficult environmental conditions, people would move further away from precious resources and arable land. The most probable reason was for protection. The elevated position offered shelter from the elements and afforded a formidable safeguard against hostile invading tribes. Some scholars have implicated the Navaho as the aggressors, but the identity of the invaders and the extent of the fighting are subject to debate. Regardless, there is clear evidence of escalating violence in the Four Corners region, as archaeologists have unearthed the remains of corpses with arrows or spearheads in them, as well as victims of cannibalism. Warfare and plundering, perhaps spawned by competition for ever-scarcer resources, could have encouraged people to seek asylum in the impregnable precipices. Access to some of the cliff dwellings is exacting even with the aid of modern climbing gear, and their lofty position no doubt provided effective lookout points to spot potential invaders.

6 ➡ Cooperative living arrangements allowed the Pueblo to remain in the region as long as possible, but the dire situation eventually reached a tipping point at the end of the 13th century. Around that time, there was a mass exodus from the Four Corners region, and it is no coincidence that this migration corresponds to the so-called Great Drought of 1276 to 1299. It seems as if the upper Rio Grande valley, with its more reliable water source, was a common destination of choice. By around 1300, the population of the Four Corners area had plummeted to almost nil, while that of the upper Rio Grande valley area had increased dramatically.

1 The word "These" in the passage refers to

(A) Products
(B) Baskets
(C) Huts
(D) Pits

2 The word "some" in the passage refers to

(A) houses
(B) communities
(C) compounds
(D) structures

3 The word "their" in the passage refers to

(A) plateaus
(B) families
(C) people
(D) arrangements

CH 01
CH 02
CH 03
CH 04
CH 05
CH 06
CH 07
CH 08
CH 09
Hackers TOEFL Reading

4 According to paragraph 4, which of the following is NOT mentioned as a drawback of a denser population?

(A) Conflict over resources
(B) Outbreaks of forest fires
(C) Erosion of farmland
(D) Degradation of woodland

Paragraph 4 is marked with an arrow [➡].

5 The word "meager" in the passage is closest in meaning to

(A) bountiful
(B) scarce
(C) untapped
(D) defiled

6 According to paragraph 5, the Pueblo built cliff dwellings in order to

(A) gain access to better agricultural land
(B) provide cover and defend against attacks
(C) show off their architectural prowess to competing tribes
(D) expand their territory and support a growing population

Paragraph 5 is marked with an arrow [➡].

7 Which of the sentences below best expresses the essential information in the highlighted sentence in the passage? *Incorrect* choices change the meaning in important ways or leave out essential information.

(A) Due to the inaccessibility and height of some cliff dwellings, invaders often reversed course upon seeing them from afar.
(B) Some of the cliff dwellings are virtually unreachable, and even climbers using modern technology have found it difficult to access them.
(C) To enter some cliff dwellings is extremely difficult, and their height made them useful as a place to scan for intruders.
(D) Even though some cliff dwellings were hard to reach, they inevitably were overtaken from time to time by skillful climbers.

8 The word "that" in the passage refers to

(A) source
(B) destination
(C) area
(D) population

9 According to paragraph 6, which of the following is true of the Rio Grande valley?

(A) It was uninhabited prior to the Pueblo migration of the late 13th century.
(B) It received more precipitation than the Four Corners area.
(C) Its population dwindled immediately after the Great Drought.
(D) Its water resources were more dependable than those in the Four Corners area.

Paragraph 6 is marked with an arrow [➡].

10 **Directions**: An introductory sentence for a brief summary of the passage is provided below. Complete the summary by selecting the THREE answer choices that express the most important ideas in the passage. Some sentences do not belong in the summary because they express ideas that are not presented in the passage or are minor ideas in the passage. **This question is worth 2 points.**

> Drag your answer choices to the spaces where they belong. To remove an answer choice, click on it. To review the passage, click on **View Text**.

For a thousand years the Pueblo lifestyle remained virtually unchanged, but between the 11th and the 13th centuries their living patterns began to shift.

-
-
-

Answer Choices

(A) In large part due to environmental pressures and issues with food production, the Pueblo formed large cooperative communities in the canyons.

(B) For some unknown reason, the Pueblo suddenly abandoned their villages in the canyon bottomlands and built houses high on cliffs.

(C) To their consternation, the Pueblo who migrated in search of peaceful conditions and a better climate arrived at the Rio Grande valley only to find drought and unrest.

(D) Their communal existence rested upon a productive division of labor, but a denser population created problems leading to social turmoil.

(E) The Pueblo built dwellings in the cliffs, presumably for protection against growing violence, and they eventually left the Four Corners region.

(F) Their intensive agriculture methods had negative consequences, such as erosion, which exacerbated the drought problem and led to food scarcity.

정답 및 해석 p.435

CH 01
CH 02
CH 03
CH 04
CH 05
CH 06
CH 07
CH 08
CH 09
Hackers TOEFL Reading

토플 빈출어휘 정리 노트

Chapter 04에 수록된 어휘들을 빈출도 순으로 정리했습니다. 음성파일을 들으며 꼭 암기하세요.

토플 최빈출어휘 [★★★]

- [ ] integral [íntigrəl] 필수적인 (=indispensable)
- [ ] consume [kənsúːm] 먹다 (=devour)
- [ ] hence [hens] 따라서 (=consequently)
- [ ] exclusive [iksklúːsiv] 특유한 (=peculiar)
- [ ] trait [treit] 특징 (=feature)
- [ ] massive [mǽsiv] 거대한 (=huge)
- [ ] staple [steipl] 주요 식품
- [ ] flourish [flə́ːriʃ] 번성하다 (=prosper)
- [ ] destruction [distrʌ́kʃən] 파괴
- [ ] allegiance [əlíːdʒəns] 충성 (=fidelity)
- [ ] phase [feiz] 단계
- [ ] exemplify [igzémplifai] 예증하다
- [ ] intentionally [inténʃənəli] 의도적으로 (=deliberately)
- [ ] refinement [riːfáinmənt] 진보 (=advancement)
- [ ] countless [káuntlis] 무수한 (=innumerable)
- [ ] distribution [dìstrəbjúːʃən] 분포 (=dispersal)
- [ ] roughly [rʌ́fli] 대략 (=approximately)
- [ ] characteristic [kæ̀rəktərístik] 특징 (=feature)
- [ ] solitary [sálətèri] 혼자 하는 (=separated)
- [ ] evoke [ivóuk] 일으키다 (=educe)
- [ ] integration [ìntəgréiʃən] 융합 (=consolidation)
- [ ] ideal [aidíːəl] 이상적인 (=optimal)
- [ ] extract [ikstrǽkt] 추출하다 (=draw)
- [ ] properly [prápərli] 적절히 (=suitably)
- [ ] derive [diráiv] 유래하다 (=originate)
- [ ] anxious [ǽŋkʃəs] 걱정하는
- [ ] alleviate [əlíːvièit] 완화시키다 (=relieve)
- [ ] conviction [kənvíkʃən] 확신 (=strong belief)
- [ ] convey [kənvéi] 전달하다 (=transmit)
- [ ] replenish [ripléniʃ] 보충하다 (=refill)
- [ ] facilitate [fəsílətèit] 용이하게 하다 (=make easy)
- [ ] exceptionally [iksépʃənəli] 예외적으로 (=extraordinarily)
- [ ] swiftly [swíftli] 신속하게 (=quickly)
- [ ] interlock [ìntərlák] 맞물리다

- [ ] proximity [prɑksíməti] 근접 (=closeness)
- [ ] pristine [prístiːn] 순수한 (=unspoiled)
- [ ] refute [rifjúːt] 반박하다 (=disprove)
- [ ] feasible [fíːzəbl] 가능성 있는 (=possible)
- [ ] plausible [plɔ́ːzəbl] 그럴싸한 (=believable)
- [ ] controversial [kàntrəvə́ːrʃəl] 논쟁의 여지가 있는 (=debatable)
- [ ] adjacent [ədʒéisnt] 인접한 (=nearby)
- [ ] complex [kəmpléks] 건물
- [ ] recurring [rikə́ːriŋ] 반복적인 (=repeated)
- [ ] meager [míːgər] 빈약한 (=scarce)
- [ ] unearth [ʌnə́ːrθ] 발굴하다 (=excavate)

토플 빈출어휘 [★★]

- [ ] enzyme [énzaim] 효소
- [ ] deceive [disíːv] 속이다
- [ ] gene [dʒin] 유전자
- [ ] inherited [inhéritid] 유전의
- [ ] reproduction [rìːprədʌ́kʃən] 생식
- [ ] replicate [réplikèit] 복제하다
- [ ] encode [inkóud] 부호화하다
- [ ] eruption [irʌ́pʃən] 분출
- [ ] fertilize [fə́ːrtəlàiz] 수정시키다
- [ ] effect [ifékt] 달성하다 (=complete)
- [ ] accuse [əkjúːz] 고발하다
- [ ] destabilize [dìːstéibəlaiz] 불안정하게 만들다
- [ ] associated [əsóuʃièitid] 관련된 (=connected)
- [ ] substitute [sʌ́bstətjùːt] 대용품 (=replacement)
- [ ] universally [jùːnivə́ːrsəli] 보편적으로
- [ ] attitude [ǽtitjùːd] 태도 (=stance)
- [ ] thrive [θraiv] 성장하다
- [ ] extremely [ikstríːmli] 몹시 (=prohibitively)
- [ ] process [práses] 가공하다
- [ ] abandon [əbǽndən] 그만두다 (=vacate)
- [ ] pollute [pəlúːt] 오염시키다
- [ ] estimate [éstəmèit] 추정하다 (=gauge)

*해커스 동영상강의의 포털 해커스인강(HackersIngang.com)에서 '토플 빈출어휘 정리 노트' 음성파일을 무료로 다운로드할 수 있습니다.

- [ ] ailment [éilmənt] 질병
- [ ] tribe [traib] 부족
- [ ] aesthetic [esθétik] 미의
- [ ] flexibility [flèksəbíləti] 융통성 (=adaptability)
- [ ] flatten [flǽtn] 납작하게 하다
- [ ] imitation [ìmətéiʃən] 가짜의
- [ ] prescribe [priskráib] 처방하다
- [ ] diagnosis [dàiəgnóusis] 진단
- [ ] allot [əlát] 배당하다
- [ ] symptom [símptəm] 증상
- [ ] approved [əprú:vd] 검증된
- [ ] exacerbate [igzǽsərbèit] 악화시키다 (=aggravate)
- [ ] vessel [vésəl] 혈관
- [ ] infectious [infékʃəs] 전염성의
- [ ] hypothesize [haipáθəsàiz] 가설을 세우다
- [ ] congregate [káŋgrigèit] 모이다
- [ ] reminiscent [rèmənísnt] 연상시키는
- [ ] point to 시사하다
- [ ] orderly [ɔ́:rdərli] 질서정연한
- [ ] downside [dáunsàid] 단점
- [ ] hygiene [háidʒi:n] 위생
- [ ] sanitation [sæ̀nətéiʃən] 위생
- [ ] escalate [éskəlèit] 증가하다

토플 기출어휘 [★]

- [ ] catalyst [kǽtəlist] 촉매
- [ ] metabolic [mètəbálik] 신진대사의
- [ ] luster [lʌ́stər] 광택
- [ ] avian [éiviən] 조류의
- [ ] resort to 기대다
- [ ] diagnostic [dàiəgnástik] 특징적인
- [ ] permanently [pə́:rmənəntli] 영구적으로
- [ ] continuous [kəntínjuəs] 계속적인 (=uninterrupted)
- [ ] injection [indʒékʃən] 주입
- [ ] chiefly [tʃí:fli] 주로

- [ ] chromosome [króuməsoum] 염색체
- [ ] civilization [sìvələzéiʃən] 문명
- [ ] rudely [rú:dli] 조잡하게 (=coarsely)
- [ ] infant [ínfənt] 유아
- [ ] harvest [há:rvist] 수확물
- [ ] newfound [njú:fàund] 새로운
- [ ] purely [pjúərli] 단지
- [ ] dietary [dáiətèri] 음식의
- [ ] additive [ǽdətiv] 첨가제
- [ ] output [áutpùt] 생산량
- [ ] byproduct [báiprà:dəkt] 부산물
- [ ] repository [ripá:zətɔ:ri] 저장소
- [ ] isolation [àisəléiʃən] 분리
- [ ] engineered [èndʒinírd] 공학적인
- [ ] fasting [fǽstiŋ] 단식
- [ ] partaker [pɑ:rtéikər] 참가자
- [ ] obstruct [əbstrʌ́kt] 막다
- [ ] restrained [ristréind] 절제하는
- [ ] placate [pléikeit] 달래다
- [ ] medicament [mədíkəmənt] 약물
- [ ] notion [nóuʃən] 개념
- [ ] tactic [tǽktik] 방책 (=strategy)
- [ ] doctrine [dáktrin] 원칙 (=principle)
- [ ] causation [kɔ:zéiʃən] 원인
- [ ] expedition [èkspədíʃən] 탐사
- [ ] fallacy [fǽləsi] 오류
- [ ] capsize [kǽpsaiz] 전복하다
- [ ] millennium [miléniəm] 천 년
- [ ] stack [stæk] 쌓다
- [ ] presence [prézns] 존재
- [ ] relent [rilént] 수그러들다
- [ ] cannibalism [kǽnəbəlìzm] 식인 풍습
- [ ] asylum [əsáiləm] 은신처
- [ ] impregnable [imprégnəbl] 난공불락의
- [ ] exodus [éksədəs] 이동

CH 01
CH 02
CH 03
CH 04
CH 05
CH 06
CH 07
CH 08
CH 09

Hackers TOEFL Reading

goHackers.com

PART 02

Making Inference

Chapter 05 Rhetorical Purpose

Chapter 06 Inference

Chapter 05
Rhetorical Purpose

OVERVIEW

Rhetorical Purpose 문제는 작가가 어떠한 의도로 특정 단어나 구 혹은 단락을 언급했는지를 묻는 유형이다. 여기서 rhetoric(수사학)이란 작가가 전달하고자 하는 바를 더욱 효과적이고 분명하게 나타내기 위하여 사용하는 여러 다양한 표현 방식을 말한다.
따라서 Rhetorical Purpose 문제를 해결하기 위해서는 작가가 특정 개념이나 정보를 언급한 의도가 무엇인지, 그리고 어떤 표현 방식을 통해 이를 언급했는지를 파악하는 연습이 필요하다.
Rhetorical Purpose 문제는 보통 한 지문당 0~3개가 출제된다.

TYPES OF QUESTIONS

대개 특정 구를 언급한 이유를 물을 때는 해당 구가 지문에 음영 처리되어 있고, 한 단락에 걸친 설명 방식을 물을 때는 단락 번호만이 표시된다. Rhetorical Purpose 문제의 전형적인 질문 유형은 아래와 같다

* Why does the author mention "⬜⬜⬜" in the passage?
* The author mentions "⬜⬜⬜" in the passage in order to
* The author mentions "⬜⬜⬜" in the passage as an example of which of the following?
* In paragraph #, why does the author give details about ____?
* What does the author conclude about ____?

또는, 본문에 언급된 특정 개념을 설명하기 위해 작가가 사용한 표현 방식(논리전개 방식) 자체를 묻기도 한다.

* In paragraph #, the author explains ____ by

간혹 단락 간의 관계, 특정 단락의 역할, 또는 단락이나 지문의 구성을 묻는 유형이 출제되기도 한다.

* What is the relationship between paragraphs # and # in the passage?
* How does paragraph # relate to the earlier discussion of ____?
* Which of the following best describes the way paragraph # is organized?

HACKERS **STRATEGY**

CH 01
CH 02
CH 03
CH 04
CH 05
CH 06
CH 07
CH 08
CH 09

Hackers TOEFL Reading

전략 1 문제의 keyword가 언급되어 있는 부분을 지문에서 찾아 전후 글의 전개방식을 파악한다.

지문에서 사용된 여러 clue 표현들을 통해서 글의 전개방식을 파악할 수 있다.

Ex Diamonds occur in a variety of hues — colorless, white, blue, yellow, orange, red, green, pink, brown, or colored black. Diamonds with a detectable hue are known as colored diamonds. Colored diamonds contain impurities or structural defects that cause the coloration, **while** pure diamonds are transparent and colorless. Most diamond impurities replace a carbon atom in the crystal lattice and the most common, nitrogen, causes a yellowish or brownish tinge.

Q: Why does the author mention "pure diamonds" in the passage?
A: To contrast ~

➡ 지문에서 pure diamonds가 언급되어 있는 문장을 보면 colored diamonds와 pure diamonds를 비교/대조하고 있는데, 이것은 접속사 while을 통해 쉽게 알 수 있다. 따라서 작가가 pure diamonds를 언급한 이유는 colored diamonds와 비교/대조하기 위해서이다.

Ex There are several stories about how the effects of the coffee bush, which was discovered around 1000 A.D., were first observed. Among them, the most prevalent is about an Ethiopian shepherd who noticed his flock was wide-awake after eating the berries off of a certain bush. When he tried the berries for himself, he found that he also became awake and energetic. With his discovery, many tribes began to take advantage of the coffee berries. **For example**, members of the Galla tribe in Ethiopia produced an energy boost from mixing a certain berry with animal fat. One path or another led people to the conclusion that the coffee bean would produce certain effects upon not only their livestock, but also themselves. The desire to capture and use the effects of coffee started the quest for cultivation and production of coffee throughout the world.

Q: The author mentions "members of the Galla tribe in Ethiopia" in the passage in order to
A: provide an example ~

➡ 지문에서 members of the Galla tribe in Ethiopia가 언급되어 있는 문장은 부족민들이 커피 열매를 활용한 예를 들고 있는데, 이것은 For example을 통해 알 수 있다. 즉, members of the Galla tribe in Ethiopia가 언급된 이유는 provide an example하기 위함이다.

해석 p.438

● 지문의 clue를 통해 파악할 수 있는 글의 전개방식

글의 전개방식		지문의 clue
설명	to explain / to describe	mean, ":"
예시	to give an example of to illustrate	for example, for instance, such as, '—'
분류	to identify types of to classify / to list	consist of, be one of the first, second
비교/대조	to compare	similarly, in the same way
	to contrast	while, on the other hand, in contrast
지지/반박	to support	be supported by
	to contradict / to criticize to refute	although (even though), despite however
부연/강조	to further develop the idea of to emphasize / to highlight	that is to say, also, in addition even, only
증명	to demonstrate / to show to give a reason for to give an evidence of	because, due to as a result, for that reason
의견/제안	to suggest / to present to propose / to argue	

TIP keyword 없이 특정 단락이나 지문에 대해 묻는 경우에도 지문의 clue를 통해 글의 전개방식을 파악할 수 있다.

전략 2 지문의 논리전개 방식을 바르게 표현한 보기가 지문과 내용면에서도 일치하는지 확인한다.

논리전개 방식을 나타내는 표현 뒤의 내용 역시 지문의 정보와 일치해야 한다.

Ex Seawater is always on the move, traveling across the planet as if a giant conveyor belt was pulling it along, and the colder, saltier, and denser the water is, the lower it sinks. Most of the water at the bottom of the North Pacific Ocean has not been exposed to sunlight in at least 800 years and some of it has been down there for two millennia. Accordingly, oceanographers have assumed the temperature of the bottom layer is stable, impervious to atmospheric warming. New evidence, **however**, shows that the lower depths there and elsewhere have warmed significantly in recent decades.

Q: Why does the author mention "New evidence" in the passage?
A: To contradict the claim that the water at the bottom of the ocean remains unaffected by a change of atmospheric temperature

➡ 우선 지문 내의 clue를 통해 전개방식을 파악하는 전략 1을 적용하였을 때, however를 통해서 앞에 나온 내용을 반박하는 전개방식임을 예상할 수 있다. 문맥을 살펴보면, 지문에서 **New evidence**는 해양학자들이 심해수에 관해 가지고 있던 기존의 생각, 즉 심해수는 대기 온도 변화에 영향을 받지 않는다는 가정을 contradict하기 위해 언급되었다. 따라서 보기는 지문에 사용된 글의 전개 방식과 내용 모두를 올바르게 표현하고 있음을 알 수 있다.

보기 중 오답을 확인한다.

지문에 사용된 논리전개 방식과 일치하지 않거나 지문의 내용과 일치하지 않는 내용을 포함한 보기는 오답으로 간주된다.

Ex In the past the lichen was considered a definitive example of mutualism, a symbiotic relationship equally beneficial to both species. The photosynthetic partner carries on photosynthesis, producing carbohydrate molecules for itself and the fungus, and the fungus obtains water and minerals for the photosynthetic partner as well as protects it against desiccation. **However**, some biologists now believe that lichen partnership is not really mutualism, but controlled parasitism of the photosynthetic partner by the fungus, as microscopic examination has revealed that some algae cells have been penetrated and destroyed by fungal hyphae.

Q: The author mentions "fungal hyphae" in the passage in order to

A: dispute the claim that photosynthetic partner and fungus have a mutually beneficial relationship (○)

➡ Fungal hyphae가 언급된 문장의 however를 통해 앞의 내용을 반박하는 전개방식임을 예상할 수 있다. 문맥을 살펴 보면, fungal hyphae는 지문에서 광합성 파트너와 곰팡이류가 공생관계라는 앞의 내용을 반박하기 위해 언급되었다. 따라서 보기의 논리전개 방식과 내용 모두 지문과 일치한다.

지문의 논리전개 방식과 일치하지 않는 오답

refute the theory that the fungus parasitizes the photosynthetic partner (×)

지문에서 일부 생물학자들이 곰팡이류가 광합성 파트너에 기생한다고 하였으므로 fungal hyphae가 곰팡이류가 광합 성 파트너에 기생한다는 이론을 refute하기 위해 언급되었다는 것은 지문에 사용된 논리전개 방식을 올바르게 표현하지 않은 것이다.

지문의 내용과 일치하지 않는 오답

clarify the process by which the fungus undergoes replication (×)

곰팡이류가 복제되는 과정은 언급되지 않았으므로 지문의 내용과 일치하지 않는다.

HACKERS STRATEGY **APPLICATION**

Great apes share about 96 percent of their DNA with humans. For chimpanzees, the figure is as high as 98.4 percent. African apes are actually more closely related to humans than they are to orangutans. According to Great Ape Survival Project(GRASP), humans' relationship with apes is so close that a taxonomist from another planet would probably classify humans as an African ape species. In a recent study by Massachusetts Institute of Technology(MIT) and Washington University, scientists compared the DNA of chimpanzees and humans. By placing the two codes side by side, scientists identified 400 million molecular changes that separate humans and chimps and pinpointed 250,000 that seem to indicate differences between the two species. All told, the gene sequences differ by four percent. However, three-quarters of the differences seem to be in even non-functional parts of the genome, suggesting that there is only a one percent difference between the two species. Researchers say the study could help explain why chimps are resistant to several human diseases such as AIDS, hepatitis, malaria, and Alzheimer's, which could help scientists find new ways to prevent or treat the diseases in humans.

1. Why does the author mention "non-functional parts" in the passage?

   (A) To compare functions of chimps' brain to those of humans'
   (B) To emphasize that humans and chimps have very few differences
   (C) To give an example of features humans share with chimps
   (D) To show that humans and chimps bear no resemblance

Reshaping the political, social, and economic climate of each country, the Revolutions of the 18th century in France and America were both turning points in history. In the American colonies, a series of altercations, political upheavals, and economic crises shook the social environment, providing impetus for a war between the British Empire and the revolutionaries between 1775 and 1783. Shortly thereafter, similar conditions among the French sparked several conflicts, beginning in 1787 and coming to a conclusion around 1799. The American and French Revolutionary periods represent a situation wherein a buildup of intersecting conditions intensified civil unrest.

2. In the passage, the author explains the Revolutions of the 18th century by

   (A) describing the ways in which they were concluded
   (B) highlighting the role of the British Empire and France
   (C) comparing similar situations in two different countries
   (D) classifying types of the primary causes for them

해석 p.438

CH 01

CH 02

CH 03

CH 04

CH 05

CH 06

CH 07

CH 08

CH 09

Hackers TOEFL Reading

1

전략 1 적용 | 강조의 부사 even을 통해 말하고자 하는 바를 강조하고 있음을 파악할 수 있다.

전략 2 적용 | 지문에서 non-functional parts가 언급된 문장의 전후 문맥을 보면, 인간과 침팬지의 유전자 염기서열은 4퍼센트 다르지만, 이 중 4분의 3은 게놈의 비기능적인 부분에 해당하므로 둘 사이에는 오직 1퍼센트의 차이만이 존재한다고 하였다. 따라서 non-functional parts는 인간과 침팬지 사이에는 차이점이 거의 없다는 것을 강조하기 위해 언급되었다. 따라서 인간과 침팬지 사이에는 차이점이 거의 없다고 진술하고 있는 (B)가 글의 전개 방식과 내용 모두 지문과 일치한다.

전략 3 적용 | (A) 지문의 논리전개 방식과 일치하지 않는 오답
지문에는 침팬지의 뇌의 기능과 인간의 뇌의 기능을 비교(compare)하는 내용이 언급되어 있지 않으므로 지문의 논리전개 방식과 일치하지 않는다.

(C) 지문의 내용과 일치하지 않는 오답
Non-functional parts가 인간과 침팬지가 공유하고 있는 특징이라는 것은 지문의 내용과 일치하지 않는다.

(D) 지문의 내용과 일치하지 않는 오답
인간과 침팬지 사이에 유사점이 전혀 없다는 것은 지문의 내용과 일치하지 않는다.

정답 | (B)

2

전략 1 적용 | 지문에서 작가는 Revolutions of the 18th century를 American colonies와 France를 통해 비교 (compare)하여 설명하고 있으며, 이는 similar 등의 표현으로 확인할 수 있다.

전략 2 적용 | 두 나라에서의 유사한 상황을 비교하여 설명하고 있다고 진술하고 있는 (C)가 논리전개 방식과 내용 모두 지문과 일치한다.

전략 3 적용 | (A) 지문의 내용과 일치하지 않는 오답
혁명이 종결된 방식은 지문에 언급되지 않았으므로 지문의 내용과 일치하지 않는다.

(B) 지문의 내용과 일치하지 않는 오답
영국과 프랑스의 역할을 강조하고 있다는 것은 지문의 내용과 일치하지 않는다.

(D) 지문의 논리전개 방식과 일치하지 않는 오답
혁명이 일어난 주요 원인들의 유형이 분류(classify)되어 있다는 것은 지문의 논리전개 방식과 일치하지 않는다.

정답 | (C)

Read each passage and answer the corresponding question for each.

1   When the colonists settled along the eastern seaboard of North America during the 17ᵗʰ century, their European traditions accompanied them. Because their domestic customs reflected this Old World heritage, it is small wonder that the style and construction of their furniture also was derived from European sources. Settlers arriving from different countries brought with them the styles of their native lands, so, for instance, 17ᵗʰ century New England furniture displays a strong English flavor, while that made in New York reveals the tastes of the Dutch.

● Why does the author mention "New England furniture" in the passage?

(A) To argue that the English settlers were unconcerned with the tastes of the Dutch

(B) To provide an example of furniture whose style originated from the colonists' native lands

(C) To support the claim that the colonists adjusted to their new homes well

(D) To note an exceptional piece of art constructed without the aid of Britain

2   Soil, which is composed of mineral particles, organic material, water, and air, is a valuable natural resource on which humans depend for food. Water, wind, ice, and other agents cause soil erosion, the wearing away, or removal of soil from the land. Water and wind are especially effective in removing soil: rainfall loosens soil particles that can then be transported away by moving water, while wind loosens soil and blows it away, particularly if the soil is exposed and dry.

● The author mentions "rainfall" in the passage in order to

(A) explain a process that can erode land

(B) contrast rainfall with mineral particles

(C) argue for the advantage of preventing erosion

(D) give an example of how moving water penetrates soil

VOCABULARY	The word ⬚ in the passage is closest in meaning to

1 heritage	(A) bounty	(B) legacy	(C) novelty	(D) sprightliness
reveals	(A) provokes	(B) adjusts	(C) shows	(D) procures
2 valuable	(A) adverse	(B) contiguous	(C) brittle	(D) precious

3   Neanderthals became extinct approximately 40,000 years ago, and their demise coincided with the emergence of *Homo sapiens*. While the extinction of Neanderthals and the emergence of modern humans were not [mutually] connected worldwide, the fossil record heavily implicates *Homo sapiens* as a contributing factor. However, not every time the two groups [encountered] one another resulted in violence, so it is likely that Neanderthals were eradicated in part because of competition for food sources.

- Why does the author mention "the fossil record" in the passage?

  (A) To indicate that Neanderthals had limited food sources
  (B) To offer proof of the date of Neanderthal extinction
  (C) To show that interspecific interactions were sometimes violent
  (D) To link *Homo sapiens* with the decline of Neanderthals

4   The source of Kawasaki disease, the foremost cause of heart damage in children, is currently unknown. However, research has determined that it occurs predominantly in young boys of East Asian descent. Experimental research indicates that the disease has genetic components that make these particular ethnic groups [susceptible] to the disease. So far, a number of gene variants located in East Asian DNA have been associated with the disease. However, an investigation of over three hundred Australian cases found that just 18.1% were of Asian ethnicity, suggesting that there are environmental factors involved, although it is not yet evident what they are.

- The author mentions "over three hundred Australian cases" in the passage in order to

  (A) identify the country with the highest affliction rate
  (B) provide an example of people with immunity
  (C) present the external components of the disease
  (D) contradict the genetic basis of the infection

VOCABULARY	The word [ ] in the passage is closest in meaning to

3	mutually	(A) reciprocally	(B) applicably	(C) cannily	(D) asymmetrically
	encountered	(A) empowered	(B) effaced	(C) faced	(D) buttressed
4	susceptible	(A) intolerable	(B) liable	(C) noticeable	(D) ineluctable

5   A community consists of the populations of various species that live together in the same place. When a natural area has been disturbed , for example, by a volcanic eruption, an earthquake, or a forest fire, a new community does not spring into existence overnight but develops gradually through a series of stages. The process of community development over time, which involves species in one stage being replaced by other species, is called ecological succession. Ecological succession is usually described in terms of the changes in the types of vegetation of an area, although each successional stage also has its own characteristic kinds of animals. The time intervals involved in ecological succession are on the order of tens, hundreds, or thousands of years, not millions of years as in the evolutionary time scale.

● Why does the author mention "evolutionary time scale" in the passage?

(A) To contrast the time required for ecological succession to that scale
(B) To visualize the scope of time needed for evolution
(C) To describe another way by which scientists measure change
(D) To clarify the rate at which geological activities occur

6   Traditionally, most American cities had fairly inflexible zoning ordinances, so developers who possessed a different vision of urban planning typically had to seek out rural plots on which to build privately regulated communities. Opponents of such regulations argued that strict zoning resulted in homogenous neighborhoods that did not meet the needs of a diverse population. This sentiment was precisely what gave rise to the New Urbanism revolution in the 1980s, which sought to create mixed-use neighborhoods that incorporated housing, shops, parks, and ample sidewalks to support foot and bicycle traffic. The town of Seaside, Florida is often cited as a place that perfectly embodies the ideals of the movement, though it is certainly not without its critics. Social activists claim that it has failed to achieve this goal because it has become a community that lacks much social or cultural variety.

● The author mentions "The town of Seaside, Florida" in the passage in order to

(A) identify the original inspiration for New Urbanism
(B) illustrate the growing need for varied neighborhoods
(C) explain why people started rejecting strict zoning practices
(D) give an example of a controversial planned community

VOCABULARY   The word ____ in the passage is closest in meaning to

5	disturbed	(A) unimpaired	(B) withered	(C) mended	(D) upset
6	meet	(A) authorize	(B) retard	(C) divulge	(D) fulfill
	incorporated	(A) dodged	(B) incommoded	(C) mingled	(D) supplanted

Read each passage and answer the corresponding question for each.

7   In the 19th century, the population of Ireland swelled, and the country turned to potato cultivation to feed the people. As much as 40 percent of the residents survived on a diet consisting almost entirely of potatoes. However, a blight lasting from 1845 to 1849 caused potatoes to become inedible, whether ⬚raw⬚ or cooked. Shortly after harvesting, the crop would rot, regardless of efforts taken to prevent decay. The collapse of the crop stemmed from low genetic variation as farmers had been using a single clone, which proved to have no resistance to the disease. The resulting famine ⬚fueled⬚ a large-scale emigration from Ireland and the deaths of over one million people.

- Why does the author give details about the genetic makeup of Irish potatoes in the passage?

   (A) To explain how Ireland effectively fed its growing population
   (B) To highlight the sophisticated breeding methods used by the Irish
   (C) To establish the reason for the failure of agriculture in Ireland
   (D) To show that the Irish took a unique crop variety overseas

8   The sociable weaver, *Philetairus socius*, is a bird species that is famous for constructing unique nesting structures. These massive nests have been likened to apartment blocks as they can accommodate up to 500 birds at a time. The outward layer of the construction is formed with large twigs angled downwards, to which grass is added to secure the ⬚foundations⬚ of the structure. These architectural marvels are comprised of dozens of linked chambers that have underside entrances surrounded by hay with sharply pointed ends to discourage predators. The entrances to the nest are akin to apartment elevators, with individual tunnels up to 25 centimeters long leading to a circular nesting chamber that contains a single breeding pair and their offspring. Each chamber is lined with soft materials, such as fur or cotton. These allow the interior to retain heat throughout the cold night. The relative security of the nest makes it attractive to several other bird species, which use it as a roosting site and coexist with the weavers.

- In the passage, the author explains the structure of sociable weaver nests by

   (A) detailing how the availability of materials dictates the design
   (B) illustrating the objects used in building nests
   (C) arguing that communal nests can be advantageous
   (D) comparing a natural construction to a manmade one

VOCABULARY	The word ⬚____⬚ in the passage is closest in meaning to			
7 raw	(A) pictorial	(B) crude	(C) provocative	(D) bearable
fueled	(A) punctured	(B) glorified	(C) spurred	(D) dipped
8 foundations	(A) bases	(B) operations	(C) allotments	(D) throngs

CH 01
CH 02
CH 03
CH 04
CH 05
CH 06
CH 07
CH 08
CH 09
Hackers TOEFL Reading

9 The most important development of antebellum American journalism came in the 1830s, when New York journalists Benjamin Day and James Gordon Bennett began appealing to mass audiences. Unlike contemporary papers, which sold for 6 cents, Day's *New York Sun* and Bennett's *New York Herald* at first sold for a penny and were peddled in the streets. In addition to the increased circulations, which would reach 77,000 for the *Herald* shortly before the Civil War, this period was noteworthy for the change in the content of newspapers. Bennett, in particular, was a pioneer in broadening the scope and sharpening the appeal of newspaper reporting. Whereas the early political papers were distinctive in their lively denunciations of opponents, the highlight of the *Herald* was its sensationalistic coverage of crime and other lurid materials.

● The author contrasts early political papers with Bennett's *Herald* in the passage in order to

(A) emphasize the increase in the popularity of newspapers
(B) describe how the charge for newspapers went down
(C) point out the importance of politics prior to the Civil War
(D) show the shift in subject matters of newspapers

10 The increasing wail of an ambulance's siren as it approaches and the corresponding decreasing pitch as it departs are common examples used to explain the Doppler effect. The sound waves in front of the siren compress when the source of the waves moves in a line. Those behind the siren are stretched out in an opposite fashion. In a parallel way, emitted light such as that from a star also changes appearance depending upon the observer's position relative to its movement. However, instead of a change in pitch like the sound of the siren, light changes color; it turns red as it recedes and blue as it approaches. The first to understand the implications of this was the eminent American astronomer Edwin Hubble.

● In the passage, the author explains the concept of light change by

(A) giving an example of various stars that change their position
(B) classifying types of sirens that constitute sound waves
(C) describing stars that shade into different colors
(D) comparing it to a familiar example of the change in sound waves

---

VOCABULARY	The word ☐ in the passage is closest in meaning to			
9 distinctive	(A) excessive	(B) special	(C) industrious	(D) continual
10 departs	(A) withdraws	(B) bickers	(C) crumbles	(D) defrosts
eminent	(A) cloistered	(B) demanding	(C) sober	(D) noted

Read each passage and answer the corresponding questions for each.

11   Kilauea is an active shield volcano that established Hawaii's largest island. It is considered moderately volatile because, despite its extensive eruptive history, the majority of explosions have been relatively weak. Kilauea originally emerged as a submarine volcano when the Pacific tectonic plate in the earth's crust moved over the Hawaiian hotspot, a convection point of intense activity in the mantle. Pressurized magma subsequently pushed through the oceanic crust repeatedly, and over time, the volcano generated height through the continual addition of a fresh layer of basalt lava until it finally breached the surface of the ocean around 100,000 years ago. Since then, Kilauea has continued to expand not only through its central vent systems but also by way of fissures that radiate in irregular patterns and propagate through linear fractures. And where there are many rift zones in proximity to each other, they sometimes produce significant new vent systems, such as during the infamous Puʻu ʻŌʻō eruption, which began in 1983 and has the distinction of being the longest-lasting discharge of any during the past 500 years.

1 Why does the author mention "a fresh layer of basalt lava" in the passage?

(A) To describe a material expelled from volcanoes
(B) To explain how a volcano has increased in size
(C) To provide an example of mantle convection
(D) To show how volcanic fissures are formed

2 The author mentions "Puʻu ʻŌʻō eruption" in the passage in order to

(A) prove that linear fractures can move in asymmetrical directions
(B) offer an example of an event that created additional vent systems
(C) highlight an eruption that lasted an extraordinarily long time
(D) indicate that rift zones often form a short distance from one another

3 What is the purpose of the passage?

(A) To compare different types of eruptions
(B) To describe the composition of a shield volcano
(C) To illustrate the development of volcanic vents
(D) To explain the formation of a volcano

VOCABULARY   The word ☐ in the passage is closest in meaning to

11	volatile	(A) untamed	(B) explosive	(C) indiscriminate	(D) plumb
	relatively	(A) comparably	(B) strikingly	(C) perpetually	(D) irreversibly
	fissures	(A) tokens	(B) dregs	(C) cracks	(D) stains

CH 01
CH 02
CH 03
CH 04
CH 05
CH 06
CH 07
CH 08
CH 09
Hackers TOEFL Reading

12   To develop healthy immune systems, infants require cellular material and nutrients from the mother. The transfer of these begins in the womb and continues postnatally via lactation, which provides many advantages to the infant. From day one, the mother produces colostrum, a preliminary form of breast milk that is particularly rich in antibodies like white blood cells (leukocytes). Initially, colostrum delivers relatively high concentrations of leukocytes to the infant. In particular, during a period of infection of the mother or child, this leukocyte conveyance will undergo a sharp acceleration. By the end of the second week, however, the quantity of leukocytes passed from mother to infant diminishes significantly, presumably because the child begins to produce enough immunological cells of his or her own. Throughout the process of lactation, the baby receives vital nutrients through the acquisition of proteins that promote the cultivation of essential intestinal bacteria. These simultaneously protect the babies against E. coli, a bacterium with the capacity to kill infants with weak immune systems.

1 In the passage, the author explains the delivery of colostrum by

(A) describing the stages of leukocyte transfer from mother to child
(B) comparing white blood cell levels in babies that were or were not breastfed
(C) detailing the various ways infants are able to fight off infection
(D) contrasting two different immune responses to a particular disease

2 Why does the author mention "E. coli" in the passage?

(A) To explain why infants require proteins from milk
(B) To describe a negative consequence of breastfeeding in newborns
(C) To provide evidence that breast milk contains beneficial bacteria
(D) To give an example of a potentially dangerous pathogen

3 The author's purpose in writing the passage is

(A) to describe why infants need certain nutrients
(B) to emphasize the value of leukocytes in breast milk
(C) to explain the benefits of breastfeeding infants
(D) to highlight the various stages of lactation

VOCABULARY   The word [   ] in the passage is closest in meaning to

12 require	(A) accord	(B) demand	(C) envision	(D) widen
lactation	(A) vein	(B) respiration	(C) molt	(D) nursing
acceleration	(A) ramification	(B) confederation	(C) facilitation	(D) duration

13 Hail develops through the accretion of ice particles in storm clouds. These clumps of ice form from water droplets that begin to freeze when the majority of the cloud is below 0 degrees Celsius. As the ice collides with water, the latter rapidly freezes and forms new layers, and these can be seen in cross section and share some similarity to an onion that is cut in half. For hail to grow in size, it requires the presence of not only abundant droplets of water but also rising air within the storm cloud that repeatedly circulates the hailstones, creating more and more collisions and perpetuating accretion. Without an updraft, frozen liquid would be dispelled from the cloud through gravity before it could develop enough mass. And because the upward air currents are strongest in intense storms, the severity of the atmospheric disturbance affects the dimensions of the hail. This is why minor storm clouds may produce hailstones only 5 millimeters in diameter, while major ones can generate hail up to 15 centimeters across.

1 Why does the author mention "an onion" in the passage?

(A) To highlight the role of accretion in the growth of layers
(B) To emphasize how large some ice particles can become
(C) To illustrate the inner structure of a hailstone
(D) To contrast the relative density of two objects

2 The author mentions "an updraft" in the passage in order to

(A) explain why some precipitation fails to freeze
(B) describe a feature that is common in storm clouds
(C) show the impact of gravity on hailstone development
(D) provide a prerequisite for hail formation

3 Which of the following best describes the organization of the passage?

(A) The process of a weather phenomenon is described.
(B) Differences between various cloud types are outlined.
(C) Competing theories of hail development are explained.
(D) The role of wind currents in storms is detailed.

CH 01
CH 02
CH 03
CH 04
CH 05
CH 06
CH 07
CH 08
CH 09
Hackers TOEFL Reading

VOCABULARY	The word ☐ in the passage is closest in meaning to			
13 rapidly	(A) fluently	(B) judiciously	(C) disinterestedly	(D) drastically
similarity	(A) hilarity	(B) durability	(C) affinity	(D) sincerity
affects	(A) impinges upon	(B) converges	(C) takes account of	(D) dilutes

14 Charles Darwin $\boxed{\text{pioneered}}$ the notion that emotions of self-consciousness are unique to humans. However, the psychological study of how these capacities arise in people occurred much later, starting with a 1932 experiment by Kathryn Bridges, who observed and recorded the daily emotional behavior of 62 babies over three or four months. This and subsequent research established that the emotional development of children proceeds in distinct stages from infancy to approximately three years of age.

Newborns display a very limited assortment of emotional behaviors. For instance, picking up or tickling a child $\boxed{\text{triggers}}$ a reaction representing contentment or happiness, and this may be exhibited through facial expressions, such as a smile. By around 18 months, babies begin to demonstrate evidence of self-awareness, which gives rise to emotions like empathy and envy. Then between years two and three, toddlers generate the capacity to understand social rules, leading to the onset of what are known as evaluative emotions. These result from the child incorporating cultural standards that allow them to analyze their own success and failure or whether they have lived up to expectations. Their contextual assessment of themselves matures and grows to include complex feelings, including pride and shame, by age three. Though the range and subtlety of feelings continue to expand and diversify beyond this point, psychologists $\boxed{\text{label}}$ this the benchmark for all ensuing emotional experience and display.

1 Why does the author mention "a 1932 experiment" in the passage?

(A) To prove that only humans are capable of self-awareness
(B) To explain how experts learned that emotion changes with age
(C) To identify what launched a new era of psychological inquiry
(D) To compare competing views on how emotions are acquired

2 The author mentions "picking up or tickling a child" in the passage in order to

(A) explain how babies were handled during a particular study
(B) describe the importance of actively interacting with newborns
(C) indicate behaviors that demonstrate self-conscious emotions
(D) give an example of actions that elicit certain emotional responses

3 Which of the following best describes the relationship of paragraph 2 to paragraph 1?

(A) Paragraph 2 analyzes the experiment outlined in paragraph 1.
(B) Paragraph 2 details the process summarized in paragraph 1.
(C) Paragraph 2 introduces supplementary research to support the claims in paragraph 1.
(D) Paragraph 2 provides contrasting evidence to the theory described in paragraph 1.

VOCABULARY The word ☐ in the passage is closest in meaning to

14 pioneered	(A) initiated	(B) sneered	(C) blended	(D) nurtured
triggers	(A) infuriates	(B) elicits	(C) vanquishes	(D) undermines
label	(A) embed	(B) cram	(C) annihilate	(D) designate

15 The Stone Age began more than 3 million years ago and continued until the discovery of the technology for forging metal tools in the ninth century BCE. As the name suggests, it was dominated by stone implements, many of which were preserved in lake beds and then later exposed after water levels dropped, allowing for their archaeological discovery. The Stone Age is mainly represented by two periods: the Oldowan and the Acheulian.

The Oldowan culture is named after the Olduvai Gorge in Tanzania, where its artifacts were originally discovered. Characteristic of this period are the crude pebble tools known as Oldowan choppers, which were made by hammering a few flakes off cobble-sized stones. These were presumably crafted for utilization in food preparation. There is also reliable evidence that the same people made tools out of bone. Some experts even speculate that they most likely also worked with wood, though no definitive examples of this have been preserved at any known Oldowan site.

By contrast, Acheulian craftsmanship was more sophisticated and gave rise to the so-called hand-axe tradition. The Acheulian axes featured two flat sides and opposing sharpened edges that met at a point. This design made them much more effective at cutting and slicing, though considerably more challenging to create. Because these implements are quite similar in appearance to a flat, open human hand — sharing the same size, symmetry, and thickness — some anthropologists believe that they may have had some sort of third-hand symbolism and, thus, might have served some function beyond the merely pragmatic.

1 What is the purpose of paragraph 1 in the overall discussion of stone tools?

  (A) It provides a broad temporal background of their development.
  (B) It proposes a theory for how early humans produced them.
  (C) It explains the archaeological methods used to discover them.
  (D) It introduces a novel approach to determining their precise age.

2 Why does the author give details about appearance and dimensions of the hand-axes in the passage?

  (A) To suggest that they were not necessarily practical tools
  (B) To cast doubt on a controversial claim by anthropologists
  (C) To indicate why their exact purpose will never be known
  (D) To support the idea that their design imitated a human hand

3 What is the relationship between paragraphs 2 and 3 in the passage?

  (A) Paragraph 2 presents a theory and Paragraph 3 addresses its plausibility.
  (B) Paragraph 2 discusses the discovery of a procedure and Paragraph 3 details its refinement.
  (C) Paragraph 3 explains why the techniques outlined in Paragraph 2 were abandoned.
  (D) Paragraph 3 provides a comparative reference for the objects described in Paragraph 2.

VOCABULARY The word ☐ in the passage is closest in meaning to

15	dropped	(A) pondered	(B) diminished	(C) compressed	(D) detoured
	evidence	(A) preoccupation	(B) precept	(C) corroboration	(D) correspondence
	quite	(A) fairly	(B) winsomely	(C) quietly	(D) dexterously

정답 및 해석 p.439

HACKERS **TEST**

1   Triggered by a stock market crash in 1929, the Great Depression was a worldwide economic downturn that negatively impacted the lives of ordinary people. This was especially true in the United States, where the depression caused staggeringly high unemployment, forcing many of the jobless out of their homes and into slums known as Hoovervilles. These groups of shacks and tents were named after President Herbert Hoover, whose inaction had been widely blamed for the situation. The devastating effects of the depression put tremendous pressure on the government to improve the economy, and following the election of President Franklin D. Roosevelt in 1932, new economic regulations were enacted to address several critical issues.

2   ➡ Regulation of securities was a preeminent concern of the Roosevelt administration because insufficient oversight in this area had been a major contributing factor to the stock market crash. Before the Great Depression, companies publicized false or misleading information about themselves, hoping to induce people to purchase their stocks. Many hopeful investors bought securities at excessive prices without really knowing the true value of the underlying companies, pushing the stock market higher and higher, which encouraged even more people to invest. This pattern of behavior continued to artificially inflate stock prices until eventually the bubble burst and the market declined dramatically.

3   ➡ In response to the problem, the government began mandating that any company issuing securities provide certain critical information to investors, including financial data about profits and losses. Additionally, a new agency called the Securities and Exchange Commission was given responsibility for implementing the new requirements and making sure that companies disclosed accurate information to prospective buyers. As a result, investors were able to make informed decisions by analyzing business data before buying a company's stock, and the prices of securities more accurately reflected actual business values, making the stock market more stable.

4   While securities regulation helped prevent another market crash, the depression also necessitated additional regulatory attention in the banking sector. As the economy began to deteriorate during the early days of the downturn, people withdrew more and more of their savings from banks, and if rumor spread that a particular bank was running out of money, depositors would flock there and demand immediate payment. These "bank runs" drove many institutions into bankruptcy, and by 1933, almost ten thousand of them had gone out of business in the United States, diminishing consumer confidence in banking. The Roosevelt administration addressed the crisis by establishing the Federal Deposit Insurance Corporation, or FDIC, which began collecting insurance premiums from financial institutions and using the proceeds to reimburse customers so that people did not lose their money if their bank became insolvent. The creation of the FDIC is widely

credited with increasing public confidence in financial institutions and reducing the frequency and negative effects of bank failures.

5 Perhaps no area of regulation was more widely felt than the increase in government oversight of the labor market, particularly with respect to labor unions. These groups had negotiated with businesses for higher pay and better working conditions in the years prior to the Great Depression, but due to skyrocketing unemployment during the downturn, companies could simply fire union employees and easily hire non-union replacements, making workers hesitant to join these organizations and greatly weakening organized labor. Consequently, firms were able to ignore worker demands, which prompted the Roosevelt administration to pass regulations that prohibited businesses from getting rid of employees merely because they joined a union and required that companies bargain with unions rather than simply ignore them.

6 The new law helped workers win concessions from their employers, but additional regulations were enacted to establish a minimum wage and a standard number of working hours per week. With so many unemployed citizens competing for a small number of job openings, many businesses were offering lower wages and demanding longer hours; the government sought to alleviate these issues by requiring that companies pay employees at least twenty-five cents per hour and provide additional compensation for any time worked in excess of forty hours per week. While the overall economic effect of the minimum wage law is debated, many economists believe that higher wages helped the economy because ordinary people were able to spend more money, increasing demand for goods and services. Moreover, the restriction on working schedules may have encouraged companies to hire more employees to make up for the lost hours.

1 Why does the author mention "Hoovervilles" in the passage?

(A) To explain why many unemployed people became homeless
(B) To give an example of a global consequence of the Great Depression
(C) To show that President Hoover was responsible for housing the jobless
(D) To illustrate how people were adversely affected by the Great Depression

2 According to paragraph 2, which of the following was a cause of the stock market crash?

(A) The government invested too heavily in the stock market.
(B) Companies did not keep accurate financial information about themselves.
(C) Stock prices underestimated the true values of companies.
(D) Securities were not regulated enough prior to the Great Depression.

Paragraph 2 is marked with an arrow [➡].

3 The author mentions the "Securities and Exchange Commission" in order to

(A) suggest that the new securities regulations were insufficient
(B) show how the new securities regulations were carried out
(C) explain the process by which securities laws were made
(D) demonstrate how information about securities was published

4 According to paragraph 3, all of the following were effects of the new securities regulations EXCEPT:

(A) The stock market grew less volatile.
(B) People were better informed about the companies they invested in.
(C) The stocks of many companies began to increase in value.
(D) Stock prices more accurately showed the value of the company.

Paragraphs 3 is marked with an arrow [➡].

5 What is the relationship between paragraphs 2 and 3 in the passage?

(A) Paragraph 3 lays out the effects of the securities regulations outlined in paragraph 2.
(B) Paragraph 2 explains a problem that was solved by the actions taken in paragraph 3.
(C) Paragraph 3 illustrates the concept of securities introduced in paragraph 2.
(D) Paragraph 2 provides arguments in favor of regulations and paragraph 3 refutes them.

6 The word "deteriorate" in the passage is closest in meaning to

(A) disappear
(B) stabilize
(C) get worse
(D) build up

7 Why does the author mention that "companies could simply fire union employees and easily hire non-union replacements"?

(A) To indicate why unemployment was so high at the time
(B) To show one of the effects of new labor regulations
(C) To explain why many workers did not join labor unions
(D) To illustrate how companies encouraged union membership

8 The word "alleviate" in the passage is closest in meaning to

(A) mitigate
(B) eradicate
(C) eliminate
(D) generate

9 Which of the sentences below best expresses the essential information in the highlighted sentence in the passage? *Incorrect* choices change the meaning in important ways or leave out essential information.

(A) Although their conclusion is debatable, many economists believe that the minimum wage regulation was responsible for ending the Great Depression.

(B) Economists continue to debate the overall economic effect of the minimum pay guideline, which increased the amount of money companies paid to their workers.

(C) Many economists believe that the minimum wage law, while controversial, helped the economy by increasing the amount of goods and services produced by workers.

(D) Although its effects on the whole are controversial, the minimum wage law is credited by many economists with fueling economic recovery since workers could afford to buy more goods and services.

10 **Directions**: An introductory sentence for a brief summary of the passage is provided below. Complete the summary by selecting the THREE answer choices that express the most important ideas in the passage. Some sentences do not belong in the summary because they express ideas that are not presented in the passage or are minor ideas in the passage. **This question is worth 2 points.**

Drag your answer choices to the spaces where they belong. To remove an answer choice, click on it. To review the passage, click on **View Text**.

The United States government created new regulations in an attempt to solve several important problems during the Great Depression.

-
-
-

Answer Choices

(A) To strengthen the bargaining power of workers, businesses were required to hire more union workers and grant them concessions on pay and working hours.

(B) Due to an increasing number of bank runs, The Federal Deposit Insurance Corporation was created to reduce problems within the banking industry.

(C) The Securities and Exchange Commission was created to write new securities regulations and limit the number of stocks companies could sell.

(D) Most economists now believe that the new regulations were successful in improving economic conditions and ending the Great Depression.

(E) Previously overlooked by the government, securities were more tightly regulated to address one of the causes of the Great Depression.

(F) The 1930s saw a significant increase in employment regulation, which was intended to lessen various hardships experienced by workers.

정답 및 해석 p.445

CH 01
CH 02
CH 03
CH 04
CH 05
CH 06
CH 07
CH 08
CH 09
Hackers TOEFL Reading

1   The fourth planet of the solar system, Mars, visible with the naked eye, waxes and wanes in the night sky during the course of the year. Due to the elliptical orbits of both the Earth and Mars, the appearance of Mars will have a very distinct reddish color when it is closest to Earth, which occurs twice every thirty-two years in alternating fifteen- and seventeen-year intervals. In contrast, it can be virtually invisible to the naked eye or masked by the Sun's glare when its orbit carries it opposite from Earth.

2   ➡ For over three thousand years, the Red Planet has been, second only to the Moon, the most studied celestial body in the universe. Its proximity to Earth has spurred a plethora of scientific studies, suggesting it could be the home of an intelligent alien life form. In the nineteenth century, two prominent astronomers, Percival Lowell and Giovanni Schiaparelli, used an advanced spectroscope to study the fine details of Mars and noted unusual topographical features, which they called *canali*, which in Italian means channels; however, at the time it was often mistranslated as canals. Since this term implies construction, there were many who took the discovery of canals to mean that intelligent life existed at one time on the remote planet. Following this, there was a spate of scientific as well as literary interest, and the public's fancy was captured by the idea that perhaps the solar system was home to more than one sentient race.

3   ➡ The attraction to Mars is much stronger than that for all other planets, which all tend to be extremely hostile to life, because the Red Planet is not only the most accessible destination but is also believed to contain topography conducive to both the development of life and long-term settlement by human explorers. The surface undergoes seasonal fluctuations in color which at one time were assumed to be caused by vegetation. Some people believed that surface flora would bloom in the summer and enter a period of inactivity in the winter. Early observers also noted the existence of polar ice caps on Mars, which hinted at the possibility of water, a prerequisite for life.

4   ➡ This image of Mars as potentially harboring life persisted until July of 1965, when the Mariner probe sent back twenty-two close-up photographs of the surface. These pictures revealed a stark and barren landscape which was a far cry from the fertile Mars envisioned by many. The canals, which had once been considered signs that an intelligent civilization was engaging in agriculture, were shown to be simply dried up natural waterways or just shadows cast by natural land features. The color changes which seemed to allude to the possibility of vegetation were, upon close inspection, revealed to be the result of dust storms on the surface, during which seasonal winds blew up huge areas of the parched surface.

5   ➡ Following the Mariner expedition, numerous other missions were sent to Mars with a few successfully landing on the surface. While it seemed that no living organism could live on the surface of the planet since the thin atmosphere would not filter enough hazardous ultraviolet light, there has been some recent evidence that the pronouncement of Mars as a dead planet may have been premature. Opportunity and Spirit, two NASA rovers

currently on the surface of Mars, have been involved in new research and have found traces of methane in the air. Since methane is unstable, it was most likely generated by methanogens, which are methane-producing bacteria. Although no conclusive evidence has yet been discovered, future research is bound to continue to focus on Mars as a possible source of extraterrestrial life.

1 The word "intervals" in the passage is closest in meaning to

(A) periods
(B) variances
(C) orbits
(D) records

2 The word "its" in the passage refers to

(A) sky
(B) Earth
(C) Mars
(D) Sun

3 Why does the author mention canals in the paragraph 2?

(A) To rebut the idea that Lowell and Schiaparelli found alien life
(B) To show that construction had taken place on Mars in the past
(C) To claim that accurate translation is important for scientists
(D) To give a reason for people's belief in the existence of life on Mars

Paragraph 2 is marked with an arrow [➡].

4 The phrase "conducive to" in the passage is closest in meaning to

(A) requisite to
(B) favorable to
(C) disadvantageous to
(D) fundamental to

CH 01

CH 02

CH 03

CH 04

CH 05

CH 06

CH 07

CH 08

CH 09

Hackers TOEFL Reading

5 Which of the following best describes the organization of paragraph 3?

(A) Reasons for the fascination with Mars and some relevant features
(B) A comparison of notable characteristics of Mars and other planets
(C) Inventions and their impact on public perception of Mars
(D) A factual description of Mars followed by a fictional account

Paragraph 3 is marked with an arrow [➡].

6 Which of the sentences below best expresses the essential information in the highlighted sentence in the passage? *Incorrect* choices change the meaning in important ways or leave out essential information.

(A) The high winds made it impossible for vegetation to exist on the surface of Mars.

(B) Dust storms were found to be the cause of the surface color variation on Mars.

(C) The likelihood of plants on Mars is reduced by the discovery of seasonal dust storms.

(D) As vegetation on Mars was stifled by strong winds, the change in surface color didn't occur.

7 What is the relationship between paragraphs 4 and 5 in the passage?

(A) Paragraph 4 introduces a tentative theory that is debunked in paragraph 5.
(B) Paragraph 4 presents an outline of the topics that are discussed in paragraph 5.
(C) Paragraph 5 provides a more updated account of an issue raised in paragraph 4.
(D) Paragraph 5 offers a solution to a problem introduced in paragraph 4.

Paragraphs 4 and 5 are marked with an arrow [➡].

8 The word "hazardous" in the passage is closest in meaning to

(A) doomful
(B) weak
(C) dangerous
(D) mysterious

9 Why does the author mention "methane" in the passage?

(A) To give the latest proof of the possibility of life
(B) To reinforce the idea that Mars is a barren world
(C) To highlight the effectiveness of the NASA rovers on Mars
(D) To describe how thin the atmosphere of Mars is

10 **Directions**: An introductory sentence for a brief summary of the passage is provided below. Complete the summary by selecting the THREE answer choices that express the most important ideas in the passage. Some sentences do not belong in the summary because they express ideas that are not presented in the passage or are minor ideas in the passage. **This question is worth 2 points.**

> Drag your answer choices to the spaces where they belong. To remove an answer choice, click on it. To review the passage, click on **View Text**.

Mars has long been considered suitable for harboring alien life.

-
-
-

Answer Choices

(A) NASA has launched a series of increasingly sophisticated Mars probes.

(B) Scientists have paid attention to Mars' potential as a space research center.

(C) Several characteristics of Mars led people to believe it was fairly conducive to life, but the pictures from the Mariner drastically conflicted with such views.

(D) Misinterpretation of astronomers' work propagated the notion that artificial waterways had been built on Mars.

(E) Findings on Mars have provided evidence that the planet is worthy of continued research in the quest to find life in outer space.

(F) Because of its vicinity to Earth, early astronomers were able to observe Mars in the sky.

정답 및 해석 p.446

CH 01
CH 02
CH 03
CH 04
CH 05
CH 06
CH 07
CH 08
CH 09
Hackers TOEFL Reading

1   In post-colonial homes with large parlors, women frequently gathered in quilting bees and helped neighbors and friends finish their needlepoint work, taking turns working on one of the four corners of the quilt frame. These weekly or monthly events constituted women's primary means of socializing in an otherwise isolated rural American environment. Expert quilters would work together, sometimes teaching novice girls, and carefully piece together a full blanket while singing, telling stories, and sharing ideas about everyday life. Based on the complexity of the design, the project could take many days to complete, or as little as one afternoon. As the craft matured and the socioeconomic status of the quilters changed, the style also became more sophisticated depending on whether the purpose was to commemorate loved ones or community milestones, or simply keep everyone in the family warm.

2   ➡ The earliest quilts were fashioned with relatively simple designs and were made to be primarily functional rather than to serve as a means of elaborate artistic expression. Parsimonious women recycled highly valued scraps of materials to make and repair the quilts. Called patchwork, the technique centered on the construction of blocks, or squares of fabric that were sewn together to make the quilt top. Once this was finished, a layer of cotton or wool batting was laid down, making the quilt soft and comfortable. Then a large piece of backing was placed underneath the batting and all three layers were sewn with small stitches. Because the tops were sewn with many different odds and ends, printing styles and color varied from block to block.

3   ➡ Patchwork quilts, in general, had utilitarian designs, but in the early 1800s, the craft was artistically enhanced by groups of affluent women who could spend their leisure time perfecting complicated new patterns by cutting out specific shapes of fabric and hand stitching these onto the foundation piece. Called appliqué, a term adopted from French which means "to apply," the technique required delicate needlework and special materials, which increased the cost of each quilt. At first, only the wealthy could afford to make appliqué quilts, but throughout the century, American textile printers stepped up production and lowered costs. The introduction of the sewing machine also reduced stitching time. By the early 1900s, appliqué had surpassed patchwork in popularity, mainly due to its versatility and integration into folk art of the era.

4   One common use of appliqué was to record local community history, popularized by the Baltimore Album motif. The Baltimore Album motif was named for the city where it first became fashionable, and perhaps the best example of how women used quilting to record aspects of their community. The design generally used elaborate floral, animal, or patriotic themes, constructed from numerous individually sewn blocks, each signed by their maker. Talented calligraphers might also write verses or messages to the intended owner of the final product, hoping to remind him or her of the many hands that were involved in the multistage undertaking. While most messages were textual, some were pictorial symbols. If a spider web pattern was stitched into a quilt, it was believed to bring the quilt maker and recipient of the quilt good fortune.

5 Eager to assimilate any new aesthetic trend into their artwork, quilters embraced asymmetric designs into their coverlets, stitching irregular patches either with appliqué or patchwork piecing. Women's magazines not only promoted the new techniques, but also coined the term crazy quilts (traditionally, "craze" meant to break or tear into splinters) to describe the use of exotic brocades, velvets, and wools, topped with embroidery, to set out kaleidoscopic or abstract arrangements. Some publications even gave away snippets of silk to encourage women to subscribe. As mass media grew, so did the interest in innovative needlework. Crazies were a perfect way for talented women to show off their skill and imagination because they were complicated by intricate stitches such as herringbone, fly, and chain. Like appliqué, these quilts were first made only by the more affluent, but as their popularity grew, women began fashioning them out of cotton, denim, and flannel. Female artisans, for the first time in American history, found their creatively charged works in galleries.

1 According to the passage, the length of the time needed to perfect a quilt

(A) was affected by the number of experts
(B) varied depending on the intricacy of the pattern
(C) increased because of the time for story telling
(D) was a foremost standard to grade it

2 Which of the sentences below best expresses the essential information in the highlighted sentence in the passage? *Incorrect* choices change the meaning in important ways or leave out essential information.

(A) Once the quilters became more wealthy and influential, they began to experiment with more sophisticated designs.

(B) As quilting techniques developed and the social position of their makers was altered, the quilts displayed a more refined style according to their intended function.

(C) Quilts were created to celebrate important events or congratulate close friends and relatives, as well as elevate women's roles in the community.

(D) Because the style of quilts reflected the status of the makers, quilters tried to elaborate their works using advanced techniques.

3 In paragraph 2, the author describes patchwork by

(A) outlining the method to obtain materials
(B) listing the types of several common designs
(C) clarifying its purpose as artistic expression
(D) showing the process by which it was made

Paragraph 2 is marked with an arrow [➡].

4 Why does the author mention "many different odds and ends" in the passage?

(A) To emphasize the diversity of techniques used in patchwork
(B) To show that suitable scraps of material were difficult to find
(C) To point out that a variety of methods were used to sew small stitches
(D) To provide the reason that blocks were not uniform in design

5 How does paragraph 3 relate to the earlier discussion of patchwork quilting?

(A) It introduces a technique of quilt making that amplified artistic expression.
(B) It describes a quilting style that is inferior to that used in a previous era.
(C) It illustrates how technological progress revolutionized the quilting industry.
(D) It explains why the upper class eschewed conventional quilting methods.

Paragraph 3 is marked with an arrow [➡].

6 The word "surpassed" in the passage is closest in meaning to

(A) exceeded
(B) outlasted
(C) fell behind
(D) replaced

7 Why does the author mention "Baltimore Album motif" in the passage?

(A) To demonstrate the prevalence of appliqué quilts in Baltimore
(B) To give a reason for women's affection for quilts
(C) To give an example of appliqué's use as a community record
(D) To contrast the Baltimore style to that of other cities

8 The word "assimilate" in the passage is closest in meaning to

(A) divide
(B) incorporate
(C) insert
(D) translate

9 Which of the following best describes the organization of the passage?

(A) A critical commentary about a time period and its artistic accomplishments
(B) A description of a craft and its development in historical perspective
(C) A historical analysis of quilting and its impact in contemporary society
(D) An analysis of the pros and cons of various traditional quilting techniques

10 **Directions**: An introductory sentence for a brief summary of the passage is provided below. Complete the summary by selecting the THREE answer choices that express the most important ideas in the passage. Some sentences do not belong in the summary because they express ideas that are not presented in the passage or are minor ideas in the passage. **This question is worth 2 points.**

> Drag your answer choices to the spaces where they belong. To remove an answer choice, click on it. To review the passage, click on **View Text**.

CH 01

CH 02

CH 03

CH 04

CH 05

CH 06

CH 07

CH 08

CH 09

Hackers TOEFL Reading

Quilts have gone through many stages of development and are now considered a form of art.

-
-
-

Answer Choices

(A) Quilts with complex patterns were produced by sewing particular shapes of individual textile onto the foundation piece.

(B) Publications helped to attract women's interest in quilts by distributing fine quality cloth to subscribers.

(C) Quilting skills were passed from experts to beginners at quilting bees in an effort to preserve traditional skills.

(D) Quilts were initially created by making use of leftover bits of fabric in consideration of practicality and had inconsistent patterns and colors.

(E) The middle layer in multi-layered quilts served as the base for the underlying batting and made the quilts more yielding to the touch.

(F) Covers were made by stitching erratic fabric scraps and were pieced together using other types of quilting techniques.

정답 및 해석 p.448

1   The evolution of the internal biological clock, which is also known as the circadian rhythm, is directly linked to the 24-hour cycle of day and night on Earth and was first recognized centuries ago when botanists saw its importance in plants due to the effect that light had on the flowering of plants and in their preparations for winter. Only in the past four decades, however, have researchers discovered that there is a biological clock in animals; following this revelation, they have endeavored to understand how it is controlled.

2   After establishing the existence of biological clocks in fauna, the results of the initial studies and new advances in neurological studies led researchers to further explore the mechanisms by which organisms were able to adjust their timing. Preliminary findings indicated that the circadian rhythm was not a true 24-hour sequence, but rather, species showed wide variation, from 20-hour to 28-hour periods in which those kept in isolation would eventually fall out of sync with the natural environment. In contrast, those that were kept in a normal environment seemed unaffected, with no exhibitions of periodic distortions, which conclusively showed the necessity of sunlight.

3   Yet the exact mechanism for the transfer of photic information to the brain remained obscured until the discovery of melanopsin, a photopigment found in retinal cells. When the retina is exposed to light, melanopsin is sent via a neural pathway to the suprachiasmatic nuclei (SCN). The SCN is a cluster of thousands of neurons and cells located in the hypothalamus, the portion of the brain responsible for a range of important metabolic processes, including those that control circadian cycles and related phenomena, such as fatigue, sleep, hunger, thirst, and body temperature. Upon receipt of the information from the retina, the SCN performs minor adjustments and ensures that the internal time is kept concurrent with the environment. Without regular exposure to sunlight in conjunction with these complex processes of photoreception and neural transmission, the side effect would be disruption of the biological clock. As a consequence, hormones in the body would become imbalanced, and the affected organism would become disoriented and experience erratic short-term sleep patterns.

4   The importance of the SCN was demonstrated in an experiment involving rats, which had their SCN removed during the experiment to prove the SCN was the control of the body's clock. These rats lost the behaviors associated with circadian rhythm, and they even stopped drinking. But some rats had only a portion of their SCN removed. After dissecting the portion, the researchers noticed that the remaining SCN in these rats continued sending forth a steady stream of proteins that functioned as messengers to the body, keeping all the visceral organs in time, diurnally raising basal temperatures, releasing cortisol, and elevating blood pressure in anticipation of a day of activity.

5   ➡ Once the SCN was recognized as the control center, the next step, in an effort to understand how to control the cycle, was to identify the genes that regulated the mechanism, and since the fruit fly was one of the most studied subjects in genetics, it was naturally the first animal in which a specific gene sequence was identified. However, it

took an additional seventeen years for the DNA sequences that control the rhythms in mammals to be discovered. The discovery resulted from an experiment in 1988. Hamsters with a defective DNA sequence known as the "clock gene" sent faulty signals to the SCN, which thus kept them from ever establishing a regular circadian rhythm. Without this internal feedback mechanism, the hamster would eat, drink, and sleep at irregular intervals, exhibiting aberrant periodicity, although surprisingly the amounts it ate, drank, and slept showed no deviation from those of a normal hamster.

6 ➡ In humans, a similar mechanism is in existence, which serves the same function, and there has been considerable research devoted to trying to understand human rhythms. For example, people who travel from one time zone to another often experience physiological symptoms such as nausea, irritability, and insomnia. Some disorders previously thought to be psychological have also recently been found to be affected by the circadian rhythm. Generally, exposure to sunlight will eventually help reset the body's inner alignment, but during the winter, the shorter days can exacerbate the problem and lead to seasonal affective disorder. A form of depression, it has been linked to increased drug and alcohol abuse as well as suicide, but due to increased understanding of the causes, treatments such as light therapy have been developed to aid those afflicted by equalizing their hormone levels.

Glossary
cortisol an adrenal-cortex hormone that is active in carbohydrate and protein metabolism

1 The word "it" in the passage refers to

(A) light
(B) flowering
(C) biological clock
(D) revelation

2 The author mentions "those kept in isolation" in the passage in order to

(A) identify which organisms are suitable for the experiment
(B) explain the role of the brain in clock regulation
(C) provide an example of species neurologists studied
(D) compare them with species exposed to sunlight

3 The word "conclusively" in the passage is closest in meaning to

(A) decisively
(B) illusorily
(C) elastically
(D) deceptively

CH 01
CH 02
CH 03
CH 04
CH 05
CH 06
CH 07
CH 08
CH 09
Hackers TOEFL Reading

4 The word "erratic" in the passage is closest in meaning to

(A) dependable
(B) insufficient
(C) imminent
(D) unpredictable

5 Why does the author discuss an experiment involving rats in the passage?

(A) To argue that the SCN affects only a few organs of the body
(B) To illustrate the link between the SCN and decreased blood pressure
(C) To suggest that the SCN's primary function is to break down proteins
(D) To provide evidence for the SCN's management of the biological clock

6 In paragraph 5, why does the author mention "Hamsters"?

(A) To contrast their gene sequence that regulates the circadian rhythm with that of the fruit fly
(B) To describe the first identification of a gene in mammals that controls the biological clock
(C) To explain how the origin of genetic research aided in the discovery of the biological clock gene
(D) To clarify which subjects are most appropriate for large-scale genetic research in biology

Paragraph 5 is marked with an arrow [➡].

7 Which of the sentences below best expresses the essential information in the highlighted sentence in the passage? *Incorrect* choices change the meaning in important ways or leave out essential information.

(A) In order for a hamster to control its internal clock, it must be able to eat, drink, and sleep at regular times like other hamsters.
(B) The biological needs of a normal hamster were much lower than those of a hamster without the circadian rhythm.
(C) A hamster with no internal biological clock differed from an ordinary one by the times it would feed and rest but not in the total amount.
(D) Differences in behavior between normal and abnormal hamsters were observed by removing their mechanism for internal control.

8 What is the purpose of paragraph 6 in the overall discussion of circadian rhythm?

(A) To dispel the notion that the biological phenomenon extends to human beings
(B) To introduce the reader to some recent revelations about biological rhythms in humans
(C) To examine some of the ways in which circadian rhythms affect people
(D) To explain that people can control their circadian rhythms through psychological training

Paragraph 6 is marked with an arrow [➡].

9 The word "eventually" in the passage is closest in meaning to

(A) ultimately
(B) inevitably
(C) undoubtedly
(D) absolutely

10 **Directions**: An introductory sentence for a brief summary of the passage is provided below. Complete the summary by selecting the THREE answer choices that express the most important ideas in the passage. Some sentences do not belong in the summary because they express ideas that are not presented in the passage or are minor ideas in the passage. **This question is worth 2 points.**

Drag your answer choices to the spaces where they belong. To remove an answer choice, click on it. To review the passage, click on **View Text**.

Like plants, animals have the circadian rhythm that helps regulate body functions.

-
-
-

Answer Choices

(A) Species exhibit various types of internal clocks and need to synchronize with each other.

(B) It was discovered that the retina works in conjunction with melanopsin and the SCN to regulate the biological clock.

(C) The role of the suprachiasmatic nuclei in maintaining internal clocks is to increase body temperature.

(D) Further experiments confirmed the crucial regulatory role of the SCN and genes in the rhythmic functions of multiple organisms.

(E) As with animals, sensitivity to light and circadian cycles can affect the moods and behavior of humans.

(F) People who have difficulty in sleeping should be placed under medical care immediately.

정답 및 해석 p.450

토플 빈출어휘 정리 노트

Chapter 05에 수록된 어휘들을 빈출도 순으로 정리했습니다. 음성파일을 들으며 꼭 암기하세요.

토플 최빈출어휘 [★★★]

☐ **reflect** [riflékt] 반영하다

☐ **heritage** [héritidʒ] 전통 (=legacy)

☐ **reveal** [riví:l] 드러내다 (=show)

☐ **wear away** 차츰 닳다 (=erode)

☐ **implicate** [ímplikeit] 시사하다

☐ **encounter** [inkáuntər] 부딪히다 (=face)

☐ **susceptible** [səséptəbl] 영향받기 쉬운 (=liable)

☐ **interval** [íntərvəl] 간격 (=period)

☐ **incorporate** [inkɔ́:rpərèit] 결합하다 (=mingle)

☐ **meet** [mi:t] 충족시키다 (=fulfill)

☐ **rural** [rúrəl] 지방의

☐ **fuel** [fju:əl] 부채질하다 (=spur)

☐ **scope** [skoup] 범위 (=extent)

☐ **distinctive** [distíŋktiv] 특색 있는 (=special)

☐ **compress** [kəmprés] 압축하다 (=crush)

☐ **implication** [ìmplikéiʃən] 의미

☐ **eminent** [émənənt] 저명한 (=noted)

☐ **relatively** [rélətivli] 상대적으로 (=comparably)

☐ **radiate** [réidieit] 퍼지다

☐ **component** [kəmpóunənt] 요소 (=factor)

☐ **affect** [əfékt] 영향을 미치다 (=impinge upon)

☐ **rapidly** [rǽpidli] 급속히 (=drastically)

☐ **pioneer** [pàiəníər] 창시하다 (=initiate)

☐ **trigger** [trígər] 야기하다 (=elicit)

☐ **mask** [mæsk] 숨기다 (=conceal)

☐ **evidence** [évədəns] 증거 (=corroboration)

☐ **devastating** [dévəstèitiŋ] 파괴적인

☐ **enact** [inǽkt] 제정하다

☐ **mandate** [mǽndeit] 요구하다

☐ **deteriorate** [ditíəriərèit] 악화되다

☐ **offspring** [ɔ́:fspriŋ] 새끼

☐ **virtually** [vɔ́:rtʃuəli] 거의 (=nearly)

☐ **remote** [rimóut] 먼 (=distant)

☐ **conducive to** 도움이 되는 (=favorable to)

☐ **hint** [hint] 암시하다 (=clue)

☐ **prerequisite** [pri:rékwəzit] 필수조건 (=requirement)

☐ **allude** [əlú:d] 암시하다 (=suggest)

☐ **hazardous** [hǽzərdəs] 위험한 (=dangerous)

☐ **surpass** [sərpǽs] 넘어서다 (=exceed)

☐ **versatility** [vɔ̀:rsətíləti] 다양한 용도

☐ **assimilate** [əsíməlèit] 흡수하다 (=incorporate)

☐ **coin** [kɔin] 신조어를 만들어내다

☐ **conclusively** [kənklú:sivli] 확연히 (=decisively)

☐ **erratic** [irǽtik] 불규칙한 (=unpredictable)

☐ **aberrant** [əbérənt] 비정상적인 (=abnormal)

토플 빈출어휘 [★★]

☐ **valuable** [vǽljuəbl] 귀중한 (=precious)

☐ **remove** [rimú:v] 제거하다 (=clear)

☐ **transport** [trænspɔ́:rt] 이동시키다

☐ **mutually** [mjú:tʃuəli] 서로 (=reciprocally)

☐ **result in** 결과를 초래하다

☐ **serve as** 역할을 하다

☐ **disturb** [distɔ́:rb] 흩트리다 (=upset)

☐ **gradually** [grǽdʒuəli] 서서히 (=slowly)

☐ **on the order of** 대략

☐ **give rise to** ~이 일어나게 하다

☐ **foundation** [faundéiʃən] 토대 (=base)

☐ **noteworthy** [nóutwɔ̀:rði] 주목할 만한

☐ **depart** [dipá:rt] 멀어지다 (=withdraw)

☐ **recede** [risí:d] 멀어지다

☐ **volatile** [válətil] 불안정한 (=unsettled)

☐ **fracture** [frǽktʃər] 균열

☐ **require** [rikwáiər] 필요로 하다 (=demand)

☐ **lactation** [læktéiʃən] 수유 (=nursing)

☐ **acceleration** [æksèləréiʃən] 촉진 (=facilitation)

☐ **symmetry** [símətri] 대칭

☐ **arise** [əráiz] 생기다

☐ **preserve** [prizɔ́:rv] 보존하다

*해커스 동영상강의 포털 해커스인강(HackersIngang.com)에서 '토플 빈출어휘 정리 노트' 음성파일을 무료로 다운로드할 수 있습니다.

☐ reliable [riláiəbl] 믿을 만한

☐ similarity [sìmələ rǽrəti] 비슷함 (=affinity)

☐ label [léibəl] 분류하다 (=designate)

☐ drop [drɑp] 낮아지다 (=diminish)

☐ archaeological [à:rkiəládʒikəl] 고고학적인

☐ preeminent [priémənənt] 주요한

☐ concession [kənséʃən] 양보

☐ definitive [difínətiv] 결정적인

☐ elliptical [ilíptikəl] 타원형의

☐ hostile [hástl] 비우호적인

☐ stark [stɑ:rk] 황량한

☐ premature [prì:mətjúər] 시기상조의

☐ novice [návis] 초보자

☐ sophisticated [səfístəkèitid] 세련된 (=urbane)

☐ parsimonious [pà:rsəmóuniəs] 검소한

☐ affluent [ǽfluənt] 부유한

☐ popularize [pápjulər àiz] 대중화하다

☐ disruption [disrʌ́pʃən] 분열

☐ dissect [disékt] 절개하다

☐ nausea [nɔ́:ziə] 구역질

☐ disorder [disɔ́:rdər] 질환

☐ eventually [ivéntʃuəli] 결과적으로 (=ultimately)

☐ depression [dipréʃən] 우울증

토플 기출어휘 [★]

☐ taste [teist] 취향

☐ particle [pá:rtikl] 입자

☐ mineral [mínərəl] 광물

☐ emergence [imə́:rdʒəns] 출현

☐ in terms of 측면에서 (=with regard to)

☐ raw [rɔ:] 원료 그대로의 (=crude)

☐ weave [wi:v] (직물을) 짜다

☐ opponent [əpóunənt] 반대하는 사람

☐ survive on ~으로 연명하다

☐ swell [swel] 증가하다

☐ cultivation [kʌ̀ltivéiʃən] 재배

☐ crop [krɑ:p] 농작물

☐ rot [rɑ:t] 썩다

☐ decay [dikéi] 부패

☐ algae [ǽldʒi:] 조류

☐ in particular 특히

☐ sharpen [ʃá:rpən] 더 분명히 하다

☐ stretch out 뻗다

☐ fissure [fíʃər] 갈라진 틈 (=crack)

☐ akin to ~과 유사한

☐ coexist [kòuigzíst] 공존하다

☐ intestinal [intéstənl] 장의

☐ neural [njúərəl] 신경의

☐ moderately [má:dərətli] 적당히

☐ scale [skeil] 규모

☐ intense [inténs] 격렬한

☐ blood pressure 혈압

☐ circulate [sə́:rkjəleit] 순환시키다

☐ dimension [dɑiménʃən] 크기

☐ quite [kwait] 상당히 (=fairly)

☐ downturn [dáuntə̀:rn] 경기 침체

☐ name after 이름을 따서 명명하다

☐ inaction [inǽkʃən] 태만

☐ oversight [óuvərsàit] 단속

☐ proceeds [próusi:dz] 수익금

☐ reimburse [rì:imbə́:rs] 배상하다

☐ insolvent [insálvənt] 파산의

☐ a spate of 많은

☐ sentient [sénʃənt] 지각 있는

☐ extraterrestrial [èkstrətəréstriəl] 외계의

☐ commemorate [kəmémər èit] 기념하다

☐ kaleidoscopic [kəlàidəskápik] 변화무쌍한

☐ side effect 부작용

☐ irritability [ìrətəbíləti] 과민성

☐ insomnia [insámniə] 불면증

Chapter 06
Inference

OVERVIEW

Inference 문제는 지문에 명백히 드러나 있지 않지만, 지문에 나타나 있는 사실을 바탕으로 추론 가능한 것을 선택하는 유형이다. 여기서 inference(추론)란 이미 알고 있는 사실을 바탕으로 지문 내에 명확히 제시되지 않은 정보를 도출해내는 과정을 말한다.

따라서 Inference 문제를 제대로 풀기 위해서는 지문에 제시된 정보를 정확하게 이해하는 것이 필수적이며 주관적인 생각은 배제하고 지문에 근거하여 추론해야 한다.

Inference 문제는 보통 한 지문당 0~2개가 출제된다.

TYPES OF QUESTIONS

대개 단락 번호가 문제에 함께 제시되며, 지문에 해당 단락이 [➡] 표시로 나타난다. 선택지에는 4개의 보기가 주어진다.

Inference 문제의 전형적인 질문 유형은 아래와 같다.

- According to paragraph #, what can be inferred about ____?
- According to paragraph #, which of the following may best represent the attitude of ____?
- Based on the information in paragraph #, what can be inferred about ____?
- Which of the following can be inferred from paragraph # about ____?
- It can be inferred from paragraph # that ____
- In paragraph #, what does the author imply about ____?

간혹 지문에 언급된 내용을 바탕으로 도출될 수 있는 결론을 묻기도 한다.

- Which of the following can be concluded from the passage?

HACKERS **STRATEGY**

CH **01**

CH **02**

CH **03**

CH **04**

CH **05**

CH **06**

CH **07**

CH **08**

CH **09**

Hackers TOEFL Reading

전략 1 문제의 keyword가 언급되어 있는 부분을 지문에서 찾는다.

지문을 scanning하여 keyword와 관련된 내용을 지문에서 찾은 후, keyword가 들어있는 문장 및 전후 문맥을 정확히 파악한다.

Ex The Aurora consists of rapidly shifting patches and dancing columns of light of various hues. Extensive auroral displays are accompanied by disturbances in the terrestrial magnetism and interference with radio, telephone, and telegraph transmission. **The period of maximum and minimum intensity of the Aurora follows almost exactly that of the sunspot cycle, which is an eleven-year cycle.**

Q: It can be inferred from the passage that **sunspots**
A: have phases of differing intensities

➡ 문제의 keyword인 sunspots(흑점)는 지문의 마지막 문장에 언급되어 있다. '오로라의 최대최소 강도 주기는 11년을 주기로 하는 태양흑점 주기의 최대최소 강도 주기를 거의 정확하게 따른다'라고 하였으므로, 태양흑점에 다른 강도를 갖는 시기가 있음을 추론할 수 있다.

전략 2 지문에서 추론의 근거가 되는 부분을 바탕으로 올바르게 추론한 보기를 답으로 선택한다.

추론의 근거로 삼을 수 있는 부분은 지문에서 한두 문장일 수도 있고, 여러 단락이 될 수도 있다.

● **Keyword가 들어있는 문장을 읽고 추론**
한 문장만을 근거로 추론이 가능할 경우, 추론된 문장은 거의 keyword가 들어있는 문장의 paraphrase 수준에 가깝다.

Ex **In some areas where electric-power demand varies sharply at different times of the day, pumped-storage hydroelectric stations are used.**

Q: According to the passage, it can be inferred that **pumped-storage hydroelectric stations**
A: could be the solution to inconsistent electric-power demand

➡ 문제의 keyword인 pumped-storage hydroelectric stations는 문장 뒷부분에 언급되어 있다. '양수식 수력 발전소는 시간대에 따라 전력 수요가 급격히 다른 일부 지역에서 사용된다'라고 하였으므로 일관되지 않은 전력 수요에 대한 해결책이 될 수 있음을 추론할 수 있다.

해석 p.453

- **Keyword가 들어있는 문장과 그 주변 문장의 내용을 통합하여 추론**

Keyword가 들어있는 문장만으로 추론의 근거가 약할 경우, 주변 문장의 정보를 조합해서 추론한다.

Ex **Most New Deal artists** were grateful to President Roosevelt for giving them work and **enthusiastically supported the new deal's liberal agenda**. Not surprisingly, **their art reflected this point of view**.

Q: According to the passage, it can be inferred that most of the works created by **New Deal artists**

A: were not politically neutral

➡ 문제의 keyword인 New Deal artists는 첫 번째 문장에 언급되어 있다. 첫 번째 문장에서 '대부분의 뉴딜 시대의 예술가들이 열정적으로 뉴딜 정책의 자유 민주 안건을 지지'했고 두 번째 문장에서 '그들의 작품이 이러한 관점을 반영했다'라고 하였다. 따라서 뉴딜 시대 예술가들이 창조해 낸 대부분의 작품은 정치적으로 중립적이지 않았다고 추론할 수 있다.

- **한 단락 또는 여러 단락의 정보를 종합하여 추론**

작가의 의견을 묻거나 한 단락 또는 여러 단락에 걸쳐 있는 전반적인 내용에 관해 추론해야 할 경우, 지문 전체 내용에 관한 이해가 필수적이다.

Ex There is another and less specific reason why caricature had to await the advent of printing and the wider dissemination of knowledge which resulted. The successful political cartoon presupposes a certain average degree of intelligence in a nation, an awakened civic conscience, a sense of responsibility for the nation's welfare. A political cartoonist would waste his time appealing to **a nation of feudal vassals; he could not expect to influence a people to whom the ballot box was closed. Caricature flourishes in an atmosphere of democracy**; there is an eternal incompatibility between its audacious irreverence and the doctrine of the divine right of kings.

Q: According to the passage, it can be inferred that a **political cartoonist** would most likely succeed

A: in a society of people who can vote against their country's ruler

➡ 문제의 keyword는 political cartoonist와 succeed이다. '풍자만화는 국민들의 선거권이 없는 봉건국가(a nation of feudal vassals)에서는 영향을 발휘하지 못하며 민주주의 풍토에서 꽃피울 수 있다'라는 것이 글의 결론이므로, 정치 풍자만화가는 사람들이 통치자에 대해 반대 투표를 할 수 있는 사회에서 가장 성공할 것임을 추론할 수 있다.

CH 01

CH 02

CH 03

CH 04

CH 05

CH 06

CH 07

CH 08

CH 09

Hackers TOEFL Reading

전략 3 보기 중 오답을 확인한다.

지문의 내용과 상반되거나 지문에 언급되지 않은 보기는 오답으로 간주된다.

Ex It was true that canals could not compete with rail. They were limited both in volume carried per unit and in speed; they were too small, too slow, and fragmented. In contrast, the railways, as they became integrated into national systems, provided a far more extensive service with greater flexibility. The canals were further handicapped because they were not, for the most part, common carriers themselves but were largely dependent on intermediate carrying companies. **Although transport via canals was initially cheaper than via rail, railways were a more popular choice for transportation.**

Q: According to the passage, it can be inferred that when choosing **a method of transportation**

A: price is not always the most important factor (○)

➡ 문제의 키워드는 a method of transportation이다. 마지막 문장에서 '운하가 철도보다 저렴했음에도 불구하고 철도가 더 인기 있는 교통수단이었다'라는 내용이 나오므로, 가격이 교통수단을 선택하는 데 있어 항상 가장 중요한 요인은 아님을 추론할 수 있다.

지문의 내용과 상반된 오답

canals were competitive in that they were managed independently by themselves (×)

지문에서 '운하가 대부분 중간 운송업체에 의존하여 불리했다'라고 하였으므로 '운하가 독립적으로 경영되어 경쟁력이 있었다'라는 것은 지문의 내용과 상반된다.

지문에 언급되지 않은 오답

most people still don't think canals are a good method of transportation (×)

'사람들이 여전히 운하가 좋은 교통수단이라고 생각하지 않는다'라는 것은 지문에 언급되지 않았다.

HACKERS STRATEGY **APPLICATION**

As trouble between the British government and the colonies grew with the approach of the American Revolution, Franklin's deep love for his native land and his devotion to individual freedom brought him back to America in 1775. There, while his illegitimate son, William Franklin, was becoming a leader of the Loyalists, Benjamin Franklin became one of the greatest statesmen of the American Revolution and of the newborn nation. He was a delegate to the Continental Congress, was appointed postmaster general, and was sent to Canada with Samuel Chase and Charles Carroll of Carrollton to persuade the people of Canada to join the patriot cause. He was appointed in 1776 to the committee that drafted the Declaration of Independence, which he willingly signed.

Late in 1776 he sailed to France to join Arthur Lee and Silas Deane in their diplomatic efforts there for the new republic. Franklin, with a high reputation in France well supported by his winning presence, did much to gain French recognition of the new republic in 1778. Franklin helped to direct U.S. naval operations and was successful agent for the United States in Europe — the sole one after suspicions and quarrels caused Congress to annul the powers of the other American commissioners.

1. What can be inferred from paragraph 1 about Benjamin Franklin?

   (A) He hesitated to sign the Declaration of Independence at first.
   (B) He returned to his country to spread ideas of individual liberty.
   (C) He didn't have close relationship with his son, William Franklin.
   (D) He criticized Great Britain for suppressing personal freedom.

2. It can be inferred from paragraph 2 that when Benjamin Franklin visited France late in 1776

   (A) he had never been to France before then
   (B) he was the first ambassador who was delegated to France
   (C) France took the initiative in Europe at the time
   (D) his personal repute played an important part in his mission

해석 p.453

1 | 전략 1 적용 | 문제의 keyword는 Benjamin Franklin으로 지문 전체에 걸쳐 언급되어 있으므로 보기에서 문제 해결의 단서를 찾아 관련 내용이 지문의 어디에 언급되어 있는지 찾는다.

(A) 단서 the Declaration of Independence → 1단락 마지막 문장에 언급됨
(B) 단서 returned to his country → 1단락 3번째 줄에 brought him back to America 언급됨
(C) 단서 William Franklin → 1단락 3번째 줄에 언급됨
(D) 단서 Great Britain → 1단락 첫 줄에 the British government 언급됨

| 전략 2 적용 | 지문의 첫 번째 문장에서 Franklin의 애국심과 개인의 자유를 향한 일념이 그를 미국으로 돌아오게 하였다고 했으므로 (B)와 같이 그가 개인의 자유에 대한 사상을 퍼뜨리기 위하여 고국으로 돌아왔음을 추론할 수 있다.

| 전략 3 적용 | (A) 지문의 내용과 상반된 오답
Franklin이 독립선언서에 자발적으로 서명했다고 하였으므로 처음에 서명하기를 주저했다는 것은 지문의 내용과 상반된다.
(C) 지문에 언급되지 않은 오답
Franklin이 아들과 사이가 좋지 않았다는 것은 지문에 언급되지 않았다.
(D) 지문에 언급되지 않은 오답
Franklin이 영국을 개인의 자유를 억압한다며 비판했다는 것은 지문에 언급되지 않았다.

| 정답 | (B)

2 | 전략 1 적용 | 문제의 keyword는 France와 1776이다. 이들은 2단락 첫 번째 문장에 언급되어 있다.

| 전략 2 적용 | 문제의 keyword가 들어있는 문장과 그 다음 문장의 정보를 조합하여 추론한다. Franklin이 1776년 후반 새로운 공화국을 위한 외교 노력에 동참하기 위해 프랑스로 갔을 때 프랑스에서의 그에 대한 높은 평판으로 1778년에 새 공화국에 대한 프랑스의 승인을 받는 데 많은 기여를 했다고 하였으므로 (D)와 같이 그의 개인적인 평판이 임무를 수행하는 데 중요한 역할을 했음을 추론할 수 있다.

| 전략 3 적용 | (A) 지문에 언급되지 않은 오답
'1776년 이전에 Franklin이 프랑스에 가본 적이 없었다'라는 것은 지문에 언급되지 않았다.
(B) 지문의 내용과 상반된 오답
'Franklin이 Arthur Lee와 Silas Deane의 프랑스에서의 외교 노력에 동참하기 위해 프랑스로 갔다'라고 하였으므로 '그가 프랑스에 파견된 최초의 대사였다'라는 것은 지문의 내용과 상반된다.
(C) 지문에 언급되지 않은 오답
'1776년에 프랑스가 유럽에서 주도권을 쥐고 있었다'라는 것은 지문에 언급되지 않았다.

| 정답 | (D)

HACKERS **PRACTICE**

Choose a statement that best describes what can be inferred from each passage.

1 Ancient Mesopotamian deities were usually depicted in human form. Early statues were simple wood carvings, but eventually artists added gold overlay and colorful adornment to represent garments of jewelry to match textual descriptions of the individual gods, such as Inanna, who according to legend wore a lapis lazuli necklace on her descent into the underworld.

(A) Sculptures were the basis of the written accounts of a god's appearance.
(B) Most of the original sculptures of Mesopotamian gods have been lost.
(C) Inanna was the most important of the ancient Mesopotamian gods.
(D) Renderings of Mesopotamian gods became more elaborate over time.

2 President Franklin Delano Roosevelt's record-breaking win with 60.8 percent of the popular vote stood for a quarter century until Lyndon Johnson's victory netted a slightly higher percentage at 61.9. However, even it would not rank first if presidential elections prior to the 1804 ratification of the 12th Amendment were considered.

(A) Roosevelt holds the largest margin of victory since the passage of the 12th Amendment.
(B) At least one president before 1804 received more than 61.9 percent of the popular vote.
(C) More than two presidents got over 60 percent of the popular vote after 1804.
(D) Johnson narrowly defeated Roosevelt in the closest presidential election in history.

3 Refrigeration in industry is carried out mostly by means of compression cooling and in some cases by absorption cooling. The basic technology has remained unchanged for many years, but recently the pace of developments has increased. The high ozone depletion potential of refrigerants has led to a major drive to replace CFCs(chlorofluorocarbons) with more environmentally acceptable refrigerants.

(A) Absorption cooling uses fewer CFCs than compression cooling.
(B) CFCs were developed in response to more eco-friendly chemicals.
(C) The use of CFCs in industry has been forbidden recently.
(D) CFCs are partially responsible for the disruption of the ozone layer.

VOCABULARY   The word ⬜ in the passage is closest in meaning to

1 deities	(A) disciples	(B) splinters	(C) divinities	(D) fillets
2 record-breaking	(A) heterogeneous	(B) regardful	(C) impartial	(D) unprecedented
3 acceptable	(A) absurd	(B) tolerable	(C) taciturn	(D) restful

4   Human skeletons convey much information that can ⸤hasten⸥ the characterization or identification of individuals by anthropologists. For example, experts can offer an approximate assessment of a person's ⸤stature⸥ by measuring one thigh bone; yet they also must consider other variables to make an accurate evaluation. One of these is age: after 40, humans tend to lose one centimeter per decade due to compression and deterioration of the spine.

(A) Unless all variables are accounted for, virtually nothing can be deduced from viewing human remains.

(B) Changes in anatomy after maturity are too minor to consider in skeletal analysis.

(C) Investigation of a single bone produces insufficient data to establish precise conclusions.

(D) Anthropologists have developed methods to pinpoint the exact age of human skeletons.

5   In nineteenth-century Paris, artists such as Édouard Manet adored the immigrant street performers known as Romani or gypsies. These ⸤itinerant⸥ "bohemians" inspired many painters to embrace the ideals of freedom and cast off traditional constraints, such as notions of social standing or adherence to traditional values. To reflect the gypsies' revolutionary ideals, artists sometimes included taboo subject matter in their work. For example, printmaker Théophile Steinlen included a black cat — a depiction previously reserved only for sinister ⸤conventions⸥ — in a marketing poster for a famous cabaret.

(A) Édouard Manet and other Parisian artists frequently depicted gypsies in their art.

(B) Many bohemians pretended to adopt personal freedom but never fully gave up old customs.

(C) The social status of the Romani people grew as their popularity in Paris rose.

(D) Steinlen did not intend for the black cat to be perceived as a menacing symbol.

VOCABULARY   The word ☐ in the passage is closest in meaning to

4	hasten	(A) founder	(B) graze	(C) speed up	(D) parcel out
	stature	(A) height	(B) imprint	(C) mixture	(D) accuracy
5	itinerant	(A) gallant	(B) traveling	(C) connate	(D) ecumenical
	conventions	(A) boundaries	(B) constellations	(C) avocations	(D) usages

If the statement for each passage can be inferred from the passage, mark T, otherwise mark F.

6   Most bat species have good eyesight that helps them effectively navigate and hunt at night, but some of them also have the capacity to utilize echolocation to get around and find prey. These mammalian aviators emit pulses of sonar that reflect off objects and send an "echo" back to their specially adapted, oversized ears. Once a bat receives this audible response, it will fly in the direction of the target and continually emit sound waves with increasing rapidity so that it can move to the exact location of its quarry. This physiological process involves a membrane in the inner ear which pulsates at the frequency of the incoming sound and transforms this signal into a neural code that is interpreted by the brain as a particular trajectory and distance.

_____ (A) Some researchers have wrongly assumed that bats hunt primarily with their eyes.

_____ (B) The large size of the bat's ears is integral to making echolocation possible.

_____ (C) Once bats pinpoint the location of their target, they fly in its direction with increased speed.

_____ (D) Returning sound waves must be encoded to make them comprehensible to the bat's nervous system.

7   Demands for a transcontinental railroad across America intensified during the 1840s and spawned numerous, often competing, proposed routes. Among the first was that put forth by merchant Asa Whitney, whose prolonged voyage to China in 1844 propelled him to seek a quicker trade route to Asia. He spent much of his own money to create maps, pamphlets, and lobby Congress; he even led an overland expedition to assess the feasibility of his plan, but his attempts failed to generate any political support. It was not until Abraham Lincoln's signing of the Pacific Railroad Act of 1862 that any concrete plans were outlined for the project. Two companies, the Central Pacific and Union Pacific, were awarded the contract for construction of two separate lines, which ultimately joined on May 10, 1869 in Utah. Although any calculation of the total cost of the enterprise would involve conjecture, some estimates suggest that it was in excess of $120 million.

_____ (A) There was no consensus in the 1840s regarding the best course for a railway to traverse the American continent.

_____ (B) While in China, Asa Whitney was impressed by the railroad networks he encountered.

_____ (C) Whitney was initially unable to convince legislators that his plan was a good idea.

_____ (D) It took two companies seven years to complete the building of the railway.

VOCABULARY   The word [____] in the passage is closest in meaning to

		(A)	(B)	(C)	(D)
6	prey	(A) plumage	(B) hole	(C) game	(D) freight
7	feasibility	(A) futility	(B) practicability	(C) stability	(D) ability
	conjecture	(A) aftermath	(B) vow	(C) combination	(D) guess

8

When the British passed the 1765 Stamp Act, which required all printed documents to include a tax stamp, American colonists were outraged. Many of them began to question or ignore their obligations as British subjects, and some simply refused to pay the taxes outlined in the act. Furthermore, radical colonists threatened to physically harm and publicly humiliate any official who tried to enforce it. British perception of this reaction brought about the abolition of the ordinance to appease the Americans. Yet this outcome also stemmed from the fact that the revenue it sought to generate did not come to fruition. Despite the overturn, the statute's legacy remained fresh in the minds of the people. Local leaders began calling for revolution and promoted rejecting rule from abroad in any form or fashion. This spirit soon permeated the colonies and ultimately led to the Declaration of Independence and war with Britain.

_____ (A) The British most likely misjudged the reactions colonists would have to the new law.

_____ (B) The British overestimated the tax revenue they would generate through the Stamp Act.

_____ (C) Some leaders in America opposed the idea that the colonies should revolt.

_____ (D) The colonists declared war on Britain as soon as the Stamp Act was passed.

9

Darwin, using previously coined terminology, popularized the concept of biological fitness. He postulated that species which can reproduce prolifically will have a higher survival rate than those that cannot, presuming that their offspring and subsequent generations are also fertile. However, this simplified "survival-of-the-fittest" view encountered justifiable criticism and had to undergo modification. Critics pointed out that focusing solely on successful procreation ignored genetic drift, which holds that some genetic changes occur simply by chance and do not necessarily promote survival or reproduction.

_____ (A) Darwin is often wrongly credited with inventing a popular biological term.

_____ (B) Fitness presupposes the high fertility of multiple generations.

_____ (C) Views about survival have undergone little change over time.

_____ (D) Most scientists deny that genetic alteration can occur by chance.

VOCABULARY	The word		in the passage is closest in meaning to	
8	obligations	(A) shards	(B) congresses	(C) duties	(D) targets
	perception	(A) cognizance	(B) context	(C) obsession	(D) commendation
	rejecting	(A) enraging	(B) renouncing	(C) endorsing	(D) impounding
9	prolifically	(A) covetously	(B) strenuously	(C) simply	(D) abundantly

CH 01
CH 02
CH 03
CH 04
CH 05
CH 06
CH 07
CH 08
CH 09
Hackers TOEFL Reading

10   A key ingredient in the settlement of the American West was the promise of cheap, fertile land. This stimulated mass internal migration as well as immigration from overseas. Whether hoping to escape from poverty or gain freedom from oppressive conditions, these pioneers pursued their "manifest destiny" — the notion that Americans were entitled by God to colonize lands all the way to the Pacific. This dream-like vision was perpetuated by extremely successful marketing campaigns undertaken by steamship companies. They advertised free transportation in European newspapers, while Western US states set up immigration bureaus overseas.

_____ (A) The arable land in Europe was too expensive for most people to afford.

_____ (B) People fleeing harsh conditions viewed Western settlement as their divine right.

_____ (C) Initial attempts to attract foreigners failed, so advertisers altered their approach.

_____ (D) US states paid steamship companies to transport immigrants from Europe to America.

11   The Indian Removal Act of 1830 ushered in one of the most hotly debated and controversial chapters in US history. It called for the forced relocation of Native Americans from their ancestral lands east of the Mississippi River to what is modern-day Oklahoma. Prior to this time, the government tended to analyze natives on a per-tribe basis. Yet according to the new law, the totality of "Native America" was treated as a single, though heterogeneous, category. Likewise, the new territory became legally viewed as a solitary domestic nation which was dependent upon and under the protection of the United States. While the majority grudgingly accepted their fate through treaty negotiations, during which they were motivated by the lure of peace with the federal government, some resisted the coerced resettlement. The Cherokee, in particular, vehemently refused to abandon their hereditary homeland. Their protest lasted until 1838, when President Martin Van Buren ordered the US Army to enter Cherokee territory and capture resistors and accompany them along the route to their eventual destination. This long march became known as the Trail of Tears because an estimated 4,000 to 5,000 people died before reaching the terminus.

_____ (A) The new law meant that the government treated each Native tribe as if it was part of one larger entity.

_____ (B) The act was merely a legal declaration of how the government had always classified Native Americans.

_____ (C) Though most tribes fought against the injunction, a few of them were pleased with the new arrangement.

_____ (D) One of the unintended consequences of the transfer of Cherokee people was a sizable refugee population.

VOCABULARY	The word ☐ in the passage is closest in meaning to			
10 ingredient	(A) element	(B) cargo	(C) allowance	(D) barge
11 forced	(A) involuntary	(B) imperiled	(C) erroneous	(D) extravagant
Likewise	(A) Actually	(B) Indeed	(C) Contrarily	(D) Similarly
lure	(A) pinion	(B) similitude	(C) enticement	(D) temperament

Read each passage and answer the corresponding questions.

12　Zuni culture had reached its peak before the Spanish conquest, which further diminished its preeminence in southwestern North America. However, some of its artistic traditions survived the foreign occupation and even persist today. For instance, Zuni pottery is regularly produced for utilitarian and ceremonial purposes, such as for carrying water or for use in religious rituals. To craft it, artisans collect local pale-colored clay, form it, and coat it with an additional thin clay layer before polishing it to a fairly smooth finish. They then color it using native plant extracts or mineral-based paint to mask any remaining trace of graininess. The secular and sacred functions of their handiwork are also evidenced by Zuni "jewelry." Silversmiths inlay silver with turquoise in mosaic designs or join small stones in delicate patterns for use in rings, which are considered to be some of the finest in the world. As such, the rings are generally sold for economic gain and are worn for personal ornamentation by the purchaser. In contrast, multicolored necklaces made up of hand-sculpted animals connected by a cord are not exclusively meant for outward adornment but are also for spiritual use in the home.

1　According to the passage, what can be inferred about Zuni culture?

(A) It placed an emphasis on religious art over practical art.
(B) Some of its traditions stemmed from foreign influence.
(C) Its presence in the region is stronger than it ever was.
(D) The Spanish invasion was not the initial cause of its decline.

2　What can be inferred about Zuni jewelry from the passage?

(A) Some of it has no significant ceremonial value.
(B) Much of it commands high prices internationally.
(C) It is always used for purely decorative purposes.
(D) It is made from locally collected materials.

CH 01
CH 02
CH 03
CH 04
CH 05
CH 06
CH 07
CH 08
CH 09
Hackers TOEFL Reading

VOCABULARY　The word _____ in the passage is closest in meaning to

12 peak	(A) apex	(B) wrath	(C) aboriginality	(D) reproof
smooth	(A) dense	(B) firm	(C) eroded	(D) sleek
trace	(A) promulgation	(B) impression	(C) stench	(D) sham

13   Biomorphic regeneration is the restoration of lost body structures and tissues that are rebuilt through a mass of adjoining cells called a *blastema*. This ability is rare among vertebrates but is present in certain reptiles, and the phenomenon is best known in lizards, geckos, and iguanas. Unlike their reptilian cousins, such as snakes, these creatures have the capacity to replace their tails with new ones. It is an adaptation designed to avoid predation, whereby part or all of the animal's terminal segment dislodges when molested. As the tail wriggles in the predator's mouth, it distracts the attacker and allows the creature to escape. The newly acquired tail is not a mere replica of the first, however. Researchers realized this after carefully studying the regrowth of tails for up to 250 days and documenting the connections and interactions between nerves and muscle tissue that cause movement. They found that the regrown tail contains a central tube of cartilage instead of vertebrae and displays a different muscular structure, features which scientists believe make the regenerated one less flexible while retaining some functional properties of the original.

1 According to the passage, which of the following can be inferred about snakes?

(A) Their anatomical structures are well suited for capturing prey.
(B) They are occasional predators of lizards, geckos, and iguanas.
(C) Their bodies lack the capacity for biomorphic regeneration.
(D) They are well adapted to a wide range of environments.

2 According to the passage, it can be inferred that original tail is different from the regenerated one because

(A) it consists mostly of muscle and cartilage
(B) it contains vertebrae
(C) it lasts approximately 250 days
(D) it has a limited range of motion

VOCABULARY   The word ☐ in the passage is closest in meaning to

13 adjoining	(A) dilapidated	(B) sensual	(C) utter	(D) bordering
rare	(A) downright	(B) uncommon	(C) pure	(D) unsparing
terminal	(A) confrontal	(B) grab	(C) last	(D) tatty

14 In order to understand the origins of writing, it is necessary to debunk a couple of once-popular theories about language and culture. First, languages are not descended from a single prototype, as many scholars have suggested. That view largely derived from a Biblical interpretation of language origins and held that writing systems emerged in ancient Mesopotamia, from where they spread and evolved throughout the world. Further, nineteenth-century sociologists who applied the biological theory of evolution to language development viewed writing as not only having a common ancestor but also exhibiting an evolutionary hierarchy in which alphabetical scripts were viewed as superior to ideographic or syllabic writing systems. In the context of the linguistic history of ancient world, that perspective presented European and Near Eastern cultures as more highly evolved than those of Asia, Africa, or Mesoamerica. Nothing could be further from the truth, as empires rich in cultural splendor, complete with magnificent architecture, art, laws, and infrastructure, were built by civilizations with non-alphabetic scripts.

Scholars now agree that writing developed independently in the Fertile Crescent, Asia, and Mesoamerica. Of these geographical areas, there is a general consensus that the earliest writing occurred in the Fertile Crescent land of Sumer, possibly as early as 8000 B.C. The ancient Sumerians originally used tokens, such as small clay triangles, spheres, and cones, to represent sheep, measures of grain, jars of oil, and other goods. Basically, the shape of the token carried its meaning. It is theorized that these tokens served communities in keeping track of goods for the purpose of pooling and redistributing resources. But they were sometimes placed in burial sites, and may have also indicated gifts to temples, tributes to rulers, or tax payments. Much later, around 3100 B.C., the Sumerians invented numerals, separating the symbol for sheep from the number of sheep, so writing and mathematics may have evolved together. Diggings at Uruk show that the Sumerian script advanced from pictographs to ideographic writing, in which a symbol represented a concept. At that point, writing was already developing into a tool that could communicate ideas.

1 According to the passage, what can be inferred about the author's view of culture?

(A) Its value is inextricably tied to a civilization's ability to use written language.
(B) It need not be associated with a civilization's particular writing system.
(C) It must be viewed in the context of how a society evolves over time.
(D) Its significance goes beyond the tangible accomplishments of empires.

2 Which of the following can be inferred about the ancient Sumerians?

(A) Their mathematical knowledge may have contributed to the refinement of their script.
(B) Their written system of language was gradually adopted by neighboring communities.
(C) Their original motive in creating a writing system was for religious purposes.
(D) Their writing system was more complex than those of Asia and Mesoamerica.

VOCABULARY   The word ☐ in the passage is closest in meaning to

14 debunk	(A) compel	(B) hover	(C) neglect	(D) uncover
consensus	(A) scrutiny	(B) impediment	(C) agreement	(D) mandate
tool	(A) implement	(B) projection	(C) proximity	(D) peril

15 After achieving its independence from imperial Spain following a prolonged resistance and much bloodshed, the Dutch Republic became a proud place eager to move on and prosper. By the mid-1600s, the young confederation had become the wealthiest nation in Europe, experiencing unprecedented economic $\boxed{\text{vitality}}$ that fueled a flowering of culture and stimulated the Golden Age of Dutch art. Artistic developments in the 17th century placed Dutch painting on the international stage as artists turned to an ultra-realistic depiction of subjects using a precision that the world had never before witnessed. Their portraiture and renditions of landscapes were almost photographic in their likeness to reality and conveyed tremendous detail.

Dutch artists became particularly well known for their genre paintings, which sought to capture scenes of everyday life. Genre art sprang both from the desire of painters to pursue new themes and customers' strong affinity for topics that were familiar. Thus, artists $\boxed{\text{readily}}$ found an audience for their paintings of peasants working in agricultural fields, ordinary citizens shopping in markets, or soldiers poised for battle.

Moreover, and notably, the new generation of artists pioneered the virtually unheard-of practice of portraying domestic scenes, such as a man writing a letter or a woman receiving a music lesson in a private home. Though this "slice-of-life" approach indicated an appreciation for the mundane, this does not presuppose that genre art was perfectly indicative of the actual lives of citizens. Like a mirror portrays the exact inverse of the reflected image, in all $\boxed{\text{probability}}$ these works conveyed only a seemingly real vision of society.

1 What can be inferred about Dutch independence in the passage?

(A) It arose from civil unrest that began in the 16th century.
(B) It would not have been likely without armed conflict.
(C) It resulted in closer economic ties with the rest of Europe.
(D) It could have been prevented if Spain had invaded earlier.

2 According to the passage, the discussion of household scenes in Dutch art implies that

(A) they were preferred to those that displayed public places
(B) they were rarely included in the work of previous artists
(C) they were typically painted in the private homes of the subjects
(D) they were initially very popular but later viewed as too mundane

---

VOCABULARY	The word ☐ in the passage is closest in meaning to			
15 vitality	(A) vigor	(B) majority	(C) premonition	(D) saturnineness
readily	(A) perilously	(B) fleetingly	(C) jointly	(D) easily
probability	(A) impetuosity	(B) likelihood	(C) peculiarity	(D) sequence

16 In the 1920s, the "Chicago School" became an academic brand of sociology promulgated by a group of professors and colleagues that developed an unusually high level of cohesion. These sociologists believed that the best way to learn about human nature was to study people in urban environments. For them, this meant Chicago, which constituted a perfect object of scrutiny as it had developed a capricious character as the fastest-growing municipality in the world — skyrocketing from a population of 30,000 in 1850 to nearly two million in 1900 — and because one-third of its people at the time were immigrants with varying cultural backgrounds. These researchers were keenly interested in understanding the proliferation of secular problems, such as drunkenness and violence, which plagued the city. To better comprehend the phenomenon, professors and students conducted studies in the "real world" by interacting with people on their own terms. For example, one sociologist might work in a neighborhood of alienated immigrants, while another might choose a district with a high homeless population. The explanation that they ultimately proposed became known as social disorganization theory, which held that the development of urban corruption in Chicago resulted from the growing variety of culturally distinct residential locales and the diversity of lifestyles that these subcultures approved of and perpetuated. Starting with the assumption that people are products of their environments, the Chicago School claimed that cultural expectations were what governed behavior, and as more and more ethnic groups competed, the weakening of traditional standards ensued. As a result, crime, delinquency, and other deviant behaviors became more prevalent.

1 According to the passage, what can be inferred about sociologists in the 1920s?

(A) They often conducted experiments in tightly controlled environments.
(B) The majority of them agreed with the assumptions of the Chicago School.
(C) It was rare for them to band together to form likeminded groups.
(D) Only a few of them pursued research outside the major cities.

2 It can be inferred from the passage that communities with high cultural diversity

(A) resulted in unprecedented number of homeless persons
(B) generated an assortment of styles in residential architecture
(C) exhibited noticeably higher rates of social vice
(D) created communication barriers between neighborhoods

VOCABULARY   The word ☐ in the passage is closest in meaning to

16	capricious	(A) fickle	(B) tragic	(C) circumspect	(D) tertiary
	secular	(A) eccentric	(B) worldly	(C) pervasive	(D) sterile
	alienated	(A) bypassed	(B) systematized	(C) estranged	(D) protested

정답 및 해석 p.454

CH 01
CH 02
CH 03
CH 04
CH 05
CH 06
CH 07
CH 08
CH 09

Hackers TOEFL Reading

1 The general principle of exponential growth is that the larger something gets, the faster it grows. For example, under ideal circumstances, a single cell of the bacterium *E. coli* can divide every twenty minutes, each time doubling in size, and while the numbers increase slowly at first, within one day it would be equal to the size and weight of the Earth. In a socioeconomic context, steam power — widely regarded as the icon of the Industrial Revolution — intertwined the processes of industrialization and urbanization that fuelled spectacular growth in Britain's economy over the course of the 19th century, the reverberations of which brought fundamental changes to all of Western civilization. While waterpower offered abundant and cheap energy, the steam engine rendered its severe geographical constraints redundant, thus serving as a catalyst for the wholesale relocation of industry away from rural areas and into large urban centers.

2 This device converted thermal energy into mechanical power by heating water in a boiler, channeling the resulting steam into a cylindrical chamber equipped with a piston, and then generating atmospheric pressure at intervals to move the piston up and down. It became a potent force that transformed commercial enterprises in the manufacturing industries. Steam-driven textile machines, for example, could spin multiple threads with the turn of a single wheel, and coordinate precise movements through levers, cams, and gears that allowed a single worker to weave more bolts in one shift than a team of pre-industrial artisans could turn out with weeks of muscle-powered toil. These machines needed fuel, coal, to create the heat necessary to make steam, and as a result the mining industry also benefited from them.

3 In transport, high horsepower steam engines gave life to ships and locomotives. With the same precision, rapidity, and reliability as the pistons pumping up and down in the bowels of the vessels themselves, urban industrialists sped outbound into previously unreachable areas with tons of finished products, while raw materials zoomed into factories. Large factories were created to centralize the manufacture of goods since it was more cost-effective to construct single large buildings rather than multiple smaller factories. These factories which were initially built on the outskirts of the towns eventually expanded into the city, developing the first metropolises, a pattern which would be followed across all parts of Western Europe and America. The lure of jobs and a higher quality of life brought more than half of the entire English population into the cities and their housing, entertainment, and other requisite needs served to further increase the importance of urban areas.

4 ➡ Sociologists believe that this kind of urbanization leads to increased literacy, a notion supported by the fact that as of the 1840s, 65 to 70 percent of the English population had

learned how to read, a progression that coincided with the advent of steam-powered printing presses. Previously, books were a rare and tightly-controlled resource because they were quite time-consuming and expensive to produce. These new machines, however, could churn out millions of pages in a single day. Printing presses quickly flooded the modern world, allowing new forms of thought in the fields of politics, philosophy, and literature to be circulated amongst a vast, hungry, and profitable new audience from such writers as Marx and Nietzsche. This dispersion led to the development in the mass consciousness of such concepts as capitalism, communism, and existentialism, and also illuminated such issues as children's and workers' rights.

5　It also resulted in the rapid acceleration of scientific exploration. College curricula were established and graduate schools appeared. Workshops turned into laboratories, tinkering became industrial research, and the theoretical concepts behind individual inventions were organized into systematic innovations. Developers began to explore ways to evolve steam-driven centralized factory architecture into a more decentralized system, so that little motors could power factory devices in the hands of each and every worker. Ultimately, by the end of the 19th century, the steam engine gave way to a new form of power production, electricity, although the latter's ascension would not have been possible without the macrocosmic trailblazing of its predecessor.

1 According to the passage, what does the author state was the effect of the steam engine on England?

(A) It incorporated Britain in international economy.
(B) It motivated factory owners to move to pastoral settings.
(C) It was the source of economic growth in England.
(D) It gave more power to those with access to water power.

2 Which of the following can be inferred from the passage about waterpower generation?

(A) It was the most popular power source before steam.
(B) It was restricted to certain locations due to topography.
(C) Water in one area tended to be dried up in an instant.
(D) The construction of waterpower plants was too expensive.

3 The word "potent" in the passage is closest in meaning to

(A) strong
(B) inept
(C) quaint
(D) cohesive

4 Why does the author mention "pre-industrial artisans" in the passage?

(A) To give an emphasis on their labor in old economy
(B) To highlight the lower quality of mass produced goods
(C) To provide an example of efficiency of muscle power
(D) To contrast mechanical production to their production

5 Which of the sentences below best expresses the essential information in the highlighted sentence in the passage? *Incorrect* choices change the meaning in important ways or leave out essential information.

(A) As more people entered the cities, the quality of life in the urban areas began to significantly decrease.
(B) The boom in the entertainment and housing sectors vastly increased the population of many urban areas.
(C) Once people drawn by the opportunity of employment and a better life moved into cities, their everyday demands continued to expand the significance of urban areas.
(D) The population of England rose as a result of the influx of the population into urban areas in search of work.

6 According to paragraph 4, the author implies that the availability of books

(A) considerably increased the workload of factory workers
(B) lessened the popularity of other forms of entertainment
(C) enabled early writers to republish their works more cheaply
(D) was closely interconnected with the people's ability to read

Paragraph 4 is marked with an arrow [➡].

7 The word "dispersion" in the passage is closest in meaning to

(A) dissemination
(B) digression
(C) decommission
(D) delusion

8 It can be inferred from the passage that electricity

(A) led to more uses of steam technology
(B) made possible the production of smaller motors
(C) could decentralize the plant system
(D) decreased the demand for laborers

9 The phrase "its predecessor" in the passage refers to

(A) system
(B) worker
(C) electricity
(D) steam engine

10 **Directions**: An introductory sentence for a brief summary of the passage is provided below. Complete the summary by selecting the THREE answer choices that express the most important ideas in the passage. Some sentences do not belong in the summary because they express ideas that are not presented in the passage or are minor ideas in the passage. **This question is worth 2 points.**

> Drag your answer choices to the spaces where they belong. To remove an answer choice, click on it. To review the passage, click on **View Text**.

The Industrial Revolution led by the steam engine drastically reshaped England in the 1800s.

- ●
- ●
- ●

Answer Choices

(A) Constructing large factories permitted factory proprietors to centralize the manufacturing process in one location.

(B) The application of steam engines in the manufacturing industries made it feasible to mass-produce goods efficiently.

(C) Due to steam-driven mass production equipment, books became widely accessible and interests in scientific research increased.

(D) The cities which had easy access to ports had advantages of shipping the finished products at a small outlay.

(E) The power needed to generate the steam came from the burning of coal for the most part.

(F) The improvement in transportation facilities powered by steam led to a better distribution of goods and the formation of big cities.

정답 및 해석 p.459

CH 01
CH 02
CH 03
CH 04
CH 05
CH 06
CH 07
CH 08
CH 09
Hackers TOEFL Reading

1 ➡ Fossils are the mineralized remains of plants and animals found in rock formations and along coasts, forming only in rare occasions when living material is covered by sediment, or falls into an anoxic environment such as a lakebed or ocean. The process of fossilization begins when the rotting organic remains are covered with layers of soil, sand, and other residue, replaced with hard minerals, and eventually compact to form solid rock.

2 As far back as the 17th century, naturalists began to use these fossil records to document the comparative anatomy of various species and develop a better understanding of the earth's eclectic biology. One of the most startling observations coming to light from this research is that while some fossils resemble organisms alive today, others are drastically different. This would indicate that there have been changes to the number and kind of species that live on the earth and that these modifications may be related to the current set of living creatures.

3 In an effort to understand how and when these changes occur, naturalists have studied mineral deposits. They offer three distinct opinions about the observed alteration of the earth's organisms, one of which is the idea that plants and animals themselves do not change, but are replaced by different species. Whenever a new geological find reveals a different group of fossils, this is attributed to a mass extinction or catastrophe whereby the older species was wiped out. The presence of the new organism is explained by repopulation of the region by species migrating in from surrounding areas. Advocates of this theory, known as Catastrophism, are generally religious scholars who accredit all organic and inorganic creations to God, suggesting all species have existed unvaried since the moment the earth came to life.

4 ➡ Another assessment, developed by Jean-Baptiste Lamarck, is that changes take place over time as species acquire new characteristics and pass these on to the next generation. Lamarck speculated, for example, on the anatomy of giraffes, suggesting that the animals acquired their extended necks over many generations as a result of the gradual increase in lengths as shorter animals stretched to reach leaves on the branches of trees. It is believed that slight elongations were passed on to calves and eventually, numerous tiny accessions added up to the present existence of long-necked giraffes. Unfortunately, "Lamarckism" fails to account for the passing down of hereditable traits that do not bestow an advantage upon the offspring, nor for the fact that maleficent traits are sometimes passed down.

5 Finally, the most contemporary opinion is that the refinement of abilities happens through natural selection, the tendency of organisms that are born with favorable adaptations to their environments to survive and produce new generations. Naturalist Charles Darwin first proposed this theory in 1859 based on a detailed and painstaking study of countless species he encountered during many ocean voyages, coupled with extensive reading on current thought in the sciences. In the Galapagos, for example, Darwin observed that each island gave way to a distinct variety of mockingbirds, which he believed had

originated from one common ancestor, and those that were better able to obtain food were more likely to live until maturity, mate, and eventually produce offspring. It is presumable that because the islands possess unique geological habitats, food sources may be different as well, meaning that dissimilar adaptations could be equitable and thus, bird populations were unmistakably diverse yet equally well-suited to their particular area. This solidified Darwin's belief in "fitness," or rather, the notion that organisms with advantageous mutations have a better chance of survival, and thus a greater opportunity to reproduce, eventually affecting a transformation in the entire population.

6 Today, researchers continue to flesh out Darwin's theory using contemporary genome studies. That is, they attempt to understand mutations at the molecular level and postulate that they arise when DNA is incorrectly translated from one organism to its offspring, wherein negative or positive effects are generated, the latter being more likely to help that animal or plant survive. Some now consider general adaptation to be organic evolution or, the accumulation of genetic mutations in populations of living organisms through many generations. Regardless of their opinion, the underlying foundation of modern science is that change itself is persistent and immutable, meaning that researchers can rely only on its presence while continuing to ponder the mechanisms.

1 Which of the following can be inferred about the fossil formation in paragraph 1?

(A) Organic matters need to contain many minerals prior to covering.
(B) Contact with air inhibits the preservation of organic material.
(C) Only species that live in water can be preserved as fossils.
(D) The creation of fossils is a somewhat common occurrence.

Paragraph 1 is marked with an arrow [➡].

2 The word "eclectic" in the passage is closest in meaning to

(A) stupendous
(B) diverse
(C) consistent
(D) enigmatic

3 The word "others" in the passage refers to

(A) species
(B) observations
(C) fossils
(D) organisms

4 According to the passage, which of the following would the proponents of Catastrophism most likely support?

(A) Species remain in the same areas in which they were generated.
(B) There is no life that has been newly created ever since the origin of the earth.
(C) The emergence of fossils leads to the change in the surrounding environment.
(D) Mass extinctions pave the way for new features to form in surviving species.

5 In paragraph 4, why does the author mention long-necked giraffes?

(A) To offer experimental proof that Lamarck's theories are superior to others
(B) To give an explanation of how new adaptations appear according to Lamarck
(C) To set up a contrast of Lamarck's opinion with Darwin's opinion
(D) To show Lamarckism's ability to contradict previously observed phenomenon

Paragraph 4 is marked with an arrow [➡].

6 The word "tendency" in the passage is closest in meaning to

(A) consensus
(B) complement
(C) remedy
(D) inclination

7 According to the passage, the type of mockingbirds in the Galapagos became diversified because

(A) they were anxious to increase the amount of offspring they had
(B) their ancestors adapted to their distinct habitats in different ways
(C) the females only wanted to mate with males with specific traits
(D) random mutations disseminated new traits through the various populations

8 Which of the sentences below best expresses the essential information in the highlighted sentence in the passage? *Incorrect* choices change the meaning in important ways or leave out essential information.

(A) Since mutations occur at the microscopic level, they are passed onto the offspring and can have numerous benefits.
(B) Only those mutations which affect the organism's DNA will be passed onto the following generations.
(C) It is believed that resulting genetic errors have pros and cons with the former aiding the survival of the species.
(D) Only changes in DNA, which help the organism survive, are passed on the next generation.

9 Which of the following can be concluded from the passage?

(A) Catastrophism's explanation of how species repopulate a region is consistent with evolutionary theory.

(B) Lamarck's theories contain elements that are incompatible with Catastrophism.

(C) Darwin based his theory of how hereditable traits are passed down to offspring on the work of Lamarck.

(D) Contemporary genome studies have cast doubt on Darwin's belief that similar species have a common ancestor.

10 **Directions**: An introductory sentence for a brief summary of the passage is provided below. Complete the summary by selecting the THREE answer choices that express the most important ideas in the passage. Some sentences do not belong in the summary because they express ideas that are not presented in the passage or are minor ideas in the passage. **This question is worth 2 points.**

> Drag your answer choices to the spaces where they belong. To remove an answer choice, click on it. To review the passage, click on **View Text**.

People can understand how organisms have evolved by looking at the fossil record.

- ●
- ●
- ●

Answer Choices

(A) Giraffes have the advantage of picking leaves of a tall tree.

(B) The appearance of new species into the area is ascribed to migration of species from other areas.

(C) Changes occur randomly with beneficial ones more likely to spread throughout the population.

(D) Fossilization is an enormously complex process that requires many different elements.

(E) Traits developed within the species' lifetime are able to be inherited by their following generations.

(F) Cross breeding is considered the most important factor of animals' mutations.

정답 및 해석 p.461

CH 01
CH 02
CH 03
CH 04
CH 05
CH 06
CH 07
CH 08
CH 09
Hackers TOEFL Reading

1   Vicious crimes can contribute to a sense of anxiety among citizens who feel defenseless against the perpetrators. Continued concern over public protection has triggered recurring discussions about violence in media, political and social arenas, and the proliferation of a plentitude of theories about the cause of violence, which attribute it variously to war, drug addiction, or class or race frustrations, even suggesting that it is inherently present in cultural identity. As part of an effort to understand the predisposition to violence, scientists have attempted to speculate on a biological explanation for this behavior.

2   ➡ Some scientists have considered a direct relationship between the likelihood a person will commit a violent crime and the level of serotonin, an organic compound believed to play an integral role in the regulation of mood, sleep, sexuality, and appetite, present in the brain. In the central nervous system, serotonin is part of the biochemistry that is related to several psychological conditions; depression, migraines, bipolar disorder, and anxiety are all linked to an overproduction or underproduction of the compound. If violent behavior could be clinically linked to an imbalance in brain chemicals, then scientists would be able to control aggressive tendencies through medication before the behavior escalates.

3   ➡ The first government-sponsored study into the possibility of an inherited propensity for violence was conducted in 1998 by the Violence Initiative Project, which was led by two Columbia University professors, covering a wide scope of interdisciplinary subjects, such as biochemistry, neurophysiology, and genetics. The team chose to examine the brains of 34 young boys, none of whom had previously committed a violent act. They were selected because each had an older sibling (all boys) who had been incarcerated for a violent crime. The scientists assumed that the younger brothers would display a similar inclination toward violence as their older siblings and thus hypothesized that they would exhibit low levels of serotonin. During the test, the subjects fasted for 12 hours, drank only water, and were administered an oral dose of fenfluramine hydroxide, a volatile chemical that, when consumed, heightens serotonin levels in normal brains and produces severe mood-related side effects, such as abnormally high incidences of fatigue, headache, and irritability. By introducing the chemical, researchers claimed that they would be capable of raising their subjects' supposedly low serotonin levels to those of average brains and that medication would, regardless of race, class, or any other environmental stressors, inhibit their desire for executing violent acts.

4   ➡ While withdrawing hourly blood samples of the subjects to test brain chemistry, the scientists disproved their own theories because the medicated younger siblings, 44-percent African-American and 56-percent Hispanic, in fact, began to show some of the side effects of the drug, indicating that fenfluramine hydroxide had not balanced serotonin levels, but actually produced a spike that was abrupt. A complete post-trial review, which compared pre-trial samples with the hourly samples, revealed that the boys did not possess the expected lower than average serotonin levels, challenging the professors' main argument.

CH 01

CH 02

CH 03

CH 04

CH 05

CH 06

CH 07

CH 08

CH 09

Hackers TOEFL Reading

5   Social scientists examining the clinical tests promptly suggested that the main reason for the failure of the professors to link serotonin to violence was because aggressive behavior is determined through a variety of mitigating factors, including a prior history of offensive behavior, childhood experiences, and socio-economic status. According to common social theories, children who are exposed to violence and situations in which they are hurt either physically or emotionally often display tendencies toward hurting others, and sociologists are quick to point out that this is based not on biology, but rather on circumstances. In fact, studies with twins raised in different households, one violent and one non-violent, evidently show that the causation is exposure, not genetic similarity. In addition, criminologists warn that heredity cannot be seen as a driving force behind the predisposition to violence because it denies personal responsibility of the perpetrator, makes judgments of individuals who have never committed a violent act based on biology, and fails to address a myriad of social agents influencing behavior.

6   According to social scientists, any scientific study that excludes data about the test subject's historical and social background should be considered reductionist, having a tendency to use an inadequately simple set of structures to explain a more complex one. In response, clinical researchers have adjusted many of their clinical trials to account for differences in social and historical context.

1   The word "anxiety" in the passage is closest in meaning to

(A) annoyance
(B) resolve
(C) worry
(D) euphoria

2   According to paragraph 2, serotonin regulates all of the following EXCEPT

(A) mood
(B) appetite
(C) concentration
(D) sleep

Paragraph 2 is marked with an arrow [➡].

3   It is implied in paragraph 2 that the goal of research into the biological cause of violent behavior is to

(A) understand how brain chemistry reacts to artificial drugs
(B) use medicines to prevent violent inclinations from worsening
(C) increase the ability of society to recognize potential threats
(D) encourage those at risk to go through an examination

Paragraph 2 is marked with an arrow [➡].

4 The word "they" in the passage refers to

(A) professors
(B) scientists
(C) younger brothers
(D) older siblings

5 It can be inferred from paragraph 3 that the researchers believed the subjects' older brothers

(A) ceased from their violent acts completely
(B) passed their traits to the subjects
(C) refused to take medicinal therapy
(D) had less than normal degree of serotonin

Paragraph 3 is marked with an arrow [➡].

6 Which of the sentences below best expresses the essential information in the highlighted sentence in the passage? *Incorrect* choices change the meaning in important ways or leave out essential information.

(A) Those exposed to the environmental triggers of violence would be affected by the increase in serotonin fenfluramine hydroxide produced.
(B) It was believed that the use of fenfluramine hydroxide would keep the subjects from employing violence by normalizing their serotonin levels.
(C) Fenfluramine hydroxide was given to the subjects from various backgrounds in the belief that it would increase their serotonin levels.
(D) Researchers had to adjust fenfluramine hydroxide according to the serotonin levels, which varied depending on a variety of factors.

7 According to paragraph 4, analysis of the subjects' blood samples

(A) led to confidence in the effectiveness of fenfluramine hydroxide on violent behavior
(B) showed their serotonin levels were not below the average at the beginning of the experiment
(C) proved that it was inappropriate for researchers to alter the serotonin levels by artificial means
(D) supported the contention that older siblings were more apt to use violence than younger ones

Paragraph 4 is marked with an arrow [➡].

8 The word "abrupt" in the passage is closest in meaning to

(A) sudden
(B) harsh
(C) gradual
(D) improper

9 According to the passage, the author implies that the research done with twins

(A) denies the argument that a combination of different elements causes violence

(B) suggests that exposure to violence fosters a genetic predisposition to aggression

(C) promotes the notion that inheritance is not a major factor in violence

(D) recommends that scientific studies should be done with no consideration of historical background

10 **Directions**: An introductory sentence for a brief summary of the passage is provided below. Complete the summary by selecting the THREE answer choices that express the most important ideas in the passage. Some sentences do not belong in the summary because they express ideas that are not presented in the passage or are minor ideas in the passage. **This question is worth 2 points.**

> Drag your answer choices to the spaces where they belong. To remove an answer choice, click on it. To review the passage, click on **View Text**.

Studies on violence have focused on finding an underlying cause.

-
-
-

Answer Choices

(A) Violence is a major concern among many people and is widely discussed in a variety of fields in society.

(B) Many scholars claim that environmental and social factors are the cause of the onset of violent conduct.

(C) People who committed a violent crime have to take responsibility under the law.

(D) The results of a government study disputed the relationship between serotonin and violence.

(E) Continued and abusive use of medicines is able to set off brute acts.

(F) One theory is that serotonin levels determine whether individuals will commit violent crimes.

정답 및 해석 p.463

CH 01
CH 02
CH 03
CH 04
CH 05
CH 06
CH 07
CH 08
CH 09
Hackers TOEFL Reading

1 ➡ The American Revolution against Britain (1775-1783) was the first modern war of liberation against a colonial power, yet it was not until half a century later that America could claim its cultural independence from English literature and art. In the immediate decades following the military revolution, American authors and artists retained an identification with England and continued to imitate English artistic models, while a complexity of economic and political factors on both sides of the Atlantic encumbered the promotion of their works. Indeed, cultural revolutions are not instantaneous and cannot be imposed, but must evolve from a new set of sensibilities and within a climate of opportunity.

2 ➡ The accomplishments and aspirations of Benjamin Franklin (1706-1790) rendered him the prime American example of the Age of Enlightenment, and his work laid the groundwork for the generations of nationalist writers that followed. Franklin's writings portrayed America as having distinct values and interests from those of England and contributed to the creation of an American national identity. Through his civic writings, personal letters, and acclaimed autobiography, Franklin touted the attributes of industry, independence, and innovativeness that helped shape the American Revolution. By the early decades of the 19th century, the first wave of distinctly American fiction writers began to benefit from Franklin's publishing activities and his promotion of American culture overseas. Inspired and inventive authors portrayed uniquely American subjects, such as westward migration, that evoked the vibrant imagery of the American landscape and the collective sentiments of the American people. But unlike Franklin, who remained fully entrenched in the Enlightenment's emphasis on scientific reason and the rationalization of nature, the new breed of writers ushered in the Age of American Romanticism by highlighting the emotional and aesthetic qualities of nature through allegory and personification. The novelist Washington Irving (1789-1859), for instance, was renowned for having devised imaginative means to humanize the vast American countryside and endow it with a set of legends all its own, ultimately recreating and helping to satisfy the young nation's sense of history and adventure.

3 ➡ The relationship between man and nature was indeed the quintessential element of American Romanticism, and this interplay became the driving theme in the burgeoning nationalistic literary and artistic identities. Furthermore, the earlier European Romantic movement's tenets of the breaking off of old traditions, the revolutionary nature of culture, as well as individualism, easily transferred to serve 19th century American society's ideals of justice, liberty, and equality as the natural rights of man. An influential set of authors in New England developed a version of Romanticism called Transcendentalism, which was a philosophic and literary movement that promoted individuality and self-reliance and affirmed the validity of intuitive truth that was available to every man. The movement's chief spokesperson, Ralph Waldo Emerson (1803-1882), has been reputed as the father of American literature and as a man who articulated the new nation's needs and potential, becoming the archetypal American artist. At a time when many in the United States remained in awe of European culture, he urged Americans to reject their deference to old

modes and values of Europe, as in his famous address American Scholar, in which he argued that Americans were self-reliant enough to develop a literature reflecting their own national character: "Our day of dependence, our long apprenticeship to the learning of other lands, draws to a close." His calls to exploit the untapped materials of the nation inspired many of his contemporaries, as well as subsequent generations of writers and artists.

4 The ideals of Transcendentalism found visual embodiment in the creations of the first so-called school of American art, the Hudson River School, led by Thomas Cole (1801-1848). Just as Emerson had claimed that Americans should write about themselves in their own place, Cole noted in an essay published in 1836 that it was not necessary for artists to turn to Europe for inspirational subjects for their paintings and declared that the most impressive source of inspiration was the scenery of the American wilderness. The School helped form the mythos of the dominant American landscape in a Romantic aesthetic that was spontaneous and sweeping. Their paintings projected optimism for the future and admiration for the New World wilderness which they considered sacred and healing for the human spirit. These artists have been credited for legitimizing landscapes that were distinctively American as a subject matter for canvas and at the same time for infusing American artists with the confidence to turn away from European subjects and models to those of their own culture and of their country's ever-expanding frontier.

1 Which of the following can be inferred about American works of art in the late 18th century in paragraph 1?

(A) They primarily described English life of the colonial period.
(B) It was quite uncommon to find British-style art in America.
(C) They were produced with the economic support of England.
(D) It was difficult to distinguish them from their British counterparts.

Paragraph 1 is marked with an arrow [➡].

2 The word "those" in the passage refers to

(A) accomplishments and aspirations
(B) generations
(C) writings
(D) values and interests

3 According to the passage, what can be inferred about literature in the early 1800s?

(A) Authors were more occupied with industry than with nature.
(B) American publications were available in foreign countries.
(C) Colonial literature was in greatest demand in the local market.
(D) Fiction writers played a vital role in the American Revolution.

CH 01
CH 02
CH 03
CH 04
CH 05
CH 06
CH 07
CH 08
CH 09
Hackers TOEFL Reading

4 According to paragraph 2, authors of American Romanticism would most likely deal with

(A) a well-known political figure in New England
(B) a sea voyage in the Atlantic Ocean
(C) a family living in log cabins on the frontier
(D) a battle between two powerful nations

Paragraph 2 is marked with an arrow [➡].

5 According to paragraph 3, all of the following elements carried over from European Romanticism to American Romanticism EXCEPT

(A) a rejection of outdated customs
(B) a belief that culture is transformative
(C) a concern with protecting nature
(D) a focus on the role of the individual

Paragraph 3 is marked with an arrow [➡].

6 In stating that many in the United States remained "in awe of European culture" the author means that a lot of people in the United States

(A) took satisfaction in European culture
(B) were in reverence of European culture
(C) deviated from European culture
(D) were in accordance with European culture

7 In the passage, why does the author quote "Our day of dependence, our long apprenticeship to the learning of other lands, draws to a close." from Emerson's speech?

(A) To illustrate the degree to which American artists were prone to exploit the literary works from other countries

(B) To demonstrate that Emerson felt that Americans still had a few things to learn from European culture

(C) To give an explanation of why Americans were unwilling to incorporate the values of Europe into their literature

(D) To emphasize Emerson's insistence that Americans should break away from the literary models of other nations

8 The word "impressive" in the passage is closest in meaning to

(A) remarkable
(B) optimal
(C) rudimentary
(D) consistent

9   Which of the sentences below best expresses the essential information in the highlighted sentence in the passage? *Incorrect* choices change the meaning in important ways or leave out essential information.

(A) The Hudson River School led American artists to use their own culture and land for inspiration as well as depicted the American landscape in their paintings.

(B) The focus on the American landscape and culture over traditional European subjects was the most significant achievement of the Hudson River School.

(C) Once landscapes were viewed as legitimate subjects of paintings, the Hudson River School and other American artists began to reject European models.

(D) The Hudson River School was given credit for their landscape paintings because their art portrayed American culture and its expanding territory.

10 **Directions**: An introductory sentence for a brief summary of the passage is provided below. Complete the summary by selecting the THREE answer choices that express the most important ideas in the passage. Some sentences do not belong in the summary because they express ideas that are not presented in the passage or are minor ideas in the passage. **This question is worth 2 points.**

> Drag your answer choices to the spaces where they belong. To remove an answer choice, click on it. To review the passage, click on **View Text**.

The independence of American literature and art from England in the 19th century was a gradual process.

- ●
- ●
- ●

Answer Choices

(A) Transcendentalism inspired writers to compose pieces based on distinct American themes and subjects.

(B) American literature incorporated European Romanticism in order to clearly express the natural rights of man.

(C) The American Revolution created an atmosphere that made English culture unpopular on American soil.

(D) America's cultural revolution came as a result of the original works of Washington Irving.

(E) American authors influenced by Benjamin Franklin produced works of American Romanticism.

(F) Painting in America was largely concerned with capturing the nation's unique physical characteristics.

정답 및 해석 p.465

CH 01
CH 02
CH 03
CH 04
CH 05
CH 06
CH 07
CH 08
CH 09
Hackers TOEFL Reading

Chapter 06에 수록된 어휘들을 빈출도 순으로 정리했습니다. 음성파일을 들으며 꼭 암기하세요.

토플 최빈출어휘 [★★★]

- [ ] **adornment** [ədɔ́ːrnmənt] 장식
- [ ] **ancient** [éinʃənt] 고대의
- [ ] **potential** [pəténʃəl] 잠재력
- [ ] **hasten** [héisn] 앞당기다 (=speed up)
- [ ] **revolutionary** [rèvəlúːʃəneri] 혁명적인
- [ ] **convention** [kənvénʃən] 관습 (=usage)
- [ ] **pinpoint** [pínpɔ̀int] 위치를 정확하게 파악하다 (=locate exactly)
- [ ] **conjecture** [kəndʒéktʃər] 추측 (=guess)
- [ ] **utilize** [júːtəlàiz] 이용하다 (=make use of)
- [ ] **transform** [trænsfɔ́ːrm] 변화시키다 (=change)
- [ ] **concrete** [káːŋkriːt] 구체적인
- [ ] **likewise** [làikwáiz] 이와 같이 (=similarly)
- [ ] **alter** [ɔ́ːltər] 변화시키다 (=change)
- [ ] **trace** [treis] 흔적 (=impression)
- [ ] **segment** [ségmənt] 부분
- [ ] **consensus** [kənsénsəs] 일치 (=agreement)
- [ ] **vitality** [vaitǽləti] 생동감 (=vigor)
- [ ] **readily** [rédəli] 쉽게 (=easily)
- [ ] **distract** [distrǽkt] 주의를 분산시키다
- [ ] **assumption** [əsʌ́mpʃən] 가설
- [ ] **potent** [póutnt] 강력한 (=strong)
- [ ] **coincide with** 일치하다 (=correspond)
- [ ] **dispersion** [dispə́ːrʒən] 전파 (=dissemination)
- [ ] **illuminate** [ilúːmənèit] 조명하다 (=light up)
- [ ] **residue** [rézədjùː] 잔류물 (=remnant)
- [ ] **eclectic** [ikléktik] 다양한 (=diverse)
- [ ] **drastically** [drǽstikəli] 완전히
- [ ] **advocate** [ǽdvəkèit] 지지자
- [ ] **speculate** [spékjulèit] 고찰하다
- [ ] **tendency** [téndənsi] 경향 (=inclination)
- [ ] **postulate** [pástʃulèit] 간주하다 (=hypothesize)
- [ ] **immutable** [imjúːtəbl] 변치 않는 (=unchangeable)
- [ ] **mechanism** [mékənìzm] 과정
- [ ] **anxiety** [æŋzáiəti] 불안감 (=worry)

- [ ] **abrupt** [əbrʌ́pt] 갑작스러운 (=sudden)
- [ ] **myriad** [míriəd] 다수 (=multitude)
- [ ] **instantaneous** [ìnstəntéiniəs] 순간적인
- [ ] **impose** [impóuz] 강제하다 (=force)
- [ ] **renowned** [rináund] 유명한 (=famous)
- [ ] **endow** [indáu] 부여하다 (=grant)
- [ ] **interplay** [íntərplèi] 상호작용 (=interaction)
- [ ] **burgeon** [bə́ːrdʒən] 싹트다
- [ ] **subsequent** [sʌ́bsikwənt] 이후의 (=succeeding)
- [ ] **embodiment** [imbádimənt] 구현
- [ ] **spontaneous** [spɑntéiniəs] 즉흥적인 (=unplanned)

토플 빈출어휘 [★★]

- [ ] **record-breaking** [rékərdbrèikiŋ] 전례 없는 (=unprecedented)
- [ ] **acceptable** [ækséptəbl] 허용 가능한 (=tolerable)
- [ ] **navigate** [nǽvigeit] 길을 찾다
- [ ] **rapidity** [rəpídəti] 속도
- [ ] **prey** [prei] 먹잇감 (=game)
- [ ] **feasibility** [fìːzəbíliti] 실행 가능성 (=practicability)
- [ ] **obligation** [àbləgéiʃən] 의무 (=duty)
- [ ] **perception** [pərsépʃən] 인식 (=cognizance)
- [ ] **reject** [ridʒékt] 거부하다 (=renounce)
- [ ] **outrage** [áutreidʒ] 격분하다
- [ ] **reproduce** [rìːprədjúːs] 번식하다
- [ ] **prolifically** [prəlífikəli] 왕성하게 (=abundantly)
- [ ] **habitat** [hǽbitæt] 서식지
- [ ] **ingredient** [ingríːdiənt] 원료 (=element)
- [ ] **poverty** [páːvərti] 가난
- [ ] **forced** [fɔːrst] 강제적인 (=involuntary)
- [ ] **smooth** [smuːð] 매끈한 (=sleek)
- [ ] **delicate** [délikət] 정교한
- [ ] **peak** [piːk] 정점 (=apex)
- [ ] **terminal** [tə́ːrmənl] 맨 끝의 (=last)
- [ ] **rare** [rɛər] 드문 (=uncommon)
- [ ] **basis** [béisis] 기반

*해커스 동영상강의 포털 해커스인강(HackersIngang.com)에서 '토플 빈출어휘 정리 노트' 음성파일을 무료로 다운로드할 수 있습니다.

☐ adjoin [ədʒɔ́in] 붙어 있다 (=border)

☐ tool [tuːl] 도구 (=implement)

☐ concept [kánsept] 의미

☐ impressive [imprésiv] 인상적인 (=imposing)

☐ probability [prɑ̀bəbíləti] 가능성 (=likelihood)

☐ alienate [éiljənèit] 떨어지게 하다 (=estrange)

☐ secular [sékjulər] 속세적인 (=worldly)

☐ literacy [lítərəsi] 읽고 쓸 줄 앎

☐ fossil [fásəl] 화석

☐ extinction [ikstíŋkʃən] 멸종

☐ catastrophe [kətǽstrəfi] 재앙

☐ inorganic [ìnɔːrgǽnik] 무생물의

☐ voyage [vɔ́iidʒ] 항해

☐ maturity [mətʃúərəti] 성숙

☐ solidify [səlídəfài] 확고하게 하다

☐ molecular [məlékjulər] 분자의

☐ ponder [pándər] 숙고하다

☐ addiction [ədíkʃən] 중독

☐ identity [aidéntəti] 정체성

☐ likelihood [láiklihùd] 가능성

☐ commit [kəmít] 저지르다

☐ inclination [ìnklənéiʃən] 경향

☐ supposedly [səpóuzidli] 추정상 (=presumably)

토플 기출어휘 [★]

☐ deity [díːəti] 신 (=divinity)

☐ rank [ræŋk] (순위를) 차지하다

☐ pace [peis] 속도

☐ depletion [diplíːʃən] 파괴

☐ stature [stǽtʃər] 크기 (=height)

☐ adore [ədɔ́ːr] 무척 좋아하다

☐ lure [luər] 유혹 (=enticement)

☐ entitle [intáitl] 자격을 주다

☐ debunk [diːbʌ́ŋk] 틀렸음을 밝히다

☐ descend [disénd] 유래하다

☐ capricious [kəpríʃəs] 변덕스러운 (=fickle)

☐ deviant [díːviənt] 일탈적인

☐ enterprise [éntərpràiz] 기업

☐ outskirt [áutskə̀ːrt] 교외

☐ decentralize [diːséntrəlàiz] 분산시키다

☐ anoxic [ænáksik] 산소가 없는

☐ elongation [ilɔ̀ːŋgéiʃən] 길이의 늘어남

☐ accession [ækséʃən] 계승

☐ painstaking [péinztèikiŋ] 치밀한

☐ presumable [prizúːməbl] 추측할 수 있는

☐ equitable [ékwətəbl] 합리적인

☐ unmistakably [ʌ̀nmistéikəbli] 분명히

☐ mutation [mjuːtéiʃən] 변이

☐ vicious [víʃəs] 잔인한

☐ plentitude [pléntitjùːd] 많음

☐ frustration [frʌstréiʃən] 좌절

☐ predisposition [prìːdispəzíʃən] 성향

☐ imbalance [imbǽləns] 불균형

☐ escalate [éskəlèit] 심해지다

☐ propensity [prəpénsəti] 경향

☐ interdisciplinary [ìntərdísəplənèri] 여러 학문이 결합된

☐ sibling [síbliŋ] 형제

☐ background [bǽkgràund] 배경

☐ account for 설명하다 (=explain)

☐ aspiration [æ̀spəréiʃən] 포부

☐ render [réndər] 되게 하다

☐ usher [ʌ́ʃər] 도래를 알리다

☐ quintessential [kwìntəsénʃəl] 정수의

☐ tenet [ténit] 신조

☐ self-reliance [sélfrilàiəns] 자주성

☐ affirm [əfə́ːrm] 확언하다

☐ intuitive [intjúːətiv] 직관적인

☐ spokesperson [spóukspə̀ːrsn] 대변자

☐ awe [ɔː] 경외

☐ untapped [ʌ̀ntǽpt] 개발되지 않은

CH 01
CH 02
CH 03
CH 04
CH 05
CH 06
CH 07
CH 08
CH 09

Hackers TOEFL Reading

goHackers.com

Hackers TOEFL READING

PART 03

Recognizing Organization

Chapter 07 Insertion

Chapter 08 Summary

Chapter 09 Category Chart

Chapter 07
Insertion

OVERVIEW

Insertion 문제는 글의 흐름을 유기적이고 자연스럽게 연결할 수 있도록 문제에 제시된 문장을 지문의 적절한 위치에 삽입하는 유형이다. 논리적 연관성이 부족한 곳에 삽입 문장을 넣음으로써 논리적으로 더욱 완벽한 글이 완성된다.
따라서 Insertion 문제를 제대로 풀기 위해서는 글의 흐름을 파악하고, 문장과 문장이 어떻게 논리적으로 연결되어 있는지 알아보는 연습이 필요하다.
Insertion 문제는 보통 한 지문당 1개가 출제된다.

TYPES OF QUESTIONS

4지선다의 질문 형태와는 달리, 지문에 4개의 [■]이 표시되어 있으며 삽입될 문장이 제시된다. 지문의 [■]를 클릭하면 그 자리에 문제로 제시된 문장이 볼드체로 삽입되어 나타난다.
Insertion 문제의 전형적인 질문 유형은 아래와 같다.

Look at the four squares [■] that indicate where the following sentence could be added to the passage.

(삽입 문장)

Where would the sentence best fit?

Click on a square [■] to add the sentence to the passage.

HACKERS **STRATEGY**

CH 01
CH 02
CH 03
CH 04
CH 05
CH 06
CH 07
CH 08
CH 09

Hackers TOEFL Reading

전략 1 삽입할 문장을 읽고 삽입 문장 내의 clue를 찾는다.

삽입 문장에는 어느 곳에 삽입되어야 논리적인지를 알려주는 clue가 들어 있다.

● **동일어구 반복**

동일한 단어가 반복될 경우 동일한 단어는 근접하여 있다.

> **Ex** The Olmecs built large earth and stone pyramids as centers for religious worship, and they produced huge sculptures and fine jade carvings. **Many of their sculptures mix human and jaguar-like features.**

➡ 볼드체 문장(삽입 문장)의 clue는 sculptures이다. 앞 문장에 sculptures가 언급되었으므로 그 문장 뒤에 위치하여야 한다.

● **지시어**

대부분의 경우, 지시어를 포함한 문장은 지시어가 가리키는 대상이 들어있는 문장 뒤에 나온다. 삽입 문장에 자주 나오는 지시어로는 it, they, this, these, the former, some이 있다.

> **Ex** Certain mechanisms prevent interbreeding between two different species, thus maintaining reproductive isolation. **These preserve the integrity of the gene pool of each species by preventing gene flow between different species.**

➡ 볼드체 문장(삽입 문장)의 clue는 These이다. 지시대명사 These가 가리키는 것은 앞 문장의 mechanisms이다.

● **연결어**

연결어는 글의 흐름을 원활히 해주는 기능을 하므로, 연결어를 통해 글의 논리적 구조를 예상할 수 있다.
삽입 문장에 자주 쓰이는 연결어를 정리하면 아래와 같다.

부연	in addition, furthermore, moreover, also, as well, besides, first/second/third
대조	but, however, in contrast, on the other hand, on the contrary
비교	similarly, likewise
인과	due to, because of, therefore, consequently, as a result, thus, hence, in conclusion
예시	for example, for instance
조건	otherwise

> **Ex** Many tropical bat species are dependent on nectar, pollen, and flowers and fruits of plants and are known to "track" the development of the plant resources. **Additionally, many bats rely on plants (especially trees) as roosting sites for varying periods of time.**

➡ 볼드체 문장(삽입 문장)의 clue는 Additionally이다. 앞 문장에서 박쥐의 초목 의존에 대해 설명하고 있고 삽입 문장 역시 '박쥐가 초목을 쉬는 장소로 이용한다'라는 내용을 담고 있으므로 삽입 문장은 박쥐의 초목 이용에 대한 추가 설명이다.

해석 p.468

● 정관사(the) + 명사

'정관사 + 명사'는 앞서 언급되는 '명사' 또는 '부정관사(a/an) + 명사'를 받는 것이므로, '정관사 + 명사'를 포함한 문장은 '명사' 또는 '부정관사 + 명사'가 있는 문장의 뒤에 위치한다.

Ex In competition, two or more organisms simultaneously require a single resource, which is usually in limited supply. **The resources for which plants commonly compete include water, light, soil minerals, and growing space.**

➡ 볼드체 문장(삽입 문장)의 clue는 The resources이다. 따라서 '부정관사 + 명사'인 a single resource가 언급된 문장 뒤에 위치하여야 한다.

● 주제문

대부분의 글은 주제문, 즉 일반적인 사실이나 주장 또는 뒤에서 다룰 내용의 개요 문장이 먼저 나오고, 그 뒤에 그에 따른 구체적인 설명, 예시, 근거가 나오는 두괄식 구조를 가지고 있다.

Ex **Chemical compounds can be divided into two broad groups, inorganic and organic.** Inorganic compounds are relatively small compounds of elements other than carbon. On the other hand, organic compounds are generally large and complex and contain carbon and usually hydrogen.

➡ 볼드체 문장(삽입 문장)의 clue는 뒷부분에서 논의될 개념들(inorganic and organic chemical compounds)을 간략히 설명하고 있다는 것이다. 따라서 도입부의 역할을 하는 주제문이므로 맨 처음에 위치하여야 한다.

전략 2 [■]가 표시된 부분의 주변 문장들을 읽으며 삽입 문장 내의 clue를 근거로 답을 찾는다.

삽입 문장에 들어있는 clue뿐만 아니라 [■]가 표시된 문장들의 내용 또한 정확히 파악하여 삽입 문장의 위치를 찾는다.

Ex In terms of usage, stained glass is commonly associated with religious purposes. For centuries, stained-glass windows, as featured in churches and cathedrals, were regarded as expressions of faith and loyalty. ■ It was not until the Renaissance era that the purpose of stained glass changed to include non-religious uses. ■ During this time, stained glass gained popularity as a fashionable decoration for homes and public buildings, in addition to churches. ■ The glass used was essentially the same as in churches. ■ **However, the colors were changed from the traditional, royal-looking colors reserved for cathedrals to softer, muted shades considered appropriate in domestic windows.**

Clue 찾기

볼드체 문장(삽입 문장)의 clue는 역접의 관계를 나타내는 접속사 However이다.

Clue를 근거로 답 찾기

앞 문장은 삽입 문장과 반대되는 내용을 담고 있어야 한다. 삽입 문장에서 '색상은 대성당에서 사용되었던 것과 달랐다'라고 하였으므로 그 앞 문장에는 교회에서 사용되었던 것과 똑같았다는 내용이 들어 있어야 한다. [■]가 표시된 문장들을 읽어보면 네 번째 [■]의 앞 문장이 그와 같은 내용을 담고 있음을 알 수 있다.

[■]를 클릭하여 문장을 삽입한 후 문맥이 자연스러운지 확인한다.

문장을 삽입한 후에는 앞뒤 문장들과의 흐름이 자연스러운지 확인해야 한다.

Ex Musical comedy theater, as seen upon the stages of New York's famed Broadway and in venues around the world, has taken many years to evolve. ■ The first traces of musical theater's origins can be found within the French and Viennese operettas of the 1800s. ■ **These musical plays achieved international popularity by offering European audiences a lighter version of full-length operas, and featured the lively integration of song, dance, music and theater.** Upon reaching the United States, however, the polished European works encountered a very different creative form: the rollicking American variety shows and bawdy musical revues of the era. ■ Although early forms of musical theater such as minstrel shows, burlesque and vaudeville often relied upon crude slapstick and racial stereotypes for their humor, it was not long until US playwrights and composers took a cue from their European neighbors. ■ Clever, witty and melodic, the new comic operettas blended America's love for exaggerated humor with the live orchestras and lyrical songs of Europe, and the Broadway musical comedy was born.

Clue 찾기
볼드체 문장(삽입 문장)의 clue는 These musical plays이다.

Clue를 근거로 답 찾기
These musical plays가 가리키는 것은 앞 문장의 French and Viennese operettas이므로 삽입 문장이 두 번째 [■] 뒤에 위치해야 함을 알 수 있다.

문맥이 자연스러운지 확인
These musical plays가 French and Viennese operettas를 가리키므로 앞 문장과의 연결이 자연스럽다. 또한, 그 뒤의 문장은 '이러한 유럽의 세련된 작품들이 미국에서 새로운 형태의 뮤지컬을 만나게 되었다'라고 하였으므로 삽입 문장에 뒤이어 나오는 문장과의 연결도 자연스럽다.

CH 01
CH 02
CH 03
CH 04
CH 05
CH 06
CH 07
CH 08
CH 09

Hackers TOEFL Reading

Water continuously circulates from the ocean to the atmosphere to the land and back to the ocean, providing a renewable supply of purified water on land. ■ Water moves from the atmosphere to the land and the ocean in the form of precipitation, such as rain, snow, sleet, or hail. ■ Water, then, evaporates from land and reenters the atmosphere directly or flows in rivers and streams to coastal estuaries, where fresh water meets the ocean. ■ The movement of water from land to the ocean is called runoff. ■ Water also seeps downward in the soil to become groundwater. Groundwater supplies water to the soil, to stream and rivers, and to plants. Ultimately, however, the water that falls on land from the atmosphere makes its way back to the ocean. Regardless of its physical form (solid, liquid, or vapor) or location, every molecule of water eventually moves through the hydrologic cycle.

1. Look at the four squares [■] that indicate where the following sentence could be added to the passage.

This complex cycle, known as the hydrologic cycle, results in a balance between water in the ocean, on the land, and in the atmosphere.

Where would the sentence best fit?

Click on a square [■] to add the sentence to the passage.

■ The tension between the nationalists and the underrepresented American merchants reached a breaking point in 1765, when a flurry of controversy arose in the colonies over the imposed Stamp Act, a law that raised the cost of postage, sending the additional profits back to Britain to pay for nationalist army services. ■ He was charged with smuggling, a move that further incited a revolutionary spirit. ■ Despite having the charges dropped, Hancock, along with colleague Samuel Adams, continued rallying against the infringing economic sanctions and coordinated a boycott on vessels carrying tea bound for the Boston harbor. ■ When the British passed the Tea Act, allowing the royalist East India Company to sell its goods to colonies directly at a lower cost than could be met by local merchants, Adams and 50 collaborators boarded the ships and smashed all cartons containing the tea, throwing them into the water. The act of vandalism, known as the Boston Tea Party, brought the struggle between the patriots and the government to light.

2. Look at the four squares [■] that indicate where the following sentence could be added to the passage.

An upset protestor, John Hancock, who was vocal about his dislike of the Act, had his ship Liberty seized by customs officials.

Where would the sentence best fit?

Click on a square [■] to add the sentence to the passage.

해석 p.468

1

| 전략 1 적용 | 삽입할 문장의 clue는 지시어가 포함된 This complex cycle이다. |

| 전략 2 적용 | 지시형용사가 포함된 This complex cycle이 가리키는 것은 첫 번째 문장에서 언급되는 바다, 대기, 육지에서의 물의 순환이다. 따라서 첫 번째 [■] 뒤에 삽입되어야 한다. |

| 전략 3 적용 | This complex cycle은 앞 문장의 내용, 즉 물은 육지에 재생 가능한 깨끗한 물을 공급하며 바다에서 대기와 육지로, 그리고 다시 바다로 계속해서 순환한다는 것을 가리키므로 앞 문장과의 연결이 자연스럽다. 또한, 뒤의 문장에서는 바다, 육지, 대기에서 물의 균형을 가져오는 과정에 대하여 자세히 언급하고 있으므로 삽입 문장에 뒤이어 나오는 문장과의 연결도 자연스럽다. |

정답 1st ■

2

| 전략 1 적용 | 삽입할 문장의 clue는 '정관사 + 명사'인 the Act와 사람 고유 명사 John Hancock이다. |

| 전략 2 적용 | The Act가 가리키는 것은 첫 번째 문장에 언급되어 있는 Stamp Act이며, 두 번째 [■]의 다음 문장의 주어 He가 가리키는 것이 삽입 문장의 John Hancock이므로 두 번째 [■] 뒤에 삽입되어야 한다. |

| 전략 3 적용 | The Act는 앞 문장의 Stamp Act를 가리키므로 앞 문장과의 연결이 자연스럽다. 또한, 뒤의 문장에서 밀수 혐의를 받은 것에 대해 언급하고 있으므로 삽입 문장에 뒤이어 나오는 문장과의 연결도 자연스럽다. |

정답 2nd ■

For each question, arrange the sentences in correct order.

1

(A) Some species achieve fertilization through the transfer of pollen within a single flower or from one bloom to another on the same plant, because the |formation| of the flower parts allows for both male and female reproductive organs.

(B) In flowering plants, also known as angiosperms, pollination is achieved by the distribution of pollen from the anther to the stigma, and if successful, it will lead to the development of an embryo that becomes a seed.

(C) In other species, individual plants are either distinctly male or female, so two separate specimens are required for successful pollination to be accomplished.

Answer _____ – _____ – _____

2

(A) The |complex| interactions between industrial emissions and the atmosphere produce a phenomenon known as acid rain.

(B) Then the pollutants mix with the moisture, and create a highly acidic liquid that falls as rain and can severely damage forests.

(C) When factories, for example, release pollutants into the air as a byproduct of production, chemicals such as sulfur dioxide are carried by clouds as they move above across the landscape.

Answer _____ – _____ – _____

3

(A) Psoriasis is a chronic skin disorder that results in the development of lesions that can produce significant itching and pain.

(B) A fact that seems to |sustain| this assertion is that the consumption of large amounts of unpasteurized milk or butter alleviates the symptoms. But consuming pasteurized dairy products does not, because pasteurization destroys the natural enzymes.

(C) Some researchers have proposed that it is related to a deficiency in enzymes that are |critical| for health and nutrition.

Answer _____ – _____ – _____

VOCABULARY	The word ☐ in the passage is closest in meaning to

		(A)	(B)	(C)	(D)
1	formation	(A) extension	(B) evolution	(C) composition	(D) placement
2	complex	(A) terse	(B) sumptuous	(C) despicable	(D) sophisticated
3	sustain	(A) decoy	(B) tease	(C) uphold	(D) proscribe
	critical	(A) crucial	(B) urgent	(C) reasonable	(D) dangerous

4

    (A) In small mammal species, the gathering and storage of food is probably just as significant, and occasional feeding during hibernation allows them to $\boxed{\text{restore}}$ the calories lost in their dormancy when sustenance is otherwise seasonally unavailable.

    (B) Perhaps the most important adaptation is the ability to $\boxed{\text{periodically}}$ adjust body temperature and heart rate to normal levels, which is believed to facilitate sleep or stimulate the immune system.

    (C) Warm-blooded animals that hibernate face many challenges and must utilize a range of physiological and behavioral strategies to ensure that they maintain the bodily functions necessary to survive the winter.

Answer _____ – _____ – _____

5

    (A) As time passed, it became increasingly common for members of the nobility to erect permanent structures for theatrical performances within their palaces. In most cases, a stage and seating area with $\boxed{\text{lavish}}$ decorations was built in a large hall. However, as the palaces had a number of other functions, they cannot be considered theaters in the modern sense of the word.

    (B) In Italy at the beginning of the sixteenth century, plays were generally not performed in buildings specifically designed as theaters. Instead, a temporary structure that included a very simple stage was erected. It was usually set up outdoors and would be taken down once the performance had ended.

    (C) The palace venues were eventually superseded by buildings that operated exclusively as theaters. The interiors of these structures usually followed the same basic design — an open seating area directly in front of a large stage was enclosed by a half-circle of raised boxes reserved for the wealthy. The fact that the theater owners generated revenue primarily by charging for admission $\boxed{\text{prompted}}$ them to include as many seats as possible.

Answer _____ – _____ – _____

VOCABULARY	The word ☐ in the passage is closest in meaning to			
4	restore	(A) rate	(B) recover	(C) ratify	(D) recast
	periodically	(A) regularly	(B) casually	(C) presently	(D) fitfully
5	lavish	(A) fascinating	(B) lucrative	(C) deluxe	(D) vivid
	prompted	(A) intrigued	(B) abided	(C) consolidated	(D) provoked

6

(A) What they all have in common is their behavior after they breach the surface. Universally, they cling to a twig or leaf at the water's edge and sit perfectly $\boxed{\text{still}}$ before shedding their shell and transforming into their mature form — a dazzling aeronautical acrobat.

(B) Whether the young dragonflies surface at the same time is determined by the season. While dragonflies that come out in spring tend to do so almost simultaneously, with members of the same population emerging together, those that wait until summer appear sporadically over the course of weeks or months.

(C) The life cycle of a dragonfly begins when an adult $\boxed{\text{deposits}}$ eggs in a body of water, such as a lake, river, or stream. The eggs develop into a nymph, which spends approximately a year living as an aquatic insect, after which it will emerge from the water when the temperature rises to a suitable level and the threat of frost has passed.

Answer _____ − _____ − _____

Choose the sentence that best completes the blank in each passage.

7

An acid is a compound that dissociates in a solution of water to form hydrogen ions and negatively charged ions. Some acids are known as strong acids because they break up almost $\boxed{\text{completely}}$ in water. Hydrochloric acid is a very strong acid because most of its molecules decompose, $\boxed{\text{producing}}$ hydrogen ions and chloride ions. _____ _____. Vinegar, which is a dilute solution of acetic acid, is an example of a weak acid.

(A) It is an important industrial chemical for many applications
(B) Each combines with a hydroxide ion of a base to form a water molecule
(C) Others, called weak acids, dissolve only slightly
(D) In a complex process and at a high energetic cost, it is secreted by parietal cells

---

VOCABULARY	The word ☐ in the passage is closest in meaning to			
6 still	(A) spotless	(B) motionless	(C) boundless	(D) artless
deposits	(A) nourishes	(B) saves	(C) hurls	(D) lays
7 completely	(A) previously	(B) resolutely	(C) possibly	(D) thoroughly
producing	(A) pausing	(B) releasing	(C) grumbling	(D) offsetting

8   Kinkajous are small tree-dwelling mammals that are exclusively nocturnal. As such, it might be ⟨expected⟩ that they have excellent night vision, though in fact their eyesight is very poor. Thus, they rely ⟨primarily⟩ on their sense of smell and touch to navigate the forest canopy and find food. Their set of extremely sharp teeth is reminiscent of that of a carnivore, but they are generally vegetarian and forage for fruit. _____.
Additionally, their long tongues help them reach nectar in flowers, which is another key source of sustenance.

(A) Due to their shy and elusive nature, they were not well known to scientists until recently

(B) Feeling their way through the treetops, they seasonally hunt for small prey like frogs and insects

(C) Their inability to see well at night sometimes leaves them vulnerable to predation

(D) Their food usually provides them with sufficient liquid for hydration, so kinkajous rarely need to drink water

9   It is well documented that the Incan people developed ⟨domesticated⟩ plants and animals that helped them form large settlements. They undertook a tremendous amount of effort to transform dry mountain terrain into land suitable for sedentary life. However, one thing that is puzzling to anthropologists is why the Inca tended to move up in altitude over time. _____ _____. As the settlements increased in elevation, the Inca encountered harsher and harsher conditions. So why did they do it? Well, one motivation for this ⟨change⟩ might have been their religion. Religion was central to Incan culture, and one of their gods that was highly revered was Inti, who represented the sun, a heavenly body. Perhaps they thought moving higher brought them closer to heaven. This could explain why the major centers like Machu Picchu were located at more than 7,000 feet above sea level.

(A) Each new colony was established at a higher location
(B) Corn was particularly well suited to cultivation at high altitude
(C) Experts think that they may have conclusively solved the mystery
(D) It became harder for the settlers to scale the mountain

VOCABULARY	The word ☐ in the passage is closest in meaning to			
8	expected	(A) anticipated	(B) emigrated	(C) surveilled	(D) survived
	primarily	(A) seldom	(B) slightly	(C) preeminently	(D) pretty
9	domesticated	(A) meddled	(B) deformed	(C) treated	(D) tamed
	change	(A) draft	(B) shift	(C) diversion	(D) achievement

CH 01
CH 02
CH 03
CH 04
CH 05
CH 06
CH 07
CH 08
CH 09
Hackers TOEFL Reading

10   In the 1960s, scientists realized that the earth's magnetic field sometimes reverses itself. This discovery was accomplished through observing rock that had been deposited by lava flows. The successive layering of volcanic rock made millions of years of geologic history available to scientists. _____. Researchers studied the pattern of iron, which exhibits strong magnetism and in modern times is predictably directed toward the North Pole. However, after conducting measurements at hundreds of locations around the world, they concluded that approximately half of the iron layers were oriented toward the south. This revelation overturned the 400-year-old assumption that the needle of a compass will forever point north.

(A) Much of the lava was too old for the scientists to draw any firm conclusions
(B) Because the rock was well preserved, its chemical composition could be determined
(C) Of particular interest to those in the investigation were layers with high levels of iron
(D) They were surprised to find that the iron deposits in the lava were so old

11   During astronomer Christiaan Huygens's 1655 observations of Saturn, it became obvious to him that the giant planet had a large moon in its orbit. This massive satellite, subsequently named Titan, is approximately 50 percent larger than Earth's moon. A notable feature of Titan is its dense atmosphere, which produces wispy clouds in its northernmost latitudes. Elsewhere, the atmosphere is characterized by a thick haze or smog that is sufficiently opaque to conceal its surface from the view of astronomers. Therefore, to find out what lies beneath, NASA launched the Cassini spacecraft. In 2004, Cassini entered Saturn's orbit, and the following year it touched down on Titan's surface. _____ _____. Cassini sent back photos that revealed informational breakthroughs about the landscape. In addition to revealing its varied topography, they showed that geological features moved up to 30 kilometers in less than two years, which suggests that the moon's crust is disassociated from the solid core and is floating on some kind of liquid subterranean ocean.

(A) It confirmed Christiaan Huygens's theories about Titan's atmosphere
(B) This was the first-ever moon landing in the outer solar system
(C) Several spacecrafts were sent to gather data about Saturn
(D) There were more moons in orbit around the planet

VOCABULARY   The word ☐ in the passage is closest in meaning to

10	accomplished	(A) kindled	(B) continued	(C) achieved	(D) faltered
	available	(A) accessible	(B) touchable	(C) plentiful	(D) liberal
11	obvious	(A) extraneous	(B) evident	(C) well-known	(D) opaque
	wispy	(A) deluding	(B) listless	(C) thin	(D) pecuniary

12   Art ⌈inevitably⌉ reflects the unique values and customs of the culture in which it arises. Tibetan art, for instance, frequently depicts Buddhist material due to Buddhism's prolonged and pervasive influence in Tibetan society, and this can be seen in the paintings that decorate the walls of monasteries and temples in the region. These works of art typically feature elaborate patterns of spiritual symbols and representations of divine beings. To create these patterns, artists used rulers to determine precisely where each image should be located relative to the others. _____. In addition, artists were influenced by the Buddhist belief that each color represents a specific attribute — for example, white stands for peace and purity. The colors used in these paintings were often selected based on their symbolic meaning to express Buddhist concepts.

(A) Due to this approach, the paintings tended to have a wide array of colors
(B) Such exactness was necessary because of the complexity of the paintings
(C) Even very old wall paintings are well preserved because of Tibet's arid climate
(D) The amount of time an individual painting took depended on the size of the wall

Read each passage and answer the corresponding question for each.

13   The Great Depression of the 1930s brought about tremendous social and economic upheaval in America, but it also inspired people. It was during this time that certain artists created the art movement "American Regionalism." ■ Leading the way were Grant Wood and Thomas Hart Benton, who sought to create a distinctive style that relied heavily on realism and highlighted rural, small-town life, particularly that of the Midwest. ■ Their goals were to capture the simplicity and hardships of the pastoral lifestyle and to distance themselves from painters who focused on 'urban' life and themes. ■ They also sought to ⌈isolate⌉ themselves from foreign influences, such as impressionism and abstract expressionism. ■

Look at the four squares [■] that indicate where the following sentence could be added to the passage.

Their paintings of rolling hills, hay bales, and cornfields reflect their own personal backgrounds, as they grew up in the area.

Where would the sentence best fit?

Click on a square [■] to add the sentence to the passage.

Answer _____

VOCABULARY   The word ☐ in the passage is closest in meaning to

12 inevitably	(A) repeatedly	(B) originally	(C) progressively	(D) unavoidably
13 isolate	(A) astound	(B) insulate	(C) explicate	(D) halt

CH 01
CH 02
CH 03
CH 04
CH 05
CH 06
CH 07
CH 08
CH 09
Hackers TOEFL Reading

14   Igneous rocks result from the cooling of hot magma or lava. As the hot liquid cools, it turns yellow and then various shades of red, solidifying completely to form several types of igneous rock. A texture that is coarse or has large crystals that can be seen by the naked eye means that the magma cooled slowly. ■ The result is a rock known as granite. ■ If the rock has small crystals or a fine texture, the rock cooled quickly. ■ Granite and basalt are two of the most abundant types of igneous rocks. ■ If the rock has very few or no crystals, the magma cooled in just a few hours or days, producing a glass known as obsidian. These different types of rock illustrate the diversity of properties igneous rocks have.

Look at the four squares [■] that indicate where the following sentence could be added to the passage.

Basalt is an example of this type of igneous rock.

Where would the sentence best fit?

Click on a square [■] to add the sentence to the passage.

Answer _____

15   Conservation in the United States has had a fairly recent history. Because America is so vast and its resources so abundant, environmental concerns did not come into question until 1900 when the excessive killing of egrets, spoonbills, and other showy birds forced Congress to enact a law against using bird feathers and stuffed birds to decorate women's hats. ■ This was considered landmark legislation for its time. ■ However, public interest in protecting birds and other animals tapered during the Second World War. ■ The war years saw the large-scale manufacture of insecticides for farming and ranching interests. ■ When dead birds began dropping out of the sky in the early 1960s, no one knew why until biologist Rachel Carson's book *Silent Spring* revealed how pesticides and other toxic chemicals move through the food chain, ultimately subjecting every human being to contact with the deadly chemicals. Suddenly, ecology became an important issue and the clamor that ensued compelled the American government to step in.

Look at the four squares [■] that indicate where the following sentence could be added to the passage.

These were also used to poison rodents, wolves, and other forms of wildlife.

Where would the sentence best fit?

Click on a square [■] to add the sentence to the passage.

Answer _____

VOCABULARY   The word ☐ in the passage is closest in meaning to

14 various	(A) assorted	(B) immune	(C) blunt	(D) indecent
15 excessive	(A) auxiliary	(B) extemporaneous	(C) meager	(D) undue
protecting	(A) defending	(B) misgiving	(C) affording	(D) merging

16 In 1860, the first overland express postal route for mail delivery to California was established: The Pony Express. The course began at St. Joseph, Missouri, which was the westernmost destination for mail delivery by train, and passed through Salt Lake City before ending in Sacramento, California. The Pony Express's founder, William H. Russell, placed ads in newspapers for young men who were excellent horse riders and willing to face the possibility of death on a daily basis. This is because the route took the riders through fairly unknown and hostile territory. ■ For their work and bravery, employees were granted good pay and benefits, and had to swear to never mistreat the horses. ■ Typically, a single rider would cover 75 to 100 miles in a day and would stop to change horses every 10 or 15 miles; however, deliveries could be performed more quickly when necessary. ■ Though successful, the Pony Express was short lived. The development of coast-to-coast telegraph made it obsolete and its operation shut down less than two years after its inception. ■

Look at the four squares [■] that indicate where the following sentence could be added to the passage.

For example, in 1861, couriers carried Abraham Lincoln's inaugural presidential address across the country in only seven days and 17 hours.

Where would the sentence best fit?

Click on a square [■] to add the sentence to the passage.

Answer _____

17 Ballet began in the courts of Italy and France in the late 16th and 17th centuries. Dancing was considered an essential part of an aristocrat's education, and figured prominently in the spectacular pageants of the age. ■ Many of these court ballets involved figured dances, in which elaborately costumed performers moved through various geometrical formations; spectators might watch the patterns from above and often joined in a general ball at the end. ■ Court ballet effectively integrated various arts, including music, and poetic declamation as well as dance. ■ Louis XIV of France, for example, danced in several court ballets, including the Ballet de la Nuit of 1653, in which he portrayed the Sun Rising to lead a corps of virtues succeeding to the creatures of the night. ■ The role made Louis the focus of a superbly ordered multitude and expressed his official character as the Roi-Soleil(Sun-King).

Look at the four squares [■] that indicate where the following sentence could be added to the passage.

It also allowed theater and reality to merge—an effect on which the period's monarchs capitalized.

Where would the sentence best fit?

Click on a square [■] to add the sentence to the passage.

Answer _____

VOCABULARY	The word ⬚ in the passage is closest in meaning to			
16 granted	(A) graded	(B) considered	(C) lent	(D) bestowed
17 integrated	(A) influenced	(B) unified	(C) interpreted	(D) performed

정답 및 해석 p.469

CH 01
CH 02
CH 03
CH 04
CH 05
CH 06
CH 07
CH 08
CH 09
Hackers TOEFL Reading

HACKERS TEST

1   In North America, several species of birds migrate excessive distances south to avoid inhospitable conditions brought about by climatic fluctuations. ■[1]They return home unerringly every spring because the route and means are pre-wired into their genetic memory. ■ Others, most notably Canadian geese, lack this advantage. ■ Therefore, they must first assimilate passage parameters into their cognizance by emulating their parents. ■

2   ■[2]The sight of large skeins of Canadian geese making grueling journeys south in autumn and north in spring is now a firmly-entrenched rite of seasonal change in multiple parts of the North American continent. ■ On a biological level, diminishing daylight hours and decreasing temperatures set off a hormonal discharge in the pituitary gland that gives geese their basic itinerant urge. ■ On a more practical level, they are herbivores and feed primarily on grass and berries, which are plentiful in summer, but inadequate later, when heavy snow cover and freezing temperatures make moving and staying warm very exacting. ■ Accordingly, flying south affords them the comfort of wintering in a better climate that has much more food available, although the preponderance of southern foxes, coyotes, and various other predators compels the geese to return in the spring to nest in safer surroundings more suitable for the raising of goslings.

3   ➡ Both ways, the marathon is extremely arduous, and many fail to survive, particularly sick or weak members susceptible to starvation or exhaustion while struggling to keep up with a flock that can ascend to as much as 2,500m in fair skies. Conversely, cloudy or stormy weather forces an entire group to significantly lower the altitude, running the risk of colliding into buildings, phone towers, airplanes, and the bullets of hunters, who often lie in wait along established migration lines to pick them off indiscriminately. An even greater nemesis, however, is land development. Rampant urbanization wipes out valuable resting spots, which forces them to fly further than they normally would, often well past reasonable thresholds of endurance.

4   Because of these multiple impediments, geese have evolved a series of special methods to withstand the taxing rigors of the journey through countless generations of habituation. The passing of the summer solstice brings gradually diminishing daylight hours, which serves as a signal for these birds to begin preparation by increasing the amount of food they eat. As a result of it, they can sustain themselves during the long flight and encase themselves in excess body fat that better insulates against the frigid temperatures of higher altitudes. During flight, they congregate in large flocks and fly in a V-formation, with the larger and stronger birds leading off to start, and then falling towards the rear as they begin to tire. This arrangement is extremely aerodynamic and drastically reduces the wind shear on the birds in the rear, where most of the young, who generally lack the strength to bear the full brunt of high winds, tend to fly. ■[9]This group coordination allows for much

longer flight times without need for as many stops along the way for rest or food. ■ For example, some that have a large number of goslings in tow will stop more frequently, while others will do the opposite if their total trip distance is relatively short. ■ One of the briefest known is the 16-hour, one day jaunt that some subspecies make from Hudson Bay to Wisconsin, while one of the longest ends up in Mexican territory. ■ As a broad generalization, the larger subspecies tend to breed further south than the smaller ones.

1 Look at the four squares [■] that indicate where the following sentence could be added to the passage.

Most are able to make the round trip instinctively.

Where would the sentence best fit?

Click on a square [■] to add the sentence to the passage.

2 Look at the four squares [■] that indicate where the following sentence could be added to the passage.

There are a number of motivations for these biannual sojourns.

Where would the sentence best fit?

Click on a square [■] to add the sentence to the passage.

3 The word "urge" in the passage is closest in meaning to

(A) excuse
(B) rationale
(C) defense
(D) impulse

4 The word "compels" in the passage is closest in meaning to

(A) trains
(B) forces
(C) convinces
(D) prepares

5 According to the passage, why do the geese fly north in the spring?

(A) There isn't enough grass in the south during the summer.
(B) The days get shorter and the temperature falls in the south.
(C) The environment in the south makes nest building difficult.
(D) A number of predators in the south put their young in jeopardy.

6 Which of the sentences below best expresses the essential information in the highlighted sentence in the passage? *Incorrect* choices change the meaning in important ways or leave out essential information.

(A) Hunters are the greatest threat since they shoot geese indiscriminately as they prepare to land.
(B) A heavy storm endangers geese since it makes them more likely to fly into objects.
(C) Geese are put into much danger when weather conditions compel them to fly at lower levels.
(D) Due to the risk of crashing into high-rise buildings, it is better for geese not to fly in bad weather.

7 In paragraph 3, why does the author mention "land development"?

(A) To describe a factor leading to overexhaustion among geese
(B) To stress the importance of sweeping up the land for geese's relaxation
(C) To compare current migration destinations with older ones
(D) To highlight the need for more environmentally friendly construction

Paragraph 3 is marked with an arrow [➡].

8 According to the passage, the advantage to flying in a V-formation is that

(A) it makes the birds more recognizable to people on the ground
(B) it lessens the degree of wind deformation on the rear birds
(C) it ensures that the birds return to the proper site every year
(D) it helps scientists follow the birds' annual migration patterns

9 Look at the four squares [■] that indicate where the following sentence could be added to the passage.

The frequency of pauses varies widely from group to group because Canadian geese learn their flight techniques from their parents, and are thus able to alter them as necessary, depending on the situation.

Where would the sentence best fit?

Click on a square [■] to add the sentence to the passage.

10 **Directions**: An introductory sentence for a brief summary of the passage is provided below. Complete the summary by selecting the THREE answer choices that express the most important ideas in the passage. Some sentences do not belong in the summary because they express ideas that are not presented in the passage or are minor ideas in the passage. **This question is worth 2 points.**

Drag your answer choices to the spaces where they belong. To remove an answer choice, click on it. To review the passage, click on **View Text**.

Canadian geese migrate according to seasonal changes from the north to the south and vice versa.

- ●
- ●
- ●

Answer Choices

(A) People have been able to teach young geese how to migrate properly.

(B) The chemical alteration in the brain and the acquisition of provisions are the main causes for geese's journeys.

(C) Flying at high altitudes is much colder than at lower ones.

(D) Serious hurdles face the geese on every journey they make.

(E) A V-formation and accumulated fat help geese to migrate successfully.

(F) The chemical alteration in the geese's brain is due to changes in weather and sunlight.

정답 및 해석 p.474

CH 01
CH 02
CH 03
CH 04
CH 05
CH 06
CH 07
CH 08
CH 09
Hackers TOEFL Reading

1   By the early 1900s, the silent movie industry had grown into a successful international business, earning a firm position in the popular culture of the day. Without sound, the audience understood plot and character through exaggerated actions or visual cue cards displaying important text that were inserted into the storyboard at appropriate times. Occasionally, movie reels traveled the country with live musicians, adding a soundtrack to enhance storytelling, and live troupes would accompany each film and speak the dialogue of the on-screen actors, providing the audio to complement the images. This satisfied some members of the audience, but what people truly craved was to hear the natural speech patterns of their favorite stars.

2   The technology to reproduce dialogue already existed in the form of the phonograph, an early record player invented by Thomas Edison, which was sold to arcades where customers could pay to listen to a piece of music or a speech through an individual ear tube. ■⁴Similarly, the elaborate device known as the Kinetoscope, which used spinning disks to play short animated films, imprinted onto cylinders or longer strips of celluloid that would turn from one spindle to another, was wildly successful in specialized movie parlors. ■ However, the images were only observable through a tiny peephole cut into the box that housed the functioning apparatus, an intentional design characteristic that ensured the sale of multiple units to one cinema. ■ Because the ratio of Kinetoscopes to customers was always 1:1, business owners were keen to purchase as many machines as they could afford to accommodate growing demand. ■

3   ➡ More than two decades later, the Kinetophone was introduced by Edison, incorporating both the phonograph and the Kinetoscope. As a recording device, it functioned by lip-syncing actors' voices after the moving pictures had been captured or by using an armature to operate both recording functions at the same time. ■⁶For playback in the theater, two operators worked together, one in the projection booth and one in the orchestra pit with the phonograph. ■ Yet, the machine could hardly be labeled as a breakthrough. ■ Because the film was produced on a completely different machine, perfect playback was often marred when one or the other component was mistimed or failed. ■ Theater owners complained about faulty synchronization of sound and picture, a consequence of Edison's poor conceptualization of its implementation in the theater environment. In addition, there were audio problems related to the phonograph's inability to produce a sound level that would fill a large space. While the film was simply projected onto a screen, the audio had to come from speakers without the aid of electronic amplification.

4   These limitations were overcome by Lee De Forest, who patented a method of amplifying sounds leading to the introduction of the monotone loudspeaker in 1925. The new speakers were able to project sound loud enough to reach all customers in a theater filled to capacity, and newly conceived electronic condenser microphones recorded better audio quality by helping to filter out background noise while capturing crisp vocalization. This new system, dubbed the Vitaphone, captured public attention in the fall of 1927 with

the release of *The Jazz Singer*, the first "talkie," or, talking picture. ■[9]Word-of-mouth spread, and soon paying customers were lining up at the cinema to get a look at this state-of-the-art technology, and more importantly, to hear the dialogue of the film's star, Al Jolson. ■

5 Despite overcoming many technical restrictions, the Vitaphone still suffered from synchronization problems as well as the burden of distribution since it had to deliver records, which could only be played for several screenings, along with all of the films. ■ As the fidelity of sound on film increased, it quickly became the media of choice for talkies, ushered in a new wave of public interest in filmed entertainment, and represented the beginning of newfound respect for the industry. ■

1 Which of the sentences below best expresses the essential information in the highlighted sentence in the passage? *Incorrect* choices change the meaning in important ways or leave out essential information.

   (A) The theaters would provide the audience with live music and instant performances to draw the audience's interest in storytelling.

   (B) Music was so important to understanding the plot that live musicians were needed to play at performances of movies.

   (C) Since there was no sound by the early 1900s, people in the audience would read the dialogue of the actors out loud with live musicians.

   (D) Musicians and troupes would sometimes go along with the films to provide the background sound or speak the parts of the actors.

2 The word "elaborate" in the passage is closest in meaning to

   (A) industrial
   (B) complex
   (C) portable
   (D) massive

3 The word "ratio" in the passage is closest in meaning to

   (A) inequity
   (B) proportion
   (C) quantity
   (D) intersection

CH 01
CH 02
CH 03
CH 04
CH 05
CH 06
CH 07
CH 08
CH 09
Hackers TOEFL Reading

4 Look at the four squares [■] that indicate where the following sentence could be added to the passage.

Attempting to maximize return received on investment, they pined for a Kinetoscope that would project the moving pictures onto a white screen for the pleasure of larger paying audiences.

Where would the sentence best fit?

Click on a square [■] to add the sentence to the passage.

5 According to paragraph 3, why was the Kinetophone not considered a breakthrough?

(A) The device required many people to operate it.
(B) The audio and video often did not match perfectly.
(C) The playback equipment tended to break down.
(D) The audio equipment played music and voices individually.

Paragraph 3 is marked with an arrow [➡].

6 Look at the four squares [■] that indicate where the following sentence could be added to the passage.

They timed their motions to start the film rolling as the needle was dropped on the record.

Where would the sentence best fit?

Click on a square [■] to add the sentence to the passage.

7 According to the passage, the main way the Vitaphone improved over the Kinetophone was

(A) the use of electronic devices for amplifying sound
(B) the time at which the movie was released to the public
(C) the amount of people who could watch the movie at one time
(D) the number of operators that were required for playback

8 According to the passage, what can be inferred about *The Jazz Singer*?

(A) Its sound was made by playing a recording.
(B) It was the first film Al Jolson appeared in.
(C) Its initial release to cinemas was delayed.
(D) It remained unknown until its overseas debut.

9 Look at the four squares [■] that indicate where the following sentence could be added to the passage.

For these reasons, the Vitaphone did not maintain its dominance of the industry for long as a newer technology, sound on film, quickly usurped it.

Where would the sentence best fit?

> Click on a square [■] to add the sentence to the passage.

10 Directions: An introductory sentence for a brief summary of the passage is provided below. Complete the summary by selecting the THREE answer choices that express the most important ideas in the passage. Some sentences do not belong in the summary because they express ideas that are not presented in the passage or are minor ideas in the passage. **This question is worth 2 points.**

> Drag your answer choices to the spaces where they belong. To remove an answer choice, click on it. To review the passage, click on **View Text**.

The development of sound film took place over a series of stages.

- ●
- ●
- ●

Answer Choices

(A) Live musicians made it possible to convey the plot of film to audiences of hundreds of spectators.

(B) The attempt for synchronizing sound and picture was of help toward the advancement of sound film.

(C) *The Jazz Singer* was the first movie to include dialogue between actors.

(D) Monotone loudspeakers and electronic condenser microphones were introduced to improve sound.

(E) Thomas Edison's design of the Kinetoscope was well received by theater owners.

(F) Early reproduction of sound in film was based on the phonograph and the Kinetoscope.

정답 및 해석 p.476

CH 01
CH 02
CH 03
CH 04
CH 05
CH 06
CH 07
CH 08
CH 09
Hackers TOEFL Reading

1 ■¹For millennia, people have observed the flight of birds and made attempts at mimicking their graceful voyage through the sky. ■ The question of how something heavier than the atmosphere could become airborne was an ostensibly insurmountable problem for these early designers. ■

2 Amazingly, it was not until the 19ᵗʰ century that the kite, a seemingly weighty object, would provide an answer to the advancement of aerodynamics. ■ The key to its flight lies in its ability to counteract gravity by managing air flow as wind pushes against the kite's flat undersurface and causes it to elevate. The pressure keeps the body aloft and is similar to that which allows birds to maintain height while soaring or hovering.

3 ➡ Based on those observations, a milestone in aviation was finally achieved in 1853, when the first successful manned flight took place in Yorkshire, England. The vessel was a glider, essentially modeled after the kite, but large enough to be fitted with cargo. Designed by British innovator, George Cayley, it was a rudderless fixed-wing aircraft with curved wings and a dihedral space for the pilot, based on the anatomy of herons that Cayley had shot down during his many hunting expeditions. During initial flights, it was pulled swiftly downhill by six workers using a rope until it caught the wind and raised up about 100 feet, flying a short distance before crashing into the field. This simple test paved the way for a watershed of subsequent research into the ability to control direction and maintain altitude.

4 The advance of directional control, allowing the pilot to better bridle the machines, would stem from a scientific inquiry into the principles of efficient aerodynamics. ■⁶Although mathematical work had been done to determine the important engineering formulas required for flight, two aviation pioneers, Orville and Wilbur Wright, began to doubt the accuracy of this data after a series of disappointing flight trials and recognized the need for control of the aircraft once aloft. ■ Consequently, they began a chain of meticulous experiments using a closed rectangular box fitted with a fan at one end, — an air tunnel to simulate pressure upon an assortment of surfaces — and model planes to establish accurate formulas for flight. ■ This caused one wing to rise and the other to fall much like modern ailerons and allowed for control over the plane's roll. ■ A later improvement, the rudder, gave the pilot additional control over the lateral movement of the craft.

5 Now that initial lift and navigation were achieved, what remained was to power the craft to provide the adequate amount of air pressure in less than optimal wind conditions and sustain momentum. The first effort came using steam engines, but despite many attempts, mastering full-scale versions proved impossible because the tremendous weight of the machinery prohibited its ability to lift off the ground. The solution came from the new lighter-weight, internal-combustion engine, which had recently been developed in the extended use of the emerging automobile industry. On December 17, 1903, the application of this gasoline powered motor contributed to the first self-propelled, manned, and piloted air flight, lasting 12 seconds and traveling at a pace of approximately 30 miles

per hour (50 kilometers per hour).

6   Although the efficiency of the combustion engine models would exponentially increase in the next fifty years, the capability of this generation of planes could not compare with modern jets. ■[9]Until the first flight of a jet powered aircraft in 1939, airplane motors spun propellers mounted on the front of the plane, pushing through a large amount of air at a relatively slow rate. ■ Engines in the jet powered aircraft, on the other hand, are placed on the wings or on the rear of an airplane and accelerate the air that is sucked into the motor by passing it through a series of circular blades that turn at an increasing rate. ■ This innovation has allowed for over a 2,000 percent increase in airspeed and the modern, efficient mode of transportation that is readily available today. ■

1   Look at the four squares [■] that indicate where the following sentence could be added to the passage.

While some have harnessed artificial wings composed of feathers, others have devised complex machinery, such as Da Vinci's ornithopter, all to no avail.

Where would the sentence best fit?

Click on a square [■] to add the sentence to the passage.

2   The word "mimicking" in the passage is closest in meaning to

(A) exploiting
(B) documenting
(C) incorporating
(D) imitating

3   The word "that" in the passage refers to

(A) wind
(B) kite
(C) pressure
(D) body

CH 01
CH 02
CH 03
CH 04
CH 05
CH 06
CH 07
CH 08
CH 09
Hackers TOEFL Reading

4 According to paragraph 3, which of the following can be inferred about the pilot of the glider?

(A) He needed to start outside the craft to help it attain speed promptly.
(B) He aided the Wright Brothers to design their own airplanes.
(C) He refused to fly far because of a possible clash into the field.
(D) He was not able to steer toward the direction he wanted to fly.

Paragraph 3 is marked with an arrow [➡].

5 The author mentions "the anatomy of herons" in the passage in order to

(A) explain how dihedrals affect flight performance
(B) show where Cayley got his inspiration from
(C) contrast an animal's flight with a glider's
(D) demonstrate that Cayley was a skilled hunter

6 Look at the four squares [■] that indicate where the following sentence could be added to the passage.

After acquiring new data from the experiments, they developed a method to warp the wings of the craft.

Where would the sentence best fit?

Click on a square [■] to add the sentence to the passage.

7 The passage states that the gasoline powered engines were more effective than steam engines because

(A) they were smaller
(B) they weighed less
(C) they didn't need water
(D) they cost less

8 According to the passage, jet powered aircrafts differ from other crafts in

(A) the moment of the wind resistance
(B) the position of the propulsion systems
(C) the need of air to give positive lift
(D) the ability to control the flying speed

9 Look at the four squares [■] that indicate where the following sentence could be added to the passage.

Before exiting, the air is raised to an incredible speed, at which point fuel is added directly to it and ignited, thus moving a smaller amount of air, but an explosively faster rate.

Where would the sentence best fit?

Click on a square [■] to add the sentence to the passage.

10 Directions: An introductory sentence for a brief summary of the passage is provided below. Complete the summary by selecting the THREE answer choices that express the most important ideas in the passage. Some sentences do not belong in the summary because they express ideas that are not presented in the passage or are minor ideas in the passage. **This question is worth 2 points.**

Drag your answer choices to the spaces where they belong. To remove an answer choice, click on it. To review the passage, click on **View Text**.

The evolution of the manned flight progressed rapidly once the basic principles of aerodynamics were discovered.

-
-
-

Answer Choices

(A) The ailerons in modern planes allow pilots to control the lateral roll.

(B) The Wright Brothers introduced mechanisms for controlling the craft in the air.

(C) A kite could stay aloft by reducing the weight of the materials to make it lighter than air.

(D) The first plane was a glider that didn't have any propulsion or steering devices.

(E) Planes were outfitted with engines that provided power in conditions with little or no wind.

(F) The steam engine was consistently considered viable despite weight constraints.

정답 및 해석 p.478

CH 01
CH 02
CH 03
CH 04
CH 05
CH 06
CH 07
CH 08
CH 09

Hackers TOEFL Reading

1 ➡ Caves are natural cavities, which occur in the Earth's topography, and feature rich geographical formations. Also called caverns, they develop in various rock types and are the end result of several different processes, including glacial recession, volcanic activity, or water abrasion. The most common type of formation, a product of mild chemical reactions, is a solution cave system, which contributes to karst terrain, a combination of geological phenomena generally characterized by rugged landscape, exposed ledges, chaotic surface drainage, and sinkholes.

2 The birth of a solution cave begins with rainwater, which absorbs CO_2 as it falls through the atmosphere, making it more acidic. Upon reaching the ground, the water acidifies further through organic reactions as it percolates through the mantle. This process forms a weak form of carbonic acid (H_2CO_3), capable of dissolving limestone anywhere the water comes in contact with it. But because the limestone is impermeable, water cannot settle within the rock, and it is forced to make its way toward the water table by pushing through tiny fractures. Erosion occurs when the acidic chemicals in the rainwater react with the slightly basic calcium carbonate, mostly in the form of mineral calcite, held in the limestone. ■[2]This kind of erosion is a form of chemical weathering known as *dissolution*. ■ Eventually, the fissures open wider and wider, allowing more water to enter and additional dissolving to occur. ■ This initial phase of opening up minute passageways may take thousands or even millions of years and is largely dependent upon climate and soil acidity. ■

3 If suitable conditions persist, certain water channels will enter a phase of enlargement, whereby expansion is considerably more rapid. ■[4]Scientists consider the critical stage to be around half a centimeter, as that is the approximate diameter at which capacity and turbulence combine to drastically increase the rate of erosion. ■ The largest conduit will draw in much of the available water and begin to exponentially outpace smaller conduits. ■ Often the pathway will become completely filled with water, and depending on local geography, a circular or elliptical passage will develop wherein the floor, walls, and ceiling deteriorate uniformly. ■

4 ➡ Further development of the cave is governed by the water table. ■[6]When the water table completely saturates the cave and flows at high volume over long periods, extensive cave networks can develop because the constant flow of water will continuously erode the inner surfaces of the cave. ■ Therefore, the largest caves are formed along the water table, and an extraordinary example is Mammoth Cave in southern Kentucky, which has been surveyed at over 500 kilometers in length, making it the longest spelunked cave tract on record. ■ But conditions are not always so stable as those under which Mammoth Cave formed. ■ A moderate drop in the water table level or ground subsidence may cause a cave to end up below the optimum level for dissolution. If the incoming water level recedes, the ceiling will be exposed to the air and no longer erode, but the walls and floor will continue to be altered by solution erosion, deepening the floor up to 30 to 50 meters and producing a canyon shape. Slowing or cessation of water movement in the

cave system typically results in small streams or stagnant pools.

5 Moreover, a severe drop in the water table or dramatic uplift from tectonic activity can completely deplete a cave of groundwater. ■[9]Such caves advance toward the stagnation phase, in which sculpting is significantly reduced. ■ However, rainwater continues to fall and makes its way downward, reacting with the limestone as it moves. ■ Dissolved in the water is calcite, a crystallized mineral similar to chalk, leached from the limestone. ■ Precipitation and deposition of calcite adds to rather than erodes the cave ceilings and floors. Gradually, as water droplets drip from the cave's upper surface, evaporation occurs, and traces of the mineral are left behind. These mineral deposits form cone-like structures, called stalactites, which hang from the roof of caves. At the same time, the water droplets that slide from the end of the stalactites onto the floor below form similar structures, called stalagmites. If a stalactite-stalagmite set becomes large enough, it can join in the middle to produce columns. Stalactites and stalagmites in mass create spectacular aesthetic displays for spelunkers.

1 According to paragraph 1, which of the following is NOT mentioned as a contributor to cave formation?

(A) receding glaciers
(B) active volcanoes
(C) aqueous wearing
(D) crustal uplifting

Paragraph 1 is marked with an arrow [➡].

2 Look at the four squares [■] that indicate where the following sentence could be added to the passage.

For instance, wet climates with acidic soils produce conduits faster than arid regions with alkaline soils.

Where would the sentence best fit?

Click on a square [■] to add the sentence to the passage.

3 The word "uniformly" in the passage is closest in meaning to

(A) sharply
(B) evenly
(C) noticeably
(D) intermittently

CH 01
CH 02
CH 03
CH 04
CH 05
CH 06
CH 07
CH 08
CH 09

Hackers TOEFL Reading

4 Look at the four squares [■] that indicate where the following sentence could be added to the passage.

Eventually, the dominant passage may expand to the extent that it swallows up all the smaller ones adjacent to it.

Where would the sentence best fit?

Click on a square [■] to add the sentence to the passage.

5 Why does the author mention "Mammoth Cave" in paragraph 4?
  (A) To illustrate the link between cave formation location and size
  (B) To counter a claim about the important role of the water table
  (C) To provide further explanation of the glacial recession process
  (D) To discredit a possible reason for the expansion of cave networks

Paragraph 4 is marked with an arrow [➡].

6 Look at the four squares [■] that indicate where the following sentence could be added to the passage.

Its impressive size has inspired a national park to share the same name and attracts 2 million visitors per year.

Where would the sentence best fit?

Click on a square [■] to add the sentence to the passage.

7 Which of the sentences below best expresses the essential information in the highlighted sentence in the passage? *Incorrect* choices change the meaning in important ways or leave out essential information.

  (A) If air is introduced into the cave, it will force the water out, allowing the size of the space to grow significantly.

  (B) The rate of the solution erosion will become faster if the water level goes down and the air comes in.

  (C) When the water level drops, the erosion of the walls and floor keeps proceeding, but not the ceiling.

  (D) As the water recedes, it brings in air that is responsible for the continued erosion of the floor and walls.

8 The word "deplete" in the passage is closest in meaning to

  (A) replenish
  (B) exhaust
  (C) bypass
  (D) shrink

9 Look at the four squares [■] that indicate where the following sentence could be added to the passage.

This stage effectively marks the death of the cave in terms of its expansion.

Where would the sentence best fit?

Click on a square [■] to add the sentence to the passage.

10 **Directions**: An introductory sentence for a brief summary of the passage is provided below. Complete the summary by selecting the THREE answer choices that express the most important ideas in the passage. Some sentences do not belong in the summary because they express ideas that are not presented in the passage or are minor ideas in the passage. **This question is worth 2 points.**

Drag your answer choices to the spaces where they belong. To remove an answer choice, click on it. To review the passage, click on **View Text**.

Solution caves display a series of distinct stages of development.

- ●
- ●
- ●

Answer Choices

(A) Rainwater aids in cavern formation by collecting in the Earth's crust and compressing the underlying limestone and bedrock.

(B) The formation of solution caves is initiated as water acidifies and reacts with limestone, dissolving the rock and exploiting small fissures.

(C) When conditions are appropriate, some passageways pass through a crucial juncture that culminates in their rapid expansion.

(D) The final stage of a cave's life occurs when dissolution erodes the cave walls so extensively that the roof of the cave collapses under its own weight.

(E) Fluctuations in water or ground levels can cause dissolution to slow or cease altogether, ultimately leading to the stagnation phase of cave development.

(F) Evaporation of any remaining water droplets results in mineral deposits which can create cone-like formations on the cave's roof.

정답 및 해석 p.480

CH 01
CH 02
CH 03
CH 04
CH 05
CH 06
CH 07
CH 08
CH 09
Hackers TOEFL Reading

토플 빈출어휘 정리 노트

Chapter 07에 수록된 어휘들을 빈출도 순으로 정리했습니다. 음성파일을 들으며 꼭 암기하세요.

토플 최빈출어휘 [★★★]

- [ ] formation [fɔːrméiʃən] 형성 (=composition)
- [ ] complex [kəmpléks] 복잡한 (=sophisticated)
- [ ] industrial [indʌ́striəl] 산업의
- [ ] rely on 의존하다 (=depend on)
- [ ] periodically [pìəriádikəli] 주기적으로 (=regularly)
- [ ] sustain [səstéin] 유지하다 (=uphold)
- [ ] critical [krítikəl] 중요한 (=crucial)
- [ ] nutrition [nutríʃən] 영양
- [ ] revenue [révənuː] 수익
- [ ] prompt [prɑmpt] 유발하다 (=provoke)
- [ ] temporary [témpərəri] 임시의
- [ ] lavish [lǽviʃ] 호화스러운 (=deluxe)
- [ ] deposit [dipázit] 알을 낳다 (=lay)
- [ ] stimulate [stímjulèit] 촉진하다 (=promote)
- [ ] domesticate [dəméstikèit] 길들이다 (=tame)
- [ ] settlement [sétlmənt] 정착지
- [ ] obvious [ábviəs] 분명한 (=evident)
- [ ] inevitably [inévətəbli] 필연적으로 (=unavoidably)
- [ ] harsh [hɑːrʃ] 혹독한
- [ ] isolate [áisəlèit] 고립시키다 (=insulate)
- [ ] diversity [divə́ːrsəti] 다양성 (=variety)
- [ ] excessive [iksésiv] 과도한 (=undue)
- [ ] enact [inǽkt] 제정하다
- [ ] protect [prətékt] 보호하다 (=defend)
- [ ] pioneer [pàiəníər] 초기의
- [ ] grant [grænt] 부여하다 (=bestow)
- [ ] spectacular [spektǽkjulər] 호화로운 (=magnificent)
- [ ] integrate [íntəgrèit] 통합하다 (=unify)
- [ ] urge [əːrdʒ] 충동 (=impulse)
- [ ] compel [kəmpél] 강요하다 (=force)
- [ ] arduous [ɑ́ːrdʒuəs] 고된 (=difficult)
- [ ] impediment [impédəmənt] 장애물 (=obstacle)
- [ ] rigor [rígər] 고초
- [ ] elaborate [ilǽbərət] 정교한 (=complex)

- [ ] ratio [réiʃou] 비율 (=proportion)
- [ ] implementation [ìmpləməntéiʃən] 실행
- [ ] conceive [kənsíːv] 고안하다 (=imagine)
- [ ] mimic [mímik] 흉내내다 (=imitate)
- [ ] milestone [máilstòun] 획기적인 사건 (=important event)
- [ ] meticulous [mətíkjuləs] 정밀한 (=detailed)
- [ ] optimal [áptəməl] 최적의 (=best)
- [ ] accelerate [æksélərèit] 가속시키다
- [ ] impermeable [impə́ːrmiəbl] 불침투성의 (=impenetrable)
- [ ] uniformly [júːnəfɔ̀ːrmli] 균일하게 (=evenly)
- [ ] deplete [diplíːt] 고갈시키다 (=exhaust)

토플 빈출어휘 [★★]

- [ ] transfer [trǽnsfər] 전이
- [ ] contribute to 기여하다
- [ ] restore [ristɔ́ːr] 회복하다 (=recover)
- [ ] occasional [əkéiʒənl] 가끔의
- [ ] exclusively [iksklúːsivli] 오직
- [ ] enclose [inklóus] 둘러싸다
- [ ] dissociate [disóuʃièit] 분리하다
- [ ] break up 분해하다 (=fragment)
- [ ] completely [kəmplíːtli] 완벽하게 (=thoroughly)
- [ ] decompose [dìːkəmpóuz] 분해시키다
- [ ] produce [prədjúːs] 생성하다 (=release)
- [ ] primarily [praimérəli] 주로 (=preeminently)
- [ ] motivation [mòutəvéiʃən] 동기
- [ ] expect [ikspékt] 예상하다 (=anticipate)
- [ ] elevation [èlivéiʃən] 고도
- [ ] revered [rivíərd] 존경받는
- [ ] change [tʃeindʒ] 변화 (=shift)
- [ ] complement [kámpləmənt] 보완
- [ ] reverse [rivə́ːrs] 역전시키다
- [ ] available [əvéiləbl] 쓰일 수 있는 (=accessible)
- [ ] accomplish [əkámpliʃ] 이루다 (=achieve)
- [ ] opaque [oupéik] 불투명한

*해커스 동영상강의 포털 해커스인강(HackersIngang.com)에서 '토플 빈출어휘 정리 노트' 음성파일을 무료로 다운로드할 수 있습니다.

☐ wispy [wíspi] 성긴 (=thin)

☐ launch [lɔːntʃ] 발사하다

☐ cessation [seséiʃən] 중단

☐ custom [kʌ́stəm] 관습

☐ divine [diváin] 신성한

☐ urban [ə́ːrbən] 도시의

☐ various [véəriəs] 다양한 (=assorted)

☐ coarse [kɔːrs] 거친

☐ step in 개입하다

☐ illustrate [íləstreit] 나타내다

☐ ordered [ɔ́ːrdərd] 질서정연한

☐ inhospitable [inháspitəbl] 척박한

☐ exacting [igzǽktiŋ] 고된

☐ withstand [wiðstǽnd] 견디다

☐ taxing [tǽksiŋ] 고생스러운

☐ crave [kreiv] 갈망하다

☐ accommodate [əkámədèit] 충족시키다

☐ ostensibly [asténsəbli] 표면적으로

☐ counteract [kàuntərǽkt] 거스르다

☐ soar [sɔːr] 날아오르다

☐ stem [stem] 유래하다

☐ topography [təpágrəfi] 지형

☐ deposition [dèpəzíʃən] 퇴적(물)

토플 기출어휘 [★]

☐ atmosphere [ǽtməsfir] 대기

☐ adaptation [ædæptéiʃən] 적응

☐ hibernate [háibərnèit] 동면하다

☐ physiological [fiziəládʒikəl] 생리적인

☐ deficiency [difíʃnsi] 결핍

☐ shed [ʃed] 벗다

☐ molecule [má:ləkju:l] 분자

☐ dilute [dailúːt] 묽은

☐ still [stil] 가만히 있는 (=motionless)

☐ carnivore [ká:rnivɔːr] 육식 동물

☐ nocturnal [nɑktə́:rnl] 야행성의

☐ magnetism [mǽgnətizm] 자성

☐ predictably [pridíktəbli] 예상대로

☐ measurement [méʒərmənt] 측정

☐ overturn [òuvərtə́:rn] 뒤집다

☐ astronomer [əstrá:nəmər] 천문학자

☐ spiritual [spíritʃuəl] 종교적인

☐ conceal [kənsíːl] 감추다

☐ latitude [lǽtitu:d] 위도

☐ orbit [ɔ́:rbit] 궤도

☐ texture [tékstʃər] 조직

☐ mistreat [mìstríːt] 학대하다

☐ conservation [kànsərvéiʃən] 보호

☐ showy [ʃoui] 화려한

☐ landmark [lǽndmà:rk] 기념비적인

☐ legislation [lèdʒisléiʃən] 법률 제정

☐ large-scale [lá:rdʒskèil] 대규모의

☐ toxic [táksik] 유독한

☐ clamor [klǽmər] 소란

☐ spectator [spékteitər] 구경꾼

☐ fidelity [fidéləti] 충실도

☐ airborne [έərbɔ̀:rn] 하늘을 나는

☐ insurmountable [ìnsərmáuntəbl] 해결할 수 없는

☐ weighty [wéiti] 무거운

☐ aloft [əlɔ́:ft] 공중에

☐ aviation [èiviéiʃən] 항공

☐ lateral [lǽtərəl] 측면의

☐ a series of 일련의

☐ abrasion [əbréiʒən] 침식

☐ rugged [rʌ́gid] 울퉁불퉁한

☐ acidic [əsídik] 산성인

☐ percolate [pə́:rkəlèit] 침투하다

☐ weathering [wéðəriŋ] 풍화작용

☐ spelunk [spilʌ́ŋk] (동굴을) 탐험하다

☐ subsidence [səbsáidns] 하강

CH 01
CH 02
CH 03
CH 04
CH 05
CH 06
CH 07
CH 08
CH 09

Hackers TOEFL Reading

Chapter 08
Summary

OVERVIEW

Summary 문제는 보기 중에서 지문의 주요한 내용을 언급하고 있는 것을 골라 지문 요약을 완성시키는 유형이다. 여기서 Summary(요약)란 글의 중심 내용을 추려내어 간략히 표현하는 것을 말한다. 따라서 Summary 문제를 제대로 풀기 위해서는 글을 읽으면서 글의 전체적인 주제 및 단락별 핵심 포인트를 파악하고, major idea와 minor idea를 구별하는 연습이 필요하다.

Summary 문제는 대개 각 지문의 마지막 문제로 출제된다. 간혹 Summary 문제가 출제되지 않는 지문에는 뒷장에서 다룰 Category Chart 문제가 출제된다.

TYPES OF QUESTIONS

4지선다의 질문 형태와는 달리, directions와 introductory sentence가 주어지고 그 아래에 지문 요약을 위한 요약표와 6개의 보기가 제시된다. 6개의 보기 중, 요약을 완성시키기에 적절한 3개를 클릭하여 요약표에 넣어야 한다. 2점 만점이며 부분 점수가 있다. (3개 – 2점, 2개 – 1점, 0~1개 – 0점)

Summary 문제의 전형적인 질문 유형은 아래와 같다.

Directions: An introductory sentence for a brief summary of the passage is provided below. Complete the summary by selecting the THREE answer choices that express the most important ideas in the passage. Some sentences do not belong in the summary because they express ideas that are not presented in the passage or are minor ideas in the passage. **This question is worth 2 points.**

Drag your answer choices to the spaces where they belong. To remove an answer choice, click on it. To review the passage, click on **View Text**.

(Introductory sentence)
-
-
-

(Answer Choices)

HACKERS **STRATEGY**

CH 01
CH 02
CH 03
CH 04
CH 05
CH 06
CH 07
CH 08
CH 09

Hackers TOEFL Reading

전략 1 Introductory sentence를 읽고 요약문의 main idea를 파악한다.

대개 Introductory sentence는 완성될 요약문의 topic sentence로서, 앞으로 서술할 내용을 대략적으로 소개하는 역할을 한다. 따라서 Introductory sentence를 통해 main idea를 파악하면, 보기가 main idea 와 부합하는지를 살펴본 후 정답이 아닐 가능성이 높은 보기들을 어느 정도 가려낼 수 있다.

Ex Plants are classified into three main groups on the basis of how photoperiodism affects their flowering. Short-day plants flower when the night length is equal to or greater than critical day length. This critical day length varies considerably from one plant species to another but falls between 12 and 14 hours for many. The initiation of flowering in short-day plants is due not to the short period of daylight but to the long, uninterrupted period of darkness. Examples of short-day plants are ragweed, and poinsettia, whose flowers appear late summer or fall.

Plants which bloom when the night time is equal to or shorter than critical day length are called long-day plants. These plants can detect the shortening nights of late spring and early summer, and their flowers emerge at that time.

Some plants, called day-neutral plants, initiate flowering not in response to seasonal changes in the amounts of daylight and darkness but responding to some other type of stimulus, external or internal. Many of these plants originated in the tropics, where day length does not vary appreciably during the year.

Flowering in response to photoperiodism varies from plant to plant.
-
-
-

Answer Choices

(A) Short-day plants bear flowers when the night length is equal to or exceeds critical day length.

(B) Critical day length generally lasts between 12 and 14 hours.

(C) Ragweed and poinsettia fall under the category of short-day plants.

(D) There are more species of long-day plants than there are of short-day plants.

(E) Long-day plants blossom while the night length is less than or equal to critical day length.

(F) Day-neutral plants develop flowers according to external or internal stimulus.

➡ Introductory sentence를 통해 요약문의 main idea는 '광주성에 따라 식물의 개화기가 다르다'이고, 앞으로 식물별 개화기가 어떻게 다른지 그 양상이 서술될 것임을 예상할 수 있다. 보기 (B)는 개화기에 대한 이해를 돕는 부가 정보인 임계일장에 대한 내용이지만, 식물별 개화기가 어떻게 다른지는 설명하지 않으므로 정답이 아닐 가능성이 높다. 보기 (C)와 (D)는 개화기에 대한 언급 없이 단순히 단일 식물의 예를 들거나, 장일 식물과 단일 식물의 종의 개수에 대해서만 말하고 있으므로 정답이 아닐 가능성이 높다.

해석 p.482

단락별 핵심 포인트를 보기와 비교 확인한 후 답을 선택한다.

Summary 문제의 정답은 보통 한 단락의 핵심 포인트일 가능성이 높은데, 간혹 두 개 이상 단락의 핵심 포인트를 포함하는 경우도 있다. 여기서 핵심 포인트란, 지문 내용의 이해를 돕기 위한 예시 및 부가 설명 등을 제외한 주요 내용이다. 따라서 지문을 읽을 때 각 단락의 핵심 포인트가 무엇인지를 생각하며 읽고 단락별로 이를 간단히 Note-taking해두면, Note-taking한 내용을 보기와 비교하며 답을 고를 수 있다.

간혹 답인지 확신할 수 없는 보기의 경우, 보기의 keyword가 지문의 어느 부분에 언급된 것인지 scanning을 통해 지문에서 다시 찾아 내용을 확인한 후 답을 선택한다.

Note-taking

- P1-1. plants – 3 grps., photoperiodism → flowering

- P1-2. short-day plant – night length ≧ critical length

- P2. long-day plant – night time ≦ critical length

- P3. day-neutral plant – responding to other stimulus

➡ 지문의 1단락에서는 광주성이 개화기에 영향을 미치는 양상에 따라 식물을 세 가지 부류로 나눌 수 있다고 언급한다. 그리고 그 첫 번째 부류인 단일 식물은 밤이 임계일장과 동일하거나 더 길 때 꽃을 피운다는 설명이 나온다. 2단락에서는 두 번째 부류인 장일 식물이 밤이 임계일장과 동일하거나 더 짧을 때 꽃을 피운다는 내용이 언급된다. 3단락에서는 세 번째 부류인 중일 식물이 밤의 길이가 아닌 다른 자극에 의해 꽃을 피운다는 내용이 나온다.

Answer Choices

(A) Short-day plants bear flowers when the night length is equal to or exceeds critical day length.

(B) Critical day length generally lasts between 12 and 14 hours.

(C) Ragweed and poinsettia fall under the category of short-day plants.

(D) There are more species of long-day plants than there are of short-day plants.

(E) Long-day plants blossom while the night length is less than or equal to critical day length.

(F) Day-neutral plants develop flowers according to external or internal stimulus.

➡ 보기 (A)는 Note-taking의 P1-2와 일치하며, Note-taking을 통해 단일 식물이 1단락에 언급됨을 알 수 있다.
보기 (E)는 Note-taking의 P2와 일치하며, Note-taking을 통해 장일 식물이 2단락에 언급됨을 알 수 있다.
보기 (F)는 Note-taking의 P3과 일치하며, Note-taking을 통해 중일 식물이 3단락에 언급됨을 알 수 있다.

보기 중 오답을 확인한다.

Minor idea를 나타내거나 지문에 전혀 언급되지 않은 보기는 오답으로 간주된다.

Flowering in response to photoperiodism varies from plant to plant.

(A) Short-day plants bear flowers when the night length is equal to or exceeds critical day length.

(E) Long-day plants blossom while the night length is less than or equal to critical day length.

(F) Day-neutral plants develop flowers according to external or internal stimulus.

Answer Choices

(B) Critical day length generally lasts between 12 and 14 hours.

(C) Ragweed and poinsettia fall under the category of short-day plants.

(D) There are more species of long-day plants than there are of short-day plants.

Minor idea를 나타낸 오답

(B) Critical day length generally lasts between 12 and 14 hours.
임계일장의 지속 시간에 대해 말하고 있는 문장으로 minor idea를 나타내므로 오답이다.

(C) Ragweed and poinsettia fall under the category of short-day plants.
단일 식물의 예를 들고 있는 문장으로 minor idea를 나타내므로 오답이다.

지문에 언급되지 않은 오답

(D) There are more species of long-day plants than there are of short-day plants.
장일 식물과 단일 식물의 종의 개수에 대한 내용은 지문에 전혀 언급되지 않았으므로 오답이다.

During the 1850s the issue of slavery caused divisions within the existing Whig and Democratic parties, bringing about the need for a third political party. Emerging in the face of political turmoil, this new party was formed to represent the interests of the North and abolitionists. A founder named Alvan Bovay decided to call the party "Republican" because it was a simple, yet historically significant name associated with equality.

The founders of the Republican Party were committed to the rights of individual states and a limited role for national government. The first stirrings of a Republican Party began in February of 1854, when defectors from the Whig party gathered secretly to discuss the creation of a new party. Anti-slavery forces then rallied together and adopted resolutions opposing the controversial Kansas-Nebraska Act, which allowed territories to determine whether slavery would be legalized by popular sovereignty, at the first public meeting in Wisconsin. In a second meeting, a small group of local citizens dissolved their political committees and chose five men to serve as the committee of the new party.

As word spread, the party formally organized itself by holding its first convention, adopting a national platform, and nominating candidates for state offices. Tensions mounted over the issue of slavery as a concerted effort was made to counter the Democrats' plan to extend slavery to new territories joining the Union. The number of anti-slavery Republicans who ran and were elected for office increased, further galvanizing the two sides. At the national convention of 1856 in Philadelphia, the party nominated John C. Freemont as president and "Free Soil, Free Labor, Free Speech, Free Men, Freemont!" became the slogan of the Republican Party. Although losing to the Democrats, Freemont managed to capture a third of the vote despite running as a third-party, boosting optimism for the 1860 elections.

Abraham Lincoln, a respected state politician from Illinois, became the first Republican to win the White House in 1860. Lincoln defeated three other candidates despite not winning a single electoral vote from any Southern states. The election of Lincoln ended sixty years of political dominance by the Democrats and barely a month following his victory, Southern states began to secede from the Union. The Civil War erupted soon thereafter and Lincoln was challenged with preserving the Union. Amid the Civil War, against the advice of his cabinet, Lincoln signed the Emancipation Proclamation that freed the slaves. He, along with the Republican Congress, worked to pass the Thirteenth and Fourteenth amendments, which outlawed slavery and guaranteed equal protection under the law. During the Reconstruction Era, Republicans were helped by the Democrats' connection with the South and ran virtually unopposed for several years.

The Republican Party evolved in the mid-nineteenth century from the existing political parties.

-
-
-

해석 p.482

CH 01
CH 02
CH 03
CH 04
CH 05
CH 06
CH 07
CH 08
CH 09

Hackers TOEFL Reading

Answer Choices

(A) Republicans were instrumental in elevating the women's status in the society.

(B) Republicans and Democrats were at odds over the issue of slavery in new territories.

(C) After a previous defeat, the party was successful when Abraham Lincoln was elected to be the first Republican president in office.

(D) Lincoln went to great length to avoid the Civil War and keep his vested interest.

(E) Whig party defectors alienated themselves from their party by holding secret meetings.

(F) The Republican Party was committed to states' rights and united in preventing the spread of slavery.

| 전략 1 적용 | Introductory sentence를 통해 요약문의 main idea는 '공화당의 등장'임을 알 수 있다. 그런데 보기 (E)는 공화당의 등장과 직접적인 관련이 없는 휘그당에 대한 내용이므로 정답이 아닐 가능성이 높다. |

| 전략 2 적용 | 단락별 핵심 포인트를 Note-taking하여 보기와 대조하면 보기 (B)는 Note-taking의 P3과 일치, 보기 (C)는 Note-taking의 P4와 일치, 보기 (F)는 Note-taking의 P2와 일치한다. |

Note-taking

P1. new party – Republican, interests of North & abolitionists

P2. Republican party – individual states > national gov't
  – anti-slavery forces

P3. party formally organized – tensions over slavery issue
  w/ Democrats

P4. Abraham Lincoln – 1st Republican president

| 전략 3 적용 | (A) 여성의 지위에 관해서는 지문에 전혀 언급되지 않았으므로 오답이다.
(D) Lincoln이 남북전쟁을 막고 기득권을 지키기 위해 노력했다는 내용은 지문에 언급되지 않았으므로 오답이다.
(E) 휘그당 탈당자들이 비밀 회합을 열었다는 것은 minor idea를 나타내므로 오답이다. |

| 정답 | (B), (C), (F) |

Read each passage and choose the main idea for each.

1   From approximately 1050 to 700 BC, Greek ceramics were characterized by the use of geometric shapes and highly stylized representations of plants and animals as decorative elements. This changed, however, when artists in Athens adopted a new technique known as black-figure pottery. Before a ceramic vessel was put into the kiln, silhouettes of human figures were added to its surface using a black pigment composed of potash and iron-rich clay. Then, an artist would employ a sharp implement to carve fine lines into the pigment. A |virtue| of this technique was that lifelike images of people could be created. Accurate portrayals of the human form came to be an important theme in Greek pottery, and later styles incorporated and improved on the methods employed in black-figure pottery.

(A) Early Greek artists decorated ceramic vessels with a wide assortment of designs.

(B) Vessels with depictions of the human form were used in religious ceremonies.

(C) Black-figure pottery marked a significant transition in the development of Greek ceramics.

(D) The black-figure technique was employed by artists living in regions other than Greece.

2   In 1997, astronomers detected several intergalactic stars located in otherwise empty regions of space. Until this discovery, it had been believed that stars existed only within galaxies. As all stars originate in galaxies, there has been a great deal of speculation about what causes intergalactic stars to take up their solitary positions. One theory is that a collision between two galaxies leads to a gravitational disturbance that |expels| an individual star. In this scenario, an intergalactic star would have likely belonged to a very small galaxy, as the gravitational pull of a large one would have prevented its escape. Another hypothesis is that intergalactic stars result from an interaction with a massive black hole, a region of space with an extremely powerful gravitational field. Proponents of this theory believe that intergalactic stars were once components of a binary star system — two stars that orbit each other. When one of the stars in the system passes too close to a black hole, it becomes trapped, causing the other to break out of orbit and begin moving away at a very high velocity. If this star reaches sufficient speed, it overcomes the gravitational force of the galaxy as a whole and moves out into intergalactic space.

(A) Various theories have been proposed to explain how a star moves out of its original galaxy.

(B) A galactic cluster includes an extremely large number of stars.

(C) A rare phenomenon leads to the destruction of binary star systems.

(D) An intergalactic star avoids the gravitational pull of a black hole.

VOCABULARY   The word [   ] in the passage is closest in meaning to

		(A)	(B)	(C)	(D)
1	virtue	(A) verse	(B) statue	(C) zone	(D) merit
2	expels	(A) chops	(B) explores	(C) spews	(D) flusters

3   Appearing in Pittsburgh in 1905 for the first time, nickelodeons were small, neighborhood movie theaters in which admission was obtained for a nickel, or five cents. Often located in converted storefronts of all kinds, the popularity of these affordable and entertaining venues was such that their numbers mushroomed to approximately 8,000 by 1908. Sparsely decorated, smoke-filled, dingy and dark, they would show "moving pictures" about 15 to 20 minutes long on a variety of subjects. They admitted nearly 200 people, all of whom sat on simple chairs and who could easily hear the accompanying music played on piano by a local girl, who would attempt to match the music to the tone of the particular scene. As urban populations grew, the number of nickelodeons declined by degrees because audiences increasingly preferred the comfortable and well-appointed surroundings of larger theaters with their first-run movies, better-quality musical accompaniments and well-dressed ushers.

(A) Nickelodeons could accommodate up to 200 people and had live music for the films.
(B) The name nickelodeon came from the cost of admission which was one nickel.
(C) Nickelodeons were famous for showing movies on a diversity of genres.
(D) Nickelodeons while popular at first eventually were supplanted by larger theaters.

4   The rapid territorial expansion of the United States in the 1800s encouraged a liberal land-grant policy that culminated in the Homestead Act of 1862. There were several requirements to fulfill for claiming the land. First, a would-be homesteader who was 21 years of age and the head of a household had to file an intention for claiming a public tract of land at the nearest Land Office. The office would then examine public records to verify that it did not have a previous claim. Second, the applicant would need to make a series of improvements to the land, such as building a dwelling on the property and cultivating the soil. After a five-year period of continual residence, it could be claimed without a fee. The act produced a new agricultural base for the new nation that today still largely supports the country's food supplies. Moreover, homesteading allowed over a million landless farmers and immigrants to attain property and the means of independent sustenance, thereby creating the basis of an unprecedented new middle class hitherto unseen in Western society. Before the act was fully repealed in 1986, over 270 million acres, or about 10 percent of all US lands, had been conferred to private individuals by the federal government. Clearly, this act played a substantial role in the shaping of the American landscape.

(A) The Homestead Act after it permitted many people to own land had a dramatic effect on America.
(B) In order to qualify for the Homestead Act, a person had to meet some requirements.
(C) The number of farms developed with the Homestead Act led to the increase in the agricultural base.
(D) The Homestead Act was created because America had acquired so much land.

VOCABULARY	The word ⬚ in the passage is closest in meaning to			
3	affordable	(A) modest	(B) exacting	(C) formidable	(D) accustomed
4	property	(A) vessel	(B) mutiny	(C) holding	(D) allusion
	conferred	(A) repulsed	(B) annexed	(C) rejoiced	(D) provided

5   The Industrial Revolution, which began in Great Britain at the end of the eighteenth century, had a significant impact on British society. It not only provided more options for consumers but also led to a decline in the quality of life of many people.

One of the benefits of the Industrial Revolution was that it greatly reduced the cost of many goods. Previously, items such as clothing, cooking implements, and furniture were created by craftspeople in small workshops, making them quite costly. However, the development of mass production methods flooded Great Britain with large quantities of inexpensive consumer goods. As a result, even people who were not wealthy could afford to furnish their entire home and clothe their family in store-bought merchandise.

Unfortunately, the factory system that made mass production possible had negative consequences for members of the working class. The rapid urbanization that occurred when large numbers of people relocated to industrial areas led to the creation of overcrowded and unsanitary slums. In these areas, pests such as rats bred quickly and water supplies became contaminated, resulting in the spread of disease. In addition, factory owners commonly required their employees to work twelve hours a day for very low wages. As employers had access to a large pool of unskilled labor, there was little motivation to offer greater compensation or to reduce working hours. Thus, for many people, the Industrial Revolution led to a life of poor health, toil, and poverty that was impossible to escape.

Topic sentence: The Industrial Revolution led to significant changes in Great Britain.

_____ (A) Workers had to cope with harsh living and working conditions.

_____ (B) Workshops employing craftspeople produced consumer goods.

_____ (C) Mass-produced items tended to be of a lower quality than handmade goods.

_____ (D) Factory owners were able to hire large numbers of unskilled laborers.

VOCABULARY   The word _____ in the passage is closest in meaning to

5	entire	(A) flimsy	(B) eerie	(C) whole	(D) lame
	bred	(A) negated	(B) multiplied	(C) corroded	(D) weakened
	escape	(A) swipe	(B) dispatch	(C) elucidate	(D) flee

6 Mercury is the only metallic chemical element that takes a liquid form at room temperature. It was once believed to have medicinal properties and was drunk in small quantities to increase longevity. Although it is now known to be highly toxic and therefore dangerous for human consumption, mercury still has a number of practical applications.

Mercury can be used to extract gold that is mixed with non-metallic substances. This is because mercury's atomic structure makes it a solvent of certain metals. Alluvial miners who search for gold in riverbeds add mercury to sand or silt. Any gold present dissolves into the mercury, forming a mixture that is called an amalgam. Later, this substance is heated until the mercury evaporates, leaving only the gold behind.

Mercury is also employed to create the massive telescopes used in observatories. These instruments have traditionally included large parabolic mirrors made of glass that redirect incoming light in a way that magnifies distant objects. The problem is that the glass mirrors are prohibitively expensive to produce. However, with a slight modification to the design of the telescope, mercury can serve as an inexpensive alternative because it is highly reflective in its liquid state. When a large pool of mercury is spun rapidly, it forms a smooth, curved surface that functions in a manner similar to the glass mirrors.

Topic sentence: The characteristics of mercury make it suitable for a variety of uses.

_____ (A) Some metals dissolve when they are mixed with mercury.

_____ (B) Consumption of mercury is hazardous to humans.

_____ (C) Liquid mercury reflects light very effectively.

_____ (D) Mercury will evaporate if it is exposed to sufficient heat.

CH 01
CH 02
CH 03
CH 04
CH 05
CH 06
CH 07
CH 08
CH 09

Hackers TOEFL Reading

VOCABULARY   The word [   ] in the passage is closest in meaning to

6	dangerous	(A) languid	(B) prodigious	(C) monotonous	(D) critical
	modification	(A) variation	(B) ratification	(C) convocation	(D) signification
	state	(A) sanitation	(B) condition	(C) scope	(D) tumult

7   In 1978, the US government launched the first of a network of satellites that would become the Global Positioning System (GPS), a navigation system that sends time and location data to devices equipped with a receiver. Since then, the US military has become increasingly dependent on this technology, leading to concerns about what would happen if GPS was unavailable during a crisis. To address this issue, the Department of Defense has developed a new navigation tool called the Timing and Inertial Measurement Unit (TIMU) that is intended to serve as an alternative to GPS.

TIMU is a miniscule device — about one third of the size of a penny — with seven key components. The first of these is an atomic clock, an instrument that keeps highly accurate time by measuring the frequency of the energy emitted by electrons — positively and negatively charged particles that orbit atoms. TIMU also includes three gyroscopes that are capable of detecting the orientation of the device and the direction of movement. Finally, TIMU has three accelerometers that calculate the rate of travel. By measuring time, direction, and speed, these instruments can track the movement of a person equipped with the device and, assuming the starting point has been identified, provide continuously updated location information without relying on data from satellites. This means that navigation assistance will be available to military units in the event that GPS has been temporarily disabled. An additional advantage of TIMU is that it can be used in environments that signals from GPS satellites cannot reach, such as under the surface of the ocean or in caves and tunnels.

Topic sentence: TIMU is a device developed by the US Department of Defense as an alternative to GPS.

_____ (A) Civilian devices capable of receiving GPS data have become increasingly common.

_____ (B) TIMU includes an atomic clock that relies on subatomic particles to measure time.

_____ (C) Movement from a known starting point is measured without the aid of a satellite.

_____ (D) Navigation in marine and subterranean environments is possible using TIMU.

VOCABULARY   The word ☐ in the passage is closest in meaning to

7	intended	(A) designed	(B) pasted	(C) intruded	(D) justified
	track	(A) trim	(B) traverse	(C) chase	(D) intercept
	temporarily	(A) ultimately	(B) transitorily	(C) magnificently	(D) initially

8   There is a widely held misconception that the hump of a camel is used to store a reserve of water that can be drawn upon when necessary. Although this animal does have a number of physical adaptations that allow it to go for long periods of time without drinking, the hump is not one of them. However, the hump has two important functions that should not be overlooked because they are necessary for the camel's survival in the harsh desert environment.

First of all, the camel's hump is composed primarily of fatty tissue. A mature camel has up to 36 kilograms of fat stored in its hump and is able to metabolize this material for energy when it is unable to locate food, a common situation in the desert. The longer the camel goes without eating, the smaller its hump will become. If the hump disappears completely, the camel is most likely on the brink of starvation and will die shortly unless it receives nourishment. Fortunately, a camel can replenish its hump very quickly once it has consumed sufficient food and has had an opportunity to rest.

Another benefit is that the hump allows the camel to cope more easily with the extreme temperatures of the desert. The hump has a couple of thermoregulatory functions that prevent the camel from overheating. To begin with, fat is an insulator that makes it difficult for heat to dissipate. As the bulk of a camel's fat is stored in the large mound on its back, the rest of its body has very little insulation, meaning that heat does not become trapped and is continuously being released into the air. Another way that the hump affects temperature is that its presence increases the surface area of the camel's body. Animals with a high surface area to volume ratio are able to radiate thermal energy more effectively, and, therefore, are less likely to overheat.

Topic sentence: The camel's hump has a number of important roles that enable it to survive in the desert.

_____ (A) The fat stored on the camel's back can be used for energy when food is scarce.

_____ (B) The camel is capable of going for extended period of time without water.

_____ (C) The camel is better able to regulate its body temperature because of its hump.

_____ (D) The tissue contained in the camel's hump is an efficient heat insulator.

| VOCABULARY | The word ☐ in the passage is closest in meaning to |

8	overlooked	(A) glimpsed	(B) abridged	(C) overshadowed	(D) neglected
	benefit	(A) smattering	(B) cache	(C) advantage	(D) deterrent
	difficult	(A) arduous	(B) confiding	(C) abstract	(D) objective

CH 01
CH 02
CH 03
CH 04
CH 05
CH 06
CH 07
CH 08
CH 09
Hackers TOEFL Reading

9 It was around the late 1930s and early 1940s that the electronic television truly came to be a part of the American public's daily life. By 1950, almost everyone owned a television set and already the dynamics of American culture had changed drastically. People were spending less time exercising, reading books, etc., and more time in their living rooms. In fact, between 1950 and 1955, the average amount of time spent viewing television went up 1,440 percent. Not only did this phenomenon affect social routine, but it also had a huge effect on other public media such as radio, newspaper, and, most of all, film. National cinema was the industry influenced most by the popularity of the home-based entertainment provided by television.

The convenience of TV created obvious competition for movie studios that relied on the public's desire to get away from their homes for entertainment. However, the television offered all of the viewing pleasure available in a theater without the hassles of purchasing tickets, getting to the movie, and having to travel home afterwards. Very simply, people wanted less and less to go outside of home. Thus, the 1950s witnessed a near "death" for the film industry as a result of the impact of TV on American entertainment culture.

Film studios nationwide were quick to come up with measures to counteract, although relatively futilely, the industry's decreasing popularity. Since televisions were still in black and white, film producers immediately focused on color films, and even attempted cinematic techniques such as Cinemascope, Technicolor, and 3D films. Other attempts included the widening of cinema screens, the introduction of reclining seats, and free snacks. While such lures drew in the crowds initially, viewers soon lost interest and returned to the ever evolving world of television entertainment.

Consequently, the film industry reacted with another try at drawing audiences by offering films of a more adult content. Violence, vulgar language, and especially sexual content became part of mainstream film. This was a great advantage for film, as television couldn't (at that time) allow such productions for the sake of the plethora of children viewers. At this point, cinematic popularity slowly began to grow again, although it never reached the pre-television per capita ratings that it once enjoyed. Unfortunately, television eventually caught up and began to produce adult-oriented shows and late night specials, so the theater audiences once again dwindled. Despite all of the attempts to reignite film's popularity, movie theaters even still today struggle to maintain their place in American entertainment culture.

VOCABULARY The word ☐ in the passage is closest in meaning to

9	convenience	(A) dereliction	(B) intervention	(C) boldness	(D) handiness
	measures	(A) affectations	(B) collaborations	(C) efforts	(D) concords
	dwindled	(A) decreased	(B) surged	(C) retrospected	(D) incinerated

Directions: An introductory sentence for a brief summary of the passage is provided below. Complete the summary by selecting the THREE answer choices that express the most important ideas in the passage. Some sentences do not belong in the summary because they express ideas that are not presented in the passage or are minor ideas in the passage. **This question is worth 2 points.**

> Drag your answer choices to the spaces where they belong. To remove an answer choice, click on it. To review the passage, click on **View Text**.

The advent of television had a widespread impact on the more traditional form of public amusement, film.

-
-
-

Answer Choices

(A) Most people preferred the comfort of remaining in their homes watching television to the inconvenience of going to the theater.

(B) Almost all of the movies shown in theaters were also shown on television.

(C) When television came out, it caused people to invest less time in exercising and reading.

(D) Children viewers were not permitted to watch adult-oriented shows on television.

(E) Film industry leaders offered fresh inventions to recover its popularity over television.

(F) Gearing movies to audiences of higher ages had only brief influence on enthusiasm for the cinema.

CH 01
CH 02
CH 03
CH 04
CH 05
CH 06
CH 07
CH 08
CH 09
Hackers TOEFL Reading

10   Plants, like any other species, are susceptible to predation that threatens their survival. Constant attacks by herbivores are a continuous threat that has prompted the development of self-defense mechanisms in plants. The study of plant defense is ridden with a number of theories dating back to the 1950s that attempt to explain why and how these defense mechanisms developed, but as of yet there are no conclusive results. What scientists do know is that types of protective measures are evolving and that plants and herbivores are locked in an arms race of sorts regarding the growth of chemical defense techniques. As fast as plants can put up protective barriers, the herbivorous predators (most notably insects) counteract them with their own adaptations that allow them to gain access to the plants.

Each plant utilizes different methods, or a combination thereof, to react to the approach or attack of its enemies. The quaking aspen, *Populus Tremuloides*, grows laterally compressed petioles that cause the leaves to vibrate with any kind of breeze. The vibration makes it difficult for insects to stay on the leaf surfaces. A number of plants develop dense mats of trichomes that abscise when the leaf expands fully, acting as a physical barrier to all kinds of insects. Both of these defenses attempt to keep away potential threats, but there are some protective measures that counterattack the invader already present. An example of this is the *Populus Deltoides* that secretes a resin through its stipular bud scales once an insect has attached itself to its stem. The resin contains a toxin that is poisonous to most enemies. In another way, the *Populus Grandidentata* has a defense in which it produces extraneous floral nectaries to ensure that the predators do not take all of its nutrient supplies.

More recent studies show that a plant's initial response to an attack by a pathogen is the most critical for the plant's survival. It is this response that triggers the defense mechanism, yet the pathway by which it occurs is still unknown. Recent work with cultured plants cells in suspension has revealed that exposure to a pathogen results in changes in the levels of cytosolic calcium concentration, the production of reactive oxygen species, the activation of protein kinases, and the release of the novel lipid second messenger phosphatidic acid. All of these reactions occur within 1-4 minutes after the plant's recognition of a foreign invader, signaling the defenses almost immediately and ensuring the plant's survival.

VOCABULARY   The word ☐ in the passage is closest in meaning to

10 threatens	(A) swells	(B) endangers	(C) aggravates	(D) terminates
cause	(A) trespass	(B) toil	(C) induce	(D) linger
present	(A) existing	(B) casual	(C) steadfast	(D) sterile

Directions: An introductory sentence for a brief summary of the passage is provided below. Complete the summary by selecting the THREE answer choices that express the most important ideas in the passage. Some sentences do not belong in the summary because they express ideas that are not presented in the passage or are minor ideas in the passage. **This question is worth 2 points.**

> Drag your answer choices to the spaces where they belong. To remove an answer choice, click on it. To review the passage, click on **View Text**.

As a response to danger, plants utilize systems of protection that fend off destructive aggressors.

-
-
-

Answer Choices

(A) The manner by which plants shield themselves against invaders is constantly evolving.

(B) Some predators take nutritive elements from floral nectaries of plants.

(C) It is vital for a plant to instantaneously respond to any sign of bacterial or viral causative agent.

(D) Plenty of plants have layers of sharp edges that pop out when attackers come near.

(E) Researchers have found a way to isolate the toxic substance released by plants.

(F) A plant's response to threats can vary widely, from keeping away hidden enemies to retaliating against existing predators.

CH 01
CH 02
CH 03
CH 04
CH 05
CH 06
CH 07
CH 08
CH 09

Hackers TOEFL Reading

11   At the beginning of the European Middle Ages, books did not exist, or at least not in the form and quantity prevalent in modern times. The majority of the population was illiterate and cultural stories, mostly related to heroic deeds or monstrosities, were passed on orally by storytellers, minstrels, and poets. However, throughout the course of that historical period, the printed book came into being and marked a turning point in European social history. The way of preserving cultural myths, stories, and historical narrations had evolved into an almost entirely written form.

The traditional way of preparing a book consisted of an arduous process that took years to complete. The first step was to cure the animal hides for pages, then make and mix the pigments for the ink, followed by the readying of quills, and finally rule each page for the actual writing. Once this entire preparatory stage was complete, every word of the book had to be written in long-hand by a scribe before the book could be illuminated with leafs of gold, silver, and copper. Thus, the labor intensiveness and high cost of producing only one copy of a book meant that very few were made and that only the elite would possess one.

Without a doubt, it was the Catholic Church that maintained control over and ensured the preservation of most books during the Middle Ages. The church at that time was the center of society, above even nobility, and was therefore in the position to elevate literature to the status of an act of God. Monks were assigned the task of copying texts and all religious servants were expected to be literate and skilled in the crafts of scribing or illustrating. By the 14th century, monasteries were set aside solely for the purpose of such tasks, as demand for copies, especially of the bible, grew rapidly. Interestingly, those monasteries kept libraries full of not only sacred texts, but also many of the literary, scientific, and philosophical works of the Greeks and Romans that otherwise might not have been preserved well enough to be read today.

In 1445, a man by the name of Johann Gutenberg forever changed the lives of people in Europe, and eventually throughout the world, with his invention of the printing press. Gutenberg's press could produce books quickly and at little cost in both materials and labor. This resulted in two major effects for European society at that time: less domination by the papal authorities and the dissemination of books to the general public. Not only could works be printed outside of the monasteries, but also were so widely available at such low prices that even the common man could purchase a copy of the bible or a literary piece.

| VOCABULARY | The word ☐ in the passage is closest in meaning to |

11 deeds	(A) fallacies	(B) components	(C) oaths	(D) exploits
sacred	(A) presumable	(B) stopgap	(C) holy	(D) rebellious
dissemination	(A) propagation	(B) abrogation	(C) disposal	(D) reputation

Directions: An introductory sentence for a brief summary of the passage is provided below. Complete the summary by selecting the THREE answer choices that express the most important ideas in the passage. Some sentences do not belong in the summary because they express ideas that are not presented in the passage or are minor ideas in the passage. **This question is worth 2 points.**

> Drag your answer choices to the spaces where they belong. To remove an answer choice, click on it. To review the passage, click on **View Text**.

During the Middle Ages, the development and spread of books affected the growth of European society.

-
-
-

Answer Choices

(A) Most people in Medieval society were devout followers of the Catholic Church.

(B) Some of the important literary works from ancient western civilizations have been lost because of poor printing practices.

(C) Written texts in the Middle Ages were governed and created by the ruling religious authorities.

(D) Books made by hand required extensive amounts of effort and time and were not for general use.

(E) The spread of books into popular culture resulted from the ability to mass-produce copies of texts.

(F) Public libraries were established by the church for people who wanted to learn to read and write.

CH 01
CH 02
CH 03
CH 04
CH 05
CH 06
CH 07
CH 08
CH 09

Hackers TOEFL Reading

12   The often misleading name Tin Pan Alley refers to the assemblage of music publishers and songwriters who congregated in New York City during the late nineteenth and early twentieth century, leading the popular music scene. Originally, there was a specific place, West 28th Street between Broadway and Sixth Avenue of Manhattan, where these music industry leaders dwelled, which is how it became referred to as an "alley." It was along this street that a number of pianists played popular songs to draw in clientele. Critics likened the sounds to the noise of tin pans. Although meant as a criticism, the cluster of shops in that area became known throughout the world as Tin Pan Alley.

The beginning of Tin Pan Alley is typically designated to be around 1885, at the time that a large number of music publishers moved into the same area. The shops on Tin Pan Alley originally arose because of the competitiveness amongst publishers that printed numerous versions of any popular songs to be sold as sheet music. Owing to extremely weak copyright control on melodies, no single publisher could keep up with the trends. For these reasons, a group of publishing shops teamed up together to form the Tin Pan Alley as a way to draw business from individual sellers in the rest of the city.

Even though those small shops became the largest music houses in the nation, they went out of business around the middle of the twentieth century due to dramatic shifts in the music industry. There are debates over exactly what caused the demise of Tin Pan Alley and when the congregation as a recognizable entity ultimately ended. Some experts believe the inevitable fate of the assemblage was determined in the 1930s when the introduction of the radio and phonograph replaced sheet music. It was also during this period that major Hollywood studios bought up several of the largest Tin Pan Alley publishers.

However, other experts contend that it wasn't until the emergence of rock and roll in the 1950s that the Tin Pan Alley finally sealed its fate. According to this view, the producers of Tin Pan Alley greatly underestimated the lasting power of this novel form of music and failed to adapt to changes in consumer preferences. Because Tin Pan Alley products did not keep up with the times, they became less popular and unprofitable to produce.

Despite the closing of the local shops, the music industry was forever marked by the widespread influence that Tin Pan Alley had on popular music. It wasn't only famous performers that used the publishing houses, but also amateur singers and song pluggers. In order to sell to the latter group, music houses had to change the more popular tunes into music readable and playable to less skilled musicians. The variations of music that arose from this situation prompted a creative explosion that was unprecedented in American popular music.

VOCABULARY	The word ⬚ in the passage is closest in meaning to

12	cluster	(A) loafer	(B) enterprise	(C) faculty	(D) group
	numerous	(A) tricky	(B) countless	(C) trivial	(D) dogmatic
	replaced	(A) retracted	(B) superseded	(C) slipped	(D) synthesized

Directions: An introductory sentence for a brief summary of the passage is provided below. Complete the summary by selecting the THREE answer choices that express the most important ideas in the passage. Some sentences do not belong in the summary because they express ideas that are not presented in the passage or are minor ideas in the passage. **This question is worth 2 points.**

> Drag your answer choices to the spaces where they belong. To remove an answer choice, click on it. To review the passage, click on **View Text**.

Tin Pan Alley, a famous collection of music shops along a particular street in Manhattan, became a leader in the popular music industry.

-
-
-

Answer Choices

(A) Sounds produced by the musicians in the street gave rise to the nickname of Tin Pan Alley.

(B) Changes in the music industry led to the downfall of Tin Pan Alley, but precisely why and when it collapsed is debated.

(C) The emergence of a less theatrical style of music caused people to turn away from Tin Pan Alley.

(D) The formation of such a district was motivated by the unrestricted system of score publishing at the time.

(E) Since not everyone could read standard sheet music, alternate versions that were devised increased inventiveness.

(F) Almost all of the customers of Tin Pan Alley were directors and producers of large theatrical performances.

정답 및 해석 p.483

CH 01
CH 02
CH 03
CH 04
CH 05
CH 06
CH 07
CH 08
CH 09
Hackers TOEFL Reading

01 ## The Potlatch

1 ➡ The potlatch was a ceremonial distribution of property practiced by the indigenous communities of the Pacific Northwest in the United States and in the province of British Columbia in Canada. This custom, usually held in longhouses or large outdoor areas, served as markers for certain social events such as the birth of a new child, the marriage of a young couple, or a successful hunting season. It could be used to commemorate the transfer of ownership or serve as a record of payment in lieu of written records in addition to providing a public display of military alliances or familial bonds. The primary purpose of the potlatch, however, was to provide a means to re-distribute wealth among the tribe in an objective and ethical manner, allowing the host to rid himself of the spiritual burden that he felt as the sole owner of material items in an essentially communal environment.

2 The potlatch consisted of three main activities, all of which are inherently tied to its comprehensive definition. The first is feasting, usually on salmon or seal meat, among numerous other foods, reflecting the tradition of sharing seasonal bounty of fish, a successful whale hunt or other surplus of food with neighboring groups. Honored guests, for example, tribal elders, those who had traveled long distances to attend, or traditional healers, were seated and served with great formality, receiving the most elaborate dishes in the largest amounts. The generosity of the host was tacit in the extravagance of the meal, served not in simple daily-use vessels but in ornate hand-carved or painted feasting platters, often of heirloom quality and sometimes as large as a small canoe.

3 ➡ Another aspect of the potlatch is dancing, usually accompanied by singing, and performed for a variety of devotional reasons such as praying for a robust harvest, honoring deceased relatives, or the celebration of special kinship associations. Since each family practiced a unique form of folk dancing, the gathering offered an unparalleled opportunity for the host to show his heritage to others, including members of outlying tribes. Should invited guests wish to present their own elaborate productions, they must first seek permission or be honored with a specific bidding. Throughout the event, some participants wore masks that depicted the supernatural being who had bequeathed the family, or one of their ancestors, with the knowledge of movement and music. For costumes, button blankets were also often worn and later given as gifts to thank the guests for coming and to ask them to remember the dances for the next potlatch.

4 ➡ The practice of gift-giving is the third and most critical factor that identifies the potlatch, although its implied generosity is not the main reason why this occurs. Not only was this an occasion to repay debts, acknowledge services rendered by neighbors, and ensure the continuance of established relationships, but also a time to purge material possessions and reassert communal values. ■ Canoes, eulachon oil, goat hair blankets, or even songs, names, and crests, were offered, diminishing the family's supplies almost to the

point of bankruptcy. ■ Sometimes, if property was anchored or too cumbersome to move to the site of the potlatch, it was simply destroyed so as to comply with the general philosophy of spiritual deliverance and cathartic revelation. ■ Once the portions were accepted, they were ordinarily painted or engraved to commemorate the passing of the potlatch. ■

5 In an effort to assimilate these indigenous populations into Western culture, where community practices that involve purging oneself of material goods are considered contrary to the underlying work ethic, both the United States and Canadian governments banned the potlatch practice in 1884. They believed it to be an irrational destruction of property, one that had grown rampant in the coastal communities now exposed to more goods. As a result, the practitioners went underground to avoid persecution, holding ceremonies in secret, until the law was lifted in 1951. In modern times, the custom has been modified to include a myriad of cultural events such as graduations, baby showers, and anniversaries. Although the level of formality has been dropped, the continuance of the custom ensures that the traditions are remembered and carry on into each passing generation.

1 According to paragraph 1, which of the following is NOT mentioned as a purpose for having a potlatch?

(A) It honored relationships between different social units.
(B) It was held to celebrate major events in people's lives.
(C) It made it mandatory for the wealthy to distribute their valuables.
(D) It served as public notice of a change in proprietorship.

Paragraph 1 is marked with an arrow [➡].

2 The word "objective" in the passage is closest in meaning to

(A) ambling
(B) unbiased
(C) astute
(D) erudite

3 Which of the following can be inferred about the society having the potlatch?

(A) Primogeniture was a very common practice.
(B) It had a rigidly hierarchical structure.
(C) It was dependent on the ocean for sustenance.
(D) The gap between the rich and the poor was great.

CH 01 CH 02 CH 03 CH 04 CH 05 CH 06 CH 07 CH 08 CH 09 Hackers TOEFL Reading

4 The word "tacit" in the passage is closest in meaning to

(A) implicit
(B) archaic
(C) vain
(D) showy

5 According to paragraph 3, which of the following is true of the dancing practice?

(A) Each family possessed a distinctive dance style.
(B) Guests often presented the dancers with commemorative gifts.
(C) Each guest was required to perform a dance in honor of an ancestor.
(D) Whoever received the host's dancing garment would hold the next potlatch.

Paragraph 3 is marked with an arrow [➡].

6 The word "their" in the passage refers to

(A) members
(B) tribes
(C) guests
(D) productions

7 In paragraph 4, why does the author mention "even songs, names, and crests"?

(A) To show that even destitute families were able to provide gifts at a potlatch
(B) To emphasize the spiritual element of the potlatch ceremony
(C) To demonstrate the significance of these concepts to a family's finances
(D) To provide examples of nonmaterial possession for the excessive potlatch

Paragraph 4 is marked with an arrow [➡].

8 Which of the sentences below best expresses the essential information in the highlighted sentence in the passage? *Incorrect* choices change the meaning in important ways or leave out essential information.

(A) The governments of both Canada and the US banned potlatches in order to destroy the indigenous populations completely.

(B) Potlatches were outlawed in the 19th century by America and Canada in order to make the indigenous communities integrate into mainstream societies.

(C) Both the US and Canada made an effort to discourage potlatches since they were deemed as a wasteful and irrational destruction of goods.

(D) The decision of Canada and America to restrict potlatches was part of an attempt to incorporate the indigenous peoples into capitalist society.

9 Look at the four squares [■] that indicate where the following sentence could be added to the passage.

Copper was one such item that was frequently brought as broken pieces, thus lowering its monetary value, but heightening its cultural significance.

Where would the sentence best fit?

Click on a square [■] to add the sentence to the passage.

10 Directions: An introductory sentence for a brief summary of the passage is provided below. Complete the summary by selecting the THREE answer choices that express the most important ideas in the passage. Some sentences do not belong in the summary because they express ideas that are not presented in the passage or are minor ideas in the passage. **This question is worth 2 points.**

Drag your answer choices to the spaces where they belong. To remove an answer choice, click on it. To review the passage, click on **View Text**.

> **The potlatch which serves various purposes consists of a diversity of activities.**
>
> ●
>
> ●
>
> ●

Answer Choices

(A) The surplus of seasonal foods was shared during a banquet.

(B) Formal dining ware was used to show the bounteousness of the host.

(C) Material items were offered to guests for a variety of reasons.

(D) Despite the inhibition of the practice, it continued to carry on in secret.

(E) Ancestral dances were performed by the host as well as the guests.

(F) Non-tribal members were invited to the potlatch, although they did not usually participate.

정답 및 해석 p.489

CH 01
CH 02
CH 03
CH 04
CH 05
CH 06
CH 07
CH 08
CH 09

Hackers TOEFL Reading

1   In 1880, the city of Los Angeles was a desolate chunk of land on the western coast of the United States. As pioneers migrated westward, they settled in the area, built widespread irrigation, planted orchards, and became some of the wealthiest farmers in the country. Over time, however, the cool fruit trees were overcome by hot pavement and tall buildings, and this massive urbanization has had a profound impact on the normal downtown temperature, often 10 degrees higher than in the suburbs and continuing to increase by about one degree every decade. Isothermic maps of a region, which show the geographic distribution of the monthly or annual average temperature values, indicate a heat spike in the location of the city that is likened to the contours of an island, and for this reason the phenomenon is called an Urban Heat Island, or UHI.

2   It often develops in tandem with metropolitan progress and appears in other major population centers. ■ Scientists are becoming more convinced that Urban Heat Islands contribute to the slow rise in the Earth's surface temperature. ■ This, in turn, leads to higher energy consumption and puts strain on local power plants that produce heat-trapping greenhouse gases. In addition, higher average temperatures can cause a startling change in wind patterns, rainfall, and the amount of artificial-ozone-producing smog in affected areas, leading to detrimental climate changes for outlying agricultural regions. ■

3   ➡ Facing such urgent environmental concerns, geologists have now delved into finding ways to combat these phenomena by looking at their root causes. ■ Tall buildings and urban structures, a city's geometrics, greatly influence the city temperature by providing surface areas that display a greater ability to trap and retain heat than their natural surroundings. Albedo, the fraction of reflected light, is diminished by the implementation of darker building material, such as asphalt and black rooftops, which due to its color, absorbs the majority of the radial spectrum and does not reflect much radiation back into the environment. This causes warmth to linger even after sunset and provides no way for the city to cool itself down. Mediterranean cultures have attempted to counter this trend by using low-absorption terracotta and fair hues of building paints, and a larger proportion of the Sun's rays are bounced back into the atmosphere. By comparison, Americans have constantly concentrated more on the aesthetic qualities of their architecture, using inefficient but visually pleasing resources. Studies now show that the importance of color is so striking that temperature differences between a light rooftop and a darker one can exceed 70 degrees.

4   The second main determinant is the lack of vegetation in urban environments. As more people move into cities and away from rural communities, trees and vegetation are displaced to make way for new roadways and other infrastructure. Planners shift their attention away from replacing lost greenery toward the construction of enough residential and commercial buildings to accommodate the increasing population. They fail to notice the obvious ways in which trees can reduce heat — by limiting wind speed or by shading buildings and intercepting sunlight by absorbing the radiation through their foliage. Covering an air-conditioning unit with vines, for example, can keep the machine cool and

allow it to function more efficiently. Deciduous trees planted on the west and south sides, which are the sunniest, of buildings can provide enough shade to cut down energy consumption by up to 30 percent. Furthermore, shrubs and bushes can neutralize atmospheric heat by releasing water through evapotranspiration, like when a person sweats during physical activity. A plant takes in groundwater through its roots and secretes it through pores in its leaves. A large tree may produce up to 40 gallons of water in a day, effectively eliminating as much heat as a 100W bulb left on for eight hours. The neutralizing effect of this process can greatly lower the temperature in an urban environment. A concentrated effort to create more green space within cities would not only enhance the city's beauty, but also most importantly, temper the conditions found in hot cities.

1 The phrase "likened to" in the passage is closest in meaning to

(A) compared to
(B) affixed to
(C) dedicated to
(D) restricted to

2 According to the passage, an Urban Heat Island is termed so because

(A) the temperature of the city is significantly greater than that of the suburbs
(B) an isotherm in the urban area resembles the contour line of an island
(C) it usually happens in heavily industrialized areas of major isles
(D) the location of the city in which it occurs is isolated from other areas

3 The word "detrimental" in the passage is closest in meaning to

(A) pointed
(B) harmful
(C) incremental
(D) flattering

4 According to paragraph 3, dark-colored buildings contribute to a rise in temperatures by

(A) increasing the amount of radiant energy reflected
(B) inhibiting the absorption of energy by nearby plants
(C) not sending back a great deal of heat into the atmosphere
(D) requiring occupants to use higher levels of energy

Paragraph 3 is marked with an arrow [➡].

CH 01
CH 02
CH 03
CH 04
CH 05
CH 06
CH 07
CH 08
CH 09

Hackers TOEFL Reading

5 The word "itself" in the passage refers to

(A) radiation
(B) warmth
(C) sunset
(D) city

6 In paragraph 3, the author mentions Mediterranean cultures in order to

(A) contrast their response to the UHI to that in America
(B) emphasize the ill effects of buildings painted in dark colors
(C) argue that America's overuse of energy causes heat islands
(D) show beauty and function can both be incorporated into design

7 According to the passage, in which of the following environments would an Urban Heat Island least likely happen?

(A) Dark-colored buildings with thick vegetation
(B) Light-colored buildings with thick vegetation
(C) Dark-colored buildings with sparse vegetation
(D) Light-colored buildings with sparse vegetation

8 Which of the sentences below best expresses the essential information in the highlighted sentence in the passage? *Incorrect* choices change the meaning in important ways or leave out essential information.

(A) If a city concentrated more upon nature, then it would look much more attractive.
(B) With the increasing temperatures, cities have been turning to green spaces as a solution.
(C) For both appearances and temperatures, urban areas need more greenery.
(D) Making green tracts of land adds to the beauty of urban areas to a great extent.

9 Look at the four squares [■] that indicate where the following sentence could be added to the passage.

One way they do this is by increasing the demand for refrigeration and air conditioning in warmer climates.

Where would the sentence best fit?

Click on a square [■] to add the sentence to the passage.

10 **Directions**: An introductory sentence for a brief summary of the passage is provided below. Complete the summary by selecting the THREE answer choices that express the most important ideas in the passage. Some sentences do not belong in the summary because they express ideas that are not presented in the passage or are minor ideas in the passage. **This question is worth 2 points.**

> Drag your answer choices to the spaces where they belong. To remove an answer choice, click on it. To review the passage, click on **View Text**.

Urban Heat Islands are created by the confluence of numerous factors that raise the ambient temperatures.

-
-
-

Answer Choices

(A) Smog in industrial cities is growing worse due to the increasing temperature.

(B) Los Angeles has suffered from Urban Heat Islands most severely.

(C) The rise in temperatures is attributed to the scarcity of plants, which have a cooling effect.

(D) High temperatures lead to human actions that exacerbate the problems.

(E) A plant absorbs water through its roots and then emits it into the atmosphere.

(F) Densely packed buildings take in much solar radiation and release it slowly.

정답 및 해석 p.491

CH 01

CH 02

CH 03

CH 04

CH 05

CH 06

CH 07

CH 08

CH 09

Hackers TOEFL Reading

1   ➡ No life on earth is isolated; survival depends on interactions with other species. The most common influential relationships involve food: competing for the same food supply, hunting for prey, and avoiding being prey. Should the reliance on another species reach a level so great the organisms are interdependent, scientists consider them to be symbiotic, or having a prolonged association that is necessary for the continued existence of either one or both.

2   Symbiotic living arrangements are commonplace in the natural environment and researchers hold a vested interest in identifying these pairs, particularly when the survival of one is critical for human employment. Agriculture and sustainable ecology, for example, require a comprehensive appreciation of species because if delicate relationships are ignorantly severed, then the organisms may perish.

3   One way organisms can form symbiotic relationships is when each partner mutually benefits from the presence of the other. This type of relationship is called mutualism and usually develops between two radically divergent samples of plants or animals. One may produce waste that feeds the other, or it may provide conditions, such as shade, protection, or shelter, indispensable to survival. The most common type of mutualism involves an organism that eats leftover food from the mouth of another larger creature, thereby keeping the oral cavity clean and assisting with general hygiene. Another kind of beneficial arrangement is nitrogen fixation, usually appearing in legumes like peas and clover, which harbor bacteria in their roots. The bacteria convert atmospheric nitrogen into ammonia, a nitrogen compound that plants can utilize, and in return the legumes furnish them with oxygen and nutrients. Nitrogen is also important to the environment as a whole since animals get the bulk of their required nitrogen from absorbing these plants.

4   However, if only one species benefits and the other neither benefits nor is harmed, then this symbiotic relationship is classified as commensalism. This literally means 'at the table together' since it was first used to describe one group of animals consuming the unused food of another. The commensal, the one that benefits from the waste or existence of the other, is often a small scavenger accompanied by a large predator, whereby the scavenger feeds off food left behind by its companion. While initially the definition was related only to food, it has now been expanded to include other benefits, such as access to sunlight. In a rainforest, the dense canopy limits the amount of light that falls to the forest floor, so shorter plants are often overshadowed by taller ones. Epiphytes are small plants that perch on tall plants for better access to the sun, but they do not take any nutrients like parasitic plants do.

5   The last type of relationship, parasitism, is the best known and also the most widely studied. ■ Parasitism is when one species is negatively affected by the other such as when diminutive parasites damage their comparatively enormous hosts in two major ways; the first is by consuming the host organism itself and using its anatomy as a nutrient supply. ■ While in some cases this entails actually ingesting tissue like the hookworm

which sucks human blood, other types hijack cells and divert their resources. ■ For example, viruses appropriate a cell causing it to replicate the virus and when all the resources have been exhausted, the cell explodes and spreads the new viruses to other cells. ■

6 ➡ The second way parasites injure their hosts is by liberating toxins. These invaders aren't purposely trying to harm their host, but the toxins produced are by-products of their cellular metabolism. Humans are constant host to a stream of bacteria, and it is by mere chance that some of the bacteria have waste that is toxic to humans. For example, exotoxin is a waste product of diphtheria that is extremely poisonous to humans, and it causes irreparable deterioration to the nervous system, inflames tissue, and damages the heart. Up to a quarter of all people infected die unless treated immediately. It is, however, better for the parasite to allow the host to survive as long as possible since this is the primary resource for its own reproductive health.

7 These relationships are not fixed and it is not uncommon for one type to evolve into another. For instance, the bacteria that live in our intestines produce vitamin K, so what was once commensalism has progressed into mutualism. Therefore, it is cardinal to remember that all life is interdependent and removing one species without acknowledging its interrelationships can potentially have severe repercussions on the biosphere as a whole.

CH 01
CH 02
CH 03
CH 04
CH 05
CH 06
CH 07
CH 08
CH 09

Hackers TOEFL Reading

1 According to paragraph 1, which of the following is true of symbiosis?

(A) The relationship is only reflected in organisms that are isolated in the distance.
(B) The relationship breaks when one species becomes independent.
(C) The relationship is seldom found in the natural environment.
(D) The relationship is indispensable to at least one of the species.

Paragraph 1 is marked with an arrow [➡].

2 The word "perish" in the passage is closest in meaning to

(A) cohere
(B) disappear
(C) abate
(D) endeavor

3 What can be inferred about nitrogen fixation in the passage?

(A) Legumes release nitrogen gas back into the atmosphere.
(B) Plants cannot directly absorb atmospheric nitrogen.
(C) Ammonia is created and has a bad effect on plants.
(D) The legumes usually benefit more than the bacteria.

4 The word "furnish" in the passage is closest in meaning to

(A) spray
(B) smear
(C) supply
(D) smother

5 The word "its" in the passage refers to

(A) existence
(B) predator
(C) scavenger
(D) food

6 Which of the following is true of diphtheria in paragraph 6?

(A) It has no limit in its growth.
(B) It forbids its host to reproduce.
(C) It has metabolic disorders.
(D) It does not attack its host directly.

Paragraph 6 is marked with an arrow [➡].

7 In stating that it "causes irreparable deterioration" the author means that it is

(A) springy
(B) curable
(C) unbeatable
(D) lethal

8 Which of the following can be inferred about a parasite in paragraph 6?

(A) It benefits if the host survives for a long time.
(B) It gains access to the host's blood where the nutrients are.
(C) It takes various forms as long as the other is uninjured.
(D) It uses the host for protection from poisons.

9 Look at the four squares [■] that indicate where the following sentence could be added to the passage.

This cycle continues until the host can no longer survive or is able to fight off the invasion.

Where would the sentence best fit?

Click on a square [■] to add the sentence to the passage.

10 **Directions**: An introductory sentence for a brief summary of the passage is provided below. Complete the summary by selecting the THREE answer choices that express the most important ideas in the passage. Some sentences do not belong in the summary because they express ideas that are not presented in the passage or are minor ideas in the passage. **This question is worth 2 points.**

> Drag your answer choices to the spaces where they belong. To remove an answer choice, click on it. To review the passage, click on **View Text**.

Symbiosis shows the importance of interspecies relationships in nature.

-
-
-

Answer Choices

(A) Once the association between two organisms is set, it is unalterable.

(B) The relationship is sometimes lopsided with one deriving some advantage and the other unaffected.

(C) It is crucial for one partner to keep up hygiene for another.

(D) It is true that two different organisms are advantageous to each other.

(E) Humans are responsible for upsetting the balance between symbiotic species.

(F) The connection is injurious to the host, but helps its partner.

정답 및 해석 p.493

CH 01
CH 02
CH 03
CH 04
CH 05
CH 06
CH 07
CH 08
CH 09

Hackers TOEFL Reading

1 ➡ Timepieces of various sorts have been in circulation since ancient times, but the history of the clock industry in the modern sense begins in the eighteenth century. Prior to then, clocks and watches were largely confined to the realms of scientists or wealthy hobbyists, and were only used to tell time in a crude way. But changes in transportation brought on by the Industrial Revolution made timekeeping a necessity and helped cement time consciousness in the minds of the masses.

2 ➡ In design, production, and trade, England was the frontrunner in the modern clock industry. The British penchant for producing accurate and portable timepieces was perfectly suited for the needs of a growing, mobile population, and the early development of the railroad in Britain provided a catalyst for Britain's market hegemony in the first half of the nineteenth century. Because the safe and predictable operation of railways was highly dependent upon keeping track of time, clocks were posted at intervals throughout the railway system to allow engineers to synchronize their chronometers, and telegraph services would periodically wire times to stations throughout the railway system so that clocks could be continually adjusted for accuracy. While this helped prevent accidents and allowed railway companies to keep tighter schedules, it also helped travelers to anticipate arrivals, departures, and connections with greater precision. These developments underpinned a burgeoning awareness of the importance of time throughout society, prompting those with sufficient means to purchase pocket watches. Thus, train travel increased the demand for timepieces and bolstered the overall clock industry in England.

3 However, there were drawbacks to the English system that would be exploited by competitors. Namely, the English market was solely devoted to handmade clocks, and avaricious craftsmen who profited from their esoteric skills viewed mechanization as a threat and actively lobbied against the use of machinery to craft "fake clocks." As a result, British timepieces remained extremely costly to produce. But while the British were antagonistic toward mechanization, this was not the case in Switzerland, where companies began to experiment with the automated manufacture of individual components, such as plates and wheels. By using machines to fashion some parts, timepieces could be fabricated more quickly and cheaply than British timepieces.

4 ➡ But the Swiss did not submit to the allure of fully mechanized production. ■ Instead, they adopted a flexible system whereby machines were used in the first stage of production to create semi-finished products, and highly skilled artisans were responsible for the final touches. ■ This approach afforded the best of both worlds, as Swiss timepieces could be produced efficiently without sacrificing the diversity and quality of hand craftsmanship. ■ State-of-the-art machinery and an expert and adaptable workforce allowed Swiss companies to respond quickly to fluctuations in market demand and consumer preferences, and Swiss timepieces, especially watches, gradually became synonymous with "top quality" in the minds of buyers. ■ Watches under the moniker "Swiss made" fetched handsome prices in jewelers and other high-end shops both at home and abroad,

and ultimately the Swiss overtook Britain as the recognized industry leader and held that position until the middle of the twentieth century.

5 ➡ Many Swiss-made timepieces ended up in US markets, where American clockmakers focused on quantity at the expense of perceived quality. Although the United States lacked the sheer numbers of skilled craftsmen of their European counterparts, American artisans paved the way for inexpensive timepieces through perfecting the art of mass production. By 1815, Eli Terry, an engineer in Connecticut, was using water-powered mills to fabricate completely uniform and interchangeable parts that were ready to be assembled without any manipulation or fine tuning by skilled laborers. As such, his clocks could be produced quickly by apprentices without the need for journeymen. Understanding the commercial value of his undertakings, Terry attempted to safeguard his methods with patents, but his legal actions did not hold back the tide of competitors for long. Other companies followed suit and by the late 1800s, Americans were producing timepieces quickly and cheaply on a massive scale. In 1899, the Ingersoll Watch Company's "Yankee" pocket watch sold for one dollar, and these dollar watches were coming off the assembly line on the order of eight thousand per day.

6 ➡ The fact that the Americans could produce timepieces virtually anyone could afford had its advantages. American clocks and watches flooded the world market, eventually overtaking Swiss brands not only in sales but also in revenues. Between 1945 and 1970, the Swiss share of the global watch market plummeted from 80 to 42 percent, and by 1970, two US watch companies, Timex and Bulova, ranked first in worldwide sales and total revenues respectively.

1 According to paragraph 1, what can be inferred about timepieces prior to the eighteenth century?

(A) Clocks were preferred to watches for telling time.
(B) Many clocks and watches were not very sophisticated.
(C) They were viewed as unnecessary by the wealthy.
(D) They were used primarily by transportation companies.

Paragraph 1 is marked with an arrow [➡].

2 According to paragraph 2, Britain's prominence in the clock industry can be largely attributed to

(A) its predilection for creating affordable timepieces
(B) its precocious development of the railway system
(C) its invention of a device to make clocks more accurate
(D) its rigorous adherence to safety regulations

Paragraph 2 is marked with an arrow [➡].

3 The word "sufficient" in the passage is closest in meaning to

(A) adequate
(B) attainable
(C) equivocal
(D) deliberate

CH 01
CH 02
CH 03
CH 04
CH 05
CH 06
CH 07
CH 08
CH 09
Hackers TOEFL Reading

4 Why does the author mention the phrase "fake clocks"?

  (A) To criticize the craftsmanship of clocks made in Britain
  (B) To emphasize the derision British craftsmen had for machine-made clocks
  (C) To point out a misconception Switzerland had about British-made clocks
  (D) To compare clocks made in Britain to those made in Switzerland

5 According to paragraph 4, which of the following questions can NOT be answered?

  (A) What was a benefit of the Swiss' approach to production?
  (B) How did the Swiss expeditiously react to changes in the market?
  (C) What kinds of shops merchandised Swiss watches?
  (D) How did Britain respond to the threat of Swiss ascendance?

  Paragraph 4 is marked with an arrow [➡].

6 Which of the sentences below best expresses the essential information in the highlighted sentence in the passage? *Incorrect* choices change the meaning in important ways or leave out essential information.

  (A) Terry knew how valuable his work was, but he was unable to secure patents to protect it.

  (B) Knowing that competitors were likely to imitate his work, Terry sought to protect his methods with patents.

  (C) Terry tried to protect his commercial interests with patents, but his efforts did not work in the long term.

  (D) Because some of Terry's competitors attempted to use his methods, he decided to take legal action.

7 According to the passage, what is the relationship between paragraphs 5 and 6?

  (A) Paragraph 6 clarifies how the circumstances delineated in paragraph 5 came to be.

  (B) Paragraph 6 illustrates how the problems recounted in paragraph 5 were solved.

  (C) Paragraph 6 details the long-term impact of the developments discussed in paragraph 5.

  (D) Paragraph 6 restates the information presented in paragraph 5 in a new way.

  Paragraphs 5 and 6 are marked with arrows [➡].

8 Which of the following can be concluded from the passage?

  (A) The number of craftsmen interested in learning how to make clocks and watches diminished during the nineteenth century.

  (B) The general quality of handmade timepieces increased steadily during the eighteenth century before tapering off in the nineteenth century.

  (C) The percentage of people who could afford to purchase timepieces increased dramatically between the eighteenth and twentieth centuries.

  (D) The timekeeping accuracy of clocks and watches produced with mechanized methods escalated rapidly in the twentieth century.

9 Look at the four squares [■] that indicate where the following sentence could be added to the passage.

As a result, a host of watchmakers were able to successfully market their watches under an encompassing national brand.

Where would the sentence best fit?

Click on a square [■] to add the sentence to the passage.

10 **Directions**: An introductory sentence for a brief summary of the passage is provided below. Complete the summary by selecting the THREE answer choices that express the most important ideas in the passage. Some sentences do not belong in the summary because they express ideas that are not presented in the passage or are minor ideas in the passage. **This question is worth 2 points.**

Drag your answer choices to the spaces where they belong. To remove an answer choice, click on it. To review the passage, click on **View Text**.

Three major players—Britain, Switzerland, and the United States—emerged as leaders in the modern clock industry.

-
-
-

Answer Choices

(A) Before the eighteenth century, demand for clocks and watches in Britain was limited to the niche markets of avid scientists and affluent individuals.

(B) The development of the railway helped Britain gain an edge in the production and sale of timepieces, but British artisans failed to embrace innovative production methods.

(C) Switzerland combined technological innovation with deft craftsmanship to take and maintain control of the watch industry into the twentieth century.

(D) America was not able to overtake Swiss dominance in the clock industry until the latter half of the twentieth century, but it had already cornered the luxury market by the late 1800s.

(E) Mastery of mass-production techniques enabled America to manufacture affordable timepieces, and their share of worldwide sales multiplied.

(F) Switzerland's zealous pursuit of mechanized production led to the degradation of their prestigious standing, and Britain's clockmakers profited as a result.

정답 및 해석 p.494

토플 빈출어휘 정리 노트

Chapter 08에 수록된 어휘들을 빈출도 순으로 정리했습니다. 음성파일을 들으며 꼭 암기하세요.

토플 최빈출어휘 [★★★]

☐ characterize [kǽrəktəraiz] 특징짓다
☐ geometric [dʒìːəmétrik] 기하학적인
☐ virtue [və́ːrtʃuː] 장점 (=merit)
☐ employ [implɔ́i] (기술·방법 등을) 이용하다
☐ hypothesis [haipɑ́ːθəsis] 가설
☐ misleading [mislíːdiŋ] 오해시키는 (=deceiving)
☐ expansion [ikspǽnʃən] 확장 (=spread)
☐ verify [vérəfài] 확인하다 (=confirm)
☐ entire [intáiər] 전체의 (=whole)
☐ merchandise [mə́ːrtʃəndais] 상품
☐ modification [màdəfikéiʃən] 변형 (=variation)
☐ temporarily [tèmpərérəli] 일시적으로 (=transitorily)
☐ track [træk] 추적하다 (=chase)
☐ overlook [òuvərlúk] 간과하다 (=neglect)
☐ secrete [sikríːt] 분비하다 (=produce)
☐ solely [sóulli] 오로지 (=only)
☐ sacred [séikrid] 종교의 (=holy)
☐ dissemination [disèmənéiʃən] 보급 (=propagation)
☐ cluster [klʌ́stər] 무리 (=group)
☐ numerous [njúːmərəs] 많은 (=countless)
☐ replace [ripléis] 대체하다 (=supersede)
☐ objective [əbdʒéktiv] 객관적인 (=unbiased)
☐ inherently [inhíərəntli] 본래 (=essentially)
☐ comprehensive [kàmprihénsiv] 포괄적인 (=thorough)
☐ surplus [sə́ːrplʌs] 잉여 (=extra)
☐ tacit [tǽsit] 암묵적인 (=implicit)
☐ cumbersome [kʌ́mbərsəm] 번거로운
☐ be likened to 비유되다 (=be compared to)
☐ in tandem with 함께
☐ consumption [kənsʌ́mpʃən] 소비
☐ detrimental [dètrəméntl] 해로운 (=harmful)
☐ striking [stráikiŋ] 두드러진 (=remarkable)
☐ perish [périʃ] 멸종하다 (=disappear)
☐ divergent [divə́ːrdʒənt] 다른

☐ indispensable [ìndispénsəbl] 필수적인 (=necessary)
☐ leftover [léftòuvər] 찌꺼기 (=remnant)
☐ furnish [fə́ːrniʃ] 공급하다 (=supply)
☐ overshadow [òuvərʃǽdou] 가리다 (=dim)
☐ entail [intéil] 수반하다 (=involve)
☐ deterioration [ditìəriəréiʃən] 손상
☐ potentially [pəténʃəli] 잠재적으로 (=possibly)
☐ repercussion [rì:pərkʌ́ʃən] 반향 (=effect)
☐ burgeon [bə́ːrdʒən] 급증하다
☐ fabricate [fǽbrikèit] 제작하다 (=produce)
☐ fluctuation [flʌ̀ktʃuéiʃən] 변동 (=change)

토플 빈출어휘 [★★]

☐ collision [kəlíʒən] 충돌
☐ expel [ikspél] 방출하다 (=spew)
☐ proponent [prəpóunənt] 지지자
☐ affordable [əfɔ́ːrdəbl] 가격이 적당한 (=modest)
☐ sparsely [spáːrsli] 빈약하게
☐ intention [inténʃən] 목적
☐ property [prápərti] 소유지 (=holding)
☐ repeal [ripíːl] 폐지하다
☐ confer [kənfə́ːr] 수여하다 (=provide)
☐ escape [iskéip] 도망치다 (=flee)
☐ breed [briːd] 번식하다 (=multiply)
☐ take up 차지하다
☐ state [steit] 상태 (=condition)
☐ flood [flʌd] 넘치게 하다
☐ intend [inténd] 목적으로 하다 (=design)
☐ be equipped with 갖추다
☐ synchronize [síŋkrənàiz] 일치시키다
☐ benefit [bénəfìt] 이점 (=advantage)
☐ convenience [kənvíːnjəns] 편리함 (=handiness)
☐ futilely [fjúːtli] 효과 없이
☐ vulgar [vʌ́lgər] 비속한
☐ dwindle [dwíndl] 감소하다 (=decrease)

*해커스 동영상강의 포털 해커스인강(HackersIngang.com)에서 '토플 빈출어휘 정리 노트' 음성파일을 무료로 다운로드할 수 있습니다.

- [ ] predation [pridéiʃən] 포식
- [ ] threaten [θrétn] 위협하다 (=endanger)
- [ ] cause [kɔːz] 초래하다 (=induce)
- [ ] present [préznt] 있는 (=exist)
- [ ] culture [kʌ́ltʃər] 배양하다
- [ ] unparalleled [ʌnpǽrəlèld] 비길 데 없는
- [ ] comply with 따르다
- [ ] rampant [rǽmpənt] 횡행하는
- [ ] delve [delv] 연구하다
- [ ] sustainable [səstéinəbl] 지속 가능한
- [ ] sever [sévər] 단절하다 (=separate)
- [ ] diminutive [dimínjutiv] 작은
- [ ] divert [divə́ːrt] 전용하다
- [ ] appropriate [əpróuprièit] 전용하다
- [ ] explode [iksplóud] 폭발하다
- [ ] liberate [líbərèit] 방출하다
- [ ] cardinal [káːrdənl] 중요한
- [ ] interdependent [ìntərdipéndənt] 상호의존적인
- [ ] cement [simént] 공고히 하다
- [ ] underpin [ʌ̀ndərpín] 지지하다
- [ ] namely [néimli] 즉
- [ ] antagonistic [æntǽgənístik] 적대적인
- [ ] manipulation [mənìpjuléiʃən] 조작

토플 기출어휘 [★]

- [ ] admission [ædmíʃən] 입장
- [ ] mushroom [mʌ́ʃruːm] 급격히 증가하다
- [ ] fulfill [fulfíl] 충족시키다
- [ ] file [fail] 제출하다
- [ ] applicant [ǽplikənt] 지원자
- [ ] contaminated [kəntǽminèitid] 오염된
- [ ] nourishment [nə́ːriʃmənt] 영양분
- [ ] thermal [θə́ːrml] 열의
- [ ] hassle [hǽsl] 번거로움
- [ ] reignite [rìːignáit] 재점화하다

- [ ] breeze [briːz] 미풍
- [ ] toxin [táksin] 유독물질
- [ ] illiterate [ilítərət] 문맹의
- [ ] deed [diːd] 행위
- [ ] narration [næréiʃən] 서술
- [ ] purchase [pə́ːrtʃəs] 구입하다
- [ ] in lieu of 대신에
- [ ] bequeath [bikwíːð] 물려주다
- [ ] purge [pəːrdʒ] 속죄하다
- [ ] spike [spaik] 급격한 상승
- [ ] intercept [ìntərsépt] 차단하다
- [ ] foliage [fóuliidʒ] 잎
- [ ] neutralize [njúːtrəlàiz] 상쇄하다
- [ ] atmospheric [ètməsférik] 대기의
- [ ] symbiotic [sìmbiátik] 공생관계의
- [ ] harbor [háːrbər] 거처를 제공하다
- [ ] perch [pəːrtʃ] 자리 잡다
- [ ] parasitic [pærəsítik] 기생하는
- [ ] hijack [háidʒæk] 납치하다
- [ ] metabolism [mətǽbəlìzm] 신진대사
- [ ] inflame [infléim] 염증을 일으키다
- [ ] reproductive [rìːprədʌ́ktiv] 번식하는
- [ ] intestine [intéstin] 창자
- [ ] interrelationship [ìntərriléiʃənʃip] 상호관계
- [ ] frontrunner [frʌ́ntrʌ̀nər] 선구자
- [ ] penchant [péntʃənt] 경향
- [ ] hegemony [hidʒéməni] 패권
- [ ] bolster [bóulstər] 북돋다
- [ ] avaricious [æ̀vəríʃəs] 탐욕스러운
- [ ] craftsman [krǽftsmən] 공예가
- [ ] esoteric [èsətérik] 소수만 아는
- [ ] state-of-the-art [stéitəvðiàːrt] 최첨단의
- [ ] high-end [hàiénd] 고급의
- [ ] interchangeable [ìntərtʃéindʒəbl] 교체 가능한
- [ ] apprentice [əpréntis] 견습생

CH 01
CH 02
CH 03
CH 04
CH 05
CH 06
CH 07
CH 08
CH 09

Hackers TOEFL Reading

Chapter 09
Category Chart

OVERVIEW

Category Chart 문제는 지문에서 비교·대조되고 있는 중요한 정보들을 문제에 제시된 각 category(범주)에 맞게 분류 및 정리하는 유형이다. 따라서 Category Chart 문제를 정확히 해결하기 위해서는 지문을 읽으며 각 category에 대한 다양한 특징들을 정확하게 파악하고 분류하여 정리하는 연습이 필요하다. Category Chart 문제는 지문당 1개가 출제되기도 하고, 아예 출제되지 않기도 한다. Category Chart 문제가 출제되지 않는 지문에는 앞장에서 다룬 Summary 문제가 출제된다.

TYPES OF QUESTIONS

4지선다의 질문 형태와는 달리 directions, 보기, category chart가 제시되는데, 보기는 category chart에 정답으로 들어갈 수 있는 개수보다 많이 주어진다. 3점 또는 4점 만점이며 부분 점수가 있다.

빈칸의 개수가 5개인 경우: 5개 – 3점, 4개 – 2점, 3개 – 1점, 2~0개 – 0점,
빈칸의 개수가 7개인 경우: 7개 – 4점, 6개 – 3점, 5개 – 2점, 4개 – 1점, 3~0개 – 0점

Category Chart 문제의 전형적인 질문 유형은 아래와 같다.

Directions: Select the appropriate phrases from the answer choices and match them to the category to which they relate. **This question is worth 3 points.**

> Drag your answer choices to the spaces where they belong. To remove an answer choice, click on it. To review the passage, click on **View Text**.

Answer Choices	Category 1
	●
	●
	●
	Category 2
	●
	●

HACKERS **STRATEGY**

전략 1 문제에 제시된 category를 확인한 후, 비교·대조되는 정보에 유의하며 지문을 읽는다.

Category Chart 문제가 나오는 지문은 두 가지 category를 비교·대조하는 내용이 나온다. 먼저 문제에 제시된 category가 무엇인지 파악한 후, 어떤 점을 비교·대조하고 있는지에 유의하며 지문을 읽는다.

Ex **Trees can be classified into two broad categories: coniferous and deciduous.**
Coniferous trees have narrow or overlapping leaves and bear their seeds in cones.
Nearly all coniferous trees are evergreens, meaning they maintain their leaves
throughout the year. They shed only the oldest leaves, which are usually on the lower
half of the tree and do not receive as much sunlight as newly developed leaves higher
up. They are either long pointed needles or small, flat scales. Cones, considered the
flower on the conifer, will disintegrate to release seeds for reproduction. Conifers are
known for their durability and size, having some of the largest and oldest living plants in
the world.

Deciduous trees, on the other hand, do not bear their seeds in cones and their foliage
drops in autumn. Before this, the leaves often turn a yellow, orange, or red color. They
are also known as broadleaf trees due to having leaves that are wider than those of the
conifers. This allows for a greater surface area for photosynthesis but also means the
leaves are too fragile to withstand cold weather. New foliage appears each spring. The
seeds of deciduous trees are protected inside a hard nut or fleshy fruit and are
dispersed when eaten by animals. Oaks and maples are two of the most common
examples of deciduous trees.

Directions: Select the appropriate phrases from the answer choices and match them
to the type of trees to which they relate. **This question is worth 3 points.**

Drag your answer choices to the spaces where they belong. To remove an
answer choice, click on it. To review the passage, click on **View Text**.

Answer Choices	Coniferous Trees
	•
	•
	Deciduous Trees
	•
	•
	•

➡ 문제에 제시된 **category**는 침엽수와 낙엽수이다. 지문에서는 각 나무의 잎 색깔 및 크기, 씨가 들어있는 장소 등이
비교·대조되고 있다.

해석 p.497

CH 01
CH 02
CH 03
CH 04
CH 05
CH 06
CH 07
CH 08
CH 09

Hackers TOEFL Reading

주어진 보기와 지문을 대조하여 지문의 정보를 올바르게 paraphrase한 보기를 고른다.

지문에서 파악한 정보를 토대로, 주어진 보기를 보며 지문에서 해당하는 부분을 scanning하여 찾은 후 내용을 대조한다. 지문의 내용이 보기에 똑같이 나오기보다는 paraphrase되어 나오는 경우가 많으므로, 보기와 지문을 대조할 때는 지문의 내용이 보기에서 어떻게 paraphrase되었는지 확인한다.

Answer Choices	Coniferous Trees
(A) Inability to produce seeds	●
(B) Narrow foliage	●
(C) Color changes in leaves	**Deciduous Trees**
(D) Extremely thin barks	
(E) Partial loss of leaves	●
(F) Vulnerability to cold	●
(G) Seeds enclosed in berries	●

➡ 보기 (B)는 침엽수를 설명하고 있는 첫 번째 문단의 narrow ~ leaves가 paraphrase되었으며, 보기 (E)는 shed only the oldest leaves가 paraphrase되었다.
보기 (C)는 낙엽수를 설명하고 있는 두 번째 문단의 the leaves often turn a yellow, orange, or red color가 paraphrase되었다. 보기 (F)는 too fragile to withstand cold weather이 paraphrase되었고, 보기 (G)는 The seeds ~ inside a hard nut or fleshy fruit이 paraphrase되었다.

TIP 단락별 핵심 포인트를 Note-taking해야 하는 Summary 유형과는 달리, Category Chart 유형에서는 detail과 관련된 보기들이 나오므로 각 보기를 지문과 직접 대조하여 확인한다.

보기 중 오답을 확인한다.

지문의 내용과 상반되거나 지문에 언급되지 않은 보기는 오답으로 간주된다.

Answer Choices	Coniferous Trees	
(A) Inability to produce seeds	(B) Narrow foliage	
(D) Extremely thin barks	(E) Partial loss of leaves	
	Deciduous Trees	
	(C) Color changes in leaves	
	(F) Vulnerability to cold	
	(G) Seeds enclosed in berries	

지문의 내용과 상반된 오답

(A) Inability to produce seeds

침엽수와 낙엽수 모두 씨를 퍼뜨릴 수 있다고 했으므로 지문의 내용과 상반된다.

지문에 언급되지 않은 오답

(D) Extremely thin barks

나무 껍질이 얇은지 두꺼운지에 대한 내용은 지문에 언급되지 않았다.

CH 01
CH 02
CH 03
CH 04
CH 05
CH 06
CH 07
CH 08
CH 09

Hackers TOEFL Reading

The Civil War that raged across the nation from 1861 to 1865 was the violent conclusion to decades of diversification. Gradually, throughout the beginning of the nineteenth century, the North and South followed different paths, developing into two distinct and very different regions.

The northern soil and climate favored smaller farmsteads rather than large plantations. Industry flourished, fueled by more abundant natural resources than in the South, and many large cities were established (New York was the largest city with more than 800,000 inhabitants). By 1860, one quarter of all Northerners lived in urban areas. Between 1800 and 1860, the percentage of laborers working in agricultural pursuits dropped drastically from 70 percent to only 40 percent. Slavery had died out, replaced in the cities and factories by immigrant labor from Europe. Transportation was easier in the North, which boasted more than two-thirds of the railroad tracks in the country and the economy was on an upswing. Northerners belonged to the Whig/ Republican political party and they were far more likely to have careers in business, medicine, or education. Northern children were slightly more prone to attend school than Southern children.

The fertile soil and warm climate of the South made it ideal for large-scale farms and crops like tobacco and cotton. Because agriculture was so profitable, few Southerners saw a need for industrial development and 80 percent of the labor force worked on the farm. There were no large cities aside from New Orleans, and most of the ones that did exist were located on rivers and coasts as shipping ports to send agricultural produce to European or Northern destinations. Only one-tenth of Southerners lived in urban areas and transportation between cities was difficult, except by water — only 35 percent of the nation's train tracks were located in the South. A slightly smaller percentage of white Southerners were literate than their Northern counterparts, and Southern children tended to spend less time in school. As adults, many Southern men joined the Democratic political party and gravitated toward military careers as well as agriculture.

Directions: Select the appropriate phrases from the answer choices and match them to the region to which they relate. **This question is worth 3 points.**

Answer Choices	The North
(A) Import of agricultural products from Europe	•
(B) Majority of train tracks present	•
(C) Employment of slave labor on farmsteads	•
(D) Economy based on agriculture	
(E) Growth of industry-based cities	**The South**
(F) Strong affiliation with the Democratic party	•
(G) Labor supplied by European immigrant	•

해석 p.497

CH 01

CH 02

CH 03

CH 04

CH 05

CH 06

CH 07

CH 08

CH 09

Hackers TOEFL Reading

| 전략 1 적용 | 지문에서는 북부에서 산업이 발전한 반면, 남부에서는 농업이 발전하게 되었던 배경과 과정을 비교·대조하고 있다. |

| 전략 2 적용 | 주어진 보기를 보며 지문에서 해당하는 부분을 scanning하여 대조한 후, 각 category에 해당하는 지문 속 정보를 올바르게 paraphrase한 보기를 고른다. |

보기 (B)는 북부를 설명하고 있는 두 번째 문단의 more than two-thirds ~ country가 paraphrase되었으며, 보기 (E)는 Industry flourished, ~ many large cities were established가 paraphrase되었다. 보기 (G)는 replaced ~ by immigrant labor from Europe이 paraphrase되었다.

보기 (D)는 남부를 설명하고 있는 세 번째 문단의 80 percent of the labor force worked on the farm이 paraphrase되었으며, 보기 (F)는 joined the Democratic political party가 paraphrase되었다.

| 전략 3 적용 | (A) 지문의 내용과 상반된 오답
지문에서 남부가 농산물을 유럽으로 보냈다고 했으므로 지문의 내용과 상반된다.

(C) 지문에 언급되지 않은 오답
농장에서의 노예의 이용은 지문에 언급되지 않았다. |

| 정답 | The North–(B), (E), (G)   The South–(D), (F) |

Read each passage and answer the corresponding question for each.

1 Mycorrhizae are symbiotic fungi that are associated with the roots of vascular plants. The plants provide the fungi with energy-rich sugars, while the fungi aid in the plant's uptake of water and absorption of essential nutrients. Mycorrhizal fungi are of two general types, endomycorrhizal and ectomycorrhizal.

Endomycorrhizae are microscopic and are the ancestral, more primitive, form of mycorrhizae. They penetrate and live within the cells of the host plant's roots. Though there are relatively few species of these fungi, they are widespread across a range of environments and can be found in the vast majority of the world's woody and herbaceous flora.

Ectomycorrhizae have evolved more recently and are large enough to be visible to the naked eye. These fungi reside outside the roots of their hosts, where they form networks in the soil between the roots. There are many species of these fungi, but they are only associated with a few thousand woody plants and confined to temperate regions.

Directions: Select the correct answer choice that corresponds to the numerical sequence designated in the table.

①	• Live within the roots of the host plant • Too small to be seen without a lens or microscope
②	• Reside in the soil externally to the plant's roots • Limited to parts of the globe with temperate climates

Answer Choices

(A) ① Endomycorrhizae ② Ectomycorrhizae
(B) ① Vascular Plants ② Host Plants
(C) ① Mychorrhizae ② Endomycorrhizae
(D) ① Herbaceous Flora ② Woody Flora

VOCABULARY	The word ☐ in the passage is closest in meaning to			
1 essential	(A) naked	(B) necessary	(C) unaided	(D) available
primitive	(A) sinister	(B) inclined	(C) uncanny	(D) rudimentary
widespread	(A) sprightly	(B) hazardous	(C) common	(D) prudent

2 An alloy is a metal and at least one other chemical element that have bonded to form a new substance. Electrum and bronze are two of the earliest recorded examples of alloys used by humans.

Both are composed primarily of two metals — electrum is a combination of gold and silver, while bronze is made up of copper and tin. However, there are also trace amounts of other metallic elements within these alloys, such as platinum in electrum and nickel in bronze. Electrum was produced by craftspeople, but it could also be mined. Its main source was ore deposits in Asia Minor. The bronze utilized by humans in ancient times was an artificial alloy.

Each of these alloys was used because of an inherent weakness of a component metal. Electrum was more durable than gold and therefore better suited for coinage. Also, the specific ratio of gold to silver could be altered to adjust the value of the coins. Bronze was used in place of copper to create implements because it was harder and yet had a lower melting point, making it easier to cast. In addition, there was little chance of it eroding due to exposure to water.

Directions: Select the correct answer choice that corresponds to the numerical sequence designated in the table.

①	● Forms naturally in some areas ● Used to create early forms of currency
②	● Allowed for the production of improved implements ● Highly resistant to corrosion

Answer Choices

(A) ① Gold　② Silver
(B) ① Electrum　② Bronze
(C) ① Copper　② Tin
(D) ① Platinum　② Nickel

VOCABULARY　The word ☐ in the passage is closest in meaning to

2	recorded	(A) documented	(B) haphazard	(C) improvised	(D) wayward
	source	(A) glue	(B) origin	(C) staple	(D) relish
	specific	(A) burly	(B) gleaming	(C) thick	(D) proper

3 While most people associate the making of cloth with women, activities of weaving and knitting were ⎡originally⎤ male-only occupations. However, the industrialization of the Western world turned most textile trades into factory processes, leaving the tasks of weaving and knitting to be picked up by the women left at home. Weaving, the process of turning two threads of yarn into cloth by way of a loom, is most commonly employed for the creation of tapestries and rugs. It involves the interlacing of the two sets of thread, the weft and the warp, at 90 degrees to one another. The material is most commonly wool, cotton, or flax.

Another popular textile art, knitting, is used for making practical daily materials, such as sweaters, socks, scarves, and other clothing items. It is performed by the ⎡connection⎤ of horizontal and parallel threads by means of interlocking loops of varying sizes. Able to be performed by machine or hand, knitting patterns can vary greatly depending on the type of stitch used. Most complex stitches are formed by some combination of the two most basic stitches, the knit and purl. For instance, the garter stitch is simply back and forth rows of knits and purls, but the ⎡alteration⎤ of knit and purl rows will produce a stockinette stitch.

Directions: Select the appropriate phrases from the answer choices to complete the table.

Weaving	• Typically used to make tapestries and rugs •
Knitting	• Can be done manually or with machinery •

Answer Choices

(A) Rarely performed by men prior to industrialization
(B) Consists of entwining two sets of threads at a set angle
(C) Involves meshing various loops to join multiple threads
(D) Considered the most-effective method of producing textiles

---

VOCABULARY   The word [   ] in the passage is closest in meaning to

3	originally	(A) insolently	(B) nearly	(C) initially	(D) ominously
	connection	(A) linking	(B) hiatus	(C) appliance	(D) pact
	alteration	(A) transformation	(B) impetus	(C) innovation	(D) momentum

4   *Spermatophyte* is a classification of plants that includes all species that reproduce through the production and dispersal of seeds. It is divided into two subcategories, *angiosperm* and *gymnosperm*.

Angiosperms are commonly referred to as flowering plants because the ovary in which their seeds develop is a part of a flower. The ovary protects seeds by keeping them at a fairly constant temperature and preventing dehydration. Eventually, the ovary will ripen and become a fruit. The primary function of the fruit is to facilitate seed dispersal. For example, it may be consumed by an animal, which then excretes the undigested seeds in areas distant from the parent plant. This is why fruits tend to be both tasty and nutritious — successful reproduction is directly related to how appealing a fruit is to animals seeking food.

In contrast, gymnosperms produce seeds that are not enclosed by an ovary. For most species, the immature seeds are instead contained within *strobili*, clusters of hard scales that have a protective role related to that of ovaries. The cones found on pine and spruce trees are examples of strobili. Depending on the species, it may take a year or longer for a seed to reach maturity, and even then it will only be dispersed if specific environmental conditions are met. Many gymnosperm species rely on the wind to transport their seeds, which have appendages shaped like small wings that allow them to maintain altitude to travel greater distances.

Directions: Select the appropriate phrases from the answer choices to complete the table.

Angiosperms	• Have seeds that mature within an ovary •
Gymnosperms	• Protect seeds with a hard, scaly structure •

Answer Choices

(A) Produce flowers to ensure adequate seed dispersal
(B) Release seeds several times over the course of a year
(C) Use other organisms to carry seeds to new areas
(D) Require a significant period of time for seeds to mature

VOCABULARY   The word ⬚ in the passage is closest in meaning to

4	constant	(A) hectic	(B) mute	(C) naive	(D) fixed
	related	(A) motivated	(B) mishandled	(C) pertinent	(D) permanent
	maintain	(A) keep up	(B) pass through	(C) overtake	(D) pare

Read each passage and answer the corresponding question for each.

5   The form versus content debate in all fields of art criticism has dominated the academic scene for over a century. The debate has produced two schools of thought, namely the Formalist and Contextualist schools, which represent differing perspectives on how art should be viewed, analyzed, interpreted, and appreciated. Essentially, the two perspectives differ in what each values as the central or important aspect of any artwork. There is the Formalist approach, with its emphasis on pure artistic qualities; the composition, color, shape, and specific techniques take top priority. Formalists argue that a piece of art is to be appreciated for its aesthetic qualities. A viewer's reaction or emotive response comes from those artistic qualities rather than from any external significance. While some view this perspective as limiting, formalists suggest that a deep understanding of art necessitates its separation from pre-designated interpretations or analyses based on historical or social context.

Incompatibly, Contextualists defend the inherent significance of the conditions that caused the production of an artwork. Contextualism contends that art's meaning is to be found in the socio-historic environment in which it was produced and even in the influence a given artwork has had from a historic or psychological perspective. It is not that contextualism denies the significance of form, but rather that it interprets form based on the external factors that Formalism is apt to negate. While a Formalist would consider the name of an artist interesting, yet insignificant, a Contextualist would purport that an understanding of that artist's social background will give meaning to the stylistic choices of that particular piece. In the end, both schools of thought fail to validate each other's point of view, resulting in a rather distinctive dichotomy in the realm of art criticism.

Directions: Select the appropriate phrases from the answer choices to complete the Contextualist's approach to art analysis.

Formalist	● Credence given to the physical properties of the painting itself ● Disregard of previous categorization for a keen appreciation of art
Contextualist	● ●

Answer Choices

(A) Understanding of the artwork as conditioned by a given environment
(B) Importance placed on the economic value of the piece of art
(C) Analysis of artistic form on the basis of exterior elements
(D) Attraction to artwork based on the name of the artist

VOCABULARY   The word ☐ in the passage is closest in meaning to

5	perspectives	(A) incentives	(B) patterns	(C) standpoints	(D) addresses
	emphasis	(A) illusion	(B) negligence	(C) patience	(D) stress
	inherent	(A) innate	(B) neat	(C) nervous	(D) obedient

6 Frequently confused and often misidentified, the piano and harpsichord are instruments that while they share many qualities, differ in fundamental ways. An important distinction is in the structure of the keys. There are 88 keys on a piano, resulting in a 7 1/4 octave range. Harpsichords, meanwhile, will only have a 4 – 4 1/2 octave range. On both instruments the keys are made of wood, but their widths differ dramatically, with the piano keys being almost twice the size. Aside from the physical structure of the keys, the manner in which the keys are played, resulting from the internal construction of the instruments, is of great importance.

The piano is designed with the idea in mind that when a key is pressed, it causes a felt-covered hammer to strike strings stretched on a rigid frame. The vibration caused by the striking of the strings results in vibrations that cause sounds. The pianist must put a good amount of weight and muscle into the action of playing, using her/his back, shoulders, arms, and hands to ensure that the proper amount of pressure results in the desired sound. Thus, the pianist finds it difficult to adjust to the sensitivity of a harpsichord. Since the latter's keys are directly in line with the framed strings, no effort or muscle is needed to produce sound. In a harpsichord, the pressing of a key causes a jack, a thin strip of wood holding a quill at the top, to pluck the string by coming up from below it until the quill slides around the string and returns below. The jack is engineered in a way that no matter how the key is pressed, the quill will pluck the string at the same pace and strength. The inflexible nature of the harpsichord ironically makes it one of the easiest to play and one of the most accurate musical instruments.

Directions: Select the appropriate phrases from the answer choices to complete the characteristics of harpsichord.

Piano	• Permits the greatest amount of regulation by the player • Produces sound as a result of striking-induced vibration
Harpsichord	• •

Answer Choices

(A) Utilizes back strength of the player
(B) Possesses strings and keys on the same linear axis
(C) Has a jack which pulls the string
(D) Has the keys made of metal

CH 01
CH 02
CH 03
CH 04
CH 05
CH 06
CH 07
CH 08
CH 09
Hackers TOEFL Reading

VOCABULARY The word ☐ in the passage is closest in meaning to

6	qualities	(A) pensions	(B) attributes	(C) antitheses	(D) intervals
	desired	(A) immense	(B) permanent	(C) expected	(D) tedious
	inflexible	(A) omnipresent	(B) intermittent	(C) perverse	(D) rigid

7　Heat transfer is the movement of thermal energy through matter. Convection and conduction are two of the main mechanisms of this phenomenon.

Convection enables heat to be transferred within a fluid — matter in a liquid or gas state. When the temperature of a fluid such as air or water $\boxed{\text{increases}}$, molecules acquire additional energy, which causes them to begin moving apart very rapidly. As the heated fluid expands, it becomes less dense and, therefore, begins to rise. This upward movement displaces colder and denser fluid, forcing it downwards. Assuming the heat source remains, the process is repeated $\boxed{\text{consecutively}}$, creating a convection current that spreads heat throughout the fluid.

For heat to pass through a solid, conduction must occur. The molecules in a solid are packed closely together in rigid arrangements, preventing them from moving away from each other as they absorb thermal energy. Instead, the molecules directly exposed to heat will begin to vibrate rapidly, which results in a rise in temperature. They will then bump into adjacent molecules, causing them to $\boxed{\text{immediately}}$ vibrate as well. This process is repeated, with molecules further and further from the heat source being set into motion. In this way, heat moves from areas with a higher temperature to those with a lower one. Conduction not only enables the transfer of energy within an object but also between two separate objects in direct contact with each other. This explains how heat can move from a frying pan to the food within it — the rapidly moving molecules in the pan impact the food molecules, which makes them begin to vibrate.

Directions: Select the appropriate phrases from the answer choices to complete the conduction.

Convection	<ul><li>A fluid becomes less dense as it absorbs heat.</li><li>A current is formed that transports energy.</li></ul>
Conduction	<ul><li></li><li></li></ul>

Answer Choices

(A) Molecules shake quickly when subjected to heat.
(B) The collision of molecules results in the transmission of energy.
(C) Thermal energy only affects molecules in direct contact with a heat source.
(D) Solid matter expands slightly as its temperature rises.

VOCABULARY　The word ☐ in the passage is closest in meaning to

7	increases	(A) multiplies	(B) pants	(C) intersects	(D) spoils
	consecutively	(A) aptly	(B) serially	(C) perfectly	(D) literally
	immediately	(A) primarily	(B) infrequently	(C) merely	(D) instantly

Native Americans have inhabited the North American continent since crossing the Bering Strait from Siberia some 17,000 to 11,000 years ago. No single event, not even the Ice Age, affected them quite as much as the arrival of the European Conquistadors. From Columbus' first step onto the New Land in 1492 until the 19th century, the slaughter and relocation of the Native Americans caused massive decreases in some populations and extinctions in others.

Prior to the entrance of the Europeans, Native Indians were tribal people that made their livings as hunters and gatherers. Historically they are remembered as a culture for their spiritual beliefs and medicinal practices, both of which were interlinked with their natural environments. Each tribe had its own unique language and customs, although the basic ways of living were very similar. For the most part, the Natives of North America lived natural and relatively peaceful lives, although warring between tribes over territorial disputes or other possessions was a routine practice.

The arrival of the Europeans interrupted the Native American way of life in almost every sector. First and foremost, a majority of the Native Americans were taken as slaves, for example, Christopher Columbus took 250,000 Arawaks from Haiti. Second, the conquistadors and subsequent settlers pushed the Indians off of their land and relocated them to remote and unfavorable settlements built specifically for the purpose of holding them. This caused the spread of a number of diseases and the loss of many cultural traditions that could not be upheld under such conditions. In fact, the Europeans brought with them a plethora of diseases to which the Native Americans were not immune.

Directions: Select appropriate phrases from the answer choices to complete the situation of native Americans after the arrival of the Europeans.

Native Americans prior to European colonization	• Earned their living by hunting and collecting food • Lived in separate tribes that had common ways of life
Native Americans after the arrival of the Europeans	• •

Answer Choices

(A) Traveled primarily by canoes along the rivers and lakes to hunt
(B) Were affected by a number of serious and foreign illnesses
(C) Practiced the Christian beliefs of the Western European conquerors
(D) Were forced to settle in residences designed for accommodating them

---

VOCABULARY   The word ☐ in the passage is closest in meaning to

8	disputes	(A) inflictions	(B) feuds	(C) aims	(D) alarms
	interrupted	(A) attenuated	(B) illustrated	(C) suspended	(D) outweighed
	unfavorable	(A) adverse	(B) outspoken	(C) parallel	(D) underlying

CH 01
CH 02
CH 03
CH 04
CH 05
CH 06
CH 07
CH 08
CH 09
Hackers TOEFL Reading

Read each passage and answer the corresponding question for each.

9   Painting and sculpture remain today two of the most popular forms of artistic expressions. Painting, outdating sculpture by about 25,000 years, was the first artistic practice employed by humans around 32,000 years ago. The first paintings were engraved and painted on the insides of cave walls in Grotte Chauvet in France and depicted a variety of mammals from that time period. However, sculpture didn't get its start until around 5,000 years back in Egypt, only to be picked up by the Greeks and refined as a form of high art.

Painting, in essence, is the practice of applying suspended pigment and a glue to a surface. It is always focused on color and the manner in which color is employed to a two or three dimensional surface to illustrate or imitate a scene, person, or object. Sculpture, on the contrary, is an expression concerned almost solely with space: how to occupy it, relate to it, and influence our perception of it. It is always in three dimensional forms and typically imitates a person, deity, mythological figure, or imaginary creature.

In regards to the materials employed, painting and sculpture differ drastically. Painting, as mentioned above, requires both a medium carrying pigment and some form of adhesive, as well as a surface onto which to place the paint. Examples of the surface include paper, canvas, and mural. Painters can use oil, water mixable oil paints, gouache, ink, pastel, and more. Then there is, of course, the need for the medium with which to apply the paint, which is typically a brush, but can also take the shape of a sponge, or any other absorption capable medium.

In contrast, the materials used in sculpture are unlimited. Since sculpture is defined by the changing of one or more of the physical or contextual attributes of an object, such as its mass, texture, etc., the possibilities are infinite. Nonetheless, there are a number of materials traditionally used, including stone, clay, wood, and many more. However, contemporary artists are beginning to experiment with the use of gasses and other less traditional materials, revitalizing the classical form of expression.

Despite all their differences, painting and sculpture share a common goal; that is to record, interpret, and pass on the human experience. The first paintings were recordings of the mammalian and animal life available to early human civilization, which made future generations aware of the bounty in that area. Sculptures of pharaohs and gods adorned the ancient pyramids to ensure that the lives of such deities and nobles were not only remembered, but continued in the next world to return someday. In both cases, art functions as more than merely aesthetic pleasure; it hands down the history and future hopes from one generation to the next.

VOCABULARY   The word ☐ in the passage is closest in meaning to

9   refined   (A) narrated   (B) grasped   (C) polished   (D) whipped
    contemporary   (A) passive   (B) cozy   (C) paramount   (D) coeval
    adorned   (A) embellished   (B) condoned   (C) shielded   (D) clove

Directions: Select the appropriate phrases from the answer choices and match them to the type of artistic expression to which they relate. **This question is worth 3 points.**

> Drag your answer choices to the spaces where they belong. To remove an answer choice, click on it. To review the passage, click on **View Text**.

Answer Choices	Painting
(A) Manipulates the characteristics of objects	•
(B) Usually illustrates animals and sea life	•
(C) Uses some form of adhesive	
(D) Utilizes unlimited types of elements	**Sculpture**
(E) Concentrates on how to treat space	•
(F) Is the most traditional form of artistic expression	•
(G) Has the role of aesthetic amusement at most	•

CH 01
CH 02
CH 03
CH 04
CH 05
CH 06
CH 07
CH 08
CH 09
Hackers TOEFL Reading

10 When energy travels through the ocean, it causes water to move in a circular motion, resulting in the creation of a wave. While most of these are not a threat to humans, highly destructive ones such as rogue waves and tsunamis may form under specific conditions. A rogue wave is any wave that is over twice the height of the ones around it, although this term is generally reserved for the massive walls of water that occasionally develop during severe storms. Until fairly recently, most scientists dismissed the idea of rogue waves, writing off reports of these types of waves as exaggerations by mariners. However, in 1995, sensors on an oil platform in the North Sea recorded that the structure had been struck by a 29.9 meter wave that was significantly larger than others in the area. With irrefutable proof that rogue waves did in fact exist, scientists made a concerted effort to acquire additional data about them.

One thing that became apparent was that rogue waves are much bigger than previously thought to be possible — the US Naval Research Laboratory tracked one during Hurricane Ivan in 2004 that exceeded 40 meters in height. The exact process by which these immense waves form is not known, but researchers suspect that interactions between the wind and ocean currents play an important role. Although all surface waves get their energy from the wind, their shape and speed is influenced by ocean currents. When the wind blows water in the direction of an oncoming current, the wave is compressed and pushed upwards. Given that wind velocity and direction fluctuate wildly during a storm, this process may occasionally produce a single wave of much greater size than normal.

In the case of tsunamis, the underlying cause is well established — energy is released underwater very suddenly, most commonly by an earthquake. This sends a series of tsunami waves outward in all directions. However, it's important to note that a tsunami travels under the water rather than on the surface. Therefore, even though a large amount of energy is moving through the ocean, there is almost no sign of it on the surface of deep water. It is when the tsunami reaches shallow areas that its height increases. Tsunamis can be higher than 30 meters, and multiple waves will strike the same area in succession causing significant harm. For example, a tsunami that occurred in the Indian Ocean in 2004 resulted in approximately 230,000 deaths and $15 billion in property damage. In response, countries in regions at risk have begun working together to develop an international tsunami warning system.

VOCABULARY The word ⬚ in the passage is closest in meaning to

10 destructive	(A) perennial	(B) ruinous	(C) pervasive	(D) infirm
acquire	(A) earn	(B) inhibit	(C) revolutionize	(D) patch
regions	(A) altitudes	(B) blinks	(C) territories	(D) ambitions

Directions: Select the appropriate phrases from the answer choices and match them to the type of wave to which they relate. **This question is worth 3 points.**

> Drag your answer choices to the spaces where they belong. To remove an
> answer choice, click on it. To review the passage, click on **View Text**.

Answer Choices	Rogue Waves
(A) Confirmed to exist for the first time in 1995	•
(B) Form only during tropical storms such as hurricanes	•
(C) Produced as the result of earthquakes	
(D) Receive its energy from moving air	**Tsunamis**
(E) Led to the creation of a global warning system in 2004	•
(F) Increase in height as it approaches the coastline	•
(G) Travel under the surface of the water	•

CH 01

CH 02

CH 03

CH 04

CH 05

CH 06

CH 07

CH 08

CH 09

Hackers TOEFL Reading

11 If there is one characteristic trait that marks the United States' place in the history of world politics, it is its presidential system. Scholars of political science call the United States the "birthplace of presidency," as it was the first nation to create such a government, which has been adopted by a number of countries, including Indonesia, the Philippines, and most of the countries in South America. In its beginnings, the presidential system was developed in reaction to the colonist's repugnance for the English monarchy. Still today, America's president-based government stands in contrast in many ways to the parliamentary cabinet system now used in the United Kingdom.

The overriding difference between the two systems lies in the respective divisions of power. The presidential system is based on the division of two equal branches, the executive and legislative. These branches are separate and neither holds power over the other ensuring stability by preventing abuses and corruption. The executive branch consists of the president, who is elected directly by the people offering the nation's citizens stronger confidence in their government, and his/her cabinet, referred to as advisors or staff. However, the president has the ultimate say in any decision. The legislative branch holds the parliament and is not controlled or influenced in any way by the executive party.

In comparison, any type of parliamentary system is based on the dependency of the executive branch on the legislative branch for support. There is no clear division between the branches and no clear leader. Unlike in the presidential system, the executive branch of a parliamentary government is made up of a cabinet and prime minister (or some other head of government) who equally contribute to the decision-making process. The head of government has the ability to use reserved rights in the case of a crisis, but in general acts as just another member of the cabinet. Then the legislative branch consists of a parliament that is highly influenced by, and requires the approval of, the cabinet in order to pass any laws or policies. Thus, there is little separation of power in such a system as compared to the presidential government.

VOCABULARY	The word ____ in the passage is closest in meaning to			
11 reaction	(A) aspect	(B) ingenuity	(C) sarcasm	(D) reply
confidence	(A) certainty	(B) injunction	(C) trance	(D) cohesion
ability	(A) immorality	(B) capacity	(C) abatement	(D) ailment

Directions: Select the appropriate phrases from the answer choices and match them to the type of political systems to which they relate. **This question is worth 3 points.**

> Drag your answer choices to the spaces where they belong. To remove an answer choice, click on it. To review the passage, click on **View Text**.

Answer Choices	Presidential
(A) The cabinet that can utilize special right in emergency situations	•
(B) Decision-making authority shared by all government sects	•
(C) Head of government chosen by the people	
(D) National finances controlled by the ruling party	•
(E) Laws passed in accordance with cabinet members	**Parliamentary Cabinet**
(F) Power split-up between distinct governmental units	•
(G) America as the first country to adopt that sort of system	•

CH 01
CH 02
CH 03
CH 04
CH 05
CH 06
CH 07
CH 08
CH 09

Hackers TOEFL Reading

12 European music can be broadly classified based on the era of its composition, and encompasses the variety of general styles that were widespread during each epoch. Baroque is the genre of vocal and instrumental music that slowly developed over the 17ᵗʰ century and came to fruition between 1700 and 1750. Its characteristics reflect two major influences, the introduction of the mechanical organ, which became the featured instrument in many compositions, and the rise in the status of the Church. Composers, in particular J.S. Bach, Handel, and Vivaldi upheld religious values of harmony with nature by writing sublime musical pieces that rarely deviated from the main melody. Intricately ornamented pieces were crafted to carefully maintain a uniform emotive response by keeping constant energy from the first note to the last, using extending techniques such as tremolo and pizzicato to emphasize a focus on the depiction of a single auditory expression.

At the same time, some composers augmented the use of voice, by mutating sacred choral structures, and capitalizing on diatonic tonality and imitative counterpoint, to enhance religious storytelling. This allowed vocal soloists to utter comprehensible text over accompanying music, a practice that swiftly grew into opera and was perhaps the most recognizable trend that came out of an age.

The roles of counterpoint and ornamentation diminished following the Baroque period and they were replaced with homophonic texture, the changing of keys, called modulation, resulting in rich dramatic compositions that carried a variety of emotional elements as opposed to one distinct feeling. The term Classical music has been applied to this subsequent era, occurring roughly from 1730 to 1850, developing in common parlance in an attempt to canonize the time between Bach and Beethoven, a significant composer of the late-Classical period. The genre is marked by the disappearance of the organ in favor of the piano. Many pieces highlighted this new type of keyboard in addition to the violin and other stringed instruments, which together with percussion comprise the Classical orchestra. The aggrandizement of instrumentation supplements the great musical complexity of the Classical genre, in which the reliance on musical development, defined as the process by which a musical idea or motif is repeated in different formats, or in an altered form, can be nurtured in an array of phrasing techniques, usually four or eight bars in length. Structurally, the works build up hierarchically from small movements to complete one large performance that can be as short as thirty minutes to as long as three hours in length.

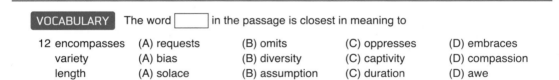

VOCABULARY The word ⬚ in the passage is closest in meaning to

12 encompasses	(A) requests	(B) omits	(C) oppresses	(D) embraces
variety	(A) bias	(B) diversity	(C) captivity	(D) compassion
length	(A) solace	(B) assumption	(C) duration	(D) awe

Directions: Select the appropriate phrases from the answer choices and match them to the type of European music to which they relate. **This question is worth 4 points.**

Drag your answer choices to the spaces where they belong. To remove an answer choice, click on it. To review the passage, click on **View Text**.

Answer Choices	Baroque
(A) Included many different types of instruments	•
(B) Got a musical motif reiterated in modified formats	•
(C) Was influenced by increased importance of religion	•
(D) Exercised restraint in the application of voice	•
	Classical
(E) Had a preference for the piano	•
(F) Composed pieces that seldom digressed from leading tunes	•
(G) Often focused on only one feeling at a time	•
(H) Created numerous musical terms	
(I) Was the precursor to opera	

정답 및 해석 p.498

HACKERS **TEST**

제한 시간: 18분

1   Archaeologists and geologists prior to the 1940s had no way to accurately date the objects they found. Then, at the University of Chicago, the Manhattan Project discovered how to precisely measure rates of radioactive decay. Even though this new technique, absolute dating, is effective in gauging the natural radioactivity of certain elements in given specimens to ascertain their specific chronological age, such as 60 million years before the present, the older method of relative dating, which assigns speculative dates to artifacts via such factors as location and association, is still in widespread use.

2   ■ The most common absolute dating tactic, called radiometric dating, works out the age of rocks from the deterioration of their radioactive elements. ■ However, rocks also contain small amounts of unstable elements, "parent" isotopes, that will break up spontaneously and degenerate into "daughter" isotopes in a process known as radioactive decay. ■ The rate of degeneration is expressed in terms of the parent's half-life or, the time it takes for one-half of its matter to decay. ■ For example, when igneous or metamorphic rocks crystallize, they may capture within themselves a supply of Uranium-238, which has a half-life of 4.5 billion years. Over that period of time, half of its matter will decay into Lead-206, and in the next 4.5 billion years, half of what is left will convert, leaving one quarter of the original, and so forth. If it contains half amounts of each, it means that one half-life has passed. Scientists can therefore determine age by measuring the ratio of one isotope to the other within a sample.

3   ➡ While this method can accurately date rock specimens right to the very beginning of Earth's life, the chronicling of organic materials such as wood or plant fibers necessitates the slightly different approach of Carbon-14 dating. Its basic concept is that when a plant dies, it no longer acquires carbon, at which point its Carbon-14 isotopes will start to decay. These are counted using an Accelerated Mass Spectrometer, which can analyze samples at 1,000 times the magnification of the Geiger Muller counters used in other radiometric procedures. The drawback of this technique is that it is only applicable with objects younger than 50,000 years, owing to the relatively short half-life of organic isotopes.

4   ➡ Before the advent of such devices, archaeologists and geologists were largely limited to using the relative dating method. This falls under a sub-discipline of geology known as stratigraphy, which is the science of rock strata, or, layers. Layering occurs in sedimentary rocks as they accumulate through time, meaning that these hold the key to deciphering the succession of historical events in the Earth's past. For example, geologists have deduced that the oldest rocks in the Grand Canyon are situated at the base of the gorge and are from the late Proterozoic period, while those overlain atop these are from the younger Paleozoic era. This inference is called the "Law of Superposition," which states

that in an undisturbed horizontal sequence of rocks, the oldest rock layers will be on the bottom, with successively younger rocks located above them. This also means that fossils found in the lowest levels of a sequence of layered rocks will represent the most ancient record of life there. In rare instances, a sequence of layers that has been deposited and compressed to form rock could literally be overturned by the thrusting of the Earth's crust as its continental plates collide, meaning that the youngest rocks in a sequence will be at the bottom. However, this can be identified by the extensive faulting and breaking of rocks that contrast sharply with the same original sequence of rocks present elsewhere in undisturbed order.

Glossary

isotopes atoms that have the same number of protons and electrons but different numbers of neutrons

CH 01

CH 02

CH 03

CH 04

CH 05

CH 06

CH 07

CH 08

CH 09

Hackers TOEFL Reading

1 According to the passage, what can be inferred about radioactive decay?

(A) It is equal for all radioactive isotopes.
(B) The pace at which it occurs is constant.
(C) Daughter isotopes undergo decay.
(D) Only uranium's rate is currently known.

2 The word "determine" in the passage is closest in meaning to

(A) develop
(B) finish
(C) care
(D) figure out

3 The word "its" in the passage refers to

(A) matter
(B) sample
(C) life
(D) plant

4 According to paragraph 3, an Accelerated Mass Spectrometer is used to

(A) determine the number of isotopes
(B) identify the types of carbon
(C) measure the level of radioactivity
(D) separate the specimens of rocks

Paragraph 3 is marked with an arrow [➡].

5 The author mentions objects younger than 50,000 years in paragraph 3 in order to

(A) explain a strong point of an Accelerated Mass Spectrometer
(B) show that the Carbon-14 method is limited in use
(C) highlight the importance of organic isotopes
(D) suggest the span the Geiger Muller Spectrometer covers

Paragraph 3 is marked with an arrow [➡].

6 The word "succession" in the passage is closest in meaning to

(A) string
(B) disturbance
(C) magnitude
(D) detriment

7 The word "deduced" in the passage is closest in meaning to

(A) implied
(B) indicated
(C) concluded
(D) contended

8 In paragraph 4, why does the author mention thrusting of the Earth's crust?

(A) To clarify the mechanism by which newer rocks are created inland
(B) To explain the process by which rocks become progressively layered
(C) To prove that relative dating is no longer useful in the modern sciences
(D) To illustrate a case in which the Law of Superposition is not applicable

Paragraph 4 is marked with an arrow [➡].

9 Look at the four squares [■] that indicate where the following sentence could be added to the passage.

Rocks are made up of crystals that contain various chemical elements such as iron, magnesium, and silicon which are stable.

Where would the sentence best fit?

Click on a square [■] to add the sentence to the passage.

10 **Directions**: Select the appropriate phrases from the answer choices and match them to the type of dating they represent. **This question is worth 3 points.**

> Drag your answer choices to the spaces where they belong. To remove an answer choice, click on it. To review the passage, click on **View Text**.

Answer Choices	Absolute Dating
(A) Takes other areas into consideration in case of geological changes	●
(B) Eliminates the need for manual excavation of specimens	●
(C) Observes rocks in layers to determine the order of historical incidents	●
(D) Is able to ascribe precise dates to artifacts	**Relative Dating**
(E) Estimates the age of vegetation using Carbon-14 isotopes	●
(F) Applies chemical substances to samples to disclose their main ingredients	●
(G) Measures the proportion of parent to daughter elements of rocks	

정답 및 해석 p.505

CH 01
CH 02
CH 03
CH 04
CH 05
CH 06
CH 07
CH 08
CH 09

Hackers TOEFL Reading

1 ➡ In 4000 BC, hunter-gatherers living along the floodplains between the Tigris and Euphrates Rivers, known as the Fertile Crescent, ceased their nomadic ways and settled into sedentary agrarian settlements. A steady supply of food triggered a period of population growth that made coordination necessary, giving birth to the concept of large-scale political organization in the form of the Mesopotamian empires. Four hundred years later, a similar shift occurred along the banks of the Nile River as Egypt passed rapidly from a state of Neolithic culture with a complex tribal character into a well-organized monarchy.

2 Although the two cultures, together known as the Cradle of Civilization, emerged almost simultaneously, there were some fundamental differences between them that were largely due to unique geographical compositions. Egypt was entirely arid, save for a fertile swath running through its center that was nourished by the Nile River. Insulated on three sides by desert and on the fourth by the Mediterranean Sea, a unanimous cultural identity developed that was unadulterated by outside influences and wholly subservient to the life-giving properties of the Nile, which formed the symbolic basis of its political system. On the other hand, Mesopotamian civilization was scattered over a wider expanse that allowed independent urban centers to take root in various locations. Because life was constantly plagued by disastrous and unpredictable floods, metropolises were often forced to invade each other in times of hardship. The result was a tempestuous sequence of upheavals that made unity and cohesion tenuous.

3 ➡ Numerous groups had control over the Fertile Crescent at one time or another during the course of the centuries. Despite the repeated rise and fall of the empires, culture of the valley remained basically the same. The first major empire was that of the Sumerian, whose control over the area began in approximately 3000 BC. Their kings, while important, were not considered divine, but rather served as the liaison between the people and the gods. One of their main duties was to determine when the best time for planting was. This need spurred the development of cuneiform, the world's first writing system, to record the changes in the wildly unpredictable floodplains and manage the resources. While religion was important to the Mesopotamians, it did not infiltrate every aspect of their lives as it did in Egypt. Because of this, there were strict laws that clearly delineated the rules and responsibilities of members of the society and the most famous of these is the Code of Hammurabi. From this code and other remains, archaeologists have found that Mesopotamian society was highly structured with distinct social classes. Individuals could own land and this contributed to the rise of a stronger business class, which acted as a check to the king's power.

4 In sharp contrast to the unstable evolution of Mesopotamia, ancient Egypt was consistently stable throughout the bulk of its empire. Egypt was first unified in 3100 BC and remained stable until it was conquered in 525 BC by Persia. This great period of stability in both the environment and the government led to its central idea that the universe functioned with regularity and predictability, just like the Nile with its remarkably

consistent cycle of floods. ■ In the moral sphere, humankind was obligated to subdue its desires and actions so that law and order could be maintained and society could continue to prosper. ■ The monarchial Pharaoh was viewed as a divine incarnation of Horus, the son of the god of the underworld and thus his power was absolute. ■ As the apex of the society, he monopolized all land, industry, and commerce, so the economy was heavily dependent upon him and there was overwhelming state control in all aspects of Egyptian life. ■

Glossary

Neolithic relating to the later part of the Stone Age, when people had started farming but still used stone for making weapons and tools

1 According to paragraph 1, what does the author imply resulted when itinerant people began to settle in one place?

(A) They did not have to hunt any longer due to plenty of food supplies.
(B) Religion based upon a respect for nature was born immediately.
(C) The need for a political system to manage a swelling population arose.
(D) They had to develop methods to deal with overflows from the rivers.

Paragraph 1 is marked with an arrow [➡].

2 The word "emerged" in the passage is closest in meaning to

(A) convened
(B) appeared
(C) operated
(D) evolved

3 Which of the sentences below best expresses the essential information in the highlighted sentence in the passage? *Incorrect* choices change the meaning in important ways or leave out essential information.

(A) A cultural identity based around life on the Nile gave rise to a political system that was highly resistant to the influences of outside cultures.

(B) The basis of the political system was a homogenous culture that was free of external influences and dependent on the Nile due to its geographical isolation.

(C) Located between the desert and the Mediterranean Sea, the culture that developed on the Nile was influential because of its complex political system.

(D) The symbolic nature of its political system forced the culture that formed on the Nile to take measures to resist the influences of outside forces.

CH 01
CH 02
CH 03
CH 04
CH 05
CH 06
CH 07
CH 08
CH 09
Hackers TOEFL Reading

4 The word "sequence" in the passage is closest in meaning to

(A) selection
(B) concentration
(C) distribution
(D) progression

5 The word "Their" in the passage refers to

(A) groups
(B) empires
(C) the Sumerian
(D) gods

6 According to paragraph 3, the development of cuneiform was prompted by the requirement to

(A) govern a nation's territory
(B) increase a king's authority
(C) regulate agricultural activities
(D) record religious ceremonies

Paragraph 3 is marked with an arrow [➡].

7 In paragraph 3, why does the author mention "the Code of Hammurabi"?

(A) To show how the king's influence was checked by a business class
(B) To give an example of the laws by which the Mesopotamians lived
(C) To define the rights that individuals had in early Mesopotamia
(D) To contrast the laws in Mesopotamia to those in ancient Egypt

Paragraph 3 is marked with an arrow [➡].

8 The word "apex" in the passage is closest in meaning to

(A) source
(B) core
(C) acme
(D) symbol

9 Look at the four squares [■] that indicate where the following sentence could be added to the passage.

In addition to his fiscal responsibilities, he performed rituals and constructed temples to honor the gods.

Where would the sentence best fit?

Click on a square [■] to add the sentence to the passage.

10 Directions: Select the appropriate phrases from the answer choices and match them to the type of civilization to which they relate. **This question is worth 3 points.**

> Drag your answer choices to the spaces where they belong. To remove an answer choice, click on it. To review the passage, click on **View Text**.

Answer Choices	Mesopotamia
(A) A king's power lessened as his country became more secularized.	•
(B) Classes who had landownership and high economic strength were present.	•
(C) Religion had an influence on all parts of individual lives.	**Egypt**
(D) An all-powerful king controlled every sphere of a society.	•
(E) Each metropolis in a diversity of areas passed through constant turmoil.	•
(F) An individual who can communicate with the gods was considered the most sacred.	•
(G) The belief that the cosmos is steady and consistent spread.	

정답 및 해석 p.506

CH 01
CH 02
CH 03
CH 04
CH 05
CH 06
CH 07
CH 08
CH 09
Hackers TOEFL Reading

1 All organisms require a source of energy in order to grow, reproduce, and carry on the daily functions necessary for life. The usual concept of the food chain has the Sun at the top giving energy to plants, which are consumed by other organisms that are in turn devoured themselves, and so on. Although this is certainly true for the bulk of species, there are some plants that — unable to use the Sun efficiently — must leech onto other greenery like vampires, in the sense that they use a root system to "bite" prey and "suck" out its life-sustaining nutrients.

2 All parasitic plants have a unique adaptation — a modified root called a haustorium — that allows them to fasten to other flora in order to extract food or water. This is an important distinction, as there are other plants called epiphytes, which also bind to host plants, but lacking haustoria, cannot derive any water or nutrients from them and so are not parasitic. Those truly parasitic plants are categorized into two groups, depending on where their haustorium penetrates the host. The first types are hemiparasites, which attach themselves to the host's root-to-stem water-transporting xylem, while the second types are holoparasites, which affix themselves to the host's nutrient-distributing phloem.

3 ➡ As hemiparasites extort only water and dissolved minerals from their victims, they must produce their own carbohydrates via photosynthesis. This process needs chlorophyll, giving these bandits a green hue that makes them visually indistinguishable from ordinary foliage. Botanists must therefore identify them by closely examining their root system, which features tiny, hair-like projections that extend into a targeted host either at the stem or root, depending on the genus of hemiparasite. These do not actually penetrate into the tissues of the victim, but rather latch on to its membranes, as their large surface areas allow for a more effective means of liquid transfer.

4 This stratagem is neatly exemplified by the mistletoe, as its red and white berries are eaten by birds, passed through their digestive tracts, and excreted onto tree branches. After these sticky seeds are deposited, they begin to grow haustoria, which penetrate into the bark of the tree and attach to the xylem. They then use the requisite water from the tree to start their growth. In this manner, mistletoe is able to grow on a wide variety of trees, and although it can eventually prove lethal if infestation is heavy, damage more commonly results only in growth reduction of the host.

5 This is not the case with the more malevolent holoparasites, as they wrest almost all of their carbohydrates from their targets by unleashing an extensive network of haustoria throughout their phloem, often rendering their victims withered and on the brink of demise. Because holoparasites do not need photosynthesis for any kind of energy production, they do not produce chlorophyll, and therefore feature leaf and stem systems in a variety of colors that, like all parasitic plants, can produce a great diversity of flowers, such as the magnificent Rafflesia, the world's largest.

6 This behemoth extracts its entire requirement from its host, the Tetrastigma vine. ■

Provided that the victim is not weakened by the loss to the point of death — a rare overindulgence — there seems to be no limit to the amount the Rafflesia may extract, and therefore no limit to the size of the flower it ultimately blooms. ■ This flower's odor, likened to that of a rotting corpse, attracts flies and beetles from miles away, which swarm forth to pollinate the flower, thus helping to produce its four million odd seeds. ■ These are spread by animals onto other vines, where the cycle continues as new plants attach to other vines and grow in stealth until ready to give rise to more mammoth blossoms, ultimately leaving in their wakes the withered husks of exhausted Tetrastigmas. ■

7 The degree of pathogenicity varies greatly among parasitic plants from the relatively benign effects of the mistletoe to the more severe effects of the Rafflesia. However, both hemiparasites and holoparasites follow the general rule in biology that a good parasite does not kill its host, at least not until it successfully reproduces.

1 The word "devoured" in the passage is closest in meaning to

(A) eaten
(B) pumped
(C) raised
(D) stored

2 According to the passage, why does the author mention "epiphytes"?

(A) To describe a different type of parasitic plant
(B) To suggest various ways plants obtain nutrients
(C) To clarify the definition of a parasitic plant
(D) To emphasize the role of the haustorium

3 According to the passage, the classification of parasitic plants as hemiparasites or holoparasites is determined by

(A) the site of attachment of the modified root to the host
(B) the rate at which they take nutrients from the host
(C) the type of species which they prey upon
(D) whether or not they have a parasitic haustorium

CH 01
CH 02
CH 03
CH 04
CH 05
CH 06
CH 07
CH 08
CH 09
Hackers TOEFL Reading

4 According to paragraph 3, hemiparasites are not visually distinguished from common plants because

(A) they have the same shape of roots
(B) they have the same shade due to chlorophyll
(C) they have small projections at the stem
(D) they send forth the same fragrance

Paragraph 3 is marked with an arrow [➡].

5 The word "lethal" in the passage is closest in meaning to

(A) fortuitous
(B) vicious
(C) fatal
(D) ephemeral

6 The word "that" in the passage refers to

(A) extravagance
(B) diameter
(C) flower
(D) odor

7 Which of the sentences below best expresses the essential information in the highlighted sentence in the passage? *Incorrect* choices change the meaning in important ways or leave out essential information.

(A) The Tetrastigma vines are visited by animals, which deprive the Rafflesia of the opportunity to develop new blossoms.
(B) New growths of the Rafflesia occur as animals bring the seeds with them and affect other Tetrastigma vines.
(C) The Rafflesia grows in cycles which allow animals to spread the seeds to other Tetrastigmas.
(D) The Tetrastigmas have yet to make blossoms which will attract many animals because their seeds are not spread.

8 The word "severe" in the passage is closest in meaning to

(A) negative
(B) extreme
(C) disruptive
(D) cumulative

9 Look at the four squares [■] that indicate where the following sentence could be added to the passage.

When it finally bursts through the bark of its ravaged prey, it shows an extravagance on a truly monumental scale, often spanning over one meter in diameter.

Where would the sentence best fit?

Click on a square [■] to add the sentence to the passage.

10 **Directions**: Select the appropriate phrases from the answer choices and match them to the type of plants to which they relate. **This question is worth 3 points.**

Drag your answer choices to the spaces where they belong. To remove an answer choice, click on it. To review the passage, click on **View Text**.

Answer Choices	Hemiparasites
(A) Are not able to blossom for reproductive purposes	●
(B) Stick to the victim's membranes with a broad surface area	●
(C) Display stems and leaves in diverse colors	●
(D) Attach to the nutrient transport cells in the host	**Holoparasites**
(E) Photosynthesize for generating their own carbohydrates	●
(F) Always kill the host by limiting nutrient supply	●
(G) Merely extract water and liquefied minerals from the victim	

정답 및 해석 p.508

CH 01
CH 02
CH 03
CH 04
CH 05
CH 06
CH 07
CH 08
CH 09
Hackers TOEFL Reading

Sources of Modern African History

1   Innumerable pundits have alleged that the presumed dearth of resources available to scholars about African history precludes a detailed understanding of Africa's past. ■ Yet while the historical record is not as complete as it is for well-documented regions such as Europe or East Asia, it is nonetheless replete with an array of insightful materials. ■ From these, historians can extract useful data with which to construct a meaningful portrayal of at least portions of Africa's bygone days. ■ These resources, whether written or oral, are essential tools for shedding light on the shadowy antiquity of one of the world's most fascinating continents. ■

2   ➡ Though scattered and largely confined to specific regions of the continent, a large body of written materials does, in fact, exist. Most of these are preserved in Arabic or European languages. The former resulted from Muslim invasions and spread over the course of twelve centuries. Works include obituaries of dignitaries, political propaganda, and travel narratives. Many of the Arabic literary works have a pronounced, polemical tone and are packed with religious objectives, but some contain a wealth of secular information related to trade routes, natural resources, and agriculture. Relatively scant are official archives, but where available, these offer comparatively objective sources, and indeed Arabic was implemented in diplomatic discourse throughout a wide swath of Northern Africa. At first glance, official archives may seem uninspiring, as they are often little more than unimaginative and tiresome accounts of judicial decisions, treaties, financial transactions, and so on, but, unlike narrative literature, archives employ an overwhelmingly matter-of-fact style that lends these official records a high degree of authenticity.

3   ➡ As for materials in European languages, the records were largely produced from the viewpoint of colonial powers. Some of the earliest were composed by Christian missionaries, who traveled to remote regions of Africa and recorded the first descriptive accounts of isolated tribes. Having lived alongside indigenous peoples and learned their native tongues, missionaries were in a unique position to convey social and cultural information to the Western world. They described local customs, ceremonies, dress, and behavior in stunning detail. However, their accounts suffered from a pronounced bias, an often pejorative attitude toward the so-called savage and primitive societies of nonbelievers. Similarly, the content and tone of documents produced by European explorers and colonial administrators were heavily slanted in favor of colonial aims.

4   The absence of accounts from the perspective of indigenous tribes can largely be explained by the fact that, despite being one of the world's foremost examples of linguistic diversity, the vast majority of Africa's languages do not have a written form. Even Swahili and Hausa, which could be transcribed, were confined to poetry and myths. As such, much of the extant indigenous material from sub-Saharan Africa is so heavily reliant upon oral resources that it should be viewed with the same caution that would be exercised when approaching oral history. In fact, communities in this area never developed a specialized literati or penchant for keeping records. And oral literature, which often

evolves quickly, is more reflective of contemporary currents and how people subjectively — whether consciously or subconsciously — construct their own histories. This limitation has led some historians to view oral history as fanciful, and indeed there have been discrepancies between the spoken word and official records or archaeological evidence.

5 ➡ But despite their pitfalls, oral records do have intrinsic worth, as they reveal the perspectives of indigenous peoples. By functioning as a living museum, they illuminate the culture of Africa and induce the historian to look at history from new angles. Unlike archives, oral tradition does not just store or reflect history; it creates it and presents it in an artistic or entertaining way. And such embellishment need not always be fiction. Some epics are filled with information or imagery that is accurately reflective of historical daily life, and these stories are passed down verbally from generation to generation. For instance, in the *Epic of Silamaka* we are told of herding communities, of shepherds who were chosen to care for the flocks of the king, and how people wore shoes made of tanned ox hides, with one leather strap over the big toe and one over the heel. Recognizing the value of oral stories, historians have enthusiastically turned to interviews, and this has led to the creation of an entirely new genre of oral literature: life histories. People are asked to share their memories of colonial and post-colonial experiences, to talk about their personal lives, and to recount tales long passed down from family to family. Juxtaposed against written sources and archaeological evidence, oral stories convey more than just a glimpse into the culture and history of Africa. Rather, they give us snapshots of Africa's living soul.

1 The word "precludes" in the passage is closest in meaning to

(A) permits
(B) prevents
(C) instigates
(D) institutes

2 Which of the following can be inferred about Muslims from paragraph 2?

(A) They were interested in exploiting Africa's natural resources.
(B) Their full impact on African culture was not immediate.
(C) They encountered strong resistance from local tribes.
(D) Their system of law conflicted with native African values.

Paragraph 2 is marked with an arrow [➡].

3 Which of the following was NOT mentioned as a form of Arabic literature?

(A) descriptions of journeys
(B) texts of political suasion
(C) death notices of luminaries
(D) annotated biographies

CH 01
CH 02
CH 03
CH 04
CH 05
CH 06
CH 07
CH 08
CH 09
Hackers TOEFL Reading

4 According to paragraph 3, which of the following is true of the accounts of Christian missionaries?

(A) They contained information previously unavailable in the West.
(B) They were critical of how colonial powers treated the local people.
(C) They included quotations from indigenous leaders.
(D) They were censored by religious authorities prior to publication.

Paragraph 3 is marked with an arrow [➡].

5 Which of the sentences below best expresses the essential information in the highlighted sentence in the passage? *Incorrect* choices change the meaning in important ways or leave out essential information.

(A) Obviously, the excessive resurgence of interest in native oral histories from sub-Saharan Africa should be viewed with admonition.

(B) Consequently, the indigenous resources from sub-Saharan Africa that are currently available result from the careful scrutiny of historians.

(C) Essentially, the same discretion given to oral history should be extended to many of the existing native resources from sub-Saharan Africa.

(D) Inevitably, the fact that so many indigenous oral resources from sub-Saharan Africa exist will be greeted with muted enthusiasm by scholars.

6 What is the purpose of paragraph 5 in the overall discussion of sources of African history?

(A) It provides a summary conclusion to the topics discussed in the other paragraphs.

(B) It introduces a new set of questions for scholars to debate and explore.

(C) It discusses the potential value of oral resources in the overall context of available materials.

(D) It explores the comparative deficiencies of written texts when compared to oral resources.

Paragraph 5 is marked with an arrow [➡].

7 The word "convey" in the passage is closest in meaning to
(A) explain
(B) provoke
(C) embrace
(D) provide

8 What can be concluded from the passage?

(A) The range of resources deemed worthy of study by historians of Africa has expanded.

(B) An indicative portrait of how Africans once lived is never likely to come to light.

(C) Africa is an example of how oral sources are more worthwhile than written resources.

(D) Accounts of Africa's history are so partial that they are fundamentally untrustworthy.

9 Look at the four squares [■] that indicate where the following sentence could be added to the passage.

Some even have ventured to question whether Africa has a verifiable history at all.

Where would the sentence best fit?

> Click on a square [■] to add the sentence to the passage.

10 **Directions**: Select the appropriate phrases from the answer choices and match them to the appropriate resource. **This question is worth 3 points.**

> Drag your answer choices to the spaces where they belong. To remove an answer choice, click on it. To review the passage, click on **View Text**.

Answer Choices	Written Resources
(A) Tend to fluctuate along with corresponding trends	●
(B) Impel scholars to examine history from novel viewpoints	●
(C) Contain valuable information about administrative affairs	Oral resources
(D) Confined to limited areas of sub-Saharan Africa	●
(E) Generated by Arabs and Christian evangelists	●
(F) Representative of the points of view of endemic peoples	
(G) Reliant upon information that is impossible to substantiate	●

정답 및 해석 p.510

토플 빈출어휘 정리 노트

Chapter 09에 수록된 어휘들을 빈출도 순으로 정리했습니다. 음성파일을 들으며 꼭 암기하세요.

토플 최빈출어휘 [★★★]

- [ ] **essential** [isénʃəl] 필수의 (=necessary)
- [ ] **primitive** [prímətiv] 미개한 (=rudimentary)
- [ ] **widespread** [wàidspréd] 널리 퍼진 (=common)
- [ ] **record** [rikɔ́:rd] 기록으로 남기다 (=document)
- [ ] **ratio** [réiʃiou] 비율
- [ ] **exposure** [ikspóuʒər] 노출
- [ ] **source** [sɔ:rs] 산지 (=origin)
- [ ] **originally** [ərídʒənəli] 원래 (=initially)
- [ ] **alteration** [ɔ̀:ltəréiʃən] 변형 (=transformation)
- [ ] **depend on** ~에 따라
- [ ] **constant** [kánstənt] 일정한 (=fixed)
- [ ] **maintain** [meintéin] 유지하다 (=keep up)
- [ ] **perspective** [pərspéktiv] 관점 (=standpoint)
- [ ] **appreciate** [əprí:ʃièit] 평가하다 (=value)
- [ ] **inherent** [inhíərənt] 본질적인 (=innate)
- [ ] **contend** [kənténd] 주장하다 (=claim)
- [ ] **incompatibly** [ìnkəmpǽtəbli] 상반되게
- [ ] **dispute** [dispjú:t] 분쟁 (=feud)
- [ ] **routine** [ru:tí:n] 일상적인 (=ordinary)
- [ ] **immune** [imjú:n] 면역의
- [ ] **refine** [ri:fáin] 세련되게 하다 (=polish)
- [ ] **attribute** [ǽtrəbjù:t] 특성 (=characteristic)
- [ ] **contemporary** [kəntémpərèri] 현대의
- [ ] **adorn** [ədɔ́:rn] 장식하다 (=embellish)
- [ ] **exaggeration** [igzæ̀dʒəréiʃən] 과장
- [ ] **suspect** [səspékt] 생각하다
- [ ] **acquire** [əkwáiər] 얻다 (=learn)
- [ ] **adopt** [ədápt] 채택하다
- [ ] **respective** [rispéktiv] 각각의
- [ ] **confidence** [kánfədəns] 믿음 (=certainty)
- [ ] **crisis** [kráisis] 위기
- [ ] **encompass** [inkʌ́mpəs] 포함하다 (=embrace)
- [ ] **determine** [ditə́:rmin] 산정하다 (=figure out)
- [ ] **drawback** [drɔ́:bæk] 단점

- [ ] **deduce** [didjú:s] 추론하다 (=infer)
- [ ] **emerge** [imə́:rdʒ] 등장하다 (=appear)
- [ ] **arid** [ǽrid] 건조한
- [ ] **sequence** [sí:kwəns] 연속 (=progression)
- [ ] **apex** [éipeks] 최고 위치 (=acme)
- [ ] **devour** [diváuər] 먹다 (=eat)
- [ ] **lethal** [lí:θəl] 치명적인 (=fatal)
- [ ] **severe** [səvíər] 심각한 (=extreme)
- [ ] **preclude** [priklú:d] 방해하다 (=prevent)
- [ ] **pitfall** [pítfɔ̀:l] 위험 (=difficulty)
- [ ] **intrinsic** [intrínsik] 고유의 (=inherent)

토플 빈출어휘 [★★]

- [ ] **specific** [spisífik] 특정한 (=proper)
- [ ] **connection** [kənékʃən] 연결 (=linking)
- [ ] **parallel** [pǽrəlèl] 평행의
- [ ] **related** [riléitid] 관련이 있는 (=pertinent)
- [ ] **dehydration** [dì:haidréiʃən] 탈수
- [ ] **debate** [dibéit] 논쟁 (=contention)
- [ ] **criticism** [krítəsìzm] 비평
- [ ] **school** [sku:l] 학파
- [ ] **emphasis** [émfəsis] 강조 (=stress)
- [ ] **priority** [praiɔ́:rəti] 우선순위
- [ ] **external** [ikstə́:rnl] 외부적인
- [ ] **significance** [signífikəns] 중요성 (=importance)
- [ ] **necessitate** [nəsésətèit] 필요로 하다
- [ ] **separation** [sèpəréiʃən] 분리
- [ ] **quality** [kwáləti] 특징 (=attribute)
- [ ] **desire** [dizáiər] 원하다 (=expect)
- [ ] **adjust** [ədʒʌ́st] 적응하다
- [ ] **inflexible** [infléksəbl] 융통성 없는 (=rigid)
- [ ] **consecutively** [kənsékjutivli] 연속적으로 (=serially)
- [ ] **immediately** [imí:diətli] 즉시 (=instantly)
- [ ] **increase** [inkrí:s] 증가하다 (=multiply)
- [ ] **absorb** [əbsɔ́:rb] 흡수하다

*해커스 동영상강의 포털 해커스인강(HackersIngang.com)에서 '토플 빈출어휘 정리 노트' 음성파일을 무료로 다운로드할 수 있습니다.

☐ interrupt [ìntərʌ́pt] 방해하다 (=suspend)

☐ unfavorable [ʌ̀nféivərəbl] 좋지 않은 (=adverse)

☐ pigment [pígmənt] 안료

☐ destructive [distrʌ́ktiv] 파괴적인 (=ruinous)

☐ bump into ~에 부딪히다

☐ contextual [kəntékstʃuəl] 문맥상의

☐ region [ríːdʒən] 지역 (=territory)

☐ proof [pruːf] 증거

☐ reaction [riǽkʃən] 반응 (=reply)

☐ division [divíʒən] 분리

☐ stability [stəbíləti] 안정 (=equilibrium)

☐ abuse [əbjúːs] 남용

☐ corruption [kərʌ́pʃən] 부패

☐ ability [əbíləti] 능력 (=capacity)

☐ approval [əprúːvəl] 승인

☐ variety [vəráiəti] 다양함 (=diversity)

☐ augment [ɔːgmént] 증대시키다

☐ supplement [sʌ́pləmənt] 보충하다

☐ length [leŋkθ] 길이 (=duration)

☐ gauge [geidʒ] 측정하다 (=measure)

☐ succession [səkséʃən] 연속 (=string)

☐ innumerable [injúːmərəbl] 무수한

☐ discrepancy [diskrépənsi] 불일치

토플 기출어휘 [★]

☐ uptake [ʌ́ptèik] 흡수

☐ microscopic [màikrəskápik] 현미경으로 봐야만 보이는

☐ metallic [mətǽlik] 금속의

☐ in place of ~을 대신하여

☐ occupation [àkjupéiʃən] 일

☐ negate [nigéit] 부인하다

☐ misidentify [mìsaidéntəfai] 오인하다

☐ distinction [distíŋkʃən] 차이점

☐ sensitivity [sènsətívəti] 민감

☐ engineer [èndʒiníər] 설계하다

☐ fluid [flúːid] 유체

☐ slaughter [slɔ́ːtər] 대량학살

☐ entrance [éntrəns] 등장하다

☐ gatherer [gǽðərər] 채집자

☐ medicinal [mədísənl] 의약의

☐ first and foremost 무엇보다도

☐ mammal [mǽməl] 포유동물

☐ revitalize [riːváitəlàiz] 활기를 불어넣다

☐ dismiss [dismís] 일축하다

☐ irrefutable [ìrifjúːtəbl] 반박할 수 없는

☐ oncoming [áːnkʌmiŋ] 다가오는

☐ shallow [ʃǽlou] 얕은

☐ repugnance [ripʌ́gnəns] 반감

☐ monarchy [mánərki] 군주제

☐ epoch [épək] 시대

☐ genre [ʒɑ́ːnrə] 장르

☐ come to fruition 결실을 맺다

☐ sublime [səbláim] 장엄한

☐ note [nout] 음

☐ mutate [mjúːteit] 변형시키다

☐ capitalize on 이용하다

☐ canonize [kǽnənàiz] 찬양하다

☐ hierarchically [hàiərɑ́ːrkikəli] 계층적으로

☐ specimen [spésəmən] 표본

☐ ascertain [æ̀sərtéin] 확인하다

☐ chronological [krànəládʒikəl] 연대순의

☐ decipher [disáifər] 해독하다

☐ collide [kəláid] 충돌하다

☐ unanimous [juːnǽnəməs] 단일적인

☐ plague [pleig] 괴롭히다

☐ fanciful [fǽnsifəl] 공상적인

☐ fiction [fíkʃən] 허구

☐ epic [épik] 서사시

☐ recount [rikáunt] 상술하다

☐ juxtapose [dʒʌ́kstəpòuz] 나란히 놓다

CH 01
CH 02
CH 03
CH 04
CH 05
CH 06
CH 07
CH 08
CH 09
Hackers TOEFL Reading

goHackers.com

Hackers **TOEFL** READING

ACTUAL
TEST

ACTUAL TEST 1
ACTUAL TEST 2

ACTUAL TEST 1

01   Earth's Energy Balance

1   According to the first law of thermodynamics, the amount of energy that enters an open system — one with a boundary that is permeable to both energy and matter — is equal to the amount that eventually exits. This fundamental principle explains why average temperatures on Earth remain relatively constant from year to year. Electromagnetic radiation emitted by the Sun, which accounts for 99.97 percent of the energy available in the atmosphere and on the surface of the planet, raises the temperature of air, water, and land as it is absorbed. However, this is compensated for by the heat the planet radiates back into space, creating a state of equilibrium that has come to be referred to as Earth's energy balance.

2   ➡ Not all of the solar energy that penetrates the outer layer of the atmosphere can be considered part of the planet's energy budget. ■ Some of this energy, which is primarily in the form of shortwave radiation such as visible and ultraviolet light, is scattered by atmospheric particles through the process of diffusion — radiation that strikes a gas molecule or miniscule piece of dust or ash suspended in the air will be deflected in a random direction. ■ The fact that lighter-colored objects are highly reflective is another factor that limits how much solar energy is available, a phenomenon known as the albedo effect. ■ Approximately 24 percent of the incoming radiation is reflected by cloud formations, and another 4 percent by areas of land with high albedo ratings — those covered with large amounts of ice and snow, such as the polar regions, or with other reflective substances like the sands of deserts. ■

3   ➡ The greatest part of the remaining radiation is absorbed by landmasses and oceans on the surface of the planet, while a smaller portion is taken in by particles in the atmosphere. As matter absorbs solar radiation, the kinetic energy of its constituent atoms increases — they begin to vibrate more quickly, which causes the temperature of the matter to rise. This means that the absorption of solar energy heats the planet. However, the extent to which this happens is limited because as its temperature rises, matter begins to emit long-wave radiation in the form of heat. The amount of thermal energy released is proportional to the temperature increase; if the temperature doubles, the energy radiated increases by a factor of sixteen. At a certain point the amount of incoming and outgoing energy will be equal, preventing the temperature of the matter from rising any further.

4   ➡ Although a small percentage of the heat radiated by the surface of Earth passes directly through the atmosphere and dissipates into space, most is absorbed by matter in the atmosphere. The temperatures of these particles rise until they begin to emit energy equally in all directions. Approximately half travels back down to the surface of the planet where it is reabsorbed by land and water. The remainder moves in the opposite direction to either escape into space or to be absorbed by matter at higher altitudes. This cycle, known as the greenhouse effect, repeats itself

until the energy reaches the outer layer of the atmosphere, where it is released into space.

5 ➡ The transfer of heat back and forth between the surface of the planet and the atmosphere plays a vital role in making Earth habitable. The recycling of energy and the delay in its transfer to space results in an average surface temperature of approximately fifteen degrees Celsius. If Earth did not have an atmosphere, this would decline by over 200 percent.

6 The energy balance of the planet can be affected by a number of factors, triggering global climate change. Known as climatic forcings, some of these alter the amount of energy entering the atmosphere, such as fluctuations in the Sun's luminosity or cyclic deviations in Earth's orbit. Others influence the other side of the equation. For instance, the burning of fossil fuels increases atmospheric levels of carbon dioxide and methane, which are effective absorbers of thermal energy. This intensifies the greenhouse effect, thereby reducing the rate at which heat is transferred back into space and gradually increasing surface temperatures. Of course, as the planet becomes warmer, it radiates an increasing amount of heat until eventually a new balance between incoming and outgoing energy is achieved.

1 The word "fundamental" in the passage is closest in meaning to

    (A) simple
    (B) essential
    (C) major
    (D) compelling

2 According to paragraph 2, diffusion occurs when

    (A) the wavelength of light is altered
    (B) energy is redirected by matter
    (C) radiation is absorbed by molecules
    (D) particles in the air are scattered

    Paragraph 2 is marked with an arrow [➡].

3 According to paragraph 2, what can be inferred about the albedo rating of the planet's surface?

    (A) It changes based on the amount of incoming solar radiation.
    (B) It increases as the temperatures of air and land decline.
    (C) It varies depending on local environmental conditions.
    (D) It remains constant in areas with extensive cloud cover.

4 The word "constituent" in the passage is closest in meaning to

(A) primary
(B) component
(C) disparate
(D) subsequent

5 According to paragraph 3, what causes atoms to vibrate more quickly?

(A) The intensity of the heat emitted by matter increases.
(B) The amount of energy that matter contains is altered.
(C) The structure of matter is transformed by kinetic force.
(D) The radiation of thermal energy by matter quickens.

Paragraph 3 is marked with an arrow [➡].

6 According to paragraph 4, what happens to the bulk of the heat emitted by Earth?

(A) It is dissipated before it enters the higher altitudes of the atmosphere.
(B) It is ejected into space immediately after being radiated into the air.
(C) It is reflected back to the surface by atmospheric molecules.
(D) It is drawn in by particles in the air before being released.

Paragraph 4 is marked with an arrow [➡].

7 What is the relationship between paragraphs 4 and 5 in the passage?

(A) Paragraph 4 explains a climatic process and paragraph 5 states one of its significant effects.
(B) Paragraph 4 presents a theory about climate change and paragraph 5 provides supporting evidence.
(C) Paragraph 4 discusses an energy phenomenon and paragraph 5 outlines its underlying causes.
(D) Paragraph 4 describes the types of atmospheric heat transfer and paragraph 5 provides an example.

Paragraphs 4 and 5 are marked with arrows [➡].

8 The word "this" in the passage refers to

(A) energy
(B) space
(C) temperature
(D) atmosphere

9 Look at the four squares [■] that indicate where the following sentence could be added to the passage.

As a result, about 7 percent of the total radiation from the Sun returns to space right away.

Where would the sentence best fit?

Click on a square [■] to add the sentence to the passage.

10 **Directions**: An introductory sentence for a brief summary of the passage is provided below. Complete the summary by selecting the THREE answer choices that express the most important ideas in the passage. Some sentences do not belong in the summary because they express ideas that are not presented in the passage or are minor ideas in the passage. **This question is worth 2 points.**

Drag your answer choices to the spaces where they belong. To remove an answer choice, click on it. To review the passage, click on **View Text**.

The energy taken in by Earth corresponds to the amount it eventually releases.

-
-
-

Answer Choices

(A) Heat radiated by the planet moves back and forth between its surface and atmosphere before entering space.

(B) Climate change is disturbing the balance between the energy entering and leaving the planet's surface.

(C) Some solar radiation is dispersed by particles in the atmosphere or reflected by clouds and planetary surface features.

(D) The temperature of the planet would decline to dangerous levels if not for the greenhouse effect.

(E) Particles in the atmosphere retain long-wave energy emitted by the Sun for an extended period of time.

(F) Most of the energy from the Sun is absorbed by matter at the planet's surface, causing it to emit heat.

정답 및 해석 p.513

1 ➡ During the nineteenth century, industrialization in America created unprecedented growth, resulting in a higher proportion of people living in urban settings: railroads bridged the gap between cities and rural areas, urban factories drew workers away from farm life in search of better pay, and waves of immigrants flooded into US cities from overseas. The collective outcome of urbanization was that cities exploded in size so rapidly that nobody had foresight or opportunity to implement any sort of comprehensive and strategic urban development plan. Instead, the organization of cities was left to market forces and disjointed government entities that lacked the will and know-how to cope with the swiftly changing circumstances. It was not until the early twentieth century, just before World War I, that a truly formal and organized form of city planning came to the forefront of the American agenda, and several key developments helped trigger its eventual establishment.

2 ➡ As more and more people crammed into confined areas, overcrowding became a concern for urban residents. Factory workers were typically provided cheap housing in run-down buildings in slums, and profit-seeking landlords usually divided houses into multiple units in an attempt to put as many people in them as possible. Immigrants often congregated in any vacant area and constructed makeshift homes, creating large clusters of communities called "shanty towns." Such places offered substandard amenities and put people in uncomfortable proximity to one another. ■ Often the streets outside were no more convenient. ■ Crowds of pedestrians shared the packed streets with railways and merchants, and the chaotic hustle and bustle made getting around town frustrating. ■ As a result of the inconvenience associated with overcrowding, people began to consider ways to organize urban areas so that they would be less densely populated. ■

3 The first clearly discernible impetus toward an organized restructuring of urban design came in the mid to late 1800s in the form of much-needed sanitation reforms, which developed out of a growing uneasiness about the filthiness of urban areas. Though American cities seldom had as much filth as their European counterparts, they were nonetheless extremely dirty places by modern standards. Noxious fumes spewed incessantly from factories, which discharged untreated chemicals directly into streams. There was no sewer system in most cities, and people dumped garbage into alleys or any other convenient spot. Even in the nation's capital, pigs roamed about freely and horses defecated on the streets, and it is said that the White House itself was infested with vermin. On top of the unsavory stench, the lack of proper sanitation allowed for the proliferation of germs and led to numerous epidemics, including deadly outbreaks of tuberculosis and cholera. In the aftermath of such morbid events, activists and government officials convened to discuss plans for cleaning up their municipalities.

4 Another development that prompted the birth of city planning was the City Beautiful Movement, which sought to make cities more aesthetically pleasing. One way in which this sentiment manifested itself was in the design and construction of more and larger green spaces. In 1850, the vast majority of city parks were no more than a few acres. Yet a bold move by the city of New York — the setting aside of 843 acres for a public park — set a precedent that would be the envy and inspiration of cities around the country. Construction on Central Park began in 1858, and the fashioning of this "green oasis for the refreshment of the city's soul and body" represented a watershed moment as cities such as Baltimore, St. Louis, and San Francisco soon boasted their

own large public green spaces. In addition to promoting parks, proponents of beautification advocated erecting public monuments, designing government buildings in classical style, and creating formal gardens.

5 ➡ By the 1910s, the term "city planning" itself had entered the vocabulary of public officials and other notable members of municipal communities. Although opinions varied about the best way to proceed, most people agreed that some kind of centralized entity was needed to oversee every facet of city growth. This responsibility was conferred upon city planning commissions, which began to appear around the 1930s. Planning commissions were given the task of drafting the overall vision and regulatory tools to ensure safe, responsible, and sustainable building for the future. Working closely with mayors and city councils, they soon began to make progress in improving the living conditions in American cities.

11 The word "unprecedented" in the passage is closest in meaning to

(A) understated
(B) unfettered
(C) unaccounted for
(D) unheard of

12 Which is NOT listed as a factor in the growing ratio of people residing in urban areas?

(A) The creation of new cities
(B) Railroads
(C) Influxes of immigrants
(D) Factory jobs

13 According to paragraph 1, what was the overall consequence of urbanization?

(A) Cities were compelled to create a new government entity.
(B) Cities began searching for leaders with a keen understanding of market forces.
(C) Cities grew so fast that no thorough plan for city development materialized.
(D) Cities swallowed up most of the surrounding communities in rural areas.

Paragraph 1 is marked with an arrow [➡].

14 Which of the sentences below best expresses the essential information in the highlighted sentence in the passage? *Incorrect* choices change the meaning in important ways or leave out essential information.

(A) Prior to World War I, city planning in America was highly unorganized, but several crucial circumstances helped to eventually formalize it after the war.

(B) Only in the early 1900s did orderly city planning become a priority in America, and a few important occurrences contributed to its later implementation.

(C) In the early twentieth century, a number of key developments caused city planning to take a back seat to other more pressing matters in America.

(D) By the time a formalized form of city planning was finally instituted in America, World War I was about to begin.

15 Which of the following can be inferred from the discussion of overcrowded housing in paragraph 2?

(A) Factories usually did not provide housing for their workers.
(B) Factory workers typically commuted long distances between home and work.
(C) Dwellings in shanty towns were not built to last very long.
(D) Landlords often had difficulty finding people to rent their run-down buildings.

Paragraph 2 is marked with an arrow [➡].

16 Why does the author mention "the White House" in the passage?

(A) To give an example of one of the few sanitary places in the country
(B) To emphasize that no place was immune to sanitation issues
(C) To highlight the main reason for the sanitation reforms
(D) To contrast the cleanliness of a special building with that of ordinary dwellings

17 The word "manifested" in the passage is closest in meaning to

(A) asserted
(B) defined
(C) transformed
(D) revealed

18 According to paragraph 5, which of the following is true about how people viewed city planning?

(A) Most of the population felt that formal city planning was unnecessary.
(B) Community leaders could not agree about who should carry out city planning.
(C) The majority of citizens accepted that one body should be responsible for city planning.
(D) Few people believed that true city planning was possible in their lifetime.

Paragraph 5 is marked with an arrow [➡].

19 Look at the four squares [■] that indicate where the following sentence could be added to the passage.

Proposals for how that might be accomplished included converting unused buildings into affordable housing as well as widening thoroughfares and adding sidewalks.

Where would the sentence best fit?

Click on a square [■] to add the sentence to the passage.

20 **Directions**: An introductory sentence for a brief summary of the passage is provided below. Complete the summary by selecting the THREE answer choices that express the most important ideas in the passage. Some sentences do not belong in the summary because they express ideas that are not presented in the passage or are minor ideas in the passage. **This question is worth 2 points.**

> Drag your answer choices to the spaces where they belong. To remove an answer choice, click on it. To review the passage, click on **View Text**.

Industrialization led to rapid urbanization in nineteenth-century America, setting up the need for a formal system of city planning.

-
-
-

Answer Choices

(A) After the continual occurrence of deadly epidemics, city governments were compelled to seek ways to clean up their cities.

(B) An early precursor of city planning came in the form of sanitation reforms, which were in reaction to the dirty conditions in American cities.

(C) Although the City Beautiful Movement gained strong support in New York, its activities had little impact in other parts of America.

(D) Public concern about overcrowded dwellings and streets prompted people to think about how cities could be designed to be more sparsely populated.

(E) Among the developments that gave rise to city planning was a social movement which encouraged activities designed to make cities more beautiful.

(F) Because living conditions were so dire, city planning commissions were granted the authority to expedite sustainable development regardless of the short-term costs.

정답 및 해석 p.515

ACTUAL TEST 2

01   **Marine Bioluminescence**

1   In his *Naturalis Historia*, Pliny the Elder (AD 23-79) described rotten wood that glows in the dark, a phenomenon that came to be known as foxfire. ■ In modern times, it was discovered that foxfire is actually an effect created by wood-dwelling fungi that are bioluminescent; that is, they produce their own light via chemical reactions. ■ Bioluminescence is not unique to fungi but is also present in various species of insects, arachnids, and worms. ■ Yet it is in the world's oceans, not on land, where the vast majority of bioluminescent creatures can be found, and nearly every major group of marine organisms has at least some members that glow. ■ Researchers believe that the relatively lengthy, stable evolutionary history of the oceans and their comparative lack of light, particularly at great depths, made them ideal environments for the emergence of bioluminescence.

2   The reaction that gives rise to bioluminescence has a number of chemical prerequisites. The primary substance involved is luciferin, a light-producing pigment. Some species have evolved biological processes to synthesize their own luciferin, while others obtain it by feeding on other bioluminescent organisms or through symbiotic relationships with them. Light is generated when the luciferin is oxidized by molecular oxygen in the presence of an enzyme called luciferase, which serves as a catalyst for the reaction, with light, oxyluciferin, and water emitted as byproducts. In some cases, a charged ion, often of calcium or magnesium, is also needed in order for bioluminescence to occur.

3   Biologists have not conclusively determined the precise evolutionary advantage bestowed by bioluminescence when it first emerged, but one clue may lie in the fact that the chemical reaction involved results in the degradation of oxygen. Since many bioluminescent organisms initially evolved in oxygen-free environments, the oxygen molecules produced through photosynthesis by plants that evolved later may have been toxic to them. This is consistent with the incidence of bioluminescence among single-celled marine organisms. Many such creatures that first existed prior to the evolution of marine plants subsequently developed bioluminescence, likely as a way of eliminating oxygen. In contrast, most unicellular organisms that emerged after plants, like diatoms, had no need to perform light-producing reactions, perhaps because oxygen was a part of their environment from the beginning of their existence as species.

4   ➡ The validity of the oxygen-elimination hypothesis remains open to debate, but it is clear that whatever the original purpose of bioluminescence, it has since taken on many other functions, and one of the more common of these is protection from other organisms. For example, many sea creatures emit light to evade predators, and the vampire squid is one such species. In the presence of a predator, it ejects glowing mucus that both startles and confuses its would-be attacker, which facilitates the squid's escape. The Atolla jellyfish is known for its "burglar alarm," using light as a signaling device of sorts; when threatened by a predator, it emits a series of bright

flashes that attract yet larger fish that eat the attacker. Other bioluminescent organisms generate light in order to avoid detection, a strategy referred to as counter-illumination. Many predators, such as sharks, hunt from below and spot the silhouettes of their targets above them against the backdrop of sunlight; to counter this, some prey species produce their own light in order to blend in with their backgrounds. By adjusting the degree of bioluminescence as light conditions vary, these species can remain virtually undetectable.

5 ➡ Counter-illumination also serves as an effective hunting mechanism, something that can be clearly seen in the case of the cookiecutter shark. Like counter-illuminating prey, it brightens itself to match light from above, but it simultaneously leaves a small patch of flesh near its pectoral fins unilluminated in order to deceive its targets. Smaller predators such as mackerel and tuna mistake the dark shape as a small fish and swim closer, giving the shark ample opportunity to devour them. Similarly, some organisms utilize the light source itself as a type of lure that is effective in attracting prey. The group of deep-sea organisms known as anglerfish is well-known for this behavior: a luminescent lump of flesh is attached to a thin filament extending from an anglerfish's forehead, much like the bait and tackle utilized by a fisherman. The anglerfish remains stationary and waves the brightly lit lure back and forth in front of its head, and as soon as an organism is drawn in by the light, the anglerfish bites down on it with its sharp teeth.

1 Which of the sentences below best expresses the essential information in the highlighted sentence in the passage? *Incorrect* choices change the meaning in important ways or leave out essential information.

(A) Scientists maintain that the persistent lack of light in the world's oceans, as well as their stability, make them ideal habitats for organisms that possess bioluminescence.

(B) Biologists think that bioluminescence is more prevalent in environments that lack sufficient levels of light and have enjoyed consistent conditions for many years.

(C) It is thought that the seas were well suited for the development of bioluminescence because they are relatively dark and have endured a long time without a great deal of change.

(D) Marine environments are darker than other biomes, which explains why bioluminescence is continuing to evolve in the world's oceans.

2 All of the following are chemicals that are needed for bioluminescence EXCEPT

(A) luciferin
(B) luciferase
(C) oxygen
(D) oxyluciferin

3 The word "them" in the passage refers to

(A) organisms
(B) environments
(C) molecules
(D) plants

4 What can be inferred about diatoms from the passage?

(A) They are presently evolving bioluminescence.
(B) They are incapable of photosynthesis.
(C) They are not affected adversely by oxygen.
(D) They are toxic to marine plants.

5 The word "facilitates" in the passage is closest in meaning to

(A) sanctions
(B) eases
(C) encourages
(D) hinders

6 According to paragraph 4, the Atolla jellyfish produces light in order to

(A) draw sizeable predators to its location
(B) identify potential attackers that could threaten it
(C) distract larger organisms before escaping
(D) entice fish that can be eaten to swim closer

Paragraph 4 is marked with an arrow [➡].

7 The word "stationary" in the passage is closest in meaning to

(A) unmoving
(B) waiting
(C) searching
(D) watching

8 The author's main purpose in paragraph 5 is to

(A) emphasize the utility of counter-illumination
(B) contrast two types of bioluminescent prey
(C) explain how aquatic hunters are able to produce light
(D) illustrate the use of bioluminescence by predators

Paragraph 5 is marked with an arrow [➡].

9 Look at the four squares [■] that indicate where the following sentence could be added to the passage.

Fireflies, for instance, produce flashes of light both to warn predators of their unpalatability as well as attract mates.

Where would the sentence best fit?

Click on a square [■] to add the sentence to the passage.

10 **Directions**: An introductory sentence for a brief summary of the passage is provided below. Complete the summary by selecting the THREE answer choices that express the most important ideas in the passage. Some sentences do not belong in the summary because they express ideas that are not presented in the passage or are minor ideas in the passage. **This question is worth 2 points.**

Drag your answer choices to the spaces where they belong. To remove an answer choice, click on it. To review the passage, click on **View Text**.

> **Bioluminescence is the creation and emission of light by living things, and it is particularly prevalent in ocean environments.**
>
> ●
>
> ●
>
> ●

Answer Choices

(A) Predators utilize bioluminescence in order to locate and identify their prey.

(B) There is an ongoing debate regarding the primary purpose of bioluminescence, with biologists split among those supporting theories of offensive and defensive functions.

(C) A chemical reaction generates light, and this may have developed initially as a way to dispose of a harmful substance.

(D) Bioluminescence enables predators to entice prey to swim closer, allowing the attacker to feed on them.

(E) A number of chemicals combine, allowing organisms to produce illumination and eliminate various toxins.

(F) Marine organisms emit light in order to make themselves less visible, escape from attackers, or lure creatures that consume predators.

정답 및 해석 p.517

1 ➡ Edwin Hubble's investigations in the early twentieth century were focused on the size and scope of the universe. At the time, it was still commonly thought that the Milky Way galaxy comprised everything in the cosmos, but Hubble believed it was possible that the universe was actually much larger. Utilizing a powerful new telescope that had been built on Mount Wilson in California, he set his sights on an astronomical object named Andromeda and saw what appeared to be a collection of many individual stars. Hubble suspected that Andromeda was its own galaxy — that is, he thought that it lay outside the Milky Way — but in order to prove this, he needed to calculate the distance of Andromeda from Earth.

2 Measuring astronomical distances was then, as now, an extremely challenging task that required something called a standard candle — a class of astronomical objects that have a known, absolute luminosity due to a characteristic inherent to all objects in the class. ■ Once an entity belonging to such a class is identified, its distance can be calculated by comparing its absolute brightness with its apparent brightness as seen from Earth. ■ Hubble found a standard candle in Andromeda in the form of a Cepheid variable, a type of star that fluctuates in brightness over a set period of days or weeks and has an absolute luminosity that corresponds to the length of the cycle of light variation. ■ By calculating the star's luminosity based on its period and then comparing it to the brightness as observed through his telescope, Hubble determined that Andromeda is located far outside the Milky Way, conclusively demonstrating that it is a galaxy. ■

3 Thereafter, Hubble expanded his observations to other galaxies, and in addition to measuring their distances from Earth, he also analyzed the spectra of light emitted by them. He found that light from galaxies is always shifted toward the red end of the light spectrum, where wavelengths are longer. This phenomenon, known as redshifting, indicates that galaxies are moving away from Earth, effectively stretching the light waves they emit, with greater redshifting being indicative of higher relative velocities. Significantly, Hubble found that galaxies that are farther from Earth are traveling away from Earth at faster speeds than galaxies that are closer. The only explanation for this observation is that the universe is expanding.

4 ➡ Hubble's work had an immediate and profound effect on cosmology. An expanding universe indicated that the cosmos had actually been smaller in the distant past, giving rise to a new model regarding the origin of the universe — the big bang theory — which states that the cosmos began in a very hot and dense state at a single point and has been growing ever since. After the initial expansion, the universe cooled enough for the formation of matter. Researchers assumed that the attractive gravitational force of this matter is slowing down the expansion, suggesting two possible futures: a "closed" universe in which the expansion is eventually reversed and the universe contracts, and an "open" universe in which expansion continues infinitely. Determining which of these possibilities is likeliest required a complex calculation in terms of how fast the universe is expanding relative to the density of matter contained within it, and for decades, cosmologists failed to reach a consensus.

5 The late twentieth century brought dramatic discoveries that changed everything. Advances in observational technology allowed astronomers to look deeper into space than ever before, and in order to learn more about universe expansion, they turned their gaze to some of the most distant

visible galaxies, more than 10 billion light years away. In these collections of stars, researchers searched for and found a number of Type Ia supernovae — massive star explosions that each have the same brightness, enabling astronomers to utilize them as standard candles and thereby measure their distances. After calculating their distances and also measuring their redshifts, researchers made a surprising discovery: the supernovae were about 15 percent farther from Earth than would have been expected under the then-existing model of universe expansion, a discrepancy suggesting that the enlargement of the universe is actually accelerating, not slowing down. Some scientists have posited an enigmatic force called dark energy that is pushing galaxies apart at ever increasing speeds; however, the exact reason for the acceleration is uncertain and remains one of the greatest mysteries of modern science.

11 According to paragraph 1, Edwin Hubble sought to calculate the distance between Andromeda and Earth in order to

   (A) show that Andromeda was an independent system of stars
   (B) determine the position of Andromeda in the Milky Way
   (C) prove that Andromeda contained as many stars as the Milky Way
   (D) resolve a debate regarding the exact size of the universe

   Paragraph 1 is marked with an arrow [➡].

12 The author mentions a "Cepheid variable" in order to

   (A) suggest that stars in Andromeda exhibit strong luminosity
   (B) demonstrate how the calculation of a distance was possible
   (C) give an example of an astronomical discovery by Hubble
   (D) illustrate how Hubble determined Andromeda's brightness

13 According to the passage, why was it concluded that the universe is expanding?

   (A) The spectra of light emitted by galaxies are unaffected by their speed.
   (B) More distant groups of stars are associated with higher relative speeds.
   (C) Light waves emitted by galaxies closer to Earth are more stretched.
   (D) Faster-moving galaxies have been observed to produce greater redshifting.

14 The word "profound" in the passage is closest in meaning to

   (A) negligible
   (B) direct
   (C) positive
   (D) intense

15 What can be inferred about matter from paragraph 4?

   (A) It originally existed in an extremely heated and dense condition.
   (B) It produced energy that was responsible for the big bang.
   (C) It was not present at the very beginning of the cosmos.
   (D) It exerts forces that are reversing the universe's expansion.

   Paragraph 4 is marked with an arrow [➡].

16 Which of the sentences below best expresses the essential information in the highlighted sentence in the passage? *Incorrect* choices change the meaning in important ways or leave out essential information.

(A) Research into the possibility of an open or closed future of the universe led to new discoveries regarding the gravitational attraction of matter.

(B) Based on their presumption that the universe is getting bigger at a decreasing rate, experts thought that it will either become smaller or expand forever.

(C) Astronomers believe that the gravity exerted by matter is causing the cosmos to shrink, and this will either continue unabated or cease.

(D) The expansion of matter within the universe is generating additional gravity that will reverse the expansion of the universe or allow it to continue forever.

17 According to the passage, all following are true of Type Ia supernovae EXCEPT

(A) They are utilized by astronomers as means of measurement.

(B) They are located in distant galaxies that are far from Earth.

(C) They produce huge explosions that cause the expansion of galaxies.

(D) They each exhibit the exact same level of luminosity.

18 The word "discrepancy" in the passage is closest in meaning to

(A) contingency
(B) fallacy
(C) inconsistency
(D) deficiency

19 Look at the four squares [■] that indicate where the following sentence could be added to the passage.

This method is possible because light becomes weaker at a consistent rate as it travels over long distances.

Where would the sentence best fit?

Click on a square [■] to add the sentence to the passage.

20 **Directions**: An introductory sentence for a brief summary of the passage is provided below. Complete the summary by selecting the THREE answer choices that express the most important ideas in the passage. Some sentences do not belong in the summary because they express ideas that are not presented in the passage or are minor ideas in the passage. **This question is worth 2 points.**

> Drag your answer choices to the spaces where they belong. To remove an answer choice, click on it. To review the passage, click on **View Text**.

A number of twentieth-century discoveries contributed to modern science's understanding of an expanding universe.

- ●
- ●
- ●

Answer Choices

(A) Research into the nature of the universe revealed that it began as a single point, and experts expect the cosmos to continue to expand indefinitely.

(B) Observations of distant galaxies showed that the rate of the universe's expansion has been accelerating, a phenomenon that might be explained by an elusive force.

(C) Edwin Hubble's research in the early 1900s demonstrated that galaxies are growing farther and farther apart.

(D) An early twentieth-century astronomer utilized a specific type of standard candle to determine the redshifts of distant galaxies.

(E) Astronomers have a number of theories as to why the rate of the universe's expansion has been increasing.

(F) A theory of cosmic origin was devised, and scientists attempted to calculate what the future holds for the universe.

정답 및 해석 p.519

MEMO

기본에서 실전까지 iBT 토플 리딩 완벽 대비

|H|A|C|K|E|R|S| TOEFL
READING

개정 5판 4쇄 발행 2025년 1월 13일
개정 5판 1쇄 발행 2023년 8월 31일

지은이	David Cho	언어학 박사, 前 UCLA 교수
펴낸곳	(주)해커스 어학연구소
펴낸이	해커스 어학연구소 출판팀

주소	서울특별시 서초구 강남대로61길 23 (주)해커스 어학연구소
고객센터	02-537-5000
교재 관련 문의	publishing@hackers.com
동영상강의	HackersIngang.com

ISBN	978-89-6542-599-1 (13740)
Serial Number	05-04-01

외국어인강 1위,
해커스인강(HackersIngang.com)
ⅢⅢ 해커스인강

전세계 유학정보의 중심,
고우해커스(goHackers.com)
ⅢⅢ 고우해커스

- 실전 감각을 극대화하는 **iBT 리딩 실전모의고사**
- 효과적인 리딩 학습을 돕는 **빈출어휘 암기&지문녹음 MP3**
- 해커스 토플 스타강사의 **본 교재 인강**

- **토플 보카 외우기, 토플 스피킹/라이팅 첨삭 게시판** 등 무료 학습 콘텐츠
- 고득점을 위한 **토플 공부전략 강의**
- **국가별 대학 및 전공별 정보, 유학 Q&A 게시판** 등 다양한 유학정보

[외국어인강 1위] 헤럴드 선정 2018 대학생 선호브랜드 대상 '대학생이 선정한 외국어인강' 부문 1위

전세계 유학정보의 중심
고우해커스

goHackers.com

|H|A|C|K|E|R|S|

TOEFL

READING

David Cho

정답 · 해석 · 정답단서

TOEFL iBT
최신출제경향
반영

해커스 어학연구소

HACKERS
TOEFL

READING

정답·해석·정답단서

해커스 어학연구소

DIAGNOSTIC TEST

01 Bluegills

p.32

1. (C)	2. (D)	3. (D)
4. (B)	5. (A)	6. (A)
7. (C)	8. (D)	9. 3rd
10. (B)–3단락, (D)–2단락, (F)–4단락		

1 낚시꾼들은 bluegill을 북아메리카에서 가장 인기 있는 낚시용 물고기의 일종으로 인정할 텐데, 그것은 민물 호수나 연못에서 자주 발견된다. 6~9인치(15~23센티미터) 이상으로는 거의 자라지 않는 이 비교적 작은 물고기는 특이한 짝짓기 습성 때문에 많은 야생 생물학자의 집중적인 연구대상이 되어오기도 했다. 수컷이 새끼들을 돌본다는 점에서는 다른 어류와 유사하지만, 암컷 및 다른 수컷들보다 큰 우두머리 수컷은 그들이 기르고 있는 새끼들이 진짜 자기 새끼인지 정확히 알 수가 없는데, 이는 짝짓기 의식을 회피하고 속임수로 알을 수정시키려 하는 다른 수컷들이 있기 때문이다.

2 번식 집단의 약 80퍼센트를 차지하는 몸집이 큰 수컷 성어는 그들의 크기, 눈 뒤에서 머리 위를 가로지르는 구릿빛 줄무늬, 산란기에 노란색이나 주황색으로 변하는 은청색의 가슴으로 구별되는데, 주로 bluegill의 생식을 담당한다. 이들은 3년에서 4년이 지나야 성적 성숙기에 도달하는데, 이 유예 기간은 그들이 섭취한 음식물을 성공적으로 영역을 지키고 포식자들을 물리치기에 유리한 큰 몸집을 발달시키는 데 쓸 수 있게 한다. Bluegill은 집단 산란어이기 때문에, [4]수컷 성어들은 20마리 혹은 30마리씩 무리를 지어 움푹한 땅을 만들기 위해 꼬리지느러미로 모래 바닥을 쓸어서 'bedding'이라 불리는 접시만 한 크기의 둥지를 판다. [3]그다음 수컷은 얕은 물에서 둥지를 맴돌며, 하나 혹은 여럿의 암컷을 유인하기 위해서 꿀꿀거리는 소리를 낸다. 수컷은 새로 낳아 수정시킨 알을 지키는데, 알이 부화해서 새끼 물고기들이 나온 후에도 스스로 생존할 수 있는 나이가 될 때까지 새끼들을 계속해서 보호한다.

3 [5]Bluegill 수컷 중 소수(약 20퍼센트)는 자신의 영역을 지킬 수 있을 만큼 자라기 전부터 생식활동을 시작한다. Cuckold 혹은 sneaker bluegill은 그들 에너지의 대부분을 정자가 들어있는 정소로부터의 분비물인 어백을 생산하는 생식선에 투입한다. 그 결과, 그들은 주변의 둥지를 이용할 필요가 있는 생식전략에 에너지를 들여왔다. Cuckold bluegill은 혼자서 성공적으로 암컷을 유인하기에는 너무 온순하다. 이들은 큰 수컷 성어를 찾아서, 그것의 번식지 근처 수초에 숨어 암컷 물고기 떼가 그곳을 지나가기를 기다린다. 암컷은 짝을 고른 다음 'dip'이라 불리는 동작을 통해 몸을 기울여 대략 30개의 난자를 방출한다. 보통은 그곳에 거주하는 수컷 성어가

자신의 어백을 이 난자에 퍼붓겠지만, 그 수컷이 모든 난자에 도달할 기회를 얻기 전에 작은 cuckold bluegill이 숨어있던 곳에서 나와 쏜살같이 위험한 둥지 부근으로 돌진하여 난자를 향해서 자신의 어백을 분출한 후, 잡히지 않고 재빨리 원래 있던 곳으로 돌아올 것이다. 이 전술로 cuckold bluegill은 난자가 둥지에 안착하기 전에 가능한 한 많은 수의 난자를 수정시키고자 하므로, 자신의 작은 몸을 이용해서 최대한 민첩하게 접근한다. 운이 좋아서 어떤 큰 상처도 입지 않고 임무를 완수한다면 cuckold bluegill은 그 번식기 내내 계속하여 다른 수컷 성어의 둥지에 몰래 접근할 것이다.

4 [8]이 신속하게 돌진하는 기술은 두 번의 번식기로 한정되는데, 이는 신체적 성장이 지연되더라도 중단될 수는 없어서 결국 민첩성이 떨어지는 큰 몸집을 갖게 되기 때문이며, 그래서 자신의 유전자를 다음 세대에 전달할 가능성을 높이기 위해 cuckold bluegill은 의태라는 새로운 방법을 개발한다. Cuckold bluegill 성어는 여전히 수컷 성어만큼은 살찌지 않아서 암컷으로 쉽게 오인될 수 있다. 보통, 암컷은 더 옅은 색의 비늘, 아감딱지의 후방 가장자리에 두드러진 검은색 반점, 그리고 등지느러미 후미 근처에 또 다른 검은색 반점을 가지고 있다. Cuckold bluegill은 나이가 들면서 비슷한 무늬를 가지게 되어, 수컷 성어들로부터 완벽하게 자신을 위장하여 눈에 띄지 않고 쉽게 암컷의 무리 속으로 끼어들 수 있게 된다. 이런 식으로 cuckold bluegill은 근처의 암컷이 이미 만들어진 둥지에 난자를 분출하기로 결정할 때까지 따뜻한 물속을 돌아다닌다. Cuckold bluegill은 급강하하여 가라앉은 난자에 충분히 가깝게 이동한 후 어백을 분출한다. 충분한 양이 cuckold bluegill의 정자와 수정된다면, cuckold bluegill은 자신의 생식 임무를 완수한 것이다.

angler[ǽŋglər] 낚시꾼 game[geim] 낚시
intense[inténs] 집중적인 offspring[ɔ́ːfspriŋ] (동식물의) 새끼
fry[frai] 물고기 새끼 circumvent[sə̀ːrkəmvént] (교묘하게) 회피하다
ritual[rítʃuəl] 의식 fertilize[fə́ːrtəlàiz] 수정시키다
deception[disépʃən] 속임수 breed[briːd] 번식하다
distinguish[distíŋgwiʃ] 구별하다 spawning season 산란기
maturity[mətʃúərəti] 성숙기 territory[tératɔ̀ːri] 영역
predator[prédətər] 포식자 excavate[ékskəvèit] 파다
sweep[swiːp] 쓸다 depression[dipréʃən] 움푹한 땅
grunt[grʌnt] 꿀꿀거리다 sneaker[sníːkər] 살금살금 움직이는 사람
gonad[góunæd] 생식선
milt[milt] 어백(魚白, 물고기 수컷의 뱃속에 든 흰 정액 덩어리)
secretion[sikríːʃən] 분비물 testes[téstiːz] (testis의 복수) 정소
spermatozoa[spə̀ːrmætəzóuə] (spermatozoon의 복수) 정자
procreative[próukrièitiv] 생식의 meek[miːk] 온순한
dip[dip] 순간적 강하 diminutive[dimínjutiv] 작은
dart[dɑːrt] 돌진하다 squirt[skwə́ːrt] 분출하다
utmost[ʌ́tmòust] 최대한의 agility[ədʒíləti] 민첩성

encounter[inkáuntər] 부닥치다   stalk[stɔːk] 몰래 접근하다
mimicry[mímikri] 의태   beefy[bíːfi] 살찐
spurt[spəːrt] 분출하다, 뿜어 나오다   swoop[swuːp] 급강하하다
maneuver[mənúːvər] (교묘하게) 이동하다
eject[idʒékt] 분출하다, 배설하다

1 지문의 단어 "their"가 가리키는 것은?

  (A) 낚시꾼
  (B) 생물학자
  (C) 우두머리 수컷
  (D) 암컷

2 지문의 단어 "deception"과 의미상 가장 유사한 것은?

  (A) 위험
  (B) 습득
  (C) 속도
  (D) 속임수

3 2단락에서, 글쓴이는 _____ 하기 위해 꿀꿀거리는 소리를 언급한다.

  (A) 움푹한 땅을 만들기 위해 필요한 노력을 강조하기 위해
  (B) 수컷 성어들이 새끼를 위해 부르는 자장가를 묘사하기 위해
  (C) 포식자들로부터 둥지를 보호하기 위한 방법의 예를 제시하기 위해
  (D) 수컷 성어들이 이성을 유인하는 방법을 보여주기 위해

4 2단락에서 다음 중 산란에 대해 사실인 것은?

  (A) 가장 큰 수컷이 암컷들에게 가장 매력적이다.
  (B) 수컷들은 암컷들을 둥지로 유혹하기 전에 미리 둥지를 준비한다.
  (C) 암컷들은 알을 낳을 장소를 선택할 때 선호를 보이지 않는다.
  (D) 둥지 주위를 선회하는 수컷의 능력은 새끼를 기르는 것에 있어서의 체력을 보여준다.

5 3단락에서, 글쓴이는 cuckold가 _____ 라는 것을 암시한다.

  (A) 수컷 성어보다 어린 나이에 난자 수정을 시도하기 시작한다
  (B) 다른 수컷들의 둥지에 몰래 들어가려고 시도하기 전에 먼저 둥지를 만들려고 시도한다
  (C) 평생 단 하나의 전략에만 제한되어 있다
  (D) 수컷 성어들보다 암컷을 유인하는 데 훨씬 더 효과적인 방법을 가지고 있다

6 지문의 단어 "agility"와 의미상 가장 유사한 것은?

  (A) 민첩함
  (B) 부주의함
  (C) 성숙함
  (D) 다양성

7 아래 문장 중 지문 속의 음영된 문장의 핵심 정보를 가장 잘 표현하고 있는 것은 무엇인가? 오답은 문장의 의미를 현저히 왜곡하거나 핵심 정보를 빠뜨리고 있다.

(A) cuckold는 번식기 동안 따라다니는 수컷 성어의 둥지에 손상을 입힌다.
(B) 성공한 cuckold는 여러 계절 동안 계속해서 같은 둥지에 몰래 접근할 것이다.
(C) cuckold는 한곳에서 성공하면 다른 곳에서 같은 전략을 사용하려고 할 것이다.
(D) cuckold는 부상을 입기 전에 임무를 완수할 수 있다면 매우 운이 좋은 것이다.

8 4단락에 따르면, 다음 중 cuckold에 대해 사실인 것은?

  (A) 결국 스스로 암컷을 유혹하기에 충분할 만큼 크게 자란다.
  (B) 커지는 크기와 느려지는 속도 때문에 늘 성공하지 못한다.
  (C) 그들의 유전자를 대대로 물려주기 위해서는 더 멀리 이동해야 한다.
  (D) 수컷 성어의 둥지에 몰래 접근하는 방법을 바꿔야 한다.

9 네 개의 네모[■]는 다음 문장이 삽입될 수 있는 부분을 나타내고 있다.

  보통, 암컷은 더 옅은 색의 비늘, 아감딱지의 후방 가장자리에 두드러진 검은색 반점, 그리고 등지느러미 후미 근처에 또 다른 검은색 반점을 가지고 있다.

  이 문장은 어느 자리에 들어가는 것이 가장 적절한가?

10 **지시:** 지문 요약을 위한 도입 문장이 아래에 주어져 있다. 지문의 가장 중요한 내용을 나타내는 보기 3개를 골라 요약을 완성하시오. 어떤 문장은 지문에 언급되지 않은 내용이나 사소한 정보를 담고 있으므로 요약에 포함되지 않는다. **이 문제는 2점이다.**

  > bluegill 수컷들은 동종이 아니고 번식 전략에 따라 구별될 수 있다.
  >
  > · (B) 몇몇 bluegill은 생식하는 쌍이 있는 둥지로 빠르게 돌진하여, 그들의 어백을 놓는다.
  > · (D) 수컷 성어는 번식하고 후손을 지키기 위한 둥지를 방어하는 데 그것의 성숙한 몸집을 이용한다.
  > · (F) 몇몇 수컷들은 나이가 들수록 암컷처럼 보이도록 적응한다.

(A) 암컷 bluegill은 수컷 성어의 둥지 속으로 연속적으로 dip을 한다.
(C) 빠른 돌진 기술은 몰래 접근하는 수컷들에 의해 이후 사용되는 의태보다는 성공적이지 않다.
(E) 수컷 성어는 cuckold 때문에 그들이 지키는 난자와 갓 부화한 새끼들이 자기 새끼인지 확신하지 못한다.

02 Incan and Mayan Civilizations

11. (C)	12. (D)	13. (A)
14. (D)	15. (B)	16. (B)
17. (D)	18. (C)	19. 4th
20. The Incan – (C), (D), (F), (I)		
The Mayan – (B), (E), (G)		

1 스페인 정복자들의 신대륙 상륙은 토착민들의 문화와 삶을 영구적으로 대폭 바꾸어 놓았고, 이는 유럽인들이 그들을 발견한 지 얼마 안 되어 아메리카 대륙의 위대한 두 문명인 잉카와 마야 문명의 소멸을 가져왔다. 이들은 주목할 만한 도시를 남겨 놓았지만, 사라진 주민들에 대한 기록이 거의 없기 때문에 고고학자들은 사라진 이들 문명에 대해 더 많이 알아내려는 시도로 남아 있는 것들을 짜 맞출 수밖에 없다.

2 ¹²수집된 정보의 대부분은 그 도시들의 유적으로부터 얻어졌는데, 도시들은 주로 돌로 지어졌기 때문에 긴 세월을 견뎌냈다. 그런데 둘은 같은 자재를 사용했지만, 도시를 주변 환경에 매우 다르게 조화시켰다. 잉카 문명은 기술 덕분에 이것을 대체로 매끄럽게 완수할 수 있었는데, ²⁰ᴵ주변의 물체를 조각하고 도시에 농장이나 정원의 용도로 경사면을 계단 모양으로 깎은 언덕을 포함시킴으로써 그렇게 했다. 이에 비하면, 마야의 도시 개발은 거의 계획성이 없어 보인다. ²⁰ᶜ잉카 도시의 대규모 도로 체계와 정돈된 설계는 없었지만, ²⁰ᴮ마야의 도시들은 왕궁, 사원, 경기장 등의 가장 중요한 건물들을 수용할 수 있는 중앙 광장으로부터 더 유기적으로 성장하는 경향이 있었으며, ¹³/²⁰ᴱ그들은 석회석을 잘게 부수어 만든 회반죽을 개발했기 때문에 돌을 깎아서 완벽하게 아귀가 들어맞게 만드는 데 같은 양의 시간을 들일 필요가 없었다.

3 ¹⁴이렇게 건물이 느슨하게 조합된 모습은 마야의 통치법을 암시한다고도 할 수 있다. 각각의 도시는 그 주변 지역과 함께 자신들의 중심이 되는 세습 군주에 의해 통치되었고, 결과적으로 마야 제국은 하나의 통일된 국가가 아니라 서로 다른 도시국가들이 하나의 유사한 문화로 묶여있는 것이었다. ²⁰ᴰ반면에 잉카에는 Sapa Inca, 즉 유일한 잉카로 알려진 한 명의 군주가 존재했는데, 그는 최초 잉카 부족의 직계 후손이어야 했고 잉카 문명권 전 지역에 대한 절대적인 권력을 가지고 있었으며, 전 지역은 네 개의 지역으로 나뉘고 각각의 총독이 하나의 지역을 다스리며 그 총독은 지방 관리를 감독했다. 이런 계층적인 행정 지역은 정부 내의 종교와 군사를 관장하던 부서가 별개의 명령 계통에 속해 있어서 서로 간의 견제, 균형이 유지되는 시스템을 효과적으로 이루고 있었다는 점에서도 특이하다. 도로망이 매우 잘 정비되어 있어서 왕국 내의 먼 변두리 지역까지 전령이 신속하게 오갈 수 있었기에, Sapa Inca는 전 영토에 자신의 영향력을 행사할 수 있었다.

4 이런 통신 네트워크를 갖추지 못했음에도 불구하고 마야인들은 한 가지 엄청난 이점을 가지고 있었는데, ²⁰ᶠ이는 많은 연구자가 잉카 제국은 200년도 채 지속하지 못했지만, ¹⁷마야 제국이 천 년이 넘는 세월 동안 존속할 수 있었던 이유라고 믿는 것이었다. 마야인들은 정식 문자 체계를 발달시켰고, ²⁰ᴳ이 문자 체계는 이집트 상형문자와 비교되는 경우가 많지만 더 음성학에 기초한 문자였고 마야인들이 막대한 양의 정보를 전달하고 저장할 수 있게 해주었다. 1,000가지 이상의 다양한 상형문자가 발견되었지만 한 번에 500개 이상의 문자가 쓰였던 적은 없었고, 그중 200개가 음성적으로 해석될 수 있었던 것과는 대조적으로 나머지는 생략 기호들이었던 것으로 보인다. ¹⁸ᴮ/¹⁸ᴰ재구성된 언어는 석재나 토기에 새겨진 글에서 많이 얻어지지만, ¹⁸ᴬ마야인들은 나무껍질을 사용해서 원시 형태의 책이라 불리는 고문서를 만들었던 것으로도 알려졌는데, 불행하게도 이것들은 스페인 선교사들에 의해서 거의 모두 파괴되었다. 잉카의 quipu, 즉 매듭 있는 색색의 끈이 메시지를 전달하는 데 쓰였을 수도 있다고 주장하는 언어학자들이 최근에 얻어낸 연구 결과가 존재하기는 하지만, 모든 증거물이 모든 정보가 전령들에 의해서 전해졌음을 암시하고 있고, 이 관점의 지지자들이 아직까지는 증거물들을 해석할 수 있는 어떤 방법도 찾아내지 못했기 때문에 이 관점은 널리 받아들여지지는 않고 있다. 최근의 연구는 패턴을 찾아내기 위해 매듭을 분석하는 데 컴퓨터를 사용하고 있다.

5 이들 문명 간의 지리적 유사성과 시대적 공통성에도 불구하고, 마야인들과 잉카인들은 매우 다른 문화를 형성했으며 둘 다 콜럼버스가 발견하기 이전의 아메리카 대륙에서 가장 장대한 건축물들 중의 일부를 지었던 것으로 알려졌다. 불행히도 스페인의 손에 의해 이들 문명이 파괴됨으로써 단순히 유물들만 손실된 것이 아니라, 위대한 두 개의 문명이 사라졌다.

conquistador[kɑnkwístədɔ̀ːr] 정복자
drastically[drǽstikəli] 대폭, 철저하게
indigenous[indídʒənəs] 토착의, 고유의   vanish[vǽniʃ] 사라지다
archaeologist[àːrkiálədʒist] 고고학자   ruin[rúːin] 유적
withstand[wiθstǽnd] 견뎌내다   integrate[íntəgrèit] 통합하다
seamlessly[síːmlisli] 매끄럽게
incorporate[inkɔ́ːrpərèit] 포함하다
terrace[térəs] 경사면을 계단 모양으로 깎은 언덕
haphazard[hæphǽzərd] 계획성이 없는
extensive[iksténsiv] 대규모의   layout[léiàut] 설계
plaza[plɑ́ːzə] 광장   mortar[mɔ́ːrtər] 회반죽
hew[hjuː] 깎다, 자르다   confederation[kənfèdəréiʃən] 조합
indicative[indíkətiv] 암시하는   hereditary[hərédətèri] 세습적인
focal point 중심   disparate[díspərət] 다른
descendant[diséndənt] 후손, 자손, 후예
exert[igzə́ːrt] (영향력을) 행사하다   far-flung[fɑ́ːrflʌ̀ŋ] 먼, 멀리 떨어진
courier[kúːriər] 통신   immeasurable[imézərəbl] 엄청난
hieroglyphic[hàiərəglífik] 상형문자
phonetically[fənétikəli] 음성학적으로   glyph[glif] 상형문자
logographic[lóugougrǽfik] 생략 기호의
inscribe[inskráib] 새기다
codices[kóudəsìːz] (codex의 복수) 고문서
linguist[líŋgwist] 언어학자   knotted[nátid] 매듭 있는
proponent[prəpóunənt] 지지자   relic[rélik] 유물

11 지문의 단어 "withstood"와 의미상 가장 유사한 것은?

(A) 구축했다
(B) 깊어졌다
(C) 저항했다
(D) 평가했다

12 2단락에 따르면, 잉카와 마야 도시들의 일부가 살아남은 이유는 _____이었다.

(A) 현대 고고학자들에 의해 수행된 보존 사업
(B) 건축물이 세워진 고도의 기술
(C) 주변 환경과의 인상적인 수준의 융합
(D) 도시들이 건설된 자재의 내구성

13 다음 중 2단락에서 잉카의 건축 관행에 대해 추론할 수 있는 것은?

(A) 서로 일치하는 돌 블록을 조각했다.
(B) 외관보다는 기능을 더 중요하게 생각했다.
(C) 도시와 도시 간의 많은 다양성을 보여주었다.
(D) 근처에서 구할 수 있는 재료들로만 작업을 했다.

14 3단락에서 글쓴이가 "This loose confederation of buildings was somewhat indicative of Mayan governance"로 의미하는 것은?

(A) 건축물의 내구성이 사회에도 반영되어 있었다.
(B) 마야인들의 통치 방식이 건물 건축 방식에도 영향을 주었다.
(C) 마야 정부는 건물 건축에 중요한 역할을 했다.
(D) 건물 설계 방식이 정부의 조직과 유사했다.

15 지문의 단어 "disparate"과 의미상 가장 유사한 것은?

(A) 연합한
(B) 다른
(C) 친밀한
(D) 양립할 수 있는

16 아래 문장 중 지문 속의 음영된 문장의 핵심 정보를 가장 잘 표현하고 있는 것은 무엇인가? 오답은 문장의 의미를 현저히 왜곡하거나 핵심 정보를 빠뜨리고 있다.

(A) 자신의 통치를 강화하기 위해, 잉카 왕은 빠른 왕래를 가능하게 하는 복잡한 도로망을 고안했다.
(B) 전갈이 왕국을 가로질러 갈 수 있는 도로망 때문에, 잉카 왕은 통치를 유지할 수 있었다.
(C) 잉카 왕은 특사들이 영토 전역을 반드시 왕래할 수 있도록 발전된 도로망을 만들었다.
(D) 도로망을 이용했던 전령들은 먼 지역에도 잉카 왕의 명령을 전달할 수 있었다.

17 지문으로부터 문자 체계는 _____라는 것을 추론할 수 있다.

(A) 일반적으로 그림에 기반한 체계에서 발달한다
(B) 효과적이기 위해서는 음성학적 기반을 필요로 한다
(C) 정부 체계를 구축하는 데 필수적이다

(D) 한 문화의 장기적인 안정성을 보장하는 데 도움을 준다

18 다음 중 마야인들이 글쓰기에 사용했던 매체로 언급되지 않은 것은?

(A) 나무껍질
(B) 마른 토기 조각
(C) 밧줄 조각
(D) 석재 조각

19 네 개의 네모[■]는 다음 문장이 삽입될 수 있는 부분을 나타내고 있다.

최근의 연구는 패턴을 찾아내기 위해 매듭을 분석하는 데 컴퓨터를 사용하고 있다.

이 문장은 어느 자리에 들어가는 것이 가장 적절한가?

20 **지시:** 주어진 선택지에서 적절한 구를 선택하여 해당하는 문명의 종류에 연결시키시오. **이 문제는 4점이다.**

보기
(A) 왕위 계승권에 대해 몇 차례 내전을 겪었다
(H) 초기 몇 세기 동안 스페인 정복자들을 막아낼 수 있었다

잉카
· (C) 사방에 발전된 주요 도로망을 고안했다
· (D) 국가에 대해 절대 권력을 가지고 있는 전제 군주가 있었다
· (F) 2세기도 안 되는 기간 동안 존재했다
· (I) 땅을 경작하기 위한 목적으로 언덕에 계단식 대지를 포함시켰다

마야
· (B) 중앙 광장에서부터 펼쳐지기 시작하는 마을을 만들었다
· (E) 분쇄한 돌로 벽돌 사이에 바르는 콘크리트 같은 재료를 만들었다
· (G) 상징을 이용하여 정보를 전송하는 복잡한 시스템을 가지고 있었다

Chapter 01 **Sentence Simplification**

HACKERS **STRATEGY**

p.43

전략 1

Ex 초기의 복잡한 샤머니즘 의식, 즉 연극으로 발전한 축복을 위한 기도에서의 근본적인 주제는 탄생과 죽음, 성적 그리고 감정적 욕구, 육체적 욕망, 그리고 물질적인 힘을 아우르는 삶의 순환이었다.

underlying[ʌ̀ndərlàiiŋ] 근본적인 **subject matter** 주제
intricate[íntrikət] 복잡한 **invocation**[ìnvəkéiʃən] 기도
encompass[inkʌ́mpəs] 아우르다

Ex 선충의 온도에 대한 내성은 주목할만하다. 온천에서, 선충은 다른 후생동물과 비슷하거나 더 높은 온도에서 산다. 비록 그들이 극한의 기후에서 살아남기 위한 방법에 적응해 왔다 할지라도, 그들의 활동은 사막토에 비가 온 후의 기간 또는 극지방의 토양이 상대적으로 따뜻한 기간 이후와 같은 더 적당한 환경이 돌아옴에 따라 자극받는다.

nematode[némətòud] 선충 **metazoan**[mètəzóuən] 후생동물
extremity[ikstréməti] 극한 **desert soil** 사막토
polar region 극지방

전략 2

Ex 초기 복잡한 샤머니즘 의식에서의 근본적인 주제는 삶의 순환이었다.
→ 고대 샤머니즘 의식은 삶을 다루었다.

ritual[rítʃuəl] 의식

Ex 비록 음식으로서의 해조류에 대한 관심이 급증해왔다 할지라도, 서양에서 소비되는 해조류의 양은 일본인들이 소비하는 양의 일부에 불과할 것이다.
→ 서양에서 음식으로서의 해조류에 대한 관심이 증가하였지만, 아마 일본인들이 서양인들보다 훨씬 더 많은 해조류를 먹을 것이다.

fraction[frǽkʃən] 일부 **upsurge**[ʌ̀psə́:rdʒ] 급증
diet[dáiət] 음식, 다이어트

Ex 건조, 훈제, 그리고 염장은 육류를 단기간 보존할 수 있게 했지만, 신선한 육류의 이용 가능성은 매우 제한적이었다.
→ 비록 건조, 훈제, 염장으로 보존된 육류는 일시적으로 이용 가능했지만, 가공되지 않은 육류를 얻을 기회는 거의 없었다.

preserve[prizə́:rv] 보존하다
unprocessed[ʌnprɑ́sest] 가공되지 않은

전략 3

Ex 산성비는 탄화수소가 연소했을 때 방출되는 산화물이 대기 중의 물과 결합하여 생산되는 황산과 질산 같은 산성 화합물을 함유하고 있고, 산림과 수중생물 같은 유기체 파괴를 초래하는 것으로 널리 여겨진다.

compound[kámpaund] 화합물 **sulfuric acid** 황산
nitric acid 질산 **oxide**[áksaid] 산화물
hydrocarbon[hàidrəkɑ́:rbən] 탄화수소
aquatic life 수중생물

HACKERS STRATEGY **APPLICATION**

p.46

건축에서 자연적이고 개방적인 공간의 개념은 곧 건물 중에서도 주거용 주택부터 고층건물, 상업용 건물, 교량 및 주유소까지 확산되었는데, 이 건물들은 모두 건축물의 본질적인 초점은 그것의 목적에서 찾아야 한다는 내재적인 믿음을 나타냈으며, 이는 예술적 표현이 의미와 질의 전달과 동일하다는 것을 암시하였다. Wright는 은행은 그리스 신전처럼 보이는 것이 아니라 은행처럼 보여야 하고, 따라서 은행의 디자인과 건축자재는 그것의 기능과 관련이 있어야 한다고 주장했다. 자연은 목적과 디자인의 온전한 통합을 보여주는 가장 좋은 예를 제공하므로 Wright는 이 새로운 이념을 '유기적 건축'이라고 불렀는데, 이것은 전통으로부터의 급진적인 일탈일 뿐만 아니라 건축물, 시간, 그리고 장소 간의 복잡한 관계를 이해하여, 이들 세 가지 모두를 주거지에 거주하는 사람들과 그것의 물리적 환경 사이에 조화가 존재하는 하나의 의미 있는 전체로서 통합시키는 것이었다.

inherent[inhíərənt] 내재적인 **tantamount**[tǽntəmàunt] 동일한
integration[ìntəgréiʃən] 통합 **radical**[rǽdikəl] 급진적인
departure[dipá:rtʃər] 일탈 **dwelling**[dwéliŋ] 주거지

아래 문장 중 지문 속의 음영된 문장의 핵심 정보를 가장 잘 표현하고 있는 것은 무엇인가? 오답은 문장의 의미를 현저히 왜곡하거나 핵심 정보를 빠뜨리고 있다.

(A) 미적 표현이 의미와 질의 전달과 동등하다는 개념은 다양한 종류의 건물에 내재되었다.

(B) 서로 다른 다양한 건축물들은 자연적이고 개방적인 공간의 개념을 채택하였고 그것의 목적이 건물을 짓는 것의 요점이 되어야 한다는 관점을 반영했다.

(C) 건축은 예술에 견주어지는데 이는 두 가지 모두 다른 종류의 건축물을 통해서 성취되는 건축의 질을 전달하고자 하는 데 초점을 맞추기 때문이다.

(D) 고층건물과 상업용 건물은 건물 내부 공간 확장과 외부 장식에 초점을 맞추었다.

HACKERS **PRACTICE**

p.48

1. (A)	2. (B)	3. (B)
4. (A)	5. (B)	6. (B)
7. (A), (D)	8. (C), (D)	9. (A), (B), (D)
10. (D)	11. (B), (C)	12. (B), (C)
13. 1 (A), 2 (C)	14. 1 (D), 2 (B)	15. 1 (B), 2 (A)
16. 1 (C), 2 (A)	17. 1 (B), 2 (B)	

VOCABULARY

1 (D)	2 (C)	3 (A)
4 (B)	5 (A)	6 (B)
7 (D), (C)	8 (A), (B)	9 (C), (B)
10 (D), (A)	11 (C), (A)	12 (D), (D)
13 (B), (C), (A)	14 (D), (B), (A)	15 (B), (D), (A)
16 (C), (B), (A)	17 (D), (C), (B)	

1 오늘날에는 퀼트가 값비싼 예술 작품으로 여겨지지만, 역사상 그것은 사람들이 더 이상 보관하려고 하지 않는 옷을 재사용하는 절약 방법에 지나지 않았다.

quilt[kwilt] 퀼트(침대 위에 장식용으로 덮는 누비이불)
frugal[frú:gl] 절약의 reutilize[rì:jú:təlàiz] 재사용하다

(A) 퀼트는 한때 불필요한 옷을 저렴하게 재사용하는 방법이었으나, 현재 그것들은 귀중한 예술 작품으로 간주된다.
(B) 퀼트가 전통적으로 그것들의 예술적 가치로 높이 평가된 데 반하여, 그것들은 대개 경제적 목적으로 사용되었다.

2 미국에 있던 영국 총독들이 주로 과세 제도 상의 문제에 집중된 항쟁에 직면했다는 사실에도 불구하고, 그들 중 소수는 어떠한 명령이든 식민지에 의한 반란으로 이어질 것이라고 런던에 보고했다.

governor[gÁvərnər] 총독 encounter[inkáuntər] 직면하다
center on ~에 집중되다 taxation[tækséiʃən] 과세 제도
handful[hǽndful] 소수 mandate[mǽndeit] 명령, 권한
insurrection[ìnsərékʃən] 반란

(A) 총독들이 직면했던 세금에 관한 저항은 식민지들이 명령을 따르느니 차라리 반란을 일으키겠다고 런던에 말했을 때 나타났다.
(B) 몇몇 영국 총독들은 식민지들이 대체로 세금 때문에 그들에게 저항하긴 했지만, 어떠한 명령이든 저항을 야기할 것이라고 주장했다.

3 그레이트베이슨에서 모하비 사막에 이르는 지역의 건조한 기후

는 주로 시에라네바다 산맥에 의해 야기되는데, 이 산맥은 태평양에서 불어오는 폭풍 전선을 붙잡음으로써 수증기가 사막에 도달하지 못하게 막는다.

arid[ǽrid] 건조한 primarily[praimérəli] 주로
water vapor 수증기 capture[kǽptʃər] 붙잡다
front[frʌnt] 전선

(A) 태평양의 강수가 시에라네바다 산맥에 결코 도달하지 않기 때문에, 그레이트베이슨에서 모하비 사막까지는 매우 건조한 상태를 유지한다.
(B) 시에라네바다 산맥은 수분이 그레이트베이슨에서 모하비 사막까지에 도달하는 것을 막기 때문에, 그 지역은 매우 건조하다.

4 인공 암초는 형편없이 설계되어 설치되면 문제를 야기할 수 있는데, 이는 차체, 타이어, 낡은 선박, 콘크리트 조각 등 불충분하게 무거운 자재가 강한 폭풍에 의해 암초가 있는 곳으로부터 수십 마일 쓸려가서 천연 암초 지역 주위에 있는 정착성의 생명체들에게 피해를 입힐 수 있기 때문이다.

artificial[ɑ̀:rtəfíʃəl] 인공의 reef[ri:f] 암초
mount[maunt] 설치하다 insufficiently[ìnsəfíʃəntli] 불충분하게
vessel[vésəl] 선박 rubble[rʌ́bl] 조각
windstorm[wíndstɔ̀:rm] 폭풍 sedentary[sédntèri] 정착성의
organism[ɔ́:rgənìzm] 생명체

(A) 부주의하게 설계된 인공 암초가 지닌 위험은 인공 암초를 세우는 데 사용된 자재가 천연 암초 주위에 있는 서식 동물들을 방해할 수 있다는 가능성에 있다.
(B) 인공 암초의 한 가지 문제점은 그것을 세우는 데 사용된 잔해의 무게가 잘못 측정되어 바람에 의해 헐거워질 가능성이 있으면 쉽게 망가진다는 데 있다.

5 최초의 Pakicetus 화석은 산산이 부서진 아래턱뼈와 소량의 이빨로 구성된 것에 불과했지만, 어금니에 대한 철저한 정밀 조사는 견본이 결코 완전하지 않았음에도, 그 생물이 잡식성이었다고 추정하는 것이 타당함을 시사했다.

fossil[fá:sl] 화석 shattered[ʃǽtərd] 산산이 부서진
mandible[mǽndibl] 아래턱뼈 scrutiny[skrú:təni] 정밀 조사
molar[móulər] 어금니 omnivorous[ɑ:mnívərəs] 잡식성의
specimen[spésimən] 견본

(A) 단순히 아래턱뼈와 소수의 이빨로부터 Pakicetus가 잡식성 식단을 가졌다고 추정하는 것은, 비록 그것이 증명될 수는 없긴 해도 합리적인 결론이다.
(B) 첫 번째 Pakicetus 화석이 불완전했음에도 불구하고, 어금니에 관한 조사로부터 그 동물이 잡식성 동물이었다고 결론을 지어도 무방하다.

6 사유 재산의 축적을 제한하는 것과 같은, 개인의 재정 문제에 관한 어떠한 정부 간섭이든 피하고자 하는 강경한 소수의 자유주의자들이 존재하는 반면, 막대한 다수의 자유주의자들은 언론의 자유를 축소시키는 것 혹은 외설법의 통과와 같은, 표현의 자유

에 관한 최소한의 권위적인 규제가 훨씬 더 마음에 들지 않는다
고 생각한다.

vocal [vóukl] 강경한   libertarian [lìbərtériən] 자유주의자
eschew [istʃúː] 피하다   interference [ìntərfírəns] 간섭
fiscal [fískl] 재정의   accumulation [əkjùːmjuléiʃən] 축적
preponderance [pripá:ndərəns] 다수, 우세
authoritative [əθɔ́ːrəteitiv] 권위적인   curtail [kəːrtéil] 축소시키다
passage [pǽsidʒ] (법안의) 통과   obscenity [əbsénəti] 외설

(A) 대부분의 자유주의자들은 정부가 시민권의 제한에 관여해
서는 안 된다는 데 동의하지만, 그들은 사람들의 재정 문
제에 개입하는 것에 관한 정부의 역할에는 좀처럼 동의하
지 않는다.

(B) 소수의 자유주의자들은 개인 재무에 관한 정부의 모든 개
입을 강력하게 거부하지만, 그들의 대부분은 자신을 표현하
는 권리를 축소하는 것에 대해서 더욱 단호하게 반대한다.

7 Taos 부족 사람들은 다른 부족들과 친밀한 관계를 유지하긴 했
지만 Taos 부족의 관습은 대부분 변하지 않았는데, 이는 부분적
으로는 강한 공동체 의식뿐만 아니라, 종족 순도, 문화적 온전함
을 유지했던, 부락 외의 결혼에 대한 엄격한 금기 때문이다.

tribal [tráibəl] 부족의   taboo [təbúː] 금기
pueblo [pwéblou] 부락   racial [réiʃəl] 종족의
purity [pjúərəti] 순도   integrity [intégrəti] 온전함, 무결성

(A) Taos 부락은 다른 부족과 호의적인 관계를 가지고 있긴 했
지만, 인접 부족 외의 결혼에 대한 금지를 통해 그들의 관습
을 온전하게 유지했다.

(B) Taos의 부족 의식은 Taos 부족이 아닌 이웃과 긍정적이고
친밀한 관계를 유지할 수 있었기 때문에 대체로 변하지 않
고 유지되었다.

(C) Taos 부족이 Taos 부족이 아닌 원주민들과 친밀한 관계였
다는 사실에도 불구하고, 그들 부족의 관습은 부족 외 결혼
에 대한 금지령이 내려진 후에 영향을 받았다.

(D) 외부인들과 친밀함을 유지한 동시에, Taos 부족은 부족 외
의 결혼을 금지함으로써 부족의 관습을 보존할 수 있었다.

8 연구들은 다양한 동물 종에서 칼로리 제한이 신진대사율을 감소
시킬 뿐만 아니라, 세포 수준에서 산화 스트레스를 억제하는 데
에도 주요 요소라는 사실을 밝혀냈는데, 이는 병을 예방하고 수
명을 연장하는 데 상당한 영향을 미친다.

metabolic rate 신진대사율   curb [kəːrb] 억제하다
oxidative stress 산화 스트레스(체내 산화 물질과 항산화 물질 사이의
균형이 파괴되어 산화 비율이 높아지며 발생하는 스트레스)
substantial [səbstǽnʃəl] 상당한   implication [ìmplikéiʃən] 영향
stave off 예방하다   longevity [lɑːndʒévəti] 수명

(A) 연구는 칼로리와 신진대사율의 감소가 많은 동물들이 산
화 스트레스를 제한하는 데 필수적이라는 것을 시사한다.

(B) 연구에 따르면, 질병을 가장 잘 예방하고 수명을 연장시킬
수 있는 동물은 칼로리 섭취를 제어하는 동물이다.

(C) 칼로리를 줄이는 것이 신진대사를 조정하고 산화 스트레스
를 낮추는 것으로 보였고, 이는 다양한 동물들이 질병을 피

하고 더 오래 살도록 돕는다.

(D) 연구는 칼로리를 제한하는 것이 많은 동물들의 세포 산화 스
트레스를 조절하고, 더 건강하고 오랜 삶으로 이어지며, 게
다가 신진대사를 더디게 한다는 것을 보여준다.

9 아리스토텔레스 시대의 전통에 따르면, 연극 공연은 일반 사람
보다 뛰어난 사람들(즉, 영웅, 왕, 신)의 높은 지위로부터 불행으
로의 몰락을 묘사하거나, 불리한 상황이 견딜만하거나 유리한
상황으로 바뀌어 더 나은 조건을 갖게 되는 평범한 사람을 나타
냄으로써 영혼의 두려움과 유감의 정화를 불러일으켰다.

dramatic [drəmǽtik] 연극의   performance [pərfɔ́ːrməns] 공연
evoke [ivóuk] ~을 불러일으키다   purge [pəːrdʒ] 정화하다
downfall [dáunfɔ̀ːl] 몰락   elevated [éləvèitid] 높은
represent [rèprizént] ~을 나타내다
indulgent [indʌ́ldʒənt] 견딜만한
advantageous [ædvəntéidʒəs] 유리한

(A) 강자가 무너지거나 약자가 부상하는 아리스토텔레스 시대
의 연극을 본 사람들은 그들의 영혼이 정화된다고 느꼈다.

(B) 아리스토텔레스 시대의 연극에서 실권자들의 몰락과 평범
한 사람들의 부상에 대한 묘사는 관객들의 두려움과 유감을
없애는 방법이다.

(C) 아리스토텔레스 시대의 전통은 부자와 빈자 모두의 인생
사를 묘사한 공연을 본 사람들의 두려움과 유감의 해소로
이어졌다.

(D) 아리스토텔레스 시대의 연극은 강자들의 쇠퇴와 평범한 사
람들의 출세 중 하나에 초점을 두어, 두려움과 유감의 영
혼을 없앴다.

10 비록 인간 대뇌의 두 반구가 두 영역을 연결시켜 주는 신경 섬유
의 큰 집성체인 뇌량을 통해 서로 복잡한 의사소통을 하는 것을
보여주지만, 두 반구 사이의 협력 관계는 대등한 것이 아니며 대
부분의 실험이 한쪽 손을 쓰는 경향, 즉 왼손이나 오른손 중 한
손을 이용할 때, 더 나은 운동 능력을 보이는 것에서 알 수 있듯
이 한쪽이 다른 쪽을 압도한다는 것을 보여준다.

cerebral [serí:brəl] 대뇌의   hemisphere [hémisfìər] 반구
demonstrate [démənstrèit] 보여주다   intricate [íntrikət] 복잡한
corpus callosum 뇌량   neural [njúərəl] 신경의
fiber [fáibər] 섬유   partnership [pá:rtnərʃìp] 협력 관계
equitable [ékwətəbl] 대등한, 동등한
experiment [ikspérəmənt] 실험
handedness [hǽndidnis] 한쪽 손을 쓰는 경향
manifestation [mæ̀nəfistéiʃən] 보이는 것, 표시

(A) 인간 뇌에 대한 실험은 뇌량이 한쪽 반구에서 반대쪽으로 정
보를 전송하는 일을 책임진다는 것을 보여주었다.

(B) 인간 뇌의 두 반구 사이의 부등한 정보 전송은 뇌량의 기능
부전으로부터 기인한다.

(C) 사람의 왼손 또는 오른손에 대한 선호는 뇌의 반구가 둘 다
정보를 교환한다면, 둘 사이의 연결 관계가 명백하다는 점
을 증명한다.

(D) 뇌량을 통한 인간 뇌의 두 반구 사이의 상호 작용에도 불구
하고, 일반적으로 한쪽이 다른 쪽을 압도한다.

11 물론 이전에도 보드빌, 연극, 강연과 같이 모두 많은 관객에게 제공되었던 대량 소비 형태가 일부 존재했으나, 영화의 상연과 그 결과로서 일어난 대중들의 열광과 인기는 대중의 수요를 만족시키기 위한 대규모의 자본 투자와 새로운 타이틀 제작을 촉진시켰다.

mass[mæs] 대량의　**consumption**[kənsʌ́mpʃən] 소비
present[prizént] 제공하다　**spectator**[spékteitər] 관객
ensue[insúː] 결과로서 일어나다　**craze**[kreiz] 열광
encourage[inkə́ːridʒ] 촉진시키다
investment[invéstmənt] 투자　**satiate**[séiʃièit] 만족시키다
demand[dimǽnd] 수요

(A) 영화가 너무 인기 있어져서 관객을 즐겁게 하는 재미있는 이전 공연 형태의 기능을 압도해버렸다.

(B) 대량 소비 형태는 이전에도 존재했지만, 영화의 상연과 대중의 열광은 그 수요를 만족시키기 위한 자금 지원과 더 많은 타이틀의 제작을 촉발했다.

(C) 대량 소비 형태는 이전에도 존재하긴 했지만, 영화 상연과 그것의 인기는 영화 제작에 많은 양의 자본을 끌어들였다.

(D) 보통 영화는 새로운 타이틀을 제작하는 데 너무 많은 투자를 필요로 하기 때문에, 그것에 대한 대중의 수요를 만족시킬 만큼의 충분한 투자가 없었다.

12 Herbert C. Hoover는 평판이 좋은 그의 후임 대통령인 Franklin D. Roosevelt의 굉장한 개입주의와 비교할 때 경제 대공황에 대응하여 조치하지 않은 것으로 가장 많이 기억되지만, 이러한 인식은 Hoover가 대통령으로서는 다소 실패자이긴 했지만 그의 일생 중 4년의 임기를 제외하고는 큰 명성을 얻은 박애주의자였기 때문에 유감스러운 일이다.

inaction[inǽkʃən] 조치하지 않음, 무활동
respond[rispánd] 대응하다　**compare**[kəmpɛ́ər] 비교하다
frenetic[frənétik] 굉장한, 열광적인
interventionism[ìntərvénʃənìzm] 개입주의
successor[səksésər] 후임　**lamentable**[lǽməntəbl] 유감스러운
humanitarian[hjuːmǽnətɛ́əriən] 박애주의자

(A) 일반 대중은 대공황에 대응한 즉각적인 조치로 Roosevelt를 높이 평가하는 반면, Hoover의 정치적 업적은 과소평가하는 경향이 있다.

(B) Hoover는 대공황에 대한 부적합한 대응으로 사람들의 기억 속에 실패한 대통령으로 남아 있지만, 사실 그는 그의 백악관 시절 전후로 관대한 자선 사업가였다.

(C) 비록 대공황에 즉각적으로 대응하는 데 실패한 것으로 대부분 기억되지만, Hoover는 그의 대통령 임기 전후로 성공한 박애주의자였다.

(D) Hoover는 Roosevelt의 조치에 반대하기에는 정치적으로 너무 약했기 때문에 Roosevelt가 대공황에 공격적으로 개입하는 것을 지켜볼 수밖에 없었다.

13 석판 인쇄술이 한 독일 극작가에 의해 우연히 발명되었을 때, 석판화에는 검은색의 한 가지 색만이 있었다. ¹하지만, 얼마 후, 검은 윤곽선으로 그림의 원판을 만들고 나서, 보통은 수채화 물감

을 이용하여, 손으로 채색을 함으로써 다색 석판화가 완성되었는데, 이것은 아이가 색칠 공부 책의 지면을 채우기 위해 사용하는 방법과 어느 정도 유사했다. 그러나 그림을 복제하기 위해 인쇄 과정 자체에서 다양한 색상을 사용하는 기술인, 진정한 다색 석판술은, 19세기 초에야 비로소 발견되었다. ²원본보다 훨씬 더 낮은 가격에 판매되는, 저렴한 복제화 상업 시장에서의 다색 석판술의 잠재적인 수익성을 예상하여, 보스턴의 Louis Prang과 같은 사업가들은 대중이 살 수 있는 복제품을 제공함으로써 그 기술을 이용했다. Prang은 다색 석판술이 그때까지 일반 대중에게는 접근이 불가능했던 세계인, 예술의 민주화를 상징한다고 말하며 다색 석판술을 성공적으로 브랜드화했다.

lithography[liθɑ́ːgrəfi] 석판 인쇄술　**playwright**[pléirait] 극작가
watercolor[wɔ́ːtərkʌ̀lər] 수채화 물감　**akin to** ~과 유사한
chromolithography[kròuməuliθɑ́grəfi] 다색 석판술
duplicate[dúːplikeit] 복제하다
transpire[trænspáiər] 발견되다, 발생하다
profitability[prɑ̀ːfitəbiləti] 수익성
reproduction[rìːprədʌ́kʃən] 복제, 생식
entrepreneur[ɑ̀ːntrəprənə́ːr] 사업가　**capitalize on** ~을 이용하다
democratization[dimɑ̀krətizéiʃən] 민주화
hitherto[hìðərtúː] 그때까지

1 아래 문장 중 지문 속의 음영된 문장의 핵심 정보를 가장 잘 표현하고 있는 것은 무엇인가? 오답은 문장의 의미를 현저히 왜곡하거나 핵심 정보를 빠뜨리고 있다.

(A) 한 가지가 넘는 색상으로 된 석판화는 검은 윤곽선으로 인쇄된 그림에 손으로 채색함으로써 이내 이루어졌다.

(B) 아이가 색칠 공부 책에 색을 더하는 것처럼, 석판 인쇄공은 다양한 색상을 사용하여 손으로 그림들을 채웠다.

(C) 다색 석판화의 인쇄는 인쇄기에 한 가지가 넘는 색상을 수동으로 채우는 작업을 수반했다.

(D) 한 가지가 넘는 색상으로 된 석판화 제작의 성취는 검은 윤곽선으로 된 그림에 대한 필요성을 없앴다.

2 아래 문장 중 지문 속의 음영된 문장의 핵심 정보를 가장 잘 표현하고 있는 것은 무엇인가? 오답은 문장의 의미를 현저히 왜곡하거나 핵심 정보를 빠뜨리고 있다.

(A) 대부분의 사람들이 원작을 살 형편이 되지 않았기 때문에, 그들은 대신 다색 석판 인쇄공으로부터 그림을 사는 것을 선택했다.

(B) 새로운 기술은 사업가들이 그들의 대량 생산된 복제물에 대해 상당한 액수의 금액을 부과하는 것을 가능하게 했다.

(C) 기업가들은 다색 석판술이 얼마나 수익성이 좋을 수 있을지 예측했고 저렴한 인쇄물 생산을 이용했다.

(D) 많은 사업가들은 다색 석판술이 실행하기에 상업적으로 수익성이 있게 된 후에야 그것으로 눈을 돌렸다.

14 상업용으로 제작된 최초의 타자기 가운데 하나가 Hansen Writing Ball인데, 이것은 보다 신속한 서면 의사소통을 가능하게 하기 위해 1865년에 Rasmus Malling-Hansen에 의해 개발된 실용적인 집필 도구이다. ¹이 기발한 기계가 특정 알파벳

문자들을 각각의 손가락에 배치했다는 사실 때문에, 그것은 보통 펜을 잉크에 담갔다가 그것을 종이에 옮김으로써 써졌던 전통적인 필기 방법보다, 초당 300퍼센트만큼이나 더 많은 음절을 쓸 수 있었다. Hansen은 바늘꽂이 모양처럼 생긴, 현란한 황동 자판을 자랑하는 반구 모양의 기계를 디자인했고, 그는 그 초기 디자인을 자주 개선했다. [2]생산성을 최대화하기 위해, 모음이 기계의 왼쪽에, 대부분의 자음은 오른쪽에 놓이는 경향을 반영해서, 총 56개였던 자판을 전략적으로 재배치했을 뿐만 아니라, Hansen은 기계에 전자 배터리를 부착하였는데, 이것은 종이를 앞으로 움직이게 하여 그의 기계를 세계 최초의 전자 타자기로 만든 혁신이었다.

typewriter[táipraitər] 타자기　expeditious[èkspədíʃəs] 신속한
ingenious[indʒí:niəs] 기발한　contraption[kəntrǽpʃən] 기계
allocate[ǽləkeit] 배치하다　boast[boust] 자랑하다
showy[ʃóui] 현란한　brass[bræs] 황동
pincushion[pínkuʃən] 바늘꽂이
rearrange[rì:əréindʒ] 재배치하다　propensity[prəpénsəti] 경향
vowel[váuəl] 모음　consonant[ká:nsənənt] 자음
affix[əfíks] 부착하다
electromagnetic[ilèktroumægnétik] 전자기의

1 아래 문장 중 지문 속의 음영된 문장의 핵심 정보를 가장 잘 표현하고 있는 것은 무엇인가? 오답은 문장의 의미를 현저히 왜곡하거나 핵심 정보를 빠뜨리고 있다.

(A) 그 기계는 의사소통하기 위해 필요한 알파벳을 한정시킬 수 있었으므로, 집필 부담을 300퍼센트 낮추었다.

(B) 전통적인 필기 방법을 더 빠르게 만들기 위해, 그 기계는 음절의 수를 약 300퍼센트 줄였다.

(C) 그 장치가 300퍼센트 더 높은 효율성을 낳는다는 점 때문에, 전통적인 필기 방법은 점점 덜 사용되었다.

(D) 1초당, 그 장치는 집필 생산성에 있어 300퍼센트의 향상을 만들어냈는데 이는 글자들이 특정 손가락에 배정되었기 때문이다.

2 아래 문장 중 지문 속의 음영된 문장의 핵심 정보를 가장 잘 표현하고 있는 것은 무엇인가? 오답은 문장의 의미를 현저히 왜곡하거나 핵심 정보를 빠뜨리고 있다.

(A) 전자 배터리의 추가는 Hansen이 자판의 재배열을 통해 종이를 움직이게 하고 최대 효율성을 낳게 했다.

(B) Hansen은 최대 효율성을 위해 전략적으로 자판을 바꿨고, 종이의 위치를 바꾸고 전자 배터리를 추가하여 그의 장치를 차별화되게 했다.

(C) 전자 배터리를 그의 장치에 부착함으로써, Hansen은 최초의 전자 타자기를 만들었으나, 이것은 최대 효율성이라는 그의 목표를 지체시켰다.

(D) Hansen의 전자 배터리의 추가는 그로 하여금 자판의 수를 56개로 늘리게 했고, 이것은 그가 기계의 효율성을 최대화하도록 도왔다.

15 Sun Dance 의식은 여러 평원 인디언 부족에 의해 행해졌지만, 주로 미국 남서부의 Hopi 인디언들에게서 기인한다. Sun Dance는 공동체의 모든 구성원과 몇몇 초대 손님들이 모여서

우주의 법칙과 삶의 초자연적인 힘에 대한 근본적인 믿음 체계를 재차 확인하는 의식이었다. [1]이 봄 축제의 복잡한 의식에서, 선택된 부족민들은 의식에 참여할 것을 서약하고 춤을 위해 화려한 의상, 구슬로 장식된 머리 장식, 북 등을 준비하면서 겨울의 일부를 보냈다. 일단 축제가 시작되면 그 선택된 일부는 의복을 입고 원을 형성하여 그 가운데에 영적인 힘과 신비한 기운을 상징하는 막대를 세웠을 것이다. 춤은 이 막대 주위에서 시작해서 춤추는 이들이 광란 상태에 빠질 때까지 간헐적으로 며칠간 이어지며, 때때로는 의식을 끝내려고 고행을 자처하거나 단순히 지쳐서 쓰러지기도 한다. [2]Sun Dance는 부족의 모든 구성원이 함께 일하도록 고무했고 영적 세계의 엄청난 힘에 다다르기 위한 방법이었기 때문에, 속세의 욕구와 신성 간의 균형을 확인하는 것뿐만 아니라 사회적 결속을 유지시키는 수단이었다.

be attributed to ~에 기인하다
reaffirm[rì:əfə́:rm] ~을 재차 확인하다
supernatural[sù:pərnǽtʃərəl] 초자연적인
commitment[kəmítmənt] 서약　costume[kástʃu:m] 의상
bead[bi:d] ~을 구슬로 장식하다　drum[drʌm] 북
don[dɑn] ~을 입다, ~을 쓰다　apparel[əpǽrəl] 의복
erect[irékt] 세우다　pole[poul] 막대
symbolize[símbəlàiz] 상징하다　mystical[místikəl] 신비한
commence[kəméns] 시작하다
intermittently[ìntərmítntli] 간헐적으로　frenzy[frénzi] 광란
rite[rait] 의식　collapse[kəlǽps] 쓰러지다
incredible[inkrédəbl] 엄청난　cohesion[kouhí:ʒən] 결속
divine[diváin] 신성의

1 아래 문장 중 지문 속의 음영된 문장의 핵심 정보를 가장 잘 표현하고 있는 것은 무엇인가? 오답은 문장의 의미를 현저히 왜곡하거나 핵심 정보를 빠뜨리고 있다.

(A) 봄 축제를 위해 여러 가지 많은 물품들이 필요했지만, 소수의 사람들만이 그것들을 만드는 데 참여했다.

(B) 부족의 선택된 일부가 봄 축제에서 춤추기로 서약한 뒤 이전 계절을 공연 준비를 하는 데 보내곤 했다.

(C) 자격이 있다고 여겨지는 사람들만이 봄 축제에서 춤추고 준비하며 겨울을 보내는 것이 허락되었다.

(D) 부족민들은 더 정성을 들여 축제를 준비하는 시간을 갖기 위해 몇 달을 미리 약정하곤 했다.

2 아래 문장 중 지문 속의 음영된 문장의 핵심 정보를 가장 잘 표현하고 있는 것은 무엇인가? 오답은 문장의 의미를 현저히 왜곡하거나 핵심 정보를 빠뜨리고 있다.

(A) 부족 전체의 참여와 신과의 관계 때문에, Sun Dance는 부족에게 사회적이고 영적인 중요성을 모두 가지고 있었다.

(B) Sun Dance의 종교적인 요소는 대부분의 부족민들이 축제 동안에는 그들의 속세적인 염려를 거부했음을 의미했다.

(C) 부족의 다양한 구성원들은 영적 세계와 조화를 이루기 위해서 Sun Dance를 성공적이고 안정되게 만들기 위해 결속해야 했다.

(D) Sun Dance의 목적은 부족 내의 우호적인 관계를 조

성하고 춤을 통해 그들의 영적인 신념을 나타내는 것이었다.

16 많은 고생물학자와 진화론적 생물학자가 표현학적 분류 방법에 대해서 가지고 있는 문제점은 이 방법이 진화적 관계를 항상 정확히 설명해 주지는 못한다는 것이다. 다르게 말하자면, 그런 범주는 전반적인 진화 단계가 비슷할 뿐인, 서로 밀접한 관련이 없는 생물들을 한 개체군으로 묶는 경우가 많다. 이 분류법은 괄목할만한 진화적 혁신을 이어 받은 일부 생물을 제외시키고, 더욱 기본적인 특성에 기초해서 다른 생물들을 같은 개체군으로 묶는 결과를 초래한다. 예를 들어, 오늘날 조류는 작은 육식 공룡에서 직접 진화한 것이라고 알려졌다. [1]중생대 조류와 Coelurosaurian 공룡 사이에 골격의 유사성이 두드러지지만, 조류는 깃털을 가지고 있다는 점 때문에 파충류로 분류되지 않는다. 깃털은 조류를 파충류와 구별시켜 주는 진화적 혁신이다. 그러므로, 공룡이 깃털을 가지고 있지 않기 때문에, 공룡이 악어보다 조류와 더 유사함에도 불구하고 악어와 같은 파충류로 분류되는 것이다. 또 다른 예는 소위 '포유류 같은 파충류'라 불리는 동물인데, 이는 현재의 포유류가 지니고 있는 몇 가지 중요한 특징을 가지고 있지 않은 멸종된 동물이다. [2]이 동물들은 파충류로 분류되는데, 엎드린 자세를 취하고 내이골이 없는 등 진화적으로 파충류 단계에 속하는 듯 보이기 때문에, 파충류와는 진화적으로 거리가 있음에도 불구하고 파충류로 분류된다.

paleontologist[pèiliəntάlədʒist] 고생물학자
evolutionary[èvəlúːʃənèri] 진화론적인
biologist[baiάlədʒist] 생물학자   phenetic[finétik] 표현학적인
classification[klæ̀səfikéiʃən] 분류   depict[dipíkt] 설명하다
category[kǽtəgɔ̀ːri] 범주   exclude[iksklúːd] 제외하다
inherit[inhérit] 이어 받다
conspicuous[kənspíkjuəs] 괄목할만한   novelty[nάvəlti] 혁신
lump together 하나로 묶다   predatory[prédətɔ̀ːri] 육식의
skeletal[skélətl] 골격의   reptile[réptil] 파충류
crocodile[krάkədàil] 악어   extinct[ikstíŋkt] 멸종된
sprawl[sprɔːl] 엎드리다   stance[stæns] 자세
lack[læk] 없음, 결핍

1 아래 문장 중 지문 속의 음영된 문장의 핵심 정보를 가장 잘 표현하고 있는 것은 무엇인가? 오답은 문장의 의미를 현저히 왜곡하거나 핵심 정보를 빠뜨리고 있다.

   (A) Coelurosaurian 공룡과 중생대 조류가 많은 공통점을 가지고 있긴 하지만, 그들은 진화론적으로는 연관이 없다.
   (B) 깃털의 소유는 중생대 조류가 파충류로 분류되지 못하게 했다.
   (C) 조류는 깃털을 가지고 있기 때문에, 그들의 유사성에도 불구하고 공룡과 같은 분류에 포함되지 않는다.
   (D) 중생대 조류는 Coelurosaurian 공룡과 유사한 골격 구조를 가지고 있기 때문에 특별하다.

2 아래 문장 중 지문 속의 음영된 문장의 핵심 정보를 가장 잘 표현하고 있는 것은 무엇인가? 오답은 문장의 의미를 현저히 왜곡하거나 핵심 정보를 빠뜨리고 있다.

   (A) 진화론에서는 파충류와 밀접한 관계를 맺고 있지 않지만, '포유류 같은 파충류'는 파충류의 몇몇 특징들 때문에 파충류로 불린다.
   (B) 포유류의 몇몇 특징이 없기 때문에, '포유류 같은 파충류'는 명확히 파충류로 분류된다.
   (C) '포유류 같은 파충류'를 파충류로 분류하는 것은 밀접한 진화론적 관계보다는 일반적인 특징에 근거를 둔다.
   (D) 엎드린 자세와 내이골이 없다는 것은 파충류의 두 가지 독특한 특징이다.

17 '은의 주'라는 별명이 붙은 Nevada주의 채광산업 역사는 그 주의 역사와 너무나도 밀접하게 연관이 되어 있어서, 역사의 어떤 시점에 대해서는 그 두 가지를 떼어놓고 보기 힘들 정도이다. 사실 광산업이 아니었다면 Nevada주는 아마도 실제로 주로 인정되었던 시기보다 수십 년 후에도 주로 승격될 수 없었을 것이다. 그때 은의 주는 유명한 Comstock 광맥에서 캐낸 은으로 연방 편입을 매수했다. 이후 Nevada주가 된 지역은 1800년대 중반에는 주로 California로 금을 캐러 가는 사람들을 위한 고속도로 역할을 했다. 하지만 1859년에 대규모의 은 광상이 발견되자 Virginia City는 빠르게 서부 지역에서 가장 유명한 탄광촌이 되었다. 채광자와 정착자들의 급격한 유입은 불과 2년 만에 Nevada Territory의 조직으로 이어졌다. 동부에서는 미국 남북 전쟁이 일어나려 하고 있었다. [1]Lincoln은 Nevada 지역의 풍부한 광물 자원이 연방에 도움이 될 것임을 깨달았고, 그가 제안했던 노예 제도를 폐지하는 헌법 개정을 지지해줄 또 다른 북부 주가 필요했으므로 Nevada의 연방 편입을 도왔다. 비록 Nevada가 주로 승격되기 위해 필요한 127,381명의 인구의 5분의 1 정도 밖에 되지 않았지만, 연방의회는 제출된 주 헌법을 승인했고 1864년에 Nevada를 미국의 36번째 주로 인정했다. '전쟁으로 인해 태어난 주'라는 Nevada의 표어는 이 격변의 시대에 Nevada주가 담당했던 역할을 보여준다. [2]그 이후로도, 광산업은 여전히 Nevada주의 경제에 막대한 영향을 미쳤는데, 호황 시기에 광산업은 많은 돈을 유입시켰고 광물의 수요가 줄어들었던 시기에는 현저한 경제 침체를 초래하기도 했다.

mining[máiniŋ] 채광
intertwine[ìntərtwàin] 밀접하게 연관시키다, 얽히다
statehood[stéithùd] 주의 지위   decade[dékeid] 10년
massive[mǽsiv] 대규모의   deposit[dipázit] 광상, 매장물
influx[ínflʌks] 유입   prospector[práspektər] 채광자
territory[térətɔ̀ːri] 지역   brew[bruː] 일어나려고 하다
mineral[mínərəl] 광물   amendment[əméndmənt] 개정
constitution[kὰnstətjúːʃən] 헌법   immense[iméns] 막대한
boom[buːm] 호황, 벼락 경기   noticeable[nóutisəbl] 현저한
downturn[dáuntə̀rn] 침체   wane[wein] 줄어들다

1 아래 문장 중 지문 속의 음영된 문장의 핵심 정보를 가장 잘 표현하고 있는 것은 무엇인가? 오답은 문장의 의미를 현저히 왜곡하거나 핵심 정보를 빠뜨리고 있다.

   (A) Lincoln은 그것의 풍부한 자원이 노예 제도 폐지 운동에 자산이 될 것이기 때문에 Nevada 지역이 연방 편입되기를 원했다.

(B) 경제 및 정치적 상황 때문에, Lincoln은 Nevada의 연방 편입 신청을 지지했다.

(C) 풍부한 자원을 사용하고 Lincoln을 지지하겠다는 약속을 통해, Nevada 지역은 연방 편입이 될 수 있었다.

(D) Nevada 지역은 연방에 노예 제도 폐지 개정에 대한 지원을 제공하고자 했기 때문에 주의 지위를 신청하도록 고무되었다.

2 아래 문장 중 지문 속의 음영된 문장의 핵심 정보를 가장 잘 표현하고 있는 것은 무엇인가? 오답은 문장의 의미를 현저히 왜곡하거나 핵심 정보를 빠뜨리고 있다.

(A) 광물 수요의 감소는 Nevada가 많은 양의 돈을 채광 산업에 지원하는 데 쓰는 것으로 이어졌다.

(B) Nevada 채광 산업의 호황과 불황은 그 지역 경제에 막대한 영향을 미쳤다.

(C) Nevada 경제는 채광 산업에서 나온 자금의 유입으로 인해 활성화되었다.

(D) Nevada 경제의 성쇠는 광물 수요에 상당한 변화를 일으켰다.

HACKERS **TEST**

01 Electric Fish

p.58

1. (C)	2. (C)	3. (B)
4. (D)	5. (D)	6. (A)
7. (B)-3단락, (C)-4단락, (D)-2단락		

1 시각적, 청각적, 화학적 의사소통은 모든 환경의 생물체에서 가능하다. 그러나 공기는 너무 효과적인 절연체라서 송신자가 수신자에게 보내는 신호를 통과시키지 못하므로, 전기를 이용한 의사소통은 물에서만 가능하다. ¹많은 물고기가 작은 전류를 감지할 수 있기는 하지만, 전기물고기는 고도로 특화된 전기 기관을 통해 전기적 신호를 송신, 수신, 처리함으로써 방향을 찾고 의사소통할 수 있다는 점에서 다른 물고기들과 구분된다. 전기물고기 중 가장 유명한 전기뱀장어는 150볼트에 달하는 전압을 방전할 수 있는 '강하게 전기적(strongly electric)'인 부류에 속한다. Black ghost knife와 같은 다른 전기 물고기들은 '약하게 전기적(weakly electric)'인 것으로 분류되는데, 이는 그들의 최대 전기 방출이 일반적으로 1볼트도 안 되기 때문이다. 전자(strongly electric 부류)가 포식을 위해 강력한 전기 공격을 가하는 것을 제외하고, 모든 전기물고기는 전기 발생기관을 비슷하게 사용한다.

2 ³전기 기관은 전기포라고 불리는 세포들로 구성되어 있는데, 이 세포는 수축 능력은 없지만 근육세포와 마찬가지로 신경축색돌기의 끝부분에 존재한다는 점에서 근육세포와 유사점을 지닌다. 뚜렷이 원반 같은 모양을 하고 있는 전기포는 건전지의 전지처럼 일렬로 정렬되어 있다. 200,000개에 이르는 세포들이 직렬로 정렬되는데, 각각은 생화학적 활동을 통해 작은 전압을 발생시킬 능력을 가지고 있다. 전류가 동시에 방전되면, (각 세포에서 방전된) 전류는 통합되어 이들 전압의 합인 전위차를 만든다. 강하게 전기적인 물고기는 적을 기절시키거나 죽이기 위해 이 전위차를 조절해서 강한 전기 충격을 발산한다. 이와 같은 경우가 아니라면, 두 부류의 전기물고기 모두 자기 몸 주위에 약하고 지속적인 전기장을 만들기 위해서 전기포를 사용한다.

3 이러한 작용은 물고기의 몸 표면에 고루 분포되어 있는 전자 수용기의 작용과 연계되어 일어난다. 각각의 전자 수용기는 표피를 따라 분포된 전압을 모니터하는 소형 전압계와 같은 역할을 하는데, 이는 감각정보를 뇌로 전달해 주위 수역에 있는 사물의 '그림'을 생성한다. 이 과정은 electrolocation이라고 불린다. 가까운 곳의 물체가 물고기의 전기장을 교란하면, 이는 전류 흐름의 패턴을 바꾼다. ⁵만약 그 물체가 돌처럼 물보다 낮은 전도율을 갖는다면 전류는 그 물체 주위를 비껴갈 것인 반면, 만약 물체가 피라미처럼 물보다 높은 전도율을 갖는다면 그 물체는 저항이 낮은 경로가 되기 때문에 전류는 그 물체를 관통하게 될 것이다. 이러한 과정은 물고기가 자신의 전기장의 변화를 탐지하게 해주는데, 이는 주위의 물체가 먹이인지, 장애물인지, 적인지 아니면 같은 편인지를 판단하는 데 이용된다.

4 전기정보는 정보가 암호화될 수 있는 전기 기관 방전(EOD)을 통하여, 번식을 위한 목적으로 물고기들이 서로 의사소통을 하는 데에도 사용될 수 있다. 각 전기 물고기의 EOD는 특정 주파수 내에서 방전된다. 수컷 물고기가 암컷의 EOD를 받으면, 수컷 물고기는 자신의 뛰어난 생식 능력을 보이고 그 암컷 물고기로 하여금 자신을 짝짓기 상대로 고르도록 장려하기 위하여 자신의 EOD 주파수에 고의적인 변화를 준다. 수컷이 짝짓기 상대로 선택되기 위한 적격성은 보통 수컷의 주파수에 의해 결정되기 때문에, 가장 극단적인 주파수로 전기적 자극을 방출할 수 있는 수컷이 암컷을 유혹하여 산란하는 데 더 좋은 기회를 가진다. 짝짓기 기회가 제한되어 있는 무리에서는, 같은 암컷을 두고 두 수컷 사이에 싸움이 일어나기도 한다. 한 수컷은 자신의 EOD를 바꾸어 다른 수컷의 EOD를 모방하며 상대방의 신호를 효과적으로 막는데, 이로써 싸움을 시작하여 둘 중 하나가 지쳐서 항복의 뜻으로 자신의 EOD를 방출하는 것을 멈출 때까지 싸움을 계속한다. 한편, 공격적인 의도가 없는데도 주파수가 비슷해지면, 물고기는 반사적으로 주파수를 조절해서 싸움을 피할 것이다. ⁶자신과 거의 같은 주파수를 가진 물고기를 발견하면 진폭을 약간 높일 수 있고, 이에 따라 상대방도 자신의 주파수를 조절하여 약간 낮출 것이다. 방해 회피 반응(Jamming Avoidance Response), 즉 JAR로 알려진 이러한 기능은 인접한 무리 내의 평화적인 결합을 공고히 한다.

visual [víʒuəl] 시각의   **auditory** [ɔ́ːdətɔ̀ːri] 청각의
correspondence [kɔ̀ːrəspándəns] 의사소통
insulator [ínsəlèitər] 절연체   **detect** [ditékt] 감지하다
current [kə́ːrənt] 전류   **discharge** [distʃáːrdʒ] 방전
emission [imíʃən] 방출   **volley** [váli] 공격, 연발
predation [pridéiʃən] 포식   **axon** [ǽksɑn] 신경축색돌기

contract[kəntrǽkt] 수축하다 align[əláin] 정렬하다
amalgamate[əmǽlgəmèit] 통합하다 potential difference 전위차
stun[stʌd] 기절시키다 modulate[mɑ́dʒulèit] 조정하다
exude[igzúːd] 발산하다 perpetual[pərpétʃuəl] 지속적인, 영속하는
in tandem with ~와 연계되어 convey[kənvéi] 전달하다
perturb[pərtə́ːrb] 교란시키다 conductive[kəndʌ́ktiv] 전도력 있는
deflect[diflékt] 비껴가다 minnow[mínou] 피라미, 작은 물고기
gauge[ɡeidʒ] 판단하다 prowess[práuis] 뛰어난 능력
eligibility[èlidʒəbíləti] 적격성 spawn[spɔːn] 산란하다
erupt[irʌ́pt] 일어나다, 발발하다 cease[siːs] 멈추다
surrender[səréndər] 항복 oscillation[ɑ̀səléiʃən] 진폭
marginally[mɑ́ːrdʒinli] 약간, 조금 cohesion[kouhíːʒən] 결합

1 아래 문장 중 지문 속의 음영된 문장의 핵심 정보를 가장 잘 표현하고 있는 것은 무엇인가? 오답은 문장의 의미를 현저히 왜곡하거나 핵심 정보를 빠뜨리고 있다.

(A) 전류를 사용하여 의사소통하고 방향을 찾는 능력은 여러 가지 다양한 종류의 물고기들의 공통적인 속성이다.

(B) 다른 물고기가 전기를 감지할 수 있다고 하더라도, 전기물고기는 이 능력을 다른 목적을 위해 사용하기 때문에 특별하다.

(C) 특수한 전기 기관의 소유는 전기물고기들이 다른 물고기들은 사용할 수 없는 다양한 기능에 전기를 사용하게 해준다.

(D) 전기물고기는 다른 물고기들이 감지하기에는 아주 약한 전류를 발생시키는 데 그들의 특화된 전기 기관을 사용한다.

2 지문의 구 "Apart from"과 의미상 가장 유사한 것은?

(A) ~ 대신에
(B) ~와 달리
(C) ~ 외에
(D) ~이 아닌

3 아래 문장 중 지문 속의 음영된 문장의 핵심 정보를 가장 잘 표현하고 있는 것은 무엇인가? 오답은 문장의 의미를 현저히 왜곡하거나 핵심 정보를 빠뜨리고 있다.

(A) 수축 기능이 없는 것을 제외하고, 전기 기관을 형성하는 전기포는 근육세포와 비슷하다.

(B) 전기 기관을 구성하는 전기포는 수축할 수는 없지만, 위치상 근육세포와 유사하다.

(C) 전기포라고 알려진 전기 기관은 신경축색돌기의 끝부분에서 발견되기 때문에 근육세포와 유사하다.

(D) 전기포는 전기물고기의 신경축색돌기 끝부분에서 흔히 발견되는 수축하는 근육세포의 한 형태이다.

4 지문의 단어 "aligned"와 의미상 가장 유사한 것은?

(A) 부푼
(B) 주장된
(C) 야유받는
(D) 정돈된

5 아래 문장 중 지문 속의 음영된 문장의 핵심 정보를 가장 잘 표현하고 있는 것은 무엇인가? 오답은 문장의 의미를 현저히 왜곡하거나 핵심 정보를 빠뜨리고 있다.

(A) 전류는 돌처럼 낮은 전도율의 물체 주위는 비껴가지만, 피라미처럼 높은 전도율의 물체는 관통한다.

(B) 물속의 물체가 전류에 반응하는 방식은 그것들이 얼마나 잘 전기를 전도하는지에 달려 있다.

(C) 물체의 전도율이 높을수록, 더 적은 저항이 물속 전류에 가해질 것이다.

(D) 전류는 물속에서 마주치는 물체의 전도율에 따라 다르게 작용할 것이다.

6 아래 문장 중 지문 속의 음영된 문장의 핵심 정보를 가장 잘 표현하고 있는 것은 무엇인가? 오답은 문장의 의미를 현저히 왜곡하거나 핵심 정보를 빠뜨리고 있다.

(A) 전기물고기는 비슷한 신호를 사용하는 다른 물고기를 만나면 진폭을 바꿀 것이다.

(B) 비슷한 주파수를 가진 전기물고기들은 서로를 감지하기 위해 진폭을 바꿔야만 한다.

(C) 비슷한 주파수를 가진 두 마리의 전기물고기가 만나면, 더 낮은 진폭이 높아질 것이다.

(D) 전기물고기는 다른 물고기들보다 높은 진폭을 갖기 위해 자주 주파수를 조정한다.

7 **지시:** 지문 요약을 위한 도입 문장이 아래에 주어져 있다. 지문의 가장 중요한 내용을 나타내는 보기 3개를 골라 요약을 완성하시오. 어떤 문장은 지문에 언급되지 않은 내용이나 사소한 정보를 담고 있으므로 요약에 포함되지 않는다. 이 문제는 2점이다.

> 전기물고기는 전기를 감각의 하나로 사용할 수 있는 독특한 유형의 동물이다.
> · (B) 전기물고기 몸 주위의 전기장은 주위 환경에 있는 물체를 인지할 수 있게 한다.
> · (C) 전기물고기는 짝짓기 의사소통을 위한 목적으로 전기 기관 방전을 사용한다.
> · (D) 전기물고기는 몸에 있는 긴 일렬의 세포를 통해 전하를 발생시키는 능력이 있다.

(A) 강하게 전기적인 물고기들은 다양한 침입자들의 공격에 대응하여 넓은 범위의 전압을 방출한다.

(E) 거의 동일한 주파수를 가진 전기물고기들은 방해 회피 반응으로 그들의 주파수를 바꾼다.

(F) 전기물고기에 의한 수많은 방출은 의사소통을 위한 제한적인 주파수를 받아들이게 한다.

---

02 The Fremont

p.62

1. (C)	2. (D)	3. (B)
4. (D)	5. (B)	6. (B)
7. (D)	8. (A)-3단락, (C)-2단락, (F)-4단락	

1 Fremont인들은 Harvard Peabody Museum의 Noel Morss에 의해서, Fremont인들이 서기 400년에서 1300년까지 정착해서 살

았던 Utah주의 Fremont 강을 따라 이름 붙여졌다. 대부분의 고고학자는 이 지역에 처음으로 자리잡고 살았던 이들이 2,500년에서 1,500년 전에 Colorado 고원에서 이 지역으로 이주해 온 수렵 채집자들이었을 것이라고 추측한다. 약 2,000년 전부터, 현재 Utah주 중부인 지역에서 옥수수 등의 식물들이 재배되기 시작했다. [1]이러한 초기 Fremont인들은 정착 마을을 짓지 않고 유목생활을 계속하며 농사 짓는 법과 토기 만드는 법을 사방에 퍼뜨렸는데, 이로부터 700년이 지나 더 적게 이동하는 생활양식이 등장하면서 다수의 농경 공동체가 발달했고, 이 농경 공동체는 목재와 진흙으로 만든 반지하식 온실과 지상의 곡물창고로 이루어져 있었다. Fremont인들은 그들의 동시대인들만큼 세련된 농경 기술도 발달시켰는데, 관개 같은 방법으로 물의 방향을 바꾸는 기술도 사용했다.

2 Fremont인들은 Utah 남부에 살았던 잘 알려진 Anasazi족의 것과 구별하기 힘든 형태와 기술로 관개수로나 가옥들을 지었는데, 이는 처음에는 Fremont인들이 Anasazi족의 분파이거나 Anasazi족으로부터 예전에 갈라져 나왔을 것이라는 생각을 불러 일으켰다. Fremont인들은 Anasazi족에 비해 훨씬 많은 수의 이종 집단들로 이루어졌다는 점에서 사회적 조직력은 부족했지만, 적응력은 훨씬 뛰어나서 그들의 조그만 촌락들은 지역 내의 모든 영역과 지형에 자리 잡고 있었다. 그들 문화의 잔재가 발굴되면서, Morss는 Fremont인들이 별개의 집단이라는 것을 증명할 수 있었다. [3]Morss가 직면했던 한 가지 어려움은, 산재되어 있는 여러 작은 집단들이 하나의 응집력 있는 문화를 이루고 있었고 그러한 지리적 산재를 넘어선 유사점을 가지고 있었다는 것을 밝히려 한 것이었다.

3 다른 고대 문명처럼 고고학적인 틀에 꼭 들어맞지는 않지만 독특한 행동과 관습이 이 이질적인 집단을 하나로 묶어주고 있다. 그 첫 번째 특징은 부들과 큰고랭이를 자주 이용한 Fremont one-rod and bundle이라는 바구니 공예 양식인데, 이는 Basketmakers라 불리는 Anasazi족 선조의 새끼를 꼬아 만든 바구니 양식과는 쉽게 구분된다. Fremont인들은 또한 들소의 무릎관절이나 사슴, 양의 앞다리로 밑이 평평한 가죽신을 만들었다. 이러한 초기의 가죽신은 짐승의 발굽이 발꿈치 부근에 꿰매어져 징 역할을 했는데, 이는 바닥이 미끄러울 때 마찰을 증가시켜 주었다. [4]대개의 경우 가죽은 잘 보존되지 못하지만, Utah 지역의 건조한 기후 덕분에 몇 개의 표본이 발견되었고, 이 표본들은 이후에 이 지역으로 이주해온 이들의 yucca 샌들과 쉽게 구별된다. 두께가 얇은 회색 도기 파편이 모든 유적지에서 발견되었는데, 부서지기 쉬운 성질 때문에 안타깝게도 온전한 견본으로 남아있지 않다. 가장 눈에 띄는 특징으로, Fremont인들은 벽에 조각할 때 주로 사용했던 그들만의 독특한 미술양식을 가지고 있었는데, 이러한 미술 양식은 목걸이로 장식된 사다리꼴 모양의 인간 형상을 나타내고 있으며, 위치나 재료에 상관없이 모든 거주지에서 공통적으로 발견된다.

4 서기 1250년 이래로, Fremont인들은 그들이 우연히 나타났을 때와 마찬가지로 불가사의하게 사라지기 시작했고, 그들의 갑작스러운 이주를 설명할 근거를 빈약하게 남겨두었다. [6]Anasazi족과 마찬가지로, 그들이 사라지게 된 정확한 이유는 알려져 있지 않지만, 한 가지 원인이 아닌 여러 가지 원인이 복합적으로 변화를 불러왔을 가

능성이 매우 높다. 가장 흔히 지적되는 원인은 강우량의 감소 등의 기후 변화가 Fremont인들로 하여금 야생 동물 사냥에 대한 의존도를 높이게 만들었을 것이라는 것이다. 또 다른 한 가지 요소는 다른 종족 사람들이 이 지역으로 이주해 들어와서, 자원을 놓고 벌인 경쟁을 통해 Fremont인들을 쫓아냈거나, 자신들의 문화에 Fremont인들을 흡수해 버렸을 가능성도 있다. 긴 시간이 지났고 남겨진 유물의 부족 때문에 그들의 소멸에 대한 정확한 이유는 영원히 알아낼 수 없을지도 모르지만, 이 영리하고 창의적인 사람들이 자신이 살던 지역에 대한 깊은 이해를 가지고 있었다는 것만은 분명하다.

archaeologist[ù:rkiáləʤist] 고고학자　plateau[plætóu] 고원
maize[meiz] 옥수수　nomadic[noumǽdik] 유목의
itinerant[aitínərənt] 이동하는
semi-subterranean[sèmisʌbtəréiniən] 반지하의
granary[grǽinəri] 곡물창고　irrigation[ìrəgéiʃən] 관개
offshoot[ɔ́:fʃù:t] 분파　disparate[díspərət] 이종의
pocket[pákit] (주위에서 고립된 이질적인) 작은 지역, 고립 지대
niche[nitʃ] 영역　remnant[rémnənt] 잔재
excavate[ékskəvèit] 발굴하다　cohesive[kouhí:siv] 응집력 있는
cattail[kǽttèil] 부들　bulrush[búlrʌʃ] 큰고랭이
precursor[prikə́:rsər] 선조
moccasin[mákəsin] 밑이 평평한 가죽신　hock[hak] 무릎관절
bison[báisn] 들소　foreleg[fɔ́:rlèg] 앞다리
dewclaw[djú:klɔ̀:] 발굽　hobnail[hábnèil] 징
traction[trǽkʃən] 마찰　discriminate[diskrímənèit] 구별하다
shard[ʃɑ:rd] 도기 파편　fragility[frəʤíləti] 부서지기 쉬움
trapezoidal[trǽpəzɔ̀idəl] 사다리꼴의　bedeck[bidék] 장식하다
inexplicably[inéksplikəbli] 불가사의하게
haphazard[hæphǽzərd] 우연의　scant[skænt] 빈약한
precipitation[prisìpətéiʃən] 강우량　displace[displéis] 쫓아내다
paucity[pɔ́:səti] 부족　relic[rélik] 유물　demise[dimáiz] 소멸

1 아래 문장 중 지문 속의 음영된 문장의 핵심 정보를 가장 잘 표현하고 있는 것은 무엇인가? 오답은 문장의 의미를 현저히 왜곡하거나 핵심 정보를 빠뜨리고 있다.

(A) Fremont인들이 농사 짓는 법과 토기 만드는 법에 대한 지식을 축적하면서, 그들은 차츰 안전한 공동체로 자리잡았다.

(B) 그 지역의 다른 사람들과 정보를 교환해야 할 필요가 있었기 때문에, Fremont인들의 정착은 지연되었다.

(C) Fremont인들이 처음에는 이곳저곳으로 돌아다녔지만, 그들은 결국 다수의 농업 사회를 세웠다.

(D) Fremont인들이 영구적인 건물을 세우는 데 필요한 방법을 알고 나서, 그들은 유목생활을 포기했다.

2 지문의 단어 "remnants"와 의미상 가장 유사한 것은?

(A) 측면
(B) 단서
(C) 신념
(D) 유물

3 아래 문장 중 지문 속의 음영된 문장의 핵심 정보를 가장 잘 표현하고 있는 것은 무엇인가? 오답은 문장의 의미를 현저히 왜곡하거나 핵심 정보를 빠뜨리고 있다.

(A) Fremont인들은 다수의 장소를 사용한 유일한 문화여서, Morss가 그들이 진정 하나라는 것을 증명하기 어렵게 만들었다.

(B) 멀리 떨어져 있는 수많은 여러 집단들이 유사한 문화를 가지고 있었다는 사실은 Morss의 연구에 장애물이었다.

(C) Morss는 각각의 위치를 고려하지 않고 유사성으로만 이종 집단을 묶으려고 시도했다.

(D) 모임을 위한 중심지가 없이는, Morss는 다양한 집단 모두가 하나의 문화에 포함된다는 점을 증명할 수 없었다.

4 아래 문장 중 지문 속의 음영된 문장의 핵심 정보를 가장 잘 표현하고 있는 것은 무엇인가? 오답은 문장의 의미를 현저히 왜곡하거나 핵심 정보를 빠뜨리고 있다.

(A) Fremont인의 가죽신은 Utah주에서 이후에 발견된 yucca 샌들에 비해 품질이 낮았지만, 날씨 때문에 좋은 상태를 유지했다.

(B) 시간이 흐르면서 가죽 보존을 위한 날씨 조건이 크게 향상되었지만 yucca 샌들은 Fremont인들의 것보다 더 잘 보존되어왔다.

(C) Utah주의 건조한 날씨 때문에, Fremont인들이 만든 모카신의 일부는 여전히 사용할 수 있다.

(D) 잘 상하는 특성에도 불구하고, Utah주의 날씨는 yucca로 만들어진 것과 뚜렷이 다른 Fremont의 가죽신이 남아 있을 수 있게 했다.

5 지문의 단어 "depicting"과 의미상 가장 유사한 것은?

(A) 불식시키는
(B) 묘사하는
(C) 지원하는
(D) 드러내는

6 아래 문장 중 지문 속의 음영된 문장의 핵심 정보를 가장 잘 표현하고 있는 것은 무엇인가? 오답은 문장의 의미를 현저히 왜곡하거나 핵심 정보를 빠뜨리고 있다.

(A) Anasazi족의 쇠락은 Fremont인들의 소멸로 이어진 많은 변화가 생기게 했다.

(B) Fremont인들의 소멸은 분명하지 않은 여러 가지 결합된 요인들의 결과였다.

(C) Anasazi족과 Fremont인의 소멸은 그 원인은 알려지지 않았지만, 어느 정도 관련이 있다.

(D) Fremont인들의 파멸은 Anasazi족이 사라진 것과 같은 방식으로 일어났다.

7 지문의 단어 "demise"와 의미상 가장 유사한 것은?

(A) 함축
(B) 합동
(C) 무리
(D) 몰락

8 **지시:** 지문 요약을 위한 도입 문장이 아래에 주어져 있다. 지문의 가장 중요한 내용을 나타내는 보기 3개를 골라 요약을 완성하시오. 어떤 문장은 지문에 언급되지 않은 내용이나 사소한 정보를 담고 있으므로 요약에 포함되지 않는다. **이 문제는 2점이다.**

Utah주의 Fremont인들은 다른 문화와 별개로 발달했던 독특한 집단이었다.

· (A) 많은 공동체들이 광범위하게 퍼져 있었던 반면, 그들은 모두 공통적인 문화적 특징이 많았다.

· (C) 그들은 많은 촌락들을 세웠고 매우 다양한 환경에 적응했다.

· (F) 그들의 문명이 끝나버린 이유를 정확하게 설명할 충분한 정보가 남지 않았다.

(B) 그들의 건축물과 농경에서 볼 수 있듯이 그들은 Anasazi족과 어떤 관계가 있었다.

(D) 그들은 지나친 수렵으로 모든 사냥감을 고갈시켰고 그들의 도시를 버려야만 했다.

(E) 그들은 특이한 형태의 사람들을 보여주는 조각으로 가장 잘 알려져 있다.

03 | Hydroelectric Power

p.66

1. (B)	2. (A)	3. (D)
4. (C)	5. (C)	6. (C)
7. (B)	8. (A)	
9. (A)–4단락, (B)–3단락, (F)–2단락		

1 증가하고 있는 인구밀도와 환경에 대한 염려는 사회에 21세기를 헤쳐나갈 원동력을 제공해 줄 실현 가능한 대체 에너지의 새로운 연구에 대한 자극이 되어왔다. 기존의 화석연료와 달리, 물은 풍부하고, 깨끗하고, 재생 가능한 동력원으로 많은 이에게 촉망받고 있다. ²터빈으로 작동되는 대규모의 수력발전 댐이 산업화된 사회의 주요 요소인데도 불구하고, 사회적, 생태적 부작용 때문에 여러 나라에서 새로운 댐의 건설을 막기도 하고 지연시키기도 하는 반대자들이 생겨났다. 그러나 터빈을 사용하는 기술은 댐을 환경에 무해하게 개조하고자 하는 환경적으로 의식있는 열망자들에게 매력적인 가능성을 제시해 주고 있다.

2 현재 전 세계적으로 약 40,000개의 대규모 수력발전소가 있는데, 이들은 전 세계 에너지 수요의 20퍼센트를 공급하고 있다. 이러한 수력발전소들은 물을 저수지에 축적했다가 수로를 따라서 변전소로 내려 보내는데, 이때 발생하는 물의 힘이 전기를 발생시키는 터빈을 돌린다. ³얻을 수 있는 에너지의 양은 저수지와 변전소 간의 거리에 직접적으로 비례하기 때문에, 엄청난 양의 물을 저장할 수 있는 높은 댐을 건설하는 것이 효율적이다. 이는 거대한 면적의 지대가 침수되어야 함을 의미한다. 이 때문에, 지난 한 세기 동안 수백만 명의 사람들이 조상으로부터 물려받은 땅과 문화적인 애착을 가진 지역을 떠나 강제적으로 이주되길 요했고, 이는 어떠한 것으로도 보상될 수 없는 추방이었다. 게다가, 인공적인 물의 포화 상태로 인해 지상의 식물군이 몰살되었고 이로 인해서 다량의 생물체가 동시적으로 변질되었다. 또한, 이러한 대규모의 몰살 사태는 바위 속에 불활성

상태로 있었던 수은의 독소가 물로 방출되는 현상을 촉진하여 많은 어류 종에게 치명적인 결과를 가져왔다. 대규모의 거주 가능 지역을 침수시킨다면 이러한 문제를 피할 수 없기 때문에, 환경학자들은 주로 조수와 파도를 통해 바닷물을 이용하는 터빈회전 방식으로 관심을 돌려 왔다.

3 조수를 이용하는 널리 알려진 신기술은 조력 발전기인데, 이 기술은 큰 강의 어귀를 가로막는 barrage라 불리는 댐을 세워서, 터빈이 설치된 수문을 통해 밀물 때는 웅덩이로 물이 흘러 들어오고 썰물 때에는 빠져 나가게 해서 쌍방의 운동으로부터 에너지를 만들어내는 기술이다. 이러한 방식의 발전소 중 가장 큰 프랑스의 La Rance 발전소는 환경에 미치는 영향이 우려되기는 하지만, 매일 240메가와트의 전기를 생산할 수 있고 프랑스의 연간 수력발전량의 10퍼센트를 담당한다. 6강 하구의 물은 다량의 침전물을 동반하여 바다로 흘러 들어가는 경우가 많기 때문에, barrage가 세워지면 침전물이 잘 분산되지 않아 웅덩이 안의 오염물질의 농도가 높아지고, 이로 인해 박테리아의 번식 속도가 증가하게 된다. 더욱이, barrage의 수문이 닫혀 있을 때, 물고기는 터빈을 통과하려고 시도한다. 가장 어류친화적인 터빈일지라도 통과하는 어류의 사망률이 거의 15퍼센트 정도에 이르는데, 이는 매일 주변을 가로지르는 그 지역의 어종에게는 치명적인 수치이다.

4 따라서 파도에너지를 조수에너지 대신 사용하여 이러한 문제점들을 통틀어 제거하는 것은 실험적인 환경론자들의 주의를 끌었는데, 그들은 또한 파도가 더 많은 장소에서 이용될 수 있다는 사실, 영국 같이 해변이 있는 지역은 전체 전기소비량의 5퍼센트을 이 방법으로 생산해낼 수 있다는 사실에 주목한다. 7현재의 파도에너지 시스템은 발전기를 바닷물의 표면에 띄워 놓고 파도에 따라 오르내리며 에너지를 만드는데, 발전기 내부 장치의 진동 운동이 터빈을 회전시키고, 이 터빈 장치에서 발생한 전기가 해저 전선을 통해서 해안가의 발전소로 보내진다. 더욱 많이 쓰이는 시스템은 굴뚝처럼 생긴 기둥을 특징으로 하는데, 이 기둥은 바다의 바닥 위에 세워져서 파도를 기저 부근에 있는 구멍을 통해 통과시킨다. 후자의 경우에는 파도가 오르내림에 따라서 기둥 내의 물도 수위가 변한다. 내부의 수위가 높아지면 공기가 상승하게 되어 터빈을 통과하여 밖으로 빠져나가는데, 이 공기에 의해서 터빈이 회전해서 발전기를 돌린다. 수위가 다시 하강하면, 이로 인해 생긴 진공을 채우기 위해서 공기가 대기로부터 다시 흡입되고 발전기가 다시 작동된다. 비용이 많이 들고 맹렬한 파도, 염수로 인한 부식으로부터 보호하기 위한 기술을 필요로 하기 때문에 이러한 원리를 이용하는 발전장치의 원형은 발전이 더디어졌다. 이 방법의 옹호자들은 만일 사회가 정말로 이런 선의의 사업으로부터 얻어지는 환경적인 이익을 가치 있게 여긴다면, 자금 환수가 불확실하고 그 시점이 언제가 될지 미리 알 수 없다 할지라도, 대규모의 초기 투자는 확실히 가치 있다고 주장한다.

demographic[dèməgrǽfik] 인구학(통계학)의
impetus[ímpətəs] 자극 **staple**[stéipl] 주요 요소
fallout[fɔ́ːlàut] 부작용 **detractor**[ditrǽktər] 반대자
tantalizing[tǽntəlàiziŋ] 매력적인 **aspirant**[ǽspərənt] 열망자
hydroelectric[hàidrouiléktrik] 수력발전의
reservoir[rézərvwàːr] 저수지 **channel**[tʃǽnl] 수로를 통해 보내다

substation[sʌ́bstèiʃən] 변전소 **relocation**[rìːloukéiʃən] 이주
attachment[ətǽtʃmənt] 애착 **diaspora**[daiǽspərə] 추방
compensation[kàmpənséiʃən] 보상 **saturation**[sæʧəréiʃən] 포화
wipe out 몰살하다 **flora**[flɔ́ːrə] 식물군
simultaneous[sàiməltéiniəs] 동시적인
decomposition[dìːkàmpəzíʃən] 변질
biomass[báiouмæs] 생물체 **inert**[inə́ːrt] 불활성의
prevalent[prévələnt] 널리 알려진 **harness**[háːrnis] 이용하다
estuary[éstʃuèri] (간만의 차가 있는) 큰 강의 어귀
sluice gate 수문 **basin**[béisn] 웅덩이
ramification[ræ̀məfikéiʃən] 영향 **sediment**[sédəmənt] 침전물
dispersal[dispə́ːrsəl] 분산 **mortality**[mɔːrtǽləti] 사망률
devastating[dévəstèitiŋ] 치명적인, 파괴적인
traverse[trǽvəːrs] 가로지르다 **churn out** 생산하다
oscillate[ásəlèit] 진동하다 **pivot**[pívət] 회전하다
power station 발전소 **breaker**[bréikər] 부서지는 파도
prototype[próutətàip] 원형 **corrosion**[kəróuʒən] 부식
benevolent[bənévələnt] 선의의, 자비심 많은
portend[pɔːrténd] ~을 미리 알다

1 지문의 단어 "impetus"와 의미상 가장 유사한 것은?

(A) 결과
(B) 자극
(C) 향기
(D) 가장자리

2 아래 문장 중 지문 속의 음영된 문장의 핵심 정보를 가장 잘 표현하고 있는 것은 무엇인가? 오답은 문장의 의미를 현저히 왜곡하거나 핵심 정보를 빠뜨리고 있다.

(A) 댐과 관련된 다양한 문제들은 산업화된 사회에서의 댐에 대한 의존에도 불구하고 새로운 댐이 건설되지 못하게 한다.
(B) 사회적 및 생태적 우려는 많은 국가에서의 새로운 수력발전 댐의 건설을 방해했다.
(C) 대규모 댐은 산업화된 국가에서 필수적이지만, 다른 국가들에서의 건설은 지연되어 왔다.
(D) 산업화된 사회는 사회적 및 생태적인 영향 때문에 수력발전 댐에 대한 의존을 줄여왔다.

3 아래 문장 중 지문 속의 음영된 문장의 핵심 정보를 가장 잘 표현하고 있는 것은 무엇인가? 오답은 문장의 의미를 현저히 왜곡하거나 핵심 정보를 빠뜨리고 있다.

(A) 대규모 댐들은 이용할 수 있는 에너지와 물 수용 능력 간의 관계 때문에 필요하다.
(B) 저수지와 변전소의 거리는 수력발전소에 대한 기본 계획에서 고려되어야 하는 사항이다.
(C) 효율성은 댐의 크기에 의해 영향을 받는 경향이 있기 때문에, 대규모 양의 물을 유지하는 댐을 건설하는 것이 좋다.
(D) 물이 더 높은 거리에서 떨어질 때 더 많은 전력이 발생하기 때문에, 높은 댐의 건설은 효율적이다.

4 지문의 단어 "simultaneous"와 의미상 가장 유사한 것은?

(A) 경솔한
(B) 고대의

(C) 동시의

(D) 활발한

5 지문의 단어 "wholesale"과 의미상 가장 유사한 것은?

(A) 보통이 아닌

(B) 세속적인

(C) 무분별한

(D) 말이 유창한

6 아래 문장 중 지문 속의 음영된 문장의 핵심 정보를 가장 잘 표현하고 있는 것은 무엇인가? 오답은 문장의 의미를 현저히 왜곡하거나 핵심 정보를 빠뜨리고 있다.

(A) barrage는 감조 하천의 토양층이 바다로 분산되는 것을 막는 오염물질들을 증가시킴으로써 박테리아 번식을 촉진한다.

(B) 하구의 침전물 양이 증가하면, 오염물질의 양이 증가하여, 박테리아의 급증이라는 결과를 낳는다.

(C) 오염물질의 축적에서 야기된 증가된 박테리아 수는 댐이 있는 하구에서 대부분 발견되는데, 이는 이것이 침전물의 분산을 방해하기 때문이다.

(D) 박테리아로 인한 높은 오염 수준으로 인해, 많은 양의 침전물이 있는 하구는 대개 barrage를 위한 위치로 적절하지 않다.

7 아래 문장 중 지문 속의 음영된 문장의 핵심 정보를 가장 잘 표현하고 있는 것은 무엇인가? 오답은 문장의 의미를 현저히 왜곡하거나 핵심 정보를 빠뜨리고 있다.

(A) 바닷물 표면에 있는 물체의 진동은 발전소에 연결된 터빈을 회전시키는 힘을 생산해내는데, 이것은 이후에 전기로 변형된다.

(B) 전기는 파도의 오르내림에 의해 떠 있는 물체의 움직임을 통한 파도 시스템에서 발생되고, 전선을 통해 해변의 발전소로 보내진다.

(C) 파도에너지 시스템은 발전소에 연결된 해저 전선을 통해 동력을 받는 터빈을 사용한다.

(D) 파도에너지는 해변 가까이에 설치되어 파도의 움직임에 영향을 받는 기기인 터빈의 움직임에 의해 발생된다.

8 지문의 단어 "stunted"와 의미상 가장 유사한 것은?

(A) 방해받은

(B) 자극받은

(C) 밀린

(D) 조종된

9 **지시:** 지문 요약을 위한 도입 문장이 아래에 주어져 있다. 지문의 가장 중요한 내용을 나타내는 보기 3개를 골라 요약을 완성하시오. 어떤 문장은 지문에 언급되지 않은 내용이나 사소한 정보를 담고 있으므로 요약에 포함되지 않는다. **이 문제는 2점이다.**

> 물은 전기를 생산하는 데 오랫동안 사용되어왔고 더 새로운 수력발전 시스템이 실험되고 있다.
>
> · (A) 파도는 오르내리는 움직임 덕분에 실질적으로 사용할 수 있는 동력원이다.

· (B) 터빈을 돌리는 데 조류가 들어가고 나갈 때의 힘을 사용하는 시스템은 가동 중이다.

· (F) 전통적인 수력발전 시스템은 댐에 물을 저장하고 낮은 곳에 있는 변전소로 물을 보냈다.

(C) 높은 유지 관리 비용 때문에, 외해에서 작동 중인 파도에너지 원형은 거의 없었다.

(D) 댐 근처의 육지들이 물에 잠기면, 수은 농도가 증가하기 때문에 전체 생태계가 파괴된다.

(E) 오늘날 가장 보편적으로 사용되는 시스템은 환경에 최소한의 영향을 주는 조력 발전기이다.

---

04 The Erie Canal

p.70

1. (B)	2. (C)	3. (A)
4. (D)	5. (D)	6. (B)
7. (C)	8. (C)	
9. (A)–3단락, (C)–4단락, (D)–2단락		

1 19세기 초, 미국은 18개의 주로 이루어져 있었는데, 그중 13개는 Appalachia 산맥의 동쪽 해안가를 따라 위치했고, 반대편에는 목재, 광물과 비옥한 농토가 풍부한 5대호 주변을 둘러싸는 여러 개의 주가 있었다. ¹해안가의 정착민들에게는 바다가 물품의 공급원이나 상품을 내다 팔 시장으로 통하는 길이 되어 주었지만, Appalachia 산맥 서쪽의 정착민들에게는 험한 길 위로 수레마차를 끌어오는 것만이 대서양에 다다를 수 있는 유일한 수단이었다.

2 New York 주지사 DeWitt Clinton이 산 사이에 난 골짜기를 따라 흐를 수 있는 운하를 이용해서 Mohawk 강 계곡을 통하여 Hudson 강 상류(대서양의 지류)와 Erie 호의 동쪽 기슭을 잇는 공사를 제안했을 당시, 그는 회의론자들의 반대에 직면하게 되었는데, 회의론자들은 복잡한 토목 공사 사업에 요구되는 경제적 부담이 그 경제적 부담에 비례하여 그 지역에 이익을 불러올 것이라는 것을 확신하지 못했다. ²게다가, Erie 호와 Mohawk 강 사이에 길게 뻗어 있는 지역은 높이가 거의 600피트(183미터)나 되는 지역도 있었고 당시의 운하 기술로는 12피트(3.5미터) 이내의 높이 차이까지만 해결할 수 있었기 때문에, 안전한 수로의 건설을 위해서는 84개의 분리된 수문을 설치해야 했는데, 수문이란 높은 곳에서 낮은 곳으로 물이 흐르지 않게 막아주면서 배가 운하의 한 구간을 통과해서 다른 수위를 갖는 다른 구간으로 이동할 수 있게 해주는 기술적 장치이다. 또한, 이 건설 공사는 물이 흐르는 방향을 바꾸기 위해서 각각 800피트가 넘는 길이를 갖는 18개의 수로를 필요로 했고, 강의 경로를 재구성하기 위해서는 900피트 규모의 댐을 필요로 했다.

3 1817년 Clinton은 Erie 운하가 될 운하의 건설을 위해 7백만 달러의 지출을 승인하도록 주 의회를 설득했는데, Erie 운하는 그 시대의 가장 성공적인 공공 사업으로 엄청난 사회적, 경제적 변화를 불

러왔고 New York을 미국에서 가장 중요한 항구도시로 만들었다. 8년 후에 Erie 운하가 개통되자, Erie 운하는 주변과 그 이상의 지역에 즉각적인 영향을 미쳤다. Buffalo에서 New York까지의 육로 화물 운송료가 1톤에 100달러였던 것에 비해, 1톤에 10달러에 불과했던 운하를 통한 화물 운송료가 엄청난 규모의 경제활동을 끌어들임에 따라, 교역량이 폭발적으로 급증할 것이라는 Clinton의 예언은 현실이 되었다. 평저선은 6일 이내에 최대 50톤의 화물을 한곳에서 다른 곳으로 운반할 수 있었기 때문에, 시장에 들어오는 상품의 양과 종류가 급증하는 동시에 가격은 급락하게 되었고, 그 결과는 미국 전역에서 나타났다. 예를 들어, 1827년에 이르자 Georgia주의 Savannah에서는 New York주의 중부지방에서 생산된 밀이 Georgia주 내에서 생산된 밀보다 싸게 팔리게 되었다. ⁵전국적으로 New York주의 생산품에 대한 수요가 치솟으면서, 10년도 채 안 되어 New York은 매일 수천 척의 배가 드나드는, 미국에서 가장 분주한 항구가 되었고 Boston, Baltimore, New Orleans를 합한 것보다 더 많은 용적톤수를 취급하게 되었다.

4 New York시의 인구는 급증했으며, Rochester, Buffalo, 그리고 다른 신흥 산업도시들이 운하의 경로를 따라 과다하게 생겨났다. 이러한 도시들의 인구가 늘어나면서 상품의 생산과 소비가 늘어났고, 이는 운하의 통행량을 증가시켰다. 또한, 점점 더 많은 수의 배가 서쪽의 5대호 지역으로 향했는데, 이 배들은 5대호 지역의 비옥하고 값싼, 넓게 펼쳐진 땅에 매혹된 New England 지방에서 이주해 가는 사람들과 유럽 이민자들의 물결을 태우고 있었다. 운하가 개통된 후 30년 이내에 밀 생산이 14,000부셸에서 800만 부셸로 기하급수적으로 급증함에 따라, 중서부 지역은 미국의 곡창지대가 되었다. ⁷이전에는 운하를 통한 운송이 서쪽으로 이루어졌지만, 5대호 지역이 국가 농업의 중심지로 자리매김하자 이러한 흐름이 바뀌었고, 19세기 중반에 이르자 운하를 따라 행해지던 교역 중 대부분이 두 배 이상 늘어난 주요산물의 용적톤수와 함께 동쪽으로 향하게 되었다.

5 엄청난 양의 상품이 New York에서 유럽과 서인도제도 그리고 미국 해안을 따라 남쪽으로 수송되었다. 상품의 수출과 수입에 대한 수요가 상당히 늘어났고, 이는 선박 제조업자로 하여금 더욱 많은 화물을 실을 수 있는 더 빠른 속도의 배를 개발하도록 촉진하였는데, 이러한 변화들로 인해서 New York주는 1918년에 Erie 운하를 재점검하게 되었다. 원래의 수문은 폭이 넓은 평저선이 지나가기에는 너무 좁았는데, 이보다 더 중요하게도, 사업체들이 이전에는 사용되지 않던 작은 강들을 준설작업을 통해 배가 다닐 수 있게 만들어서 수송시간을 단축시킬 것을 요구했다. Erie 운하의 여러 구간을 포함하는 새로운 시설인 New York Barge 운하는 곧 완공되었으며, 1950년대 중반에 대규모의 도로 시설과 장거리 트럭의 도입이 북미 대륙 내의 선박 운송업무를 대신하게 될 때까지 이용되었다.

timber[tímbər] 목재 haulage[hɔ́ːlidʒ] 끌기
onerous[ánərəs] 힘한, 성가신 tributary[tríbjutèri] 지류
skeptic[sképtik] 회의론자 undertaking[ʌ̀ndərtéikiŋ] 사업
proportionally[prəpɔ́ːrʃənli] 비례하여
implementation[ìmpləməntéiʃən] 설치, 수행 lock[lɑk] 수문
contraption[kəntrǽpʃən] 장치 aqueduct[ǽkwədʌ̀kt] 수로

legislature[lédʒislèitʃər] 의회 immediate[imíːdiət] 즉각적인
prophecy[práfəsi] 예언 freight[freit] 화물 운송
flatboat[flǽtbòut] 평저선 tonnage[tʌ́nidʒ] (선박의) 용적톤수
plethora[pléθərə] 과다
boom town (경제화나 공업화로 인해 급격히 발달한) 신흥 도시
expanse[ikspǽns] 넓게 펼쳐진 공간
breadbasket[brédbæ̀skit] 곡창지대
exponentially[èkspounénʃəli] 기하급수적으로
bushel[búʃəl] 부셸(곡식 따위의 계량 단위)
staple[stéipl] 주요산물 dredge[dredʒ] 준설하다

1 아래 문장 중 지문 속의 음영된 문장의 핵심 정보를 가장 잘 표현하고 있는 것은 무엇인가? 오답은 문장의 의미를 현저히 왜곡하거나 핵심 정보를 빠뜨리고 있다.

(A) 해안가 정착민들은 해안가에 도착하기 위해서 추가적인 운송수단이 필요했던 서쪽 사람들에 비해 대서양의 혜택을 받았다.
(B) 동부 해안 지방의 사람들은 상품을 거래하는 데 바다를 이용했던 반면, Appalachian 산맥 서쪽의 거주민들은 대서양에 이르는 데 마차에 의존했다.
(C) 해안에 가까운 지역에 거주하는 사람들은 바다를 통해 물건을 수송할 수 있었기 때문에 먼 내륙에 살았던 사람들보다 상당한 이점이 있었다.
(D) Appalachian 산맥 서쪽 지역에 사는 사람들은 바닷길에 접근할 수 없었기 때문에, 상품의 수송을 위해 마차를 이용했다.

2 아래 문장 중 지문 속의 음영된 문장의 핵심 정보를 가장 잘 표현하고 있는 것은 무엇인가? 오답은 문장의 의미를 현저히 왜곡하거나 핵심 정보를 빠뜨리고 있다.

(A) 운하의 건설은 한 구간의 수위를 올려 다른 구간의 수위와 맞춰주는 많은 수문을 사용하는 것에 달려 있었다.
(B) 운하를 통한 선박들의 안전한 통로를 확보하기 위해, 기술자들은 수문이 물에 잠기는 것을 막는 신기술을 개발하도록 강요받았다.
(C) 두 물줄기의 큰 높이 차이와 그것을 해결하기 위한 기술의 한계로 인해, 수많은 수문들이 필요했다.
(D) 제안된 운하 위치의 지형적인 조건은 기존 운하 기술의 한계를 넓혔고 의미 있는 공학적 도전을 제기했다.

3 지문의 단어 "primary"와 의미상 가장 유사한 것은?

(A) 뛰어난
(B) 훌륭한
(C) 임박한
(D) 태만한

4 지문의 단어 "consequences"와 의미상 가장 유사한 것은?

(A) 규모
(B) 견적
(C) 대치
(D) 결과

5 아래 문장 중 지문 속의 음영된 문장의 핵심 정보를 가장 잘 표현하고 있는 것은 무엇인가? 오답은 문장의 의미를 현저히 왜곡하거나 핵심 정보를 빠뜨리고 있다.

(A) New York 상품이 가장 인기 있어지면서, 많은 수의 배가 전국으로 상품을 수송했다.

(B) Erie 운하의 경제적인 영향은 너무 거대해서 New York은 미국의 중요한 항구 도시가 되었다.

(C) New York 항구를 통해 이동하는 엄청난 양의 선박들은 새로운 상품에 대한 국내 수요를 충족시킬 수 있었다.

(D) New York은 New York 상품에 대한 증가된 수요 때문에 미국의 하천 운수의 막대한 양을 담당할 만큼 성장했다.

6 지문의 단어 "prolific"과 의미상 가장 유사한 것은?

(A) 척박한

(B) 풍부한

(C) 경작할 수 있는

(D) 거리가 먼

7 아래 문장 중 지문 속의 음영된 문장의 핵심 정보를 가장 잘 표현하고 있는 것은 무엇인가? 오답은 문장의 의미를 현저히 왜곡하거나 핵심 정보를 빠뜨리고 있다.

(A) 1800년대 중반의 5대호 지역의 농업적 중요성은 동쪽으로 향하는 운하 운송량의 급증을 초래했다.

(B) 5대호 지역의 농산품을 운반해야 하는 필요성은 운하로 수송되는 상품의 무게가 두 배로 늘어나는 결과를 초래했다.

(C) 운하 운송의 흐름은 전통적으로 동쪽에서 서쪽으로 향하는 것이었지만, 5대호 지역의 농산품 증가로 인해 추세가 바뀌었다.

(D) 5대호 주변 땅이 중요한 농업 지역이 되자 운하 운송의 대부분은 동쪽으로 향하는 무역으로 이루어졌다.

8 지문의 단어 "spurred"와 의미상 가장 유사한 것은?

(A) 허가했다

(B) 가능하게 했다

(C) 자극했다

(D) 초래했다

9 **지시:** 지문 요약을 위한 도입 문장이 아래에 주어져 있다. 지문의 가장 중요한 내용을 나타내는 보기 3개를 골라 요약을 완성하시오. 어떤 문장은 지문에 언급되지 않은 내용이나 사소한 정보를 담고 있으므로 요약에 포함되지 않는다. **이 문제는 2점이다.**

> **Erie 운하의 건설은 전국의 경제 성장에 중요한 역할을 했다.**
>
> · (A) 상업 중심지로서의 New York의 부상과 성장은 운송 상황의 직접적인 결과였다.
>
> · (C) 운하 주변의 많은 지역이 인구와 무역 증가를 겪었다.
>
> · (D) 운하의 건설은 엄청난 비용과 기술적인 제약 때문에 처음에는 방해를 받았다.

(B) 5대호 주변 지역에 사는 사람들은 대서양 근처의 주에서 상품을 받았다.

(E) 5대호로 보내졌던 상품의 양은 그 지역들이 자급자족하게 되면서 급격히 감소했다.

(F) Clinton은 New York시가 운하 사업을 위해 공공 자금을 확대해야 한다고 주장했다.

HACKERS **STRATEGY** p.77

전략 1

Ex 뮬사슴은 주로 오전, 저녁, 달빛이 비치는 밤에 활동적이다. 뜨거운 낮 동안에 활동이 없는 것은 살기에 적합한 정도로 물을 보존하고 체온을 유지하기 위한 사막환경에의 행동적 적응이다. 특질상 뮬사슴은 시원하고 외딴곳에서 잔다. 암사슴과 새끼 사슴은 탁 트인 공간에서 많이 자는 반면, 성숙한 수사슴은 바위가 많은 산등성이를 잠자리로 선호하는 것으로 보인다.

moonlit[múːnlìt] 달빛이 비치는 **livable**[lívəbl] 살기에 적합한
characteristically[kæ̀riktərístikəli] 특질상 **bed down** 자다
secluded[siklúːdid] 외딴 **buck**[bʌk] 수사슴
ridge[ridʒ] 산등성이 **doe**[dou] (사슴, 토끼의) 암컷
fawn[fɔːn] 새끼 사슴

전략 2

Ex 오존층 파괴 과정은 프레온 가스 및 기타 오존층 파괴 물질이 설비에서 샐 때 시작된다. 바람이 능률적으로 대류권 공기를 혼합하고 가스를 고르게 분산시킨다. 프레온 가스는 극도로 안정적이기 때문에 비에도 용해되지 않는다. 여러 해가 지난 후 오존층 파괴 물질 분자들은 성층권에 도달하고 강한 자외선으로 인해 분해된다.

ozone depletion 오존층 파괴 **troposphere**[trápəsfìər] 대류권
stratosphere[strǽtəsfìər] 성층권

Ex 살충제에 민감한 수중생물이 화학물질에 노출되면 그 수는 엄청나게 줄어들 것이다. 전체 먹이사슬이 바뀌게 되고, 미생물과 그 천적을 먹이로 하는 잡식 동물과 육식 동물이 먹이 부족으로 차례로 고통받게 될 것이다.

aquatic life 수중생물 **susceptible**[səséptəbl] 민감한
omnivore[ámnivɔ̀ːr] 잡식 동물 **carnivore**[káːrnəvɔ̀ːr] 육식 동물
microorganism[mài kro uɔ́ːrgənìzm] 미생물

전략 3

Ex 인구증가율은 1980년대 후반에 주춤하기 시작했으며 그 이후로 지속적으로 줄고 있다. 국제연합의 통계에 따르면 인구증가율이 감소하고 있기는 하지만, 세계 인구는 여전히 1.3퍼센트에서 1.9퍼센트씩 해마다 증가하고 있다. 최초의 농경사회가 형성되어 많은 사람이 존속할 수 있게 되었던 고대로부터 시작하여 여러 요소가 세계 인구 증가의 원인이 되어 왔다.
18세기에는 다른 큰 요인이 작용하였는데, 산업혁명이 생활 수준을 끌어올리면서 14세기에서 17세기 사이에 특히 유럽에서 인류를 괴롭혔던 기근과 전염병이 줄게 되었다. 개발도상국의 인구가 증가함에 따라 제2차 세계대전 이후에도 이러한 추세는 계속되었다. 개발도상국의 경우 균형 잡힌 출산율 유지에 필수적인 출산 제한에 대한 인식이 결여되어 있었다. 선진국에 비해 높은 사망률과 상당히 짧은 기대 수명에도 불구하고, 개발도상국의 출산율은 사망률보다 높았다. 이러한 많은 인구는 미래의 잠재적 가치에 대한 지분을 확보하기를 원하는 선진국으로부터의 음식 공급과 의료 구호를 통해 경제적으로 뒷받침되었다.

agricultural community 농경사회 **famine**[fǽmin] 기근
epidemic[èpədémik] 전염병 **plague**[pleig] 괴롭히다
life expectancy 기대 수명

HACKERS STRATEGY **APPLICATION** p.80

약 10억 년 전에, 현재의 Oklahoma에서부터 Lake Superior에 이르는 지역에 발생한 균열로 인해 북아메리카를 거의 분열시킨 화산 활동이 일어났다. 2천만 년이 넘는 기간 동안, 균열된 틈에서 용암이 간헐적으로 흘러나왔다. 이런 지형학적 시기로 인해 현재 Wisconsin 북부와 Minnesota로 알려진 지역에 이르는 산맥이 형성되었고, 로렌시아 산맥이 캐나다 동부에 형성되었다. 간헐적인 화산 활동이 계속되는 가운데 시간이 흐르면서 산의 침식작용이 발생하였다. 지금의 Lake Superior에 해당하는 산악 지대 밑에 있는 녹은 마그마가 옆으로 분출되었고, 이로 인해 산악 지대가 침몰되어 훗날 Lake Superior가 자리할 거대한 바위 분지가 형성되었다. 결국, 시간이 지남에 따라 균열이 안정되었고 바위는 북쪽에서 남쪽으로 기울게 되었다.

fracture[frǽktʃər] 균열 **lava**[láːvə] 용암
intermittently[ìntərmítntli] 간헐적으로
geomorphic[dʒìːəmɔ́ːrfik] 지형학적인 **erode**[iróud] 침식시키다
molten[móultən] 녹은 **highland**[háilənd] 산악 지대
spew[spjuː] 분출되다 **mammoth**[mǽməθ] 거대한
basin[béisn] 분지 **tilt**[tilt] 기울다

1. 지문에 따르면, 로렌시아 산맥의 형성은 _____ 시기의 결과이다.

 (A) 북아메리카 내부의 틈으로 인해 화살이 폭발했던
 (B) 북아메리카가 극심한 지진으로 인해 거의 분열되었던
 (C) 북아메리카를 가로지르는 거대한 암반이 함께 밀집되어 있던
 (D) 북아메리카를 가로지르는 산악 지대가 크게 가라앉았던

부유하고 교양 있는 가정에서 태어난 Jane Addams는 가난한 사람들이 겪는 고통에 가슴 아파했고, 그리하여 집을 떠나 여생을 시카고의 빈민가에서 보냈다. 그녀는 1889년에 Hull House라고 불리는 '사회복지관'을 설립하여 그곳에서 여러 인도주의적인 사업을 시작했

다. 그중에는 공장 근로자들을 위한 따뜻한 점심식사와 어린아이들을 대상으로 한 탁아소, ᶜ청년과 성인에게 제공되는 무료강의 등도 있었다. 이주민들은 교육의 기회뿐만 아니라 조언과 도움을 얻기 위해 Hull House를 찾았다. ᴰAddams는 아동 노동 착취에 맞서 싸우는데도 적극적이었으며 여성의 참정권 획득을 위해서도 노력했다. 하지만 모든 사람이 Jane Addams의 업적을 반겼던 것은 아니었다. 실제로 Addams가 다른 사람들의 용무에 참견한다고 여기며 이를 못마땅해 하는 사람들도 있었다. 그럼에도 불구하고 Addams는 미국뿐만 아니라 세계 여러 지역의 사회 복지 사업 발달에 엄청난 영향을 미쳤다. Addams는 사회적 약자를 위한 복지에 책임을 져야 한다는 개념을 고취시켰고, 그녀가 고안한 사회 복지 프로그램은 널리 채택되었다. Hull House를 모델로 한 사회복지관이 많은 빈민가에 세워져 아이와 어른의 삶을 더 의미 있게 만드는 데 일조했다. ᴬJane Addams는 사회에의 공헌을 인정받아 1931년에 노벨 평화상을 수상하였다.

well-to-do[wéltədù:] 부유한 **cultured**[kʌ́ltʃərd] 교양 있는
distressed[distrést] 가슴 아파하는 **slum**[slʌm] 빈민가
settlement house 사회복지관 **suffrage**[sʌ́fridʒ] 참정권
meddling[médliŋ] 참견 **social work** 사회 복지 사업
be awarded 수상하다

2. 지문에 따르면, 다음 중 Jane Addams에 대해 사실이 아닌 것은?

(A) 그녀의 사회 공헌을 인정받아 노벨 평화상을 수상했다.
(B) 모든 사람에 의해 큰 존경을 받았다.
(C) 대가 없이 사람들에게 교육을 베풀었다.
(D) 아동과 여성의 삶의 질을 향상시키는 데 열중했다.

HACKERS **PRACTICE**   p.82

1. Unfortunately, two separate Patent Office fires destroyed the majority of these models, as well as all records of early U.S. patent history.
2. After that, the textile is put into boiling water to remove the wax, and the process can be repeated.
3. Optical fibers eventually became utilized in applications in telecommunication, computer networking, and remote sensing, and flexible fiber-optic cables helped usher in the information revolution.
4. However, others, particularly jazz purists, claimed that Davis had gone too far and even abandoned his musical roots in classical jazz for a commercially inspired replacement.
5. It determined that the lands governed by the National Park Service remove approximately 17.5 million metric tons, which amounts to an annual economic savings of around $707 million in averted carbon costs.
6. He also made eggs for private clientele who were quite eager to copy the members of Russia's Imperial court and own one of the popular art objects.
7. (F), (F), (T), (F)   8. (F), (T), (T), (T)
9. (F), (T), (T), (F)   10. (F), (T), (F), (T)
11. (T), (F), (T), (F)   12. (T), (T), (T), (F)
13. 1 (B), 2 (D)   14. 1 (A), 2 (C)
15. 1 (C), 2 (D)   16. 1 (A), 2 (B)

VOCABULARY

1 (C), (B)	2 (C)	3 (D), (A)
4 (A), (B)	5 (A), (C)	6 (B), (D)
7 (C)	8 (B), (D)	9 (B), (A)
10 (A), (C)	11 (D), (B)	12 (D)
13 (B), (C), (A)	14 (B), (D), (C)	15 (B), (C), (A)
16 (D), (A), (A)		

1 1790년에 특허법이 통과되었을 때, 특허법에는 모든 새로운 발명품은 반드시 작동하는 축소 모형과 함께 제작되어야 한다는 조항이 포함되어 있었다. 미국 특허 역사의 독특한 유물인 특허 모형은 제작 후 특허청에 공개적으로 전시되었다. 1836년, 2차 특허법이 특허 모형 제작에 대해 '특허 모형은 12평방인치를 초과해서는 안 되고, 깔끔하게 제작되어야 하며, 발명가의 이름이 영구적인 방법으로 발명품 위에 인쇄, 각인, 혹은 부착되어야 한다'라는 지침을 제정하였다. 안타깝게도 두 번에 걸쳐서 특허청에 발생했던 화재로 인해서 미국의 초기 특허 역사의 모든 기록뿐만 아니라 이 모형도 대부분도 소실되었다. 1880년에 모형 제작 요건이 실효가 없다고 공표되어, 모형이 더는 제작되지 않게 되었다.

Patent Act 특허법 **provision**[prəvíʒən] 조항
miniature[míniətʃər] 축소 모형 **artifact**[ɑ́:rtəfækt] 유물
publicly[pʌ́blikli] 공개적으로
establish[istǽbliʃ] (제도·법률 등을) 제정하다
guideline[gàidláin] 지침 **square**[skwɛər] 평방
affix[əfíks] 부착하다, 붙이다 **durable**[djúərəbl] 영구적인

declare[dikléər] 공표하다   impractical[impræktikəl] 실효 없는

다수의 초기 특허 모형들이 오늘날에는 존재하지 않는 이유를 설명하는 문장을 찾으시오.

2 바틱은 여러 가지 복잡한 무늬를 만들어내기 위해 납염을 사용하는 인도네시아의 직물 염색법이다. 그 과정은 canting이라 불리는 주둥이가 달린 도구 또는 cap이라고 일컬어지는 구리 도장을 사용하여 직물에 밀랍으로 된 점과 선 무늬를 만드는 것으로 시작한다. 그다음, 천이 염색제 속에 완전히 담가진다. 밀랍이 입혀진 부분의 천은 염색이 되지 않는다. 그 후, 직물은 밀랍을 제거하기 위해 끓는 물에 넣어지며, 이 과정이 반복될 수 있다. 이것은 장인들이 선택적으로 다른 색상과 무늬를 추가하는 것을 가능하게 한다. 바틱 작품이 더 복잡하고 다채로울수록, 더 많은 횟수로 납염 과정을 거친 것이다.

batik[bətí:k] 바틱(염색이 안 되게 할 부분에 왁스를 발라 무늬를 내는 염색법) dyeing[dáiiŋ] 염색
wax resistance 납염(밀랍을 써서 물들임)
intricate[íntrikət] 복잡한 spouted[spáutid] 주둥이가 달린
copper[ká:pər] 구리 immerse[imə́:rs] 담그다 dye[dai] 염색제
artisan[á:rtəzn] 장인

다양한 색상과 무늬의 추가를 가능하게 하는 행위를 나타내는 문장을 찾으시오.

3 광섬유 기술의 시작은 20세기 초에 행해진 한 연구에 있는데 이때 물리학자들은 상이 광섬유 다발을 통해 전달될 수 있다는 것을 발견하고 입증했다. 수십 년간, 초기 연구들은 차후의 연구가 착수되어 1960년의 논문에서 '광섬유'라는 용어가 처음 나오기 전까지는 보통 과학자들에게 무시되었다. 광섬유는 '전반사'에 의존하는데, 이것은 섬유 다발과 같이 밀도가 높은 매질에서 빛이 완전히 반사되는 것으로, 이것에 의해 빛이 가파른 각도로 매질에 부딪히고 중심부를 통해 퍼진다. 광섬유는 마침내 전기 통신, 컴퓨터 네트워킹, 그리고 원격 탐사에서의 응용에 활용되었고, 유연 광섬유 케이블은 정보 혁명이 시작되게 하는 데 일조했다.

fiber optics 광섬유 inception[insépʃən] 시작, 시초
physicist[fízisist] 물리학자 transmit[trænsmít] 전달하다
subsequent[sʌ́bsikwənt] 차후의
undertake[ʌ̀ndərtéik] 착수하다
total internal reflection 전 (수)반사
medium[mí:diəm] 매질, 매체 encounter[inkáuntər] 부딪히다
steep[sti:p] 가파른 propagate[prá:pəgeit] 퍼지다
telecommunication[tèləkəmjù:nikéiʃən] 전기 통신
remote sensing 원격 탐사 usher in ~이 시작되게 하다

광섬유가 어떻게 실용적인 방법으로 사용되는지 설명하는 문장을 찾으시오.

4 많은 음악가들은 1960년대의 문화 혁명을 자신들의 음악에 급진적인 변화를 개입시킬 기회로 보았다. 예를 들어, 마일스 데이

비스는 퓨전 재즈의 창조에 일조했는데, 이 장르는 재즈와 록의 요소를 혼합하여 전에 들어본 적도 녹음된 적도 없는 소리의 조합을 만들어냈다. 그러나 그와 그의 동료들이 진보라고 여긴 것은 논란의 여지가 있는 것으로 드러났다. 몇몇 비평가들은 이 소리의 합성을 전례 없는 음악적 혁명이라고 칭찬했다. 하지만, 다른 이들, 특히 재즈 순수주의자들은, 데이비스가 도를 넘었으며 심지어 상업적 동기에 의한 대체물을 위해 그의 음악적 뿌리인 고전 재즈를 버렸다고 주장했다. 두 평가 모두 지지자들이 있었고, 퓨전 재즈는 이후에 사실상 상업적으로 한물가게 되었지만, 대부분의 평론가들은 마일스 데이비스가 역대 가장 훌륭한 재즈 연주자 중 한 명이었다는 것에 동의한다.

interject[ìntərdʒékt] 개입시키다 radical[rǽdikl] 급진적인
controversial[kà:ntrəvə́:rʃl] 논란의 여지가 있는
laud[lɔ:d] 칭찬하다 synthesis[sínθəsis] 합성
unprecedented[ʌnprésidəntid] 전례 없는
purist[pjúrist] 순수주의자 abandon[əbǽndən] 버리다
commercially[kəmə́:rʃəli] 상업적으로
replacement[ripléismənt] 대체물
assessment[əsésmənt] 평가 adherent[ədhíərənt] 지지자
subsequently[sʌ́bsikwəntli] 이후에 obsolete[à:bsəlí:t] 한물간
commentator[ká:mənteitər] 평론가

퓨전 재즈에 대한 부정적인 관점을 나타내는 문장을 찾으시오.

5 식물이 탄소 제거에 있어 결정적인 역할을 한다는 관념이 처음으로 떠오르면서, 환경운동가들은 식물 바이오매스의 제거에 세심한 주의를 기울이기 시작했다. 그들은 정부에게 식물이 생명체에 적합한 정상적인 생태계를 유지하는 데에 가지는 매우 귀중한 역할을 인지할 것뿐만 아니라 초목으로 덮인 땅을 영속적으로 보호하기 위한 규제를 추진할 것도 촉구했다. 하지만, 궁극적으로, 과학자들은 대기의 탄소를 없애는 것이 경제적으로 이롭다는 사실을 정치 지도자들에게 납득시켜야 한다는 것을 깨달았다. 하버드 대학의 한 연구는 탄소 피해에 대해 미터톤당 40달러가 조금 넘는 표준 사회적 비용 측정값을 사용했다. 이 연구는 국립 공원 관리국에 의해 관리되고 있는 땅이 대략 1천 7백5십만 미터톤의 탄소를 없앤다는 것을 알아냈으며, 이 감면된 탄소 비용은 연간 약 7억7천만 달러의 경제적 절감이 된다.

notion[nóuʃən] 관념 sequestration[sì:kwestréiʃən] 제거
environmentalist[invàiərənméntəlist] 환경운동가
botanical[bətǽnikl] 식물의
biomass[báioumæs] 바이오매스(어떤 지역 내의 동식물의 총량)
urge[ə:rdʒ] 촉구하다 ecosystem[í:kousistəm] 생태계
perpetually[pərpétʃuəli] 영속적으로
vegetation[vèdʒətéiʃən] 초목 social cost 사회적 비용
govern[gʌ́vərn] 관리하다
National Park Service 국립 공원 관리국

대기 중 탄소를 제거하는 것이 좋은 경제적 영향을 발생시킨다는 것을 나타내는 문장을 찾으시오.

6 Peter Carl Fabergé에 의해 만들어진 최초의 보석으로 장식된

달걀은 러시아의 Tsar Alexander 3세가 그의 아내인 Maria 여제에게 주기 위한 기념일 선물로서 만들어졌다. 결과적으로, Maria가 선물에 너무 기뻐하여 Tsar는 Fabergé를 국왕의 공식 금세공인으로 임명했고, 그는 매년 왕실을 위해 정교한 작품 중 하나를 만들기 시작했다. 이 달걀들은 황실 달걀로 알려지게 되었고, 디자인은 계속해서 더욱 정교해졌다. Fabergé는 각각의 달걀이 왕실 마차, 장미, 혹은 심지어 코끼리 같은 뜻밖의 선물을 담고 있도록 의도했다. 물론, 각각의 깜짝 선물 또한 귀중한 금속과 원석으로 만들어졌다. 그러나, Fabergé의 달걀에 대한 관심이 오직 왕실에서만 있는 것은 아니었다. 그는 러시아 황실의 일원들을·따라하고 유명 예술 작품 중 하나를 소유하기를 아주 갈망하는 개인 고객들을 위해서도 달걀을 만들었다.

Empress[émprəs] 여제, 황후　appoint[əpɔ́int] 임명하다
goldsmith[góuldsmiθ] 금세공인　dainty[déinti] 정교한
elaborate[ilǽbəreit] 정교한　gemstone[dʒémstòun] 원석
solely[sóulli] 오직　clientele[klàiəntél] 고객들
Imperial court 황실

Fabergé의 달걀이 평민의 손에 도달하게 되었다고 말하는 문장을 찾으시오.

7　중세 시대에는, 필사본에 삽화와 장식을 더하는 것이 유행이었다. 이 과정은 사본장식으로 알려졌고, 그것은 책에 다채로운 예술적 기교를 더했을 뿐만 아니라 필사본의 주제와 관련 있는 시각적 보조물도 제공했다. 사본장식을 하는 책에서 사용된 중요한 기법은 도금이었는데, 이것에 의해서 반짝임 효과를 얻기 위해 금박 혹은 금가루가 종이에 붙여졌다. 금이 발라지면, 그것은 닦였고, 이 탁본을 통한 연마 과정은 책을 반짝반짝 빛나게 해주었다. 이탈리아 예술가인 Cennino에 의하면, 나무 손잡이에 고정된 개의 이빨이 종종 이러한 목적으로 사용되었다. ᶜ예술가들, 대개 수도승들은 달걀 흰자위와 빻은 미네랄 혹은 식물 염료를 섞어서 얻은 선명한 색상을 첨가하기도 했는데, 이것이 템페라 페인트 형태가 되었다. 사본장식은 매우 인기 있어져서 소비자들의 요구는 모든 이윤을 남길 수 있는 인쇄물들에 사본장식이 사실상 필수이게 만들었다.

embellishment[imbéliʃmənt] 장식
manuscript[mǽnjuskript] 필사본, 원고
illumination[ilù:minéiʃən] 사본장식(필사본 제본 시 장식 삽화나 귀금속으로 책 표지를 장식하는 것)　artistry[á:rtistri] 예술적 기교
relevant[réləvənt] 관련 있는　gilding[gíldiŋ] 도금
affix[əfíks] 붙이다　burnish[bá:rniʃ] 닦다, 광을 내다
brilliantly[bríljəntli] 반짝반짝하게
mounted[máuntid] 고정된　grind[graind] 빻다
tempera paint 템페라 페인트(화가의 그림 물감으로 사용되는 보통 무기적인 건조 색소)

(A) 사본장식은 독자들이 어려운 주제를 이해하는 데 도움을 주기 위해 사용되었다.
(B) 광을 내는 기술은 Cennino라고 하는 이탈리아 예술가에 의해 개발되었다.
(C) 예술가들은 여러 가지 천연 소재를 혼합하여 그들이 사용했

던 형형색색의 페인트를 만들었다.
(D) 사본장식된 작품들은 처음에 유행했는데 시간이 지나면서 경제적으로 실행할 수 없게 되었다.

8　돌고래 등의 해양 포유동물은 생리학적으로 인간보다 바닷속 상당히 깊은 곳까지 잠수하기에 좋은 조건을 가지고 있다. 이러한 동물들의 혈액은 인간의 혈액보다 대략 30퍼센트 높은 산소 수송 및 저장 능력을 갖추고 있다. ᴮ그들은 또한 근육에 더 많은 호흡색소를 가지고 있는데, 이 호흡색소들은 이 동물들의 높은 산소 저장량에 크게 기여한다. 모든 포유동물의 호흡운동을 조절하는 뇌의 호흡중추는 주변 혈액 내의 이산화탄소에 의해 자극받는다. ᶜ돌고래 및 기타 해양 포유동물의 호흡중추는 다른 포유동물보다 혈액 속 이산화탄소에 덜 민감하다. 결과적으로 그들은 상당히 높은 이산화탄소 농도를 견뎌낼 수 있다. ᴰ게다가 새에서 파충류, 포유류에 이르는 모든 잠수동물은 잠수 시에 급격한 심장박동의 저하를 겪게 된다. 육지에서의 정상적인 심장박동이 1분에 70~80회인 물개의 경우, 잠수 중에는 심장박동률이 1분에 6~10회 정도로 낮아진다.

porpoise[pɔ́:rpəs] 돌고래
physiologically[fìziəládʒikəli] 생리학적으로
considerable[kənsídərəbl] 상당한
approximately[əpráksəmətli] 대략　capacity[kəpǽsəti] 능력
respiratory pigment 호흡색소　regulate[régjuleit] 조절하다
tolerate[tálərèit] 견디다　concentration[kànsəntréiʃən] 농도
drastic[drǽstik] 급격한　seal[si:l] 물개

(A) 돌고래 등의 해양 포유동물은 인간보다 산소를 대략 30퍼센트 더 많이 가지고 있다.
(B) 근육에 함유된 많은 양의 호흡색소는 돌고래가 산소를 저장하는 것을 도울 수 있다.
(C) 이산화탄소에 대한 호흡중추의 저하된 민감성 때문에, 돌고래는 더 높은 수준의 이산화탄소를 견딜 수 있다.
(D) 돌고래가 물 아래로 들어가면, 그들의 심장박동이 느려진다.

9　바람자루는 원뿔과 같은 모양의 천 관이다. 그것은 보통 공항과 같은 장소에서 수직 기둥에 부착되어 있으며, 바람의 방향과 속력을 모두 알아내는 데 사용된다. 이 물체가 바람에 노출되면, 그것은 돌풍의 세기에 따라 전체적으로 또는 부분적으로 부풀게 된다. 이러한 현상이 발생할 때, 바람자루의 끝부분은 바람이 현재 불고 있는 방향을 나타내어, 그쪽을 가리킬 것이다. ᴮ바람의 속도는 자루가 걸려 있는 기둥에 대한 자루의 각도를 살펴봄으로써 계산될 수 있다. ᶜ약한 바람이 불 때는 바람자루가 전체적으로 부풀어오르지 않을 것이고 아래로 처지는 경향이 있는 반면, 강한 돌풍은 바람자루를 채우고 그것을 수평으로 펄럭이게 할 것이다. 보통, 바람자루는 밝은 주황색의 나일론 재질로 만들어지지만, 몇몇은 더 명확한 바람 속도의 추정치가 측정될 수 있게 하기 위해 주황색과 흰색의 줄무늬로 이루어진다. 각각의 줄무늬는 3노트를 나타내며, 속도는 바람자루가 어디로 처지는지를 살펴봄으로써 계산된다.

windsock[wíndsɑ:k] 바람자루　vertical[vá:rtikl] 수직의

inflate[infléit] 부풀다 gale[geil] 돌풍 tip[tip] 끝부분
droop[dru:p] 아래로 처지다
knot[nɑ:t] 노트(1시간에 1해리의 속도 단위)
velocity[vəlá:səti] 속도

(A) 바람자루는 돌풍이 불어오는 방향을 가리킬 것이다.
(B) 풍속은 기둥에서의 바람자루의 각도를 봄으로써 계산된다.
(C) 부분적으로 바람이 빠져있는 바람자루는 현재 바람의 세기가 약하다는 것을 나타낸다.
(D) 바람자루의 밝은 주황색은 높은 가시성 때문에 선택되었다.

10 천왕성은 활성 가스 구름으로 둘러싸여 있으며, 연구자들은 그 구름이 암모니아(NH_3)로 혹은 황화수소(H_2S)로 이루어져 있는지에 대해 오랫동안 논쟁을 벌였다. 그러나, 그들은 두 가지 가설을 입증할 방법이 없었는데, 심지어 1986년 NASA의 우주 탐사선 Voyager 2에 의한 천왕성으로의 우주 비행 후에도 그 구름의 화학적 구성은 여전히 확인될 수 없었다. 하지만 새로운 분광학적 기술, 구체적으로는 근적외선 영역 분광기(NIFS)를 사용해서, 한 천문학자 팀은 자료를 수집할 수 있었고 마침내 그 수수께끼를 풀었다. [B]하와이에서 Gemini North 망원경으로 관측한 학자들은 천왕성의 주요 가시 구름층 바로 위에서 반사된 태양 빛을 측정한 다음, 광 흡수율을 계산하여 화학적 구성을 추론하였다. [D]그들은 천왕성의 상층부 대기는 썩은 달걀을 연상시키는 유독성의 악취를 풍기는 화합물인 황화수소를 높은 수준으로 함유하고 있다는 것을 알아냈다. 이러한 화합물의 존재는 천왕성을 가스 내행성인 토성 및 목성과 구별 짓는데, 이들 각각은 암모니아의 존재가 지배적인 대기를 가지고 있다.

Uranus[júrənəs] 천왕성 ammonia[əmóuniə] 암모니아
hydrogen sulfide 황화수소 corroborate[kərá:bəreit] 입증하다
hypothesis[haipá:θəsis] 가설
spectroscopic[spèktrəskóupik] 분광학적인
Near-Infrared Field Spectrometer 근적외선 영역 분광기
absorption rate 흡수율 noxious[nɑ́:kʃəs] 유독성의
odor[óudər] 악취 reminiscent of ~을 연상시키는
Saturn[sǽtərn] 토성 jupiter[dʒú:pitər] 목성

(A) NASA의 Voyager 2의 주요 목표는 구름의 화학 성분을 알아내는 것이었다.
(B) 과학자들은 천왕성 상층부 대기의 주요 가스를 알아내기 위해 망원경을 사용했다.
(C) 황화수소의 수준은 대기에서의 위치에 따라 다르다.
(D) 토성과 목성을 둘러싸고 있는 높은 수준의 암모니아는 그것들을 천왕성과 구별 짓는다.

11 자유의 여신상 원본의 복제품은 파리에 세워졌고 1889년 7월 4일에 들어섰다. [A]1885년에 프랑스가 미국에 준 동상의 4분의 1 크기 복제품은 프랑스에 거주하는 미국 시민들에 의해 파리에 기증되었다. 그것은 프랑스 혁명의 100주년을 기념하기 위한 것이었다. 그 조각품의 밑부분에 미국 독립기념일과 프랑스 대혁명의 날짜가 쓰인 명판이 있다. 이 동상은 센강의 작은 인공섬에 위치해 있으며 원래 에펠탑을 향해 동쪽을 바라보고 있었으

나, 1937년 만국 박람회를 위해 옮겨졌다. 그때 이래로, 그것은 뉴욕의 원본 동상의 방향으로 서쪽을 바라보고 있다. [C]미국에 있는 300피트짜리 원본과는 다르게, 프랑스에 있는 것은 겨우 70피트를 넘는 높이로, 이는 운반을 덜 어렵게 만든다. 1998년에, 이 동상은 파리에서 일본으로 옮겨져 도쿄 만의 인공섬에 전시되었다. 그것은 두 국가 간의 문화 교류 프로그램의 일환으로 1년 동안 그곳에 있었지만 그 이후로는 줄곧 파리에 남아 있다.

replica[réplikə] 복제품 Statue of Liberty 자유의 여신상
erect[irékt] 세우다 inaugurate[inɔ́:gjəreit] 들어서다, 취임하다
commemorate[kəméməreit] 기념하다
centennial[senténiəl] 100주년 French revolution 프랑스 혁명
plaque[plæk] 명판 France's Bastille Day 프랑스 대혁명의 날
World's Fair 만국 박람회 transit[trǽnzit] 운반
Tokyo Bay 도쿄 만

(A) 뉴욕 조각품의 복제품은 그 시기에 프랑스에 살던 미국계 이주민들에 의해 기증되었다.
(B) 파리 조각상이 에펠탑을 향할 수 있게 하기 위해, 그것은 1937년에 만국 박람회 중에 옮겨졌다.
(C) 유럽에 있는 복제품은 미국의 것보다 작고 옮기기 쉽다.
(D) 문화 교류 프로그램의 일환으로 일본에서 전시되는 동안, 그 조각상은 많은 방문객을 끌어들였다.

12 [A]일반적인 의견과 달리, '토템'이라는 단어는 북아메리카 북서쪽 원주민들의 화려하게 장식된 목재 장대를 의미하는 것이 아니라, 사실 영적인 존재를 의미한다. 이 토템들은 유럽에서 사용된 문장들과 마찬가지로 부족, 씨족 집단, 또는 가문의 정체성을 나타내는 수단의 역할을 하였다. [B]조각가들은 각각의 토템 장대를 조각하기 위해 낱개의 통나무를 사용했으며, 그들은 전통적으로 지역에서 채취한 돌, 뼈, 조개껍데기들을 사용해 그것들을 공들여 만들었다. 하지만, 1700년대부터는 유럽 식민지 개척자들로부터 획득한 금속 도구들이 일반적으로 사용되었다. 어떠한 조각도 시작하기 전에, 통나무들의 껍질을 벗기고 토템 생명체들은 숯을 이용해 그 목재 위에 새겨졌다. 각각의 장대는 조각된 여러 개의 토템들로 구성되었으며 하나의 토템 위에 다른 하나가 위치했고, [C]공동체와 부족, 그리고 가문에게 가장 중요한 토템은 맨 아래에 조각되었다. 각각의 토템은 축전이나 부족 축제 기간에 전해지는 이야기들을 묘사하였는데, 이때 관객들이 대개 부족 오두막 앞에 똑바로 놓여 있는 토템 장대를 보고 앉아있곤 했으며, 부족 지도자나 장로들은 이 토템을 설명하는 역사적인 이야기들을 전했다.

totem[tóutəm] 토템(아메리카 원주민 사회에서 신성시되는 상징물)
denote[dinóut] 의미하다 ornate[ɔ:rnéit] 화려하게 장식된
clan[klæn] 씨족 집단 crest[krest] 문장(紋章)
carve[kɑ:rv] 조각하다 craft[kræft] 공들여 만들다
implement[ímpləmənt] 도구 commence[kəméns] 시작하다
debark[dibá:rk] 나무껍질을 벗기다 charcoal[tʃá:rkoul] 숯
recount[rikáunt] 말을 전하다 lodge[lɑ:dʒ] 오두막
narrative[nǽrətiv] 이야기

(A) 많은 사람들이 '토템'이라는 단어가 목재로 만든 물건을 나

타낸다고 잘못 생각한다.

(B) 원주민들은 개척자들에게서 다른 것들을 얻기 전에는 고유의 도구를 관습적으로 사용했다.

(C) 장대의 맨 아래에 조각된 토템은 부족 일원에게 더 의미가 있었다.

(D) 축제 기간 중에는, 부족 전체가 이야기를 듣기 위해 오두막 주위에 모이곤 했다.

13 사구는 고 건조 지역과 밀접하게 연관되어 있으며, 그것들의 형성은 바람의 지속적인 공급, 촘촘하지 않은 퇴적물, [1]퇴적물이 자리를 잡고 축적되도록 만드는 어떠한 형태의 장애물에 달려있다. 사구의 확장은 몇 가지 상호 연관된 종류의 부식에 의해 이루어지는데, 도약 시, 중간 크기의 입자들이 공중으로 날려지고 수평으로 운반되며, 이때 일반적으로 그 길을 따라 '튕기기'를 하면서 그것들의 고도의 약 4배만큼의 거리를 이동한다. 중간 크기의 입자들이 표면에 격렬하게 충돌하면서, 그것들은 바람에 의해 움직이기엔 너무 큰 입자들과 부딪히고, 큰 입자들을 그 자리에서 움직이게 하여 포행이라고 알려진 과정으로 이를 땅을 따라 굴린다. 추가적으로, 약간의 모래가 현탁을 거치며 움직이는데, 이로 인해 모래가 공중에 높이 떠서 하늘, 수평선, 그리고 지구의 구분을 완전히 모호하게 할 수 있는 거대한 먼지 폭풍을 형성한다. 이러한 각각의 운송 방식은 지속적인 사구의 증대에 기여하는데 이는 우세풍이 바람이 불어가는 쪽의 사구가 무너질 때까지 끊임없이 바람이 불어오는 쪽의 사구로 퇴적물을 몰고 가기 때문이다. [2]이러한 침하가 주로 30도에서 34도의 경사를 발생시킨다는 사실은 사구의 영구적 확장이 가능하게 하는 안정의 각도라고 불리는 이상적인 각도가 존재한다는 주장을 뒷받침한다.

sand dune 사구, 모래 언덕 **aridity**[ərídəti] 건조
loose[luːs] 촘촘하지 않은 **sediment**[sédimənt] 퇴적물
erosion[iróuʒən] 부식
saltation[sæltéiʃən] 도약(跳躍, 모래가 개별적으로 길게 뛰면서
이동하는 것) **catapult**[kǽtəpʌlt] 날리다 **altitude**[ǽltituːd] 고도
collide[kəláid] 충돌하다
dislodge[dislá:dʒ] 자리에서 움직이게 하다
creep[kriːp] 포행(匍行, 토양물질이 주로 중력에 의해서 천천히 아래
방향으로 이동하는 현상) **suspension**[səspénʃən] 현탁(懸濁)
loft[lɔːft] 뜨다 **obscure**[əbskjúr] 모호하게 하다
mode[moud] 방식 **persistent**[pərsístənt] 지속적인
accretion[əkríːʃən] 증대 **prevailing**[privéiliŋ] 우세한
windward[wíndwərd] 바람이 불어오는 쪽
leeward[líːwərd] 바람이 불어가는 쪽
subsidence[səbsáidns] 침하 **assertion**[əsə́ːrʃən] 주장
repose[ripóuz] 안정 **perpetual**[pərpétʃuəl] 영구적인, 지속적인
feasible[fíːzəbl] 가능한

1 지문에 따르면, 퇴적물이 자리를 잡고 축적되는 것은 _____ 때문이다.

(A) 경사의 부족
(B) 장애물의 존재
(C) 바람의 정지

(D) 부식력의 부재

2 지문에 따르면, 사구의 확장에 최적인 각도가 존재한다는 주장은 _____에 의해 강화된다.

(A) 사구가 보통 특정 환경 조건이 갖춰졌을 때만 발생한다는 현실
(B) 사구의 바람이 불어가는 쪽과 불어오는 쪽은 다른 성분을 갖고 있다는 것을 밝힌 연구
(C) 사구는 우세풍이 끊임없는 지역에서 특히 형성된다는 것을 시사하는 자료
(D) 사구의 침하한 면이 상당히 예측 가능한 경사를 야기한다는 경향

14 Temple 대학교의 심리학자인 Margo Gardner와 Laurence Steinberg에 의해 시행된 연구는 10대들의 또래 압력의 힘을 분명히 보여주었다. 연구진은 조사에서 14세 이하 청소년, 19세 이하 청소년, 그리고 성인의 3개 그룹을 평가하였다. 실험을 위해, 참가자들은 한 컴퓨터상의 운전 시뮬레이션 과제를 맡게 되었다. 시뮬레이션이 진행되면서 그들은 여러 노란 불의 신호등을 직면했고, 이들을 지나쳐 갈지 말지에 대해 결정해야 했다. 지나쳐 가면 그들은 점수를 얻었지만, 안 보이는 차와 사고가 날 위험이 있었다. 더 많은 위험이 있을수록, 참가자들은 더 많은 점수를 축적할 수 있었지만, 사고 발생 시 점수를 잃을 것이었다. 심리학자들은 각 참가자들에게 시뮬레이션을 두 번 수행하도록 했다. [1]처음에는, 운전자들이 관찰되지 않는 상황에서 어떻게 행동할지 알아보기 위해 각자의 방에서 혼자 시뮬레이션을 시행했다. 이 경우에는, 각 그룹은 비슷한 수의 위험을 감수했다. 그러나, 두 번째 시뮬레이션에서, 연구진은 같은 나이 그룹의 사람들을 방에 함께 짝지어 배치하여 참가자들이 또래가 보이는 곳에서 시뮬레이션을 완료하도록 했다. 이 경우들에서는 결과가 뚜렷하게 달랐다. [2]14세 이하의 청소년들은 짝지어졌을 때 혼자 했던 것보다 2배 더 많은 위험을 감수한 반면, 19세 이하의 청소년들은 이전보다 50퍼센트 더 많은 위험을 감수했다. 대조적으로, 어른들은 위험을 감수하는 행동에 거의 변화를 보이지 않았다. 이 연구는 어린 10대들 사이의 또래에 순응하는 힘이 다른 어떤 연령층보다 훨씬 더 강하다는 것을 보여주었다. 더 나아가 이는 또래 압력이 의사결정에 미치는 영향이 나이가 들어감에 따라 감소한다는 증거를 제시했다. 성인들은 그들이 또래에서 목격한 행동을 맹목적으로 따를 필요를 훨씬 덜 느낀다.

psychologist[saikáːlədʒist] 심리학자 **peer pressure** 또래 압력
assess[əsés] 평가하다 **accumulate**[əkjúːmjəleit] 축적하다
comparable[káːmpərəbl] 비슷한 **markedly**[máːrkidli] 뚜렷하게
risk-taking[rísktèikiŋ] 위험을 감수하는
conformity[kənfɔ́ːrməti] 순응 **blindly**[bláindli] 맹목적으로
witness[wítnəs] 목격하다

1 지문에 따르면, 연구진은 _____하기 위해 참가자들이 첫 시뮬레이션을 수행하도록 했다.

(A) 혼자 있을 때 위험을 감수하는 반응을 알아내기 위해
(B) 그룹으로 참가자들을 나누는 방법을 알아내기 위해

(C) 다른 사람들이 방에 있는 것의 영향을 연구하기 위해

(D) 시뮬레이션의 점수 체계가 어떻게 작동하는지 보여주기 위해

2 지문에 따르면, 어린 10대들이 시뮬레이션에서 관찰되었을 때

(A) 그들은 나이가 더 많은 10대들보다 영향을 덜 받았다

(B) 다른 연령층과 비슷한 결과를 보였다

(C) 전보다 두 배로 위험을 감수했다

(D) 50퍼센트 더 위험을 감수할 가능성이 있었다

15 일벌은 꽃에서 꽃으로 꿀과 꽃가루를 찾아 날아다닌다. 그것이 꽃에 착지하면서, 무의식적으로 꽃가루를 수집한다. 이러한 이동은 벌의 다리와 몸에 있는 강모의 도움을 받는데, 몇 알의 꽃가루가 강모에 달라붙게 된다. 그러고 나서, 그 꽃가루는 벌에 의해 다른 꽃으로 옮겨져 수분 작용을 일으킨다. 이런 점에서, 이 보잘것없는 벌은 농부들에게 중요한 생명체이다. 일벌은 충분한 꿀과 꽃가루를 모으면, 그들의 벌통으로 돌아온다. 벌통의 내부는 벌집들로 구성되는데, 벌집은 밀랍으로 만들어진 빽빽하게 배치된 육각형의 칸으로 이뤄진 덩어리이다. 벌들은 칸 안으로 꿀을 역류시키는데, [1]그곳에서 침의 효소가 당분의 화학적 분해를 시작하고, 이후의 증발이 액체를 꿀로 전환시킨다. 꿀은 벌통의 윗부분에 영양분으로 저장되는 반면, 아래 몇 줄의 칸은 꽃가루 저장용으로 남겨진다. 그 아래에는 알, 유충, 그리고 번데기를 수용하기 위한 부가적인 두 층의 칸이 있다. [2]이 중 첫 번째 층은 일벌이 될 수정란을 보관하고, 두 번째는 수벌이 될 미수정란을 위해 남겨둔다. 여왕벌은 일반적으로 맨 아래는 아니지만 벌집 아랫부분에 위치한 자신만의 칸을 가지고 있다. 이러한 전반적인 배치는 자연 벌통에서는 거의 차이가 없는데, 이것들은 일반적으로 속이 빈 나무, 동굴, 또는 바위의 구멍 옆에 고정되어 있어, 상대적으로 침해로부터 안전하다.

nectar[néktər] 꿀 pollen[pɑ́lən] 꽃가루 bristle[brísl] 강모
latch onto ~에 달라붙다 grain of 한 알의
pollination[pàlənéiʃən] 수분 작용 humble[hʌ́mbl] 보잘것없는
hive[haiv] 벌통 honeycomb[hʌ́nikoum] 벌집
mass[mæs] (정확한 형체가 없는) 덩어리
hexagonal[heksǽgənl] 육각형의 beeswax[bíːzwæks] 밀랍
regurgitate[rigʌ́ːrdʒiteit] 역류시키다 salivary[sǽləveri] 침
enzyme[énzaim] 효소 decomposition[dìːkɑ̀mpəzíʃən] 분해
evaporation[ivæ̀pəréiʃən] 증발
nourishment[nʌ́riʃmənt] 영양분 larva[lɑ́ːrvə] 유충
pupa[pjúːpə] 번데기 fertilized egg 수정란 drone[droun] 수벌
anchor[ǽŋkər] 고정시키다 hollow[hɑ́lou] 속이 비게 하다
disturbance[distʌ́ːrbəns] 침해

1 지문에 따르면, 벌의 침에 있는 효소는

(A) 꿀과 꽃가루의 소화를 가능하게 한다

(B) 벌집의 구조적 완성에 기여한다

(C) 당분을 분해하는 과정을 시작시킨다

(D) 꿀에서 습기가 증발하는 것을 촉진한다

2 지문에 따르면, 꿀벌 알의 수정은

(A) 인공 벌통보다 자연 벌통에서 더 많이 일어난다

(B) 수벌과 일벌에 의해 이루어진다

(C) 벌집의 아래쪽에서 발생한다

(D) 어떤 벌이 될지 결정한다

16 피라미드 모양의 꼭대기를 가진, 높은 사면의 단일체인 오벨리스크는 고대 이집트에서 유래되었는데, 그곳에서 오벨리스크들은 일반적으로 파라오의 무덤 앞에 쌍으로 위치해 있었다. 이집트 오벨리스크는 붉은 화강암으로부터 채석되어 하나의 돌로 조각되었는데 그것은 어떤 경우에는 수백 톤의 무게가 나갔다. 오벨리스크 건설의 엄청난 어려움과 석공들이 이용했던 원시적인 도구들 때문에, 정확히 어떤 방법으로 고대인들이 이 거대한 기둥을 만들었는지는 오랜 기간 동안 이집트 학자들의 흥미를 끌었다.

이 난제를 풀기를 바라며, 고대 도구 전문가인 Denys Stocks는 구리로 만들어진 톱으로 화강암을 자르려 함으로써 고대의 기술적 한계를 실험적으로 모방하려 했다. 처음에, 그는 구리 톱만을 이용하여 단단한 바위를 잘라내려고 시도했지만 이 무른 금속은 빠르게 분해된다는 것을 알았고, 이는 그 방법을 실행 불가능하게 했다. 그러나, 그는 용접 홈에 모래를 더하면 이 두 가지가 함께 사용될 때 완벽한 직선의 절단면을 내는 것이 가능하다는 것을 발견했다. 이것은 모래 결정체가 화강암처럼 단단하며 본질적으로 톱을 도와 절단을 하기 때문이다. [1]그의 실험은 단단한 화강암이 기본적인 물질과 수단으로 채석될 수 있다는 것을 성공적으로 보여줬지만, 이집트인들이 정확히 어떻게 이것을 해냈는지는 여전히 수수께끼로 남아 있다.

이집트인에 의한 오벨리스크 생산은 기원전 2300년부터 1300년까지만 이어졌지만, 오벨리스크의 유산은 널리 퍼져 있었다. 사실상 모든 이집트의 정복자나 외국인 통치자는 기념물로 오벨리스크를 가져갔고, 많은 위대한 세계적 지도자들은 후에 오벨리스크의 건설을 의뢰하거나 그것에 의해 추모되었다. 두 가지 주목할 만한 예가 미국에 존재하는데, 각각은 미국의 초대 대통령인 George Washington과 남부 연합의 유일한 대통령인 Jefferson Davis를 기념한다. [2]전자는 워싱턴 DC에 위치하는데, 555피트로 수도 상공에 높이 솟아 있어 지구상에서 가장 높은 오벨리스크인 반면, 후자는 켄터키 주 외곽의 조용한 마을에 위치하며 세계에서 가장 높은 보강되지 않은 콘크리트 구조물이라는 명성을 가지고 있다.

monolith[mɑ́ːnəliθ] 단일체 quarry[kwɔ́ːri] 채석하다
granite[grǽnit] 화강암 stonemason[stóunmeisn] 석공
stupendous[stuːpéndəs] 거대한 pillar[pílər] 기둥
Egyptologist[ìːdʒiptɑ́ːlədʒist] 이집트 학자
conundrum[kənʌ́ndrəm] 난제
emulate[émjuleit] 모방하다 archaic[ɑːrkéiik] 고대의, 낡은
saw[sɔː] 톱 copper[kɑ́ːpər] 구리 degrade[digréid] 분해되다
groove[gruːv] 용접 홈 linear[líniər] 직선의
concurrently[kənkɑ́ːrəntli] 함께
rudimentary[rùːdiméntri] 기본적인
prevail[privéil] 널리 퍼져 있다 conqueror[kɑ́ːŋkərər] 정복자
commission[kəmíʃən] 의뢰하다 erection[irékʃən] 건설

memorialize[məmɔ́:riəlaiz] 추모하다
commemorate[kəméməreit] 기념하다
Confederate States 남부 연합
unassuming[ʌ̀nəsú:miŋ] 조용한 hold distinction 명성을 가지다
non-reinforced[nánri:infɔ:rst] 보강되지 않은

1 지문에 따르면, 다음 중 Denys Stocks에 의해 수행된 실험에 대해 사실인 것은?

(A) 화강암이 기본적인 수단과 도구로 모양이 잡힐 수 있다는 것을 증명했다.
(B) 고대 이집트인들이 사용한 조각 방법을 밝혀냈다.
(C) 단단한 바위는 모래와 구리만으로 채석될 수 없음을 보여줬다.
(D) 고대에 오벨리스크를 조각하는 것이 얼마나 고된 일이었는지를 보여줬다.

2 지문에 따르면, 미국에 있는 오벨리스크는 _____ 때문에 주목할 만하다.

(A) 미국에서 대통령에게 헌정된 유일한 비석이기 때문에
(B) 높이와 관련된 범주에서 각각 정상을 차지했기 때문에
(C) 이집트에서 미국으로 운송되었기 때문에
(D) 둘 다 천연 바위가 아닌 소재로 건설되었기 때문에

HACKERS **TEST**

01 **The Automobile Boom**

p.92

1. (A)	2. (C)	3. (A)
4. (B)	5. (C)	6. (D)
7. (D)	8. (C)	9. (B)
10. (C)-2~3단락, (D)-5단락, (F)-4단락		

1 1900년대 초, 회사들이 앞다투어 대량 생산기술을 시행했는데, 이는 고품질의 규격 제품을 저렴한 개당 생산비용으로 대량 생산하는 새로운 제조 공정으로의 급격한 전환을 포함했다. 이처럼 정밀하게 만들어진 호환성 있는 부품들을 이용하면서 조립 공정 절차가 표준화되었고, 원자재의 흐름이 일련의 제작 단계를 따르도록 공장의 구조가 조심스럽게 재구성되었다. 이러한 제조 공정의 혁신은 특히 미국 자동차 산업의 대단한 발전을 가져왔는데, 이는 자동차 회사인 Henry Ford사에서 가장 두드러졌다. [2]대량 생산 철학에 기초한 Henry Ford의 사업 전략은 자동차 붐을 일으켰고, 전반적인 국가 경제를 상승 상태로 고양시켰다.

2 [3]원래 Ford의 회사는 내연기관을 만들고 자동차의 외형을 설계하는 공정 전반에 대해 교육받은 전문적인 엔지니어를 고용하고 있었고, 작업장은 고정된 조립 장소에 근간을 두었는데, 그곳으로 조수들이

각각의 차에 필요한 부품을 운반하였다. [4C]하지만 Ford의 조립 라인 설치는 제조 공정을 여러 개의 세부 단계로 분할했으며, 원료가 컨베이어 벨트를 따라 운반되어 오면 직원들은 나란히 서서 개개의 작업에만 집중했다. 여러 작업을 해야 하는 경우와 달리, 하나의 작업만을 수행하는 경우에 필요한 훈련의 양은 최소화되었고, Ford사는 숙련된 고용인들을 비숙련자이거나 불완전한 숙련자라서 고용 비용이 많이 들지 않는 사람들로 대체할 수 있었다. [4D]임금에 대한 지출 절감과 더불어, [4A]이러한 변화는 숙달하기 쉬운 반복적인 단순노동만을 할당함으로써 생산 시간을 절감하였다. 이러한 두 가지 변화가 결합되어 품질 저하 없는 생산성의 급격한 증대라는 결과를 낳았다.

3 전체적으로, 새로운 제조방법은 작업장의 구조를 완전히 변화시켜서, 미국 공장의 작업 환경의 개념을 바꾸어 놓았다. [6A]이전의 산업 모델은 기술자들에게 지속적으로 교육을 제공했을 뿐 아니라 작업의 전 과정을 흥미를 가지고 일할 수 있도록 해준 것에 반해, 조립 라인은 각각의 고용인이 하나의 지루한 업무를 수행하는 세분화된 분업을 요구했다. [6B]노동자들은 곧게 그들의 작업을 지겨워했고, 흥미를 잃었으며, 이는 최종 생산품의 품질을 하락시킬 조짐을 보였다. [6C]기대 생산량 유지를 보장하기 위해서 새로운 공장이 노동자들에 대한 엄격한 감시를 필요로 한다는 것을 깨달은 Ford는 최고 수준으로 생산성을 유지하도록 위계 감독 체계를 세웠고 초기에 직업을 잃었던 많은 전문가가 이제는 엄격해지고 통제된 회사 구조의 고위직으로 들어오도록 유도하였다.

4 Ford 공장이 이룬 성공은 성장하는 자동차 산업을 수용하기 위한 새로운 주변 산업의 발달을 촉진했을 뿐 아니라 산업 전반에 혁명적인 영향을 미쳤다. 즉, 조립 라인은 자원으로서의 원자재를 필요로 하였고, 이에 따라 제철소, 유리 공장, 금속 주물공장 등이 거대 생산 공장 가까이에 밀집되어 나타났다. [7]이와 동시에, 기술이 진보함에 따라 공장 시설에 필요한 정밀부품이나 기계설비 등을 제공하던 기계 장치와 주형 제조업도 번창했으며 이는 다양한 흥미로운 새 일자리가 창출되는 결과를 초래했는데, 특히 그 무렵 군대에서 돌아온 다수의 젊은이의 흥미를 자극하고 전체적인 소비는 증진시키는 한편 실업률은 낮게 유지했다. 결과적으로 경제 호황과 자동화 공정의 발전으로 인해 Ford사는 자동차의 판매가를 1908년의 850달러에서 1925년의 300달러에도 못 미치는 가격으로 낮출 수 있었는데, 그 무렵에는 일반 사람들도 자동차를 구입할 수 있게 되어 전체적인 판매량이 급증했고, 이는 다시 자동차 관련 기업의 전반적인 번영으로 되돌아왔다.

5 궁극적으로 자가용의 급등하는 인기는 도시와 교외 지역에 영향을 미쳤는데, 그 지역들은 놀라울 정도로 증가된 자동차를 위한 공간을 마련하기 위해 급속도로 변화했다. 비포장도로는 포장도로와 고속도로로 교체되었고, 도시공학자는 이전에는 필요 없었던 배수로, 연석, 교통 표지판 및 기타 기반 시설 등을 서둘러 건설했다. [9]여가 시간이 이제 자동차 소유 중심으로 바뀌면서 자동차 전용 극장과 같은 여가용 장소가 생기고 새로 건설된 고속도로에서 드라이브를 즐기게 되었는데, 이 고속도로는 주유소, 휴게소, 광고 게시판, 심지어는 가는 길에 지친 운전자가 숙박할 모텔까지 갖추고 있었다. 전반적인

문화의 형태가 자가용 운전과 자동차 소유자의 요구에 중점을 두어 변화되었고, 이는 국가의 경제 회생에 엄청난 영향을 미쳤다.

implement [ímpləmənt] 시행하다   changeover [tʃéindʒòuvər] 전환
assembly [əsémbli] 조립
interchangeable [ìntərtʃéindʒəbl] 호환성이 있는
sequential [sikwénʃəl] 일련의   notably [nóutəbli] 특히
elevate [éləvèit] 고양시키다   upswing [ʌ́pswìŋ] 상승
combustion [kəmbʌ́stʃən] 연소   stationary [stéiʃənèri] 고정된
payroll [péiròul] 임금   chore [tʃɔːr] 단순노동
compromise [kʌ́mprəmàiz] 저하시키다
minute [mainjúːt] 세분화된   monotonous [mənátənəs] 지루한
necessitate [nəsésətèit] 필요로 하다
hierarchical [hàiərάːrkikəl] 위계의   peripheral [pərífərəl] 주변의
accommodate [əkάmədèit] 수용하다   spring up 나타나다
cluster [klʌ́stər] 밀집   boost [buːst] 증진시키다
skyrocket [skáirὰkit] 급증하다   mounting [máuntiŋ] 급등하는
repercussion [rìːpərkʌ́ʃən] 영향
astounding [əstáundiŋ] 놀라운   paved [péivd] 포장된
gutter [gʌ́tər] 배수로(차도와 인도 사이의 도랑)   curb [kəːrb] 연석
lodge [ladʒ] 숙박시키다   weary [wíəri] 지친
reverberation [rivὰːrbəréiʃən] 영향

1 지문의 단어 "rapid"와 의미상 가장 유사한 것은?

(A) 빠른
(B) 전략적인
(C) 넓은
(D) 영리한

2 다음 중 1단락의 미국 자동차 산업에 대해 사실인 것은?

(A) 진보적인 사업 전략이 더 적은 공장의 필요로 이어졌다.
(B) 품질에서의 상당한 상승이 비용 절감과 함께 이뤄졌다.
(C) 대량 생산 과정에서 자동차 붐이 시작되었다.
(D) 원자재 유입 증가가 자동차 비용을 낮췄다.

3 아래 문장 중 지문 속의 음영된 문장의 핵심 정보를 가장 잘 표현하고 있는 것은 무엇인가? 오답은 문장의 의미를 현저히 왜곡하거나 핵심 정보를 빠뜨리고 있다.

(A) 초기 공장은 작업의 모든 측면에서 훈련받은 직원에 의해 지정된 장소에서 조립되는 각각의 차가 있도록 설계되었다.
(B) 고정된 생산 시설 때문에, Ford는 자동차 조립의 모든 측면을 완료하는 데 필요한 기술을 가진 사람들을 고용했다.
(C) 제조 과정은 모든 차량이 같은 직원에 의해 조립되는 것을 필요로 했는데, 이들은 수많은 장소로 부품을 운반하곤 했다.
(D) Ford의 첫 번째 회사는 전 제조 공정을 완료할 수 있는 각각의 직원들에게 의존했다.

4 지문에 따르면, 다음 중 조립 라인의 도입이 불러온 것이 아닌 것은?

(A) 상품을 생산하는 데 필요한 시간의 단축
(B) 단축된 작업 시간
(C) 여러 개의 세부 단계를 가진 제조 공정
(D) 인건비의 감소

5 지문의 단어 "monotonous"와 의미상 가장 유사한 것은?

(A) 기본적인
(B) 반사적인
(C) 지루한
(D) 짧은

6 다음 중 지문에 제시된 정보에 근거해 대답할 수 없는 것은?

(A) 조립 라인 이전의 작업장의 특징은 무엇이었는가?
(B) 단기 분업 시행의 결과는 무엇이었는가?
(C) Ford는 어떻게 공장에서 직원의 생산성을 파악했는가?
(D) 관리자들은 무능하고 비생산적인 직원들에게 어떻게 대응했는가?

7 아래 문장 중 지문 속의 음영된 문장의 핵심 정보를 가장 잘 표현하고 있는 것은 무엇인가? 오답은 문장의 의미를 현저히 왜곡하거나 핵심 정보를 빠뜨리고 있다.

(A) 군대에서 돌아온 젊은이들이 전동 공구와 주형 생산을 포함한 기술 분야에 고용되었다.
(B) 자동차 산업에 의해 만들어진 새로운 일자리들은 일반 대중의 소비 증가로 이어졌다.
(C) 자동화 절차는 경제에 크게 기여한 다수의 새로운 산업이 생기게 했다.
(D) 자동차 공장 기반 시설을 뒷받침하는 산업이 지속적인 일자리를 제공하며 번영했다.

8 지문의 단어 "figures"와 의미상 가장 유사한 것은?

(A) 비용
(B) 가격
(C) 숫자
(D) 주장

9 아래 문장 중 지문 속의 음영된 문장의 핵심 정보를 가장 잘 표현하고 있는 것은 무엇인가? 오답은 문장의 의미를 현저히 왜곡하거나 핵심 정보를 빠뜨리고 있다.

(A) 교통망의 급속적인 확장은 운전자들이 새로운 여가용 시설에 쉽게 접근할 수 있게 해주었다.
(B) 여러 신생 기업들이 차 중심으로 돌아가는 여가 활동을 가진 새로운 인구를 수용하기 위해 생겨났다.
(C) 개인 소유 차량 수의 증가는 제3차 산업의 확장으로 이어졌다.
(D) 차에 대한 관심의 증가는 고속도로를 따라 새롭고 수익성이 있는 여러 서비스 산업의 발전으로 이어졌다.

10 **지시:** 지문 요약을 위한 도입 문장이 아래에 주어져 있다. 지문의 가장 중요한 내용을 나타내는 보기 3개를 골라 요약을 완성하시오. 어떤 문장은 지문에 언급되지 않은 내용이나 사소한 정보를 담고 있으므로 요약에 포함되지 않는다. **이 문제는 2점이다.**

> **미국의 자동차 붐은 경제를 크게 고양시켰다.**
> · (C) Ford의 조립 라인 활용은 작업장의 생산성을 크게 향상시켰다.

- (D) 자가용 사용의 증가는 관련 사업 분야가 발전하도록 하는 원인이 되었다.
- (F) 조립 라인의 적용은 공장의 배치와 구조에 주요한 영향을 끼쳤다.

(A) Ford는 고품질 상품을 만들기 위해 전문 기술자를 썼다.
(B) 대량 생산 방식은 1920년대 중반 신차 비용을 상당히 감소시켰다.
(E) 감독의 필요는 공장에 계층의 도입을 낳았다.

02 Skyscrapers

1. (D)	2. (B)	3. (B)
4. (A)	5. (D)	6. (C)
7. (B)	8. (D)	9. (C)
10. (C)-4단락, (D)-5단락, (F)-3단락		

1 1800년대 후반의 급속한 산업화는 당시의 경제 호황에 이끌려 농촌으로부터 모여든 많은 이주민 때문에 갑자기 조밀해진 도심지로 경제활동을 집중시켰다. 비록 부동산 시세는 치솟았지만 수요가 공급을 앞질렀으며, 이 문제는 수직적으로 설계된 건물이라는 새로운 개념을 이용해 제한된 공간을 최대 활용할 수 있게 되면서 해결되었고, 따라서 개발업자들에게 비교적 좁은 땅에서 막대한 수익을 짜내는 만족을 주었다.

2 초기에는 더욱 높은 건물을 짓기 위해 필요한 기술 대부분이 아예 존재하지 않았기 때문에 높은 건물을 짓는 것은 특정 높이로 한정되어 있었다. ²ᶜ우선, 초기 엘리베이터 시스템은 사용하기 불편했으므로, 매일 수십 개의 층계를 오르내리는 발상은 정신이 나간 짓으로 보였다. ²ᴰ게다가, 당시 유효한 수압으로는 물을 약 50피트 높이까지만 퍼 올릴 수 있어서 높이 뻗은 배관시설은 꿈에서나 가능한 것으로 여겨졌다. 마지막으로, 구조적 지지대의 중요성에 대한 부족한 인식은 대부분의 초기 건물이 튼튼한 벽돌로 된 두꺼운 내력벽에 의해 전적으로 지탱되었음을 의미했다. ²ᴬ이로 인해, 4, 5층 건물을 짓는 경우, 1층은 가용 공간을 최소화하고 비정상적으로 두꺼운 벽으로 이루어져야 했다.

3 이러한 상황은 영국인 발명자의 이름을 따서 'Bessemer 철강법'이라는 호칭이 붙은 대량생산 강철의 저비용 체제의 등장에 따라 변화하였으며, 강철의 대량생산은 건축가들에게 가벼운 지지 골조에 의해 지탱되는 얇은 벽으로 더욱 높은 구조물을 설계할 수 있는 자유를 주었고, 벽돌 기반과 주철 구조물을 전적으로 불필요하게 하였다. ⁵1883년에, 미국의 진정한 첫 고층빌딩으로 널리 여겨지는 시카고의 10층짜리 Home Insurance Building이 기존의 석판 기반보다 훨씬 더 뛰어난 구조적 완성도를 제공하지만 무게가 3분의 1밖에 되지 않는 수직의 강철 기둥과 수평의 들보로 이루어진 골조를 사용하며 최초로 Bessemer의 독창성을 선보였다. 기능적

로, 이 내부 지지구조는 외벽이 더는 본질적인 받침대 역할을 하지 않아도 된다는 것을 의미했고, 미적인 효과를 위해 창문을 추가하는 것을 가능하게 했다. 이 설계법의 우수성을 입증하듯이 내부 철강구조의 기본 원리는 지금까지도 널리 사용되고 있다.

4 생산 비용이 저렴해지자, 강철은 콘크리트라는 다른 건축 재료와 함께 한층 더 높은 고층빌딩을 짓는 데 사용되었다. 건축가들과 엔지니어들은 화재에 대한 강한 저항력과 우수한 방음효과 때문에 오래전부터 콘크리트를 선호했지만, 콘크리트는 잘 부서지기 때문에 창고나 공장 또는 기타 저층 건물을 짓는 용도로만 사용되어왔다. 그러나 새로운 발명으로 인해, 엔지니어들은 철근을 혼합물에 결합시킴으로써 콘크리트를 강화할 수 있었다. ⁸ᴮ1903년, Ingalls Building의 건설에 이 혼합재가 사용되었고, 이는 고온에서 녹는 강철의 성향과 고압에서 (구부러지기보다는) 부러지는 콘크리트의 성향 사이에 이상적인 절충안임이 입증되었다. 얽혀있는 강철 근으로 이루어진 내부 골격에 도포된 단단한 콘크리트는 15층 높이의 거대한 건물을 세우는 데 사용되었는데, ⁸ᶜ이는 당시 지역 언론들로 하여금 건물 외부에 임시로 설치된 지지대가 철거되자마자 빌딩이 무너져 내릴 것이라는 추측을 하게 했지만, 그들의 기대와는 달리 이 건물은 손상되지 않은 채 있었다. ⁸ᴬ이 건물은 1974년에 National Historical Civil Engineering Landmark로 지정되었고 바로 오늘까지도 여전히 그 자리를 지키고 있다.

5 비록 그 당시에는 대단한 업적으로 여겨졌지만, 층간을 가로지르는 어떤 종류의 이동수단 없이는 15층이라는 층수는 별 의미가 없었기 때문에 이러한 건축적 업적은 축소되었다. 따라서 열정적인 건축가들 사이에서는 신뢰할 만한 엘리베이터 시스템의 완성은 성배와 같은 것으로 여겨졌다. 1850년부터 증기와 수압을 이용하는 엘리베이터 시스템이 사용되었지만, 느리고 소음이 많으며 통제하기 어렵다고 알려졌다. 그러던 중 1903년, Otis Elevator사가 빠른 속도의 기어 없는 전기장치를 고안했는데, 이는 우물 안으로 밧줄을 단 양동이를 내리는 도르래 장치와 유사한, 비교적 단순한 디자인에 기초한 것이었다. ⁹이 시스템은 케이블이 감겨 있고 홈이 패인 톱니바퀴를 이용하는 전기장치를 활용했는데, 케이블의 한쪽 끝은 엘리베이터에, 다른 한쪽은 평형추에 연결되어 있었다. 뉴욕시에 있는 49층짜리 Tower Building에서 실행 가능성이 입증되자, 어떤 높이의 고층빌딩도 지을 수 있게 되었다.

6 오늘날, 고층빌딩의 놀라운 진화는 여전히 지속되고 있다. 현재 1,670피트의 놀라운 높이에 달하는 대만의 Taipei 101 빌딩이 세계에서 가장 높은 빌딩이지만, 건축가와 기술자들이 끊임없이 새로운 건축 기술과 양식을 실험하고 있는 것을 보면 '세계에서 가장 높은'이라는 칭호는 오래가지 못할 것이다.

teeming [tíːmiŋ] 많은 outpace [àutpéis] 앞지르다
conundrum [kənʌ́ndrəm] (수수께끼 같은) 문제
unprecedented [ʌnprésədèntid] 새로운, 선례가 없는
luxury [lʌ́kʃəri] 만족 dub [dʌb] 호칭을 붙이다
buttress [bʌ́tris] 지지하다 redundant [ridʌ́ndənt] 불필요한
authentic [əːθéntik] 진정한, 진짜의
premiere [primíər] 최초로 선보이다
ingenuity [ìndʒənjúːəti] 독창성, 독창력 integrity [intégrəti] 완성도

CH 02

Hackers TOEFL Reading

Chapter 02 Fact & Negative Fact | **405**

slab[slæb] 석판   scaffolding[skǽfəldiŋ] 지지구조
intrinsic[intrínsik] 본질적인   abutment[əbʌ́tmənt] 받침대
testament[téstəmənt] 입증, 계약   entrails[éntreilz] 내부
reinforce[rì:infɔ́:rs] 강화하다   incorporate[inkɔ́:rpərèit] 결합하다
compromise[kámprəmàiz] 절충안   snap[snæp] 부러지다
smother[smʌ́ðər] 도포하다   speculate[spékjulèit] 추측하다
collapse[kəlǽps] 무너지다   intact[intǽkt] 손상되지 않은
designate[dézignèit] 지정하다   feat[fi:t] 업적
traverse[trǽvə:rs] 가로지르다   hydraulic[haidrɔ́:lik] 수압의
contraption[kəntrǽpʃən] 새로운 장치   pulley[púli] 도르래
grooved[grú:vd] 홈이 패인   counterweight[káuntərwèit] 평형추

1 지문의 단어 "unprecedented"와 의미상 가장 유사한 것은?

(A) 상징적인
(B) 쓸모없는
(C) 전통적인
(D) 새로운

2 2단락에 따르면, 다음 중 고층빌딩을 짓는 것의 기술적인 제한이 아닌 것은?

(A) 낮은 층에 대한 과도한 지지가 가용 공간을 제한했다.
(B) 많은 수의 층계에 대한 큰 필요가 있었다.
(C) 사람들을 위아래로 운반할 수 있는 장치가 비효율적이었다.
(D) 양수기로는 높은 층에 배관 시설을 공급할 수 없었다.

3 지문의 단어 "redundant"와 의미상 가장 유사한 것은?

(A) 생산적인
(B) 불필요한
(C) 위엄 있는
(D) 터무니없는

4 지문의 단어 "authentic"과 의미상 가장 유사한 것은?

(A) 진짜의
(B) 화려한
(C) 합성의
(D) 독점적인

5 3단락에 따르면, 다음 중 시카고의 Home Insurance Building 에 대해 사실인 것은?

(A) 내부 구조가 그것을 10층보다 더 높게 지어지지 않게 만들었다.
(B) 건물에 내장된 들보가 건물의 무게 대부분을 지탱했다.
(C) 내벽은 건물 골조를 유지하도록 설계되었다.
(D) 가벼운 강철 골조로 지어졌다.

6 아래 문장 중 지문 속의 음영된 문장의 핵심 정보를 가장 잘 표현하고 있는 것은 무엇인가? 오답은 문장의 의미를 현저히 왜곡하거나 핵심 정보를 빠뜨리고 있다.

(A) 공사 현장 인부들은 건물을 세우는 데 콘크리트를 이용하려고 노력했지만, 콘크리트는 건물 자재로서 한정적인 성공만을 거두었다.

(B) 콘크리트는 잘 부서지곤 했기 때문에, 여러 가지 이점에도 불구하고 중요한 산업 건물의 건축 자재로는 적합하지 않았다.

(C) 콘크리트는 방화 및 방음 효과 때문에 인기 있었지만, 잘 부서지는 성질 때문에 널리 쓰이지는 않았다.

(D) 부러지는 성질에도 불구하고, 콘크리트는 불을 견디고 소리를 차단할 수 있었기 때문에 다양한 저층 건물용으로서 확실한 선택이었다.

7 지문의 단어 "intact"와 의미상 가장 유사한 것은?

(A) 평평한
(B) 손상되지 않은
(C) 결함이 있는
(D) 수직의

8 4단락에 따르면, 다음 중 콘크리트와 강철의 혼합물에 대해 사실이 아닌 것은?

(A) 이 방식으로 건축된 건물이 오늘날에도 여전히 존재한다.
(B) 이 방식은 강철과 콘크리트 각각의 단점을 보완했다.
(C) 이 방식을 사용한 건물에 대해 언론은 회의적이었다.
(D) 건축가들은 이 방식으로 건물을 건립하기를 오랫동안 바랐다.

9 5단락에 따르면, 다음 중 Otis 엘리베이터에 대해 사실인 것은?

(A) 전동 장치가 있는 평범한 장치였다.
(B) 도르래를 본떠서 만들어졌다.
(C) 전기로 조정되었다.
(D) 무거운 평형추가 필요했다.

10 지시: 지문 요약을 위한 도입 문장이 아래에 주어져 있다. 지문의 가장 중요한 내용을 나타내는 보기 3개를 골라 요약을 완성하시오. 어떤 문장은 지문에 언급되지 않은 내용이나 사소한 정보를 담고 있으므로 요약에 포함되지 않는다. **이 문제는 2점이다.**

> 기술이 발전하면서, 건축은 위쪽으로 관심을 집중하기 시작했다.
> · (C) 강철로 강화된 콘크리트는 건축가들에게 높은 빌딩을 세울 수 있는 좋은 기회를 주었다.
> · (D) 효율적이고 믿을 만한 엘리베이터가 개발되자, 그것들은 건물을 더 높이 짓는 것에 대한 장애물을 제거했다.
> · (F) 강철 골조는 다른 종류의 기반보다 더 강력한 지지를 제공했다.

(A) 고층 빌딩에 대한 수요는 도심 지역에서의 인구 집중화로부터 발전했다.

(B) Ingalls Building은 처음으로 건축에 강화 콘크리트를 사용한 빌딩이었다.

(E) 현재 가장 높은 건물은 대만에 있지만 예측할 수 있는 미래에 더 새로운 것으로 대체될 가능성이 높다.

03 Loie Fuller

p.100

1. (D)	2. (A)	3. (A)
4. (B)	5. (D)	6. (C)
7. (B)	8. (C)	
9. (C)−5단락, (D)−3단락, (F)−2단락		

1 Illinois주의 Chicago 교외의 Fullersburg에서 태어난 Marie Louise Fuller는 4살에 시카고에서 데뷔하였을 때 아역 배우로서 연기자 생애를 시작하였다. 그 이래로 25년 동안 그녀는 다양한 전속 극단과 함께 미국 지방을 순회하면서 유명한 Buffalo Bill의 Wild West Show에 참여하였을 뿐 아니라 풍자극이나 가벼운 희가극을 공연했다. [1]안무에 대한 정식 교육을 받지 못했다는 이유로 한때 기술이 부족하다는 비판을 자주 받았지만, 그녀는 실험을 통해서, 그리고 그 시대의 다른 현대무용 선구자들을 관찰함으로써 기술을 연마하였다. 1888년에 이르러 그녀의 웅장한 'natural movement' 공연은 그녀에게 뉴욕과 런던에서 어느 정도의 성공을 가져다 주었으며, 여기에서 그녀는 후에 잘 알려질 이름이 될 Loie Fuller라는 가명을 사용하도록 그녀에게 권유했던 몇몇 유명한 연기자들과 같은 무대에 올랐다.

2 Fuller에게 명성을 가져다준 것은 색깔 있는 빛을 위에서 비추면서, 풍성한 비단 주름을 능숙하게 다루는 그녀만의 방법이었다. 그녀는 최면술에 걸린 여인 역을 연기할 'Quack, M.D.'라는 멜로드라마 공연을 준비하면서, 무대 조명을 강화하여 볼륨감과 우아한 광채를 자아내도록 치마 의상에 빛을 비추는 기술적 효과를 실험하기 시작했다. 소문에 의하면 중국의 초롱에서 영감을 받아, [4]그녀는 빛의 경로에 있는 스포트라이트나 투광조명기를 포함한 각 조명 장치의 빛이 나오는 입구 위에 색깔 있는 비단 천을 덮어서, 무대 전체에 채색된 빛이 밀려 들어오는 효과를 창출하는 아이디어를 냈다. 빛을 특정한 방향으로 유도하기 위해서, 원하는 방향으로 광선을 반사할 거울이 무대의 양옆에 효과적으로 배치되어, 색색의 빛을 연기자의 의상에서 반사시켰다.

3 자신의 의상을 종종 직접 만들었던 Fuller는 이런 마술 같은 신기술에 고무되어, 의상에 빛을 잘 반사하는 소재를 사용하는 것의 효과를 시험해 보기 시작하였다. 그녀는 결국 빛을 매우 잘 반사하는 성질을 가진 반투명 비단 조각들을 자신의 긴 물결 모양의 치마에 붙여 귀신이나 유령처럼 보이게 하는 효과를 얻었다. 이는 비평가들에게 깊은 감명을 주어, Fuller를 당대의 가장 혁신적인 무용가라고 부르게 하였다. 그녀는 비평가들의 호평에 힘입어, 특정한 분위기를 불러일으키고 특정한 등장인물에게 초점을 맞추거나, 공연의 시간과 장소에 대한 느낌을 바꾸기 위하여 색과 의상의 조합을 다루는 새로운 방법을 찾아 나섰다. 관객의 반응을 끌어내는 방법 중 하나로 옷에 인광성 물체를 부착하는 방법이 있었는데, 이 인광성 물체는 표면에 닿는 모든 빛을 이용하여, 역동적인 색상을 띠도록 빛을 굴절시켰다.

4 자신의 기술적 참신함이 획기적 발견이라는 것을 깨달은 Fuller는, 계속해서 새로운 디자인을 고안하면서 자신의 발명에 대한 여러 미국 특허를 신청하여 등록하였다. 그녀는 화학자이자 방사능 연구의 선구자였던 친구 Marie Curie에게 라듐을 극장 안에서 사용할 수 있는 방법에 대한 조언을 구하기도 했지만, Curie는 라듐이 일상에서 사용하기에는 너무 위험한 원소라고 경고하며 곧 이를 거절했다. 그녀는 굽히지 않고, [6]화학 염을 이용한 실험을 계속했는데, 이 실험으로 인해서 그녀의 가내 실험실에 폭발이 일어났다. 그녀는 다치지는 않았지만, 새로운 춤을 고안하는 것으로 재빨리 그녀의 관심을 돌렸는데, 이 춤은 무대 조명과 의상 분야에서 그녀가 이루어낸 진보를 가장 돋보이게 했다.

5 점차 Fuller의 혁신적인 기법들은 그녀가 'The Serpentine Dance'라고 부르던 공연으로 형상화되었으며, 1892년 2월에 뉴욕에서 공연된 'Uncle Celestin'이라는 시사 풍자극에서 그녀는 자유로운 춤사위를 선보였고 상당한 호평을 받았다. 이 쇼는 파리로 옮겨져서 공연되었는데, 그녀는 따뜻한 환대를 받았고, 이로 인해 실험적인 공연에 있어서는 으뜸가는 국제적인 장소였던 Folies Bergere의 정규 공연자가 되어 프랑스에 머무르게 되었다. 유럽에서 공연을 하는 최초의 현대 무용가였던 Fuller는, Folies Bergere에서 다수의 쇼에 주역으로 등장했고, 특히 그녀가 밑에서 조명을 받는 유리 바닥 위에서 춤을 추었던 'Fire Dance'에서 가장 깊은 인상을 남겼다. Art Nouveau 사조가 대유행하던 시기에, [8]그녀는 Art Nouveau의 살아있는 화신처럼 무대에 등장했고, 그녀를 위해서 다수의 광고 포스터를 그려 주었던 Henri de Toulouse-Lautrec과 이후에 Fuller를 자신의 조소 작품의 모델로 사용했던 Auguste Rodin과 같은 많은 프랑스 예술가의 경의를 얻었다. 과학자들도 아방가르드한 조명 디자인을 직접 눈으로 확인하기 위해서 파리로 모여들었다. 1908년에 이르러, 그녀가 자신의 natural movement를 가르치는 학원을 열었을 때 유럽 사회는 물론, 그녀의 미국 동포들까지도 어느 정도 그녀의 발명과 재능이 한 개의 진지한 예술 형태로 합쳐진 free dance를 인정하고 있었다.

hence[hens] 그 이래로 burlesque[bərlésk] 풍자극
vaudeville[vɔ́ːdəvil] 가벼운 희가극
choreography[kɔ̀ːriágrəfi] 안무, 무용술 hone[houn] 연마하다
era[írə]시대 grandiose[grǽndiòus] 웅장한
pseudonym[súːdənìm] 가명 household name 잘 알려진 말
manipulate[mənípjulèit] 능숙하게 다루다
voluminous[vəlúːmənəs] 풍성한, 볼륨감 있는
hypnosis[hipnóusis] 최면술 ethereal[iθíriəl] 우아한
splendor[spléndər] 광채 rumor[rúːmər] 소문내다
inspire[inspáiər] 영감을 주다
aperture[ǽpərtʃər] (조명기 등에서 빛이 나오는) 입구, 틈
fixture[fíkstʃər] 장치, 시설 floodlight[flʌ́dlàit] 투광조명기
attire[ətáiər] 의상 translucent[trænslúːsnt] 반투명의
apparition[æ̀pəríʃən] 유령 dub[dʌb] ~를 −라고 부르다
evoke[ivóuk] 불러 일으키다
phosphorescent[fὰsfərésnt] 인광성의 exploit[éksploit] 이용하다
novelty[návəlti] 참신함 breakthrough[bréikθrùː] 획기적인 발견
patent[pǽtnt] 특허 chancy[tʃǽnsi] 위험한
undaunted[ʌndɔ́ːntid] 굽히지 않고

revue[rivjúː] 시사 풍자극   acclaim[əkléim] 호평
venue[vénjuː] 장소   all the rage 대유행하는
embodiment[imbádimənt] 화신   garner[gáːrnər] 얻다, 모으다
compatriot[kəmpéitriət] 동포   coalesce[kòuəlés] 합치다, 뭉치다

1 지문에 따르면, 다음 진술 중 Loie Fuller의 초기 경력에 대해 사실인 것은?

(A) Fuller는 Wild West Show에 사용된 혁신적인 방식에 의해 영감을 받았다.
(B) Fuller는 자연스러운 스타일의 춤과 기술적인 능숙함으로 찬사를 받았다.
(C) Fuller는 뉴욕의 작품에서 그녀의 첫 번째 중요 공연을 했다.
(D) Fuller는 혁신적인 무용수들을 연구함으로써 교육의 부족함을 보완했다.

2 지문의 단어 "manipulating"과 의미상 가장 유사한 것은?

(A) 조절하는
(B) 검사하는
(C) 층을 이루는
(D) 분리시키는

3 지문의 단어 "splendor"와 의미상 가장 유사한 것은?

(A) 웅장
(B) 투명
(C) 공허
(D) 선의

4 2단락에 따르면, 무대 조명의 색은

(A) 중국 초롱 빛의 색과 유사했다
(B) 천으로 덮어서 다른 색으로 바뀔 수 있었다
(C) 빛의 경로에 따라 변했다
(D) 그것들을 반사하기 위해 사용된 거울에 의해 부분적으로 발생될 수 있었다

5 아래 문장 중 지문 속의 음영된 문장의 핵심 정보를 가장 잘 표현하고 있는 것은 무엇인가? 오답은 문장의 의미를 현저히 왜곡하거나 핵심 정보를 빠뜨리고 있다.

(A) 긍정적인 평가를 얻기 위한 방법을 찾은 끝에, Fuller는 관객들의 변화를 불러일으킬 빛과 의상을 만들기로 결심했다.
(B) 호의적인 의견에 고무되어, Fuller는 그녀의 공연이 주는 감동을 장악할 수 있는 더 많은 기술을 찾았다.
(C) Fuller는 그녀의 안무의 질을 높이기 위해 무대 조명과 의상에 대한 실험을 진행하도록 장려되었다.
(D) 좋은 반응을 얻은 후, Fuller는 관객들에게 특정 효과를 주기 위해 색상과 옷을 조화시키는 새로운 방법을 찾았다.

6 지문에 따르면, Fuller는 _____ 때문에 그녀의 연구실 실험을 버리고 새로운 춤을 고안했다.

(A) 방사능 물질은 너무 위험하다고 경고를 받았기 때문에
(B) 춤을 추는 동안 연출 기법 혁신을 더 발전시킬 수 있었기 때문에
(C) 화학 염으로 실험하던 도중에 폭발을 일으켰기 때문에

(D) 그녀의 발견에 대한 몇 개의 특허를 이미 받았었기 때문에

7 지문의 단어 "chancy"와 의미상 가장 유사한 것은?

(A) 담대한
(B) 위험한
(C) 무분별한
(D) 현존하는

8 지문에 따르면, Art Nouveau의 사조는

(A) 18세기에 널리 퍼졌다
(B) 미국 예술가들에게 받아들여졌다
(C) Fuller의 춤에 나타났다
(D) 현대 무용의 본질적인 부분이었다

9 지시: 지문 요약을 위한 도입 문장이 아래에 주어져 있다. 지문의 가장 중요한 내용을 나타내는 보기 3개를 골라 요약을 완성하시오. 어떤 문장은 지문에 언급되지 않은 내용이나 사소한 정보를 담고 있으므로 요약에 포함되지 않는다. 이 문제는 2점이다.

> **Loie Fuller는 평범하게 시작하여 세계적으로 유명한 무용수가 되었다.**
>
> · (C) 그녀의 혁신적인 기술로, Loie Fuller는 센세이션을 일으킨 free dance를 소개했다.
> · (D) Loie Fuller는 반사되는 천으로 다양한 색상을 만들어냄으로써 이뤄지는 원하던 효과를 만들기 위해 노력했다.
> · (F) Loie Fuller는 색깔 있는 빛이 그녀의 옷에 반사되는 실험 때문에 잘 기억되었다.

(A) Loie Fuller의 첫 번째 주연은 그녀가 환자를 연기했던 'Quack, M.D.'라는 제목의 멜로드라마였다.
(B) Loie Fuller는 일반 대중과 비평가들에게서 인정을 받았지만, 동시대 예술가들에게는 무시받았다.
(E) Fuller는 파리에서 natural movement의 전통을 따르는 그녀의 춤 학원을 시작했다.

---

04 | Land Policy in Medieval Japan

p.104

1. (C)	2. (B)	3. (D)
4. (C)	5. (C)	6. (D)
7. (A)	8. (C)	
9. (B) −3단락, (E) −4단락, (F) −5~6단락		

1 서기 645년, 일본 황실 정부는 다이카 개신을 실시하여 일본의 통치를 천황 아래로 중앙집권화하였다. 개혁의 일환으로 정부는 '리츠료'라고 불리는, 토지소유권과 관련된 일련의 규정을 제정했다. 이 규정은 유교의 영향을 받았으며 중국의 율법주의자 관습에 근거를 두고 있는데, 이는 중국에서도 중앙집권화의 도구로 사용되었던 것이다. [1]리츠료 체제하에서 토지는 강제적인 등록제에 따라 엄격하

게 할당되었다. 등록한 사람들은 성별, 나이, 그리고 사회적 지위에 따라 토지를 받았다. 할당된 토지에 대한 대가로 각 가정에는 세금이 부과되었고 남자들은 군대에서 복무하게 되었다.

2 나라 시대(710-794)의 대부분의 기간 동안 이 할당 체제는 잘 작동하였다. 토지의 사적 소유는 일반적으로 주요 사찰과 황실 귀족에게 한정되어 있었다. 이에 따라 사실상 모든 재산은 엄밀히 말해 천황의 소유였다. 그러나 헤이안 시대(794-1185)의 초기 무렵에는 관료적인 리츠료 체제가 결국 제 기능을 잃게 되었다.

3 토지 할당 체제의 실패에는 여러 가지 요인이 있었다. 많은 농부는 세금을 내고 자기 가족들을 먹여 살리는 데 충분한 작물을 거의 생산해내지 못했다. ³ᴬ생산성은 길어진 건기 동안 특히 영향을 받았고, 가뭄은 끊임없는 걱정거리였다. 모든 농부가 강 근처의 비옥한 양질의 토지를 할당받을 만큼 운이 좋았던 것은 아니었고, 관개 기술이 충분치 않았던 이들은 가뭄이 든 해에 충분한 수확을 하기 어려웠기 때문에, 종종 감시를 피해 개울 근처의 토지를 몰래 경작할 수 있는, 숨겨진 산골짜기의 사람이 살지 않는 지역으로 이동했다. ³ᶜ다른 경작자들은 어업이나 직물 생산과 같은 더 안정적인 일을 위해 그냥 농사를 포기했다. 공식적인 기록은 한 지역에서만 할당된 토지의 70퍼센트 가까이가 경작되지 않고 있었음을 보여준다. 설상가상으로 유행병이 끊임없이 전국을 초토화시켰고, 천연두와 독감 같은 전염병이 현지 주민들을 망연자실하게 하였다. ³ᴮ이러한 문제의 최종 결과는 경작 가능한 토지에 대한 포기 증가와 정부의 세입 감소였다. 정부가 수천 명의 개별적인 토지 포기자를 추적하는 것은 그야말로 불가능했다.

4 이러한 딜레마에 대처하기 위해 정부는 토지 정책과 관련해 어느 정도 양보를 하였고, 관리들은 민간 집단의 토지 획득 및 개발에 대해 느슨한 태도를 취하기 시작했다. 사유지를 획득하는 방식은 다양했다. 지방 관리와 군벌 같은 부유한 귀족은 공공연히 토지를 매입할 수 있었고, 일부 가문은 거대한 사유지를 관리하게 되었으며 그 사유지에 대한 권리는 영속적이고 세습적이었다. ⁵소규모 토지 소유자는 보호와 지원을 받기 위해 종종 자발적으로 자신의 소유지를 거대 사찰이나 부유한 가문에 기증하기도 했는데, 권력이 있는 지주들은 농업 기술 제공은 물론이고 전사를 고용하는 데 필요한 자원이 있었기 때문이다. 사람들은 또한 개간을 통해 토지에 대한 권리를 가질 수 있었다. 정부는 경작한다는 조건 하에, 농사가 지어진 적이 없는 새로운 황무지와 불모지를 획득할 수 있도록 허용하였다. 마찬가지로 오랫동안 버려졌던 토지는 양도할 수 있는 것으로 여겨졌고 경작할 의향이 있는 사람들에게 주어졌다. 정부는 때때로 개간지에 대해 세금 면제와 같은 유인책을 제공하기도 하였다.

5 지배 엘리트 계층 내의 이러한 달라진 태도는 '쇼엔'의 확산을 낳았다. 쇼엔은 법 개정이나 중앙정부와의 공식 협상을 통해 전액 또는 일부 세금 면제가 승인된 사유지였다. 사찰이든 부유한 가문이든, 쇼엔의 소유자들은 소작료 및 소유지 경계 내에서 나온 모든 농작물의 일부를 징수할 수 있을 뿐만 아니라 소유지 내의 모든 거주자에 대해 완전한 지배권을 행사할 수 있는 권리를 가지고 있었다. 소유자들은 흔히 소유지에서 멀리 떨어져 살았기 때문에 종종 토지를 감독할 관리자를 필요로 했다. 성공적인 관리자들은 할당된 경작지 사

용에 따른 납세 의무를 피하기를 갈망하는 소작농 인력을 쉽게 구할 수 있었다. 비록 소유지 영역 내의 경작자들은 중앙정부에 세금을 낼 필요는 없었지만, 그들의 소작료와 수수료는 종종 할당 체제하에서 지불했어야 했을 액수를 초과했다.

6 ⁸중앙정부의 토지 정책 자유화의 지속적인 영향은 소작농이 궁극적으로 권력이 있는 지주의 지배하에 들어갔다는 것이다. 리츠료 체제 하에서는 토지의 분배가 비교적 공평했지만, 사유화는 특권층의 개인과 가문이 거대한 구획의 토지뿐만 아니라 그곳의 주민도 지배하게 하였다. 사람과 토지에 대한 이러한 이중 지배는 지방 지주에 의해 이용될 수 있는 군신 관계를 가능하게 했고, 12세기에 일본 내 정치적 지배력을 장악한 사무라이 계급을 만들어냈다.

establish [istǽbliʃ] 제정하다 Confucianism [kənfjúʃənìzm] 유교
legalist [líːgəlist] 율법주의자
deteriorate [ditíəriərèit] 제 기능을 잃다, 타락하다
continual [kəntínjuəl] 끊임없는 fertile [fə́ːrtl] 비옥한
irrigation [ìrəgéiʃən] 관개 covertly [kóuvərtli] 몰래
textile [tékstail] 직물 ravage [rǽvidʒ] 초토화하다, 유린하다
devastate [dévəstèit] 망연자실하게 하다 tax revenue 세입
concession [kənséʃən] 양보, 용인 perpetual [pərpétʃuəl] 영속적인
hereditary [hərédətèri] 세습적인 reclamation [rèkləméiʃən] 개간
deserted [dizə́ːrtid] 버려진 alienable [éiljənəbl] 양도할 수 있는
inducement [indjúːsmənt] 유인책, 장려책
proliferation [prəlìfəréiʃən] 확산 produce [prádjuːs] 농작물
peasant [péznt] 소작농 exceed [iksíːd] 초과하다
lasting [lǽstiŋ] 지속적인, 오래가는 equitable [ékwətəbl] 공평한
parcel [páːrsəl] 구획 lord-vassal relationship 군신 관계

1 1단락에 따르면, 다음 중 '리츠료' 체제에 대해 사실인 것은?
   (A) 일본에서 중국 법 전통에 대한 인식을 높였다.
   (B) 중국에서의 민족주의의 부활을 촉진했다.
   (C) 토지 수혜자들을 당국에 등록하도록 했다.
   (D) 주지들이 토지를 정부에 양도하게 만들었다.

2 아래 문장 중 지문 속의 음영된 문장의 핵심 정보를 가장 잘 표현하고 있는 것은 무엇인가? 오답은 문장의 의미를 현저히 왜곡하거나 핵심 정보를 빠뜨리고 있다.
   (A) 건기 동안 충분한 작물을 생산하지 못한 농부들은 다른 농부들에게 할당된 땅을 침범하기 시작했고, 이것은 물 사용에 대한 분쟁으로 이어졌다.
   (B) 일부 농부들은 이상적인 경작지와 가뭄 동안 생산할 수 있는 기술이 없었기 때문에, 그들은 적막한 산골짜기 저지대의 개울 근처에서 종종 농사를 지었다.
   (C) 일부 농부들은 다행히 물이 풍부한 비옥한 땅으로부터 이익을 얻었지만, 그렇지 못한 대다수의 사람들은 가뭄 동안 충분한 작물을 생산하는 데 종종 실패했다.
   (D) 물을 찾아, 많은 농부들이 산을 내려가서 오직 그들만 존재를 알고 있는 개울 주변의 땅을 경작하기 시작했다.

3 3단락에 따르면, 다음 중 대답할 수 없는 것은?
   (A) 생산성 감소의 결정 요인은 무엇이었는가?
   (B) 토지 포기의 재정적인 결과는 무엇이었는가?

(C) 왜 일부 농부들은 토지를 경작하는 것을 그만뒀는가?

(D) 왜 정부는 경작 가능한 토지에 대한 세금을 올렸는가?

4 지문의 단어 "perpetual"과 의미상 가장 유사한 것은?

(A) 절대적인

(B) 취소할 수 있는

(C) 영구적인

(D) 순식간의

5 4단락에 따르면, 일부 사람들은 자신의 땅을 자발적으로 _____ 양도했다.

(A) 관직에 대한 답례로

(B) 상속세를 지불하는 것을 피하기 위해

(C) 보호에 대한 대가로

(D) 위험에 직면한 황야 지역을 보존하기 위해

6 지문의 단어 "deserted"와 의미상 가장 유사한 것은?

(A) 증여된

(B) 분열된

(C) 보유된

(D) 버려진

7 지문의 단어 "proliferation"과 의미상 가장 유사한 것은?

(A) 증가

(B) 부재

(C) 창조

(D) 촉진

8 6단락에 따르면, 다음 중 정부의 더욱 유동성 있는 토지 정책의 결과인 것은?

(A) 중앙 정부를 전복하기 위해 지주들이 지역 군벌들과 손을 잡았다.

(B) 지주들과 소작인들 간의 점점 늘어나는 갈등이 전개되었다.

(C) 광범위한 토지 소유가 특권을 가진 소수의 손에 들어갔다.

(D) 지주들은 그들의 봉신들에게 토지 일부를 분배해야 했다.

9 **지시:** 지문 요약을 위한 도입 문장이 아래에 주어져 있다. 지문의 가장 중요한 내용을 나타내는 보기 3개를 골라 요약을 완성하시오. 어떤 문장은 지문에 언급되지 않은 내용이나 사소한 정보를 담고 있으므로 요약에 포함되지 않는다. **이 문제는 2점이다.**

> 9세기 무렵, 토지 사유화는 한 세기 넘게 자리잡아왔던 할당 체제를 점차 대체하기 시작했다.
>
> · (B) 정부는 토지 사용을 감독하는 것이 점점 어렵다는 것을 알게 되었고, 토지 할당 체제는 흐트러지기 시작했다.
>
> · (E) 관료들은 토지 사용에 대한 규정을 완화함으로써 변화하는 환경에 대응했고, 그 결과 사유화의 길을 열었다.

· (F) 토지 사유화의 확장은 소유자들이 소작 문제에 대한 완전한 관할권을 가지는 대규모 사유지의 조성으로 이어졌다.

(A) 토지 할당 체제는 중국 선례에 기초를 두었지만, 일본에서는 중국에서 그랬던 것만큼 성공하지 못했다.

(C) 사유지에 대한 소작권은 경작자에게 궁극적으로 그들의 재정적 상황을 개선시켜준 상당한 절세를 제공했다.

(D) 비옥한 토지를 할당받은 농부들은 가치가 떨어지는 토지를 버릴 수밖에 없었던 사람들에게 일을 제공했다.

Chapter 03 **Vocabulary**

HACKERS **STRATEGY** p.111

전략 1

Ex 오직 커뮤니케이션을 통해서만 한 동물이 다른 동물의 행동에 영향을 줄 수 있다. 하지만 인간의 발화가 갖는 커뮤니케이션 잠재력이 막대한 것에 비해, 인간이 아닌 생물의 커뮤니케이션은 지극히 제한되어 있다.

restricted[ristríktid] 제한된

Ex 별들이 시간이 지남에 따라 성운 내에서 형성되고 진화함으로써, 주변 가스를 밝게 빛나게 하는 높은 에너지 방출을 일으키며, 놀랄만큼 아름다운 색채를 만들어낸다. 이 이온화된 가스는 다양한 모양과 크기를 가질 수 있으며, 일부 발광 성운은 긴 필라멘트 구조를 형성하는 반면, 다른 것들은 더 불규칙하거나 얼룩 같은 모양을 띠기도 한다.

nebulae[nébjələ] 성운 **stunning**[stʌ́niŋ] 놀랄만큼 아름다운
ionize[áiənàiz] 이온화하다 **emission nebulae** 발광 성운
filamentary[fìləméntəri] 필라멘트의, 섬유 모양의
blob[blab] 얼룩, 작은 덩이

TIP 1950년대 미국은 전 세계 총 수출량의 25퍼센트를 차지했다. 하지만 최근에는 중국과 인도 같은 국가들이 세계의 상품과 서비스의 주요 원천으로 부상하고 있다.

account for ~을 차지하다 **emerge**[imə́ːrdʒ] 부상하다

TIP 의사는 전문용어를 사용하는데, 이는 특정 집단이나 직업의 사람들이 사용하는 특별한 언어로, 환자들이 알 필요가 없는 내용을 이해하지 못하게 한다.

jargon[dʒáːrgən] 전문용어

TIP 그 요새는 황량한 것처럼 보였으나, 내부는 정부 군사와 관리들로 가득 차 있었다.

deserted[dizə́ːrtid] 황량한

전략 2

Ex 관개와 경작 기술의 진보로 인간의 정착 규모가 증가하면서 재화 및 인력 순환을 개선시킬 필요성이 그 어느 때보다 중대해졌다. 끝없는 식량 수색을 위해 유목생활을 한 구석기 시대의 인간들은 주로 걸어서 이동하였으며, 가족들의 도움을 받아 필수물품을 소지하고 다녔다.

settlement[sétlmənt] 정착 **nomadic**[noumǽdik] 유목의

Ex 에너지 분배는 모든 유기체가 포식자로부터 자신을 방어하고, 충분한 식량을 획득하고, 생산하며, 정해진 신체구조대로 성장하기에 충분한 힘을 비축하면서 특정 물리적 환경에서 살아남을 수 있도록 보장하는 평형을 유지해야 한다. 대부분의 경우에, 특정 기능에 지정된 에너지의 비율은 의식적으로 지정된 것이 아니라 유전적으로 결정되며, 한 종의 모든 구성원은 비교적 비슷한 생리학적 상태를 나타낸다.

allocation[æ̀ləkéiʃən] 분배 **procreate**[próukrièit] 생산하다
consciously[kánʃəsli] 의식적으로
physiological[fìziəládʒikəl] 생리학적인

전략 3

Ex Inuit족이 살았던 지역은 극히 사람이 살기 힘든 지역이었고, 그 지역의 인구는 생존을 위해 전통적인 사냥과 채집 기술에 크게 의존했다. 충분한 공급을 얻기 위해 Inuit족은 임시 거주지에 살았고, 풍부한 자원을 찾아 이동하여 그 자원을 고갈시키고 다른 곳으로 이동했다.

inhospitable[inháspitəbl] 사람이 살기 힘든
acquire[əkwáiər] 얻다 **temporary**[témpərèri] 임시의
bountiful[báuntifəl] 풍부한

HACKERS STRATEGY **APPLICATION** p.114

비록 성인 암컷 침팬지 수가 성인 수컷 침팬지 수의 두세 배가 넘을 수 있지만, 모든 침팬지 사회는 환경과 상관없이 가부장제이거나 수컷이 지배한다. 수컷 침팬지들의 서열은 마치 공동체 회원 자격처럼 매우 융통성이 있는데, 수컷들은 서로 어울리며 마음대로 소집단에 들어오거나 나간다. 수컷 서열은 다소 직선적인 한편, 하나의 우두머리 수컷에 의해 지배된다. 우두머리는 종종 '우월함을 과시'함으로써 공격 행동, 힘, 또는 지능을 통해 권력을 취할 수 있다. 그러한 과시적 행동은 소음을 내며 수컷 집단을 공격하는 것도 포함할 수 있다. 혹은 수컷 침팬지 한 마리가 다른 침팬지들 앞에서, 군림하는 우두머리 수컷의 자리에 도전하여 우두머리를 정면으로 공격할 수 있다. 이는 어떻게 낮은 서열의 침팬지가 우두머리 수컷의 자리를 차지할 수 있는지를 정확히 보여준다.

patriarchal[pèitriáːrkəl] 가부장제의 **hierarchy**[háiərὰːrki] 서열
at will 마음대로 **linear**[líniər] 직선의 **alpha**[ǽlfə] 우두머리의
head-on[hédɔ̀ːn] 정면으로

1. 지문의 단어 "flexible"과 의미상 가장 유사한 것은?

(A) 신중한
(B) 완고한

(C) 완전한
(D) 가변적인

Smart dust는 개별적으로 mote라고 불리는, 밀리미터 눈금을 가진 다수의 마이크로 전자기계 장치로 구성되어 있다. mote는 먼지 입자만큼이나 작으며 원거리 센서를 포함한 양방향 무선 수신기로 구성되어 있다. 수천 개의 mote는 자료를 수집하고 감시하기 위해 건물 전체나 대기로 분산될 수 있다. Smart dust를 주목하게 만드는 것은 네트워크를 가능하게 하는 힘을 가지고 있기 때문이다. mote 하나는 아주 적은 정보만 제공할 수 있지만 서로 통신하는 수백 개의 mote는 어디에서 무슨 일이 일어나는지에 대한 상세한 화면을 구성할 수 있다. 따라서 smart dust 기기는 군사에서부터 기상 및 의학 분야에 이르기까지 모든 분야에 응용할 수 있다.

consist of ~로 구성되다 **compose**[kəmpóuz] 구성하다
remote[rimóut] 원거리의 **atmosphere**[ǽtməsfìər] 대기
noteworthy[nóutwə̀ːrði] 주목할 만한 **detailed**[ditéild] 상세한
application[æ̀pləkéiʃən] 응용

2. 지문의 단어 "composed"와 의미상 가장 유사한 것은?

(A) 완성된
(B) 인위적인
(C) ~로 이루어진
(D) 소비된

HACKERS **PRACTICE** p.116

1. 1 waste, 2 (B)
2. 1 damage, 2 (C)
3. 1 emitted, 2 (C)
4. 1 execute, 2 (A)
5. 1 volatility, 2 (D)
6. 1 brightness, 2 (B)
7. 1 moved, 2 (B)
8. 1 fundamentals, 2 (B)
9. 1 adapt, 2 (B)
10. (D)
11. (B)   12. (B)   13. (B)
14. (D)   15. (B)   16. (B)
17. (C)   18. 1 (B), 2 (C), 3 (B)
19. 1 (B), 2 (C), 3 (A)   20. 1 (D), 2 (B), 3 (B)
21. 1 (A), 2 (A), 3 (C)   22. 1 (D), 2 (A), 3 (B)

VOCABULARY

1 (B)   2 (D)   3 (C)
4 (A)   5 (A)   6 (B)
7 (B)   8 (D)   9 (B)

---

10 (C)   11 (D)   12 (B)
13 (C)   14 (A)   15 (C)
16 (B)   17 (A)   18 (D), (C), (B)
19 (B), (A), (D)   20 (C), (A), (D)   21 (C), (A), (B)
22 (B), (D), (A)

1 공기 중으로 높게 물을 뿌리는 전통적이고 매우 비효율적인 진동 살수장치는 바람과 증발작용으로 물을 낭비할 수 있고, 안개나 미세한 물보라를 만드는 살수장치도 마찬가지로 많은 양의 물을 증발작용으로 낭비할 수 있다.

inefficient[ìnifíʃənt] 비효율적인
oscillate[ásəlèit] 진동하다, 왕복하다
sprinkler[spríŋklər] 살수장치, 물뿌리개
spray[sprei] 뿌리다; 물보라 **lavish**[lǽviʃ] 낭비하다
evaporation[ivæ̀pəréiʃən] 증발작용 **mist**[mist] 안개

2 "lavishes"의 동의어 묶음인 것은?

(A) 희생하다, 포기하다, 인정하다
(B) 낭비하다, 소비하다, 버리다
(C) 감염시키다, 오염시키다, 더럽히다
(D) 잃어버리다, 잘못 두다, 양도하다

2 인체의 가장 거대한 조직인 피부는, 신체 외부의 표면을 미생물에 의한 침투와 손상으로부터 보호하는 한편, 면역 체계는 백혈구와 같은 특수한 세포들을 이용하여 감염성 침입 인자들로 인한 신체 내부의 손상을 막는다.

organ[ɔ́ːrgən] 조직, 기관 **penetration**[pènitréiʃən] 침투
microorganism[màikrouɔ́ːrgənìzm] 미생물
leukocyte[lúːkəsàit] 백혈구 **thwart**[θwɔːrt] 막다
devastation[dèvəstéiʃən] 손상 **infectious**[infékʃəs] 감염성의

2 "devastation"의 동의어 묶음인 것은?

(A) 결과, 성과, 영향
(B) 장벽, 장애물, 방해물
(C) 상해, 파괴, 상처
(D) 자국, 얼룩, 반점

3 신생 지구의 대기 중 초기 이산화탄소는 화산 활동에 의해 방출되었다. 이것은 생명체에 도움이 되는 따뜻하고 안정된 기후에 필수적이었다. 화산 활동은 현재 매년 약 130~230테라그램의 이산화탄소를 방출하고 있다.

initial[iníʃəl] 초기의 **carbon dioxide** 이산화탄소
emit[imít] 방출하다 **volcanic**[vɑlkǽnik] 화산의
stable[stéibl] 안정된 **conducive**[kəndjúːsiv] 도움이 되는
exude[igzúːd] 방출하다
teragram[térəgræ̀m] 테라그램(10의 12제곱 그램)

2 "exudes"의 동의어 묶음인 것은?

(A) 이용하다, 활용하다, 적용하다
(B) 우세를 차지하다, 우위에 서다, 능가하다
(C) 발산하다, 방출하다, 내보내다
(D) 버리다, 제거하다, 치우다

4 미 대법원과 의회는 미 대통령이 정부에 행사할 수 있는 권력의 크기를 제한하지만, 의원내각제는 일반적으로 수상이 미 대통령보다 더 많은 권한을 행사하는 것을 허용한다.

Supreme Court 대법원 Congress[ká:ŋgrəs] 의회
wield[wi:ld] 행사하다 parliamentary system 의원내각제
prime minister 국무총리 execute[éksikju:t] 행사하다
authority[əθɔ́:rəti] 권한
counterpart[káuntərpɑ:rt] (동일한 지위나 기능을 가진) 상대, 상응하는 사람(것)

2 "wield"의 동의어 묶음인 것은?

(A) 행사하다, 발휘하다, 사용하다
(B) 기대하다, 예상하다, 예측하다
(C) 소집하다, 소환하다, 부르다
(D) 창조하다, 형성하다, 발명하다

5 유가는 수출국의 유지추출법에서의 규제 상황과 같은 요인들로 인해 변동을 거듭하지만, 수입국들은 가격 변동에 대항하는 능력에 한계가 있다.

fluctuate[flʌ́ktʃueit] 변동을 거듭하다
regulatory[régjələtɔ:ri] 규제의 oil extraction 유지추출법
volatility[vàlətíləti] 변동

2 "fluctuates"의 동의어 묶음인 것은?

(A) 빛나가다, 벗어나다, 헤매다
(B) 가만히 있다, 제자리걸음 하다, 그대로 있다
(C) 가라앉다, 완화되다, 잦아들다
(D) 바뀌다, 변하다, 흔들리다

6 대부분의 별은 거의 일정한 실광도(實光度)를 가진다. 태양은 비교적 광도에 거의 변화가 없는 별의 좋은 예(보통 11년의 태양 활동 주기 동안 약 0.1퍼센트)이다. 그러나 많은 별은 발광성에 있어서 주목할만한 변화를 겪으며 이러한 별들은 변광성(變光星)으로 알려져 있다.

constant[kánstənt] 일정한
luminosity[lù:mənásəti] 실광도(實光度)
relatively[rélətivli] 비교적, 상대적으로
significant[signífikənt] 주목할만한 variable star 변광성(變光星)

2 "luminosity"의 동의어 묶음인 것은?

(A) 부피, 크기, 양
(B) 광채, 광명, 광휘
(C) 평온, 고요, 침착
(D) 운동, 동작, 몸짓

7 대초원에 말이 출현하기 전에 원뿔형 천막집은 여성과 개에 의해서 여기저기로 운반되기에 충분한 크기여야 했다. 하지만 말이 등장하면서 이것은 극적으로 변했다. 그 결과 중 하나는 원래 5~6피트 정도의 높이였던 천막집 장대가 이제는 평균 15피트로 높아졌다는 것이다. 말 세 마리를 이용해서 이제 천막집은 꽤 쉽게 운반될 수 있었다.

prior to ~ 전에 arrival[əráivəl] 출현
tipi[tí:pi:] (북미 원주민의) 원뿔형 천막집
sufficient[səfíʃənt] 충분한 lodge[lɑdʒ] 천막집
dwelling[dwéliŋ] 집

2 "carried"의 동의어 묶음인 것은?

(A) 버려진, 포기된, 버림받은
(B) 전달된, 옮겨진, 수송된
(C) 해체된, 분해된, 붕괴된
(D) 강화된, 증감된, 보강된

8 몸의 움직임과 음악 이론의 결합인 Dalcroze 방식은 사람의 몸을 음악 도구로 사용함으로써 학생들이 음악적인 표현을 위해 자연스러운 감정을 취하도록 장려한다. 전체적으로, Dalcroze 방식은 똑같이 중요한 세 개의 원칙으로 이루어져 있는데, 이는 도레미파 발성 연습, 즉흥 연주, 유리드믹스이며, 이 세 개가 합쳐져 결과적으로 Jacque-Dalcroze가 완전한 음악 교육이라고 여긴 것이 된다. 이론적으로 이러한 원칙들의 융합이 창조적이고 예술적인 개인을 만들어낸다.

Dalcroze Method Dalcroze 방식(스위스 음악가 Dalcroze에 의해 창안된 음악 교육법) combination[kàmbənéiʃən] 결합, 조합
as a whole 전체적으로, 전체로서
fundamental[fʌ̀ndəméntl] 원칙, 원리
solfege[sɑlféʒ] 도레미파 발성 연습
improvisation[imprɑ̀vəzéiʃən] 즉흥 연주
eurhythmics[juːríðmiks] 유리드믹스(음악 리듬을 몸놀림으로 표현하는 리듬 교육법) amount to 결과적으로 ~이 되다
ideally[aidíːəli] 이론적으로 amalgamation[əmæ̀lgəméiʃən] 융합

2 "principles"의 동의어 묶음인 것은?

(A) 상태, 단계, 기간
(B) 기준, 기초, 표준
(C) 영향, 효과, 작용
(D) 솜씨, 소질, 재능

9 노동의 분화는 연령에 따라 상당히 뚜렷하지만, 연구 결과는 어떤 대이변의 사건으로 초래된, 균형이 깨진 연령 구조를 가진 일벌 개체군에서 각 일벌이 순응하여 그들의 나이에 맞지 않는 임무를 맡는다는 것을 밝혔다. 일벌들이 이러한 방식으로 행동을 변경할 때, 그들은 정상적인 발달 순서에 따라 행동할 때보다 덜 효율적으로 일을 수행한다.

fairly[féərli] 상당히 clear-cut[klíərkʌ̀t] 뚜렷한
catastrophic[kæ̀təstráfik] 대이변의 adapt[ədǽpt] 순응하다

assume[əsúːm] 맡다 modify[mάdəfài] 변경하다
fashion[fǽʃən] 방식 perform[pərfɔ́ːrm] 수행하다
sequence[síːkwəns] 순서

2 "modify"의 동의어 묶음인 것은?

  (A) 인정하다, 알다, 인지하다
  (B) 수정하다, 조절하다, 바꾸다
  (C) 정복하다, 압도하다, 진압하다
  (D) 버티다, 맞서다, 반항하다

10 안정 상태에 있는 것으로 묘사되는 인구는 출생률과 동일한 사
    망률을 지녀서 변하지 않는 인구이다.

delineate[dilínieit] 묘사하다 death rate 사망률
birth rate 출생률

  (A) 유동성
  (B) 수단
  (C) 무게
  (D) 안정

11 비록 꿀벌과 말벌은 생물학적으로 밀접하게 연관되어 있지는 않
    지만, 그들은 몇 가지 해부학적 특성들을 공유하는데, 이를테면
    그들이 '촉수'로 사용하는 앞 더듬이와 위험이 임박했음을 인지
    했을 때 복부 뒤쪽에서 뻗어 나가는 독침과 같은 것들이다.

wasp[wɑːsp] 말벌 anatomical[ænətάmikəl] 해부학적인
anterior[æntíriər] 앞의, 앞쪽에 있는 antenna[ænténə] 더듬이
feeler[fíːlər] 촉수 venomous[vénəməs] 독성의
stinger[stíŋər] 침 abdomen[ǽbdəmən] 복부
imminent[íminənt] 임박한

  (A) 이전의
  (B) 뒤쪽의
  (C) 우수한
  (D) 열등한

12 원자와 분자는 음전기로 대전된 전자의 수가 양전기로 대전된
    양자의 수와 정확하게 같다는 점에서 전기적으로 중성을 띤다.

atom[ǽtəm] 원자 molecule[mάləkjùːl] 분자
neutral[njúːtrəl] 중성의 in that ~라는 점에서
negatively[négətivli] 음전기적으로 charged[tʃɑ́ːrdʒd] 대전된
electron[iléktrɑn] 전자 positively[pάzətivli] 양전기적으로
proton[próutɑn] 양자

  (A) 사본
  (B) 같은 것
  (C) 한 쌍
  (D) 반대

13 'Tyrannosaurus rex'로 알려진 악명 높은 육식 공룡은 엄청난
    급성장을 겪어 결국 약 5,000킬로그램에 육박하였으나, 너무 크

고 무거워져 빨리 움직일 수 없게 되었고 더 효율적인 육식 동물
의 먹이를 훔치기 위해 그들을 위협하여 쫓아버려야 했다.

notorious[noutɔ́ːriəs] 악명 높은 massive[mǽsiv] 엄청난
spurt[spəːrt] 급성장 eventually[ivéntʃuəli] 결국
hefty[héfti] 크고 무거운 scare away 위협하여 쫓다
predator[prédətər] 육식 동물

  (A) 밝은
  (B) 크고 무거운
  (C) 부족한
  (D) 작고 맵시 있는

14 Arabica 커피콩과 Robusta 커피콩은 모양으로 명확히 구별할
    수 있다. Arabica 콩은 납작하고 장방형이며 구부러진 홈이 있
    는 데 비해, Robusta 콩은 볼록하고 둥글며 중심에 일직선의
    홈이 있다.

distinguishable[distíŋgwiʃəbl] 구별할 수 있는 flat[flæt] 납작한
oblong[άblɔ̀ːŋ] 장방형의 crooked[krúkid] 구부러진
furrow[fə́ːrou] 홈 convex[kɑnvéks] 볼록한

  (A) 적응할 수 있는
  (B) 변덕스러운
  (C) 지속 가능한
  (D) 구별할 수 있는

15 무의식적이든 의식적이든 간에, 필연적으로 신체 및 생리적인
    변화를 수반하는 청소년의 행동 변화는 심리학자들에게 큰 관심
    사다.

automatic[ɔ̀ːtəmǽtik] 무의식적인 behavioral change 행동 변화
inevitably[inévitəbli] 필연적으로, 반드시
accompany[əkʌ́mpəni] 수반하다
physiological[fìziəlάdʒikəl] 생리적인
alteration[ɔ̀ːltəréiʃən] 변화 adolescent[ǽdəlésnt] 청소년

  (A) 희미한
  (B) 의식적인
  (C) 무의식의
  (D) 끊임없는

16 Mount Rushmore에 있는 네 명의 대통령들의 이상은 그들의
    모습이 조각된 바위처럼 미국의 견고한 초석이 되었다.

ideal[aidíːəl] 이상 foundation[faundéiʃən] 초석
solid[sάlid] 견고한 figure[fígjər] 모습, 형상
carve[kɑːrv] 조각하다

  (A) 인상적인
  (B) 견고한
  (C) 엄격한
  (D) 예측할 수 없는

17 키네토스코프는 일반적으로 불연속적인 영화를 보여주었지만, 가끔 유명한 권투 시합의 경우에는 연속 라운드를 보여주곤 했다.

Kinetoscope[kiní:təskòup] 키네토스코프(에디슨이 발명한 활동 사진 영사기) discrete[diskrí:t] 불연속적인 boxing match 권투 시합 display[displéi] 보여주다 successive[səksésiv] 연속적인

(A) 기본적인
(B) 간결한
(C) 불연속적인
(D) 초현실적인

18 북극광은 지구의 북극에서 보이는 아름다운 빛의 전시이다. 하늘의 북부에 나타나며, 때맞추어 변화하고 희미하게 반짝이는 리본 모양을 가지고 있다. 색은 매우 옅은 흰색부터 녹색, 푸른색, 그리고 때로는 보라색에 이른다. 충분히 환하고 큰 경우에는 멀리 남쪽의 Florida에서도 식별할 수 있지만, 일반적으로 그것은 Canada와 Alaska 등의 북쪽 지역에서 가장 잘 보인다. 남반구에는 같은 방식으로 작용하는, 남극광이라 불리는 비슷한 현상이 있다.

aurora borealis 북극광 shimmer[ʃímər] 반짝이다 hue[hju:] 색 latitude[lǽtətjù:d] (위도상으로 본) 지역 discernible[disə́:rnəbl] 식별할 수 있는 aurora australis 남극광 hemisphere[hémisfìər] 반구 behave[bihéiv] 작용하다

1 지문의 단어 "exhibition"과 의미상 가장 유사한 것은?

(A) 잡동사니
(B) 전시
(C) 연속물
(D) 흐름

2 지문의 단어 "visible"과 의미상 가장 유사한 것은?

(A) 수단이 되는
(B) 잠재하는
(C) 눈에 띄는
(D) 장관의

3 지문의 단어 "discernible"과 의미상 가장 유사한 것은?

(A) 격렬한
(B) 인지할 수 있는
(C) 관대한
(D) 엉뚱한

19 우주의 비밀을 밝혀내고자 하는 천문학자들의 연구는 고대에 시작됐다. 하지만 현대 과학의 도래와 복잡한 과학 기술, 수학, 그리고 근거 있는 가설들의 발전이 있기 전까지, 천체를 연구하던 사람들은 이 수수께끼를 풀기 위해 고군분투하였다. 천문학자들이 풀기 위해 애썼던 가장 널리 알려진 논점 중 하나는 태양계와 그 밖의 기타 물리적 현상들이 애초에 어떻게 생겨났는지에 관한 것이었다. 거의 모든 현대 천문학적 의견에 따르면, 그 답은, 우주의 시작이 하나의 거대한 폭발 사건으로부터 비롯되었는데,

이는 특이점이라고 알려진 무한한 밀도의 영역에서 시작하여, 매우 뜨겁고 많은 양의 양성자, 중성자, 광자, 그리고 다른 아원자입자들이 사방으로 발사된 것이다. 이 최초의 '원생액'으로부터 우주의 모든 별, 행성, 그리고 생명체가 뒤이어 형성된 것이었다.

stargazer[stá:rgeizər] 천문학자 advent[ǽdvent] 도래 rigorous[rígərəs] 근거 있는, 엄격한 celestial body 천체 prevalent[prévələnt] 널리 알려진 wrestle with ~하기 위해 애쓰다 phenomenon[fəná:minən] 현상 contemporary[kəntémpəreri] 현대의 onset[á:nset] 시작 commence[kəméns] 시작하다 singularity[sìŋgjulǽrəti] 특이점(중력의 고유 세기가 무한대로 발산하는 시공의 영역) proton[próutɑn] 양성자 neutron[nú:trɑn] 중성자 photon[fóutɑn] 광자 sub-atomic particle 아원자입자 primordial soup 원생액(지구상에 생명을 발생시킨 유기물의 혼합 용액)

1 지문의 단어 "prevalent"와 의미상 가장 유사한 것은?

(A) 경박한
(B) 지배적인
(C) 간결한
(D) 변함없는

2 지문의 단어 "onset"과 의미상 가장 유사한 것은?

(A) 결말
(B) 중심점
(C) 시작
(D) 결과

3 지문의 단어 "subsequently"와 의미상 가장 유사한 것은?

(A) 나중에
(B) 더 오래
(C) 동시에
(D) 드물게

20 빙하 작용은 내리는 눈에서 시작되고, 각 눈송이는 일반적으로 자유롭게 갈라진 줄기로 된 육각형 구조를 지니기 때문에, 눈송이들이 쌓이면서 미세한 공기 기포가 그 사이에 갇히게 된다. 충분한 눈이 내리면, 중력으로 인한 그 자체의 무게하에 압축이 되기 쉬워진다. 눈과 얼음 사이의 과립 모양의 중간 형태는 '싸라기눈'이라 불리고, 지속적인 압축을 통해, 그것은 밀도 높은, 바위 모양의 빙하로 변할 수 있다. 빙하 표면에서, 얼음은 깨지기 쉽지만, 하층부 근처에서는, 매우 튼튼하고 단단하여 아래에 있는 기반암을 갈아서 빙하 찰흔을 남긴다. 빙하는 흘러가면서, 퇴적물을 집어 올리고 하류로 운반하여, 결국 빙하가 녹으면 그 퇴적물이 쌓여 종종 그에 따른 비옥한 땅을 남긴다. 빙하가 후퇴한 후에 남겨진 표면은 특유의 빙하곡과 같이 극적으로 변할 수 있는데, 그것은 보통 빙하가 산비탈을 깎아낸 가파르고 거의 수직에 가까운 절벽을 가진 골의 모양이다. 바다와 인접한 지역에서

는, 빙하의 후퇴에 따라 계곡이 때때로 바닷물에 잠기는데, 이는 '협만'으로 알려진 길고 좁은 해안 만을 형성한다. '협만'은 노르웨이 말에서 유래된 용어인데, 이는 노르웨이의 해안이 거의 1,200여 개의 이러한 지형적 특징의 존재로 두드러지기 때문이며, 이 지형은 그 나라 해안선의 31,500킬로미터 중 총 29,000킬로미터를 차지한다.

glaciation [gléisiéiʃən] 빙하 작용
hexagonal [heksǽɡənl] 육각형의   branch [brǽntʃ] 갈라지다
minute [mainjúːt] 미세한   subject to ~하기 쉬운
compaction [kəmpǽkʃən] 압축   granular [grǽnjələr] 과립 모양의
firn [fiərn] 싸라기눈, 만년설   compression [kəmpréʃən] 압축
brittle [brítl] 깨지기 쉬운   grind [graind] 갈다
bedrock [bédrɑːk] 기반암
striation [straiéiʃən] 빙하 찰흔(빙하의 이동에 의해 암석 표면에 생긴 홈 자국)   sediment [sédimənt] 퇴적물
deposit [dipɑ́ːzit] 쌓다, 퇴적시키다   fertile [fə́ːrtl] 비옥한
recede [risíːd] 후퇴하다   trough [trɔːf] (산등성이 사이의) 골
chisel [tʃízl] 깎다, 새기다   adjacent to ~에 인접한
submerge [səbmə́ːrdʒ] (물속에) 잠그다, 잠기다
retreat [ritríːt] 후퇴   inlet [ínlet] (바다 또는 호수의) 만
shoreline [ʃɔ́ːrlain] 해안선

1 지문의 구 "subject to"와 의미상 가장 유사한 것은?

(A) ~을 목격한
(B) ~을 연습한
(C) ~ 안에 몸을 숨긴
(D) ~에 영향을 받기 쉬운

2 지문의 단어 "brittle"과 의미상 가장 유사한 것은?

(A) 견고한
(B) 부서지기 쉬운
(C) 치명적인
(D) 격노한

3 지문의 구 "adjacent to"와 의미상 가장 유사한 것은?

(A) 내려다보는
(B) 인접한
(C) 마주한
(D) 도달한

21 그의 대통령 임기 동안, 앤드류 잭슨은 끊임없이 국법 은행과 그 지지자들을 공격했다. 그는 미 국법 은행의 유통 중인 통화량을 규제하는 기능이 지역 금융기관들이 신용을 늘리는 것을 저해하는 역할을 했다고 주장했다. 그에 따라, 잭슨은 1832년에 국법 은행의 설립 재허가에 대한 의회의 승인을 거부하는 것으로 즉시 응했고, 이는 실질적으로 미 연방 정부의 은행 제도의 폐지를 시작시켰다. 이것이 가져온 결과 중 하나는 지역적으로 화폐를 인쇄하는 관행을 재개한 것이었고, 은행들은 그것을 대규모로 진행했다. 총통화량은 1832년의 5천9백만 달러에서 1836년에는 1억4천만 달러로 급등했다. 자유로운 대출 관행, 부동산 투기, 그리고 비축된 금과 은으로 통화량을 충분히 환원하지 못한 것은 빠른 속도의 인플레이션과 결합하여 경제를 무너뜨리고 미국 최악의 경제 불황을 야기했다. 강력한 중앙은행을 지지했던 사람들은 시장의 급격한 악화를 초래한 경제 쇼크에 관해 노골적으로 잭슨을 비난했다.

presidency [prézidənsi] 대통령 임기
national bank 국법 은행(미국 연방 정부의 인가를 받은 상업은행)
circulation [sə̀ːrkjəléiʃən] 유통   inhibit [inhíbit] 저해하다
swiftly [swíftli] 즉시   endorsement [indɔ́ːrsmənt] 승인, 지지
re-charter [riːtʃɑ́ːrtər] 설립 재허가   veto [víːtou] 거부하다
dismantle [dismǽntl] 폐지하다   federal [fédərəl] 연방 정부의
renew [rinúː] 재개하다, 갱신하다   skyrocket [skáirɑ̀kit] 급등하다
lending [léndiŋ] 대출   speculation [spèkjuléiʃən] 투기
real estate 부동산   in reserve 비축된, 보유한
devastate [dévəsteit] 무너뜨리다   depression [dipréʃən] 불황
central bank 중앙은행   explicitly [iksplísitli] 노골적으로
downturn [dáuntəːrn] 악화, 감소

1 지문의 단어 "inhibit"과 의미상 가장 유사한 것은?

(A) 억제하다
(B) 자극하다
(C) 연장하다
(D) 예견하다

2 지문의 단어 "endorsement"와 의미상 가장 유사한 것은?

(A) 지지
(B) 거절
(C) 훈련
(D) 비판

3 지문의 단어 "vast"와 의미상 가장 유사한 것은?

(A) 작은
(B) 평균의
(C) 거대한
(D) 선택적인

22 지난 15년 정도에 걸쳐 태양의 내부 구조와 역학, 그리고 궁극적으로 다른 항성들 역시 직접적으로 수량화하기 위한 새로운 접근법이 나왔다. 1960년대의 태양의 전파되는 음파의 발견과 1970년대의 그에 대한 설명은 태양 지진학이라는 흥미로운 신기술의 발달로 이어졌다. 이 접근법은 사실상 태양 지진파에 응용되는 음향 분광학의 한 형태이다. 태양 지진학은 최초로 눈에 보이지 않는 항성의 내부 구조와 역학을 측정하기 위해, 태양 곳곳에 흩어지는 파동을 연구한다. 뚜렷한, 공명하는 수백만의 음파가 태양 표면에서 방출되는 빛의 도플러 이동에 의해 보여진다. 이 파동 주기는 전파 속도와 공진 공동의 깊이에 좌우되며, 다른 공진 공동과 함께 많은 공진 방식은 기온, 화학 구성, 그리고 태양 표면 바로 아래에서부터 태양의 중심핵까지의 움직임에 대한 매우 정밀한 조사를 가능하게 한다.

approach [əpróutʃ] 접근법   emerge [imə́ːrdʒ] 나오다
quantification [kwɑ̀ntəfikéiʃən] 수량화

dynamics[dainǽmiks] 역학 ultimately[ʌ́ltəmətli] 궁극적으로
propagate[prápəgèit] 전파하다 acoustical[əkúːstikəl] 음향의
spectroscopy[spektrάskəpi] 분광학 seismic wave 지진파
strew[struː] 흩어지다 distinct[distíŋkt] 뚜렷한
resonate[rézənèit] 공명하다 Doppler shift 도플러 이동
resonant cavity 공진 공동 mode[moud] 방식
narrow[nǽrou] 정밀한 probe[proub] 조사
composition[kàmpəzíʃən] 구성 core[kɔːr] 핵

1 지문의 단어 "quantifications"와 의미상 가장 유사한 것은?

(A) 배열
(B) 모방
(C) 개정
(D) 측량

2 지문의 단어 "strewn"과 의미상 가장 유사한 것은?

(A) 뿔뿔이 흩어진
(B) 짜여진
(C) 깨진
(D) 중지된

3 지문의 단어 "composition"과 의미상 가장 유사한 것은?

(A) 형판
(B) 구성
(C) 부속품
(D) 층

HACKERS TEST

01 Tundra

p.126

1. (B)	2. (D)	3. (C)
4. (A)	5. (A)	6. (D)
7. (C)	8. (C)	9. (B)

10. Alpine Tundra – (A), (E), (G)
    Arctic Tundra – (C), (D)

1 툰드라라는 용어는 나무가 없는 평원이라는 뜻을 가진 'tundar'라는 핀란드 단어에서 온 것으로, 영하의 온도 때문에 수목의 성장이 억제되는 물리적 지형의 지대를 나타낸다. 갈록색을 띠며 종의 천이가 평균보다 느리게 일어나는 경향이 있는 이끼, 허브, 관목 등의 저지대 식물들이 이 지대에서 일반적으로 발견되는 식물군의 특징을 나타낸다.

2 [2]툰드라의 생태계는 평원의 위치에 따라서 크게 두 가지 종류로 분류된다. 극지방에서는 북극을 둘러싸면서 남쪽으로는 수목 생장 한계선에까지 이어지는 완만하거나 평평한 지역에서 북극권 툰드라가 특징적으로 나타나고, [10E]고산성 툰드라는 정상적인 나무의 생장이 저해될 만큼 고도가 높은 모든 위도에서 나타난다.

3 고산성 툰드라가 나타나는 고도에서는 아고산대에서 자라는 가문비나무와 전나무가 작은 나무로 대체되는데, 토양이 잘 발달되어 있다면 경사가 완만한 휜히 트인 초원이 나타나거나, 풍화작용이 극심한 지역에서는 완충 식물이 왕성하게 자라는 바람받이 경사면이 나타난다. [10A]많은 양의 연 강수가 초목의 성장을 촉진시키고, 산 측면의 경사도 봄에 눈이 녹은 물과 여름 폭우의 배수가 잘 이루어지게 해주어 성장을 촉진한다. 이는 겨울의 영하 20도에서 따뜻한 계절에는 20도까지 올라가는 온난한 기후와 더불어서, 특히 냇가나 바람 반대 방향의 능선이나 얕은 계곡처럼 눈이 깊게 쌓이는 곳에서, 관목이 자랄 수 있는 환경을 제공하기도 한다. 보편적으로 환경이 가혹한 곳에서도, [10G]식물들은 평균 180일이라는 긴 성장 기간을 가질 수 있을 만큼 충분히 운이 좋으며, 밤에 끼는 서리의 위협에도 불구하고 이끼류는 존속할 수 있다.

4 [5]굴 근처에 있는 식물들도, 동물들의 변에서 토양으로 스며든 질소 등의 영양소에 의해서 추가적으로 성장이 촉진되는 효과를 받아 번성한다. 얼룩다람쥐와 마르모트 같은 일부 동물들은 한 해의 대부분을 이런 굴에서 가까운 곳에서 보내는데, 여름과 초가을에는 먹이를 모으고 겨울에는 겨울잠을 자러 굴로 돌아온다. 토끼 같은 다른 동물들은 겨울 동안에도 계속해서 먹을 것을 찾아 떠돌면서, 혹은 가능한 한 오랫동안 저장된 지방에 의지하면서 눈 속에서 살아간다. 산양과 살쾡이, 그리고 많은 새는 추운 환경에 부분적으로만 적응되어 있어서 종적인 이주를 하게 되는데, 겨울 내내 더욱 따뜻한 경사면으로 내려와서 먹이와 더욱 쾌적한 날씨를 찾는다.

5 조류를 제외하면 북극권 툰드라의 동물들은 추운 환경을 벗어나지 못하는데, 이는 지구의 총 표면의 10분의 1을 차지하는 면적을 덮고 있는 광활한 툰드라는 철에 따른 이동이 쉽게 일어나기에는 너무 넓기 때문이다. 대신 이들은 여름철에는 빨리 새끼를 낳아 기르고, 툰드라 지역이 눈으로 덮일 때에는 천적으로부터 위장하기 위한 하얀 털을 자라게 하거나, 에너지를 저장하고 체온을 유지하기 위한 지방층을 발달시키는 방법으로 넓은 지역에 펼쳐진 극한의 한랭 기후에 적응해 왔다. 순록은 큰 체표면적을 통해서 많은 열량이 분산되지 못하게 막음으로써 섭씨 영하 35도에서 5도에 이르는 낮은 기온에 대처한다. 이들은 한데 모여 난 짧은 풀들을 대량으로 섭취하여 거대한 몸집을 지탱하는데, 이 풀들은 대부분 거의 얼어붙어 있는 토양의 상층부를 뚫고 나와서 혹독한 추위를 견디기 위해서 군생하는 이끼와 작은 허브이다. 일반적으로 식물은 50일에서 60일에 불과한 짧은 성장 기간, 미미한 강우량, [10C]수 주 간 낮에도 지속되는 어둠에 의해서 성장이 억제되고, 고산성 툰드라와는 달리 생물의 다양성이 상당히 적다. 관목과 큰 허브류는 배수가 잘되지 않는 양분이 부족한 토양을 견뎌낼 수 있다 해도, 큰 폭으로 오르내리는 기온과 일조량의 심한 변동에 적응할 수 없는 경우가 많다. [10C]지구의 토양에 갇힌 탄소 중 거의 3분의 1에 달하는 양이 북극권 툰드라에 있다는 사실이 전반적 환경에 아주 중요한데, 영구동토, 즉 동결된

강우가 쌓여서 생겨난 얼어붙은 늪이 비정상적으로 높은 온도의 영향을 받게 되면 지구 온난화의 영향을 크게 가중시킬 가능성이 있기 때문이다.

lichen[láikən] 이끼 **moss**[mɔːs] 이끼 **shrub**[ʃrʌb] 관목
flora[flɔ́ːrə] 식물군 **ecosystem**[ékousìstəm] 생태계
Arctic tundra 북극권 툰드라 **rolling**[róuliŋ] (땅이) 완만한
equatorial timberline 수목의 생장 한계선
alpine tundra 고산성 툰드라 **altitude**[æltətjùːd] 고도
cripple[krípl] 저해하다 **spruce**[spruːs] 가문비나무
fir[fəːr] 전나무 **krummholz**[krúmhòults] 고산(高山)의 수목 한계
부근의 눈잣나무 따위의 작은 나무 숲 **meadow**[médou] 초원
windswept[wíndswèpt] 바람받이의 **foster**[fɔ́ːstər] 촉진하다
lee side 바람 반대 방향(바람이 가로막혀서 불어오지 않는 쪽)
subsist[səbsíst] 존속하다 **burrow**[bə́ːrou] 굴
leach[liːtʃ] 스며들다 **fauna**[fɔ́ːnə] 동물
hibernate[háibərnèit] 겨울잠을 자다
forage[fɔ́ːridʒ] 찾아 떠돌다 **camouflage**[kǽməflàːʒ] 위장하다
reindeer[réindìər] 순록 **dispersal**[dispə́ːrsəl] 분산
bulky[bʌ́lki] 거대한 **inclement**[inklémənt] 혹독한
stifle[stáifl] 억제하다 **aggravate**[ǽgrəvèit] 가중시키다
be subject to ~의 영향을 받다

1 지문의 단어 "suppressed"와 의미상 가장 유사한 것은?

   (A) 균형 잡힌
   (B) 저지된
   (C) 정신이 없는
   (D) 수리된

2 2단락에 따르면, 툰드라의 두 가지 유형은 어떻게 구별되는가?

   (A) 연간 강수량에 따라
   (B) 식물의 종류에 따라
   (C) 토양의 유형에 따라
   (D) 발생하는 장소에 따라

3 지문의 단어 "fosters"와 의미상 가장 유사한 것은?

   (A) 선언하다
   (B) 되찾다
   (C) 증진하다
   (D) 그만두다

4 지문의 단어 "subsist"와 의미상 가장 유사한 것은?

   (A) 지속되다
   (B) 소멸되다
   (C) 달아나다
   (D) 끓어오르다

5 지문에 따르면, 고산성 툰드라의 동물들은 _____ 함으로써 식물의 성장을 돕는다.

   (A) 영양 성분을 함유하고 있는 변을 퇴적함으로써
   (B) 식물을 덮은 얼음을 제거함으로써

   (C) 겨울 동안 굴에 씨앗을 보관함으로써
   (D) 경쟁 초목 지역을 제거함으로써

6 아래 문장 중 지문 속의 음영된 문장의 핵심 정보를 가장 잘 표현하고 있는 것은 무엇인가? 오답은 문장의 의미를 현저히 왜곡하거나 핵심 정보를 빠뜨리고 있다.

   (A) 북극권 툰드라의 가혹한 환경 때문에, 새들만이 겨울 동안 그 지역을 떠나려는 시도를 한다.
   (B) 북극권 툰드라의 기상 환경은 대부분의 동물들이 계절에 따른 이주 패턴을 따르는 것을 불가능하게 한다.
   (C) 북극권 툰드라는 지구 표면의 상당히 많은 부분을 덮고 있기 때문에, 동물들의 이주 경로는 넓다.
   (D) 북극권 툰드라의 거대한 크기는 거의 모든 동물들이 겨울 동안 그 지역을 떠나는 것을 막는다.

7 지문의 구 "cope with"와 의미상 가장 유사한 것은?

   (A) 계산하다
   (B) 부유하게 하다
   (C) 대처하다
   (D) 제외하다

8 지문의 단어 "dispersal"과 의미상 가장 유사한 것은?

   (A) 점화
   (B) 전율
   (C) 분배
   (D) 주기

9 지문의 단어 "aggravate"와 의미상 가장 유사한 것은?

   (A) 완화하다
   (B) 악화시키다
   (C) 재촉하다
   (D) 달래다

10 **지시**: 주어진 선택지에서 적절한 구를 선택하여 관계 있는 지형의 종류에 연결시키시오. **이 문제는 3점이다.**

보기
(B) 머지 않아 인간 활동에 의해 파괴될 위험에 놓여 있다
(F) 능선 위에 대규모의 가문비나무와 전나무 숲이 있다
고산성 툰드라
· (A) 식물의 성장을 빠르게 하는 많은 연강수량이 있다
· (E) 특정한 고도에 있는 어떠한 지역에서도 발견될 수 있다
· (G) 대략 반 년 동안 식물이 자랄 수 있게 한다
북극권 툰드라
· (C) 지구 기온을 높일 수 있는 가스의 저장소로 기능한다
· (D) 수 주의 기간 중 주간에 빛이 부족하다

02 Baroque and Rococo Art

p.130

1. (C) 2. (D) 3. (A)
4. (D) 5. (D) 6. (B)
7. (C) 8. (A) 9. (D)
10. Baroque Art – (C), (E), (G), (H)
    Rococo Art – (B), (D), (I)

1 긴 기간 동안 이어진 보수적, 전통주의적인 예술에서 벗어나면서, [10H]바로크 시대는 르네상스 양식의 진부성에 대한 반발로 1600년 무렵에 이탈리아 로마에서 시작되었다. 이 명칭은 포르투갈어 명사로 일그러진 진주를 의미하는 'barroco'에서 따온 것이고, 기교가 많이 들어간 기법이나 무절제한 주제 등 바로크 시대의 유행뿐 아니라 그 시대를 망라하는 특징을 가리키는 데 쓰인다. 바로크의 인기가 정점에 달했을 때, 이 양식의 과시적인 장대함을 비판하던 이들은 로코코라는 단어를 사용해서 프랑스와 그 주변에서 주목을 끌던, 더욱 가볍고 친근감이 느껴지는 형태의 장식을 가리키기 시작했다. 18세기 중반에 이르자 로코코는 그 자체로 건축, 회화, 조소, 음악을 아우르는 예술적인 흐름이 되었다. 현대의 예술사학자들은 한 장르의 다른 점으로 나머지 한 장르의 독특한 특징을 정의하는 등, 이 두 개의 장르를 서로에 비교해서 분류하는 경우가 많다.

2 역사적으로, 바로크 이전 시대의 예술 작품은 로마 가톨릭 교회의 엄격한 틀 속에서 고안되었다. 이 교단은 종교 개혁 때 재조직되었는데, 종교 개혁이란 성직자의 중재 없이도 일반 대중이 성경을 읽을 수 있게 하자고 선동한, 16세기 내내 지속되었던 정치적인 운동이었다. 성직자가 아닌 사람도 새롭게 성서에 대한 개인적인 관심을 가질 수 있게 되자, [2]교회 예술은 교회에 의해서 통제되던 비밀스러운 표현을 잃어버렸고, 이로 인해 예술가들은 최초로 비종교적 기관이나 개인으로부터 교회 외의 공간을 장식하기 위해 의뢰받은, 회화, 벽화, 조각 같은 작품들을 만들게 되었다. 전반적으로 그 예술의 내용은 성경의 내용에 익숙한 학식 있고 글을 읽을 수 있는 성직자들에게는 잘 맞지 않았고, 오히려 글을 모르는 일반인이 대중적으로 향유할 수 있도록 의도되었다. [10E]이러한 이유로 바로크 예술은 광범위한 관람객들을 위해서 잘 알려진 내용을 그림으로써, 특히 성인들과 성모 마리아에게 초점을 맞추는 경향이 있다.

3 바로크 예술의 대중적인 접근 가능성 때문에, 17세기 말에 이르자 바로크 예술은 유럽의 정체성에 깊이 자리 잡아서 Louis 14세가 이를 프랑스의 공식적인 양식으로 선포하여 베르사유 궁을 이 양식으로 꾸미고 화려한 응접실, 왕실, 대기실 등을 짓게 되기에 이른다. [3]이런 사업들은 왕의 방종에 염증을 느끼게 된 반 군주제주의자들을 의도적으로 바로크 양식에서 멀어지게 하고, 그들이 로코코라 부른 완전히 다른 모티프를 이용하는 그들만의 장식적인 예술을 발전시켜서 이에 대응하게 했다.

4 로코코 양식의 시초에는 건축 디자인만 그 영향을 받았다. [10I]주택의 벽, 천장, 소조물, 조각 등은 조개와 식물에서 얻은 자연적인 모티프와 결합된 추상적인 S자형의 곡선과 C자형의 소용돌이무늬로 장식되었고, 파스텔 색조와 상아색이 가장 자주 나타났다. [10B]공간감과 거룩함을 자아내기 위해서 거울이 사용되었는데, 이 거울은 보통 금은 장식이 박힌 화려한 장식의 진주 틀에 끼워져 있었다. 이런 가벼운(거품 같은) 느낌은, [10G]성경의 위대하고 진지한 장면을 풍부하고 짙은 색채 및 뚜렷한 명암과 조합한 왕의 무겁고 강렬한 디자인과 뚜렷한 대비를 이루고 있었다. 바로크 예술이 명료한 정교함으로 동작을 과장하여 엄숙한 종교적 저의를 표현했던 반면, 로코코 예술은 이러한 긴장을 완화시켰다.

5 로코코가 건축에서 시각 예술로 전이되면서 회화와 조각은 쾌활함과 가벼움을 나타내기 시작했는데, 느긋하게 나들이를 즐기는 걱정 없는 귀족 커플이나 사랑의 신화를 나타내는 아기 천사들의 모습이 주로 그려졌으며, 동양적인 디자인과 비대칭적인 구성 등의 다양한 특징이 가미되었다. [10C]수학과 기하학 발전의 시대에 등장한 바로크 양식의 중요한 측면 중 하나였던 균형은 바로크의 반대를 취하고자 하는 취향에 의해서 버림받았다. 이와 동시에, 의심할 여지 없이 바로크 양식의 가장 돋보이는 예인 Bernini의 대리석 조각 분수나 세심한 비례로 제작된 흉상, 인물상 등의 바로크 예술 작품들은 유행에 뒤처지게 되었다. [10D]기형적인 샹들리에, 형상이 일그러진 조가비 세공품, 일부 형상들을 다른 형상들보다 크게 그린 회화가 로코코 장르를 대표하게 되었고, 본질적으로 너무 진지하거나 무게 있는 작품들은 꺼려지게 되었다.

6 로코코 작가들이 심오하다고 여겨질 수 있는 어떤 작품도 제작하기를 거부했던 점은 이 장르가 오랫동안 문화에 미친 영향에 대한 의미 있는 논의를 하고자 하는 미술사학자들 사이에 논란을 불러일으켰다. 일부는 로코코가 바로크 양식의 명백한 스타일에 대한 순간적인 반발에 불과하다고 주장하는 데 반해서, 다른 이들은 로코코 양식의 본질이 덜 뚜렷한 것은 아니라고 주장한다.

banality [bənǽləti] 진부성 extravagance [ikstrǽvəgəns] 무절제함
ostentatious [ɑ̀stentéiʃəs] 과시하는 grandeur [grǽndʒər] 장대함
prominence [prɑ́mənəns] 주목 agitate [ǽdʒitèit] 선동하다
ecclesiastical [iklì:ziǽstikəl] 종교의 esoteric [èsətérik] 비밀의
embellish [imbéliʃ] 장식하다 magnificent [mæɡnífəsnt] 화려한
reception room 응접실 overindulgence [òuvərindʌ́ldʒəns] 방종
outset [áutsèt] 시초 engraving [ingréiviŋ] 조각
ornament [ɔ́:rnəmənt] 장식하다 scroll [skroul] 소용돌이 무늬
etherealness [iθíəriəlnis] 거룩함
mother-of-pearl [mʌ́ðərəvpə̀:rl] 진주의
effervescence [èfərvésns] 거품 같은 느낌
undercurrent [ʌ́ndərkə̀:rənt] 저의 alleviate [əlí:vièit] 완화시키다
aristocratic [ərìstəkrǽtik] 귀족의 cherub [tʃérəb] 천사
asymmetric [èisəmétrik] 비대칭의 discard [diskɑ́:rd] 버리다
antithesis [æntíθəsis] 반대 conspicuous [kənspíkjuəs] 돋보이는
meticulously [mətíkjuləsli] 세심하게
disfigured [disfíɡjərd] 형상이 일그러진 profound [prəfáund] 심오한
provoke [prəvóuk] 불러일으키다 manifest [mǽnəfèst] 명백한

1 지문의 단어 "prominence"와 의미상 가장 유사한 것은?

(A) 일치

(B) 관용

(C) 명성

(D) 붕괴

2 지문에 따르면, 종교 개혁 이전에 종교 예술은

(A) 성경을 읽을 수 없는 사람들을 가르치기 위해 사용되었다

(B) 장식적인 목적으로 교회에 의해 요청되었다

(C) 오직 성서를 연구함으로써만 이해될 수 있었다

(D) 교회에 의해 제작된 작품에 한정되었다

3 3단락에 따르면, 반 군주제주의자들이 _____ 에 대응하여 로코 코를 발전시켰다.

(A) 당시 왕의 방탕한 태도

(B) 베르사유 궁을 장식할 필요성

(C) 일반적으로 용인된 유럽 정체성의 부재

(D) 국가 양식으로서의 바로크 양식의 채택

4 지문의 단어 "outset"과 의미상 가장 유사한 것은?

(A) 변덕

(B) 개요

(C) 고려

(D) 시작

5 아래 문장 중 지문 속의 음영된 문장의 핵심 정보를 가장 잘 표현 하고 있는 것은 무엇인가? 오답은 문장의 의미를 현저히 왜곡하 거나 핵심 정보를 빠뜨리고 있다.

(A) 바로크와 로코코의 차이점은 종교적 주제를 다루는 방식이 었다.

(B) 바로크 회화에 표현되었던 긴장이 로코코 작품에는 없었다.

(C) 세부 묘사와 정확성에 주력했던 바로크는 로코코 양식과 매 우 달랐다.

(D) 로코코는 종교적 주제의 엄숙함을 줄임으로써 바로크와 대 조를 이루었다.

6 지문의 단어 "discarded"와 의미상 가장 유사한 것은?

(A) 적합한

(B) 받아들여지지 않는

(C) 분리된

(D) 채택된

7 지문의 단어 "profound"와 의미상 가장 유사한 것은?

(A) 얄팍한

(B) 성의 없는

(C) 깊은

(D) 의기양양한

8 지문의 단어 "provoked"와 의미상 가장 유사한 것은?

(A) 유발했다

(B) 슬퍼했다

(C) 밝혔다

(D) 깎았다

9 지문의 단어 "manifest"와 의미상 가장 유사한 것은?

(A) 숨겨진

(B) 동일한

(C) 칭찬하는

(D) 명백한

10 지시: 주어진 선택지에서 적절한 구를 선택하여 제시된 예술의 종 류에 연결시키시오. **이 문제는 4점이다.**

보기
(A) 로마 가톨릭 교회 부활의 선봉이었다
(F) 학식 있고 글을 읽고 쓸 줄 아는 성직자들에 의해 사용 되는 것으로 계획되었다
바로크 예술
· (C) 균형을 크게 강조했다
· (E) 대중의 관심을 끌기 위해 유명한 인물을 강조했다
· (G) 짙은 색채와 몹시 극적인 디자인을 혼합시켰다
· (H) 처음에는 평범한 르네상스 양식에 대응하여 고안된 이탈리아 예술이었다
로코코 예술
· (B) 공간감과 거룩함을 불러일으키기 위해 유리를 사용 했다
· (D) 일그러진 형상과 조각으로 특징지어졌다
· (I) 주제에 자연에서 가져온 여러 곡선을 적용했다

---

03 Cichlids

p.134

1. (C)	2. (B)	3. (A)
4. (C)	5. (B)	6. (A)
7. (C)	8. (C)	9. (B)
10. (A)-2~3단락, (C)-5단락, (E)-4단락		

1 세계에서 Lake Superior 다음으로 가장 큰 담수 호수인 Lake Victoria에는 놀랄 만큼 다양한 종류의 열대어들이 살고 있는데, 가 장 놀라운 것은 크기가 3센티미터부터 1미터에 이르는 어류 집단인 cichlid 500여 종이다. 서유럽 전체에 총 60여 종만이 살고 있다는 점을 고려해보면 이러한 다양성은 훨씬 더 놀랍다.

2 Lake Victoria는 빙하 형성과 심각한 가뭄 때문에 과거에 여러 번 완전히 말라붙은 적이 있기 때문에, 호수 내 cichlid의 엄청난 범위 의 다양성은 상대적으로 짧은 진화 주기 동안 발달한 것이 틀림없 다. 사실상 호수 바닥에서 채취한 퇴적물 표본은 가장 최근의 빙하

기 말인 12,000년 전만큼 최근에도 호수가 말라붙었었다는 것을 보여준다. 이는 이 지역 고유의 모든 cichlid가 죽어버렸거나 이 지역의 물이 남아 있는 다른 곳으로 도피한 것이 틀림없다는 것을 뜻한다. 살아남은 몇 안 되는 cichlid는 심각한 상황을 견디면서 계속 줄어드는 시내 또는 물웅덩이에 갇혀 있었고, 이러한 환경적 제약은 급속한 종 분화를 방해했을 것이다. 기후가 따뜻해지고 주기적인 비가 마침내 이 지역에 돌아왔을 때, 강물이 차올라 Lake Victoria를 차차 다시 채우기 시작했고 이는 물고기가 다시 한번 호수에 정착하는 것을 가능하게 했다. 아마도 cichlid의 단 하나의 종만을 포함했을 이 선구어종이 오늘날 Lake Victoria에서 발견되는 모든 cichlid 종의 조상이다.

3 이 최초의 물고기는 자원을 놓고 경쟁을 벌이지 않아도 되는 이점을 가졌기 때문에, 급속도로 늘어나 비교적 안정적이고 제약이 없는 새로운 환경을 차지하였다. 처음에는 대부분의 선구어종이 아마도 호수의 가장 좋은 지역에 모여있었을 것이다. ⁴하지만 수가 늘어나면서 동족상잔 분쟁이 불가피하게 일어났고, 많은 cichlid가 무리에서 떨어져 다양한 미소 서식지에서 개별적인 집단을 형성해야 했다. 일부 물고기는 바닥이 바위투성이거나 침적토인 물속 깊이 들어갔고, 다른 물고기는 초목이 풍부한 얕은 물에 자리 잡았다. 이러한 다양한 환경은 각각의 집단이 생태적 지위를 더욱 효과적으로 개척할 수 있도록 습성, 해부학적 구조, 형태에서의 급속한 적응을 필요로 했다. 이러한 새로운 형태로의 급속한 변화는 '적응 방산'으로 알려졌다.

4 cichlid가 이렇게 빨리 분화할 수 있었던 주요 요인 중 하나는 cichlid가 가지고 있는 여러 개의 턱이었다. 대부분의 다른 물고기와는 달리, cichlid의 목에는 인두 기관으로 알려진 뼈로 된 조직이 하나 있는데, 이는 이빨과 매우 유사한 기능을 하는 한편 입안의 이빨은 오히려 손과 유사한 역할을 한다. 인두의 턱은 상당히 민첩한데, 위턱은 위아래로 움직이거나 탈구될 수 있는 반면, 아래턱은 앞뒤로 움직일 수 있다. 인두 기관은 먹이를 먹는 데 사용되기 때문에, 입안의 이빨은 물고기의 음식물을 섭취하는 기능을 방해하지 않으면서 자유롭게 적응할 수 있다. Lake Victoria에서 발견되는 cichlid의 이빨은 삽 모양의 굵은 이빨과 핀셋 모양의 죄는 이빨 같이, 먹는 수단의 다양한 모습으로 변화되어 왔다.

5 그러나 먹는 방식만이 이 물고기의 무수한 종이 발견되는 것을 설명하는 데 필수적인 선택압으로 작용하는 것은 아니다. 급속한 종 분화에 대한 추가적인 원동력 한 가지는 cichlid의 색깔에 따라 제한되는 짝짓기 의식이었다. 수컷이 새끼를 거의, 혹은 아예 돌보지 않고 철마다 여러 번의 짝짓기를 시도하는 종에서는, 암컷의 선택이 강력한 진화적 역할을 할 수 있다. 암컷이 고를 수 있는 짝이 많을 때, 그들은 짝 선택에 있어서 좀 더 까다로워질 수 있다. 한편, 수컷은 엄청난 경쟁을 극복하기 위해 무엇인가 방법을 찾아야 한다. cichlid의 경우에는, 암컷이 알을 낳도록 유혹하기 위해 디자인된 색깔을 이용하는 수컷의 멋진 구애 양식을 발달시켰다. Lake Victoria 지역 고유의 암컷들은 특정한 모습을 가진 짝을 선택하기 때문에, 이는 다른 특징을 선호하는 집단이 같은 지역에서 각각의 종으로 나뉠 가능성을 높여준다.

6 안타깝게도, 이 놀라운 종의 다양성이 줄어들고 있으며, 오늘날에는 250종 이상의 고유종들이 Lake Victoria에서 더는 발견되지 않는다. 1950년대에 영국 식민정부는 야생 생태학자들의 반대에도 불구하고 지역 어장에서 더 큰 물고기를 잡게 할 생각으로, 외래어종인 나일 강 농어를 호수에 들여왔다. 보통 왕성한 포식자로 불리는 나일 강 농어는 6피트, 200파운드까지 거대하고 무겁게 자랄 수 있다. 당시에는 그 거대한 포식자가 수많은 작은 cichlid와 같은 더 조그만 물고기를 먹고 자라서, 그 지역 수산업의 엄청난 성장을 가져올 것이라고 생각되었다. 나일 강 농어는 급속도로 자리 잡았고, cichlid 종의 최소 반이 멸종에 이를 만큼 먹어 치우며 호수의 생태계를 근본적으로 변형시켰다. 현재 cichlid는 Lake Victoria에 사는 물고기 수의 1퍼센트도 되지 않는다.

freshwater[fréʃwɔ̀ːtər] 담수   astonishing[əstániʃiŋ] 놀라운
desiccate[désikèit] 마르게 하다, 건조시키다
endemic[endémik] 지역 고유의   take refuge in ~으로 도피하다
constraint[kənstréint] 제약   deter[ditə́ːr] 방해하다
speciation[spìːʃiéiʃən] 종(種) 분화   colonize[kálənàiz] 정착하다
pioneer[pàiəníər] 선구(先驅) 생물
conspecific[kànspisífik] 같은 종의
internecine[ìntərníːsiːn] 서로 죽이는
inevitably[inévətəbli] 불가피하게
microhabitat[màikrouhǽbitæt] 미소 서식지(미생물·곤충 등의 서식에 적합한 곳)   silt[silt] 침적토
morphology[mɔːrfálədʒi] 형태   niche[nitʃ] 생태적 지위
adaptive radiation 적응 방산(放散)
pharyngeal[fəríndʒiəl] 인두의   apparatus[æ̀pərǽtəs] 기관
ingest[indʒést] 섭취하다   sustenance[sʌ́stənəns] 음식물
scraper[skréipər] 긁는 도구   tweezer[twíːzər] 핀셋
pincher[píntʃər] 죄는 것   requisite[rékwəzit] 필수적인
parenting[pέərəntiŋ] (새끼를) 돌봄, 양육
courtship[kɔ́ːrtʃìp] 구애   entice[intáis] 유혹하다
sympatrically[simpǽtrikəli] 같은 지역에서
indigenous[indídʒənəs] 고유의   perch[pəːrtʃ] 농어

1 지문의 단어 "severe"과 의미상 가장 유사한 것은?

   (A) 변덕스러운
   (B) 불모의
   (C) 가혹한
   (D) 건조한

2 지문의 단어 "deterred"와 의미상 가장 유사한 것은?

   (A) 탄식했다
   (B) 막았다
   (C) 임명했다
   (D) 연장했다

3 지문의 단어 "colonize"와 의미상 가장 유사한 것은?

   (A) 정착하다
   (B) 버리다
   (C) 함께 하다
   (D) 따르다

4 3단락에 따르면, cichlid는 왜 개별적인 집단으로 분리되었는가?

(A) 다른 침입종들로부터의 격렬한 저항에 직면했다.

(B) 호수의 변동하는 수위에 의해 서로에게서 단절되었다.

(C) 증가하는 개체 수가 종 내의 파멸적인 경쟁을 일으켰다.

(D) 호수에 있는 그들의 초기 서식지가 살아남기에 알맞지 않았다.

5 지문의 구 "interfering with"와 의미상 가장 유사한 것은?

(A) 위반하는

(B) 방해하는

(C) 왜곡하는

(D) 희생하는

6 지문의 단어 "requisite"과 의미상 가장 유사한 것은?

(A) 필수적인

(B) 못쓰게 되는

(C) 불쌍한

(D) 고무하는

7 지문의 단어 "entice"와 의미상 가장 유사한 것은?

(A) 성가시게 하다

(B) 유쾌하게 하다

(C) 유혹하다

(D) 되살리다

8 아래 문장 중 지문 속의 음영된 문장의 핵심 정보를 가장 잘 표현하고 있는 것은 무엇인가? 오답은 문장의 의미를 현저히 왜곡하거나 핵심 정보를 빠뜨리고 있다.

(A) Lake Victoria 수컷의 구애 행동의 특수함 때문에, 고유종이 아닌 cichlid는 고유종과 짝짓기를 할 수 없다.

(B) 수컷 cichlid의 구애 행동은 암컷의 교호 반응을 일으키고, 새로운 cichlid 종의 발전으로 이어진다.

(C) 암컷 cichlid는 짝짓기 상대의 특정한 특징을 선택하기 때문에, 한 장소에서 독특한 종이 만들어질 가능성이 더 크다.

(D) 암컷 cichlid는 같은 종의 수컷의 구애 행동에만 반응하기 때문에, 밀접한 관계의 cichlid 종과 이종 교배 없이 공존할 수 있다.

9 지문의 단어 "immense"와 의미상 가장 유사한 것은?

(A) 정확한

(B) 막대한

(C) 경솔한

(D) 난해한

10 **지시:** 지문 요약을 위한 도입 문장이 아래에 주어져 있다. 지문의 가장 중요한 내용을 나타내는 보기 3개를 골라 요약을 완성하시오. 어떤 문장은 지문에 언급되지 않은 내용이나 사소한 정보를 담고 있으므로 요약에 포함되지 않는다. 이 문제는 2점이다.

> Lake Victoria cichlid는 마지막 빙하기 이후 급속한 다양화를 겪었다.

- (A) 호수에 들어가자, cichlid는 경쟁의 부재 덕분에 번성하기 시작했고 다수의 다양한 종으로 빠르게 나뉘었다.
- (C) 암컷 cichlid는 짝을 정선하기 때문에, 수컷들은 암컷의 마음을 끌기 위해 광범위한 색상을 개발해야 했다.
- (E) 여러 개의 턱의 존재로 인해 발생한 cichlid 이빨 구조의 변형은 많은 섭식 적응으로 이어졌다.

(B) cichlid의 신속한 적응의 한 가지 이유는 여러 가지 종류의 먹이를 씹을 수 있는 턱의 기능이었다.

(D) 12,000년 전 Lake Victoria 지역의 모든 cichlid 종은 이미 서로에게서 분리되어 있었다.

(F) Lake Victoria의 빠르게 변화하는 환경에 적응해야 할 필요성은 cichlid의 독특한 진화 패턴이라는 결과를 낳았다.

04 Changes in Lion Populations and Distribution

p.138

1. (D)	2. (C)	3. (D)
4. (B)	5. (D)	6. (D)
7. (B)	8. (C)	9. (A), (C)
10. (A)−1~2단락, (E)−3단락, (F)−4단락		

1 선사 시대에, 사자들은 유럽의 넓은 지역들을 돌아다녔다. 그 시대의 다른 거대 동물들과 마찬가지로 유럽 사자는 마지막 빙하기 동안 엄청난 감소를 겪었고, 약 10,000년 전에 유럽의 사자 개체는 사실상 멸종되었다. [1]과학자들은 예전부터 부족한 먹이 공급이 유럽 사자의 감소를 가져온 단 하나의 이유라고 생각해왔다. 하지만 사냥감이 전보다 덜 흔해지긴 했어도, 화석 기록들은 순록과 사향 소 같이 사자가 좋아하는 먹이 중 일부가 그들의 거대한 고양잇과 포식자가 줄어든 후에도 살아남았음을 보여준다. 이는 사자 감소의 이유들이 이전에 생각했던 것보다 더 복잡할지도 모름을 암시한다. 지금은 먹이 부족과 함께 기후와 식물 생장 변화의 조합이 대부분의 유럽에서의 그들의 멸종으로 이끌었다고 여겨진다. 세계적으로 기후가 따뜻해짐에 따라, 유럽 사자들이 의존했던 거대한 스텝 지대들이 점차 숲으로 대체되었고, 사냥에 이용 가능한 공간을 심각하게 제한하였다. 사용할 수 있는 공간과 먹이가 더 적어서 사자들은 선사 시대의 개체 수를 유지할 수 없었다.

2 하지만 유사 시대 동안 남부 유럽에서 사자를 목격한 기록이 이따금 있는데, 이는 몇몇 지역에 살아남은 개체가 있었거나, 인근 지역에서 새로 유입된 사자들이 있었음을 시사한다. 그리스 역사학자인 Herodotus에 따르면, 페르시아 지휘관 Xerxes가 기원전 5세기에 그리스를 침범했을 때, 그의 짐 나르는 낙타들이 사자에 의해 공격을 당했다. Herodotus는 또한 사자들이 대부분 Achelos와 Nestos 강 사이의 지역에 국한되어 있었다고 지적하는데, 이는 그들의 지리적인 분포가 심각하게 제한되어 있었고 위험에 처한 상태

였다는 것을 보여준다. 그리고 약 이천 년 전부터 유럽 남부의 야생 사자에 대한 기록이 없다. 만약 사자가 정말로 이 지역에서 다시 살게 된 것이라면 그 기간은 짧았고, 그들의 멸종은 알렉산더 대왕과 같은 그리스 지도자 사이의 사냥에 의해, 그리고 그보다 정도는 덜하지만 로마인의 경기장에서 싸울 사자에 대한 수요에 의해 앞당겨진 것이 틀림없다.

3 아프리카와 아시아에서 사자는 현대까지도 상당한 수가 살아남았다. 그리고는 19세기에 아프리카와 아시아의 사자 개체 수의 급격한 감소가 있었다. [6C]주된 이유는 산업 기술의 출현과 인구수의 폭발이었다. [6B]현대의 기계는 사람들로 하여금 인간의 거주, 삼림 관리, 농사를 위해 황무지를 이용할 수 있도록 하였다. 그 결과 인간과 사자의 접촉이 증가했고, [6A]현대의 화기와 화학 성분의 살충제는 놀랍도록 신속하게 사자들을 대량으로 죽이는 것을 더 쉽게 했다. 간단히 말하면, 사자들은 사냥할 공간이 훨씬 더 적었고, 만약 그들이 사람들에 의해 점령된 지역에 들어가면 흔히 총에 맞거나 독살되었다. 1800년과 2000년 사이에 사자 개체 수가 95퍼센트 줄어든 반면, 인구수는 600퍼센트 증가하였다.

4 [8A]세계의 사자 대부분이 현재 아프리카 사하라 사막 이남 지대에 국한되어 있다. 그들은 아대륙에 걸쳐 흩어져 있는 대지 지역에 산다. 아프리카에 남은 약 3만 마리 정도 되는 사자 중에서 많은 사자가 사냥꾼의 밀렵과 농장주에 의한 독살에 의해 여전히 위험에 처해 있다. 아시아에 있는 사자들의 상황은 더 위험하다. 살아남은 유일한 아시아의 사자 개체가 현재 인도의 Gir 사자 보호구역에 살고 있는데, 이곳은 단 몇백 마리의 사자가 사는 곳이다. 보호받는 상태임에도 불구하고, 이 마지막 남은 아시아 사자들은 두 가지 이유로 인해 멸종될 심각한 위험에 처해 있다. [8B]첫째로, 그들은 부유한 인도 왕자에 의해 살아남게 된 단 열두 마리 정도의 사자들의 후손들이다. [8D/9A]그들의 공유된 유전 형질은 그들의 유전자 공급원이 아주 적으며 크게 근친 교배되었다는 의미이다. 근친 교배가 그들을 유전적으로 약하고 질병에 매우 취약하게 만들었을 우려가 있다. 만약 전염병이 이 동물들 안에서 발판을 마련한다면, 많은 사자가 죽을 수 있고, 그들의 수는 회복 불가능한 수준까지 떨어질 것이다. [8D/9C]둘째로, 여전히 공원에 거주하며 가축을 키우는 것에 생계를 의존하는 몇 안 되는 거주자와의 이따금의 충돌이 남아 있다. 사자들이 가축을 잡아먹을 때, 이것은 지역 주민 사이에 사자에 대한 경멸을 일으킨다. 공원에서의 사자의 미래를 보장하기 위해서는, 사자가 먹이로 삼는 야생 유제류의 수를 충분히 유지해야 할 뿐만 아니라 가축들을 보호하려는 진행 중인 노력을 계속할 필요가 있다.

prehistoric[prìːhistɔ́ːrik] 선사 시대의 roam[roum] 돌아다니다
megafauna[mégafɔ̀ːnə] 거대 동물
extinguish[ikstíŋgwiʃ] 멸종시키다 sole[soul] 단 하나의
quarry[kwɔ́ːri] 사냥감 prey[prei] 먹이 feline[fíːlain] 고양이과
steppe[step] 스텝 지대 sighting[sáitiŋ] 목격
tenure[ténjər] 기간, 재임 기간 hasten[héisn] 앞당기다
arena[əríːnə] 경기장 harness[háːrnis] 이용하다
firearm[fáiəràːrm] 화기 poaching[póutʃiŋ] 밀렵
perilous[pérələs] 위험한 sanctuary[sǽŋktʃuèri] 보호구역
heredity[hərédəti] 유전 형질 inbreed[ínbriːd] 근친 교배하다

vulnerable[vʌ́lnərəbl] 취약한
unrecoverable[ʌ̀nrikʌ́vərəbl] 회복 불가능한
resident[rézədənt] 거주자 livelihood[láivlihùd] 생계
livestock[láivstàk] 가축 disdain[disdéin] 경멸
ungulate[ʌ́ŋgjulət] 유제류(소·말처럼 발굽이 있는 동물)

1 1단락에 따르면, 과학자들의 전통적인 관점은 선사 시대 유럽의 사자 개체 수가 _____ 때문에 감소했다는 것이었다.

(A) 다른 거대 포식자와의 경쟁 때문에
(B) 선사 시대 사람들의 남획 때문에
(C) 저체온증과 전염병 때문에
(D) 자양물의 줄어드는 이용 가능성 때문에

2 지문의 단어 "sole"과 의미상 가장 유사한 것은?

(A) 그럴듯한
(B) 주요한
(C) 유일한
(D) 사소한

3 지문의 단어 "status"와 의미상 가장 유사한 것은?

(A) 작용
(B) 기능
(C) 성격
(D) 위치

4 아래 문장 중 지문 속의 음영된 문장의 핵심 정보를 가장 잘 표현하고 있는 것은 무엇인가? 오답은 문장의 의미를 현저히 왜곡하거나 핵심 정보를 빠뜨리고 있다.

(A) 그리스와 로마 시대의 기록은 역사의 짧은 기간만을 나타낸다는 부분적인 이유 때문에 사자가 그 지역을 차지하고 있었는지 아닌지는 알 수 없다.
(B) 그 지역의 어떠한 사자의 점령이라도 오래가지 못했을 것이고, 사자의 감소는 틀림없이 그리스와 로마 스포츠에 의해 촉발되었다.
(C) 사자들이 그 지역을 차지한 후 얼마 되지 않아 그들은 그리스 지도자들에 의해 빠르게 몰살되거나 로마 경기장에서 싸우기 위해 보내졌다.
(D) 사자들의 그 지역 서식은 그들의 개체 수가 그리스인들과 로마인들에 의해 제거되지 않았다면 더 광범위했을 것이다.

5 지문의 단어 "harness"와 의미상 가장 유사한 것은?

(A) 제한하다
(B) 최대화하다
(C) 막다
(D) 이용하다

6 다음 중 3단락에서 인간이 현대의 사자들에 가하는 위협으로 언급된 것이 아닌 것은?

(A) 독극물의 사용
(B) 사람이 살지 않는 지역의 개발
(C) 치솟는 인구

(D) 총기 규제의 완화

7 지문의 단어 "commonly"와 의미상 가장 유사한 것은?

(A) 아마도
(B) 일반적으로
(C) 전하는 바에 따르면
(D) 실제로

8 4단락에 따르면, 다음 중 답할 수 없는 질문은?

(A) 어떤 구체적인 지역이 현재 세계의 사자 대부분을 보유하고 있는가?
(B) Gir 사자들의 조상을 구하는 책임은 누구에게 있었는가?
(C) 사자를 보호하기 위해 아프리카에 이뤄졌던 변화는 무엇인가?
(D) 왜 인도 사자는 여전히 멸종 위기에 처해 있는가?

9 4단락에서 아시아 사자들이 위험에 처한 이유로 언급된 **보기 두 개를 고르시오. 점수를 얻으려면, 답 두 개를 선택해야 한다.**

(A) 그들은 고립된 유전적 계통의 후손들이다.
(B) 그들을 보호하기 위해 만들어진 법규가 무시되고 있다.
(C) 공원의 인간 거주자들의 적대를 직면하고 있다.
(D) 보호구역 안에 그들에게 영향을 주기 쉬운 병이 흔하다.

10 **지시:** 지문 요약을 위한 도입 문장이 아래에 주어져 있다. 지문의 가장 중요한 내용을 나타내는 보기 3개를 골라 요약을 완성하시오. 어떤 문장은 지문에 언급되지 않은 내용이나 사소한 정보를 담고 있으므로 요약에 포함되지 않는다. **이 문제는 2점이다.**

> **시간이 지나면서, 사자들은 개체 수 감소 시기를 겪었다.**
>
> · (A) 한때 사자들이 유럽 대부분의 지역을 돌아다녔지만, 환경 변화가 선사 시대에 그들을 거의 말살시켰고, 그들은 그리스와 로마 시대에 유럽에서 사라졌다.
> · (E) 사자들은 인간들의 활동이 사자들에게 점점 해를 끼치기 시작했던 19세기까지 대부분 아시아와 아프리카에 남아 있었다.
> · (F) 대부분의 사자들은 현재 아프리카 사하라 사막 이남 지대에 살고 있으며, 거의 남아 있지 않은 아시아 사자들은 유전적 고립과 농업 종사자들의 적대감 때문에 특히 취약하다.

(B) 19세기와 20세기 동안, 전 세계의 사자 개체 수는 급격히 감소한 반면 인구 수는 몇 배 증가했다.
(C) 그리스에서의 사자에 관한 소량의 역사 기록에도 불구하고, 고대에 유럽 남부에 사자들이 실제로 다시 살았는지는 불확실한 채로 남아 있다.
(D) 인도의 Gir 보호구역의 아시아 사자들은 거의 필연적인 멸종에 직면했지만, 보존 노력은 그들의 개체 수를 유지 가능한 수준으로 증가시켰다.

Chapter 04 **Reference**

HACKERS **STRATEGY**

p.145

전략 1

Ex 인간의 뇌는 많은 작업을 동시에 수행한다. 그것은 한꺼번에 신체의 기능을 감시하고, 환경을 감지하며, 발화를 생산한다.

perceive [pərsíːv] 감지하다

Ex 생명공학 기업들은 그들의 보고서에서 향상된 기술이 유전자 변형 작물의 심각한 문제점에 대한 해결책이라고 주장한다.

drawback [dróːbæ̀k] 문제점
genetically modified crop 유전자 변형 작물

전략 2

Ex 무역풍은 시간당 11마일에서 13마일의 속도로 대양을 통과하면서, 그것이 통과하는 길에 더 따뜻한 표층수 일부를 옮겨놓고, 서태평양의 해수면에 0.5미터의 차이를 발생시킨다.

trade wind 무역풍   displace [displéis] 옮겨놓다
surface water 표층수   sea level 해수면

Ex 잭슨의 두 번째 임기 동안, 잭슨의 인기 때문에 그의 대항 세력은 휘그당으로 알려지게 된 단체로 통합하였는데, 이는 여당의 이념과 뚜렷이 대조적인 것을 제안한 집단이다.

opponent [əpóunənt] 대항 세력   ruling party 여당
collective [kəléktiv] 집단

Ex 베틀에는 두 가지 종류가 있는데, ground loom(수평으로 된 베틀)과 warp-weighted loom(수직으로 된 베틀)이다. 전자는 북아프리카에서 처음 사용되었다.

loom [luːm] 베틀   the former 전자

Ex 갑각류 동물의 세계는 특이한 모양과 적응의 세계이다. 이 동물들은 딱딱한 외피로 가장 잘 알려졌다.

crustacean [krʌstéiʃən] 갑각류 동물   bizarre [bizáːr] 특이한

Ex 천을 생산하는 과정에서, 벨트는 일부 날실은 들어 올리고 다른 것들은 낮춘다.

harness [háːrnis] 벨트   warp [wɔːrp] (베틀의) 날실

Ex 많은 동물에게 있어서, 한 장소에서 다른 곳으로 신체를 움직이는 것은 가장 중요한 일과 중의 하나이다.

Ex 북반구 지역은 겨울철에 곤충들이 부족해지므로, 먹이를 곤충에 의존하는 식충성 조류들은 적도 근처로 이동해야 한다.

northern latitudes 북반구 지역
insectivorous [ìnsektívərəs] 식충성의   equator [ikwéitər] 적도

Ex Einstein은 연구와 강의를 계속하기 위해 부인 및 두 아들과 함께 1914년에 베를린으로 이주했다. 그곳에서의 불행한 삶 때문에 부인 Mileva는 스위스로 돌아갔다.

전략 3

Ex 선태류 식물은 가장 단순한 식물로 여겨지는데, 부분적으로는 도관이 없는 유일한 식물이기 때문이다. 선태류 식물의 내부에는 물, 필수 광물 및 용해된 당분을 멀리 운반할 어떠한 수단도 없기 때문에 선태류 식물은 일반적으로 꽤 작다. 비록 일부 선태류 식물은 상피를 가지고 있지만, 다른 것들은 그렇지 않고 대신 잎이 무성한 싹의 표면을 통해 물을 직접 흡수한다. 비록 일부 선태류 식물이 건조한 지역에서 잘 견딜지라도, 일반적으로 선태류 식물은 왕성한 성장과 번식을 위해 습한 환경을 필요로 한다.

bryophyte [bráiəfàit] 선태류 식물
nonvascular [nɑnvǽskjulər] 도관이 없는   cuticle [kjúːtikl] 상피층
absorb [æbsɔ́ːrb] 흡수하다   leafy [líːfi] 잎이 무성한   shoot [ʃuːt] 싹

HACKERS STRATEGY **APPLICATION**

p.148

산악 환경에서 삼림이 생존할 수 있는 지리적 한계로 널리 정의된 수목한계선은 위로는 알프스 지방, 아래로는 북쪽 수림대 사이에 존재하는 이행대이다. 수목한계선은 일반적으로 여름 평균 낮 온도가 꽤 선선한 지역에서 나타나기 때문에, 북극해 주변으로 원을 형성하는 북극 수목한계선에서 볼 수 있는 것처럼 적도에 대한, 그리고 고도에 대한 근접성을 기반으로 한 위도 위치가 변동을 거듭할 수 있다. 그러므로 강수량의 감소에도 불구하고, 수목한계선은 적도 지역의 산악지대에서 약간 더 높게 나타나야 한다. 그러나 북미에서는 더 선선한 대기 때문에 이러한 점이지대가 비교적 낮고, 해발 약 3,500미터(11,500피트)에 나타나 인간의 연구를 위한 접근이 더 용이하다. 진행 중인 연구는 수목한계선의 생성을 자극하는 여러 요인이 있다는 것을 보여준다. 생물학적으로 유용한 열에너지의 양에 영향을 미치는 해발고도의 차이는 분명히 나무의 성장을 억제하는 주된 요소이다. 여름 최저 온도는 계절의 길이 또는 식물이 자랄 수 있는 일수를 좌우한다. 지형 또한 한몫하는데, 예를 들면, 온도 변화는 더욱 나은 태양 복사 포화도와 함께 볼록한 남향 산맥에 의해 영향을 받거나 북부 직선 유역에서 강하하는 한랭 전선에 의하여 영향을 받기 때문이다.

timberline[tímbərlàin] 수목한계선
ecotone[ékətòun] 이행대(2개의 생물군집이 접하는 부분)
alpine region 알프스 지방 boreal forest 북쪽 수림대
fluctuate[flʌ́ktʃuèit] 변동을 거듭하다
latitudinal[lætətjú:dənl] 위도의 proximity[prɑksíməti] 근접성
altitude[ǽltətjù:d] 고도 mitigating[mítəgèitiŋ] 감소시키는
precipitation[prisìpətéiʃən] 강수량 transitional zone 점이지대
elevation[èləvéiʃən] 해발고도 thermal energy 열에너지
inhibit[inhíbit] 억제하다 maturation[mæ̀tʃuréiʃən] 성숙
dictate[díkteit] 좌우하다 topography[təpɑ́grəfi] 지형
play a role 한몫을 하다 convex[kɑnvéks] 볼록한
range[reindʒ] 산맥 solar radiation 태양복사
saturation[sæ̀tʃəréiʃən] 포화도 descend[disénd] 강하하다
reach[ri:tʃ] (강의 굽이와 굽이 사이의) 직선 유역

1. 지문의 구 "this transitional zone"이 가리키는 것은?

(A) 적도
(B) 원
(C) 고도
(D) 수목한계선

2. 지문의 단어 "that"이 가리키는 것은?

(A) 미터
(B) 연구
(C) 인간
(D) 요인

HACKERS PRACTICE

p.150

p.150

1. vitamins   2. (cookie cutter) sharks
3. Clamshells 4. Archaeopteryx
5. genes   6. substances 7. barley
8. geysers   9. eggs   10. residents
11. experience 12. flattened surface
13. festivals 14. 1 (D), 2 (C) 15. 1 (A)
16. 1 (B)   17. 1 (B), 2 (A) 18. 1 (A), 2 (C)
19. 1 (D), 2 (D)

VOCABULARY

1 (C)	2 (B)	3 (D)
4 (C)	5 (A)	6 (B)
7 (A)	8 (B)	9 (C)
10 (A), (D)	11 (A)	12 (B), (C)

13 (D)	14 (C), (B)	15 (A)
16 (A), (D)	17 (B)	18 (B), (C), (A)
19 (D), (B), (A)		

1 비타민은 화학적 구조가 다양하고 사용 가능한 에너지를 직접 생산하지는 않지만, 효소로 하여금 탄수화물, 단백질, 지방으로 부터 에너지를 방출할 수 있게 한다. 그것들은 보조효소이거나 보조효소의 필수적인 부분인데, 이는 비타민이 세포 내의 특정 신진대사 작용에서 촉매로 기능한다는 것을 의미한다.

enzyme[énzaim] 효소 coenzyme[kouénzaim] 보조효소
integral[íntigrəl] 필수적인 catalyst[kǽtəlist] 촉매
metabolic[mètəbálik] 신진대사의

2 어두운색을 띤 목과 함께 이용되는 녹색의 발광 세포들은 쿠키 커터 상어들이, 작은 물고기를 흉내 냄으로써, 향유고래와 참치 를 포함한 사냥감을 속일 수 있게 해준다. 이것은 그들이 특유의 오해하게 만드는 표시에 의해 속는 다양한 생물들을 먹을 수 있 게 해준다.

light-emitting[láitimìtiŋ] 발광의 cell[sel] 세포
deceive[disí:v] 속이다 sperm whale 향유고래
imitate[ímiteit] 흉내 내다 consume[kənsú:m] 먹다, 소비하다
fool[fu:l] 속이다 misleading[mìslí:diŋ] 오해하게 만드는
display[displéi] 표시

3 사실상 대합조개를 포함한 모든 쌍각류 연체동물은 보잘것없는 석회질 진주를 만들어낼 수 있지만, 진주층으로 알려진 무지개 빛의 진주층을 포함한 종만이 상업적인 가치를 지닌 진주를 만 들어낼 수 있다. 대합조개의 껍질은 진주층을 갖고 있지 않다. 따라서 그것들의 진주는 광택이 부족하며 상대적으로 가치가 작다.

virtually[və́:rtʃuəli] 사실상 bivalved[báivæ̀lvd] 쌍각류의
mollusk[mɑ́ləsk] 연체동물 calcareous[kælkɛ́əriəs] 석회질의
of sorts 보잘것없는 iridescent[ìrədésnt] 무지개 빛의, 진주색의
nacre[néikər] 진주층 mother-of-pearl[mʌ́ðərəvpə̀:rl] 진주층
luster[lʌ́stər] 광택

4 깃털은 조류의 특징적인 신체 부위이므로 시조새를 조류로 보는 사람들은 주요 근거로 깃털에 기대는데, 이는 이 돌출부가 조류 에게 독점적이기 때문이다. 이들은 세부 조사에 따르면 대부분 의 파충류는 가지고 있지도 않은 그것의 쇄골이 현대의 조류와 유사한 차골로 융합되었다고 주장한다.

diagnostic[dàiəgnǽstik] 특징적인, 진단의 avian[éiviən] 조류의
resort to ~에 기대다 protrusion[proutrú:ʒən] 돌출부
exclusive[iksklú:siv] 독점적인
ornithological[ɔ̀:rnəθəlάdʒikəl] 조류학의
clavicle[klǽvikl] 쇄골 wishbone[wíʃbòun] 차골
latter-day[lǽtərdèi] 현대의

5 인간은 2만 개에서 2만 5천 개 사이의 유전자를 지니는데, 이는 생물학적 작용을 수행하도록 세포들을 부호화하는 염색체의 일부를 형성하는 뉴클레오타이드의 구별되는 배열이다. 이것들은 특정한 질병에 대한 민감성, 키의 잠재력, 그리고 머리색과 같은 특성들을 결정한다. 유전자들은 변형에 의해 영구적으로 바뀔 수도 있는데, 변형은 유전되거나 환경적인 요인에 의해 일어날 수 있다.

gene[dʒiːn] 유전자　distinct[distíŋkt] 구별되는, 뚜렷한
sequence[síːkwəns] 배열
nucleotide[njúːkliətàid] 뉴클레오타이드(핵산의 구성 성분)
chromosome[króuməsoum] 염색체
encode[inkóud] 부호화하다
susceptibility[səsèptəbíləti] 민감성, (병에) 걸리기 쉬움
permanently[pə́ːrmənəntli] 영구적으로　alter[ɔ́ːltər] 바꾸다
mutation[mjuːtéiʃən] 변형, 돌연변이
inherit[inhérit] 유전되다, 물려받다　factor[fǽktər] 요인

6 생물은 몸통이 흐늘흐늘한 아주 작은 원생생물에서부터 거대한 골격을 가진 큰 생물에 이르기까지 다양하다. 생물은 매우 다양한 물질로 이루어져 있으며, 그것들은 모두 생존을 위해 정선된 것들이다.

protist[próutist] 원생생물　subsistence[səbsístəns] 생존

7 고대 메소포타미아 사람들은 주로 농업에 기반을 두었던 발전된 경제 덕분에 고정된 정착지를 발달시킨 최초의 인류 중 하나였다. 수렵 채집 생활 방식에 의존했던 이전의 사회들과는 대조적으로, 메소포타미아 문명은 주요 식량원으로 보리를 경작했다. 농경법이 발전하면서, 수확량의 잉여가 뒤따랐고, 잉여 수확물은 제품과 서비스에 대한 지불 수단으로 이용되었다. 점차, 작은 마을들은 인근 지역들과 무역 관계를 수립한 소도시로 변모했다. 그 주요 산물이 지역에 믿을 만한 경제 자원을 부여하면서 문화는 곧 융성했다.

settlement[sétlmənt] 정착지　advanced[ədvǽnst] 발전된
primarily[praimérəli] 주로　agriculture[ǽgrikʌltʃər] 농업
hunter-gatherer[hʌntərgǽðərər] 수렵 채집
civilization[sìvələzéiʃən] 문명　cultivate[kʌ́ltiveit] 경작하다
barley[báːrli] 보리　farming method 농경법
surplus[sə́ːrpləs] 잉여, 과잉　ensue[insúː] 뒤따르다
harvest[háːrvist] 수확물　employ[implɔ́i] 이용하다
transform[trænsfɔ́ːrm] 변모하다　flourish[flə́ːriʃ] 융성하다
staple[stéipl] 주요 산물　endow[indáu] 부여하다

8 간헐천은 지구 표면의 분화구로부터 발달하는 희귀한 자연 지형이다. 이러한 분화구들은 물줄기와 증기를 공중으로 내뿜을 수 있고, 그 분출의 높이는 1.5미터에서 거의 100미터까지에 이른다. 간헐천은 강하게 압축된 물과 증기를 배출하는 지면의 갈라진 틈에서뿐만 아니라, 뜨거운 암석들과 지하 저수지의 결합이 있는 곳에서도 형성된다. 대부분의 간헐천은 드물게 그리고 예측할 수 없게 분출하지만, 옐로스톤 국립공원의 'Old Faithful'

과 같은 몇몇의 간헐천은 규칙적인 분출로 알려져 있다. 마찬가지로 옐로스톤에 있는 'Clepsydra'와 같은 다른 것들은, 거의 지속적인 분출 상태를 유지한다.

geyser[gáizər] 간헐천　feature[fíːtʃər] 지형, 특색
vent[vent] 분화구　eject[idʒékt] 내뿜다
expulsion[ikspʌ́lʃən] 분출　combination[kàːmbinéiʃən] 결합
reservoir[rézərvwɑːr] 저수지　fissure[fíʃər] 갈라진 틈, 균열
deliver[dilívər] 배출하다　pressurize[préʃəraiz] 압축하다
discharge[distʃɑ́ːrdʒ] 분출하다
infrequently[infríːkwəntli] 드물게
unpredictably[ʌnpridíktəbli] 예측할 수 없게
eruption[irʌ́pʃən] 분출, 폭발

9 인공수정이 성공적으로 이루어졌던 어류 종의 경우에, 인공수정 과정은 때때로 정자와 난자의 성숙을 유도하기 위해 주로 포유류의 호르몬과 연어의 뇌하수체 추출물인 다양한 혼합물의 주입을 필요로 한다. 주입되는 물질의 양과 종류는 사용되는 어류의 크기와 종에 좌우된다. 난자가 수정될 준비가 되면, 복부에 가해진 압력에 의해 추출되어 작은 용기에 담긴다. 정자도 수컷에게서 유사하게 추출되고, 수정 작용을 수행하기 위해 정자와 난자가 합쳐진다. 제대로 되었을 경우, 보통 높은 비율의 난자가 수정된다. 이것들은 부화할 때까지 산소를 공급받고 배양된다.

artificial fertilization 인공수정　injection[indʒékʃən] 주입
compound[kámpaund] 혼합물　chiefly[tʃíːfli] 주로
mammalian[məméiliən] 포유류의
pituitary[pitjúːətèri] 뇌하수체의　extract[ikstrǽkt] 추출물
induce[indjúːs] 유도하다　sperm[spərm] 정자　egg[eg] 난자
strip[strip] 추출하다　abdomen[ǽbdəmən] 복부
effect[ifékt] 수행하다　fecundation[fìːkəndéiʃən] 수정 작용
inseminate[insémənèit] 수정시키다
aerate[ɛ́əreit] 산소를 공급하다　incubate[ínkjubèit] 배양하다

10 캘리포니아 골드러시는 한 지역 신문이 금 덩어리 한 개의 발견을 보도한 후 1848년에 시작되었다. 당시에, 샌프란시스코에는 겨우 1,000명의 사람들만이 살았지만, 2년 사이에 25,000명의 거주민들로 빠르게 불어났고, 대부분은 조잡하게 지어진 판잣집이나 텐트에서 살았다. 골드러시는 해외로부터의 꾸준한 이주도 발생시켰다. 예를 들어, 캘리포니아 주에 있는 중국인의 수는 1849년의 약 50명에서 1876년 무렵에는 150,000명보다 많게 증가했다. 처음에, 그들은 값싼 노동력의 원천으로 환영받았지만, 쉽게 채굴되는 금이 희귀해지자, 현지 광부들은 그들과 함께 일했던 중국인들과 다른 외국인들에게 등을 돌리기 시작했는데, 그들을 나라에 대한 충성이 없다는 이유로 고발하고 미국의 부를 빼앗는다고 비난했다.

nugget[nʌ́git] 덩어리　populate[pá:pjuleit] 살다
swell[swel] 불어나다　rudely[rúːdli] 조잡하게
construct[kənstrʌ́kt] 짓다, 건설하다　shanty[ʃǽnti] 판잣집
immigration[ìmigréiʃən] (다른 나라에 살러 오는) 이주
extract[ikstrǽkt] 채굴하다　scarce[skers] 희귀한, 부족한
turn on 등을 돌리다, ~를 공격하다　accuse[əkjúːz] 고발하다

allegiance[əlíːdʒəns] 충성 blame[bleim] 비난하다

11 기억 연구자들에 의한 최근의 연구는 서파수면의 중요성을 강조했는데, 이것은 보통 꿈을 꾸는 것과 잠결에 걸어 다니는 것에 관련된 단계이다. 그들은 그것이 최적의 기억 강화에 필수적이라는 것을 알아냈는데, 이것은 기억을 장기 저장고에 할당될 수 있는 심상으로 변형시키는 과정이다. 이 작용에서, 뇌는 경험에 능동적으로 관여하고 그것을 손쉽게 상기될 수 있는 형태로 부호화한다. 하지만, 이러한 회상들은 시간이 지나면서 불안정해지고 강화를 필요로 할 수 있는데, 이는 급속 안구 운동 수면 주기에 발생하며, 더욱 긴 수면이 더욱 강한 기억을 만들어낸다는 것을 시사한다.

slow-wave sleep 서파수면(느린 뇌파가 나타나는 깊은 수면)
sleepwalk[slíːpwɔːk] 잠결에 걸어 다니다
optimal[ɑ́ptəməl] 최적의 consolidation[kənsɑ̀lədéiʃən] 강화
representation[rèprizentéiʃən] 심상, 묘사
allocate[ǽləkeit] 할당하다 storage[stɔ́ːridʒ] 저장고, 보관
recall[rikɔ́ːl] 상기하다 recollection[rèkəlékʃən] 회상
destabilize[diːstéibəlaiz] 불안정하게 만들다
enhancement[inhǽnsmənt] 강화
rapid-eye-movement 급속 안구 운동, 렘수면(REM)

12 북부 캘리포니아의 미웍 부족은 하나의 획일적인 집단을 나타내지 않는데 이는 그들이 각기 다른 기후를 가진 다양한 생태계에서 거주했기 때문이고, 이는 구별되는 특징들을 낳았다. 예를 들어, 따뜻한 지역에서 살았던 부족들은 옷을 거의 걸치지 않았던 반면, 더 추운 지역의 부족들은 보통 외투와 레깅스를 입었고, 특히 몹시 추운 날씨나 밤에는, 담요가 의복의 대체물로 기능했을 것이다. 그러나 때때로 문화적인 획일성은 풍습을 통해 예증되었는데, 예를 들어 의도적으로 유아의 머리를 판자에 묶는 널리 퍼진 관행에서, 판자는 머리의 뒤쪽을 꽉 눌러서 납작해진 표면을 만들었다. 미웍 부족은 보편적으로 이 특징을 매력적으로 여겼다.

represent[rèprizént] 나타내다 uniform[júːnifɔːrm] 획일적인
inhabit[inhǽbit] 거주하다 ecosystem[íːkousistəm] 생태계
vary[vέri] 각기 다르다 climate[kláimət] 기후
distinguishing[distíŋgwiʃiŋ] 구별되는 tribe[traib] 부족
don[dɑːn] 입다 frigid[frídʒid] 몹시 추운
serve as ~으로 기능하다 substitute[sʌ́bstituːt] 대체물
attire[ətáiər] 의복 exemplify[igzémplifai] 예증하다, 예가 되다
custom[kʌ́stəm] 풍습, 관습 practice[prǽktis] 관행, 실행
intentionally[inténʃənli] 의도적으로 bind[baind] 묶다
rear[rir] 뒤쪽 flatten[flǽtn] 납작하게 하다
universally[jùːnivə́ːrsəli] 보편적으로

13 고대 그리스에서 주요 종교 전통은 옥수수 파종과 수확, 포도의 생산, 도취와 관련 있는 구세신인 디오니소스를 중심으로 전개되었다. 후원자들은 그를 기리며 계절마다 축제를 벌였는데 그 중 가장 중요한 것은 디오니소스 축제로 알려진 가을에 열리는 포도주 시음 의식이었고, 이는 합창곡의 시와 찬가 암송을 포함

했다. 취객들이 그들의 저명한 신에게 디오니소스 찬양가로 불리는 송시를 노래하면, 사제가 인간과 신 사이에서 상징적인 대화로 이에 답창했다. 상류층과 하류층에서 두루 얻은 인기에 힘입어, 기원전 6세기경 코린트 왕은 디오니소스 찬양가 대회를 만들어서 모조 드라마를 만들고 상연하기 위해 엄선된 시인들을 초대했다. 처음으로 연극이 그 바탕을 이루고 있던 종교의식에서 해방되어 충분히 발달된 예술작품으로 변모하였다. 이러한 변화하는 극예술 환경은 일반 대중의 견해를 바꾸었고, 예술 형식의 진보를 시작하게 한 새로운 일반 대중의 관심을 불러일으켰다.

intoxication[intɑ̀ksikéiʃən] 도취, 취함 wine tasting 포도주 시음
celebration[sèləbréiʃən] 의식, 축전 choric[kɔ́ːrik] 합창곡의
hymn[him] 찬가 reveler[révlər] 취객, 술 마시고 흥청대는 사람
chant[tʃænt] 노래하다 ode[oud] 송시
dithyramb[díθəræmb] 디오니소스 찬양가
illustrious[ilʌ́striəs] 저명한 priest[priːst] 제
full-fledged[fúlflèdʒd] 충분히 발달된
attitude[ǽtitjùːd] 견해 trigger[trígər] 시작하게 하다
newfound[njúːfàund] 새로운, 새로 발견된
refinement[riːfáinmənt] 진보, 정제

14 무수한 종류의 박테리아가 해양 전체에 걸쳐 발견되지만, 박테리아는 해수면과 해저에 가장 많이 밀집해 있으며 중간층에는 가장 적게 존재한다. 그 이유는 박테리아가 성장하는 곳인 분해 중인 유기 물질의 분포가 이 깊이에 가장 밀집되어 있기 때문이다. 해양 박테리아는 그것들이 해양 식물의 기본적인 영양원이 되어 해양 동물을 위한 먹이의 원천을 형성하는 수용성 물질로의 유기 물질의 분해를 돕는 한에서는 몹시 중요하다.

countless[káuntlis] 무수한 distribution[dìstrəbjúːʃən] 분포
decompose[dìːkəmpóuz] 분해하다 organic[ɔːrgǽnik] 유기의
thrive[θraiv] 성장하다, 번성하다 cluster[klʌ́stər] 밀집시키다
extremely[ikstríːmli] 몹시 insofar[ìnsəfɑ́ːr] ~하는 한에서는
decomposition[diːkɑ̀mpəzíʃən] 분해
water-soluble[wɔ́ːtərsɑ̀ljubl] 수용성의

1 지문의 단어 "which"가 가리키는 것은?

(A) 해저
(B) 이유
(C) 분포
(D) 유기 물질

2 지문의 단어 "they"가 가리키는 것은?

(A) 물
(B) 깊이
(C) 박테리아
(D) 물질

15 많은 사람에게 단지 음식 재료로 생각되는 옥수수는 사실 미국과 그 외 여러 나라에서도 널리 이용되는 많은 제품의 주성분이

기도 하다. 총 연간 생산량의 약 60퍼센트 정도인 대부분의 옥수수는 소와 돼지 같은 가축의 사료로 가공된다. 대략 그것의 8퍼센트가 화학 감미료나 옥수수 전분 등의 첨가제에 사용되는 반면, 겨우 약 3퍼센트만이 통 옥수수알이나 시리얼의 형태로 사람들이 섭취할 수 있게 마련된다. 옥수수 연간 생산량의 나머지는 수출되거나 휘발유보다 훨씬 오염을 덜 일으키는 연료인 알코올 에탄올을 만들기 위해 발효된다.

purely[pjúərli] 단지　**dietary**[dáiətèri] 음식의
basis[béisis] 주성분　**process**[práses] 가공하다
consumption[kənsʌ́mpʃən] 섭취, 소비　**ear**[iər] 옥수수알
roughly[rʌ́fli] 대략　**sweetener**[swíːtnər] 감미료
additive[ǽdətiv] 첨가제　**output**[áutpùt] 생산량
ferment[fərmént] 발효시키다　**fuel**[fjúːəl] 연료

1 지문의 단어 "it"이 가리키는 것은?

　(A) 옥수수
　(B) 사료
　(C) 섭취
　(D) 시리얼

16 발전용 원자로에서 나오는 핵폐기물의 궁극적인 환경적 영향은 추정하는 것이 불가능하지만, 분명한 것은 원자로의 봉쇄가 중대한 생태상의 과제를 야기한다는 것이다. 핵 부산물은 수천 년 동안 계속 높은 방사성을 가지기 때문에, 조금의 누출이라도 주변 지역이 영구적으로 버려지는 것을 불가피하게 할 수 있다. 전통적인 저장 방법은 보통 단기 및 장기 저장소를 이용하는 두 가지 과정을 필요로 한다. 임시적으로, 다 쓴 핵연료는 현장의 웅덩이나 그것의 누출을 막도록 고안된 특수한 통에 보관될 수 있다. 하지만, 사용 가능한 공간이 가득 차면, 위험한 물질은 지하수와의 어떤 접촉으로부터든 보호하기 위해 공학적 방벽과 함께 자연적인 지질학적 분리를 이용하는 지하 시설로 옮겨져야 한다.

eventual[ivéntʃuəl] 궁극적인, 최종적인　**nuclear**[núːkliər] 핵의
electricity-generating reactor 발전용 원자로
containment[kəntéinmənt] 원자로의 봉쇄, 억제
ecological[ìːkəláːdʒikl] 생태상의, 생태계의
byproduct[báiprʌ̀ːdəkt] 부산물
radioactive[rèidiouǽktiv] 방사성을 가진　**leakage**[líːkidʒ] 누출
abandon[əbǽndən] 버리다　**indefinitely**[indéfinətli] 영구적으로
conventional[kənvénʃənl] 전통적인
necessitate[nəsésiteit] 필요로 하다
repository[ripáːzətɔ̀ːri] 저장소　**onsite**[ɔ́ːnsáit] 현장의
specialized[spéʃəlaizd] 특수한, 전문화된　**cask**[kæsk] 통
escape[iskéip] 누출　**hazardous**[hǽzərdəs] 위험한
geological[dʒìːəláːdʒikəl] 지질학적인　**isolation**[àisəléiʃən] 분리
in conjunction with ~과 함께　**engineered**[èndʒinírd] 공학적인

1 지문의 단어 "its"가 가리키는 것은?

　(A) 과정
　(B) 연료
　(C) 웅덩이

　(D) 통

17 'Achillea millefolium'이라고도 불리는 서양톱풀은, 수천 년 동안 약초로 이용되어 왔다. 그것 특유의 지혈시키는 속성들은 고대부터 인정받아 왔으며, 최근에 영양학자들은 그것이 미량 원소의 원천임을 밝혔다. 서양톱풀은 '폴리페놀'이라고 불리는 유기 화학 물질을 함유하며, 이것은 식물을 해로운 박테리아나 다른 병원체로부터 보호한다. 낮은 농도에서, 이러한 화합물들은 점막을 불침투성으로 만들 수 있어, 미생물의 침투를 막는다. 그것들은 또한 효과적인 효소 억제제로서의 역할을 하며, 이것은 해로운 병원체의 번식이나 성장을 막을 수 있다. 게다가, 서양톱풀의 생잎은 약초 재배자들에 의해 사용되며, 이들은 막자 사발과 막자로 그것들을 빻아 약을 상처 위에 직접 바른다. 그것들은 또한 뜨거운 물에 10분에서 15분간 담가지면 아로마 차를 만드는 데에도 사용될 수 있다.

yarrow[jǽrou] 서양톱풀　**medicinal**[mədísinl] 약의, 약효가 있는
millennium[miléniəm] 천 년
astringent[əstríndʒənt] 지혈시키는
nutritionist[nutríʃənist] 영양학자
micronutrient[màikrounjúːtriənt] 미량 원소
harmful[háːrmfl] 해로운　**pathogen**[pǽθədʒən] 병원체
concentration[kàːnsntréiʃən] 농도
compound[káːmpaund] 화합물　**mucous membrane** 점막
impermeable[impə́ːrmiəbl] 불침투성의
penetration[pènitréiʃən] 침투, 관통
microorganism[màikrouɔ́ːrgənizəm] 미생물
enzyme[énzaim] 효소　**inhibitor**[inhíbitər] 억제제
obstruct[əbstrʌ́kt] 막다　**reproduction**[rìːprədʌ́kʃən] 번식
herbalist[hə́ːrbəlist] 약초 재배자　**grind**[graind] 빻다, 갈다
mortar[mɔ́ːrtər] 막자사발　**pestle**[pésl] 막자
poultice[póultis] 약　**wound**[wuːnd] 상처　**steep in** ~에 담그다

1 지문의 구 "these compounds"가 가리키는 것은?

　(A) 미량 원소
　(B) 폴리페놀
　(C) 해로운 박테리아
　(D) 병원체

2 지문의 단어 "They"가 가리키는 것은?

　(A) 생잎
　(B) 약초 재배자
　(C) 약
　(D) 상처

18 영적 세계와의 교감은 개인 차원에서 일어날 수 있고, 이는 영계(靈界)와의 교류를 구하는 의식에서 나타나는데, 이 의식에서는 한 명의 젊은 남성(드물게 여성)이 단독 철야 기도에 보내지고 단식과 기도문 암송을 통해 초자연적 세계를 방문하게 되는 꿈 같은 최면 상태에 빠지게 되며, 이 초자연적 세계의 특질은 예술에 반복해서 나타난다. 대부분의 경우, 이 특이한 상태는 초자연

적인 반응을 일으키게 되고 그 사이 참가자는 보통 조언을 해주고 노래를 가르쳐 주는 수호신으로 여겨지는 동물과 중요한 상호작용을 하게 된다. 일단 의식이 끝나면, 그는 현실 세계로 돌아와서 바위의 벽, 동물 가죽, 또는 나무에 그림을 그림으로써 이러한 환영을 재현하려고 한다. 미적 우수성은 각 예술가의 재능에 따라 다양했지만, 경험을 그림으로 나타내는 것은 이 의식의 핵심요소이며 부족의 종교와 속세의 특징 간의 완전한 융합이 이루어질 수 있게 한다.

spiritual [spírit∫uəl] 영적인 manifest [mǽnəfèst] 나타나다
vision quest 영계(靈界)와의 교류를 구하는 의식(북미 인디언 부족에서 행해진 남자의 의례) solitary [sálətèri] 단독의, 혼자 하는
vigil [víd3əl] 철야 기도 fasting [fǽstiŋ] 단식
trance [træns] 최면 상태 evoke [ivóuk] 일으키다, 불러내다
metaphysical [mètəfízikəl] 초자연적인, 형이상학적인
partaker [pɑːrtéikər] 참가자 aesthetic [esθétik] 미의
integration [ìntəgréi∫ən] 융합 temporal [témpərəl] 속세의

1 지문의 단어 "this"가 가리키는 것은?

(A) 교감
(B) 세계
(C) 차원
(D) 철야 기도

2 지문의 구 "this unusual state"가 가리키는 것은?

(A) 단식
(B) 기도문
(C) 최면 상태
(D) 상호작용

19 피카소와 세잔의 영향력 있는 작품들이 예시가 되는 입체파는, 20세기의 가장 의미 있는 예술 운동 중 하나로 여겨진다. 그것은 1900년대 초기 짧은 기간의 이상적인 표상으로 여겨지며, 이 시기에 현대 예술, 문학, 그리고 건축이 그것들의 기본 원칙을 발달시켰다. 입체파 예술에서, 대상은 배경으로부터 추출, 해체되어, 다양한 원근과 각진 면들을 강조했던 추상적인 형태로 재구성되었다. 여러 시기로 나눠지는 입체파는, 처음에는 파리 지역의 몇몇 예술가들로만 한정되어 있었는데 이들은 피카소의 1907년 작품인 'Les Demoiselles d'Avignon'에서 신봉된 기하학적인, 단순화된 형태를 모방했다. 새로운 양식들이 이후 몇 년간 출현했으며, 거기서 화가들은 대상들을 제대로 형상화하는 대신 완전한 추상화에 파고들었고, 이러한 요소들을 작품으로부터 완전히 전이시켰으며, 단기 예술 분파를 만들었다. 오르피스트로 알려진 이러한 예술가들은, 밝은 색상의 사용을 선호했으며, 그들 이전 화가들의 단색 기법에 강하게 반대했다. 그들의 추상적인 구조와 선명한 색상의 결합은 거대한 기하학적 형태와 색 대비로의 전반적인 전환을 촉발했다. 1925년부터, 입체파는 예술 운동의 최전선에 있던 예술가들이 기하학적 추상과 초현실주의를 포함한 기발한 표현 방법을 탐구하기 시작하면서 하락세를 겪었다.

cubism [kjúːbizəm] 입체파 exemplify [igzémplifai] 예시를 들다
representation [rèprizentéi∫ən] 표상
fundamental [fʌ̀ndəméntl] 기본 원칙, 근본
extract [ikstrǽkt] 추출하다
deconstruct [dìːkənstrʌ́kt] 해체하다
reassemble [rìːəsémbl] 재구성하다
abstract [ǽbstrækt] 추상적인 emphasize [émfəsaiz] 강조하다
perspective [pərspéktiv] 원근, 관점 angled [ǽŋgld] 각진
geometric [d3ìːəmétrik] 기하학적인 espouse [ispáuz] 신봉하다
delve into ~에 파고들다
dislocate [dísloukeit] 전이시키다, 위치를 바꾸다
splinter group 분파 Orphist [ɔ́ːrfist] 오르피스트(입체파의 한 분파)
monochromatic [mànəkroumǽtik] 단색의
predecessor [prédəsesər] 이전 것, 전임자
prompt [prɑːmpt] 촉발하다 contrast [kɑntrǽst] 대비하다
forefront [fɔ́ːrfrənt] 최전선 novel [nɑ́ːvl] 기발한
avenue [ǽvənuː] 방법 surrealism [səríːəlizəm] 초현실주의

1 지문의 단어 "that"이 가리키는 것은?

(A) 원근
(B) 면
(C) 시기
(D) 예술가

2 지문의 구 "these elements"가 가리키는 것은?

(A) 형태
(B) 양식
(C) 화가
(D) 대상

HACKERS **TEST**

01 Placebo Effect

p.158

1. (D)	2. (B)	3. (C)
4. (A)	5. (C)	6. (D)
7. (D)	8. (C)	9. (D)
10. (C)-3단락, (D)-2단락, (F)-4단락		

1 '위약'이라는 단어의 어원은 '기쁘게 해드리겠습니다'라는 라틴어 동사에서 유래된 것으로 전통적인 의미에서 위약은 걱정하는 환자를 안정시키기 위해서, 혹은 의사가 투여하기를 꺼리는 알약을 요구하는 고집스러운 환자를 달래기 위해서 주는 가짜 약이다. [2]위약은 약물 성분을 전혀 포함하고 있지 않으므로 엄밀히 말하면 약물로 분류되지 않는다. 하지만 환자는 질병을 완화하거나 심지어 고치기 위해서 단순한 설탕 덩어리 이상의 무언가가 처방되었다고 믿게 되

며, 이는 그것이 궁극적인 회복에 대한 환자의 믿음의 힘과 결부된 암시의 힘과 더욱 큰 관련이 있다는 것을 보여준다.

2 위약을 나누어 주는 것에 찬성하는 의사들은 환자에 대한 그들의 실제 진단보다 더 강한 효과를 내는 것은 환자에게 특정한 질병이 극복될 수 있다고 안심시켜주는 처방전이라고 확신한다. 연구들은 치료를 받고자 하는 환자 중 90퍼센트에 달하는 사람들이 신체 자체의 치유 능력의 범주 안에서 회복될 수 있는 자기 제어 방식의 질환을 겪고 있다는 것을 보여줌으로써 이러한 확신을 뒷받침한다. 위약의 효능을 지지하는 연구자들과 의사들 모두 위약을 효과 있게 만드는 사람의 마음에 달린 심리적인 힘에 대해서는 아직도 확인되지 않은 채로 남아 있는 것이 많다는 것을 시인하지만, 분명히 가짜 약에 대한 환자의 전적인 신뢰를 얻어내는 의사의 능력을 포함한 환자의 믿음과 의사의 태도는 함께 중요한 역할을 하는 것으로 보인다. 이러한 것들은 위약의 효과를 극대화하는 데 있어서 모두 필수적인 요소이다.

3 미국 식품의약청(FDA)의 기록에 따르면, 임상 시험을 통해서 위약을 배당받은 환자의 35퍼센트가 장기적으로 증상이 완화되었다고 말하였고, 이는 질병에 대항하는 데 있어서 상당히 높은 성공률로 연구자들을 놀라게 했다. 이러한 결과에 대한 분석 및 설명은 환자가 사전에 알지 못하게 위약을 투여하는 간단한 절차가 직접적이고 종종 이로운 결과를 가져온다는 것을 나타내지만, 이런 보고서들이 보여주는 결과에도 불구하고 대부분의 의학 연구자는 이러한 치료가 의사-환자 간의 관계 규범을 위반한다는 점을 들어 강력하게 반대한다. 의료 윤리 규범은 신뢰의 개념이 최우선시 되어야 한다는 입장을 내세우고 의사는 진실을 전달하도록 요구받지만, 가끔은 환자들의 최선의 이익을 위해 행동하면서도 어떻게 치료를 받고 있는 사람들에게 전적으로 진실될 수 있을지에 대한 딜레마에 직면한다. 다수의 연구자는 일부 의사들이 특정 증상을 치료하는 데 사용하는 임의적인 방책의 타당성을 문제 삼고 있다. 화학 요법과 같은 더욱 적극적인 치료를 받기를 꺼리는 환자들을 설득하기 위한 목적으로 더욱 낙관적인 상황을 보여주려는 유혹에 빠지는 개업 의사들의 예에서와 같이, 거짓된 정보는 위약과 반대의 방향으로 작용한다고 보고되는데, 돌이켜보면 환자들은 만일 그들의 암의 진전도와 몸의 실제 상태를 알았더라면, 아마도 이러한 치료를 받기를 선택하지 않았을 것이다.

4 이어진 연구는 임상 검사가 끝난 검증된 의약품 대신에 위약을 투여받았다는 것을 알게 된 일부 환자들이 의사들에게 형성되어 있던 신뢰가 깨진 경우, 그리고 반대되는 'nocebo' 효과가 유발된 경우의 사례들을 보고하고 있다. 이는 환자의 건강상태를 악화시켜서 어떤 경우에는 사망으로 이어지는 요인을 촉진하기도 한다. [9]의료과실 소송의 대상이 될 가능성 때문에 치료 행위에서 위약을 실제로 사용하는 경우는 점점 더 드물어지고 있으며, 위약은 이제 실험 대상자들이 치료의 이점과 발생 가능한 위험성에 대하여 사전에 통지를 받았을 만한 연구에서만 거의 배타적으로 사용되고 있다. 이와 함께 충분한 설명에 입각한 동의가 준수되었는지를 확인하기 위한 원칙과 방침들이 이행되고 있으며, 이는 위약 효과라고 일컬어지는 것에 대한 더욱 깊은 연구의 필요성과 함께 의학적 연구 및 실행을 위한

규범과 보조를 같이 한다.

etymology [ètəmálədʒi] 어원　**placebo** [pləsí:bou] 위약(僞藥)
derive [diráiv] 유래하다　**imitation** [ìmətéiʃən] 가짜의, 모조의
anxious [ǽŋkʃəs] 걱정하는　**placate** [pléikeit] 달래다
persistent [pərsístənt] 고집스런
administer [ædmínistər] 투여하다
pharmacological [fà:rməkəládʒikəl] 약물의
categorize [kǽtəgəràiz] 분류하다
medicament [mədíkəmənt] 약물
prescribe [priskráib] 처방하다　**alleviate** [əlí:vièit] 완화시키다
suggestion [səgdʒéstʃən] 암시　**ultimate** [ʌ́ltəmət] 궁극적인
medical practitioner 의사　**dole** [doul] 나누어 주다
diagnosis [dàiəgnóusis] 진단　**conviction** [kənvíkʃən] 확신
vouch [vautʃ] 지지하다　**concede** [kənsí:d] 시인하다
unverified [ʌnvérəfaid] 확인되지 않은　**dummy** [dʌ́mi] 가짜
vital [váitl] 필수적인　**allot** [əlát] 배당하다
symptom [símptəm] 증상　**astonish** [əstániʃ] 놀라게 하다
notion [nóuʃən] 개념　**convey** [kənvéi] 전달하다
legitimacy [lidʒítəməsi] 타당성
discretionary [diskréʃənèri] 임의의　**tactic** [tǽktik] 방책
indisposed [ìndispóuzd] 꺼리는, 마음이 내키지 않는
chemotherapy [kì:mouθérəpi] 화학 요법　**in retrospect** 돌이켜보면
clinically [klínikəli] 임상적으로, 의학적으로
approved [əprú:vd] 검증된　**breach** [bri:tʃ] 깨다
induce [indjú:s] 유발하다　**exacerbate** [igzǽsərbèit] 악화시키다
malpractice suit 의료과실 소송
exclusively [iksklú:sivli] 배타적으로
doctrine [dáktrin] 원칙　**implement** [ímpləmənt] 이행하다
informed consent 설명에 입각한 동의　**observe** [əbzə́:rv] 준수하다

1 지문의 단어 "one"이 가리키는 것은?

(A) 의미
(B) 위약
(C) 의사
(D) 환자

2 1단락에 따르면, 다음 중 위약이 진짜 약으로 분류되지 않는 이유는?

(A) 개업 의사에 의해 처방되지 않는다.
(B) 어떠한 약물 성분도 없다.
(C) 환자의 건강에 영향을 미치지 않는다.
(D) 단지 환자의 믿음에 의존한다.

3 지문의 단어 "alleviate"과 의미상 가장 유사한 것은?

(A) 위반하다
(B) 짜증나게 하다
(C) 경감하다
(D) 되살리다

4 지문의 단어 "it"이 가리키는 것은?

(A) 위약
(B) 약물

(C) 질병

(D) 회복

5 지문의 단어 "that"이 가리키는 것은?

(A) 치료

(B) 성공

(C) 심리적인 힘

(D) 사람의 마음

6 지문의 구 "this practice"가 가리키는 것은?

(A) 위약을 제거하는 것

(B) 질병에 대항하는 것

(C) 결과에 대한 분석 및 설명

(D) 위약을 투여하는 것

7 지문의 단어 "they"가 가리키는 것은?

(A) 연구자

(B) 의사

(C) 개업 의사

(D) 환자

8 지문의 단어 "others"가 가리키는 것은?

(A) 연구

(B) 의약품

(C) 경우

(D) 효과

9 지문에 따르면, 소송의 위협 때문에, 위약은

(A) 잠재적인 의료과실의 위험을 감수하는 의사들에 의해서만 사용된다

(B) 환자에 대해 예상되는 역효과를 줄이도록 요구된다

(C) 의사들에 의해 성분이 철저히 조사되고 있다

(D) 환자의 직접적인 치료 행위에서 거의 투여되지 않는다

10 지시: 지문 요약을 위한 도입 문장이 아래에 주어져 있다. 지문의 가장 중요한 내용을 나타내는 보기 3개를 골라 요약을 완성하시오. 어떤 문장은 지문에 언급되지 않은 내용이나 사소한 정보를 담고 있으므로 요약에 포함되지 않는다. **이 문제는 2점이다.**

> 위약의 사용은 특정한 상황에서 효과가 있는 것으로 보이는 논란의 여지가 있는 치료 방법이다.
>
> · (C) 의사가 환자 모르게 위약을 치료제로 사용하면 윤리 문제가 발생한다.
>
> · (D) 위약의 성공은 그것이 신체 자체의 치유 능력에 긍정적으로 영향을 미치는 것으로 보인다는 사실에서 기인한다.
>
> · (F) 환자들은 자신이 위약을 투여받아왔다는 것을 알게 되면, 간혹 치명적인 역반응이 일어난다.

(A) 위약이 효과적으로 질병을 치료할 수 있는지의 여부는 어떤 재료가 포함되었는지에 달려 있다.

(B) 의료 행위의 투명성의 바람직함에도 불구하고, 개업 의사들이 환자들과 정보를 공유하는 것은 어렵다.

(E) 위약을 사용하는 것에 대한 한 가지 우려는 환자가 그들의 질병이 그리 심각하지 않다고 생각하게 만든다는 것이다.

02 Blood Cells

p.162

1. (D)	2. (C)	3. (D)
4. (B)	5. (A)	6. (A)
7. (B)	8. (B)	9. (D)
10. Erythrocytes – (A), (D), (G)		
Leukocytes – (B), (E)		

1 단세포 생물은 기체를 직접 흡입하고 노폐물을 주변에 버릴 수 있지만, 더욱 복잡한 생명체들은 외부 환경에 대한 직접적인 노출과는 거리가 먼 체내의 세포들이 영양소를 보충할 수 있게 해주는 시스템을 갖추어야 한다. 침상체를 이용하여 내부 세포들을 곧바로 외부 공기에 노출시키는 체내 관 방법은 효율적이지 않고 개체의 크기를 제한하기 때문에, 큰 동물들은 체내 환경을 조절하기 위해서 다른 정밀한 네트워크를 필요로 한다. 큰 동물들은 신체를 탈수로부터 막아주는 액체로 채워진 폐쇄적인 순환계를 가지고 있는데, 더 중요하게도 이 큰 동물들은 특수한 세포들을 이용해서 생명 유지에 필요한 기체 교환을 용이하게 하고, 바이러스와 박테리아의 공격으로부터 자신들을 방어한다.

2 혈액 내에 가장 많이 존재하는 세포는 erythrocyte로 일반적으로 적혈구라 불리는데, 생명체가 오랫동안 저산소 환경에 노출되지 않는 이상 적혈구의 농도는 일정하게 유지되며, 적혈구는 체내의 다른 세포들보다 크기가 눈에 띄게 작다. [10D]이 양면이 오목한 원반들은 사실은 담황색의 색깔을 띠고 있으며, 산소와 화합한 헤모글로빈의 존재에 의해서만 적혈구의 특징적인 붉은색으로 변한다. 적혈구는 혈액 생성 줄기세포에 의해 골수에서 생성되며, 세포핵을 가지고 있지 않기 때문에 스스로 복제하지 못한다. [10A]적혈구는 일반적으로 100일에서 120일 이상 유지되지 못하므로 끊임없이 생성된다. 그리고 일부는 스트레스가 고조되었을 때 방출되기 위하여 비장에 저장되기도 하지만, 대부분은 혈관계에서 끊임없이 순환한다.

3 [10G]수백만 개의 헤모글로빈 분자로 이루어진 각 적혈구 세포는 신체의 곳곳을 이동하면서 산소를 체내의 모든 세포에 전달하고 이산화탄소를 제거하는 역할을 한다. 작은 크기와 극도의 유연성 덕분에 적혈구는 모세 혈관(미세한 혈관)과 같이 예외적으로 좁은 공간에도 들어갈 수 있는데, [4]모세 혈관에서 적혈구는 호흡에 필요한 산소를 방출하고 세포에 의해서 분비된 노폐물인 이산화탄소와 결합하며, 적혈구가 허파로 돌아가면 이 과정은 거꾸로 진행된다.

4 Leukocyte, 즉 백혈구는 적혈구보다 훨씬 크지만 수가 적은 세포로, 면역 체계의 일부로서 외부의 침입자와 전염병을 막아주고 다수

의 하위 범주로 나뉠 수 있다. 적혈구와 마찬가지로, 이것도 골수의 줄기세포에서 만들어지지만, [10B]백혈구는 소수의 매우 제한된 환경에서 자기복제를 가능하게 하는 세포핵을 가지고 있다. 체내의 박테리아 활동 정도에 따라 더 오랜 수명을 갖는 다른 형태가 있기도 하지만, 일부 백혈구는 고작 일주일에 불과한 수명을 가지고 있다. 신체는 임파선과 흉선에 백혈구를 비축해 두는데, 신체가 직면한 위협의 정도가 얼마나 큰지에 따라 백혈구의 수는 큰 폭으로 변화한다.

5 [10E]백혈구는 침입자가 감지되었을 때 신체를 보호하기 위한 여러 가지의 메커니즘들을 가지고 있는데, 호중성 백혈구는 이것의 좋은 예를 보여준다. 호중성 백혈구는 박테리아와 같은 항원을 공격하는 두 단계의 방법을 갖는다. 첫 단계는 식균 작용으로, 이는 말 그대로 호중성 백혈구가 침입 세포를 완전히 에워싸는 것이다. 호중성 백혈구는 항원에 연결하고 자신의 세포막 일부를 사용하여 항원 주변에 일종의 기포를 생성함으로써 식균 작용을 하는데, 이는 세포 외부에 있는 신체 나머지를 보호하면서 박테리아를 무력화시킨다. 또 다른 단계는 '기포'에 달라붙는 리소좀 효소를 분비하는 것이다. 리소좀 효소의 분비는 박테리아를 분해하며, 이 모든 과정은 백혈구와 침입자의 죽음으로 끝이 난다.

6 호중성 백혈구는 자신의 임무를 수행하고 나면 더는 쓸모가 없는데, 호중성 백혈구가 독성 물질을 함유하고 있기 때문에, 소모된 세포를 여과하여 방출하는 림프계를 통해서, 또는 보다 직접적으로 감염부위에서 노란 진액을 분비하고 허파에서 가래를 뱉는 것을 통해 체내에서 신속하게 제거되어야 한다. 이와는 대조적으로 적혈구는 유용한 철분을 함유하고 있다. 적혈구가 순환 주기가 끝나게 되면 순환을 멈추지만 모든 철분이 없어지는 것은 아니다. [9]다시 사용되기 위하여, 적혈구가 파괴되기 전에 철분의 일부가 떨어져 나와 비장에 저장된다. 그리고 나서 이 철분은 새롭게 만들어지는 적혈구로 향하게 된다.

cellular [séljulər] 세포의   dispose of ~을 버리다
removed [rimú:vd] 먼, 떨어진   replenish [ripléniʃ] 보충하다
tube [tju:b] 관을 달다
spicule [spíkju:l] 침상체(동물 체내의 작은 석회질 침)
circulatory system 순환계   dehydration [dì:haidréiʃən] 탈수
facilitate [fəsílətèit] 용이하게 하다   vital [váitl] 생명 유지에 필요한
viral [váiərəl] 바이러스의   erythrocyte [iríθrəsàit] 적혈구
biconcave [baikánkeiv] 양면이 오목한   straw [strɔ:] 담황색의
oxygenate [áksidʒənèit] 산소와 화합시키다   bone marrow 골수
nuclei [njú:kliài] 세포핵   spleen [spli:n] 비장
vascular [væskjulər] 혈관의   capillary [kǽpəlèri] 모세 혈관
vessel [vésəl] 혈관   respiration [rèspəréiʃən] 호흡
leukocyte [lú:kəsàit] 백혈구   infectious [infékʃəs] 전염성의
thymus [θáiməs] 흉선   neutrophil [njú:trəfil] 호중성 백혈구
antigen [ǽntidʒən] 항원   phagocytosis [fæ̀gəsaitóusis] 식균 작용
expectorate [ikspéktərèit] ~을 뱉다   phlegm [flem] 가래

1 지문의 단어 "their"가 가리키는 것은?

  (A) 기체
  (B) 노폐물
  (C) 체내의 세포
  (D) 동물

2 지문의 단어 "some"이 가리키는 것은?

  (A) 줄기세포
  (B) 세포핵
  (C) 적혈구
  (D) 혈관계

3 지문의 단어 "which"가 가리키는 것은?

  (A) 유연성
  (B) 산소
  (C) 호흡
  (D) 이산화탄소

4 3단락에 따르면, 적혈구가 폐에 있을 때

  (A) 외부 공격으로부터 안전하다
  (B) 노폐물 기체를 방출하고 산소를 흡수한다
  (C) 헤모글로빈을 주변 조직에 내보낸다
  (D) 크기를 줄일 필요가 없다

5 지문의 단어 "these"가 가리키는 것은?

  (A) 백혈구
  (B) 침입자
  (C) 질병
  (D) 적혈구

6 아래 문장 중 지문 속의 음영된 문장의 핵심 정보를 가장 잘 표현하고 있는 것은 무엇인가? 오답은 문장의 의미를 현저히 왜곡하거나 핵심 정보를 빠뜨리고 있다.

  (A) 백혈구의 수는 외부 위협의 정도에 따라 달라지며 신체의 일부 부위에 여분이 보관되어 있다.
  (B) 감염으로 인해 줄어든 백혈구의 수를 보완하기 위해, 신체는 다른 조직에 백혈구를 저장한다.
  (C) 백혈구를 초과로 저장하는 방법이 없다면, 그 수가 너무 많이 달라져서 유기체를 위험에 처하게 할 것이다.
  (D) 백혈구의 양은 신체 상태와 보관 수준에 따라 급격한 변동을 하기 쉽다.

7 지문의 구 "The other"가 가리키는 것은?

  (A) 항원
  (B) 단계
  (C) 세포막
  (D) 신체

8 지문의 단어 "swiftly"와 의미상 가장 유사한 것은?

  (A) 전적으로
  (B) 빨리
  (C) 마침내
  (D) 쉽게

9 지문에 따르면, 철분은 _____ 적혈구에서 제거된다.

(A) 허파로 몰아내어 지기 전에

(B) 비교적 짧은 수명 때문에

(C) 독성을 띠기 전에 호중성 백혈구에 의해서

(D) 다시 사용될 목적으로

10 지시: 주어진 선택지에서 적절한 구를 선택하여 관계 있는 혈구의 종류에 연결시키시오. **이 문제는 3점이다.**

보기
(C) 손상되면 자동으로 재생될 수 있다
(F) 위험 요소를 마주하면 독성 물질을 방출한다

적혈구
· (A) 최대 3분의 1년 정도 생존한다
· (D) 산소와 결합한 헤모글로빈이 존재하면 다른 색을 띤다
· (G) 허파와 다른 신체 기관 간의 기체 교환을 담당한다

백혈구
· (B) 드문 경우에 그들을 복제할 수 있게 하는 세포핵을 가지고 있다
· (E) 외부의 유해한 생물의 침입을 막는다

---

03 Green Glaciers

p.166

1. (B)	2. (D)	3. (D)
4. (C)	5. (A)	6. (D)
7. (A)	8. (C)	9. (D)

10. (A)-4단락, (C)-3단락, (D)-2단락

1 때때로 지구의 공전궤도가 변해서 보통 때보다 지구가 태양에서 조금 더 멀어지게 되는 경우가 있는데, 이는 더욱 한랭한 기후가 지면을 덮게 하여 일반적으로 봄철에 일어나는 통상적인 계절적인 해빙이 일어나지 못하게 한다. 이러한 더 추운 기간에는 강수가 계속되어 수 밀리미터에서 1센티미터에 이르는 크기를 가진 기묘한 모양의 서로 맞물리는 결정체가 집합체를 이루는데, 이러한 집합체가 합쳐져서 점점 더 두꺼운 얼음층을 만든다.

2 위에 덮이는 얼음층의 압력과 무게가 얼음을 더욱 조밀한 만년설로 압축시키는데, 이는 수년의 기간이 지나면 빙하가 된다. 압력은 또한 물의 빙점을 낮추어, 빙하 전역에 걸쳐 흐르면서 빙하의 흐름을 원활하게 해주는 해빙수를 생성한다. 유효한 해빙수가 산 아래로 졸졸 흐르면서 거대한 얼음층이 높은 고도에서 낮은 고도로 이동하고, 이동하면서 지표면으로부터 자갈이나 퇴적물 입자를 굵어모음으로써 얼음층은 더러워지게 된다. 빙하가 바다에 쓸려 내려가게 되면 바다 위로 높이 솟은 능선을 형성하는 빙붕이 되는데, [4]빙붕의 10에

서 12퍼센트에 해당하는 부분만이 겉으로 드러나고 나머지는 해수면 밑에 있기 때문에 해상 교통에 상당한 위험을 초래한다. 빙붕은 인간의 거주지와 근접하고 순수한 구성을 이루고 있기 때문에, 빙하 생성물 중 가장 널리 연구되는 경향이 있다. Amery 빙붕은 남극 주변 인도양의 Prydz Bay의 상부에 떠 있으며, Lambert Glacier의 끝자락에 있다. 1933년에 탐험가 Douglas Mawson에 의해서 호주 영토로 선언된 이 지역에는 보기 드문 암녹색의 얼음 구조물이 존재한다. 증거 부족으로 곧 배제된 초기의 연구결과는 일부 Amery 빙산의 특이한 녹색조의 원인을 얼음 내의 높은 금속 화합물 함량에 돌리고 있는데, 빙붕의 색이 나타나는 원인을 논쟁의 대상으로 남기고 일련의 탐사 연구에 불을 지폈다.

3 이러한 탐사 중 하나는 이 색조가 바다에 내리쬐는 햇빛의 반사로 인하여 푸른 색조를 띤 보통의 얼음이 수평선 너머로 지는 낮게 깔린 붉은 태양에 비치서 나타나는 시각적 오류의 결과라는 가설을 세웠다. 가설을 검증하기 위해서, 빙하학자들은 평균적인 여름의 낮 동안 일정한 간격을 두고 무수한 분광 분석 관찰을 하면서 다양한 빛의 세기에서 빙하의 색을 측정했고, 해가 하늘의 다른 위치에서 나타나는 봄과 가을에도 이 실험을 반복했다. 실험이 완결되었을 때, 빙하학자들은 햇빛의 변화에 따라 눈에 띌 만큼 초록 색조가 옅어지거나 더 뚜렷해지지 않는 것을 발견하며 색조가 시각적인 환상이라는 가설을 반박하였다.

4 최근에 일단의 빙하학자들은 빙하의 색깔이 있는 부분은 사실 떠 있는 빙붕의 해수면 아랫부분이 노출된 것으로, 지구의 공전궤도가 태양에 더욱 가까운 평상시의 위치로 돌아오면서 녹은 보통의 얼음이 전복하여 녹색을 띠는 해양 얼음을 남긴 후에야 보인다는 주장을 제시하며 새로운 이론을 내놓았다. 이 이론은 해양 얼음이 조밀화 과정을 겪게 될 때, 다른 빙하가 형성될 때처럼 크릴새우의 사체와 공기 방울이 없는 얼음 덩어리 기저부에 서식하는 수중 식물을 포함한 생물학적 물질을 굵어 모은다는 사실을 제기하였다. 붉은색의 눈이 Phyllophora라는 적조류가 눈의 층에 포함되어 생기는 현상이라는 사실은 이미 잘 알려졌고, 그 까닭에 비슷한 생물체가 녹색 빙하의 묘한 색채를 띠게 하는 주된 요인일 수 있다는 것 또한 가능성이 있다. 실제로 Amery 빙붕 주변의 바다에서 가장 흔한 조류는 얼음 속에 사는 단세포의 유글레나이며, [9]이는 다수의 녹색 엽록소 분자를 포함하는 원생 생물계에 속하는 광합성 생물이다. 고농도의 유글레나를 함유한 해양 얼음의 노출부는 조류의 색을 띠게 되고 녹색의 빙하로 나타날 것이다.

5 해양 생물로 인해 발생했다는 견해가 아무리 그럴싸하게 들릴지라도 이는 여전히 논쟁의 여지가 있으며 증명되지 않고 있다. 신비한 녹색 얼음의 존재에 대한 어떠한 최종적인 결론이 추론되기 전에, Amery 빙붕과 이를 에워싸는 지형에 대한 철저한 조사가 선행되어야 할 것이다.

interlock [ìntərlák] 맞물리다 **trickle** [tríkl] 졸졸 흐르다
ice shelf 빙붕 **proximity** [praksíməti] 근접
pristine [prísti:n] 순수한 **bottle-green** [bátlgrì:n] 암녹색의
discard [diská:rd] 버리다 **causation** [kɔːzéiʃən] 원인
contention [kənténʃən] 논쟁 **expedition** [èkspədíʃən] 탐사
hypothesize [haipáθəsàiz] 가설을 세우다 **fallacy** [fǽləsi] 오류

tinge [tindʒ] (옅은) 색조   illuminate [ilúːmənèit] 비추다
glaciologist [glèiʃiálədʒist] 빙하학자   spectral [spéktrəl] 분광의
illusion [ilúːʒən] 환상   capsize [kǽpsaiz] 전복하다, 뒤집히다
incorporation [inkɔ̀ːrpəréiʃən] 포함   ergo [əːrgou] 그 까닭에
feasible [fíːzəbl] 가능성 있는
photosynthetic [fòutousinθétik] 광합성의
chlorophyll [klɔ́ːrəfil] 엽록소   manifest [mǽnəfèst] 나타나다
plausible [plɔ́ːzəbl] 그럴싸한   notion [nóuʃən] 견해
controversial [kàntrəvə́ːrʃəl] 논쟁의 여지가 있는
encompass [inkʌ́mpəs] 에워싸다   deduce [didjúːs] 추론하다

1 아래 문장 중 지문 속의 음영된 문장의 핵심 정보를 가장 잘 표현하고 있는 것은 무엇인가? 오답은 문장의 의미를 현저히 왜곡하거나 핵심 정보를 빠뜨리고 있다.

(A) 기온 하락 때문에, 기묘한 모양의 결정체는 두꺼운 얼음층을 야기한다.

(B) 추운 날씨에 내린 눈은 덩어리져서 얼음층을 형성한다.

(C) 눈무더기로 인한 높아진 압력으로, 거대한 눈덩어리가 만들어진다.

(D) 한랭한 기후가 계속되면 쌓인 눈은 지표에 언 상태로 남는다.

2 지문의 단어 "which"가 가리키는 것은?

(A) 압력
(B) 무게
(C) 얼음
(D) 만년설

3 지문의 단어 "one"이 가리키는 것은?

(A) 빙점
(B) 물
(C) 빙하
(D) 고도

4 2단락에 따르면, 바다의 빙붕은 _____ 때문에 선박들에 대해 장애물이 될 수 있다.

(A) 침수된 부분이 인간의 거주지에 가까이 위치하기 때문에

(B) 갈라질 수 있는 능선을 바다 위로 형성하기 때문에

(C) 대부분이 수면 아래에 있어 보이지 않기 때문에

(D) 빙붕의 덩어리가 선박의 프로펠러를 방해하기 때문에

5 지문의 단어 "pristine"과 의미상 가장 유사한 것은?

(A) 훼손되지 않은
(B) 부드러운
(C) 손상된
(D) 상한

6 지문의 단어 "it"이 가리키는 것은?

(A) 오류
(B) 얼음
(C) 색조
(D) 햇빛

7 지문의 단어 "refuting"과 의미상 가장 유사한 것은?

(A) 반증하는
(B) 보완하는
(C) 다시 말하는
(D) 단언하는

8 지문의 단어 "it"이 가리키는 것은?

(A) 일단
(B) 공전궤도
(C) 해양 얼음
(D) 조밀화

9 4단락에 따르면, 유글레나는 _____ 바다의 얼음 색깔에 영향을 미친다.

(A) 얼음 안에서 많은 수로 증가하기 때문에

(B) 얼음 속으로 들어오는 빛을 분산시키기 때문에

(C) 수중에서 녹색 파장을 흡수할 때

(D) 많은 녹색 물질을 포함하기 때문에

10 지시: 지문 요약을 위한 도입 문장이 아래에 주어져 있다. 지문의 가장 중요한 내용을 나타내는 보기 3개를 골라 요약을 완성하시오. 어떤 문장은 지문에 언급되지 않은 내용이나 사소한 정보를 담고 있으므로 요약에 포함되지 않는다. 이 문제는 2점이다.

> 남극 주변 바다에서의 녹색 얼음의 출현은 그것의 기원을 설명하는 많은 이론으로 이어졌다.
>
> · (A) 특정 생물이 얼음에 포함되는 것은 얼음 색깔 변화의 원인일 수 있다.
>
> · (C) 푸른 얼음이 석양에 빛을 받으면 녹색을 띠게 된다는 가설이 제시되었다.
>
> · (D) 일부 사람들은 얼음 내에 묻힌 금속이 얼음을 녹색으로 보이게 할 것이라는 이론을 제시했다.

(B) 모든 빙하가 응결될 때 잔해를 모으며 어떤 종류의 색을 띤 식물을 포함한다는 것은 사실이다.

(E) 얼음 상층부의 압력은 빙하가 색깔을 바꾸는 속도에 영향을 미칠 가능성이 있다.

(F) 지구가 태양을 공전하는 궤도의 변화는 광합성 해조류가 받는 빛을 확장하는 것을 돕는다고 주장된다.

04   Ancient Pueblo Indians

p.170

1. (C)	2. (D)	3. (C)
4. (B)	5. (B)	6. (B)
7. (C)	8. (D)	9. (D)
10. (A)−2~3단락, (D)−4단락, (E)−5~6단락		

1 고대의 푸에블로 인디언은 콜로라도 평원의 Four Corners 지역에

천 년 넘게 거주했다. 그곳에서 그들은 조그만 농가 주변의 땅을 경작했고 바구니, 도자기와 같은 물품을 만들어 그들 사이에서 그리고 이웃 부족들 간에 교역했다. 역사의 대부분을, 그들은 땅을 판 구덩이에 지은 낮고 원시적인 오두막에 거주했다. 이 오두막들은 주로 흩어져 있는 단일 가구 주택들이었다. 그러나 10세기 이후 Four Corners 지역에 사는 푸에블로족의 생활 방식은 크게 진화했고, 그 변화들은 두 가지의 연속적인 단계를 거쳐 발생했다.

2 11세기와 12세기에 푸에블로 인디언들은 협곡의 낮은 지대에 있는 마을에 모이기 시작했고, 그곳에 광범위한 다가구 지상 주택을 지었는데, 그 주택은 '마을'을 뜻하는 푸에블로라 불렸으며 스페인 사람들이 푸에블로족을 다른 유목 부족과 구분하기 위해 그들에게 지어준 이름이었다. 마을들을 둘러싼 것은 길과 도로망으로서, 이것이 보조 농지와 주택을 중앙 연합과 연결해 주었다. 이러한 공동체 유형의 가장 주목할만한 사례는 Chaco Canyon에 있었으며, 그곳에는 수백 개의 방이 있는 다층 구조물의 광대한 복합체들이 있었고, 그중 일부는 높이가 5층에 달했다. 필요할 경우 인접 구조물이 가로 방향으로 추가되었고, 추가적인 방들이 세로 방향으로 쌓아 올려졌으며, 이는 어느 정도 현대 아파트 건물을 연상시킨다. 이러한 새롭고 광범위한 다층 건물들은 질서정연하고 안정적이며 협동적인 문명의 존재를 시사한다.

3 그러면 푸에블로 인디언은 왜 공동체 생활을 시작했을까? 주요한 요인은 환경적인 스트레스였다. 산림학자들은 나무 나이테의 분석을 통해 그 지역 전체에 걸쳐 극심한 반복적인 가뭄이 있었다는 것을 증명했다. 적은 강수량 때문에 사람들은 경작 가능한 좁은 땅으로 몰려들 수밖에 없었다. 이 오아시스들은 종종 협곡의 낮은 지대에 위치했는데 이곳에서는 가뭄 때에도 샘과 물줄기가 흘렀다. 과학자들은 또한 강바닥의 화분 분석을 통해 그 지역이 기온이 하강하고 식물의 성장 기간이 단축되는 소규모의 빙하기를 겪었다는 것을 추론했다. 높은 고원에서 가족들을 부양할 충분한 음식을 생산할 수 없자, 사람들은 낮은 지대에서 협동적인 방식을 형성하기 시작했다.

4 인구 밀도가 높은 공동체에서 함께 일하고 생활하는 것은 사람들로 하여금 노동으로부터 얻는 수익을 최대화하게 해주었다. 노동의 분배가 이루어졌고 어느 정도의 전문화가 생겼다. 어떤 사람들은 경지를 관개했고, 다른 이들은 집을 짓고 불을 피우기 위한 나무를 추수했다. 그들은 또한 자원을 비축하기 위해 공동체 저장 시설을 지었다. 그러나 인구 밀도가 높은 것에는 단점도 있었다. 4C집약 농업은 땅을 침식시켰고, 과도한 쓰레기는 위생 문제를 발생시켰으며, 4D나무를 지나치게 많이 추수하는 것은 근방의 산림을 고갈시켰다. 더욱이, 불리한 기후 조건은 수그러들지 않았고, 4A이는 빈약한 자원에 대한 경쟁과 사회적 불안을 초래했다.

5 13세기에 푸에블로족은 벼랑 전면에 거주지를 짓기 시작했고, 이는 그들이 이룬 건축적 성취의 절정을 드러낸다. 이 절벽 거주지들은 통상적으로 절벽에서 튀어나온 바위 위나 원래 있던 동굴 주변, 혹은 고원의 정상에 지어졌다. 그렇다면 이 어려운 환경 조건 하에 사람들이 왜 귀중한 자원과 경작 가능한 경지에서 멀리 떠나왔는지에 대한 질문이 대두된다. 6가장 개연성 있는 근거는 보호를 위해 그렇게 했다는 것이다. 높이 솟은 위치는 악천후로부터의 피난처와 적

대적인 침입 부족들에 대비하여 가공할만한 보호 장치를 제공하였다. 어떤 학자들은 나바호족이 공격자들이라고 암시하였으나, 침입자의 정체성과 전투의 범위는 논의되어야 할 대상이다. 이와 관계없이, 고고학자들이 활과 창을 지닌 시체의 유해와 식인 풍습의 희생자들을 발굴했던 것과 같이, Four Corners 지역 내의 증가하는 폭력에 대한 분명한 증거가 있다. 그 어느 때보다도 부족한 자원에 대한 경쟁으로 인해 번져나갔을 전쟁과 약탈이 사람들이 난공불락의 절벽에 은신처를 찾도록 장려했을 수도 있다. 어떤 절벽 거주지들에 접근하는 것은 심지어 현대 등반 장비의 도움으로도 매우 어렵고, 그들의 높은 위치는 의심의 여지 없이 잠재적 침입자들을 발견할 수 있는 효과적인 망보기 위치를 제공했다.

6 협동적 거주 방식은 푸에블로족이 그 지역에 가능한 한 오래 남아있을 수 있도록 했지만, 참담한 상황은 결국 13세기 말에 일촉즉발의 상태에 이르렀다. 그 당시에 Four Corners 지역으로부터 대이동이 일어났고, 이 이동이 1276년부터 1299년까지 소위 대가뭄이라 불리는 시기와 맞아떨어지는 것은 우연이 아니다. 9더욱 의존 가능한 수자원이 있는 Rio Grande 계곡의 상부가 일반적인 목적지였던 것으로 보인다. 1300년대 경에 Four Corners 지역의 인구는 거의 0명으로 곤두박질친 반면에, Rio Grande 계곡 상부의 인구는 크게 증가했다.

plateau[plætóu] 고원 millennium[miléniəm] 천 년
homestead[hóumstèd] 농가 sunken[sʌ́ŋkən] (주변 지역보다) 낮은
excavate[ékskəvèit] (구멍 등을) 파다 pit[pit] 구덩이
transpire[trænspáiər] 발생하다 successive[səksésiv] 연속적인
congregate[káŋgrigèit] 모이다 canyon[kǽnjən] 협곡
bottomland[bátəmlæ̀nd] (강변의) 낮은 지대
expansive[ikspǽnsiv] 광범위한
aboveground[əbʌ́vgràund] 지상의 ancillary[ǽnsəlèri] 보조의
confederation[kənfèdəréiʃən] 연합 notable[nóutəbl] 주목할만한
adjacent[ədʒéisnt] 인접한 stack[stæk] 쌓다
reminiscent[rèmənísnt] 연상시키는
complex[kəmpléks] 건물, 단지 point to ~을 시사하다
presence[prézns] 존재 orderly[ɔ́ːrdərli] 질서정연한
dendrologist[dendrάlədʒist] 산림학자 tree ring 나이테
recurring[rikə́ːriŋ] 반복적인 spring[spriŋ] 샘
stream[striːm] 물줄기 pollen[pálən] 화분
growing season (식물의) 성장 기간
specialization[spèʃəlizéiʃən] 전문화 irrigate[írəgèit] 관개하다
stockpile[stάkpàil] 비축하다 downside[dáunsàid] 단점
erode[iróud] 침식시키다 hygiene[háidʒiːn] 위생
sanitation[sæ̀nətéiʃən] 위생 adverse[ædvə́rs] 불리한
relent[rilént] 수그러들다 meager[míːgər] 빈약한
height[hait] 절정 ledge[ledʒ] 절벽에서 튀어나온 바위
the elements 악천후 formidable[fɔ́ːrmidəbl] 가공할만한
safeguard[séifgɑ̀ːrd] 보호 장치 escalate[éskəlèit] 증가하다
unearth[ʌnə́ːrθ] 발굴하다 cannibalism[kǽnəbəlìzm] 식인풍습
asylum[əsáiləm] 은신처 impregnable[imprégnəbl] 난공불락의
precipice[présəpis] 절벽 exodus[éksədəs] 이동

1 지문의 단어 "These"가 가리키는 것은?
   (A) 물품

(B) 바구니
(C) 오두막
(D) 구덩이

2 지문의 단어 "some"이 가리키는 것은?

(A) 주택
(B) 공동체
(C) 복합체
(D) 구조물

3 지문의 단어 "their"가 가리키는 것은?

(A) 고원
(B) 가족
(C) 사람들
(D) 방식

4 4단락에 따르면, 다음 중 밀집 인구의 단점으로 언급되지 않은 것은?

(A) 자원을 둘러싼 갈등
(B) 산불의 발생
(C) 농지의 침식
(D) 산림의 퇴화

5 지문의 단어 "meager"와 의미상 가장 유사한 것은?

(A) 풍부한
(B) 부족한
(C) 미개발의
(D) 더럽혀진

6 5단락에 따르면, 푸에블로족은 _____ 하기 위해 절벽 거주지를 지었다.

(A) 더 좋은 농경지에 접근하기 위해
(B) 피난처를 제공하고 공격을 방어하기 위해
(C) 그들의 건축 솜씨를 경쟁 부족에게 과시하기 위해
(D) 그들의 영토를 확장하고 증가하는 인구를 부양하기 위해

7 아래 문장 중 지문 속의 음영된 문장의 핵심 정보를 가장 잘 표현하고 있는 것은 무엇인가? 오답은 문장의 의미를 현저히 왜곡하거나 핵심 정보를 빠뜨리고 있다.

(A) 일부 절벽 거주지의 나쁜 접근성과 높이 때문에, 침입자들은 멀리서 그것들을 보고 종종 길을 바꾸곤 했다.
(B) 일부 절벽 거주지들은 실제로 도달할 수 없으며, 현대 장비를 이용하는 등반가들조차 그곳에 접근하는 것을 어려워했다.
(C) 어떤 절벽 거주지들은 들어가기가 매우 어려우며, 그것의 높이는 그곳을 침입자들을 살피는 장소로 유용하게 만들었다.
(D) 어떤 절벽 거주지들은 도달하기가 어려웠지만, 불가피하게도 가끔씩 노련한 등반가들에 의해 정복되었다.

8 지문의 단어 "that"이 가리키는 것은?

(A) 자원

9 6단락에 따르면, 다음 중 Rio Grande 계곡에 대해 사실인 것은?

(A) 13세기 후반 푸에블로족의 이주 이전에는 사람이 살지 않았다.
(B) Four Corners 지역보다 강수량이 더 많았다.
(C) 대가뭄 직후에 인구가 점차 감소했다.
(D) 수자원이 Four Corners 지역의 것들보다 더 의존 가능했다.

10 지시: 지문 요약을 위한 도입 문장이 아래에 주어져 있다. 지문의 가장 중요한 내용을 나타내는 보기 3개를 골라 요약을 완성하시오. 어떤 문장은 지문에 언급되지 않은 내용이나 사소한 정보를 담고 있으므로 요약에 포함되지 않는다. **이 문제는 2점이다.**

> 천년 동안 푸에블로족의 생활 방식은 사실상 계속 변하지 않았지만, 11세기와 13세기 사이에 그들의 생활 양식이 변하기 시작했다.
>
> · (A) 크게 환경의 압박과 식량 생산과 관련된 문제 때문에, 푸에블로족은 협곡에 대규모 협동 공동체를 형성했다.
> · (D) 그들의 공동체는 노동의 생산적인 분배에 달려 있었지만, 밀집된 인구가 문제를 발생시켜 사회적 혼란으로 이어졌다.
> · (E) 푸에블로족은 아마 증가하는 폭력에 대한 보호책으로 절벽에 거주지를 만들었고, 결국 Four Corners 지역을 떠났다.

(B) 몇몇 알려지지 않은 이유로, 푸에블로족은 갑자기 협곡 낮은 지대의 마을을 버리고 절벽 높은 곳에 집을 지었다.
(C) 실망스럽게도, 평화로운 환경과 더 나은 기후를 찾아 이주한 푸에블로족은 Rio Grande 계곡에 도착했지만 가뭄과 불안만을 발견하게 되었다.
(F) 그들의 집약적인 농업 기술은 가뭄 문제를 악화시키고 식량 부족을 일으킨 침식과 같은 부정적인 결과를 낳았다.

Chapter 05 **Rhetorical Purpose**

HACKERS **STRATEGY**

p.179

전략 1

Ex 다이아몬드에는 무색, 흰색, 파란색, 노란색, 주황색, 빨간색, 초록색, 분홍색, 갈색, 검은색 등 여러 가지 색이 있다. 알아볼 수 있는 색을 지닌 다이아몬드는 유색 다이아몬드로 알려졌다. 순다이아몬드는 투명한 무색인 반면, 유색 다이아몬드는 색깔을 만드는 불순물이나 구조적 결함을 지니고 있다. 대부분의 다이아몬드 불순물은 결정 격자의 탄소 원자를 대체하고, 가장 흔한 불순물인 질소는 연한 노란색이나 갈색을 띠게 한다.

hue[hju:] 색 **impurity**[impjúərəti] 불순물
nitrogen[náitrədʒən] 질소 **tinge**[tindʒ] 연한 색

Ex 서기 1000년경에 발견된 커피나무의 효능이 어떻게 최초로 발견되었는지를 둘러싸고 여러 가지 설이 있다. 그중에서 가장 일반적인 설은 에티오피아의 한 양치기가 자신이 관리하는 양 떼가 특정 나무의 열매를 먹고 난 후 잠이 바짝 깼다는 사실을 발견했다는 것이다. 양들이 먹은 그 열매를 먹어본 그는 자신도 잠이 깨고 힘이 생겼다는 사실을 깨달았다. 그의 발견으로 많은 부족이 커피 열매를 이용하기 시작했다. 예를 들어, 에티오피아의 Galla 부족민들은 특정 열매와 동물의 지방을 혼합하여 에너지 보조식품을 생산했다. 이런저런 경로를 통하여 사람들은 커피 열매가 가축뿐만 아니라 그들 자신에게도 어떤 영향을 미친다는 결론에 이르게 되었다. 커피의 효능을 이해하고 이를 이용하려는 욕구가 전 세계의 커피 재배와 생산을 향한 탐구의 계기가 되었다.

wide-awake[wàidawéik] 잠이 바짝 깬 **quest**[kwest] 탐구

전략 2

Ex 해수는 마치 거대한 컨베이어 벨트가 잡아당기기라도 하듯이 전 지구를 돌며 계속해서 이동하며, 차갑고 염도와 밀도가 높은 해수일수록 더욱 밑으로 가라앉는다. 북태평양의 심해수 대부분은 최소 800년 동안 햇빛에 노출된 적이 없으며, 이 중 일부는 2000년간 심해에 머물러 있었다. 따라서 해양학자는 심해층의 온도가 안정적이며 대기 온난화에도 영향을 받지 않을 것이라고 추정해왔다. 하지만 새로운 증거에 따르면, 최근 몇십 년간 이곳저곳의 심해층의 온도가 상당히 따뜻해졌다.

oceanographer[ðuʃənágrəfər] 해양학자
impervious[impə́:rviəs] ~에 영향받지 않는

전략 3

Ex 과거에 이끼류는 상호 간에 동일하게 유익한 공생관계인 상리 공생의 확실한 예로 여겨졌다. 광합성 파트너는 광합성을 함으로써 그 자신과 곰팡이류를 위한 탄수화물 분자를 생산하고, 이 곰팡이류는 광합성 파트너를 위해 물과 미네랄을 흡수해 광합성 파트너가 건조해지지 않도록 막는 역할을 한다. 하지만 현미경을 이용한 실험이 곰팡이 균이 일부 조류 세포를 관통해 이를 파괴한다는 사실을 밝혀냄에 따라, 이끼류의 관계가 상리 공생이 아니라 곰팡이류가 광합성 파트너에 기생하는 것으로 보는 생물학자들도 있다.

lichen[láikən] 이끼류 **mutualism**[mjú:tʃuəlìzm] 상리 공생
symbiotic[sìmbiátik] 공생의
photosynthetic[fòutousinθétik] 광합성의
carbohydrate[kà:rbəháidreit] 탄수화물
desiccation[dèsikéiʃən] 건조 **parasitism**[pǽrəsaitìzm] 기생
algae[ǽldʒi:] 조류 **fungal**[fʌ́ŋgəl] 곰팡이에 의한

HACKERS STRATEGY **APPLICATION**

p.182

유인원의 유전자는 인간의 유전자와 96퍼센트 정도 일치한다. 침팬지의 경우 그 수치는 98.4퍼센트나 된다. 아프리카 유인원은 사실상 오랑우탄보다는 인간과 더 밀접한 관계를 지니고 있다. 유인원 생존 프로젝트에 따르면, 유인원과 인간의 관계는 매우 가까워서 다른 행성에서 온 분류학자는 아마도 인간을 아프리카 유인원의 한 종으로 분류할 것이다. 매사추세츠 공과 대학과 워싱턴 대학의 최근 연구에서 과학자들은 침팬지와 인간의 유전자를 비교했다. 과학자들은 두 유전자 코드를 나란히 나열함으로써, 인간과 침팬지를 구분하는 4억 개의 분자의 차이를 밝혀내고, 두 종간의 차이점을 보여주는 듯한 25만 개의 분자의 차이를 정확히 지적했다. 모두 합하여 유전자 염기 서열은 4퍼센트 달랐다. 하지만 이 차이 중 4분의 3은 게놈의 비기능적인 부분에 해당하는 것이어서, 두 종간 차이는 1퍼센트에 불과하다고 할 수 있다. 연구자들은 이 연구가 침팬지가 에이즈, 간염, 말라리아, 노인성 치매와 같은 인간의 질병에 내성을 지니고 있는 이유를 밝혀내는 데 도움이 될 수 있을 것이라고 말하는데, 이는 과학자들이 인간의 질병을 예방하거나 치료하는 새로운 방법들을 찾아내는 데 도움을 줄 것이다.

great ape 유인원 **taxonomist**[tæksánəmist] 분류학자
pinpoint[pínpòint] 정확히 나타내다 **all told** 모두 합하여
gene sequence 유전자 염기서열 **hepatitis**[hèpətáitis] 간염

1. 지문에서 글쓴이는 왜 "non-functional parts"를 언급하는가?
   (A) 침팬지의 뇌 기능과 인간의 뇌 기능을 비교하기 위해
   (B) 인간과 침팬지 사이에 차이점이 거의 없다는 것을 강조하기 위해
   (C) 인간과 침팬지가 공유하고 있는 특징의 예를 제시하기 위해

(D) 인간과 침팬지 사이에 유사점이 전혀 없다는 것을 보여주기 위해

18세기에 프랑스와 미국에서 있었던 혁명은 각 나라의 정치적, 사회적, 경제적 분위기를 개조하는 역사상의 전환점이었다. 미국 식민지에서 일련의 논쟁, 정치적 격변, 경제적 위기가 사회환경을 뒤흔들었고, 이는 1775년부터 1783년 사이에 대영제국과 혁명가들 간에 전쟁이 일어나도록 자극했다. 그 후에 곧 프랑스에서의 비슷한 상황들이 1787년에 시작하여 1799년경에 종결된 여러 분쟁의 도화선이 되었다. 미국과 프랑스의 혁명시기는 교차하는 환경들의 축적이 시민의 불만을 심화시킨 상황을 보여준다.

turning point 전환점 altercation[ɔ̀:ltərkéiʃən] 논쟁
upheaval[ʌphíːvəl] 격변 impetus[ímpətəs] 자극
thereafter[ðɛ̀ərǽftər] 그 후에 buildup[bíldʌ̀p] 축적, 증강
revolutionary[rèvəlúːʃənèri] 혁명가
intersect[ìntərsékt] 교차하다 unrest[ʌnrést] 불만

2. 지문에서, 글쓴이는 _____으로써 18세기의 혁명들을 설명한다.

(A) 혁명이 종결된 방식을 설명함으로써
(B) 영국과 프랑스의 역할을 강조함으로써
(C) 서로 다른 두 나라에서의 유사한 상황을 비교함으로써
(D) 혁명이 일어난 주요 원인들의 유형을 분류함으로써

HACKERS **PRACTICE** p.184

1. (B)	2. (A)	3. (D)
4. (D)	5. (A)	6. (D)
7. (C)	8. (D)	9. (D)
10. (D)		11. 1 (B), 2 (B), 3 (D)
12. 1 (A), 2 (D), 3 (C)		13. 1 (C), 2 (D), 3 (A)
14. 1 (C), 2 (D), 3 (B)		15. 1 (A), 2 (A), 3 (D)

VOCABULARY

1 (B), (C)	2 (D)	3 (A), (C)
4 (B)	5 (D)	6 (D), (C)
7 (B), (C)	8 (A)	9 (B)
10 (A), (D)	11 (B), (A), (C)	12 (B), (D), (C)
13 (D), (C), (A)	14 (A), (B), (D)	15 (B), (C), (A)

1 식민지 이주자들이 17세기에 북아메리카 동해안에 정착했을 때, 유럽의 전통도 그들에게 딸려갔다. 그들의 가내 풍습이 이러한 구세계의 전통을 반영했으므로, 가구의 스타일과 양식 또한 유럽의 전통으로부터 파생되었다는 것은 그리 놀라운 일이 아니다. 여러 다른 나라에서 온 정착민들은 모국의 스타일을 들여왔는데, 그 예로 17세기 뉴잉글랜드의 가구는 강한 영국풍의 멋을 보여주는 반면, 뉴욕에서 만들어진 가구는 네덜란드인의 취향을 드러내는 것을 들 수 있다.

colonist[kάlənist] 식민지 이주자 eastern seaboard 동해안
accompany[əkʌ́mpəni] 딸려가다 reflect[riflékt] 반영하다
Old World 구세계(유럽 대륙) construction[kənstrʌ́kʃən] 양식
derive from ~로부터 파생되다 reveal[rivíːl] 드러내다
taste[teist] 취향

지문에서 글쓴이는 왜 "New England furniture"를 언급하는가?

(A) 영국 정착민들이 네덜란드인의 취향에 무관심했음을 주장하기 위해
(B) 식민지 이주자들의 모국에서 유래된 가구 스타일의 예를 제공하기 위해
(C) 식민지 이주자들이 그들의 새로운 거주지에 잘 적응했다는 주장을 뒷받침하기 위해
(D) 영국의 도움 없이 만들어진 특별한 예술 작품을 언급하기 위해

2 광물 입자, 유기물질, 물, 공기 등으로 구성된 토양은 인간이 음식을 얻기 위해 의존하는 귀중한 천연자원이다. 물, 바람, 얼음 등의 동인이 토양을 차츰 닳게 만드는 토양 침식이나 육지로부터의 토양 유실을 초래한다. 물과 바람은 특히 토양 유실에 효과적인데, 강우는 토양 입자를 느슨하게 만들어서 유수에 의해 이동될 수 있게 하고, 바람은 특히 토양이 노출되어 건조할 때 토양을 느슨하게 만들어 불어 날려버린다.

be composed of ~로 구성되다 mineral[mínərəl] 광물
particle[pάːrtikl] 입자 agent[éidʒənt] 동인
soil erosion 토양 침식 wear away 차츰 닳다
removal[rimúːvəl] 유실, 제거 rainfall[réinfɔ̀ːl] 강우
loosen[lúːsn] 느슨하게 하다 transport[trænspɔ́ːrt] 이동시키다
blow away (바람에) 불어 날아가다 exposed[ikspóuzd] 노출된

글쓴이는 지문에서 _____하기 위해 "rainfall"을 언급한다.

(A) 토양을 침식시킬 수 있는 과정을 설명하기 위해
(B) 강우와 광물 입자를 대조하기 위해
(C) 침식 예방의 이점을 주장하기 위해
(D) 유수가 땅을 침투하는 방법의 예를 제시하기 위해

3 네안데르탈인은 약 40,000년 전에 멸종되었고, 그들의 종말은 '호모 사피엔스'의 출현과 동시에 일어났다. 네안데르탈인의 멸종과 현대 인류의 출현이 전 세계적으로 서로 이어지지는 않았지만, 화석 기록은 '호모 사피엔스'가 기여 요인이라고 강하게 시사한다. 하지만, 두 집단이 서로 만날 때마다 폭력을 야기했던 것은 아니므로, 네안데르탈인은 식량 자원에 대한 경쟁 때문에 멸종되었을 가능성이 어느 정도 있다.

extinct[ikstíŋkt] 멸종된 demise[dimáiz] 종말

coincide[kòuinsáid] 동시에 일어나다, 일치하다
emergence[imə́:rdʒəns] 출현   mutually[mjú:tʃuəli] 서로
implicate[ímplikeit] 시사하다   contribute[kəntríbju:t] 기여하다
encounter[inkáuntər] 만나다   eradicate[irǽdikeit] 멸종시키다

지문에서 글쓴이는 왜 "the fossil record"를 언급하는가?

(A) 네안데르탈인이 한정적인 식량 자원을 가지고 있었다는 것을 나타내기 위해
(B) 네안데르탈인의 멸종 시기에 대한 증거를 제공하기 위해
(C) 종 사이의 상호작용이 때때로 폭력적이었다는 것을 보여주기 위해
(D) '호모 사피엔스'를 네안데르탈인의 쇠퇴와 관련시키기 위해

4 아동 심장 손상의 가장 주요한 원인인, 가와사키병의 근원은 현재 알려져 있지 않다. 하지만, 연구는 그것이 동아시아 혈통의 남아에게서 주로 발생한다는 것을 밝혔다. 실험 연구는 가와사키병이 이러한 특정 인종 집단이 이 병에 감염되기 쉽게 만드는 유전적 요소를 지닌다는 것을 보여준다. 지금까지, 동아시아인의 DNA에 있는 많은 유전자 변형들이 이 병과 연관되어 왔다. 하지만, 300건이 넘는 호주 사례들에 대한 조사는 18.1퍼센트만이 아시아 민족이었다는 것을 밝혀냈고, 비록 요인들이 무엇인지 여전히 분명하지 않지만, 환경적인 요인들이 관련되어 있음을 시사했다.

foremost[fɔ́:rmoust] 가장 주요한   determine[ditə́:rmin] 밝히다
predominantly[pridá:minəntli] 주로   descent[disént] 혈통
indicate[índikeit] 보여주다   genetic[dʒənétik] 유전적인
component[kəmpóunənt] 요소, 요인   ethnic[éθnik] 인종의
susceptible[səséptəbl] 감염되기 쉬운
variant[vέəriənt] 변형, 변종   associated with ~과 연관된
investigation[invèstigéiʃən] 조사   evident[évidənt] 분명한

글쓴이는 지문에서 _____하기 위해 "over three hundred Australian cases"를 언급한다.

(A) 그 나라가 가장 높은 고통 비율을 가진다는 것을 밝히기 위해
(B) 면역력이 있는 사람들의 예를 제공하기 위해
(C) 질병의 외부 요인을 제시하기 위해
(D) 감염의 유전적 근거를 반박하기 위해

5 한 개의 군락은 한 지역에 같이 살고 있는 다양한 종으로 이루어져 있다. 화산 폭발, 지진, 또는 산불 등으로 인해서 자연 지역이 흐트러졌을 때, 새로운 군락은 갑자기 생겨나는 것이 아니라 일련의 단계를 거쳐서 서서히 발달한다. 장기간에 걸쳐서 한 단계의 종이 다른 종으로 대체되면서 군락이 발달해 가는 과정을 생태천이라고 한다. 비록 연속적인 각 단계에는 특유의 동물 종도 있기는 하지만, 생태천이는 일반적으로 한 지역의 식물 형태의 변화의 측면에서 설명된다. 생태천이는 진화의 시간 척도처럼 수백만 년 단위의 시간에 걸쳐서 일어나는 것이 아니라 대략 수십 년, 수백 년, 혹은 수천 년 단위의 간격을 두고 일어난다.

community[kəmjú:nəti] 군락   species[spí:ʃi:z] 종
disturb[distə́:rb] 흐트러뜨리다   volcanic eruption 화산 폭발

spring into 갑자기 ~이 되다   gradually[grǽdʒuəli] 서서히
replace[ripléis] 대체하다   ecological succession 생태천이
in terms of ~의 측면에서   vegetation[vèdʒətéiʃən] 식물
characteristic[kæ̀riktərístik] 특유의   interval[íntərvəl] 간격
on the order of 대략   evolutionary[èvəlú:ʃənèri] 진화의
time scale 시간의 척도

지문에서 글쓴이는 왜 "evolutionary time scale"을 언급하는가?

(A) 생태천이에 필요한 시간을 그 척도와 비교하기 위해
(B) 진화에 필요한 시간의 범위를 가시화하기 위해
(C) 과학자들이 변화를 측정하는 또 다른 방법을 설명하기 위해
(D) 지질 활동이 일어나는 정도를 명확하게 하기 위해

6 전통적으로, 대부분의 미국 도시들은 상당히 융통성 없는 지역제 법령을 가지고 있었으므로, 도시 계획에 대한 색다른 관점을 가지고 있던 개발업자들은 보통 민간 통제 지역사회를 만들기 위해 지방 부지를 찾아내야 했다. 그러한 규제에 대해 반대하는 사람들은 엄격한 지역제가 다양한 인구의 수요를 충족시키지 않는 단일 지역을 야기할 것이라고 주장했다. 바로 이 정서가 1980년대에 신도시주의 혁명이 일어나게 한 것이었고, 이는 주택, 상점, 공원, 그리고 도보와 자전거 통행을 제공하기 위한 충분한 보도를 포함한 다목적 지역을 조성하고자 했다. 플로리다 주의 해안 마을은, 비록 이 곳을 비판하는 사람들이 확실히 없지는 않지만, 그 운동의 이상을 완벽하게 구현한 장소로 종종 언급된다. 사회 운동가들은 그곳이 많은 사회적 또는 문화적 다양성이 없는 마을이 되었기 때문에 이 목적을 달성하는 것에 실패했다고 주장한다.

inflexible[infléksəbl] 융통성 없는   zoning[zóuniŋ] 지역제
ordinance[ɔ́:rdinəns] 법령   rural[rúrəl] 지방의
opponent[əpóunənt] 반대하는 사람
regulation[règjuléiʃən] 규제, 통제
homogenous[həmádʒənəs] 단일의, 동종의
diverse[daivə́:rs] 다양한   population[pà:pjuléiʃən] 인구
sentiment[séntimənt] 정서   give rise to ~이 일어나게 하다
mixed-use[míkstjù:s] 다목적의
incorporate[inkɔ́:rpəreit] 포함하다   ample[ǽmpl] 충분한
embody[imbá:di] 구현하다

글쓴이는 지문에서 _____하기 위해 "The town of Seaside, Florida"를 언급한다.

(A) 신도시주의 혁명의 최초의 영감을 밝히기 위해
(B) 다채로운 지역에 대한 증대되는 요구를 설명하기 위해
(C) 사람들이 왜 엄격한 지역제의 실행을 거부하기 시작했는지 설명하기 위해
(D) 논란이 있는 계획된 지역사회의 예를 제시하기 위해

7 19세기에, 아일랜드의 인구가 증가했고, 그 나라는 사람들에게 식량을 공급하기 위해 감자 재배에 의존했다. 40퍼센트에 달하는 국민들이 거의 오직 감자로만 이루어진 식단으로 연명했다. 하지만, 1845년부터 1849년까지 지속된 병충해는 감자를, 날

것이든 조리된 것이든, 먹을 수 없게 만들었다. 수확 직후, 부패를 막기 위해 들인 노력에 상관없이, 농작물이 썩곤 했다. 수확량의 폭락은 적은 유전적 변형으로부터 생겨났는데 이는 농부들이 질병에 내성이 없다고 밝혀진, 단일한 개체만을 사용해왔기 때문이었다. 이로 인한 기근은 아일랜드로부터의 대규모 이주와 백만 명이 넘는 사람들의 죽음을 부채질했다.

swell[swel] 증가하다, 부풀다 **cultivation**[kÀltivéiʃən] 재배
feed[fi:d] ~에게 식량을 공급하다 **resident**[rézidənt] 국민, 거주자
survive on ~으로 연명하다 **blight**[blait] 병충해
inedible[inédəbl] 먹을 수 없는 **harvesting**[há:rvistiŋ] 수확
crop[krɑ:p] 농작물, 수확량 **rot**[rɑ:t] 썩다 **decay**[dikéi] 부패
collapse[kəlǽps] 폭락, 붕괴 **stem from** ~에서 생겨나다
genetic[dʒənétik] 유전적인 **variation**[vèriéiʃən] 변형
clone[kloun] 개체, 복제 생물 **resistance**[rizístəns] 내성, 저항
famine[fǽmin] 기근 **fuel**[fjú:əl] 부채질하다

지문에서 글쓴이는 왜 아일랜드 감자의 유전적 구성에 대해 자세히 설명하는가?

(A) 아일랜드가 어떻게 증가하는 인구에게 효율적으로 식량을 공급했는지 설명하기 위해
(B) 아일랜드 사람들에 의해 사용된 세련된 육종 방법을 강조하기 위해
(C) 아일랜드의 농업 실패에 대한 이유를 밝히기 위해
(D) 아일랜드 사람들이 독특한 해외 농작물 품종을 들여왔다는 것을 보여주기 위해

8 'Philetairus socius'라고도 불리는 집단베짜기새는, 독특한 둥지 구조물을 만드는 것으로 유명한 조류이다. 이러한 거대 둥지들은 한꺼번에 500마리의 새들까지 수용할 수 있기 때문에 아파트 건물에 비유되어 왔다. 구조물의 바깥 층은 아래쪽으로 비스듬히 놓인 큰 나뭇가지들로 만들어지고, 여기에 구조물의 토대를 고정시키기 위해서 풀이 더해진다. 이러한 건축학적 경이는 수십 개의 연결된 공간으로 구성되어 있으며 이 공간은 포식자를 막기 위해 날카롭게 뾰족한 가장자리를 가진 건초들로 둘러싸여 있는 아래쪽 출입구를 가지고 있다. 둥지로의 출입구는 아파트 엘리베이터와 유사하며, 한 쌍의 새와 그들의 새끼를 수용하는 원형의 둥지 공간으로 이어지는 최대 25센티미터 길이의 개별 터널들이 있다. 각각의 공간은 털이나 솜과 같은 부드러운 재료들로 대어져 있다. 이러한 것들은 추운 밤 내내 내부가 열기를 유지할 수 있게 한다. 둥지의 적절한 보안은 몇몇 다른 조류들에게 둥지를 매력적으로 만들고, 이것들은 둥지를 보금자리로 사용하며 베짜기새들과 공존한다.

construct[kənstrÁkt] 만들다 **nest**[nest] 둥지를 틀다; 둥지
massive[mǽsiv] 거대한 **be likened to** ~에 비유되다
accommodate[əká:mədeit] 수용하다 **twig**[twig] 나뭇가지
secure[səkjúr] 고정시키다 **foundation**[faundéiʃən] 토대
marvel[má:rvl] 경이, 불가사의 **chamber**[tʃéimbər] 공간
surround[səráund] 둘러싸다 **hay**[hei] 건초
discourage[diská:ridʒ] 막다 **predator**[prédətər] 포식자
akin to ~과 유사한 **circular**[sə́:rkjələr] 원형의
a breeding pair (함께 새끼를 기르는) 한 쌍(의 동물·새)

offspring[ɔ́:fspriŋ] 새끼, 자손 **line**[lain] (안을) 대다
retain[ritéin] 유지하다 **relative**[rélətiv] 적절한, 상대적인
roosting site 보금자리 **coexist**[kòuigzíst] 공존하다

지문에서, 글쓴이는 _____으로써 집단베짜기새 둥지의 구조를 설명한다.

(A) 재료의 유용성이 어떻게 설계에 영향을 주는지 상세히 열거함으로써
(B) 둥지를 짓는 데 사용된 물체들을 설명함으로써
(C) 공동의 둥지가 이로울 수 있다고 주장함으로써
(D) 자연적 구조를 인공의 것과 비교함으로써

9 남북전쟁 전의 미국 저널리즘은 1830년대에 가장 중요한 발전을 이루었는데, 그때는 뉴욕 저널리스트인 Benjamin Day와 James Gordon Bennett이 대중의 흥미를 끌기 시작할 무렵이었다. 6센트에 팔렸던 당대의 신문과 달리 Day의 New York Sun지와 Bennett의 New York Herald지는 처음으로 길거리에서 단돈 1페니에 팔렸다. 남북 전쟁 직전에 Herald지가 기록한 77,000부에 이르는 늘어난 발행 부수뿐만 아니라, 이 시기는 신문 내용의 변화 면에서도 주목할만하다. 특히, Bennett은 신문 내용의 범위를 확대하고 신문 보도의 호소력을 더 분명히 한 선구자였다. 초기의 정치 신문이 상대방을 신랄하게 비난하는 특색이 있었던 반면, Herald지는 범죄 및 다른 선정적인 소재에 대한 선정적 보도에 중점을 뒀다.

antebellum[æ̀ntibéləm] 남북전쟁 전의
appeal to ~의 흥미를 끌다 **contemporary**[kəntémpərèri] 당대의
peddle[pédl] 팔고 다니다 **circulation**[sə̀:rkjuléiʃən] 발행 부수
noteworthy[nóutwə̀:rði] 주목할만한 **in particular** 특히
pioneer[pàiəníər] 선구자 **scope**[skoup] 범위
sharpen[ʃá:rpən] 더 분명히 하다
distinctive[distíŋktiv] 특색 있는
denunciation[dinÀnsiéiʃən] 비난
sensationalistic coverage 선정적 보도 **lurid**[lúərid] 선정적인

글쓴이는 지문에서 _____하기 위해 Bennett의 Herald지와 초기 정치 신문을 대조한다.

(A) 신문의 인기 증가를 강조하기 위해
(B) 신문 구독료가 어떻게 감소했는지 설명하기 위해
(C) 남북전쟁 이전 정치의 중요성을 언급하기 위해
(D) 신문의 소재 변화를 보여주기 위해

10 구급차가 가까이 다가오면 사이렌 소리가 커지고 또 멀어지면 이에 대응해 음조가 줄어드는 것은 도플러 효과를 설명하기 위해 사용되는 흔한 예이다. 파원이 일직선으로 이동할 때 사이렌 전면의 음파는 압축된다. 이와 반대로 사이렌 뒤쪽의 음파는 펼쳐진다. 유사한 방식으로, 별빛과 같은 방사되는 빛도 그것의 이동에 대한 관찰자의 상대적인 위치에 따라 다르게 보인다. 하지만 사이렌 소리처럼 음조의 변화가 일어나는 대신, 빛은 색을 바꾼다. 즉, 멀어지면 붉은색으로 변하고, 가까워지면 푸른색으로 변한다. 이 현상이 갖는 의미를 처음으로 이해했던 사람은 미국

의 저명한 천문학자 Edwin Hubble이었다.

wail of a siren 사이렌 소리
corresponding [kɔ̀ːrəspándiŋ] 대응하는　**pitch** [pitʃ] 음조
depart [dipáːrt] 멀어지다　**sound wave** 음파
compress [kəmprés] 압축하다　**source of the wave** 파원
stretch out 펼쳐지다, 뻗다　**in an opposite fashion** 반대로
in a parallel way 유사한 방식으로　**depending upon** ~에 따라
recede [risíːd] 멀어지다　**implication** [ìmplikéiʃən] 의미
eminent [émənənt] 저명한

지문에서, 글쓴이는 _____ 으로써 빛 변화의 개념을 설명한다.

(A) 위치를 바꾸는 여러 가지 별들의 예를 제시함으로써
(B) 음파를 구성하는 사이렌의 종류를 분류함으로써
(C) 다른 색깔로 서서히 바뀌는 별들을 묘사함으로써
(D) 그것을 음파의 변화라는 비슷한 예와 비교함으로써

11 킬라우에아 산은 하와이의 가장 큰 섬을 만든 순상 활화산이다. 그것은 적당히 불안정하다고 여겨지는데, 이는 그것의 대규모 폭발 전력에도 불구하고, 대다수의 폭발은 상대적으로 약했기 때문이다. 킬라우에아 산은 처음에 지구 표면층의 태평양 지각 판이 맨틀의 격렬한 활동의 대류 지점인 하와이 열점 위를 이동 했을 때 해저 화산으로 생겨났다. 압력이 가해진 마그마는 그 후 에 대양 지각을 반복적으로 뚫고 나아갔고, [1]시간이 흘러, 화산 은 새로운 현무암 용암층의 끊임없는 추가를 통해 고도를 만들 어내 결국 10만여 년 전에 대양의 표면을 마침내 돌파했다. 그 때부터, 킬라우에아 산은 그것의 중앙 분출구를 통해서뿐만 아 니라 불규칙한 패턴으로 퍼지며 선형의 균열을 거쳐 증식하는 분열 방법으로도 계속해서 확장해왔다. 그리고 서로에게 근접한 균열 지역이 많은 곳에서는, [2]그것들은 악명 높은 푸우오오 폭발 때와 같은 새로운 거대한 분출구를 가끔 만들어내는데, 이것은 1983년에 시작되어 지난 500년 동안 그 어떤 것보다 가장 오래 지속된 폭발이라는 특징을 가지고 있다.

active shield volcano 순상 활화산　**establish** [istǽbliʃ] 만들다
moderately [máːdərətli] 적당히　**volatile** [váːlətl] 불안정한
extensive [iksténsiv] 대규모의　**eruptive** [irʌ́ptiv] 폭발의
submarine volcano 해저 화산　**tectonic plate** 지각판
crust [krʌst] 표면층, 껍질　**hotspot** [háːtspàt] 열점
convection [kənvékʃən] 대류　**intense** [inténs] 격렬한
pressurize [préʃəraiz] 압력을 가하다
subsequently [sʌ́bsikwəntli] 그 후에
push through ~을 뚫고 나아가다　**oceanic** [òuʃiǽnik] 대양의
continual [kəntínjuəl] 끊임없는　**basalt** [bəsɔ́ːlt] 현무암
lava [láːvə] 용암　**breach** [briːtʃ] 돌파하다
expand [ikspǽnd] 확장하다　**vent** [vent] 분출, 통풍
fissure [fíʃər] 분열　**radiate** [réidieit] 퍼지다, 내뿜다
propagate [prɑ́ːpəgeit] 증식하다　**linear** [líniər] 선형의
fracture [frǽktʃər] 균열　**rift** [rift] 균열
proximity [prɑːksíməti] 근접　**infamous** [ínfəməs] 악명 높은
distinction [distíŋkʃən] 특징　**discharge** [dístʃɑːrdʒ] 폭발, 배출

1 지문에서 글쓴이는 왜 "a fresh layer of basalt lava"를 언

급하는가?

(A) 화산으로부터 분출된 물질을 묘사하기 위해
(B) 화산이 어떻게 크기가 커져 왔는지 설명하기 위해
(C) 맨틀 대류의 예를 제공하기 위해
(D) 화산 분열이 어떻게 형성되는지 보여주기 위해

2 지문에서 글쓴이는 왜 "Pu'u 'Ō'ō eruption"을 언급하는가?

(A) 선형의 균열이 비대칭적인 방향으로 이동할 수 있음을 증 명하기 위해
(B) 추가적인 분출구를 만들어내는 사건의 예를 제공하기 위해
(C) 이례적으로 긴 시간 지속했던 폭발을 강조하기 위해
(D) 균열 지역이 종종 서로 간의 짧은 거리를 형성한다는 것 을 나타내기 위해

3 지문의 목적은 무엇인가?

(A) 여러 종류의 폭발들을 비교하기 위해
(B) 순상 화산의 구성 요소를 묘사하기 위해
(C) 화산 분출구의 발달을 보여주기 위해
(D) 화산의 형성을 설명하기 위해

12 건강한 면역 체계를 발달시키기 위해서, 유아들은 어머니로부터 세포 물질과 영양분을 필요로 한다. 이러한 것들의 이동은 자궁 에서 시작하고 출생 후에 수유를 통해 계속되는데, 이는 유아에 게 많은 이점들을 제공한다. 첫째 날부터, 어머니는 특히 백혈구 (leukocyte)와 같은 항체들이 풍부한 모유의 시초 형태인 초유 를 생산한다. [1]처음에, 초유는 비교적 높은 농도의 백혈구들을 유아에게 전달한다. 특히, 어머니나 아이의 감염 기간 동안에는, 이 백혈구의 운반은 급격한 가속을 겪을 것이다. 그러나, 둘째 주 후반에는, 어머니로부터 유아에게 전해지는 백혈구의 양이 상당히 줄어드는데, 이는 아마 아이가 스스로 충분한 면역 세포 들을 생산하기 시작하기 때문이다. 수유 과정 내내, 아기는 필수 적인 장 박테리아의 함양을 촉진시키는 단백질의 획득을 통해 필수적인 영양분들을 받는다. [2]동시에 이것들은 약한 면역 체계 를 가진 유아들을 죽일 능력이 있는 박테리아인 대장균으로부터 아기들을 보호한다.

immune system 면역 체계　**infant** [ínfənt] 유아
cellular [séljələr] 세포의　**nutrient** [núːtriənt] 영양분
transfer [trǽnsfər] 이동　**womb** [wuːm] 자궁
postnatally [pòustnéitli] 출생 후에　**lactation** [læktéiʃən] 수유
colostrum [kələ́ːstrəm] 초유(출산 후 3일경까지 분비되는 모유)
preliminary [prilímineri] 시초의, 예비의　**breast milk** 모유
antibody [ǽntibɑ̀di] 항체　**leukocyte** [lúːkəsàit] 백혈구
concentration [kɑ̀ːnsntréiʃən] 농도　**infection** [infékʃən] 감염
conveyance [kənvéiəns] 운반　**undergo** [ʌ̀ndərgóu] 겪다
acceleration [əksèləréiʃən] 가속　**diminish** [dimíniʃ] 줄어들다
presumably [prizúːməbli] 아마, 추측상
immunological [ìmjunəlɑ́dʒikəl] 면역의
acquisition [æ̀kwizíʃən] 획득　**protein** [próutiːn] 단백질
promote [prəmóut] 촉진시키다　**cultivation** [kʌ̀ltivéiʃən] 함양
intestinal [intéstənl] 장의, 창자의

simultaneously[sàiməltéiniəsli] 동시에 E. coli[íːkóulai] 대장균

1 지문에서, 글쓴이는 _____으로써 초유의 전달을 설명한다.

  (A) 어머니로부터 아이로의 백혈구 이동의 단계를 묘사함으로써

  (B) 모유 수유를 했거나, 하지 않았던 아기들의 백혈구 수준을 비교함으로써

  (C) 유아들이 감염과 싸울 수 있는 다양한 방법들을 자세히 설명함으로써

  (D) 특정 질병에 대한 두 개의 다른 면역 반응을 대조함으로써

2 지문에서 글쓴이는 왜 "E. coli"를 언급하는가?

  (A) 유아들이 왜 모유의 단백질을 필요로 하는지 설명하기 위해

  (B) 신생아들의 모유 수유의 부정적인 결과를 묘사하기 위해

  (C) 모유가 유익한 박테리아를 함유한다는 증거를 제공하기 위해

  (D) 잠재적으로 위험한 병원체의 예를 제시하기 위해

3 글쓴이가 지문을 쓴 목적은 _____하기 위해서이다.

  (A) 유아에게 왜 특정 영양분이 필요한지 묘사하기 위해

  (B) 모유에 있는 백혈구의 가치를 강조하기 위해

  (C) 유아 모유 수유의 이점들을 설명하기 위해

  (D) 수유의 다양한 단계들을 강조하기 위해

13 우박은 먹구름 내 얼음 결정들의 착빙을 통해 생긴다. 이러한 얼음 덩어리는 구름의 대부분이 섭씨 0도 미만일 때 얼기 시작하는 물방울들로부터 형성된다. 얼음이 물과 충돌하면, 물은 빠르게 얼고 새로운 층들을 형성하며, [1]이것들은 단면에서 보일 수 있고 반으로 잘린 양파와 몇몇 유사점을 공유한다. 우박의 크기가 커지려면, 그것은 풍부한 물방울의 존재뿐만 아니라 먹구름 안에서 반복적으로 우박을 순환시키는 상승 대기를 필요로 하는데, 이는 점점 더 많은 충돌을 일으키며 착빙을 영구화한다. [2]상승 기류 없이는, 언 액체는 그것이 충분한 크기를 만들 수 있기도 전에 중력에 의해 구름으로부터 떨어질 것이다. 그리고 상승하는 대기 흐름은 강력한 폭풍 안에서 가장 세기 때문에, 공전 방해의 격렬함이 우박의 크기에 영향을 미친다. 이것이 작은 먹구름들은 겨우 지름 5밀리미터의 우박만 만들어낼 수 있는 반면, 큰 먹구름들은 지름 15센티미터까지의 우박을 만들어낼 수 있는 이유이다.

hail[heil] 우박 accretion[əkríːʃən] 착빙, 부착
particle[páːrtikl] 결정, 입자 storm cloud 먹구름
clump[klʌmp] 덩어리 water droplet 물방울 freeze[friːz] 얼다
Celsius[sélsiəs] 섭씨의 collide with ~과 충돌하다
latter[lǽtər] 후자 cross section 단면 presence[prézns] 존재
abundant[əbʌ́ndənt] 풍부한, 충분한
circulate[sə́ːrkjəleit] 순환시키다
perpetuate[pərpétʃueit] 영구화하다 updraft[ʌ́pdrӕft] 상승 기류
dispel[dispél] 떨어지게 하다, 떨쳐버리다 mass[mӕs] 크기, 덩어리
upward[ʌ́pwərd] 상승하는 current[kə́ːrənt] 흐름
intense[inténs] 강렬한 severity[səvérəti] 격렬함

atmospheric disturbance 공전 방해
dimension[diménʃən] 크기 diameter[daiǽmitər] 지름

1 지문에서 글쓴이는 왜 "an onion"을 언급하는가?

  (A) 층의 성장에 있어서 착빙의 역할을 강조하기 위해

  (B) 몇몇 얼음 결정이 얼마나 커질 수 있는지 강조하기 위해

  (C) 우박의 내부 구조를 예를 들어 설명하기 위해

  (D) 두 대상의 상대적인 밀도를 대조하기 위해

2 글쓴이는 지문에서 _____하기 위해 "an updraft"를 언급한다.

  (A) 일부 강수가 왜 얼지 못하는지 설명하기 위해

  (B) 먹구름의 흔한 특징을 묘사하기 위해

  (C) 우박 발달에 있어 중력의 영향을 보여주기 위해

  (D) 우박 형성의 전제 조건을 제공하기 위해

3 다음 중 지문의 구조를 가장 잘 설명한 것은?

  (A) 기상 현상의 과정이 묘사되고 있다.

  (B) 다양한 구름 종류의 차이점들이 약술되고 있다.

  (C) 우박 발달에 대한 상충되는 이론들이 설명되고 있다.

  (D) 폭풍에서 바람 흐름의 역할이 자세히 설명되고 있다.

14 찰스 다윈은 자의식이라는 감정은 인간에게만 유일무이하다는 관념을 개척했다. 그러나, 어떻게 이러한 능력이 사람에게 생기는지에 대한 심리 연구는 훨씬 나중에 나왔는데, 이 연구는 삼사 개월이 지난 아기들 62명의 일별 감정적 행동을 관찰하고 기록했던 Kathryn Bridges에 의한 1932년 실험에서 시작되었다. [1]이 실험과 차후의 연구는 아이들의 감정적 발달이 유아기부터 약 세 살의 나이까지 뚜렷한 단계들로 진행된다는 것을 밝혔다. 갓난아이들은 매우 제한된 감정적 행동의 모음을 보인다. [2]예를 들어, 아이를 들어 올리거나 간지럼을 태우는 것은 만족이나 행복을 표현하는 반응을 유발하고, 이것은 미소와 같은 얼굴 표정을 통해 드러낼 수 있다. 약 18개월 무렵에는, 아기들은 자기 인식의 증거들을 보여주기 시작하는데, 이는 공감이나 질투와 같은 감정들을 일으킨다. 그다음 이삼 년 사이에, 유아들은 사회 규칙들을 이해하는 능력을 생성하고, 이는 자기평가적 정서라고 알려진 것의 시작으로 이어진다. 이것들은 유아들이 그들 자신의 성공과 실패 또는 그들이 기대에 부응하여 살아왔는지를 분석할 수 있게 해주는 문화적 기준을 받아들이는 것으로부터 기인한다. 그들의 자신에 대한 맥락상의 평가가 세 살 무렵에는, 자존심이나 부끄러움을 포함한 복잡한 감정들을 포괄하도록 성숙하고 성장하게 된다. 감정의 폭과 섬세함은 이 시점이 지나도 계속해서 확장되고 다양해지지만, 심리학자들은 이것을 뒤따르는 모든 감정적 경험과 표현에 대한 기준으로 정한다.

pioneer[pàiənír] 개척하다 notion[nóuʃən] 관념
self-consciousness[sèlfkáːnʃəsnəs] 자의식
psychological[sàikəláːdʒikl] 심리의 arise[əráiz] 생기다
proceed[prousíːd] 진행되다 infancy[ínfənsi] 유아기
assortment[əsɔ́ːrtmənt] 모음 tickle[tíkl] 간지럼을 태우다
contentment[kənténtmənt] 만족 exhibit[igzíbit] 드러내다

self-awareness[sèlfəwérnəs] 자기 인식
empathy[émpəθi] 공감 toddler[tɑ́:dlər] 유아
onset[ɑ́:nset] 시작 evaluative emotion 자기평가적 정서
incorporate[inkɔ́:rpəreit] 받아들이다, 포함하다
contextual[kəntékstʃuəl] 맥락상의
assessment[əsésmənt] 평가 mature[mətʃúr] 성숙하다
subtlety[sʌ́tlti] 섬세함 diversify[daivə́:rsifai] 다양해지다
label[léibl] ~으로 정하다, 꼬리표를 붙이다
benchmark[béntʃmɑ:rk] 기준 ensue[insú:] 뒤따르다

1 지문에서 글쓴이는 왜 "a 1932 experiment"를 언급하는가?

(A) 오직 인간만이 자기 인식을 할 수 있다는 것을 증명하기
위해

(B) 전문가들이 어떻게 감정이 나이에 따라 변한다는 것을 알
게 되었는지 설명하기 위해

(C) 무엇이 심리 연구의 새로운 시대를 열었는지 밝히기 위해

(D) 감정이 어떻게 습득되는지에 대한 상충되는 관점들을 비
교하기 위해

2 글쓴이는 지문에서 _____ 하기 위해 "picking up or
tickling a child"를 언급한다.

(A) 특정 연구에서 아기들이 어떻게 다루어졌는지를 설명하
기 위해

(B) 신생아들과 활발하게 상호작용하는 것의 중요성을 서술
하기 위해

(C) 자의식의 감정들을 보여주는 행동들을 나타내기 위해

(D) 특정한 감정적 반응을 끌어내는 행동들의 예를 제시하기
위해

3 다음 중 2단락과 1단락의 관계를 가장 잘 설명한 것은?

(A) 2단락은 1단락에서 약술된 실험을 분석한다.

(B) 2단락은 1단락에서 요약된 과정을 자세히 설명한다.

(C) 2단락은 1단락의 주장을 뒷받침하기 위한 추가 연구를 소
개한다.

(D) 2단락은 1단락에서 묘사된 이론에 대한 대조적인 증거를
제공한다.

15 석기시대는 300만 년도 더 이전에 시작되었고 기원전 9세기에
금속 도구들을 버리는 기술의 발견 이전까지 지속되었다. 이름
이 암시하듯이, 석기시대에는 석기 도구들이 두드러졌는데, 그
것들 중 다수는 호수 바닥에 보존되었고 이후에 수위가 낮아지
자 드러나, 고고학적 발견을 가능하게 했다. 석기시대는 주로 올
두바이와 아슐리안의 두 시기로 대표된다.

올두바이 문화는 탄자니아의 올두바이 협곡의 이름을 따서 명명
되는데, 그곳에서 올두바이 공예품들이 최초로 발견되었다. 이
시기의 특징은 올두바이 도끼라고 불리는 미가공의 조약돌 도구
인데, 이것은 자갈 크기의 돌들을 몇 개의 조각으로 망치질함으
로써 만들어졌다. 이것들은 아마 음식 준비에 활용하기 위해 만
들어졌을 것이다. 또한 동일 종족이 뼈로 도구를 만들었다는 믿
을 만한 증거도 있다. 몇몇 전문가들은 심지어 그들이 목재로도
작업했을 가능성이 높다고 추측하지만, 그 어떤 알려진 올두바
이 유적에서도 결정적인 사례가 보존되지 않았기는 하다.

[3]반면, 아슐리안의 솜씨는 더욱 세련되었고 소위 주먹 도끼라는
전통을 탄생시켰다. 아슐리안 도끼는 두 개의 평평한 면과 한 점
에서 만나는 서로 다른 날카로운 모서리를 특징으로 삼는다. 이
디자인은 만들기 상당히 더 어렵기는 했지만, 자르고 얇게 써는
데에 도끼를 훨씬 더 효과적으로 만들었다. [2]이러한 도구들은 같
은 크기, 대칭, 그리고 두께를 가진다는 점에서 납작한, 펼친 사
람의 손과 외관상 꽤 비슷했기 때문에, 몇몇 인류학자들은 그것
들이 일종의 제3의 손이라는 상징을 가졌을 수 있고, 따라서, 그
저 실용적인 것을 넘어서는 어떤 기능을 했을 수도 있다고 믿
는다.

forge[fɔ:rdʒ] 버리다 dominate[dɑ́:mineit] 두드러지다, 지배하다
implement[ímpləmənt] 도구 preserve[prizə́:rv] 보존하다
expose[ikspóuz] 드러내다 drop[drɑ:p] 낮아지다
archaeological[ὰ:rkiəlɑ́dʒikəl] 고고학적인
represent[rèprizént] 대표하다 artifact[ɑ́:rtəfækt] 공예품
crude[kru:d] 미가공의 pebble[pébl] 조약돌
cobble[kɑ́:bl] 자갈 craft[kræft] 만들다
reliable[riláiəbl] 믿을 만한 evidence[évidəns] 증거
speculate[spékjuleit] 추측하다 definitive[difínətiv] 결정적인
craftsmanship[krǽftsmənʃip] 솜씨
sophisticated[səfístikeitid] 세련된 ax[æks] 도끼
considerably[kənsídərəbli] 상당히 symmetry[símətri] 대칭
anthropologist[æ̀nθrəpɑ́:lədʒist] 인류학자
symbolism[símbəlizəm] 상징 pragmatic[prægmǽtik] 실용적인

1 석기 도구들에 대한 전반적인 논의에서 1단락의 목적은?

(A) 도구 발달의 폭넓은 시간적 배경을 제공한다.

(B) 인간이 도구를 얼마나 일찍 생산했는지에 대한 이론을 제
안한다.

(C) 도구를 발견하는 데 사용된 고고학적 방법을 설명한다.

(D) 도구의 정확한 시대를 결정하는 기발한 접근을 소개한다.

2 지문에서 글쓴이는 왜 주먹 도끼의 외관과 크기에 대해 자세히
설명하는가?

(A) 주먹 도끼가 반드시 실용적인 도구는 아니었음을 시사하
기 위해

(B) 인류학자들에 의한 논란이 있는 주장에 대해 의구심을 제
기하기 위해

(C) 왜 주먹 도끼의 정확한 목적이 결코 알려지지 않을 것인
지를 알리기 위해

(D) 주먹 도끼의 디자인이 사람의 손을 본떴다는 견해를 지지
하기 위해

3 지문에서 2단락과 3단락의 관계는 무엇인가?

(A) 2단락은 이론을 제시하고 3단락은 그것의 타당성을 진술
한다.

(B) 2단락은 절차의 발견을 논의하고 3단락은 그것의 개선을
자세히 설명한다.

(C) 3단락은 2단락에서 약술된 기술들이 왜 버려졌는지 설명
한다.

(D) 3단락은 2단락에서 묘사된 물건과 비교되는 대상을 제시
한다.

p.194

1. (D)	2. (D)	3. (B)
4. (C)	5. (B)	6. (C)
7. (C)	8. (A)	9. (D)

10. (B)-4단락, (E)-2~3단락, (F)-5~6단락

1 1929년 주식 시장의 붕괴로 인해 촉발된 대공황은 평범한 사람들의 삶에 부정적인 영향을 끼친 세계적인 경제 침체였다. 이는 특히 미국에서 그러했는데, ¹미국에서 대공황은 충격적일 정도로 높은 실업률을 야기했으며, 많은 실업자를 집으로부터 Hooverville로 알려진 빈민가로 내몰았다. 이 판잣집과 텐트 지역들은 태만으로 인해 이 사태를 만들었다고 크게 비난받았던 Herbert Hoover 대통령의 이름을 따서 명명되었다. 대공황의 파괴적인 효과는 정부에 경제를 부흥시키라는 굉장한 압박을 주었고, 1932년 Franklin D. Roosevelt 대통령의 당선 후, 몇 가지 심각한 문제들을 다루기 위해 새로운 경제 법규가 제정되었다.

2 ²증권에 대한 규제는 Roosevelt 정부의 한 가지 주요 사안이었는데, 이는 이 분야의 불충분한 감독이 주식 시장 붕괴에 기여한 주요 원인이었기 때문이다. 대공황 전에 회사들은 자사에 대해 거짓이거나 호도하는 정보를 알리며, 사람들이 그들의 주식을 매입하도록 유도하기를 바랐다. 희망에 찬 수많은 투자자는 자회사들의 실제 가치를 잘 모르는 채로 과도하게 높은 가격에 증권을 매입하여 주식 시장이 점점 더 높이 치솟도록 했고, 이는 훨씬 더 많은 사람이 투자하도록 조장했다. 이러한 행동 양식은 마침내 거품이 꺼져 시장이 급락하기 전까지 계속해서 인위적으로 주가를 상승시켰다.

3 ⁵이 문제에 대응하기 위해, 정부는 증권을 발행하는 모든 회사가 투자자들에게 손익에 대한 재무 자료를 포함한 특정한 중요 정보를 제공하도록 요구하기 시작했다. ³추가로, 증권거래위원회라고 불리는 신설 기관이 새로운 요건들을 실행하고, 회사들이 잠재적 구매자들에게 반드시 정확한 정보를 공개하도록 만드는 책임을 맡게 되었다. ⁴ᴮ결과적으로, 투자자들은 어떤 회사의 주식을 구매하기 전에 기업정보를 분석함으로써 정보에 근거한 결정을 내릴 수 있었고, ⁴ᴰ증권의 가격은 기업의 실제 가치를 더욱 정확하게 반영하였는데, ⁴ᴬ이는 주식 시장을 한층 더 안정적으로 만들었다.

4 증권 규제가 또 다른 시장 붕괴를 방지하는 데 도움이 된 한편, 대공황은 금융 부문에서도 추가적인 규제 처리를 필요하게 했다. 경기 침체 초기에 경제가 악화되기 시작하자 사람들은 은행에서 예금을 점점 더 많이 인출하였고, 어떤 특정한 은행에 돈이 부족하다는 소문이 돌면 예금자들은 그곳에 떼로 몰려들어 즉각적인 지급을 요구하였다. 이 '예금인출사태'는 수많은 기관을 파산에 이르게 했고, 1933년까지 미국 내 거의 10,000 군데의 은행이 파산하여 은행업

에 대한 소비자의 신뢰가 하락했다. Roosevelt 정부는 FDIC라고도 불리는 연방예금보험공사를 설립함으로써 이 위기에 대처했는데, 이 기관은 금융기관으로부터 보험료를 징수하고 그 수익금을 고객에게 상환하는 데 사용하기 시작하여 은행이 파산하더라도 사람들이 돈을 잃지 않도록 하였다. FDIC의 설립은 금융기관에 대한 대중의 신뢰를 향상시키고 은행 도산의 빈도와 부정적 효과를 감소시킨 것으로 널리 인정받고 있다.

5 아마도 노동 시장만큼, 특히 노동조합에 관해서, 정부 감시의 증가가 크게 느껴진 규제 분야는 없을 것이다. 이 조합들은 대공황 전에도 수년 동안 더 높은 임금과 더 좋은 근무 환경을 위해 기업과 협상해왔지만, ⁷경기 침체 동안의 치솟는 실업률 때문에 회사들은 간단하게 노동조합원들을 해고하고 대신 비조합원들을 쉽게 고용할 수 있었고, 이는 노동자들이 이러한 조합에 가입하기를 주저하게 만들었으며 노동조합의 힘은 대단히 약해졌다. 결과적으로 회사들은 노동자들의 요구를 무시할 수 있게 되었고, 이는 Roosevelt 정부가 단지 노동조합에 가입했다는 이유로 기업이 직원을 해고하는 것을 금지하고, 회사가 노동조합을 그냥 무시하기보다는 노동조합과 협상할 것을 요구하는 법규를 통과시키도록 촉구하였다.

6 신설된 법은 노동자들이 고용주의 양보를 얻어내도록 도왔으나, 최저임금제와 주당 표준 근로 시간을 확립하기 위해 추가적인 규제가 제정되었다. 소수의 일자리를 두고 수많은 실업자가 경쟁했기 때문에, 많은 기업은 더 낮은 임금을 제공하면서 더 많은 근로 시간을 요구하고 있었다. 정부는 회사가 직원들에게 시간당 최소 25센트를 지급하고 주당 40시간을 초과해서 근무한 시간에 대해 추가 수당을 제공할 것을 요구함으로써 이 문제들을 완화하려고 노력했다. 최저임금제의 전반적인 경제 효과는 논란의 대상이지만, 많은 경제학자는 더 높은 임금이 경제를 부흥시켰다고 생각하는데 이는 일반인들이 더 많은 돈을 소비할 수 있어서 재화와 용역의 수요를 증가시켰기 때문이다. 더욱이, 근로 시간의 제한은 회사들이 축소된 시간을 보충하기 위해 더 많은 직원을 고용하도록 촉진했을 것이다.

The Great Depression (경제) 대공황
downturn[dáuntə̀ːrn] 경기 침체
staggeringly[stǽgəriŋli] 충격적일 정도로   **shack**[ʃæk] 판잣집
name after ~의 이름을 따서 명명하다
inaction[inǽkʃən] 태만, 활동 부족
devastating[dévəstèitiŋ] 파괴적인   **enact**[inǽkt] 제정하다
preeminent[priémənənt] 주요한   **oversight**[óuvərsàit] 감독, 단속
misleading[mislíːdiŋ] 호도하는   **underlying company** 자회사
mandate[mǽndeit] 요구하다
Securities and Exchange Commission(SEC) 증권거래위원회
deteriorate[ditíəriərèit] 악화되다   **bank run** 예금인출사태
Federal Deposit Insurance Corporation(FDIC) 연방예금보험공사
insurance premium 보험료   **proceeds**[próusiːdz] 수익금
reimburse[rìːimbə́ːrs] 상환하다   **insolvent**[insálvənt] 파산의
concession[kənséʃən] 양보   **alleviate**[əlíːvièit] 완화시키다

1 지문에서 글쓴이는 왜 "Hoovervilles"를 언급하는가?

(A) 왜 많은 실업자들이 노숙자가 되었는지 설명하기 위해

(B) 대공황의 전 세계적인 결과의 예를 제시하기 위해

(C) Hoover 대통령이 실업자들에게 거처를 제공하는 것에 책임이 있었음을 보여주기 위해

(D) 대공황에 의해 얼마나 사람들이 부정적으로 영향을 받았는지 설명하기 위해

2 2단락에 따르면, 다음 중 주식 시장 붕괴의 원인이었던 것은?

(A) 정부가 주식 시장에 너무 많이 투자했다.

(B) 회사들이 자신들에 대한 정확한 재정 정보를 기록하지 않았다.

(C) 주가가 회사의 실제 가치를 평가절하했다.

(D) 대공황 이전에는 증권이 충분히 규제되지 않았다.

3 글쓴이는 _____ 하기 위해 "Securities and Exchange Commission"을 언급한다.

(A) 새로운 증권 규제가 불충분함을 시사하기 위해

(B) 새로운 증권 규제가 어떻게 실행되었는지 보여주기 위해

(C) 증권 법이 만들어졌던 과정을 설명하기 위해

(D) 증권에 대한 정보가 어떻게 발표되었는지 설명하기 위해

4 3단락에 따르면, 다음 중 새로운 증권 규제의 효과가 아닌 것은?

(A) 주식 시장이 덜 불안정해졌다.

(B) 사람들은 그들이 투자한 회사에 대해 더 많은 정보를 알게 되었다.

(C) 많은 회사 주식의 가치가 올라가기 시작했다.

(D) 주가가 회사의 가치를 더 정확하게 보여주었다.

5 지문에서 2단락과 3단락의 관계는 무엇인가?

(A) 3단락은 2단락에서 약술된 증권 규제의 효과를 제시한다.

(B) 2단락은 3단락에서 취해진 행동에 의해 해결된 문제를 설명한다.

(C) 3단락은 2단락에서 소개된 증권의 개념을 설명한다.

(D) 2단락은 규제를 옹호하는 주장을 제시하고 3단락은 그것을 반박한다.

6 지문의 단어 "deteriorate"과 의미상 가장 유사한 것은?

(A) 사라지다

(B) 안정되다

(C) 악화되다

(D) 점점 커지다

7 글쓴이는 왜 "companies could simply fire union employees and easily hire non-union replacements"를 언급하는가?

(A) 당시에 실업률이 왜 그렇게 높았는지 나타내기 위해

(B) 새로운 노동 규제의 효과 중 하나를 보여주기 위해

(C) 왜 많은 노동자들이 노동조합에 참여하지 않았는지 설명하기 위해

(D) 회사들이 어떻게 노동조합을 장려했는지 설명하기 위해

8 지문의 단어 "alleviate"과 의미상 가장 유사한 것은?

(A) 완화하다

(B) 근절하다

(C) 제거하다

(D) 발생시키다

9 아래 문장 중 지문 속의 음영된 문장의 핵심 정보를 가장 잘 표현하고 있는 것은 무엇인가? 오답은 문장의 의미를 현저히 왜곡하거나 핵심 정보를 빠뜨리고 있다.

(A) 결과는 논쟁의 여지가 있지만, 많은 경제학자들은 최저임금제가 대공황을 끝낸 원인이었다고 생각한다.

(B) 경제학자들은 최저임금제의 전반적인 경제 효과에 대해 계속해서 논의하고 있는데, 그것은 회사가 노동자에게 지급하는 금액을 증가시켰다.

(C) 많은 경제학자들은 최저임금법이 논쟁의 여지는 있지만, 노동자들에 의해 생산되는 재화와 서비스의 양을 증가시킴으로써 경제에 도움이 되었다고 생각한다.

(D) 그것의 효과는 전체적으로 논쟁의 여지가 있지만, 최저임금법은 노동자들이 더 많은 재화와 서비스를 구입할 수 있었기 때문에 경제 회복을 자극했다는 점에서 많은 경제학자들에게 인정받는다.

10 **지시:** 지문 요약을 위한 도입 문장이 아래에 주어져 있다. 지문의 가장 중요한 내용을 나타내는 보기 3개를 골라 요약을 완성하시오. 어떤 문장은 지문에 언급되지 않은 내용이나 사소한 정보를 담고 있으므로 요약에 포함되지 않는다. 이 문제는 2점이다.

> 미국 정부는 대공황 동안 여러 가지 중요한 문제를 해결하기 위해 새로운 규제들을 만들었다.
>
> · (B) 증가하는 예금인출사태의 수로 인해, 은행 산업 내의 문제를 줄이기 위한 연방예금보험공사가 만들어졌다.
>
> · (E) 이전에는 정부에 의해 간과되었지만, 대공황의 한 가지 원인을 해결하기 위해 증권은 더 엄중히 규제되었다.
>
> · (F) 1930년대는 고용 규제에 의미 있는 증진을 목도했는데, 이는 노동자들이 겪은 여러 가지 고충을 줄이기 위한 목적이었다.

(A) 노동자들의 협상 능력을 강화하기 위해, 회사들은 더 많은 노동조합원을 고용하고 봉급과 노동 시간에 대해 그들에게 양보하도록 요구받았다.

(C) 증권거래위원회는 새로운 증권 규제를 작성하고 회사가 팔 수 있는 주식의 수를 제한하기 위해 만들어졌다.

(D) 오늘날의 대부분 경제학자들은 새로운 규제가 경제 환경을 개선하고 대공황을 끝내는 데 성공을 거두었다고 생각한다.

02 Mars

p.198

1. (A)	2. (C)	3. (D)
4. (B)	5. (A)	6. (B)

7. (C)   8. (C)   9. (A)
10. (C)−3~4단락, (D)−2단락, (E)−5단락

1 태양계의 네 번째 행성인 화성은 육안으로 볼 수 있으며, 계절이 변함에 따라 밤하늘에서 차고 기울기를 반복한다. 지구와 화성의 궤도가 모두 타원형이기 때문에 화성은 지구에 가장 가까울 때 매우 뚜렷한 불그스름한 색을 띠는데, 이는 15년, 17년의 간격으로 번갈아 32년마다 두 차례 나타난다. 대조적으로, 화성이 궤도상 지구의 정반대편에 있게 되면 육안으로 거의 볼 수 없거나 태양광에 가려서 보이지 않을 수 있다.

2 3천 년이 넘도록, 이 붉은 행성은 우주에서 달 다음으로 가장 많이 연구되어 온 천체이다. 화성의 지구와의 근접성은 대량의 과학적 연구의 원동력이 되었고, 화성에 지능을 가진 외계 생명체가 있을지도 모른다는 설이 제기되었다. 19세기에 두 명의 저명한 천문학자, Percival Lowell과 Giovanni Schiaparelli는 고성능 분광기를 사용해서 화성의 세부적인 모습을 연구했고 특이한 지형적 특징을 지적했는데, 그들은 이것을 이탈리아어로 channel(물길)이라는 뜻의 'canali'라고 불렀다. [3]하지만 당시에는 'canal(운하)'로 오역되는 경우가 많았다. 운하라는 용어는 인위적으로 건설되었다는 의미를 함축하고 있기 때문에, 운하의 발견을 이 먼 행성에 한때 지능을 가진 생명체가 존재했다는 뜻으로 받아들인 사람들이 많았다. 이에 뒤따라 과학적, 문학적 관심이 많아졌고, 대중의 환상은 태양계에 또 다른 지각이 있는 종족이 존재할지도 모른다는 생각에 사로잡혔다.

3 [5]사람들은 생명체에 극히 비우호적인 다른 모든 행성보다도 화성에 훨씬 더 매료되었는데, 왜냐하면 이 붉은 행성이 가장 도달하기 쉬운 목적지였을 뿐만 아니라, 생명의 발달과 인간 탐험가들의 장기 거주에 도움이 되는 지형을 가지고 있을 것으로 생각되었기 때문이다. 화성의 표면은 계절에 따라서 색이 변하는데, 한때 이것이 초목에 의해 발생한 현상이라고 추측되기도 했다. 어떤 사람들은 지표면의 식물이 여름에는 꽃을 피우고 겨울에는 비활성기에 들어간다고 생각했다. 초기의 관측자들은 생명의 필수조건인 물의 가능성을 암시하는 화성 극지방의 만년설의 존재를 발견하기도 했다.

4 이렇게 잠재적으로 생명체를 품고 있는 화성의 이미지는 Mariner호가 22장의 클로즈업된 화성 표면의 사진을 보내온 1965년 7월까지 유지되었다. 이 사진들은 황량한 불모지를 보여주었는데, 이는 많은 사람이 그려왔던 비옥한 화성과 전혀 다른 것이었다. 한때 지적인 문명사회가 농경 생활을 하고 있었다는 징조로 여겨지던 운하는 단지 자연적으로 생긴 물길이 말라버린 것이거나, 자연적인 지형에 의해 드리워졌던 그림자일 뿐인 것으로 드러났다. 초목의 존재 가능성을 암시하는 것으로 보였던 색의 변화는 가까이서 살펴보니 표면의 모래 폭풍의 결과인 것으로 드러났는데, 이는 바짝 마른 넓은 표면에 계절풍이 부는 것이다.

5 Mariner호 원정 이후에도 다른 수많은 탐사선이 화성으로 보내졌고, 그중 일부는 표면에 성공적으로 착륙했다. 희박한 대기가 위험한 자외선을 충분히 걸러주지 못하기 때문에 이 행성의 표면에는 어

떤 생명체도 살지 못할 것으로 보였지만, [7]화성을 죽은 행성으로 공표한 것은 시기상조였을지도 모른다는 몇몇 증거들이 최근에 나타났다. [9]현재 화성의 표면에 있는 NASA의 두 개의 탐사로봇 Opportunity와 Spirit은 새로운 조사를 수행 중이며, 공기 중의 메탄의 흔적을 발견했다. 메탄은 불안정하기 때문에 메탄을 생성하는 박테리아인 메탄 생성 미생물에 의해서 생성되었을 가능성이 크다. 결정적인 증거는 아직 발견되지 않았지만, 앞으로의 연구는 외계 생명체가 존재할 수 있는 장소로서의 화성에 초점을 맞추고 진행될 것이다.

wax and wane 차고 기울다   elliptical[ilíptikəl] 타원형의
reddish[rédiʃ] 불그스름한   alternate[ɔ́:ltərnèit] 번갈아 일어나다
interval[íntərvəl] 간격   virtually[vɔ́:rtʃuəli] 거의
celestial body 천체   proximity[prɑksíməti] 근접(성)
spur[spə:r] ~의 원동력이 되다   plethora[pléθərə] 대량
spectroscope[spéktrəskòup] 분광기   note[nout] 지적하다
topographical[tὰpəgrǽfikəl] 지형의   remote[rimóut] 먼
a spate of 많은   sentient[sénʃənt] 지각 있는
hostile[hάstl] 비우호적인   conducive to ~에 도움이 되는
vegetation[vèdʒətéiʃən] 초목   flora[flɔ́:rə] 식물
ice cap 만년설   hint[hint] 암시하다
prerequisite[pri:rékwəzit] 필수조건
potentially[pəténʃəli] 잠재적으로   stark[stɑ:rk] 황량한
a far cry from ~과 전혀 다른 것   allude[əlú:d] 암시하다
parched[pά:rtʃt] 바짝 마른   expedition[èkspədíʃən] 원정
hazardous[hǽzərdəs] 위험한   ultraviolet light 자외선
pronouncement[prənáunsmənt] 공표
premature[prì:mətjúər] 시기상조의   rover[róuvər] 탐사로봇
methanogen[meθǽnədʒən] 메탄 생성 미생물
conclusive[kənklú:siv] 결정적인
extraterrestrial[èkstrətəréstriəl] 외계의

1 지문의 단어 "intervals"와 의미상 가장 유사한 것은?

(A) 주기
(B) 변화
(C) 궤도
(D) 기록

2 지문의 단어 "its"가 가리키는 것은?

(A) 하늘
(B) 지구
(C) 화성
(D) 태양

3 2단락에서 글쓴이는 왜 운하를 언급하는가?

(A) Lowell과 Schiaparelli가 외계 생명체를 찾았다는 의견을 반박하기 위해
(B) 과거에 화성에서 공사가 일어났다는 것을 보여주기 위해
(C) 과학자들에게 정확한 번역이 중요하다는 것을 주장하기 위해
(D) 화성에 생명체가 있다는 사람들의 믿음의 이유를 설명하기 위해

4 지문의 구 "conducive to"와 의미상 가장 유사한 것은?

(A) ~에 필요한

(B) ~에 호의적인

(C) ~에 불리한

(D) ~에 기본적인

5 다음 중 3단락의 구조를 가장 잘 설명한 것은?

(A) 화성에 대한 강한 흥미의 이유와 몇몇 관련 특징

(B) 화성과 다른 행성들의 주목할 만한 특징들의 비교

(C) 발견들과 그것이 화성에 대한 대중의 인식에 미친 영향

(D) 화성에 대한 사실적인 설명의 뒤를 잇는 허구적인 설명

6 아래 문장 중 지문 속의 음영된 문장의 핵심 정보를 가장 잘 표현하고 있는 것은 무엇인가? 오답은 문장의 의미를 현저히 왜곡하거나 핵심 정보를 빠뜨리고 있다.

(A) 강풍은 화성 표면에 식물들이 살 수 없게 만들었다.

(B) 모래 폭풍이 화성 표면 색 변화의 원인으로 밝혀졌다.

(C) 화성에 식물이 살 가능성은 계절성 모래 폭풍의 발견으로 줄어든다.

(D) 화성의 식물이 강풍에 의해 억제되었기 때문에, 표면 색의 변화는 일어나지 않았다.

7 지문에서 4단락과 5단락의 관계는 무엇인가?

(A) 4단락은 5단락에서 비난받는 잠정적인 이론을 소개한다.

(B) 4단락은 5단락에서 논의되는 주제에 대한 개요를 제시한다.

(C) 5단락은 4단락에서 제기된 문제에 대해 더 최신의 설명을 제공한다.

(D) 5단락은 4단락에서 소개한 문제에 대한 해결책을 제시한다.

8 지문의 단어 "hazardous"와 의미상 가장 유사한 것은?

(A) 불길한

(B) 약한

(C) 위험한

(D) 신비한

9 지문에서 글쓴이는 왜 "methane"을 언급하는가?

(A) 생명체의 가능성에 대한 최신 증거를 제시하기 위해

(B) 화성은 불모지라는 의견을 강화하기 위해

(C) NASA 화성 탐사 로봇들이 효과적임을 강조하기 위해

(D) 화성의 대기가 얼마나 희박한지 설명하기 위해

10 **지시:** 지문 요약을 위한 도입 문장이 아래에 주어져 있다. 지문의 가장 중요한 내용을 나타내는 보기 3개를 골라 요약을 완성하시오. 어떤 문장은 지문에 언급되지 않은 내용이나 사소한 정보를 담고 있으므로 요약에 포함되지 않는다. **이 문제는 2점이다.**

> **화성은 외계 생명체가 살기에 적합하다고 오랫동안 여겨져 왔다.**
>
> · (C) 화성의 몇몇 특징은 사람들이 화성이 생명체에 상당히 좋다고 생각하게 만들었지만, Mariner호가 보낸 사진들은 그러한 생각과 철저하게 상반되었다.

> · (D) 천문학자들의 연구 결과에 대한 잘못된 해석이 인공적인 물길이 화성에 만들어졌었다는 생각을 전파시켰다.
>
> · (E) 화성에 대한 발견들은 그 행성이 외계에서 생명체를 찾기 위한 탐사로 연구를 지속할 만한 가치가 있다는 증거를 제공하고 있다.

(A) NASA는 고도로 정교한 일련의 화성 탐사선을 발사해왔다.

(B) 과학자들은 우주 연구 센터로서의 화성의 잠재력에 주목해 왔다.

(F) 지구와의 근접성 때문에, 초기 천문학자들은 화성을 하늘에서 관찰할 수 있었다.

---

03 **American Quilts**

1. (B)	2. (B)	3. (D)
4. (D)	5. (A)	6. (A)
7. (C)	8. (B)	9. (B)

10. (A)−3~4단락, (D)−2단락, (F)−5단락

1 독립 전쟁 후 커다란 응접실을 갖춘 집에서 여성들은 종종 퀼트 모임을 갖고, 돌아가면서 퀼트 조각의 네 귀퉁이를 하나씩 꿰매면서 이웃들과 친구들의 바느질거리를 완료하는 것을 도왔다. 이렇게 매주 또는 매월 열렸던 모임은 이런 모임이 아니었더라면 서로 간에 왕래가 없었을 미국 농촌 환경에서 여성들이 사회활동에 참여하는 주요 수단이 되었다. 퀼트에 능숙한 여성들은 함께 일하면서 때때로 초보 여자아이들을 가르치고, 노래를 부르고 이야기를 하며 일상생활에 대한 생각을 나누면서 이불 전체를 정성 들여서 꿰매곤 했다. [1]퀼트 작업은 디자인의 복잡한 정도에 따라서 완성하는 데 며칠이 걸리기도 하고 반나절밖에 걸리지 않기도 했다. 퀼트 공예 기술이 발달하고 퀼트를 만들던 여성들의 사회경제적 지위가 변화함에 따라, 퀼트의 목적이 사랑하는 사람이나 사회의 중요한 사건들을 기념하기 위해서인지, 아니면 단순히 가족의 보온용인지에 따라서 퀼트의 양식도 정교해졌다.

2 초기의 퀼트는 상대적으로 단순한 디자인으로 만들어졌고, 정교한 예술적 표현 수단으로서 기능하기보다는 주로 실용적인 목적으로 만들어졌다. 검소한 여성들은 퀼트를 만들고 수선하는 데 가격이 높은 천 조각을 재활용했다. [3]patchwork(쪽모이 세공)라고 불리는 이 기법은 퀼트의 겉감을 만들기 위해 함께 꿰매지는 사각형 모양의 천 조각, 즉 블록을 만드는 것에 집중하였다. 이것이 끝나면, 면이나 모로 된 솜 층을 깔아서 퀼트를 부드럽고 편하게 만들었다. 그리고 나서는 커다란 안감 조각을 솜 밑에 대고, 이 세 층을 모두 작은 땀으로 꿰맸다. [4]겉감은 많은 다양한 자투리 천을 꿰매서 만들었기 때문에, 무늬와 색깔이 블록마다 천차만별이었다.

3 [5]patchwork 퀼트는 일반적으로 실용적인 디자인이었으나, 1800년대 초에 특정한 형태의 천 조각을 잘라내 바탕천에 손바느

448 | 무료 토플자료·유학정보 제공 goHackers.com

질로 붙여 복잡한 새로운 무늬를 완성하면서 여가를 보낼 수 있었던 부유한 여성들에 의해서 퀼트 기술이 예술적으로 승화되었다. '적용시키다'라는 뜻의 프랑스어에서 따온 용어인 appliqué라고 불린 기술은 정교한 바느질과 특별한 재료를 필요로 했기 때문에 각 퀼트 조각의 가격을 인상시켰다. 처음에는 부유한 사람들만이 appliqué 퀼트를 만들 여유가 있었지만, 한 세기가 지나면서 미국 직물 제조업자들의 생산력이 증가하여 가격이 하락했다. 재봉틀의 도입 또한 바느질 시간을 줄여 주었다. 1900년대 초반 즈음에는 appliqué가 patchwork의 인기를 넘어섰는데, 이는 대체로 appliqué의 다양한 용도와 그 시대의 민속 예술로의 통합 덕분이었다.

4 ⁷appliqué는 지역 사회의 역사를 기록하는 데 흔히 사용되었고, Baltimore Album motif에 의해 대중화되었다. Baltimore Album motif는 그것이 처음으로 유행했던 도시의 이름을 따서 명명되었고, 여성들이 퀼트를 이용해서 사회의 단면을 기록했던 가장 좋은 예일 것이다. 디자인은 일반적으로 정교한 꽃, 동물, 또는 애국적인 주제를 사용했으며, 만든 사람들이 각각 서명하여 개별적으로 꿰매어 여러 개의 블록으로 구성되었다. 유능한 달필가들이 최종 완성품을 소유할 사람에게 시나 메시지를 적어 넣기도 했는데, 여러 단계의 일에 참여한 많은 이를 상기시켜 주기 위함이었다. 대부분의 메시지는 문자 형태였지만, 어떤 것들은 그림 기호였다. 만약 거미줄 무늬가 퀼트에 수놓아졌다면, 퀼트를 만든 사람과 퀼트를 받는 사람에게 행운을 가져다 줄 것으로 생각되었다.

5 자신들의 예술작품에 새로운 미적 유행을 몹시 흡수하고 싶어 했던 퀼트 장인들은 덮개에 비대칭적인 디자인을 도입했고, appliqué 또는 patchwork 기법으로 서로 어울리지 않는 조각들을 이어 붙였다. 여성잡지들은 이 새로운 기법을 홍보했을 뿐만 아니라, 변화무쌍하거나 추상적인 무늬를 만드는 데 자수가 놓인 이국적인 양단, 벨벳, 모직을 이용하는 기법을 묘사하기 위해 crazy 퀼트(전통적으로, 'craze'는 조각으로 분열하거나 찢어지는 것을 뜻했다)라는 신조어를 만들어내기까지 했다. 어떤 잡지사들은 여성의 정기 구독을 촉진하기 위해서 비단 조각을 경품으로 주기도 했다. 대중매체가 성장함에 따라 혁신적인 재봉법에 대한 관심도 커졌다. crazy 퀼트는 능력 있는 여성들이 자신들의 재주와 상상력을 과시하는 최고의 방법이었는데, 그 이유는 crazy 퀼트가 청어 가시, 낚시, 체인 등 복잡한 무늬의 바느질 때문에 어려웠기 때문이다. appliqué와 마찬가지로, 이런 퀼트도 처음에는 부유한 사람들에 의해서만 만들어졌지만, 인기가 높아지면서 면, 데님, 플란넬 등을 이용해서도 만들어지기 시작했다. 미국 역사상 최초로, 여류 장인들이 만든 창조성으로 충만한 작품들이 갤러리에 전시되었다.

parlor [páːrlər] 응접실, 거실   quilting bee 퀼트를 만드는 모임
novice [návis] 초보자
socioeconomic [sòusiəèkənámik] 사회경제적인
sophisticated [səfístəkèitid] 정교한, 세련된
commemorate [kəmémərèit] 기념하다
milestone [máilstòun] 중요한 사건   elaborate [ilǽbərət] 정교한
parsimonious [pàːrsəmóuniəs] 검소한
patchwork [pǽtʃwə̀ːrk] 쪽모이 세공

batting [bǽtiŋ] (이불 등에 넣는) 탄 솜   odds and ends 자투리 천
utilitarian [juːtìlətɛ́əriən] 실용주의의   affluent [ǽfluənt] 부유한
surpass [sərpǽs] 넘어서다   versatility [və̀ːrsətíləti] 다양한 용도
integration [ìntəgréiʃən] 통합   popularize [pápjuləràiz] 대중화하다
floral [flɔ́ːrəl] 꽃무늬의   patriotic [pèitriátik] 애국적인
calligrapher [kəlígrəfər] 달필가, 글씨 잘 쓰는 사람
multistage [mʌ́ltistèidʒ] 여러 단계의
undertaking [ʌ̀ndərtéikiŋ] 일   assimilate [əsíməlèit] 흡수하다
aesthetic [esθétik] 미적인   embrace [imbréis] 도입하다
asymmetric [èisəmétrik] 비대칭적인   coverlet [kʌ́vərlit] 덮개
coin [kɔin] 신조어를 만들어내다   splinter [splíntər] 조각
brocade [broukéid] 양단   embroidery [imbrɔ́idəri] 자수
kaleidoscopic [kəlàidəskápik] 변화무쌍한
snippet [snípit] 작은 조각   intricate [íntrikət] 복잡한
herringbone [hériŋbòun] 청어 가시 무늬
flannel [flǽnl] 플란넬(면이나 양모를 섞어 만든 얇은 모직물)

1 지문에 따르면, 퀼트를 완벽하게 하기 위해 필요한 시간은

   (A) 전문가의 수에 영향을 받았다
   (B) 양식의 복잡성에 따라 달랐다
   (C) 이야기하는 시간 때문에 늘어났다
   (D) 퀼트의 등급을 나누기 위한 가장 중요한 기준이었다

2 아래 문장 중 지문 속의 음영된 문장의 핵심 정보를 가장 잘 표현하고 있는 것은 무엇인가? 오답은 문장의 의미를 현저히 왜곡하거나 핵심 정보를 빠뜨리고 있다.

   (A) 퀼트를 만드는 사람들이 더 부유해지고 영향력이 있게 되자, 그들은 더 복잡한 디자인을 시도하기 시작했다.
   (B) 퀼트 기법이 발전하고 제작자들의 사회적 지위가 변화하면서, 퀼트는 의도된 기능에 따라 더 정교한 스타일을 보여주었다.
   (C) 퀼트는 공동체에서 여성의 역할을 승격시키기 위해서뿐만 아니라, 중요한 사건을 기념하거나 가까운 친구 및 친척을 축하하기 위해 만들어졌다.
   (D) 퀼트의 스타일은 제작자의 신분을 반영했기 때문에, 퀼트를 만드는 사람들은 선진 기술을 사용하여 자신들의 작품을 정교하게 하려고 노력했다.

3 2단락에서, 글쓴이는 _____으로써 patchwork를 설명한다.

   (A) 재료를 얻는 방법을 서술함으로써
   (B) 몇몇 일반적인 디자인의 유형을 나열함으로써
   (C) 예술적 표현으로서의 목적을 뚜렷하게 함으로써
   (D) 그것이 만들어지는 과정을 보여줌으로써

4 지문에서 글쓴이는 왜 "many different odds and ends"를 언급하는가?

   (A) patchwork에 사용된 기법의 다양성을 강조하기 위해
   (B) 적합한 재료 조각을 찾기 어려웠다는 것을 보여주기 위해
   (C) 작은 땀을 꿰매는 데 다양한 방법이 사용되었다는 것을 언급하기 위해
   (D) 디자인에서 블록이 균일하지 않았던 이유를 제공하기 위해

5 3단락은 patchwork 퀼트에 대한 초반의 논의와 어떻게 연결되

는가?

(A) 예술적 표현을 증대시킨 퀼트 제작 기법을 소개한다.

(B) 이전 시대에 사용된 것보다 열등한 퀼트 스타일을 설명한다.

(C) 기술적인 진보가 어떻게 퀼트 산업에 급격한 변화를 가져왔는지 설명한다.

(D) 왜 상류층이 전통적인 퀼트 방법을 피했는지 설명한다.

6 지문의 단어 "surpassed"와 의미상 가장 유사한 것은?

(A) 초과했다

(B) 오래 갔다

(C) 뒤처졌다

(D) 대신했다

7 지문에서 글쓴이는 왜 "Baltimore Album motif"를 언급하는가?

(A) Baltimore에서의 appliqué 퀼트의 유행을 설명하기 위해

(B) 여성들의 퀼트에 대한 애정의 이유를 제시하기 위해

(C) 지역 사회의 기록으로서 appliqué가 사용된 예를 제시하기 위해

(D) Baltimore 스타일과 다른 도시의 것을 대조하기 위해

8 지문의 단어 "assimilate"와 의미상 가장 유사한 것은?

(A) 나누다

(B) 혼합하다

(C) 끼워 넣다

(D) 번역하다

9 다음 중 지문의 구조를 가장 잘 설명한 것은?

(A) 시대와 시대의 예술적 업적에 대한 비평

(B) 공예와 그것의 발전에 대한 역사적 관점에서의 설명

(C) 퀼트 및 그것의 현대 사회에서의 영향력에 대한 역사적 분석

(D) 여러 가지 전통 퀼트 기법의 장단점에 대한 분석

10 **지시:** 지문 요약을 위한 도입 문장이 아래에 주어져 있다. 지문의 가장 중요한 내용을 나타내는 보기 3개를 골라 요약을 완성하시오. 어떤 문장은 지문에 언급되지 않은 내용이나 사소한 정보를 담고 있으므로 요약에 포함되지 않는다. **이 문제는 2점이다.**

> 퀼트는 여러 단계의 발전을 겪었고 지금은 예술의 한 형태로 여겨진다.
>
> · (A) 복잡한 양식의 퀼트는 기본 조각 위에 개개 직물의 특정 모양을 꿰매어 만들어졌다.
> · (D) 처음에 퀼트는 실용성을 생각해서 남은 천 조각을 사용하여 만들어졌고 일관되지 않은 양식과 색을 가지고 있었다.
> · (F) 겉감은 불규칙한 천 조각을 꿰매어 만들어졌고 다른 종류의 퀼트 기법을 사용하여 하나로 이어졌다.

(B) 출판물들은 구독자들에게 고급 천을 나눠 줌으로써 여성의 관심을 끄는 것을 도왔다.

(C) 퀼트 기법은 전통 기법을 보존하기 위한 노력으로 퀼트 모임

에서 전문가에게서 초보자에게 전수되었다.

(E) 여러 겹으로 된 퀼트의 중간 층은 기본적인 솜 층의 바탕으로 작용했고 퀼트의 촉감을 더 좋게 만들었다.

04 Biological Clock

p.206

1. (C)	2. (D)	3. (A)
4. (D)	5. (D)	6. (B)
7. (C)	8. (C)	9. (A)
10. (B)–3단락, (D)–4~5단락, (E)–6단락		

1 24시간 주기 리듬으로도 알려진 체내 생체 시계의 발전은 지구에서 24시간 주기로 낮과 밤이 반복되는 현상과 직접적인 연관이 있고, 식물학자들이 식물이 꽃을 피우고 겨울나기를 준비하는 데 빛이 미치는 영향 때문에 식물의 생체 시계의 중요성을 이해하게 된 수 세기 전에 처음으로 발견되었다. 하지만 학자들이 동물에게 생체 시계가 존재한다는 것을 발견한 것은 고작 40년밖에 되지 않았다. 이러한 새로운 사실에 뒤이어 학자들은 생체 시계가 어떻게 통제되는가를 이해하기 위해 노력해왔다.

2 동물에게도 시계가 존재한다는 것이 사실로 확립된 후, 최초의 연구 결과와 신경학 분야의 새로운 진척으로 인해 학자들은 유기체가 자신의 신체 시간을 조절하는 메커니즘을 더욱 깊이 연구할 수 있게 되었다. 사전에 발견된 바로는 24시간 주기 리듬이 실제로는 24시간 순환이 아니라 종마다 20시간에서 28시간의 폭넓은 변형을 보여주고, [2]이런 주기 하에, 격리된 생물들은 결국에는 자연환경과 조화되지 못하는 것으로 나타났다. 이와는 대조적으로 정상적 환경에서 자란 생물은 간헐적인 왜곡 현상 없이 아무 영향을 받지 않은 것으로 나타났으며, 이는 햇빛의 필요성을 확인해 보여준다.

3 그러나 망막 세포에서 발견되는 광색소인 멜라놉신이 발견되기 전까지, 빛에 대한 정보가 뇌로 전달되는 정확한 메커니즘은 알려지지 않은 채로 남아있었다. 눈이 밝은 빛에 노출되면, 멜라놉신이 신경의 경로를 통해 시교차상핵(SCN)에 보내진다. SCN은 시상하부에 있는 수천 개의 뉴런과 세포의 다발이며, 시상하부는 24시간 주기 및 피로, 수면, 공복, 갈증, 그리고 체온과 같은 관련 현상을 통제하는 것들을 포함한 다양한 중요 신진대사 과정을 관장하는 뇌의 일부분이다. 눈으로부터 정보를 받으면, SCN은 미세한 조정들을 수행하고 체내시간이 환경과 일치할 수 있도록 한다. 광감수성과 신경전달의 복합적인 과정과 함께 햇빛에 대한 정기적인 노출이 없다면, 생체시계의 혼란이라는 부작용이 일어난다. 결과적으로 체내 호르몬은 불균형해지고 이에 영향을 받은 유기체는 혼란에 빠져 불규칙한 단기적 수면 패턴을 겪게 된다.

4 [5]SCN의 중요성은 SCN이 체내시계를 조절한다는 것을 증명하기 위해 SCN이 제거된 쥐를 사용한 실험에서도 관찰되었다. 이 쥐들은 24시간 주기 리듬과 연관된 행동을 하지 않았고 심지어 물 마시

기를 중단했다. 그러나 몇몇 쥐들은 SCN의 일부만 제거되었다. SCN의 일부를 절개한 후 연구자들은 이 쥐들에 남아 있던 SCN이 체내로의 전달자 기능을 하는 단백질을 지속적으로 방출하며, 이는 모든 내장 기관들의 리듬을 유지하고, 낮 동안에 기초 체온을 높이고, 코티솔 호르몬을 분비하며, 낮의 활동에 대비하여 혈압을 높인다는 것을 발견했다.

5 SCN이 조절 중추인 것으로 알려지자, 신체 주기를 조절하는 방법을 이해하기 위한 다음 단계는 메커니즘을 조절하는 유전자를 확인하는 것이었고, 초파리가 유전학에서 가장 많이 연구된 대상 중 하나였기 때문에, 특정한 유전자 배열이 확인된 첫 동물도 예상대로 초파리였다. [6]하지만 포유류의 체내 리듬을 조절하는 DNA 배열이 발견되기까지는 17년이 더 걸렸다. 그 발견은 1988년에 행해진 실험에서 비롯되었다. "생체 시계 유전자"로 알려진 결함이 있는 DNA 배열을 가진 햄스터는 SCN에 잘못된 신호를 보냈고, 이것은 결과적으로 그 쥐들이 정상적인 24시간 주기 리듬을 형성하지 못하게 했다. 이러한 체내의 피드백 메커니즘이 없이, 햄스터는 비정상적인 주기성을 보이며 불규칙적인 간격으로 먹고 마시고 수면을 취했지만, 놀랍게도 먹고 마시고 잠자는 양은 정상적인 햄스터와 차이를 보이지 않았다.

6 [8]같은 기능을 하는 비슷한 메커니즘이 인간에게도 존재하며, 인간의 생체 리듬을 이해하는 것을 주제로 하는 상당한 연구가 진행되어 왔다. 예를 들어 한 표준시간대에서 다른 표준시간대에 속하는 지역으로 여행하는 사람들은 종종 구역질, 과민성, 불면증 등의 생리학적인 증상을 겪는다. 예전에는 심리적인 것으로 여겨지던 일부 질환도 24시간 주기 리듬에 영향을 받는 것으로 밝혀졌다. 일반적으로 햇빛에 노출되면 결과적으로 신체 내부의 리듬을 재조정하는 데 도움이 되는데, 겨울 동안에는 짧아진 낮이 문제를 악화시킬 수 있고 계절에 따른 정서장애를 유발할 수 있다. 우울증의 한 형태인 정서장애는 자살뿐만 아니라 약물 사용의 증가나 알코올 남용과 연관이 있으나, 그 원인에 대해 더욱 잘 이해하게 되면서, 호르몬 수치를 일정하게 함으로써 병을 앓고 있는 사람들을 돕기 위한 빛 요법과 같은 치료법들이 개발되고 있다.

circadian rhythm 24시간 주기 리듬
revelation [rèvəléiʃən] 새로운 사실 fauna [fɔ́ːnə] 동물군
neurological [njùərəládʒikəl] 신경학의 adjust [ədʒʌ́st] 조절하다
concurrent [kənkə́ːrənt] 일치하는
photoreception [fòutourisépʃən] 광감수성 side effect 부작용
disruption [disrʌ́pʃən] 분열, 혼란 erratic [irǽtik] 불규칙한
dissect [disékt] 절개하다 visceral [vísərəl] 내장의
diurnally [daiə́ːrnli] 낮 동안에 basal [béisəl] 기초의
cortisol [kɔ́ːrtəsɔ̀ːl] 코티솔(부신 피질에서 분비되는 호르몬의 일종)
gene [dʒiːn] 유전자 fruit fly 초파리
defective [diféktiv] 결함이 있는 aberrant [əbérənt] 비정상적인
periodicity [pìəriədísəti] 주기성 time zone (표준)시간대
physiological [fìziəládʒikəl] 생리학적인 symptom [símptəm] 증상
nausea [nɔ́ːziə] 구역질 irritability [ìrətəbíləti] 과민성
insomnia [insámniə] 불면증 disorder [disɔ́ːrdər] 질환, 장애
exacerbate [igzǽsərbèit] 악화시키다 affective disorder 정서장애
depression [dipréʃən] 우울증 abuse [əbjúːs] 남용

equalize [íːkwəlàiz] 일정하게 하다

1 지문의 단어 "it"이 가리키는 것은?

(A) 빛
(B) 꽃을 피움
(C) 생체 시계
(D) 새로운 사실

2 지문에서 글쓴이는 왜 "those kept in isolation"을 언급하는가?

(A) 어떤 생물이 실험에 적합한지 확인하기 위해
(B) 시간 규제에서 뇌의 역할을 설명하기 위해
(C) 신경학자들이 연구했던 종의 예를 제시하기 위해
(D) 햇빛에 노출된 종과 그것을 비교하기 위해

3 지문의 단어 "conclusively"와 의미상 가장 유사한 것은?

(A) 결정적으로
(B) 착각을 일으키게 하여
(C) 탄력적으로
(D) 기만하여

4 지문의 단어 "erratic"과 의미상 가장 유사한 것은?

(A) 의존할 수 있는
(B) 불충분한
(C) 임박한
(D) 예측할 수 없는

5 지문에서 글쓴이는 왜 쥐를 사용한 실험을 논의하는가?

(A) SCN이 신체의 몇몇 기관에만 영향을 미친다는 것을 주장하기 위해
(B) SCN과 낮아진 혈압 사이의 연관성을 설명하기 위해
(C) SCN의 주요 기능이 단백질을 분해하는 것임을 제시하기 위해
(D) SCN의 생체 시계 조절에 대한 증거를 제시하기 위해

6 5단락에서, 글쓴이는 왜 "Hamsters"를 언급하는가?

(A) 24시간 주기 리듬을 조절하는 햄스터의 유전자 배열을 초파리의 것과 대조하기 위해
(B) 생체 시계를 조절하는 포유류 유전자의 첫 발견을 서술하기 위해
(C) 유전자 연구의 발단이 어떻게 생체 시계 유전자의 발견을 도왔는지 설명하기 위해
(D) 생물학에서 어떤 주제가 대규모 유전자 연구에 가장 적합한지 명백하게 하기 위해

7 아래 문장 중 지문 속의 음영된 문장의 핵심 정보를 가장 잘 표현하고 있는 것은 무엇인가? 오답은 문장의 의미를 현저히 왜곡하거나 핵심 정보를 빠뜨리고 있다.

(A) 햄스터가 체내 시계를 조절하기 위해서는, 햄스터는 다른 햄스터들처럼 규칙적으로 먹고, 마시고 수면을 취할 수 있어야 한다.
(B) 정상적인 햄스터의 생물학적 욕구는 24시간 주기 리듬이 없는 햄스터들보다 훨씬 더 낮았다.

(C) 체내 생체 시계가 없는 햄스터는 먹이를 먹고 쉬는 시간에 있어서는 정상적인 햄스터와 달랐지만 전체적인 양에서는 그렇지 않았다.

(D) 정상적인 햄스터들과 비정상적인 햄스터들 간의 행동의 차이점이 체내 조절에 대한 메커니즘을 제거함으로써 관찰되었다.

8 24시간 주기 리듬에 대한 전반적인 논의에서 6단락의 역할은?

(A) 생물학적 현상이 인간에게까지 영향을 미친다는 개념을 없애기 위해

(B) 독자에게 인간의 생물학적 리듬에 대한 몇몇 최신의 새로운 사실을 소개하기 위해

(C) 24시간 주기 리듬이 사람들에게 영향을 미치는 몇몇 방법을 검토하기 위해

(D) 사람들이 심리적인 훈련을 통해 그들의 24시간 주기 리듬을 조절할 수 있음을 설명하기 위해

9 지문의 단어 "eventually"와 의미상 가장 유사한 것은?

(A) 마침내

(B) 불가피하게

(C) 의심할 여지없이

(D) 완전히

10 **지시:** 지문 요약을 위한 도입 문장이 아래에 주어져 있다. 지문의 가장 중요한 내용을 나타내는 보기 3개를 골라 요약을 완성하시오. 어떤 문장은 지문에 언급되지 않은 내용이나 사소한 정보를 담고 있으므로 요약에 포함되지 않는다. **이 문제는 2점이다.**

> 식물과 마찬가지로, 동물들은 신체 기능을 조정하는 것을 돕는 24시간 주기 리듬을 가지고 있다.
>
> · (B) 망막이 생체 시계를 조절하기 위해 멜라놉신 및 SCN과 함께 작용한다는 것이 발견되었다.
>
> · (D) 이후 연구들은 다수 생명체의 주기적인 기능에서 SCN과 유전자의 결정적인 조절 역할을 입증했다.
>
> · (E) 동물과 마찬가지로, 빛 민감도와 24시간 주기 리듬은 인간의 기분과 행동에 영향을 미칠 수 있다.

(A) 종들은 여러 가지 종류의 체내 시계를 보이고 서로 일치시킬 필요가 있다.

(C) 체내 시계를 유지하는 데 있어 시교차상 핵의 역할은 체온을 높이는 것이다.

(F) 잠자는 데 어려움이 있는 사람들은 즉시 치료를 받아야 한다.

Chapter 06 **Inference**

HACKERS **STRATEGY**   p.213

전략 1

Ex 오로라는 빠르게 이동하는 조각과 춤을 추듯 움직이는 다양한 색의 빛의 기둥으로 이루어져 있다. 광범위한 오로라의 출현은 지구 자기장에 대한 방해 및 라디오, 전화, 전신 전송에 대한 간섭을 동반한다. 오로라의 최대최소 강도 주기는 11년을 주기로 하는 태양흑점 주기의 최대최소 강도 주기를 거의 정확히 따른다.

hue [hju:] 색   **terrestrial magnetism** 지구 자기장
sunspot cycle 태양흑점 주기

전략 2

Ex 양수식 수력 발전소는 시간대에 따라 전력 수요가 급격히 다른 일부 지역에서 사용된다.

hydroelectric [hàidrouiléktrik] 수력 발전의

Ex 대부분의 뉴딜 시대의 예술가들은 그들에게 일거리를 준 것에 대해 Roosevelt 대통령에게 감사하였고, 열정적으로 뉴딜 정책의 자유 민주 안건을 지지했다. 당연히 그들의 작품은 이러한 관점을 반영했다.

enthusiastically [inθù:ziǽstikəli] 열정적으로

Ex 풍자만화가 인쇄술의 도래와 그로 인한 지식의 더욱 광범위한 전파를 기다려야 했던 또 다른 덜 구체적인 이유가 있다. 성공한 정치 풍자만화는 국가 내부의 어느 정도의 평균 지성, 깨어있는 시민 의식, 그리고 국가의 복지에 대한 책임감을 전제로 한다. 정치 만화가가 봉건 제도 하의 노예들로 구성된 국가에 호소하는 것은 시간을 낭비하는 것이다. 투표 상자가 닫힌 국민에게 영향을 발휘하는 것을 기대할 수는 없기 때문이다. 풍자만화는 민주주의 풍토에서 꽃피울 수 있다. 민주주의의 대담한 불손과 신성왕권 제도는 영원히 양립할 수 없기 때문이다.

caricature [kǽrikətʃər] 풍자만화   **advent** [ǽdvent] 도래
dissemination [disèmənéiʃən] 전파
presuppose [prìːsəpóuz] 전제하다   **feudal** [fjúːdl] 봉건 제도의
vassal [vǽsəl] (봉건 시대의) 노예
incompatibility [ìnkəmpætəbíləti] 양립할 수 없음
audacious [ɔːdéiʃəs] 대담한   **the divine right of kings** 신성왕권

전략 3

Ex 운하가 철도와 경쟁할 수 없었던 것은 사실이었다. 운하는 단위당 운반할 수 있는 부피와 속도의 두 가지 면에서 제한적이었다. 운하는 너무 작고, 너무 느리며, 분열되어 있었다. 반면 철도는

국가 시스템에 통합됨에 따라 더 큰 유연성을 가진 더욱 광범위한 서비스를 제공했다. 운하는 보통 그 자체가 일반적인 운송수단이 아니고 중간 운송업체에 대부분 의존하였기 때문에 더욱 불리했다. 비록 운하를 이용한 운송이 처음부터 철도보다 저렴했음에도 불구하고, 철도가 더 인기 있는 교통수단이었다.

canal [kənǽl] 운하   **fragmented** [frǽgməntid] 분열된
handicap [hǽndikæp] 불리하게 하다

HACKERS STRATEGY **APPLICATION**   p.216

미국 독립혁명이 다가옴에 따라 영국 정부와 식민지들 사이에 분쟁이 생기고 있었을 때, [1]Franklin의 깊은 애국심과 개인의 자유를 향한 일념이 1775년에 그를 미국으로 돌아오게 하였다. 미국에서 사생아로 태어난 그의 아들 William Franklin이 국왕파의 지도자가 되고 있을 때, Benjamin Franklin은 미국 독립혁명 및 신생 국가의 훌륭한 정치가 중 한 명이 되었다. 그는 대륙회의의 대리인이었으며, 우정공사 총재로 임명되었고, Samuel Chase, Charles Carroll of Carrollton과 함께 캐나다인들을 애국 운동에 참여하도록 설득하기 위해 캐나다로 보내졌다. 1776년에는 그가 자발적으로 서명한 독립선언서의 초안 작성을 맡은 위원회에 임명되었다.

1776년 후반에는 Arthur Lee와 Silas Deane의 새로운 공화국을 위한 외교 노력에 동참하기 위해 프랑스로 배를 타고 건너갔다. [2]매력 있는 존재감으로 큰 지지를 받아 프랑스에서 높은 평판을 얻은 Franklin은 1778년 새로운 공화국에 대한 프랑스의 승인을 받는 데 많은 기여를 했다. Franklin은 미국 해군 작전의 지휘를 도왔으며 유럽 내의 성공한 미국 대리인이자, 불신과 다툼이 미국 의회가 다른 미국 위원회 위원들의 권력을 무효화하도록 만들었던 이후에도 남아있던 단 한 사람이었다.

illegitimate [ìlidʒítəmət] 사생아로 태어난   **Loyalist** [lɔ́iəlist] 국왕파
statesman [stéitsmən] 정치가   **delegate** [déligət] 대리인
continental congress 대륙회의(독립 전쟁 당시 열린 영국 식민지 각 주의 대표자 회의)   **cause** [kɔːz] (사회적인) 운동, 주의
winning [wíniŋ] 매력 있는   **annul** [ənʌ́l] 무효화하다

1. Benjamin Franklin에 대해 1단락으로부터 추론할 수 있는 것은?

   (A) 처음에 독립선언서에 서명하기를 주저했다.
   (B) 개인의 자유에 대한 사상을 퍼뜨리기 위해 고국으로 돌아왔다.
   (C) 그의 아들 William Franklin과 사이가 좋지 않았다.
   (D) 영국이 개인의 자유를 억압한다며 비판했다.

2. 2단락으로부터 Benjamin Franklin이 1776년 후반에 프랑스를 방문했을 때 _____ 라는 것을 추론할 수 있다.

(A) 이전에 프랑스에 가본 적이 없었다
(B) 프랑스에 파견된 최초의 대사였다
(C) 당시 프랑스가 유럽에서 주도권을 쥐고 있었다
(D) 그의 개인적인 평판이 그의 임무에서 중요한 역할을 했다

HACKERS **PRACTICE**

p.218

1. (D)	2. (B)	3. (D)
4. (C)	5. (D)	
6. (F), (T), (F), (T)		7. (T), (F), (T), (F)
8. (T), (T), (F), (F)		9. (F), (T), (F), (F)
10. (F), (T), (F), (F)		11. (T), (F), (F), (F)
12. 1 (D), 2 (A)	13. 1 (C), 2 (B)	14. 1 (B), 2 (A)
15. 1 (B), 2 (B)	16. 1 (C), 2 (C)	

VOCABULARY

1 (C)	2 (D)	3 (B)
4 (C), (A)	5 (B), (D)	6 (C)
7 (B), (D)	8 (C), (A), (B)	9 (D)
10 (A)	11 (A), (D), (C)	12 (A), (D), (B)
13 (D), (B), (C)	14 (D), (C), (A)	15 (A), (D), (B)
16 (A), (B), (C)		

1 고대 메소포타미아의 신들은 보통 인간의 모습으로 묘사되었다. 초기의 조각상들은 단순한 나무 조각품들이었지만, 머지않아 예술가들은, 전설에 따르면 지하 세계로 내려갈 때 청금석 목걸이를 착용했던 이난나와 같이, 각 신의 원문 묘사에 일치하는 장신구 의상을 나타내기 위해 도금과 형형색색의 장식을 추가했다.

ancient[éinʃənt] 고대의 deity[díːəti] 신
depict[dipíkt] 묘사하다 statue[stǽtʃuː] 조각상
gold overlay 도금 adornment[ədɔ́ːrnmənt] 장식
garment[gáːrmənt] 의상 lapis lazuli 청금석
descent[disént] 내려가기 underworld[ʌ́ndərwəːrld] 지하 세계

(A) 조각상들은 신의 모습에 관해 서술된 자료의 근거였다.
(B) 대부분의 메소포타미아 신들의 기존 조각상들은 분실되었다.
(C) 이난나는 고대 메소포타미아의 신들 중에서 가장 중요했다.
(D) 메소포타미아 신의 묘사는 시간이 지나면서 더 정교해졌다.

2 프랭클린 델라노 루즈벨트 대통령의 국민 총 투표수 60.8퍼센트를 차지한 전례 없는 승리는 린든 존슨의 승리가 약간 더 높은 61.9퍼센트를 차지했을 때까지 25년 동안 유효했다. 하지만, 그

것조차도 1804년 미국 헌법 수정 조항 제12조 승인 이전의 대통령 선거가 고려된다면 1위를 차지하지 못할 것이다.

record-breaking[rékərdbrèikiŋ] 전례 없는 vote[vout] 총 투표수
stand[stænd] 유효하다 net[net] 차지하다
rank[ræŋk] (순위를) 차지하다 ratification[rætəfikéiʃən] 승인
Amendment[əméndmənt] 미국 헌법 수정 조항

(A) 루즈벨트는 미국 헌법 수정 조항 제12조의 통과 이래로 가장 큰 득표 차 승리 기록을 가지고 있다.
(B) 1804년 이전의 최소 한 명의 대통령은 61.9퍼센트보다 많은 국민 총 투표수를 받았다.
(C) 두 명 이상의 대통령이 1804년 이후 60퍼센트보다 많은 국민 총 투표수를 얻었다.
(D) 존슨은 역사상 가장 최근의 대통령 선거에서 루즈벨트를 가까스로 이겼다.

3 산업에서 냉각은 대부분 압축 냉각법으로 이루어지고, 어떤 경우에는 흡수 냉각법에 의해 이루어지기도 한다. 근본적인 기술은 오랜 기간 변하지 않았지만, 최근 들어 발전 속도가 빨라지고 있다. 냉각제의 높은 오존 파괴 잠재력은 프레온 가스를 좀 더 환경적으로 허용 가능한 냉각제로 교체시키는 주요한 원인이 되었다.

refrigeration[rifrìdʒəréiʃən] 냉각
compression[kəmpréʃən] 압축 absorption[æbsɔ́ːrpʃən] 흡수
pace[peis] 속도 depletion[diplíːʃən] 파괴, 소모
potential[pəténʃəl] 잠재력

(A) 흡수 냉각법은 압축 냉각법보다 더 적은 프레온 가스를 사용한다.
(B) 프레온 가스는 더 환경친화적인 화학물질에 대응하여 개발되었다.
(C) 산업에서의 프레온 가스 사용은 최근에 금지되었다.
(D) 프레온 가스는 부분적으로 오존층 파괴의 원인이 된다.

4 인간의 뼈는 인류학자들에 의한 개체의 특성화나 식별을 촉진할 수 있는 많은 정보를 전달한다. 예를 들어, 전문가들은 허벅지 뼈 하나를 측정함으로써 한 사람의 키에 대한 거의 정확한 평가를 제공할 수 있다. 그러나 그들이 정확한 평가를 하기 위해서는 다른 변수들 또한 고려해야 한다. 그중 하나는 나이인데, 40세 이후에, 인간은 척추의 압축과 퇴화로 인해 10년당 1센티미터씩 줄어드는 경향이 있다.

skeleton[skélitn] 뼈 convey[kənvéi] 전달하다
hasten[héisn] 촉진하다, 서둘러 하다
characterization[kæ̀rəktəraizéiʃən] 특성화
identification[aidèntifikéiʃən] 식별
anthropologist[æ̀nθrəpáːlədʒist] 인류학자
approximate[əprɑ́ːksimeit] 거의 정확한, 근사치인
assessment[əsésmənt] 평가 stature[stǽtʃər] 키
thigh[θai] 허벅지 variable[vériəbl] 변수
evaluation[ivæ̀ljuéiʃən] 평가 compression[kəmpréʃən] 압축
deterioration[ditìəriəréiʃən] 퇴화, 퇴보 spine[spain] 척추

(A) 모든 변수들이 설명되지 않는 한, 사실상 인간의 유해를 보는 것으로 추론될 수 있는 것은 없다.
(B) 성숙기 이후의 해부학적 구조의 변화는 너무 적어서 골격 분석에 고려되지 않는다.
(C) 하나의 뼈에 대한 연구는 정확한 결론을 수립하기에는 불충분한 정보를 제시한다.
(D) 인류학자들은 인간 뼈의 정확한 나이를 특정할 수 있는 방법들을 개발했다.

5 19세기 파리에서, 에두아르 마네와 같은 예술가들은 로마니 혹은 집시라고 알려진 이민자 거리 공연자들을 무척 좋아했다. 이 떠돌아다니는 '보헤미안'들은 많은 화가들이 자유의 이상을 받아들이고 사회적 신분에 대한 관념이나 전통적 가치에 대한 고수와 같은 전통적 제약들을 벗어버리도록 고무하였다. 집시들의 혁명적인 이상을 반영하기 위해서, 예술가들은 때때로 그들의 작품에 금기의 소재들을 포함시켰다. 예를 들어, 판화 제작자인 테오필 스탱랑은 예전에는 불길한 관습으로만 여겨졌던 묘사인 검은 고양이를 한 유명한 카바레의 마케팅 포스터에 포함시켰다.

adore[ədɔ́ːr] 무척 좋아하다 **immigrant**[ímigrənt] 이민자
itinerant[aitínərənt] 떠돌아다니는 **inspire**[inspáiər] 고무하다
embrace[imbréis] 받아들이다 **cast off** 벗어버리다
constraint[kənstréint] 제약 **adherence**[ədhírəns] 고수
revolutionary[rèvəlúːʃəneri] 혁명적인 **taboo**[təbúː] 금기의
depiction[dipíkʃən] 묘사 **sinister**[sínistər] 불길한

(A) 에두아르 마네와 다른 파리의 예술가들은 자신들의 작품에 집시를 자주 묘사했다.
(B) 많은 보헤미안들은 개인의 자유를 받아들인 척했지만 절대로 오랜 관습을 완전히 버리지는 않았다.
(C) 로마니들의 사회적 지위는 파리에서 그들의 인기가 올라가면서 성장했다.
(D) 스탱랑은 검은 고양이가 위협적인 상징으로 여겨지는 것을 의도하지 않았다.

6 대부분의 박쥐 종들은 그것들이 밤에 효과적으로 길을 찾고 사냥하도록 돕는 좋은 시력을 가지고 있지만, 그것들 중 일부는 돌아다니고 먹잇감을 찾기 위해 반향 정위를 활용하는 능력을 가지고 있기도 하다. 이러한 포유류 비행사는 음파의 파동을 방출하는데 [B]이것은 물체에 반사되어 그것들의 특별하게 변형된, 매우 큰 귀로 '반향'을 보낸다. 박쥐가 이 가청 응답을 받으면, 그것은 사냥감의 정확한 위치로 이동할 수 있도록 목표물의 방향으로 날아가면서 증대하는 속도로 끊임없이 음파를 방출할 것이다. 이 생리학적 과정은 내이의 막과 관련되어 있는데 이것은 [D]귀로 들어오는 소리의 빈도에 따라 진동하고 이 신호를 뇌에서 특정 궤도와 거리로 해석되는 신경 부호로 변환한다.

navigate[nǽvigeit] 길을 찾다
echolocation[èkouloukéiʃən] 반향 정위(동물이 소리나 초음파를 내어서 그 돌아오는 메아리 소리로 상대와 자기의 위치를 확인하는 방법)
aviator[éivieitər] 비행사 **emit**[imít] 방출하다 **pulse**[pʌls] 파동
sonar[sóunɑːr] 음파, 음파 탐지 **rapidity**[rəpídəti] 속도

quarry[kwɔ́ːri] 사냥감 **physiological**[fìziəlɑ́dʒikəl] 생리학적인
membrane[mémbrein] 막 **pulsate**[pʌ́lseit] 진동하다
neural code 신경 부호 **trajectory**[trədʒéktəri] 궤도

(A) 일부 연구자들은 박쥐가 주로 시각을 이용하여 사냥한다고 잘못 추측했다.
(B) 박쥐 귀의 큰 크기는 반향 정위를 가능하게 만드는 데 필수적이다.
(C) 박쥐가 목표물의 정확한 위치를 알고 나면, 그들은 증대하는 속도로 그쪽을 향해 날아간다.
(D) 돌아오는 음파는 박쥐의 신경계에서 이해 가능하게 만들기 위해 부호화되어야 한다.

7 [A]미국을 가로지르는 대륙 횡단 철도에 대한 수요는 1840년대에 심화되었고 보통 대립되는, 수많은 후보 노선들을 낳았다. 최초의 노선 중 하나는 상인 Asa Whitney에 의해 제안되었는데, 그의 1844년 중국으로의 장기 항해는, 그가 아시아로의 더 빠른 교역 경로를 찾도록 이끌었다. 그는 자신의 많은 재산을 지도, 소책자들을 만들고, 의회에 로비하는 데 사용했다. 그는 심지어 계획의 실현 가능성을 가늠하기 위해 육로 탐험을 주도하기도 했지만, [C]그의 시도들은 어떠한 정치적 지원도 이뤄내지 못했다. 에이브러햄 링컨의 1862년의 유니언 퍼시픽 철도법 서명 이후에야 비로소 프로젝트를 위한 어느 정도 구체적인 계획들의 윤곽이 잡혔다. 두 회사 Central Pacific 사와 Union Pacific 사는, 두 개의 개별 노선 공사에 대한 계약을 따냈으며, 이 노선은 마침내 1869년 5월 10일 유타 주에서 연결되었다. 이 대규모 사업에 대한 어떤 총비용 견적이든 추측을 포함하긴 하겠지만, 몇몇 추정치는 그것이 1억 2천만 달러를 초과했음을 시사한다.

transcontinental[trænzkɑ̀ːntinéntl] 대륙 횡단의
intensify[inténsifai] 심화되다 **spawn**[spɔːn] 낳다
put forth 제안하다 **prolonged**[prəlɔ́ːŋd] 장기의
voyage[vɔ́iidʒ] 항해, 여행 **overland**[óuvərlænd] 육로의
expedition[èkspədíʃən] 탐험 **feasibility**[fìːzəbíliti] 실현 가능성
concrete[kɑ́ːŋkriːt] 구체적인
enterprise[éntərpraiz] 대규모 사업
conjecture[kəndʒéktʃər] 추측

(A) 1840년대에는 미국 대륙을 가로지르는 철도의 최적 노선에 대한 합의가 없었다.
(B) 중국에 있는 동안, Asa Whitney는 그가 마주한 철도망에 감명을 받았다.
(C) Whitney는 처음에 그의 계획이 좋은 생각이라는 것을 입법자들에게 설득시킬 수 없었다.
(D) 두 회사가 철로 건설을 완료하기까지는 7년이 걸렸다.

8 영국이 모든 인쇄된 문서에 대하여 인지세를 포함하도록 요구하는 1765년의 인지 조례를 통과시켰을 때, 미국 식민지인들은 격분했다. 그중 다수는 영국 국민으로서의 의무에 대해 이의를 제기하거나 무시하기 시작했고, 몇몇은 해당 조례에 서술된 세금을 지불하는 것을 단순히 거부해버렸다. 뿐만 아니라, 급진적인 식민지인들은 그것을 집행하려는 어떤 공무원에게든 물리적으

로 해를 끼치고 공개적으로 망신을 줄 것이라고 협박했다. ᴬ이 반응에 대한 영국의 인식은 미국인들을 달래기 위한 조례 폐지를 초래했다. 그러나 이 결과는 ᴮ조례가 창출하고자 했던 세입이 달성되지 못했다는 사실에서도 역시 기인했다. 번복에도 불구하고, 법령의 흔적은 사람들의 마음속에 생생하게 남았다. 지역 지도자들은 변혁을 선언하기 시작했고 해외로부터 온 그 어떠한 형태나 방식의 규율도 거부할 것을 선동했다. 이 정신은 곧 식민지에 퍼졌고 결국 미국의 독립 선언 및 영국과의 전쟁으로 이어졌다.

stamp[stæmp] 인지, 도장 outrage[áutreidʒ] 격분하다
obligation[à:blìgéiʃən] 의무 refuse[rifjú:z] 거부하다
humiliate[hju:mílieit] 망신을 주다 enforce[infɔ́:rs] 집행하다
perception[pərsépʃən] 인식 abolition[æ̀bəlíʃən] 폐지
ordinance[ɔ́:rdinəns] 조례 appease[əpí:z] 달래다
come to fruition 달성되다 overturn[òuvərtə́:rn] 번복
statute[stǽtʃu:t] 법령 legacy[légəsi] 흔적, 유산
reject[ridʒékt] 거부하다 permeate[pə́:rmieit] 퍼지다

(A) 영국인들을 아마 새로운 법에 대해 식민지인들이 가질 반응들을 잘못 판단했을 것이다.
(B) 영국인들은 인지 조례를 통해 창출할 세입을 과대평가했다.
(C) 미국의 몇몇 지도자들은 식민지가 반란을 일으켜야 한다는 생각에 반대했다.
(D) 식민지인들은 인지 조례가 통과되자마자 영국에 전쟁을 선포했다.

9 다윈은, 이전에 만들어진 전문 용어를 사용하여, 생물학적 적응도라는 개념을 대중화했다. ᴮ그는 다산할 수 있는 종들이 다산하지 못하는 종들보다 더 높은 생존율을 가질 것이라고 상정했는데, 이는 그것들의 새끼들과 그다음 세대들 또한 번식력이 있다고 추정했기 때문이다. 하지만, 이 단순화된 '적자생존'의 관점은 타당한 비판에 직면했고 수정을 거쳐야 했다. 비평가들은 단지 성공적인 생식에만 초점을 맞추는 것은 유전적 부동을 무시하는 것이라고 지적했는데, 이는 일부 유전적 변화가 단순히 우연에 의해 발생하며 생존 혹은 번식을 반드시 촉진시키는 것은 아니라고 주장한다.

coin[kɔin] 만들다 terminology[tə̀:rmənáːlədʒi] 전문 용어
popularize[pá:pjələraiz] 대중화하다
postulate[pástʃulèit] 상정하다 offspring[ɔ́:fspriŋ] 새끼, 후손
fertile[fɔ́:rtl] 번식력이 있는 encounter[inkáuntər] 직면하다
justifiable[dʒʌ́stifaiəbl] 타당한 procreation[pròukriéiʃən] 생식
genetic drift 유전적 부동(개체군 내에서 자연 선택 이외의 요인에 의해
대립 유전자의 빈도가 매 세대마다 기회에 따라 변동하는 현상)

(A) 다윈은 대중적인 생물학적 용어를 개발한 공이 있는 것으로 종종 잘못 믿어진다.
(B) 적응도는 여러 세대의 뛰어난 번식 능력을 전제로 삼는다.
(C) 생존에 대한 관점은 시간이 흘러도 거의 변화를 겪지 않았다.
(D) 대부분의 과학자들은 유전적 변형이 우연히 발생할 수 있음을 부정한다.

10 미국 서부 정착의 주요 요소는 값싸고, 비옥한 땅에 대한 전망이었다. 이것은 해외로부터의 이민뿐만 아니라 대규모의 국내 이주도 활성화시켰다. ᴮ가난에서 벗어나는 것을 바라든 억압적인 상황으로부터 자유를 얻기를 바라든, 이러한 개척자들은 자신의 '명백한 사명'을 추구했는데, 이것은 미국인들에게 태평양까지도 식민지화할 자격이 신에 의해 주어졌다는 신념이었다. 이러한 꿈 같은 환상은 증기선 회사들에 의해 착수된 대단히 성공적인 마케팅 캠페인에 의해 영속되었다. 그들이 유럽 신문에 무료 교통수단을 광고하는 동안, 미국 서부의 주들은 해외 출입국관리국을 설립했다.

ingredient[ingrí:diənt] 요소 settlement[sétlmənt] 정착
promise[prá:mis] 전망 fertile[fɔ́:rtl] 비옥한
stimulate[stímjuleit] 활성화시키다
internal[intə́:rnl] 국내의, 내부의 migration[maigréiʃən] 이주
poverty[pá:vərti] 가난 oppressive[əprésiv] 억압적인
pioneer[pàiənír] 개척자 manifest[mǽnifest] 명백한
entitle[intáitl] 자격을 주다 perpetuate[pərpétʃueit] 영속시키다
undertake[ʌ̀ndərtéik] 착수하다

(A) 유럽에 있는 경작 가능한 땅은 너무 비싸서 대부분의 사람들은 매입할 여유가 되지 않았다.
(B) 열악한 상황을 피하는 사람들은 서부 정착이 신이 내린 권리라고 보았다.
(C) 외국인들을 끌어모으려는 초기 시도가 실패하여, 광고주들은 접근법을 바꿨다.
(D) 이주민들을 유럽에서 미국으로 수송하기 위해 미국의 주 정부는 증기선 회사들에 돈을 지불했다.

11 1830년의 인디언 이주법은 미국 역사상 가장 열띤 논쟁이 이뤄지고 논란이 많았던 시기들 중 하나가 시작되게 했다. 그것은 아메리카 원주민들이 미시시피강 동쪽의 조상의 땅으로부터 오늘날의 오클라호마로의 강제 이주를 요구했다. 이 시기 이전에는, 정부는 부족 단위 기반으로 원주민들을 분석하는 경향이 있었다. ᴬ그러나 새로운 법에 따르면, '아메리카 원주민' 전체는, 여러 부족들로 이루어짐에도 불구하고, 하나의 범주로 취급되었다. 마찬가지로, 새로운 영토는 미국의 보호에 의존하고 보호 하에 놓여지는 하나의 국토로서 법적으로 간주되었다. 대다수가 연방 정부와의 평화라는 미끼에 의해 동기 부여가 되면서 조약 협상을 통한 자신의 운명을 마지못해 받아들이는 동안, 몇몇 사람들은 강제 재정착에 저항했다. 특히, 체로키 인디언은 대대로 내려오는 고향을 버리고 떠나는 것을 격렬하게 거부했다. 그들의 저항은 대통령 마틴 밴 뷰런이 미군에게 체로키 인디언 영토에 들어가 저항자들을 체포하고 최종 목적지까지 가는 길에 그들과 동행하라고 명령했던 1838년까지 이어졌다. 이 긴 행렬은 눈물의 길이라고 알려지게 되었는데 이는 약 4,000명에서 5,000명으로 추산되는 사람들이 목적지에 도착하기 전에 죽었기 때문이다.

usher in 시작되게 하다 controversial[kà:ntrəvə́:rʃl] 논란이 많은
relocation[rì:loukéiʃən] 이주 ancestral[ænséstrəl] 조상의
heterogeneous[hètərədʒí:niəs] 여러 다른 종류들로 이루어진

territory[térətɔːri] 영토 solitary[sáːləteri] 하나의
domestic[dəméstik] 국내의 grudgingly[grʌ́dʒiŋli] 마지못해
treaty[tríːti] 조약 federal government 연방 정부
resist[rizíst] 저항하다 vehemently[víːəməntli] 격렬하게
abandon[əbǽndən] 버리고 떠나다
hereditary[hərédɪtri] 대로 내려오는, 세습의
protest[prətést] 저항 terminus[tɔ́ːrminəs] 목적지

(A) 새로운 법은 정부가 각 원주민 부족을 마치 하나의 큰 실체의 일부처럼 취급한다는 뜻이었다.
(B) 그 법은 그저 정부가 늘 아메리카 원주민들을 분류했던 방식의 법적 공표일 뿐이었다.
(C) 대부분의 부족들은 그 명령에 맞서 싸웠지만, 그들 중 몇몇은 새로운 합의에 기뻐했다.
(D) 체로키 사람들의 이동으로 의도하지 않은 결과 중 하나는 상당한 난민 인구였다.

12 [1]주니족의 문화는 스페인의 정복 이전에 정점에 이르렀고, 이 정복은 북미 남서부에서 그것의 우세를 더욱 약화시켰다. 그러나, 그것의 예술 전통 중 일부는 외부의 점령을 견뎌내어 심지어 오늘날까지도 잔존한다. 예를 들어, 주니족의 도자기는 물을 실어 나르거나 종교 의식에서의 사용을 위한 것과 같이, 실용적이고 의례적인 목적을 위해 자주 만들어진다. 그것을 만들기 위해, 장인들은 지역의 연한 색 점토를 모아, 빚고, 추가적인 얇은 점토 겹으로 표면을 코팅한 뒤 아주 매끈한 마감을 위해 그것을 다듬는다. 그다음 그들은 남아있는 모든 오돌토돌한 흔적을 없애기 위해 야생 식물의 추출물이나 광물 기반의 물감을 사용해 그것을 색칠한다. 작품의 세속적이고 성스러운 기능은 주니족의 '보석'에 의해서도 입증된다. 은세공인들은 반지에 사용하기 위해 은에 터키석으로 모자이크식 무늬를 새기거나 정교한 문양으로 된 작은 돌멩이를 붙였는데, 이것들은 세계에서 가장 훌륭한 것들 중 일부로 간주된다. [2]이와 같이, 반지들은 일반적으로 경제적 이득을 위해서 판매되거나 구매자의 개인 장식품으로 착용된다. 반면, 끈으로 연결되어 있는 손으로 조각한 동물들로 구성된 다색의 목걸이는 가정에서 외관 장식을 위한 것일뿐만 아니라 종교적 용도를 갖기도 한다.

conquest[káːŋkwest] 정복 diminish[dimíniʃ] 약화시키다
preeminence[priémənəns] 우세 occupation[àːkjupéiʃən] 점령
persist[pərsíst] 잔존하다 pottery[páːtəri] 도자기
utilitarian[jùːtilitériən] 실용적인 ritual[rítʃuəl] 의식, 의례
craft[kræft] 만들다 artisan[áːrtəzn] 장인
pale-colored[péilkʌlərd] 연한 색의
graininess[gréininis] 오돌토돌함 secular[sékjələr] 세속적인
turquoise[tɔ́ːrkwɔiz] 터키석 delicate[délikət] 정교한
ornamentation[ɔ̀ːrnəmentéiʃən] 장식품
adornment[ədɔ́ːrnmənt] 장식

1 지문에 따르면, 주니족 문화에 대해 추론할 수 있는 것은?
(A) 실용적인 예술보다는 종교적인 예술에 중점을 두었다.
(B) 그것의 전통들 중 일부는 외래 영향에서 기인했다.
(C) 종교에서 그것의 영향력은 여태까지 중 가장 강하다.

(D) 스페인의 침략은 그것의 쇠퇴의 초기 원인이 아니었다.

2 지문으로부터 주니족의 보석에 대해 추론할 수 있는 것은?
(A) 그것의 일부는 중요한 의례적 가치가 없다.
(B) 그것의 다수는 국제적으로 높은 가격이 책정된다.
(C) 항상 오직 장식 목적으로 사용된다.
(D) 현지에서 수집된 재료들로 만들어진다.

13 생물학적 재생이란 상실된 신체 구조와 조직의 복원인데 이는 '아체'라고 불리는 많은 인접한 세포들에 의해 재건된다. 이 능력은 척추동물에게는 흔하지 않지만 특정 파충류에는 존재하며, 이 현상은 도마뱀, 도마뱀붙이, 그리고 이구아나에서 가장 잘 알려져 있다. [1]뱀과 같은 그들의 파충류 종형과는 달리, 이러한 생물들은 그들의 꼬리를 새것으로 교체하는 능력을 가진다. 이것은 포식을 피하기 위해 고안된 적응인데, 이로써 공격을 당할 때 동물의 끝부분의 일부 혹은 전체가 분리된다. 꼬리가 포식자의 입속에서 꿈틀거리면서, 공격자의 주의를 분산시키고 그 생물이 달아날 수 있게 한다. 하지만, 새롭게 얻어진 꼬리는 첫 꼬리의 단순 복제물이 아니다. 연구원들은 꼬리의 재성장을 250일 동안 신중히 연구하고 움직임을 일으키는 신경과 근육 조직 사이의 연결과 상호 작용을 기록한 뒤에 이를 알아냈다. [2]그들은 다시 자란 꼬리는 척추뼈 대신 연골의 중심관을 가지고 있으며 다른 근육 구조를 보인다는 것을 알아냈는데, 과학자들은 이 특성들이 재생된 꼬리가 원래의 것보다 덜 유연하지만 일부 기능적 특성은 원래의 것을 유지하게 만드는 것이라고 믿는다.

biomorphic[bàioumɔ́ːrfik] 생물학적인
regeneration[ridʒènəréiʃən] 재생 restoration[rèstəréiʃən] 복원
tissue[tíʃuː] 조직 adjoining[ədʒɔ́iniŋ] 인접한
vertebrate[vɔ́ːrtibrət] 척추동물 reptile[réptail] 파충류
phenomenon[fənáːmənən] 현상 adaptation[æ̀dæptéiʃən] 적응
terminal[tɔ́ːrminl] 끝의 segment[ségmənt] 부분
dislodge[dislɑ́ːdʒ] 분리하다 molest[məlést] 공격하다
wriggle[rígl] 꿈틀거리다 distract[distrǽkt] 주의를 분산시키다
replica[réplikə] 복제물 cartilage[káːrtilidʒ] 연골
vertebra[vɔ́ːrtibrə] 척추뼈 property[práːpərti] 특성

1 지문에 따르면, 다음 중 뱀에 대해 추론할 수 있는 것은?
(A) 그들의 해부학적 구조는 먹이를 포획하는 데 제격이다.
(B) 그들은 주로 도마뱀, 도마뱀붙이, 그리고 이구아나의 포식자이다.
(C) 그들의 몸은 생물학적 재생 능력이 없다.
(D) 그들은 넓은 범위의 환경에 잘 적응한다.

2 지문에 따르면, _____ 때문에 원래의 꼬리가 재생된 꼬리와는 다르다는 것을 추론할 수 있다.
(A) 주로 근육과 연골로 구성되기 때문에
(B) 척추뼈를 가지고 있기 때문에
(C) 약 250일 동안 지속되기 때문에
(D) 제한된 범위의 움직임을 가지기 때문에

14 문자의 기원을 이해하기 위해서는, 한때 유명했던 언어와 문화에 대한 두 가지 이론이 틀렸음을 밝힐 필요가 있다. 첫째로, 언어는 많은 학자가 주장해온 것처럼 하나의 원형에서 유래된 것이 아니다. 그러한 견해는 주로 언어의 기원에 대한 성서의 해석에서 비롯된 것으로, 문자 체계가 고대 메소포타미아에서 발생했으며 그곳에서 전 세계로 퍼져나가고 진화했다고 주장했다. 더욱이 진화의 생물학적 이론을 언어 발달에도 적용한 19세기 사회학자들은 문자에 공통된 조상이 있다고 보았을 뿐 아니라 문자가 진화적인 계층 구조를 나타낸다고 보았는데, 그 구조 내에서 알파벳 문자들은 표의 문자나 음절 문자 체계보다 더 우월한 것으로 여겨졌다. 고대의 언어학적 역사의 맥락에서 이러한 관점은 유럽과 근동의 문화가 아시아, 아프리카, 혹은 중앙아메리카의 문화보다 더 크게 진화한 것으로 묘사했다. [1]이보다 더 진실에서 거리가 먼 이야기는 없는데, 이는 장대한 건축, 예술, 법률, 그리고 사회기반시설을 갖춘, 문화적인 탁월함이 풍부한 제국들이 알파벳 문자를 쓰지 않는 문명에 의해 건설되었기 때문이다.

오늘날의 학자들은 비옥한 초승달 지대, 아시아, 그리고 중앙아메리카에서 문자가 독립적으로 발달했다는 데 동의한다. 이러한 지역 중에서도, 가장 초기의 문자가 아마도 일찍이 기원전 8000년에 수메르의 비옥한 초승달 지대에서 발생했다는 데 대체로 의견이 일치한다. 고대 수메르인들은 원래 양, 일정량의 곡물, 기름병, 그리고 그 외의 물품들을 표현하기 위해 진흙으로 된 작은 삼각형, 구, 원뿔 모양의 상징물들을 사용했다. 기본적으로 이 상징물의 형태가 그것의 의미를 전달했다. 이러한 상징물들이 자원을 모으고 재분배하기 위한 목적으로 물품의 출납을 기록하는 데 쓰이며 공동체에 기여했다는 이론이 정설화되었다. 그러나 그것들은 가끔 무덤에 놓이기도 했고, 사원에 바친 선물, 군주에게 바친 공물 혹은 세금을 나타냈을 수도 있다. [2]먼 훗날, 기원전 3100년에 이르러 수메르인들은 숫자를 발명하며 양의 상징을 양의 숫자로부터 독립시켰고, 이에 따라 문자와 수학이 함께 진화해왔을 것이다. Uruk 지방의 출토품은 수메르의 문자가 상형 문자에서 표의 문자로 발전했음을 보여주는데, 표의 문자에서 상징은 의미를 나타냈다. 이 시점에 이르러 문자는 이미 생각을 전달할 수 있는 도구로 발전하고 있었다.

debunk[diːbʌ́ŋk] (생각, 믿음 등이) 틀렸음을 밝히다
descend[disénd] (언어가) ~에서 유래하다
prototype[próutətàip] 원형 derive[diráiv] ~에서 비롯되다
ideographic[ìdiəgrǽfik] 표의 문자의 syllabic[silǽbik] 음절의
Near Eastern 근동의
Mesoamerica[mèzouəmérikə] 중앙아메리카
splendor[spléndər] 탁월, 현저 consensus[kənsénsəs] 일치
token[tóukən] 상징물 sphere[sfiər] 구 cone[koun] 원뿔
keep track of ~을 기록하다 pictograph[píktəgræf] 상형 문자
concept[kánsept] 의미, 개념
communicate[kəmjúːnəkèit] 전달하다

1 지문에 따르면, 문화에 대한 글쓴이의 관점에 대해 추론할 수 있는 것은?

(A) 문화의 가치는 문자 언어를 사용할 수 있는 문명의 능력과 불가분하게 연결되어 있다.

(B) 문명의 특별한 문자 체계와 관련될 필요는 없다.

(C) 시간이 흐르면서 한 사회가 어떻게 발전하는지에 대한 맥락에서 보아야 한다.

(D) 문화의 중요성은 제국의 실체적인 업적을 넘어선다.

2 다음 중 고대 수메르인에 대해 추론할 수 있는 것은?

(A) 그들의 수학 지식은 문자의 진보에 기여했을 것이다.

(B) 그들의 언어 문자 체계는 이웃 공동체에 의해 점차 받아들여졌다.

(C) 그들의 문자 체계를 만든 원래의 의도는 종교적인 목적이었다.

(D) 그들의 문자 체계는 아시아와 중앙아메리카의 것보다 더 복잡했다.

15 [1]장기적인 저항과 많은 유혈 사태 끝에 스페인 제국으로부터의 독립을 쟁취한 후, 네덜란드 공화국은 열심히 성장하고 번영하는 훌륭한 곳이 되었다. 1600년대 중반 무렵, 이 신생 연방은 유럽에서 가장 부유한 국가가 되었는데, 이때 문화의 전성기에 불을 지피고 네덜란드 예술의 황금기를 촉진시킨 전례 없는 경제적 활력을 경험했다. 17세기의 예술적 발전은 네덜란드 그림을 국제 무대에 오르게 했는데 이는 예술가들이 세계가 이제껏 목도한 적이 없는 정밀함을 사용하는 대상의 극현실적인 묘사 기법으로 전향함에 따른 것이었다. 그들의 초상화와 풍경화에서의 표현은 현실과의 유사성에 있어서 마치 사진 같았고 굉장한 세부 묘사를 보였다.

네덜란드 예술가들은 특히 풍속화로 잘 알려지게 되었는데, 이것은 일상생활의 장면들을 포착하고자 했다. 풍속화는 새로운 주제를 추구하려는 화가들의 욕구와 익숙한 주제에 대한 고객의 강한 친밀감에서 비롯되었다. 따라서, 예술가들은 농경지에서 일하고 있는 농부들, 시장에서 물건을 사고 있는 평범한 시민들, 혹은 전투태세를 갖추고 있는 군인들을 그린 그림들의 애호가들을 손쉽게 발견했다.

게다가, 특히, [2]새로운 세대의 예술가들은 개인 가정집에서 편지를 쓰고 있는 남자나 음악 교습을 받고 있는 여자와 같은, 가정의 모습들을 묘사하는 사실상 전대미문의 풍습을 개척했다. 이 '생활의 단면' 접근법이 일상적인 것들에 대한 감상을 보여주긴 했지만, 이것이 풍속화가 시민들의 실생활을 완벽하게 보여준다는 것을 상정하지는 않는다. 거울이 반사된 이미지의 정확한 반대를 보여주는 것처럼, 십중팔구로 이러한 작품들은 단지 사회의 표면상 실제 모습만을 전달했다.

independence[ìndipéndəns] 독립 imperial[impíriəl] 제국의
resistance[rizístəns] 저항 bloodshed[blʌ́dʃed] 유혈 사태
confederation[kənfèdəréiʃən] 연방
unprecedented[ʌnprésidentid] 전례 없는
vitality[vaitǽləti] 활력 ultra-realistic[ʌ̀ltrəriːəlístik] 극현실적인
portraiture[pɔ́ːrtrətʃər] 초상화 rendition[rendíʃən] 표현
affinity[əfínəti] 친밀감 agricultural[æ̀grikʌ́ltʃərəl] 농경의
poised[pɔizd] 전투태세를 갖추고 있는 notably[nóutəbli] 특히

unheard-of[ʌnhə́:rdʌv] 전대미문의
appreciation[əpri:ʃiéiʃən] 감상 mundane[mʌndéin] 일상적인
presuppose[pri:səpóuz] 상정하다 inverse[ìnvə́:rs] 반대
in all probability 십중팔구로 seemingly[sí:miŋli] 표면상

1 지문에서 네덜란드 독립에 대해 추론할 수 있는 것은?
   (A) 16세기에 시작된 국내적 불안으로부터 발생했다.
   (B) 무력 충돌 없이는 가능하지 않았을 것이다.
   (C) 나머지 유럽과의 더 밀접한 경제적 유대로 이어졌다.
   (D) 스페인이 더 일찍 침략했다면 방지될 수도 있었을 것이다.

2 지문에 따르면, 네덜란드 예술에서 가정의 모습에 대한 논의는 _____라는 것을 암시한다.
   (A) 공공 장소를 보여주는 것보다 선호되었다
   (B) 이전 예술가들의 작품 속에서는 거의 포함되지 않았다
   (C) 전형적으로 대상들의 개인 가정집에서 그려졌다
   (D) 초기에는 매우 인기 있었으나 나중에는 너무 평범하다고 여겨졌다

16 [1]1920년대에, '시카고 학파'는 보통과는 달리 높은 수준의 응집력을 보인 교수들 및 동료들의 집단에 의해 보급된 사회학의 한 학파가 되었다. 이러한 사회학자들은 인간 본성에 대해 알기 가장 좋은 방법은 도시 환경에 있는 사람들을 연구하는 것이라고 믿었다. 그들에게, 이러한 환경은 시카고를 의미했는데, 그곳은 1850년의 30,000명에서 1900년에는 거의 2백만 명으로 인구가 급등하며 세계에서 가장 빠르게 성장하는 자치 도시로서의 변덕스러운 특성을 발전시켜왔고, 그 당시 사람들의 3분의 1이 다양한 문화적 배경을 가진 이민자들이었기 때문에 완벽한 정밀 조사의 대상이라고 여겨졌다. 이 연구원들은 도시를 괴롭히는 취기와 폭력과 같은 세속적인 문제들의 급증을 이해하는 것에 대해 매우 관심을 가졌다. 이 현상을 더 잘 이해하기 위해서, 교수들과 학생들은 '현실 세계'에서 그들만의 방식으로 사람들과 소통함으로써 연구를 시행했다. 예를 들어, 한 사회학자는 소외된 이주민들의 근처에서 일했을 것이고, 또 다른 사회학자는 높은 노숙자 인구 밀도의 지역을 선택했을 것이다. 그들이 궁극적으로 제시했던 설명은 사회해체이론으로 알려지게 되었는데, [2]이는 시카고의 도시 부패 발생이 문화적으로 구분된 주거 현장의 다양화와 이러한 하위 문화들이 승인하고 영속시키는 생활 방식의 다양성에서 기인했다고 여겼다. 사람들이 그들 환경의 산물이라는 가정으로부터 시작하여, 시카고 학파는 문화적 기대치가 행동을 좌우하는 것이며, 더 많은 인종 집단이 경쟁하면서, 전통적 기준의 약화가 뒤따른다고 주장했다. 결과적으로, 범죄, 비행, 그리고 다른 일탈적 행위들은 더욱 만연하게 되었다.

promulgate[prá:mlgeit] 보급하다 cohesion[kouhí:ʒn] 응집력
scrutiny[skrú:təni] 정밀 조사 capricious[kəpríʃəs] 변덕스러운
municipality[mju:nìsipǽləti] 자치 도시
skyrocket[skáirɑ:kit] 급등하다 varying[vέəriŋ] 다양한
proliferation[prəlìfəréiʃən] 급증 secular[sékjələr] 세속적인
plague[pleig] 괴롭히다 comprehend[kɑ:mprihénd] 이해하다

phenomenon[fənú:minən] 현상 alienate[éiliəneit] 소외시키다
district[dístrikt] 지역 corruption[kərʌ́pʃən] 부패
locale[loukǽl] 현장 subculture[sʌ́bkʌ̀ltʃər] 하위 문화
assumption[əsʌ́mpʃən] 가정 govern[gʌ́vərn] 좌우하다
ethnic[éθnik] 인종의 ensue[insú:] 뒤따르다
delinquency[dilíŋkwənsi] 비행 deviant[dí:viənt] 일탈적인

1 지문에 따르면, 1920년대 사회학자들에 대해 추론할 수 있는 것은?
   (A) 보통 엄격하게 통제되는 환경에서 실험을 실시했다.
   (B) 그들 중 다수는 시카고 학파의 가정에 동의했다.
   (C) 그들이 비슷한 생각을 가진 집단을 형성하여 함께 뭉치는 것은 드물었다.
   (D) 그들 중 소수만이 주요 도시 밖에서 연구를 수행했다.

2 지문으로부터 높은 문화적 다양성을 띠는 지역사회는 _____라는 것을 추론할 수 있다.
   (A) 전례 없는 수의 노숙자들을 낳았다
   (B) 주거 건축에서 여러 가지 양식을 만들어냈다
   (C) 현저하게 더 높은 사회 범죄 비율을 보였다
   (D) 이웃들 간 의사소통의 장벽을 만들었다

HACKERS **TEST**

01 Steam Power

p.228

1. (C)	2. (B)	3. (A)
4. (D)	5. (C)	6. (D)
7. (A)	8. (C)	9. (D)

10. (B)-2단락, (C)-4~5단락, (F)-3단락

1 기하급수적인 성장의 일반 원리는 어떤 것이 커지면 커질수록 더 빨리 성장한다는 것이다. 예를 들어, 이상적인 환경 하에서, 하나의 'E. coli(대장균)' 세포는 20분마다 한 번씩 분열을 일으키고 그때마다 크기가 두 배로 커지는데, 처음에는 세포 수가 느리게 증가하더라도 하루 이내에 지구의 크기와 무게에 맞먹게 될 것이다. [1]사회경제학적 맥락에서 볼 때 산업혁명의 상징물로 널리 여겨지는 증기 엔진은 19세기 영국 경제에 엄청난 성장을 불러일으켰던 산업화와 도시화를 밀접히 연관시켰는데, 그 영향은 서구 문명 전반에 걸친 근본적 변화를 불러왔다. 수력이 풍부하고 값싼 에너지를 제공했지만, [2]증기기관은 수력의 극심한 지형적인 제약을 불필요하게 했고, 따라서 산업이 시골 지역에서 대도시 지역으로 대대적으로 재배치되는 데 촉매 역할을 했다.

2 증기기관은 보일러 안의 물을 가열시켜서 발생하는 증기를 피스톤이 달린 원통으로 흘려보낸 후, 간격을 두고 증기압을 발생시켜서

피스톤을 위아래로 움직이게 하는 방식으로 열에너지를 동력으로 전환했다. 이는 제조업에 종사하는 기업의 모습을 변모시키는 강력한 동력원이 되었다. 예를 들어, 증기로 움직이는 방직기는 한 개의 물레만을 돌려도 여러 가닥의 실을 자을 수 있었고, 레버, 캠, 기어 등을 통해 정확한 작동을 유도할 수 있었으며, [4]이로 인해서 산업혁명 이전에 여럿의 장인들이 수 주에 걸친 힘든 육체노동 끝에 짜냈던 옷감보다 많은 양을 단 한 명의 노동자가 하루의 근무 시간 동안 짜낼 수 있게 되었다. 이 기계들은 증기를 만드는 데 필요한 열을 발생시키기 위해서 연료, 즉 석탄을 필요로 했기 때문에 결과적으로 채광업계도 증기기관으로부터 이득을 얻게 되었다.

3 운송 면에서는, 높은 마력의 증기기관이 선박과 기차에 생명을 불어넣어 주었다. 피스톤이 선박의 심장부에서 상하로 움직이면서 펌프운동을 할 때와 같은 정확도, 속도, 신뢰도로, 도시의 제조업자들은 엄청난 양의 공산품을 앞세워서 이전에는 닿을 수 없었던 곳까지 외부로 급격히 시장을 넓혀 갔고, 동시에 원료는 공장으로 집중되었다. 제품의 생산을 집중시키기 위해서 대규모의 공장이 생겨났는데, 이는 하나의 큰 공장을 짓는 것이 다수의 작은 공장을 건설하는 것보다 더 경제적이었기 때문이다. 처음에는 교외에 지어졌던 이 공장들은 결국에는 도시 내부로 확장되어 들어와 최초의 거대도시를 탄생시켰는데, 이러한 패턴은 서유럽과 미국 전역에서 이어지게 되었다. 전체 영국 인구의 절반 이상이 일자리와 더 높은 삶의 질에 매료되어 도시로 모여들었고, 주택, 오락 및 다른 삶의 필수 요소에 대한 수요가 도시 지역의 중요성을 더욱 증가시키는 데 일조했다.

4 사회학자들은 이러한 도시화는 식자율을 증가시킨다고 믿는데, [6]1840년대 시점에서, 영국 인구의 65퍼센트에서 70퍼센트가 읽는 법을 배운 상태였다는 사실이 이 주장을 뒷받침하며, 이러한 진보는 증기기관을 이용한 인쇄기의 등장과 그 시점이 일치한다. 이전에는 책이 만드는 데 시간이 오래 걸리고 비쌌기 때문에 심한 통제를 받는 귀한 자원이었다. 하지만 이 새로운 기계는 하루 만에 수백만 장의 페이지를 대량으로 생산해낼 수 있었다. 인쇄기는 현대 사회에서 급속도로 홍수를 이루어, 다수의 간절한, 돈벌이가 되는 새로운 독자층에 Marx나 Nietzsche와 같은 작가들에게서 나온 정치, 철학, 문학 분야의 새로운 사상을 퍼뜨렸다. 이러한 사상의 전파는 자본주의, 공산주의, 실존주의 등의 개념에 대한 대중의 자각으로 이어졌고, 또한 어린이와 노동자의 권리 같은 문제들을 조명했다.

5 이것은 또한 과학 연구 활동이 급격히 촉진되는 결과를 가져왔다. 대학 교과과정이 확립되었고 대학원이 등장했다. 작업장은 실험실로, 수리 작업은 공학적 연구로 변모했으며 개개의 발명에 깔린 이론적인 원리들이 체계적인 신기술로 정리되었다. [8]개발자들은 증기기관을 이용하는 중앙집중식의 공장 구조를 더욱 분산된 시스템으로 발전시키는 방법을 연구하기 시작했으며, 결과적으로 작은 전동기가 각각의 노동자가 다루는 장비들에 동력을 제공할 수 있었다. 최종적으로 19세기 말에 이르자, 증기기관은 새로운 전력 생산의 형태인 전기에 자리를 내어 주었다. 비록 후자의 이런 지위 상승은 종합적 혁신이었던 선조(증기기관)가 없었다면 불가능했을 테지만 말이다.

---

exponential [èkspounénʃəl] 기하급수적인
E. coli [í:kòulai] 대장균(Escherichia coli)
intertwine [ìntərtwáin] 밀접히 연관되게 하다
reverberation [rivə̀:rbəréiʃən] 영향
redundant [ridʌ́ndənt] 필요가 없어진, 여분의
catalyst [kǽtəlist] 촉매제   thermal [θə́:rməl] 열의
cylindrical [silíndrikəl] 원통 모양의
at intervals 간격을 두고, 띄엄띄엄   potent [póutnt] 강력한
enterprise [éntərpràiz] 기업   spin [spin] (실을) 잣다
lever [lévər] 레버
cam [kæm] 캠(회전 운동을 왕복 운동으로 바꾸는 장치)
weave [wi:v] 짜다   toil [tɔil] 힘든 노동
industrialist [indʌ́striəlist] 제조업자
outbound [áutbàund] 외부로 가는   outskirt [áutskə̀:rt] 교외
literacy [lítərəsi] 식자, 읽고 쓸 줄 앎   coincide with ~과 일치하다
advent [ǽdvent] 등장, 출현   churn out 대량 생산하다
circulate [sə́:rkjulèit] 퍼뜨리다   dispersion [dispə́:rʒən] 전파
consciousness [kánʃəsnis] 자각
capitalism [kǽpətəlìzm] 자본주의
communism [kámjunìzm] 공산주의
existentialism [ègzisténʃəlìzm] 실존주의
illuminate [ilú:mənèit] 조명하다
acceleration [æksèləréiʃən] 촉진   curricula [kəríkjulə] 교과과정
tinker [tíŋkər] 수리하다   theoretical [θì:ərétikəl] 이론적인
decentralize [di:séntrəlàiz] 분산시키다
ascension [əsénʃən] 지위 상승
macrocosmic [mæ̀krəkázmik] 종합적인
trailblazing [tréilblèiziŋ] 혁신

1 지문에 따르면, 증기기관이 영국에 미친 영향에 대해 글쓴이가 진술한 것은?

(A) 영국을 국제 경제에 통합시켰다.
(B) 공장주들이 시골 환경으로 이동하도록 자극했다.
(C) 영국의 경제 성장의 원천이었다.
(D) 수력을 이용할 수 있는 사람들에게 더 많은 권력을 주었다.

2 다음 중 수력 발전에 대해 지문에서 추론할 수 있는 것은?

(A) 증기 이전에 가장 인기 있는 전력원이었다.
(B) 지형 때문에 특정 위치에 제한되었다.
(C) 한 지역의 물은 즉시 마르는 경향이 있었다.
(D) 수력 발전소의 건설은 너무 비쌌다.

3 지문의 단어 "potent"와 의미상 가장 유사한 것은?

(A) 강한
(B) 부적당한
(C) 기이한
(D) 결합력 있는

4 지문에서 글쓴이는 왜 "pre-industrial artisans"를 언급하는가?

(A) 이전 경제에서의 그들의 노동을 강조하기 위해
(B) 대량 생산되는 제품의 낮은 품질을 강조하기 위해

(C) 근력의 효율성의 예를 제공하기 위해

(D) 기계 생산과 그들의 생산을 대조하기 위해

5 아래 문장 중 지문 속의 음영된 문장의 핵심 정보를 가장 잘 표현하고 있는 것은 무엇인가? 오답은 문장의 의미를 현저히 왜곡하거나 핵심 정보를 빠뜨리고 있다.

(A) 더 많은 사람들이 도시로 가면서, 도시 지역에서의 삶의 질은 현저히 떨어지기 시작했다.

(B) 오락과 주택 지구의 급격한 증가는 많은 도시 지역의 인구를 크게 증가시켰다.

(C) 고용 기회와 더 나은 삶에 이끌린 사람들이 도시로 이동하자, 그들의 일상의 수요는 도시 지역의 중요성을 계속해서 확장시켰다.

(D) 영국의 인구는 일자리를 찾아 도시 지역으로 들어온 인구 유입의 결과로 증가했다.

6 4단락에 따르면, 글쓴이는 책의 보급이 _____ 라는 것을 암시한다.

(A) 공장 노동자들의 작업량을 크게 증가시켰다

(B) 다른 형태의 오락의 인기를 줄였다

(C) 초기 작가들이 그들의 작품을 더 저렴하게 다시 출판할 수 있도록 했다

(D) 사람들의 독해력과 밀접하게 서로 연결되었다

7 지문의 단어 "dispersion"과 의미상 가장 유사한 것은?

(A) 보급

(B) 탈선

(C) 휴업

(D) 기만

8 지문에서 전기는 _____ 라는 것을 추론할 수 있다.

(A) 증기 기술의 더 많은 사용을 이끌었다

(B) 더 작은 전동기의 생산을 가능하게 했다

(C) 공장 체계를 분산시킬 수 있었다

(D) 노동자들에 대한 수요를 줄였다

9 지문의 구 "its predecessor"가 가리키는 것은?

(A) 시스템

(B) 노동자

(C) 전기

(D) 증기기관

10 **지시:** 지문 요약을 위한 도입 문장이 아래에 주어져 있다. 지문의 가장 중요한 내용을 나타내는 보기 3개를 골라 요약을 완성하시오. 어떤 문장은 지문에 언급되지 않은 내용이나 사소한 정보를 담고 있으므로 요약에 포함되지 않는다. **이 문제는 2점이다.**

> 증기기관에 의해 시작된 산업혁명은 1800년대 영국을 대폭 변화시켰다.
>
> · (B) 제조업에서 증기기관의 적용은 효율적으로 제품을 대량 생산하는 것을 가능하게 했다.

· (C) 증기기관을 이용하는 대량 생산 장비 때문에, 책은 매우 손에 넣기 쉬워졌고 과학 연구에 대한 관심이 증가했다.

· (F) 증기로 동력을 얻는 수송 시설의 개발은 제품의 더 나은 유통과 대도시 형성으로 이어졌다.

(A) 대규모 공장 건설은 공장주들이 제조 공정을 하나의 장소로 집중시키는 것을 허용했다.

(D) 항구에 접근하기 쉬운 도시들은 적은 비용으로 완제품을 선적하는 혜택이 있었다.

(E) 증기를 발생시키는 데 필요한 힘은 대부분 석탄을 태움으로써 얻었다.

02 Species

p.232

1. (B)	2. (B)	3. (C)
4. (B)	5. (B)	6. (D)
7. (B)	8. (C)	9. (B)
10. (B)−3단락, (C)−5단락, (E)−4단락		

1 화석은 암석 퇴적층에서, 또는 해안을 따라서 발견되는 광물화된 동식물의 잔해로, [1]생물이 퇴적물로 덮이거나 호수 바닥 또는 해저 등 산소가 없는 환경으로 떨어지는 드문 경우에만 형성된다. 화석화 과정은 부패하는 유기체 잔해가 흙, 모래, 그리고 다른 잔류물로 여러 겹 덮이면서 시작되는데, 유기체는 딱딱한 무기물로 변형되고 결국 굳어 암석을 형성한다.

2 일찍이 17세기 때부터, 박물학자들은 이러한 화석 증거물들을 이용해 비교학적 관점에서 다양한 종의 해부 구조를 기록하고, 지구의 다양한 생물에 대한 더 나은 이해를 발전시키기 시작했다. 이런 연구를 통해 밝혀지고 있는 가장 놀라운 발견 중 하나는, 어떤 화석들은 오늘날 살아있는 생물들과 닮은 반면, 어떤 화석들은 완전히 다른 모습을 하고 있다는 것이다. 이것은 지구에 사는 생물 종의 수와 종류가 변화해왔고, 이러한 변형이 현존하는 생물들과 관련이 있을지도 모른다는 것을 암시한다.

3 박물학자들은 언제, 어떻게 이러한 변화가 생겼는지 알아내기 위해서 광상을 연구해왔다. 이들은 지구 생물의 변천에 대해서 서로 다른 세 가지의 학설을 제시하고 있는데, 그중 하나는 동식물이 그들 스스로 변화한 것이 아니라 다른 종에 의해서 대체되었다는 의견이다. 새로운 지질학적 발견이 새로운 화석 집단을 밝힐 때마다, 이러한 종의 변화는 이전의 종들을 싹쓸이한 대규모 멸종 현상이나 재앙 때문인 것으로 여겨졌다. 그리고 새로운 생물의 존재는 주변 지역의 종이 이주해 와서 그곳에 자리 잡게 된 것으로 설명된다. [4/9]대재앙 이론이라고 알려진 이 이론의 지지자는 일반적으로 종교학자들로, 이들은 모든 종이 지구가 탄생한 최초의 날부터 변함없이 존재해왔다고 주장하며, 모든 생물 및 무생물의 창조를 신의 업적으로 여긴다.

4 [9]Jean-Baptiste Lamarck에 의해 전개된 다른 한 가지 해석은 종이 새로운 형질을 얻어서 다음 세대에 물려주면서, 시간이 흐름에 따라 생물의 변천이 일어났다는 것이다. 예를 들어, Lamarck는 기린의 해부학적 특징에 대해 고찰하면서, 키가 작은 기린이 나뭇가지의 잎사귀를 향해 몸을 뻗으면서 점차적으로 목의 길이가 늘어난 결과 기린이 여러 세대에 걸쳐서 길어진 목을 갖게 되었다는 설을 제시했다. [5]약간씩 길어진 목의 형질이 새끼들에게 유전되면서, 결과적으로는 수많은 작은 변화가 계승되어 오늘날 긴 목을 가진 기린이 존재하게 되었다고 생각된다. 불행히도, 'Lamarckism (Lamarck의 이론)'은 새끼에게 이득을 주지 않는 유전 형질을 물려주는 현상이나, 해로운 형질이 종종 전해지기도 한다는 사실을 설명하지 못한다.

5 마지막으로, 가장 현대에 나온 학설은 자연선택을 통해 능력이 개량된다는 것인데, 이는 환경에 유리한 적응을 타고난 생물이 살아남아서 후손을 남기는 경향을 말한다. 박물학자 Charles Darwin은 여러 번의 항해 동안 접한 셀 수 없이 많은 생물에 대해 행한 자세하고 치밀한 연구를 바탕으로, 당대의 과학 이론에 대한 광범위한 연구를 결부시켜 1859년에 이 이론을 최초로 제시하였다. 예를 들어, Galapagos 제도에서 Darwin은 각각의 섬마다 독특한 특징을 가진 흉내지빠귀가 살고 있는 것을 관찰했는데, Darwin은 이들이 공통된 조상으로부터 유래했으며, 먹이를 더 잘 구할 수 있었던 새가 성숙할 때까지 살아남아 짝을 짓고 결국에는 후손을 남길 가능성이 더 많다고 믿었다. [7]각각의 섬은 지질학적으로 뚜렷하게 다른 서식지이므로 먹이도 서로 다를 것이라 추측할 수 있는데, 이는 각 섬의 환경에 각각 다르게 적응하는 것이 합리적일 수 있다는 것을 의미하므로, 흉내지빠귀는 분명히 Darwin이 관찰한 대로 종류가 다양하면서 동시에 각각의 특수한 환경에 적응하도록 변했을 것이다. 이러한 관찰 결과는 '적합성', 즉 유리한 변이를 거친 생물이 생존할 가능성이 더 높아 번식할 기회를 더 많이 갖게 되고, 결국에는 종 전체의 변형에 영향을 미친다는 개념에 대한 Darwin의 믿음을 확고히 해주었다.

6 오늘날, 과학자들은 현대 게놈 연구를 통해서 계속적으로 Darwin의 이론을 보완하고 있다. 즉, 과학자들은 분자 수준에서 돌연변이를 이해하려 노력하고 있고, 돌연변이는 한 생물체의 DNA가 자손에게 잘못 전해질 때 발생하고, 그 결과 부정적 혹은 긍정적인 효과가 나타날 수 있는데, 후자 쪽이 그 동식물의 생존에 도움을 줄 가능성이 더 높다고 간주하고 있다. 일부 과학자들은 이제 일반적인 적응 과정을 생명체의 진화, 혹은 여러 세대에 걸친 생명체의 유전적 변이의 축적으로 여긴다. 그들의 주장에 관계없이, 현대과학의 밑바탕이 되는 이론은 변화 자체는 끊임없이 지속되며 변치 않는다는 것인데, 이는 연구자들이 진화 과정에 대한 숙고를 계속하는 동안에도 변화가 존재한다는 것만 신뢰할 수 있음을 의미한다.

fossil[fásəl] 화석 mineralize[mínərəlàiz] 광물화하다
sediment[sédəmənt] 퇴적물 anoxic[ænáksik] 산소가 없는
residue[rézədjù:] 잔류물 compact[kəmpækt] 굳다, 압축되다
naturalist[nætʃərəlist] 박물학자 anatomy[ənætəmi] 해부 구조
eclectic[ikléktik] 다양한 drastically[dræstikəli] 완전히
modification[màdəfikéiʃən] 변형, 변이

deposit[dipázit] 광상(광물이 묻혀있는 땅속 부분)
alteration[ɔ̀:ltəréiʃən] 변천 attribute to ~ 때문으로 여기다
extinction[ikstíŋkʃən] 멸종 catastrophe[kətæstrəfi] 재앙
advocate[ædvəkèit] 지지자
accredit to ~의 공적(또는 원인)을 -탓으로 간주하다
inorganic[ìnɔːrgænik] 무생물의 assessment[əsésmənt] 해석
speculate[spékjulèit] 고찰하다
elongation[ilɔ̀:ŋgéiʃən] 길이의 늘어남 calf[kæf] 새끼
accession[ækséʃən] 계승
contemporary[kəntémpərèri] 현재의, 동시대의
painstaking[péinztèikiŋ] 치밀한, 공들인 voyage[vɔ́iidʒ] 항해
mockingbird[mákiŋbə̀:rd] 흉내지빠귀 maturity[mətʃúərəti] 성숙
presumable[prizú:məbl] 추측할 수 있는
equitable[ékwətəbl] 합리적인, 적당한
unmistakably[ʌ̀nmistéikəbli] 분명히
solidify[səlídəfài] 확고하게 하다 mutation[mju:téiʃən] 변이
reproduce[rì:prədjú:s] 번식하다
transformation[trænsfərméiʃən] 변형 flesh[fleʃ] 보완하다
genome[dʒí:noum] 게놈 molecular[məlékjulər] 분자의
postulate[pástʃulèit] 간주하다 genetic[dʒənétik] 유전적인
immutable[imjú:təbl] 변치 않는 ponder[pándər] 숙고하다
mechanism[mékənìzm] 과정, 절차

1 다음 중 화석 형성에 대해 1단락으로부터 추론할 수 있는 것은?
   (A) 유기체는 덮이기 전에 많은 광물을 포함할 필요가 있다.
   (B) 공기와의 접촉은 유기물의 보존을 방해한다.
   (C) 물에 사는 종들만 화석으로 보존될 수 있다.
   (D) 화석의 생성은 다소 일반적인 발생이다.

2 지문의 단어 "eclectic"과 의미상 가장 유사한 것은?
   (A) 엄청난
   (B) 여러 가지의
   (C) 일관된
   (D) 수수께끼의

3 지문의 단어 "others"가 가리키는 것은?
   (A) 종
   (B) 발견
   (C) 화석
   (D) 생물

4 지문에 따르면, 다음 중 대재앙이론의 옹호자들이 지지할 것 같은 것은?
   (A) 종은 그들이 생성되었던 곳과 같은 지역에 계속 남는다.
   (B) 지구의 탄생 이래 새롭게 창조된 생명체는 없다.
   (C) 화석의 출현은 주변 환경의 변화로 이어진다.
   (D) 대규모 멸종은 살아남은 종들에게서 새로운 특징이 형성되는 것을 용이하게 한다.

5 4단락에서, 글쓴이는 왜 긴 목을 가진 기린을 언급하는가?
   (A) Lamarck의 이론이 다른 것들보다 뛰어나다는 실험적 증거를 제공하기 위해

(B) Lamarck에 따르면 어떻게 새로운 적응이 나타나는지 설명하기 위해

(C) Lamarck의 의견과 Darwin의 의견을 대조하기 위해

(D) 이전에 관찰된 현상을 반박하는 Lamarckism의 능력을 보여주기 위해

6 지문의 단어 "tendency"와 의미상 가장 유사한 것은?

(A) 합의

(B) 보완

(C) 구제책

(D) 경향

7 지문에 따르면, Galapagos 제도의 흉내지빠귀의 종류는 _____ 때문에 다양해졌다.

(A) 그것들이 낳은 후손의 수를 늘리고 싶어했기 때문에

(B) 그것들의 조상은 서로 다른 방식으로 그것들의 독특한 서식지에 적응했기 때문에

(C) 암컷들은 특유의 특징이 있는 수컷들하고만 짝짓기를 하고 싶어했기 때문에

(D) 임의적인 변이가 여러 개체들을 통해 새로운 특징을 퍼뜨렸기 때문에

8 아래 문장 중 지문 속의 음영된 문장의 핵심 정보를 가장 잘 표현하고 있는 것은 무엇인가? 오답은 문장의 의미를 현저히 왜곡하거나 핵심 정보를 빠뜨리고 있다.

(A) 변이가 미시적인 수준에서 발생하기 때문에, 그것들은 후손에게 전해져서 수많은 이득을 본다.

(B) 생물의 DNA에 영향을 주는 변이만이 다음 세대에 전해질 것이다.

(C) 결과적인 유전적 오류는 장점과 단점이 있으며 전자는 종의 생존을 돕는다고 여겨진다.

(D) 생물이 생존하도록 돕는 DNA상의 변화만이 다음 세대에 전해진다.

9 다음 중 지문에서 결론 내릴 수 있는 것은?

(A) 종이 어떻게 한 지역에서 재번식하는지에 대한 대재앙이론의 설명은 진화론과 일관된다.

(B) Lamarck의 이론은 대재앙이론과 맞지 않는 요소들을 포함한다.

(C) Darwin은 어떻게 유전성 특징이 후손에게 전해지는지에 대한 이론의 근거를 Lamarck의 연구에 두었다.

(D) 현대의 게놈 연구는 유사한 종은 공통의 조상을 가진다는 Darwin의 믿음에 의구심을 제기한다.

10 지시: 지문 요약을 위한 도입 문장이 아래에 주어져 있다. 지문의 가장 중요한 내용을 나타내는 보기 3개를 골라 요약을 완성하시오. 어떤 문장은 지문에 언급되지 않은 내용이나 사소한 정보를 담고 있으므로 요약에 포함되지 않는다. **이 문제는 2점이다.**

> 사람들은 화석 기록을 관찰함으로써 어떻게 생물이 진화했는지 이해할 수 있다.
> - (B) 지역에서의 새로운 종의 출현은 다른 지역으로부터의 종 이동의 결과이다.

> - (C) 변이는 개체 가운데 퍼지기 더 쉬운 유리한 종에서 임의로 발생한다.
> - (E) 종의 일생 동안 발달되는 특징은 다음 세대에 유전될 수 있다.

(A) 기린들은 키가 큰 나무의 잎사귀를 뜯어 먹기에 유리하다.

(D) 화석화는 서로 다른 많은 요소가 필요한 엄청나게 복잡한 과정이다.

(F) 이종 교배는 동물 변이의 가장 중요한 요소로 여겨진다.

03 Violence

p.236

1. (C)	2. (C)	3. (B)
4. (C)	5. (D)	6. (B)
7. (B)	8. (A)	9. (C)
10. (B)–5~6단락, (D)–3~4단락, (F)–2단락		

1 잔인한 범죄는 범죄자들에게 무방비 상태로 노출되었다고 느끼는 시민들에게 불안감을 유발할 수 있다. 대중 보호에 대한 지속적인 관심은, 대중 매체와 정계, 사회계에서 폭력에 대해 반복적인 논의를 불러일으키고, 폭력의 원인에 대한 많은 이론을 증식시켰는데 이러한 이론들은 폭력의 원인으로 전쟁, 마약 중독, 또는 계급이나 인종 차별로 인한 좌절을 들었고, 폭력성이 문화적 정체성에 내재해 있다고 주장하기까지 한다. 폭력적 성향을 이해하려는 노력 하에, 과학자들은 폭력성을 생물학적으로 통찰하고자 노력해 왔다.

2 일부 과학자들은 어떤 한 사람이 폭력적인 범죄를 저지를 가능성과 체내의 세로토닌 농도 간에 직접적인 관계가 있을 것이라 생각해왔는데, [2]여기서 세로토닌이란, 심리 상태, 수면, 성욕, 식욕의 조절에 있어서 절대적인 역할을 한다고 알려진, 뇌 속에 존재하는 유기 화합물이다. 중추신경계에서 세로토닌은 몇 가지 정신적인 상태와 관련된 생화학 시스템의 일부분을 이루고 있는데, 우울증, 편두통, 양극성 장애, 불안감은 모두 이 유기화합물의 과다 및 과소 분비와 관련되어 있다. [3]만일 폭력적인 행동이 뇌 내의 화학물질의 불균형과 연관된다는 것을 임상적으로 확인한다면, 과학자들은 난폭한 행동이 더 심해지기 전에 약물치료를 통해서 폭력적인 성향을 조절할 수 있게 될 것이다.

3 최초로 정부의 지원을 받은 선천적인 경향으로서의 폭력성에 대한 연구는 1998년에 Columbia 대학교수 2명이 이끈 Violence Initiative Project 팀에 의해서 수행되었으며, 생화학, 신경생리학, 유전학 등의 여러 학문이 결합된 분야를 광범위하게 다루었다. 연구팀은 폭력적인 행동을 아직 나타내지 않은 어린 소년 34명의 뇌를 관찰하는 방법을 택했다. 이 소년들이 선택된 이유는 이들이 모두 폭력 범죄로 투옥된 적이 있는 형제를 두고 있었기 때문이었다. [5]과학자들은 동생들도 형들과 비슷한 폭력적 경향을 나타낼 것이라고 추측했으므로 동생들의 세로토닌 농도도 낮은 수치를 나타낼 것이라고 가정했다. 실험 기간 동안, 실험대상자들은 12시간 동안 굶었

고 물만 마셨으며 수산화 펜플루라민이 경구 투여되었는데, 수산화 펜플루라민이란 휘발성 물질로, 섭취하면 정상적인 뇌의 세로토닌 농도를 증가시켜서 심리 상태와 관련된 심한 부작용, 즉 비정상적으로 잦은 피로, 두통, 과민 반응 등을 유발한다. 연구자들은 이 물질을 도입함으로써 낮을 것으로 추정되는 대상자들의 세로토닌 농도를 평균적인 뇌의 세로토닌 농도로 끌어올릴 수 있게 될 것이며, 이 약물치료로 인종, 계층, 또는 환경에 의한 기타 스트레스 요인과 상관없이, 이들의 폭력적인 행동을 하려는 욕구를 억제할 수 있을 것이라고 주장했다.

4 한 시간마다 연구대상자들의 혈액 표본을 채취해서 뇌의 화학 작용을 검사한 결과, 과학자들은 자신들의 이론이 틀렸음을 확인했는데, 왜냐하면 44퍼센트가 흑인이고 56퍼센트가 히스패닉 계통인, 약물을 투여한 이 동생들이 사실상 약에 대한 부작용을 보이기 시작했는데 이는 수산화 펜플루라민이 세로토닌 농도를 적당하게 조절한 것이 아니라 갑작스럽게 증가시켰다는 것을 나타냈기 때문이다. [7]실험 후에 종합적인 검토를 하면서 실험 전에 채취한 표본을 매시간 채취한 표본들과 비교한 결과, 예측했던 바와는 달리 소년들이 평균보다 낮은 세로토닌 수치를 가지고 있지 않았다는 것이 밝혀졌고 이는 교수들의 주된 주장에 반하는 것이었다.

5 이 임상 실험을 관찰했던 사회과학자들은 즉각적으로 교수들이 세로토닌을 폭력과 연관시키고자 했던 실험에 실패한 주된 이유가 공격적인 행동이 과거의 난폭한 행동, 어린 시절의 경험, 사회경제적 상태 등 많은 참작할만한 요소를 통해 결정되기 때문이라고 주장했다. 일반적인 사회 이론에 따르면, 폭력 또는 자신이 물리적이거나 정신적인 상처를 입을 상황에 노출된 아이들은 다른 사람에게 해를 입히는 경우가 많은데, 사회학자들은 이런 행동들이 생물학적인 요인에 의한 것이 아니라 오히려 상황에 의한 것이라는 점을 재빨리 지적한다. [9]실제로, 다른 가정에서, 즉 한 명은 폭력적인 가정에서, 다른 한 명은 폭력적이지 않은 가정에서 자란 쌍둥이에 대한 연구는 유전적인 유사성이 아닌 주변 환경에의 노출에 인과 관계가 있다는 것을 명백히 보여준다. 또한, 범죄학자들은 유전적 요인을 폭력성이 나타나게 하는 원동력으로 볼 수 없다고 경고하는데, 이는 이로 인해 범죄자의 개인적인 책임을 간과하고, 폭력적인 행동을 하지 않은 사람에 대해서도 생물학적인 요인에 근거하여 판단하게 되며, 행동에 영향을 미치는 다수의 사회적 동인을 다룰 수 없기 때문이다.

6 사회과학자들에 따르면, 실험대상자의 과거와 생활 배경에 대한 자료를 배제한 과학적인 연구는 모두 과도한 단순화, 즉 부적절하게 단순한 구조를 이용해서 더욱 복잡한 구조를 설명하려는 경향을 가지는 것으로 간주되어야 한다. 이에 대응해서 임상 연구자들은 사회적, 역사적 맥락에서 차이를 설명할 수 있도록 다수의 임상 실험을 바로잡아 왔다.

vicious[víʃəs] 잔인한 perpetrator[pə́:rpətrèitər] 범죄자
arena[ərí:nə] 계 proliferation[prouìfəréiʃən] 증식
plentitude[pléntitjù:d] 많음, 풍부함 addiction[ədíkʃən] 중독
frustration[frʌstréiʃən] 좌절 identity[aidéntəti] 정체성
predisposition[prì:dispəzíʃən] 성향

likelihood[láiklihùd] 가능성 commit[kəmít] 저지르다
integral[íntigrəl] 절대적인, 필수의 depression[dipréʃən] 우울증
migraine[máigrein] 편두통 bipolar disorder 양극성 장애
clinically[klínikəli] 임상적으로 imbalance[imbǽləns] 불균형
medication[mèdəkéiʃən] 약물 치료
escalate[éskəlèit] 심해지다 propensity[prəpénsəti] 경향
interdisciplinary[ìntərdísəplənèri] 여러 학문이 결합된
neurophysiology[njùəroufiziálədʒi] 신경생리학
sibling[síbliŋ] 형제 incarcerate[inká:rsərèit] 투옥하다
inclination[ìnklənéiʃən] 경향 hypothesize[haipáθəsàiz] 가정하다
fast[fæst] 굶다 fenfluramine hydroxide 수산화 펜플루라민
volatile[válətl] 휘발성의 fatigue[fətí:g] 피로
irritability[ìritəbíləti] 과민 반응
supposedly[səpóuzidli] 추정상, 아마 spike[spaik] 증가, 급증
abrupt[əbrʌ́pt] 갑작스러운 mitigating[mítəgèitiŋ] 참작할만한
causation[kɔːzéiʃən] 인과 관계
criminologist[krìmənálədʒist] 범죄학자 myriad[míriəd] 다수
agent[éidʒənt] 동인 background[bǽkgràund] 배경
reductionist[ridʌ́kʃənist] 과도한 단순화 account for ~을 설명하다

1 지문의 단어 "anxiety"와 의미상 가장 유사한 것은?

(A) 불쾌함
(B) 결의
(C) 걱정
(D) 행복

2 2단락에 따르면, 다음 중 세로토닌이 조절하는 것이 아닌 것은?

(A) 심리 상태
(B) 식욕
(C) 집중력
(D) 수면

3 폭력적인 행동의 생물학적 원인에 대한 연구의 목적은 _____ 라고 2단락에서 암시된다.

(A) 뇌의 화학 작용이 어떻게 인공 약물에 반응하는지 이해한다
(B) 폭력적인 성향이 악화되는 것을 막기 위해 약물을 사용한다
(C) 잠재적인 위협을 알아보는 사회의 능력을 높인다
(D) 위험에 처한 사람들이 검사를 받도록 장려한다

4 지문의 단어 "they"가 가리키는 것은?

(A) 대학교수들
(B) 과학자들
(C) 동생들
(D) 형들

5 과학자들은 실험대상자들의 형들이 _____ 라고 생각했다는 것을 3단락으로부터 추론할 수 있다.

(A) 그들의 폭력적인 행동을 완전히 그만두었다
(B) 그들의 특징을 실험대상자들에게 전달했다
(C) 약물 치료를 받기를 거부했다
(D) 세로토닌 수치가 정상보다 낮았다

6 아래 문장 중 지문 속의 음영된 문장의 핵심 정보를 가장 잘 표현하고 있는 것은 무엇인가? 오답은 문장의 의미를 현저히 왜곡하거나 핵심 정보를 빠뜨리고 있다.

(A) 폭력의 환경적 자극에 노출된 사람들은 수산화 펜플루라민이 생산하는 세로토닌의 증가에 의해 영향을 받을 것이다.

(B) 수산화 펜플루라민의 사용은 세로토닌 수치를 정상화시킴으로써 실험대상자들이 폭력을 휘두르지 않게 할 것이라고 생각되었다.

(C) 수산화 펜플루라민은 그것이 세로토닌 수치를 높일 것이라 생각하고 여러 환경의 실험대상자들에게 주어졌다.

(D) 연구원들은 다양한 요소에 따라 달라지는 세로토닌 수치에 따라 수산화 펜플루라민을 조절해야 했다.

7 4단락에 따르면, 실험대상자들의 혈액 표본에 대한 분석은

(A) 폭력적인 행동에 대한 수산화 펜플루라민의 영향에 대한 확신으로 이어졌다

(B) 실험 시작 시 그들의 세로토닌 수치가 평균 이하가 아니었음을 보여주었다

(C) 연구원들이 인위적인 수단으로 세로토닌 수치를 바꾸는 것은 부적절함을 증명했다

(D) 형들이 동생들보다 폭력을 사용하기 더 쉽다는 주장을 뒷받침했다

8 지문의 단어 "abrupt"와 의미상 가장 유사한 것은?

(A) 갑작스러운
(B) 거친
(C) 점진적인
(D) 부적절한

9 지문에 따르면, 글쓴이는 쌍둥이들에게 한 연구가 ＿＿＿＿라는 것을 암시한다.

(A) 다른 요소들의 결합은 폭력을 유발한다는 주장을 부정한다

(B) 폭력에의 노출은 공격의 유전적 성향을 촉진함을 나타낸다

(C) 유전은 폭력의 주요한 요인이 아니라는 개념을 조성한다

(D) 과학적인 연구는 역사적인 배경을 고려하지 않고 행해져야 한다고 제안한다

10 지시: 지문 요약을 위한 도입 문장이 아래에 주어져 있다. 지문의 가장 중요한 내용을 나타내는 보기 3개를 골라 요약을 완성하시오. 어떤 문장은 지문에 언급되지 않은 내용이나 사소한 정보를 담고 있으므로 요약에 포함되지 않는다. **이 문제는 2점이다.**

> 폭력에 대한 연구는 근본적인 원인을 찾는 것에 초점을 두고 있다.
>
> · (B) 많은 학자들이 환경적 그리고 사회적 요소가 폭력적인 행동의 시작 원인이라고 주장한다.
> · (D) 정부 연구의 결과가 세로토닌과 폭력 간 관계에 이의를 제기했다.
> · (F) 한 이론은 세로토닌 수치가 개인이 폭력적인 범죄를 저지를 것인지의 여부를 결정한다는 것이다.

(A) 폭력은 많은 사람들의 주요 관심사이고 사회의 여러 분야에

서 널리 논의된다.

(C) 폭력적인 범죄를 저지르는 사람들은 법률에 의한 책임을 져야 한다.

(E) 약물의 지속적이고 남용하는 사용은 폭력적인 행동을 유발할 수 있다.

---

04 American Art and Literature

1. (D)	2. (D)	3. (B)
4. (C)	5. (C)	6. (B)
7. (D)	8. (A)	9. (A)
10. (A)-3단락, (E)-2단락, (F)-4단락		

1 영국에 대항해서 일어난 미국 독립혁명(1775-1783)은 식민통치 권력에 대항한 최초의 근대적 독립전쟁이었으나, 미국이 영국 문학과 예술로부터 문화적인 독립을 이룰 수 있었던 것은 이로부터 반세기가 지난 후였다. 군사 혁명 직후의 수십 년 동안, 대서양 양쪽에서 복잡하게 얽힌 경제적, 정치적 요인들이 미국 작가와 예술가들의 작업을 방해했지만, [1]미국 작가와 예술가들은 영국과의 일체감을 계속 유지했고 영국의 예술적 모델을 지속적으로 모방했다. 실제로, 문화적 혁명은 즉시 일어나지 않고, 강제로 이루어질 수 없으며, 반드시 새로운 정서와 기회가 보장되는 풍조 속에서 서서히 나타나야 한다.

2 Benjamin Franklin(1706-1790)의 업적과 포부는 그를 계몽주의 시대의 주된 미국인의 전형이 되게 했으며, 그의 작품은 그의 뒤를 이은 국가주의 작가 세대들의 토대를 마련했다. Franklin의 글은 미국이 영국과 뚜렷이 구분되는 가치와 관심사를 가지는 것으로 묘사했고, 미국의 국가 정체성을 창조하는 데 기여했다. Franklin은 그의 시민적 글쓰기, 사적인 편지들, 그리고 호평받는 자서전을 통해 미국 독립 혁명을 발생시킨 근면, 독립, 혁신성의 장점을 내세웠다. [3]19세기 초에 이르자, 최초의 뚜렷하게 미국적인 색채를 띠는 소설가들이 Franklin의 출판 활동과 해외에서의 미국 문화 홍보의 덕을 보기 시작했다. [4]영감을 받은 창조적인 작가들은 서부로의 이주 같은 독자적인 미국적 주제를 묘사했고, 이는 미국 풍경의 활기 넘치는 이미지와 미국인들의 집단적인 정서를 떠오르게 하는 것들이었다. 그러나 과학적 이상과 자연의 합리화를 강조하는 계몽주의적 시각을 견지했던 Franklin과 달리, 새로운 부류의 작가들은 풍자와 의인화를 통해 자연의 정서적이고 심미적인 특성들을 강조하며 미국 낭만주의 시대의 도래를 알렸다. 예를 들어, 소설가 Washington Irving(1789-1859)은 광활한 미국의 토지를 인간적으로 표현하고, 이에 고유한 전설을 부여하는 창조적인 방법을 고안한 것으로 유명한데, 이는 궁극적으로 이 신흥 국가의 역사와 모험 의식을 재현하고 만족시키는 것을 도왔다.

3 인간과 자연의 관계는 미국 낭만주의의 본질적인 요소이고, 이 상호작용은 싹트는 국가주의의 문학적, 예술적 정체성에 큰 영향을 미치

CH 06

Hackers TOEFL Reading

Chapter 06 Inference | **465**

는 주제가 되었다. [5]게다가 초기 유럽 낭만주의 운동의 신조였던 오랜 전통의 파괴, 문화의 혁명적 성향, 그리고 개인주의는 쉽게 전해져서, 정의, 자유, 평등을 인간의 자연적인 권리로 삼는 19세기 미국 사회의 이상을 받들었다. New England 지방에서 영향력을 가지고 있던 일단의 작가들은 초월주의라 불리는 낭만주의의 한 갈래를 발전시켰는데, 이는 개성과 자주성을 장려하고 모든 이들에게 통용되는 직관적인 진리가 있음을 확언한 철학적, 문학적인 운동이었다. 이 운동의 대표적 대변인인 Ralph Waldo Emerson(1803-1882)은 미국 문학의 아버지로, 또 새로운 국가가 필요로 하는 것과 잠재력을 표명한 사람으로 일컬어지며 전형적인 미국 예술인이 되었다. [6]아직 미국의 많은 사람이 유럽 문화에 대한 경외를 가지고 있던 시기에, Emerson은 '미국의 학자'라는 유명한 강연에서 주장했듯이 미국인들에게 옛날의 방식과 유럽의 가치에 대한 존경심을 버릴 것을 촉구했는데, [7]이 강연에서 그는 미국인은 자신만의 국가적인 성격을 반영하는 문학을 발전시키기에 충분한 자립성을 가졌다고 주장했다: '의존의 시대, 오랫동안 다른 나라 학문의 제자 역할을 하던 시대는 끝나가고 있다.' 미국 내의 아직 개발되지 않은 소재들을 적극적으로 이용하라는 그의 권유는, 동시대의 많은 사람만이 아니라 이후 세대의 작가와 예술가들에게도 영감을 주었다.

4 초월주의의 이상은 Thomas Cole(1801-1848)에 의해 주도되었던, 소위 최초의 미국 화파인 Hudson River 화파의 작품들에서 그 시각적인 구현을 찾았다. Emerson이 미국인들은 자신들의 나라에서 자신에 대한 글을 써야 한다고 주장했던 것과 마찬가지로, Cole은 1836년에 발표했던 에세이에서 예술가들은 그림에 영감을 줄 주제를 유럽에서 찾을 필요가 없다고 주장했고, 영감의 가장 인상적인 원천은 미국 황야의 풍경이라고 단언했다. 이 화파는 미국에서 지배적으로 나타나는 지형의 양식이 즉흥적이고 거침없는 낭만주의적 미학으로 형성되는 것을 도왔다. 이들의 그림은 미래에 대한 낙관과 성스럽고 인간의 영혼을 치유해 준다고 여겼던 신대륙의 황야에 대한 경외심을 그렸다. 이 화가들은 독특한 미국적인 풍경을 캔버스에 담을 대상으로 인정하는 동시에 미국의 작가들로 하여금 유럽적인 주제와 모델로부터 그들 자신의 문화와 국가의 나날이 확장되어 가는 변경지대의 주제와 모델로 눈을 돌리도록 자신감을 불어넣어 줬다는 점에서 그 공적을 인정받아 오고 있다.

identification[aidèntəfikéiʃən] 일체감
encumber[inkʌ́mbər] 방해하다
instantaneous[ìnstəntéiniəs] 순간적인
impose[impóuz] 강제하다   evolve[ivɑ́lv] 서서히 나타나다
aspiration[æ̀spəréiʃən] 포부   render[réndər] ~가 되게 하다
Age of Enlightenment 계몽주의 시대
usher[ʌ́ʃər] ~의 도래를 알리다
romanticism[roumǽntəsìzm] 낭만주의
renowned[rináund] 유명한   endow[indáu] 부여하다
quintessential[kwìntəsénʃəl] 본질적인, 정수의
interplay[íntərplèi] 상호작용   burgeon[bə́:rdʒən] 싹트다
tenet[ténit] 신조
transcendentalism[trænsendéntəlìzm] 초월주의
self-reliance[sélfriláiəns] 자주성   affirm[əfə́:rm] 확언하다

intuitive[intjú:ətiv] 직관적인
spokesperson[spóukspə̀:rsn] 대변자
be reputed as ~로 일컬어지다   articulate[ɑ:rtíkjulət] 표명하다
archetypal[ɑ́:rkitàipəl] 전형적인   awe[ɔ:] 경외
deference[défərəns] 존경   untapped[ʌ̀ntǽpt] 개발되지 않은
subsequent[sʌ́bsikwənt] 이후의
embodiment[imbɑ́dimənt] 구현
mythos[míθɑs] (어떤 집단·문화에 특유한) 양식, 가치관
spontaneous[spɑntéiniəs] 즉흥적인   infuse[infjú:z] 불어넣다

1 다음 중 18세기 후반 미국 예술 작품에 대해 1단락으로부터 추론할 수 있는 것은?
   (A) 주로 식민지 시대의 영국의 삶을 묘사했다.
   (B) 미국에서 영국풍의 예술 작품을 찾는 것은 상당히 보기 드문 일이었다.
   (C) 영국의 경제적인 지원으로 생산되었다.
   (D) 영국의 것들과 구별하기 어려웠다.

2 지문의 단어 "those"가 가리키는 것은?
   (A) 업적과 포부
   (B) 세대
   (C) 글
   (D) 가치와 관심사

3 지문에 따르면, 1800년대 초반 문학에 대해 추론할 수 있는 것은?
   (A) 작가들은 자연보다는 산업에 더 열중했다.
   (B) 미국의 책들을 외국에서 구할 수 있었다.
   (C) 식민지 문학은 지역 시장에서 가장 수요가 많았다.
   (D) 소설가들은 미국 혁명에 중대한 역할을 수행했다.

4 2단락에 따르면, 미국 낭만주의 시대의 작가들은 _____을 다루었을 것이다.
   (A) New England의 유명한 정치적 인물
   (B) 대서양으로의 항해
   (C) 국경의 통나무집에 사는 가족
   (D) 두 강국 사이의 전쟁

5 3단락에 따르면, 다음 중 유럽 낭만주의에서 미국 낭만주의로 이어진 요소가 아닌 것은?
   (A) 낡은 관습에 대한 거부
   (B) 문화가 변혁적이라는 믿음
   (C) 자연 보호에 대한 관심
   (D) 개인의 역할에 대한 초점

6 많은 미국인들이 "in awe of European culture"에 남아 있었다는 진술에서 글쓴이는 미국의 많은 사람들이 _____라는 것을 의미한다.
   (A) 유럽 문화에 만족했다
   (B) 유럽 문화를 우월하게 여겼다
   (C) 유럽 문화에서 벗어났다

(D) 유럽 문화에 따랐다

7 지문에서, 글쓴이는 왜 Emerson 연설의 "Our day of dependence, our long apprenticeship to the learning of other lands, draws to a close."를 인용하는가?

(A) 미국 예술가들이 다른 나라의 문학 작품을 이용했던 경향의 정도를 설명하기 위해

(B) Emerson은 미국인들이 유럽 문화로부터 여전히 배울 것이 있다고 생각했음을 증명하기 위해

(C) 왜 미국인들이 유럽의 가치를 그들의 문학에 통합시키기를 꺼렸는지 설명하기 위해

(D) 미국인들이 다른 나라의 문학적 모델에서 독립해야 한다는 Emerson의 주장을 강조하기 위해

8 지문의 단어 "impressive"와 의미상 가장 유사한 것은?

(A) 주목할 만한

(B) 최적의

(C) 기본의

(D) 일관된

9 아래 문장 중 지문 속의 음영된 문장의 핵심 정보를 가장 잘 표현하고 있는 것은 무엇인가? 오답은 문장의 의미를 현저히 왜곡하거나 핵심 정보를 빠뜨리고 있다.

(A) Hudson River 화파는 미국의 풍경을 그림에 묘사했을 뿐 아니라 미국 화가들이 그들의 문화와 땅을 영감으로 사용하도록 이끌었다.

(B) 전통적인 유럽 주제가 아닌 미국의 풍경과 문화에 주력한 것은 Hudson River 화파의 가장 중요한 업적이었다.

(C) 풍경화가 회화의 적합한 주제로 여겨지자, Hudson River 화파와 다른 미국 화가들은 유럽의 모델을 거부하기 시작했다.

(D) Hudson River 화파는 그들의 예술이 미국의 문화와 그것의 확장되는 영토를 표현했기 때문에 그들의 풍경화에 대한 공로를 인정받았다.

10 지시: 지문 요약을 위한 도입 문장이 아래에 주어져 있다. 지문의 가장 중요한 내용을 나타내는 보기 3개를 골라 요약을 완성하시오. 어떤 문장은 지문에 언급되지 않은 내용이나 사소한 정보를 담고 있으므로 요약에 포함되지 않는다. 이 문제는 2점이다.

> **19세기의 미국 문학과 예술의 영국으로부터의 독립은 점진적인 과정이었다.**
>
> · (A) 초월주의는 작가들이 독특한 미국의 테마와 주제에 근거한 작품을 만들도록 영감을 주었다.
> · (E) Benjamin Franklin에게 영향을 받은 미국 작가들은 미국 낭만주의 작품을 만들었다.
> · (F) 미국의 그림은 국가의 독특한 자연 특징을 포착하는 것에 크게 관심이 있었다.

(B) 미국 문학은 인간의 자연권을 명확히 표현하기 위해 유럽의 낭만주의를 통합했다.

(C) 미국 혁명은 영국 문화가 미국 땅에서 인기가 없어지도록 만드는 분위기를 조성했다.

(D) 미국의 문화 혁명은 Washington Irving의 원저작물의 결과로 일어났다.

HACKERS **STRATEGY**

p.249

전략 1

Ex 올메카인들은 종교적 예배의 중심지로서 흙과 돌로 만든 거대한 피라미드를 세웠고, 크나큰 조각상과 정교한 옥 조각품들을 제작했다. 그 조각품 중 다수가 인간과 재규어의 형상을 섞어놓았다.

earth[ə:rθ] 흙, 토양 **jade**[dʒeid] 옥 **carving**[káːrviŋ] 조각품
jaguar[dʒǽgwɑːr] 재규어

Ex 특정 메커니즘은 서로 다른 두 종 간의 교배를 막고, 따라서 생식 격리를 유지한다. 이것은 다른 종 간의 유전자 유동을 막음으로써 각 종의 유전자 공급원의 무결성을 보존한다.

interbreed[ìntərbríːd] 교배하다 **reproductive isolation** 생식격리
integrity[intégrəti] 무결성 **gene pool** 유전자 공급원
gene flow 유전자 유동

Ex 많은 열대성 박쥐 종은 초목의 꿀, 화분, 그리고 꽃과 열매에 의존하고, 초목 자원의 성장을 '추적'하는 것으로 알려졌다. 게다가, 많은 박쥐는 다양한 시간대에 쉬는 장소로서 초목(특히 나무)에 의존한다.

nectar[néktər] 꿀 **pollen**[pálən] 화분 **roost**[ruːst] 쉬다

Ex 경쟁 관계에서, 두 개 이상의 유기체는 일반적으로 제한적으로 공급되는 하나의 자원을 동시에 필요로 한다. 식물들이 얻기 위해 경쟁하는 자원은 보통 물, 빛, 광물 자원, 그리고 성장할 공간을 포함한다.

soil mineral 광물 자원

Ex 화합물은 무기물과 유기물의 두 그룹으로 크게 나누어질 수 있다. 무기 화합물은 탄소 외에 상대적으로 작은 화합물 성분이다. 반면, 유기 화합물은 일반적으로 크고 복잡하며, 탄소를 포함하고 보통 수소도 포함한다.

chemical compound 화합물 **inorganic**[ìnɔːrgǽnik] 무기물의
organic[ɔːrgǽnik] 유기물의 **carbon**[káːrbən] 탄소

전략 2

Ex 관례상 스테인드글라스는 보통 종교적 목적과 관련이 있다. 수 세기에 걸쳐 스테인드글라스 창은 교회와 대성당에서 나타났듯이 신앙심과 충성의 표현으로 여겨졌다. 르네상스 시대가 되어서야 스테인드글라스의 목적이 비종교적인 용도까지 포함하는 것으로 바뀌었다. 이 기간에, 스테인드글라스는 교회는 물론이고

가정집과 공공건물에서까지 유행하는 장식으로서 인기를 얻었다. 사용된 유리는 기본적으로 교회에서 사용된 것과 같은 것이었다. 그러나 색상은 대성당 전용의 전통적이고 장엄한 색에서 가정용 창에 적절하게 여겨졌던 좀 더 부드럽고 밝지 않은 색상으로 바뀌었다.

usage[júːsidʒ] 관례, 관습 **cathedral**[kəθíːdrəl] 대성당
muted[mjúːtid] 밝지 않은

전략 3

Ex 뉴욕의 유명한 브로드웨이와 전 세계 공연장의 무대에서 만나게 되는 뮤지컬 극은 수년 동안 발달해왔다. 뮤지컬 극의 기원에 대한 최초의 흔적은 1800년대의 프랑스와 빈의 오페레타에서 발견될 수 있다. 이 뮤지컬 극들은 유럽 관객들에게 장편 오페라의 짧은 버전을 제공함으로써 국제적인 인기를 얻었고, 노래, 춤, 음악, 극의 생생한 통합을 특색으로 했다. 그러나 미국에 이르자, 세련된 유럽 작품들은 매우 색다른 창조적인 형태를 접했다. 그것은 흥겨운 미국 버라이어티 쇼와 그 시대의 외설적인 뮤지컬 시사 풍자극이었다. 비록 버라이어티 쇼, 벌레스크, 그리고 보드빌과 같은 뮤지컬 극의 초기 형태가 종종 극의 유머를 위해 상스런 익살이나 인종적 편견에 의존하기는 했지만, 미국 극작가와 작곡가들이 이웃한 유럽인들을 본받기까지는 그리 오래 걸리지 않았다. 똑똑하고 재치 있는 아름다운 선율의 새로운 희극 오페레타가 과장된 유머에 대한 미국인들의 애정을 유럽의 라이브 오케스트라 및 서정적 노래와 조합하여 브로드웨이 뮤지컬이 탄생했다.

famed[féimd] 유명한 **evolve**[iválv] 발달하다
operetta[àpərétə] 오페레타(짧은 오페라)
integration[ìntəgréiʃən] 통합 **polished**[páliʃt] 세련된
encounter[inkáuntər] 접하다 **rollicking**[rálikiŋ] 흥겨운
bawdy[bɔ́ːdi] 외설적인 **revue**[rivjúː] 시사풍자극
minstrel show (흑인으로 분장한 백인 연예인에 의한) 버라이어티 쇼
burlesque[bərlésk] 벌레스크, 통속적 희가극
vaudeville[vɔ́ːdəvil] 보드빌(희극 배우, 가수, 곡예사 등이 출연하는 쇼)
crude[kruːd] 상스런 **slapstick**[slǽpstìk] 익살
racial stereotype 인종적 편견

HACKERS STRATEGY **APPLICATION** p.252

물은 육지에 재생 가능한 깨끗한 물을 공급하면서 바다에서부터 대기로, 육지로, 그리고 다시 바다로 돌아가며 계속해서 순환한다. 물의 순환이라고 알려진 이 복잡한 주기는 바다, 육지, 그리고 대기에 존재하는 물 사이의 균형을 가져온다. 물은 비, 눈, 진눈깨비 또는 우박과 같은 강수 형태로 대기에서 육지와 바다로 이동한다. 그 후 물은

땅으로부터 증발하고 직접 대기 중으로 다시 들어가거나 강과 개울로 유입되어 해안 하구에 이르는데, 이곳에서는 담수와 바다가 만난다. 육지에서 바다로 향하는 물의 흐름은 유거수라고 불린다. 물은 또한 지하수가 되기 위해 땅속으로 스며든다. 지하수는 땅, 개울, 강, 그리고 식물에 물을 제공한다. 그러나 궁극적으로 대기 중에서 육지로 떨어지는 물은 바다로 돌아간다. 물 분자의 물리적 형태(고체, 액체 또는 기체) 또는 위치에 상관없이, 모든 물 분자는 결국 물의 순환에 따라 이동한다.

hydrologic cycle 물의 순환 precipitation[prisìpətéiʃən] 강수
sleet[sli:t] 진눈깨비 hail[heil] 우박
evaporate[ivǽpərèit] 증발하다 reenter[rì:éntər] 다시 들어가다
estuary[éstʃuèri] 하구 runoff[rʌ́nɔ̀:f] 유거수 seep[si:p] 스미다
groundwater[gráundwɔ̀:tər] 지하수
ultimately[ʌ́ltəmətli] 궁극적으로 molecule[máləkjù:l] 분자

1. 네 개의 네모[■]는 다음 문장이 삽입될 수 있는 부분을 나타내고 있다.

   물의 순환이라고 알려진 이 복잡한 주기는 바다, 육지, 그리고 대기에 존재하는 물 사이의 균형을 가져온다.

   이 문장은 어느 자리에 들어가는 것이 가장 적절한가?

국수주의자들과 지위가 미약한 미국 상인들 사이의 갈등은 1765년에 한계점에 다다랐는데, 이때 식민지에서 우편요금을 인상하여 발생하는 추가 수입을 국군의 유지비 충당을 위해 영국으로 보내는 강제된 법인 인지 조례에 관한 논쟁의 분란이 일어났다. 화가 나 이 조례에 대한 혐오를 강경하게 밝힌 항의자 John Hancock은 그의 선박 Liberty가 통관 관리에 의해 압수되게 만들었다. 그는 밀수와 더 나아가 혁명정신을 선동한 혐의로 기소되었다. 고소가 취하되었음에도 불구하고, Hancock은 동료 Samuel Adams와 함께 경제적 제재 침해에 반대하는 집회를 계속했고, 차를 싣고 보스턴 항구로 향하는 선박에 대한 거부 운동을 조직화했다. 영국이 왕정주의적인 동인도회사가 지역 상인들보다 더 낮은 가격으로 상품을 식민지에 직접 팔 수 있도록 허용하는 다세법을 통과시켰을 때, Adams와 50명의 협력자는 배에 올랐고 차가 든 모든 상자를 박살 내고 물속으로 던졌다. 보스턴 차 사건으로 알려진 이 공공 기물 파손 행위는 애국자들과 정부 간의 싸움을 폭로했다.

underrepresented[ʌ̀ndərrèprizéntid] 지위가 미약한
breaking point 한계점 flurry[flə́:ri] 분란, 동요
Stamp Act 인지 조례 smuggling[smʌ́gling] 밀수
economic sanction 경제적 제재 boycott[bɔ́ikɑt] 거부 운동
bound for ~로 향하는 Tea Act 다세법
collaborator[kəlǽbərèitər] 협력자
vandalism[vǽndəlìzm] 공공 기물 파손 행위
Boston Tea Party 보스턴 차 사건 patriot[péitriət] 애국자
bring something to light ~을 폭로하다

2. 네 개의 네모[■]는 다음 문장이 삽입될 수 있는 부분을 나타내고 있다.

   화가 나 이 조례에 대한 혐오를 강경하게 밝힌 항의자 John

Hancock은 그의 선박 Liberty가 통관 관리에 의해 압수되게 만들었다.

이 문장은 어느 자리에 들어가는 것이 가장 적절한가?

HACKERS **PRACTICE** p.254

1. (B) – (A) – (C)	2. (A) – (C) – (B)
3. (A) – (C) – (B)	4. (C) – (B) – (A)
5. (B) – (A) – (C)	6. (C) – (B) – (A)
7. (C)	8. (D)	9. (A)
10. (C)	11. (B)	12. (B)
13. 2nd	14. 3rd	15. 4th
16. 3rd	17. 3rd	

VOCABULARY

1 (C)	2 (D)	3 (C), (A)
4 (B), (A)	5 (C), (D)	6 (B), (D)
7 (D), (B)	8 (A), (C)	9 (D), (B)
10 (C), (A)	11 (B), (C)	12 (D)
13 (B)	14 (A)	15 (D), (A)
16 (D)	17 (B)	

1 (A) 몇몇 종은 하나의 꽃 안에서 혹은 같은 식물 내 하나의 꽃에서 다른 꽃으로의 꽃가루 전이를 통해 수정을 이뤄내는데, 이는 꽃 부분의 구조가 암수의 생식 기관을 둘 다 준비해두기 때문이다.
   (B) 속씨식물이라고도 알려진 현화식물에서, 수분은 꽃밥에서 암술머리로의 꽃가루 분포를 통해 이루어지며, 만약 성공적이면, 그것은 씨앗이 되는 배아의 발달로 이어질 것이다.
   (C) 그 밖의 종에서는, 개개의 식물은 각각 암수가 뚜렷하며, 따라서 성공적인 수분이 이뤄지기 위해서는 두 가지 별개의 표본이 필요하다.

species[spíːʃiːz] 종 fertilization[fə̀ːrtəlizéiʃən] 수정
transfer[trǽnsfəːr] 전이 pollen[pálən] 꽃가루
bloom[bluːm] 꽃 formation[fɔːrméiʃən] 구조, 형성
allow for 준비하다 reproductive organ 생식 기관
angiosperm[ǽndʒiəspə̀ːrm] 속씨식물(씨방 속에 씨가 들어있는 식물)
pollination[pàlənéiʃən] 수분 anther[ǽnθər] 꽃밥
stigma[stígmə] 암술머리 development[divéləpmənt] 발달
embryo[émbriou] 배아 individual[ìndivídʒuəl] 개개의
distinctly[distíŋktli] 뚜렷하게 separate[séprət] 별개의
specimen[spésimən] 표본

2 (A) 산업 배출물과 대기의 복잡한 상호 작용은 산성비라고 알려진 현상을 만들어낸다.

(B) 그다음 오염 물질은 수증기와 섞이고, 비로 내려 숲을 심각하게 파괴할 수 있는 매우 강한 산성 액체를 만든다.

(C) 예를 들어, 공장이 생산의 부산물로 오염 물질을 공기 중에 배출하면, 아황산가스와 같은 화학 물질은 지역을 가로질러 떠다니는 구름에 의해 옮겨지게 된다.

complex[kəmpléks] 복잡한　interaction[ìntərǽkʃən] 상호 작용
industrial[indʌ́striəl] 산업의　emission[imíʃən] 배출물
atmosphere[ǽtməsfìr] 대기　phenomenon[fənɑ́:minən] 현상
acid[ǽsid] 산성의　pollutant[pəlú:tənt] 오염 물질
moisture[mɔ́istʃər] 수증기　liquid[líkwid] 액체
byproduct[báiprʌ̀dəkt] 부산물
chemical[kémikl] 화학 물질　sulfur dioxide 아황산가스

3 (A) 건선은 만성 피부 질환인데 이는 상당한 가려움과 고통을 초래할 수 있는 병변의 발달을 야기한다.

(B) 이 주장을 뒷받침하는 것으로 보이는 사실은 많은 양의 저온 살균을 하지 않은 우유나 버터를 섭취하는 것이 증상을 완화시킨다는 것이다. 하지만 저온 살균된 유제품을 섭취하는 것은 그렇지 않은데, 이는 저온 살균이 천연 효소를 파괴하기 때문이다.

(C) 몇몇 연구원들은 그것이 건강과 영양에 중요한 효소의 결핍과 연관되어 있음을 제시했다.

psoriasis[səráiəsis] 건선, 마른버짐　chronic[krɑ́:nik] 만성의
disorder[disɔ́:rdər] 질환
lesion[lí:ʒn] 병변(병이 원인이 되어 일어나는 생체의 변화)
itching[ítʃiŋ] 가려움　sustain[səstéin] 뒷받침하다
assertion[əsə́:rʃən] 주장
consumption[kənsʌ́mpʃən] (체내) 섭취
unpasteurized[ʌ̀npǽstəràizd] 저온 살균을 하지 않은
alleviate[əlí:vieit] 완화시키다
pasteurize[pǽstʃəraiz] 저온 살균하다　dairy product 유제품
enzyme[énzaim] 효소　propose[prəpóuz] 제시하다
deficiency[difíʃənsi] 결핍　critical[krítikl] 중요한
nutrition[nutríʃən] 영양

4 (A) 작은 포유동물 종에서는, 먹이를 모으고 저장하는 것도 대개 그만큼 중요하고, 동면 중에 가끔 먹이를 먹는 것은 그들이 휴면 중 잃은 열량을 회복할 수 있게 하는데 이렇게 하지 않았더라면 계절에 따라 자양물을 구할 수 없었을 것이다.

(B) 어쩌면 가장 중요한 적응은 주기적으로 체온과 심박수를 정상 수준으로 조절하는 능력인데, 이것은 수면을 용이하게 하거나 면역 체계를 활발하게 한다고 믿어진다.

(C) 동면하는 온혈동물은 많은 문제에 직면하며 겨울을 견뎌내기 위해 필수적인 육체 기능을 확실히 유지하기 위해 다양한 생리적 전략과 행동적 전략을 활용해야 한다.

mammal[mǽml] 포유동물　gather[gǽðər] 모으다
significant[signífikənt] 중요한　occasional[əkéiʒənl] 가끔의

hibernation[hàibərnéiʃən] 동면　restore[ristɔ́:r] 회복하다
dormancy[dɔ́:rmənsi] 휴면　sustenance[sʌ́stənəns] 자양물
adaptation[æ̀dəptéiʃən] 적응
periodically[pìəriɑ́:dikli] 주기적으로
facilitate[fəsíliteit] 용이하게 하다
stimulate[stímjuleit] 활발하게 하다　immune system 면역 체계
challenge[tʃǽləndʒ] 문제, 도전　utilize[jú:təlaiz] 활용하다
physiological[fìziəlɑ́dʒikəl] 생리적인
behavioral[bihéivjərəl] 행동적인　strategy[strǽtədʒi] 전략

5 (A) 시간이 흐르면서, 귀족의 일원에게는 그들의 궁전 안에 연극 공연을 위한 상설 구조물을 건립하는 것이 점점 더 보편화되었다. 대부분의 경우, 호화로운 장식이 된 무대와 관객석이 큰 강당에 지어졌다. 하지만, 궁전은 다른 많은 기능을 가지고 있었기 때문에, 단어의 현대적 의미로서의 극장으로는 여겨질 수 없다.

(B) 16세기 초기 이탈리아에서, 연극은 대개 특별히 극장으로 디자인된 건물에서 공연되지 않았다. 대신에, 매우 단순한 무대를 포함한 임시 구조물이 건립되었다. 그것은 보통 야외에 설치되었으며 공연이 끝나면 철거되곤 했다.

(C) 궁전 장소는 결국 오직 극장으로만 운영되는 건물로 대체되었다. 이러한 구조물들의 내부는 보통 같은 기본 디자인을 따랐는데, 큰 무대 바로 앞에 탁 트인 관객석이 부자들을 위해 예약된 반원 형태의 높은 특별석으로 둘러싸여 있었다. 극장 소유주들이 입장료를 징수하는 것으로 주로 수익을 냈다는 점은 그들이 가능한 한 많은 좌석을 넣도록 유도했다.

nobility[noubíləti] 귀족　erect[irékt] 건립하다
permanent[pə́:rmənənt] 상설의, 영구적인
theatrical[θiǽtrikl] 연극의　lavish[lǽviʃ] 호화로운
specifically[spəsífikli] 특별히　temporary[témpəreri] 임시의
take down 철거하다, 해체하다　supersede[sù:pərsí:d] 대체하다
exclusively[iksklú:sivli] 오직, 독점적으로
enclose[inklóuz] 둘러싸다　raised[reizd] (주변보다) 높은
box[bɑks] 특별석　revenue[révənu:] 수익
primarily[praimérəli] 주로　admission[ədmíʃən] 입장료
prompt[prɑmpt] 유도하다

6 (A) 그것들 모두가 공통으로 가진 특징은 수면 위로 뛰어오른 이후의 습성이다. 일반적으로, 그것들은 물가에 있는 잔가지나 나뭇잎에 매달려 완전히 가만히 있다가 허물을 벗고 성충의 형태로 변태하여, 눈부신 항공 곡예사가 된다.

(B) 어린 잠자리들이 같은 시기에 수면 위로 올라오는지의 여부는 계절에 따라 결정된다. 봄에 나오는 잠자리들은 거의 동시에 수면 위로 올라오는 경향이 있어서, 같은 개체의 구성원들이 함께 모습을 드러내는 데 반해, 여름까지 기다리는 것들은 몇 주에서 몇 달에 걸쳐 산발적으로 나온다.

(C) 잠자리의 생활 주기는 성충이 호수, 강, 혹은 개울과 같은 물줄기에 알을 낳으면 시작된다. 알은 유충으로 성장하는데, 이것은 수생 곤충으로 살면서 약 1년을 보낸 뒤, 기온이

적절한 수준으로 올라가고 추위의 위협이 지나가고 나면 물에서 나올 것이다.

behavior[bihéivjər] 습성 breach[briːtʃ] (수면 위로) 뛰어오르다
surface[sə́ːrfis] 수면; 수면 위로 올라오다 cling[kliŋ] 매달리다
twig[twig] 잔가지 shed[ʃed] 벗다
transform[trænsfɔ́ːrm] 변태하다 dazzling[dǽzliŋ] 눈부신
aeronautical[èrənɔ́ːtikəl] 항공의 acrobat[ǽkrəbæt] 곡예사
simultaneously[sàiməltéiniəsli] 동시에
emerge[imə́ːrdʒ] 모습을 드러내다, 나오다
sporadically[spərǽdikli] 산발적으로 life cycle 생활 주기
deposit[dipázit] (알을) 낳다, 두다 nymph[nimf] 유충
aquatic[əkwǽtik] 수생의 suitable[súːtəbl] 적절한
frost[frɔːst] 추위, 서리

7 산은 수용액에서 분리되어 수소 이온과 음이온을 형성하는 화합물이다. 어떤 산은 물속에서 거의 완벽하게 분해되기 때문에 강산이라 알려졌다. 염산은 매우 강한 산인데, 이는 대부분의 분자가 분해되어 수소 이온과 염화 이온을 생성하기 때문이다. 약산이라 불리는 다른 산들은 거의 용해되지 않는다. 묽은 초산 용액인 식초는 약산의 한 예이다.

dissociate[disóuʃièit] 분리하다 solution of water 수용액
hydrogen ion 수소 이온 negatively charged ion 음이온
break up 분해하다 hydrochloric acid 염산
molecule[máləkjùːl] 분자 decompose[dìːkəmpóuz] 분해시키다
vinegar[vínigər] 식초 dilute[dailúːt] 묽은, 약한
acetic acid 초산

(A) 그것은 많은 용도의 중요한 산업 화학물질이다
(B) 각각은 물 분자를 형성하기 위해 염기성의 수소 이온과 결합한다
(C) 약산이라 불리는 다른 산들은 거의 용해되지 않는다
(D) 복잡한 과정과 높은 에너지 손실 끝에, 그것은 벽세포에 의해 분비된다

8 킨카주는 전적으로 야행성인 나무에 사는 작은 포유동물이다. 그 때문에, 그것들이 훌륭한 야간 시력을 갖고 있다고 예상될지도 모르지만, 사실 그것들의 시력은 매우 안 좋다. 따라서, 그것들은 숲속에서 길을 찾고 먹이를 찾기 위해 주로 후각과 촉각에 의존한다. 그것들의 극도로 날카로운 이빨은 육식 동물의 이빨을 연상시키지만, 그것들은 일반적으로 초식 동물이며 열매를 찾아 돌아다닌다. 그것들의 먹이는 보통 수화 작용을 위한 충분한 수분을 제공하기 때문에, 킨카주는 좀처럼 물을 마실 필요가 없다. 게다가, 그것들의 긴 혀는 꽃 속의 꿀에 닿을 수 있게 도와주며, 이는 자양물의 또 다른 주요 원천이다.

exclusively[iksklúːsivli] 전적으로
nocturnal[nɑːktə́ːrnl] 야행성의 rely on ~에 의존하다
navigate[nǽvigeit] 길을 찾다
reminiscent[rèminísnt] 연상시키는
carnivore[kɑ́ːrnivɔːr] 육식 동물
vegetarian[vèdʒətériən] 초식 동물 forage[fɔ́ːridʒ] 먹이를 찾다
nectar[néktər] (꽃의) 꿀

(A) 겁이 많고 잘 달아나는 본성으로 인해, 그것들은 최근까지 과학자들에게 잘 알려지지 않았다
(B) 나무 꼭대기에서 더듬어가며 길을 찾으면서, 그것들은 개구리나 곤충처럼 작은 먹이를 정기적으로 사냥한다
(C) 밤에 잘 보지 못하는 것은 종종 그것들을 포식에 취약하게 한다
(D) 그것들의 먹이는 보통 수화 작용을 위한 충분한 수분을 제공하기 때문에, 킨카주는 좀처럼 물을 마실 필요가 없다

9 잉카 부족민들이 재배용 작물과 가축 동물을 발달시켰고 이는 그들이 큰 정착지를 형성하도록 도왔다는 것은 잘 기록되어 있다. 그들은 메마른 산간 지역을 정착 생활에 적합한 땅으로 바꾸기 위해 엄청난 양의 노력을 들였다. 하지만, 인류학자들에게 당혹스러운 한 가지는 왜 잉카 부족민들은 시간이 흐르면서 고도가 높은 곳으로 올라가는 경향이 있었냐는 것이다. 각각의 새로운 거주지는 더 높은 위치에 자리 잡고 있었다. 정착지의 고도가 높아지면서, 잉카 제국은 더욱더 혹독한 상황에 직면했다. 그런데 그들은 왜 그랬을까? 자, 이 변화의 한 가지 동기는 그들의 종교였을지도 모른다. 잉카 문화에서 종교는 가장 중요했으며, 그들의 신 중 매우 존경받던 신은 인티였고, 그는 천체인 태양을 상징했다. 아마 그들은 더 높이 이동하는 것이 자신을 천국으로 더 가깝게 데려간다고 생각했을 것이다. 이것은 마추픽추와 같은 주요 중심지가 해발 7,000피트가 넘는 높이에 위치했던 이유를 설명할 수 있었다.

document[dɑ́ːkjument] 기록하다
domesticated[dəméstikèitid] 재배용의, 가축의
settlement[sétlmənt] 정착지
tremendous[trəméndəs] 엄청난 terrain[təréin] 지역
sedentary[sédnteri] 정착하는
anthropologist[ænθrəpɑ́ːlədʒist] 인류학자
altitude[ǽltituːd] 고도가 높은 곳, 고도 elevation[èlivéiʃən] 고도
encounter[inkáuntər] 직면하다 harsh[haːrʃ] 혹독한
motivation[mòutəvéiʃən] 동기 religion[rilídʒən] 종교
central[séntrəl] 가장 중요한 revered[rivírd] 존경 받는
heavenly[hévnli] 천국의, 하늘의

(A) 각각의 새로운 거주지는 더 높은 위치에 자리 잡고 있었다
(B) 옥수수는 높은 고도에서의 경작에 특히 적절했다
(C) 전문가들은 자신들이 아마도 그 수수께끼를 결정적으로 해결했다고 생각한다
(D) 정착자들이 산을 오르는 것이 더 어려워졌다

10 1960년대에, 과학자들은 지구의 자기장이 가끔 스스로 역전한다는 것을 깨달았다. 이 발견은 용암류에 의해 퇴적되어 있던 암석을 관찰함으로써 이루어졌다. 화산암의 연속적인 층은 과학자들이 수백만 년의 지질학적 역사를 연구할 수 있게 만들었다. 연구에 참여한 사람들에게 특히 흥미를 불러일으킨 것은 철의 성분이 높은 지층이었다. 연구원들은 철의 양상을 연구했는데, 이것은 강한 자성을 드러내며 현대에는 예상대로 북극을 향해 있었다. 하지만, 전 세계 수백 곳의 장소에서 측정한 후, 그들은 철 광층의 거의 절반은 남쪽을 향해 있었다고 결론을 내렸다. 이 새

로운 사실은 나침반의 바늘이 언제나 북쪽을 가리킬 것이라는 400년 된 가설을 뒤집었다.

magnetic field 자기장　**reverse**[rivə́ːrs] 역전하다
deposit[dipάːzit] 퇴적하다　**lava flow** 용암류
successive[səksésiv] 연속적인
geologic[dʒìːəládʒik] 지질학적인　**exhibit**[igzíbit] 드러내다
magnetism[mǽgnətizəm] 자성
predictably[pridíktəbli] 예상대로
measurement[méʒərmənt] 측정
conclude[kənklúːd] 결론을 내리다　**orient**[ɔ́ːrient] ~을 향하다
revelation[rèvəléiʃən] 새로운 사실　**overturn**[òuvərtə́ːrn] 뒤집다
assumption[əsʌ́mpʃən] 가설

(A) 과학자들이 어떤 확고한 결론을 끌어내기에는 대부분의 용암이 너무 오래되었다

(B) 암석이 잘 보존되었기 때문에, 그것의 화학적 구성이 밝혀질 수 있었다

(C) 연구에 참여한 사람들에게 특히 흥미를 불러일으킨 것은 철의 성분이 높은 지층이었다

(D) 그들은 용암 속 철광상이 매우 오래되었다는 것을 발견하고 놀랐다

11 천문학자 크리스티안 하위헌스의 1655년 토성 관측 중에, 이 대행성의 궤도에는 커다란 위성이 있다는 것이 그에게 분명해졌다. 이 거대한 위성은, 그 후에 타이탄이라고 명명되었고, 지구의 달보다 약 50퍼센트 더 크다. 타이탄의 두드러진 특징은 그것의 밀도 높은 대기이며, 이것은 그 행성의 최북단 위도에 가느다란 구름을 만들어낸다. 다른 곳에서, 대기는 두꺼운 실안개나 스모그로 특징지어지며 그것은 천문학자들로부터 표면을 감추기에 충분할 만큼 불투명하다. 그러므로, 그 아래에 무엇이 있는지 알아내기 위해서, NASA는 우주선 카시니 호를 발사했다. 2004년에, 카시니 호는 토성의 궤도에 진입했고, 이듬해에 타이탄의 표면에 착륙했다. 이것은 역대 최초의 외행성계에서의 위성 착륙이었다. 카시니 호는 그 지형에 대한 정보를 담은 새로운 발견을 드러내는 사진들을 보내주었다. 그것의 다양한 지형을 드러낼 뿐만 아니라, 그 사진들은 지형이 2년에 30킬로미터까지 이동한다는 것을 보여주었으며, 이는 위성의 지각이 단단한 중심부와 분리되어 있고 일종의 액체로 된 지하 바다 위를 떠다니고 있다는 것을 시사한다.

astronomer[əstrάːnəmər] 천문학자
observation[ὰːbzərvéiʃən] 관측　**obvious**[άːbviəs] 분명한
moon[muːn] 위성, 달　**orbit**[ɔ́ːrbit] 궤도
massive[mǽsiv] 거대한　**satellite**[sǽtəlait] 위성
subsequently[sʌ́bsikwəntli] 그 후에
notable[nóutəbl] 두드러진　**dense**[dens] 밀도 높은
atmosphere[ǽtməsfìr] 대기　**wispy**[wíspi] 가느다란
northernmost[nɔ́ːrðərnmoust] 최북단의　**latitude**[lǽtitudː] 위도
haze[heiz] 실안개　**sufficiently**[səfíʃəntli] 충분할 만큼
opaque[oupéik] 불투명한　**conceal**[kənsíːl] 감추다
surface[sə́ːrfis] 표면　**launch**[lɔːntʃ] 발사하다
breakthrough[bréikθrùː] 새로운 발견
topography[təpάːgrəfi] 지형　**geological feature** 지형, 지질

crust[krʌst] 지각　**disassociate**[dìsəsóuʃieit] 분리하다
subterranean[sʌ̀btəréiniən] 지하의

(A) 그것은 타이탄의 대기에 대한 크리스티안 하위헌스의 이론을 입증했다

(B) 이것은 역대 최초의 외행성계에서의 위성 착륙이었다

(C) 토성에 대한 자료를 수집하기 위해 몇몇 우주선이 보내졌다

(D) 그 행성 주변의 궤도에 더 많은 위성들이 있었다

12 예술은 필연적으로 그것이 발생한 문화 고유의 가치와 관습을 반영한다. 예를 들어, 티베트 예술은 티베트 사회에서 오랜 기간 계속된 만연한 불교의 영향 때문에 불교의 소재를 흔히 묘사하며, 이것은 그 지역의 수도원과 절의 벽을 장식하는 그림에서 볼 수 있다. 이러한 예술 작품들은 보통 종교적인 상징과 신성한 존재의 초상에 대한 정교한 원형을 특징으로 삼는다. 이러한 원형들을 만들기 위해, 예술가들은 다른 것들에 호응하여 각 그림이 정확히 어디에 위치해야 할지를 결정하기 위해 자를 사용했다. 이러한 정확성은 그림의 복잡성 때문에 필수적이었다. 게다가, 예술가들은 각 색깔이 특정한 속성을 상징한다는 불교의 신념에 영향을 받았는데, 예를 들어, 흰색은 평화와 순결을 상징한다. 이러한 그림에 사용된 색깔은 종종 불교의 개념들을 나타내기 위해 그것들의 상징적 의미에 따라 선택되었다.

inevitably[inévitəbli] 필연적으로　**reflect**[riflékt] 반영하다
value[vǽljuː] 가치　**custom**[kʌ́stəm] 관습
arise[əráiz] 발생하다　**depict**[dipíkt] 묘사하다
Buddhist[búːdist] 불교의　**material**[mətíriəl] 소재
prolonged[prəlɔ́ːŋd] 오랜 기간 계속되는
pervasive[pərvéisiv] 만연하는　**monastery**[mάːnəstèri] 수도원
temple[témpl] 절, 신전　**elaborate**[ilǽbərət] 정교한
pattern[pǽtərn] 원형, 무늬　**spiritual**[spíritʃuəl] 종교적인
symbol[símbl] 상징　**representation**[rèprizentéiʃən] 초상, 묘사
divine[diváin] 신성한　**precisely**[prisáisli] 정확히
belief[bilíːf] 신념　**attribute**[ətríbjuːt] 속성
stand for ~을 상징하다　**purity**[pjúrəti] 순결

(A) 이런 접근으로 인해, 그림들은 다양한 색을 가지는 경향이 있었다

(B) 이러한 정확성은 그림의 복잡성 때문에 필수적이었다

(C) 티베트의 건조한 날씨 때문에 매우 오래된 벽화들조차도 잘 보존되어 있다

(D) 각각의 그림을 그리는 데 걸리는 시간은 벽의 크기에 달려 있었다

13 1930년대의 대공황은 미국에서 엄청난 사회적 그리고 경제적 격변을 초래했지만, 사람들에게 영감을 주기도 했다. 일부 예술가들이 '미국 지역주의' 예술 운동을 일으킨 것도 이때였다. 이것을 이끈 사람은 그랜트 우드와 토머스 하트 벤턴이었는데, 그들은 사실주의에 크게 의존했고 특히 중서부에서의 시골 작은 동네에서의 삶을 강조한 독특한 방식을 만들어내고자 했다. 그들의 구불구불한 언덕, 건초 더미, 그리고 옥수수밭 그림은 그들 자신의 개인적인 배경을 반영하는데, 이는 그들이 그 지역에서 자

랐기 때문이다. 그들의 목표는 목가적 생활 방식의 소박함과 어려움을 담아내고 '도시' 생활과 주제에 중점을 두는 화가들과 거리를 두는 것이었다. 그들은 또한 자신들을 인상주의와 추상적 표현주의와 같은 외세로부터 분리하고자 했다.

Great Depression 대공황 bring about ~을 초래하다
tremendous [trəméndəs] 엄청난 upheaval [ʌphíːvl] 격변
inspire [inspáiər] 영감을 주다 regionalism [ríːdʒnəlìzm] 지역주의
seek to ~을 하고자 하다 distinctive [distíŋktiv] 독특한
realism [ríːəlìzm] 사실주의 highlight [háilait] 강조하다
rural [rúrəl] 시골의 capture [kǽptʃər] (화폭에) 담아내다
simplicity [simplísəti] 소박함 hardship [háːrdʃip] 어려움
pastoral [pǽstərəl] 목가적인 distance [dístəns] 거리를 두다
urban [ə́ːrbən] 도시의 foreign influence 외세
impressionism [impréʃənìzm] 인상주의
abstract [ǽbstrækt] 추상적인
expressionism [ikspréʃənìzm] 표현주의

네 개의 네모[■]는 다음 문장이 삽입될 수 있는 부분을 나타내고 있다.

그들의 구불구불한 언덕, 건초 더미, 그리고 옥수수밭 그림은 그들 자신의 개인적인 배경을 반영하는데, 이는 그들이 그 지역에서 자랐기 때문이다.

이 문장은 어느 자리에 들어가는 것이 가장 적절한가?

14 화성암은 뜨거운 마그마 또는 용암의 냉각으로부터 생긴다. 뜨거운 액체가 냉각되면서 노랗게, 그다음에는 다양한 색조의 붉은색으로 변하면서 몇 가지 종류의 화성암을 형성하며 완전히 응고된다. 육안으로 볼 수 있는 거칠거나 큰 결정체가 있는 조직은 마그마가 천천히 식었다는 것을 의미한다. 이 결과물이 바로 화강암이라는 암석이다. 만약 암석이 작은 결정이나 미세한 구조를 가지고 있다면, 그 암석은 빠르게 식은 것이다. 현무암은 이런 종류의 화성암의 한 예이다. 화강암과 현무암은 화성암 중 가장 풍부한 종류 두 가지이다. 만약 암석이 결정이 거의 없거나 아예 없다면, 마그마는 몇 시간 혹은 며칠 만에 냉각되어 흑요암이라 알려진 유리질의 물질을 생성한 것이다. 이런 여러 종류의 암석은 화성암이 가진 다양한 특성을 나타낸다.

igneous rock 화성암 result from ~으로부터 생기다
cooling [kúːliŋ] 냉각 magma [mǽgmə] 마그마 lava [láːvə] 용암
solidify [səlídəfài] 응고시키다, 결정시키다
completely [kəmplíːtli] 완전히 texture [tékstʃər] 조직, 짜임
coarse [kɔːrs] 거친, 조잡한 crystal [krístl] 결정체
naked eye 육안 granite [grǽnit] 화강암 basalt [bəsɔ́ːlt] 현무암
abundant [əbʌ́ndənt] 풍부한 obsidian [əbsídiən] 흑요암
illustrate [íləstrèit] 나타내다 diversity [divə́ːrsəti] 다양성
property [prápərti] 특성

네 개의 네모[■]는 다음 문장이 삽입될 수 있는 부분을 나타내고 있다.

현무암은 이런 종류의 화성암의 한 예이다.

이 문장은 어느 자리에 들어가는 것이 가장 적절한가?

15 미국의 환경보호주의는 꽤 최근에 생겨난 것이다. 미국은 땅이 아주 크고 자원이 풍부해서 1900년에 이르기까지 환경에 대한 우려가 제기되지 않았는데, 1900년에는 백로, 노랑부리저어새 등 화려한 조류가 과도하게 사냥되어 의회가 새의 깃털과 박제된 조류로 여성의 모자를 장식하지 못하도록 하는 법을 제정하기에 이르렀다. 이 법은 그 당시에는 기념비적인 법률 제정으로 인식되었다. 하지만 조류와 다른 동물들을 보호하려는 대중의 관심은 제2차 세계 대전 동안 차츰 줄어들었다. 전쟁 시기에는 농업과 목장 경영에 쓰일 대규모의 살충제가 제조되었다. 이것은 또한 설치류, 늑대, 그리고 다른 종류의 야생생물을 독살하는 데도 이용되었다. 1960년대 초에 죽은 새가 하늘에서 떨어지기 시작했을 때, 생물학자 Rachel Carson이 저서 '침묵의 봄'에서 살충제 등의 유독 화학물질이 어떻게 먹이사슬을 통해 이동해서 최종적으로 모든 인간이 이런 치명적인 화학물질에 노출당하기 쉽게 하는지를 밝히기 전에는 아무도 그 이유를 알지 못했다. 갑자기 환경 보존은 중요한 문제로 대두하였고, 이에 뒤따른 소란은 미국 정부를 개입시켰다.

conservation [kànsərvéiʃən] 보호 fairly [féərli] 꽤
vast [væst] 큰, 막대한 resource [ríːsɔːrs] 자원
environmental [invàiərənméntl] 환경적인
concern [kənsə́ːrn] 우려 excessive [iksésiv] 과도한
egret [íːgrit] 백로 spoonbill [spúːnbìl] 노랑부리저어새
showy [ʃóui] 화려한 enact [inǽkt] (법을) 제정하다
stuffed [stʌft] 박제한 landmark [lǽndmàːrk] 기념비적인
legislation [lèdʒisléiʃən] 법률 제정 taper [téipər] 차츰 줄어들다
large-scale [láːrdʒskèil] 대규모의
manufacture [mǽnjufǽktʃər] 제조, 생산
insecticide [inséktəsàid] 살충제 ranching [rǽntʃiŋ] 목장 경영
pesticide [péstəsàid] 살충제 toxic [táksik] 유독한, 독성의
food chain 먹이사슬 subject to ~을 당하기 쉬운
ecology [ikálədʒi] 환경 보존 clamor [klǽmər] 소란
ensue [insúː] 뒤따르다 compel [kəmpél] 강요하다
step in 개입하다

네 개의 네모[■]는 다음 문장이 삽입될 수 있는 부분을 나타내고 있다.

이것은 또한 설치류, 늑대, 그리고 다른 종류의 야생생물을 독살하는 데도 이용되었다.

이 문장은 어느 자리에 들어가는 것이 가장 적절한가?

16 1860년에, 캘리포니아 주로의 우편 배달을 위한 최초의 육상 속달 우편 경로가 확립되었는데, 이것이 포니 익스프레스이다. 노선은 기차 우편 배달의 최서단 도착지인 미주리 주의 세인트 조세프에서 시작했고, 솔트레이크시티를 지나 캘리포니아 주의 새크라멘토에서 끝이 났다. 포니 익스프레스의 창립자인 윌리엄 헌팅턴 러셀은, 말을 잘 타고 매일 죽음의 가능성을 마주할 용의가 있는 젊은 남자들을 구인하는 신문 광고를 냈다. 이것은 그 경로가 배달원들이 상당히 알려지지 않은 비우호적인 지역을 거치도록 했기 때문이다. 그들의 업무와 용감함에 대해, 직원들은

좋은 보수와 혜택을 받았고, 말을 절대로 학대하지 않겠다고 맹세해야 했다. 보통, 한 명의 배달원은 하루에 75마일에서 100마일을 이동하며 10마일에서 15마일마다 말을 교대하기 위해 멈춰 서고는 했지만, 필요할 때는 배달이 더 빠르게 수행될 수도 있었다. **예를 들어, 1861년에, 배달원들은 에이브러햄 링컨의 대통령 취임 연설문을 단 7일 17시간 만에 국토를 횡단하여 운반했다.** 포니 익스프레스는 성공적이었음에도 불구하고, 오래가지 못했다. 대륙 횡단 전신의 발달은 그것이 더 이상 쓸모가 없게 만들었으며 개시 이후 2년도 되지 않아 그것의 운영은 중단되었다.

overland[óuvərlænd] 육상의
westernmost[wéstərnmoust] 최서단의
destination[dèstinéiʃən] 도착지 founder[fáundər] 창립자
on a daily basis 매일 hostile[hástl] 비우호적인
territory[térətɔːri] 지역 bravery[bréivəri] 용감함
grant[grænt] 주다 swear[swer] 맹세하다
mistreat[mìstríːt] 학대하다
coast-to-coast[kóustəkòust] 대륙 횡단의
telegraph[téligræf] 전신 obsolete[ὰːbsəlíːt] 더 이상 쓸모가 없는
inception[insépʃən] 개시

네 개의 네모[■]는 다음 문장이 삽입될 수 있는 부분을 나타내고 있다.

예를 들어, 1861년에, 배달원들은 에이브러햄 링컨의 대통령 취임 연설문을 단 7일 17시간 만에 국토를 횡단하여 운반했다.

이 문장은 어느 자리에 들어가는 것이 가장 적절한가?

17 발레는 16세기 말과 17세기에 이탈리아와 프랑스의 궁정에서 시작되었다. 춤은 귀족 교육의 필수적인 요소로 여겨졌고 그 시대의 호화로운 구경거리로 시선을 끌며 나타났다. 이러한 궁중 발레 중 대부분은 특정한 모양을 형상화한 춤을 포함했는데, 화려한 복장을 갖춘 공연자들이 다양한 기하학적인 대열을 이루면서 움직였다. 구경꾼들은 위에서 그러한 모양을 구경했고 종종 쇼가 끝날 때 열리는 일반 무도회에 참가하기도 했다. 궁중 발레는 춤뿐 아니라 음악, 시 낭송 등을 망라하는 다양한 예술분야를 효과적으로 통합했다. **그것은 또한 극과 현실이 하나가 될 수 있게 해주었는데 이러한 효과를 그 시대의 군주들은 이용했다.** 예를 들어 프랑스의 루이 14세는 여러 궁정 발레에서 춤을 추었고, 그중 하나로 1653년의 Ballet de la Nuit(밤의 발레)가 있었는데, 그 공연에서 그는 Sun Rising(떠오르는 태양)을 연기해서 밤의 괴물들을 몰아내는 천사의 무리를 이끌었다. 이 배역은 루이 14세를 최고로 질서정연한 군주의 구심점으로 만들어주었고, 루이 14세의 공식적인 명칭이었던 Roi-Soleil(태양왕)을 실제로 구현해냈다.

court[kɔːrt] 궁정, 궁중 essential[isénʃəl] 필수적인, 중요한
aristocrat[ərístəkræt] 귀족 figure[fígjər] 나타나다
prominently[prάmənəntli] 시선을 끌며
spectacular[spektǽkjulər] 호화로운
pageant[pǽdʒənt] 장대한 구경거리, 행사
performer[pərfɔ́ːrmər] 공연자

geometrical[dʒìːəmétrikəl] 기하학적인
spectator[spékteitər] 구경꾼, 관람객
pattern[pǽtərn] 모양, 형식 ball[bɔːl] 무도회
integrate[íntəgrèit] 통합하다 declamation[dèkləméiʃən] 낭송
corps[kɔːr] 무리, 집단, 군단 virtue[vɔ́ːrtʃuː] 선
succeed[səksíːd] ~의 뒤를 잇다 superbly[suːpɔ́ːrbli] 최고로
ordered[ɔ́ːrdərd] 질서정연한 multitude[mʌ́ltitjùːd] 군중, 집단
official[əfíʃəl] 공식적인

네 개의 네모[■]는 다음 문장이 삽입될 수 있는 부분을 나타내고 있다.

그것은 또한 극과 현실이 하나가 될 수 있게 해주었는데 이러한 효과를 그 시대의 군주들은 이용했다.

이 문장은 어느 자리에 들어가는 것이 가장 적절한가?

HACKERS TEST

01 Geese

p.262

1. 1st	2. 2nd	3. (D)
4. (B)	5. (D)	6. (C)
7. (A)	8. (B)	9. 2nd
10. (B)−2단락, (D)−3단락, (E)−4단락		

1 북미에서는 여러 종의 새들이 기후 변동에 의한 척박한 환경을 피하기 위해 남쪽으로 엄청난 거리를 이동한다. **이 새들의 대부분은 본능적으로 왕복 여행을 할 수 있다.** 대부분의 새는 매년 봄마다 어김없이 고향으로 돌아오는데, 이는 경로와 방법이 유전적인 기억 안에 선천적으로 각인되어 있기 때문이다. 어떤 새들은, 그중에서도 특히 캐나다 기러기는 이러한 이점을 가지고 있지 않다. 따라서 그 새들은 우선 부모를 모방하면서 경로의 특성들을 인식 범위 안에 받아들여야만 한다.

2 가을에는 남쪽으로, 봄에는 북쪽으로의 힘겨운 이동을 하는 캐나다 기러기의 거대한 무리가 이루는 광경은 지금은 북미대륙의 여러 지역에서 계절변화시기의 확립된 의식이다. **이렇게 반년마다 이동하여 체류하는 것에는 많은 동기가 있다.** 생물학적 관점에서 보면, 줄어드는 일조시간과 낮아지는 온도가 그들의 근본적인 방랑 충동을 불러일으키는 호르몬을 뇌하수체에서 방출하게 한다. 좀 더 실제적인 관점에서 보면, 캐나다 기러기들은 초식동물이고 주로 풀이나 과실을 먹이로 삼는데, 풀이나 과실은 여름에는 풍성하지만, 후에 폭설과 추운 기온이 움직이고 몸을 따뜻하게 유지하는 것을 매우 고되게 만드는 때가 되면 부족해진다. 따라서 남쪽으로의 비행은 기러기들이 먹을 것이 훨씬 더 풍부한 좋은 환경에서 겨울을 날 수 있는 안락함을 제공한다. [5]비록 다수의 남부 여우, 코요테, 그리고 다른 다

양한 육식동물들이 기러기가 봄에는 새끼를 기르기에 적합한 안전한 환경에서 둥지를 짓기 위해 돌아가지 않을 수 없게 만들지만 말이다.

3 갈 때와 돌아올 때 모두 이 장거리 이동은 매우 고되어서 많은 새가 살아남지 못하는데, 특히 맑은 날에는 2,500미터 상공까지 올라가는 무리를 따라잡기 위해 고군분투하는 동안 굶주림과 피로에 영향 받기 쉬운 병들거나 약한 기러기들이 그러하다. 이와는 반대로, 구름 낀 날이나 폭풍우 치는 날씨는 기러기 무리 전체의 비행 고도를 상당히 낮추게끔 하여, 기러기들이 건물이나 전화송신탑, 비행기에 충돌하고 무차별적으로 사냥하기 위해 고정된 이주 경로를 따라 기다리는 사냥꾼의 총알에 맞을 위험에 처하게 한다. ⁷그러나 이보다 더한 강적은 토지 개발이다. 횡행하는 도시화는 소중한 휴식처를 없애버리기 때문에 기러기들로 하여금 평상시보다 더 먼 거리를 비행하게 하여, 종종 지구력의 적당한 한계를 넘게 만든다.

4 이러한 다양한 장애물 때문에, 기러기들은 수 세대에 걸친 습관화를 통해 여행의 고초를 견뎌내기 위한 일련의 특별한 방법을 진화시켜 왔다. 하지가 지나면 일조시간이 서서히 줄어들고, 이는 기러기들에게 섭취하는 음식의 양을 늘림으로써 준비를 시작하라는 신호가 된다. 그 결과, 기러기들은 장거리 여행 동안 생명을 유지할 수 있으며, 여분의 체지방으로 그들의 몸을 덮는데, 이 체지방은 높은 상공의 혹한 기온으로부터 그들을 더 잘 보호해준다. 비행 중에, 기러기들은 군집해서 V자 모양으로 날아가는데, 이때 몸집이 크고 강한 새들이 시작점으로 나서고 피곤해지기 시작하면 뒤쪽으로 내려간다. ⁸이러한 배열은 매우 공기역학적이며 대개 높은 풍속에 정면으로 맞설 힘이 부족한 대부분의 어린 새가 날고 있는 뒤쪽에 가해지는 풍속 변화를 급격하게 줄여준다. 이러한 단체 협동은 쉬거나 먹기 위해 멈춰야 할 필요를 없애, 비행시간을 훨씬 더 연장해준다. 캐나다 기러기는 비행 기술을 부모로부터 배우고, 따라서 상황에 따라 필요한 대로 비행 기술을 조정할 수 있기 때문에 휴식의 빈도는 무리에 따라 매우 다양하다. 예를 들어, 딸린 새끼들이 많은 무리는 더 자주 휴식을 취할 것이고, 전체 비행 거리가 비교적 짧은 무리는 휴식을 별로 취하지 않을 것이다. 알려진 것 중 가장 짧은 이동 중 하나는 16시간으로 캐나다 기러기의 어떤 아종이 Hudson Bay에서 Wisconsin주까지 행하는 하루만의 짧은 여행이며, 가장 긴 이동 중 하나는 멕시코 영토에까지 이르기도 한다. 일반적으로, 몸집이 큰 아종들이 작은 종들보다 더욱 먼 남쪽에서 번식하는 경향이 있다.

inhospitable[inháspitəbl] 척박한   climatic fluctuation 기후 변동
unerringly[ʌnə́:riŋli] 어김없이
pre-wired[prí:wàiərd] 선천적으로 각인된
assimilate[əsíməlèit] 받아들이다
cognizance[kágnəzəns] 인식 범위   emulate[émjulèit] 모방하다
skein[skein] (날짐승의) 무리   grueling[grú:əliŋ] 힘겨운
rite[rait] 의식   set off ~하게 하다   pituitary gland 뇌하수체
itinerant[aitínərənt] 방랑하는   urge[ə:rdʒ] 충동
herbivore[hə́:rbəvɔ̀:r] 초식동물   exacting[igzǽktiŋ] 고된
preponderance[pripándərəns] 다수
gosling[gázliŋ] 새끼   arduous[á:rdʒuəs] 고된
susceptible[səséptəbl] 영향 받기 쉬운
nemesis[néməsis] 강적, 정복할 수 없는 것

rampant[rǽmpənt] 횡행하는   urbanization[ə̀:rbənizéiʃən] 도시화
threshold[θréʃhould] 한계   impediment[impédəmənt] 장애물
withstand[wiθstǽnd] 견디다   taxing[tǽksiŋ] 고생스러운
rigor[rígər] 고초   habituation[həbìtʃuéiʃən] 습관화
summer solstice 하지   congregate[káŋgrigèit] 모이다
aerodynamic[ɛ̀əroudainǽmik] 공기역학의   wind shear 풍속 변화
bear the full brunt of ~에 정면으로 맞서다
coordination[kouɔ̀:rdənéiʃən] 협동   in tow 따라다니는
jaunt[dʒɔ:nt] 짧은 여행   subspecies[sʌ́bspì:si:z] 아종

1 네 개의 네모[■]는 다음 문장이 삽입될 수 있는 부분을 나타내고 있다.

   이 새들의 대부분은 본능적으로 왕복 여행을 할 수 있다.

   이 문장은 어느 자리에 들어가는 것이 가장 적절한가?

2 네 개의 네모[■]는 다음 문장이 삽입될 수 있는 부분을 나타내고 있다.

   이렇게 반년마다 이동하여 체류하는 것에는 많은 동기가 있다.

   이 문장은 어느 자리에 들어가는 것이 가장 적절한가?

3 지문의 단어 "urge"와 의미상 가장 유사한 것은?

   (A) 이유
   (B) 원리
   (C) 방어
   (D) 충동

4 지문의 단어 "compels"와 의미상 가장 유사한 것은?

   (A) 훈련하다
   (B) 강요하다
   (C) 설득하다
   (D) 준비하다

5 지문에 따르면, 봄에 기러기들은 왜 북쪽으로 날아가는가?

   (A) 남쪽에는 여름 동안 충분한 풀이 없다.
   (B) 남쪽에서는 낮이 짧아지고 기온이 떨어진다.
   (C) 남쪽의 환경이 둥지를 짓는 것을 어렵게 만든다.
   (D) 남쪽의 많은 포식자들이 그들의 새끼를 위험에 빠뜨린다.

6 아래 문장 중 지문 속의 음영된 문장의 핵심 정보를 가장 잘 표현하고 있는 것은 무엇인가? 오답은 문장의 의미를 현저히 왜곡하거나 핵심 정보를 빠뜨리고 있다.

   (A) 사냥꾼들은 기러기들이 착륙하기 위해 준비할 때 무차별적으로 총을 쏘기 때문에 가장 큰 위험이다.
   (B) 폭풍우는 기러기들이 사물에 더 잘 부딪히게 하기 때문에 기러기들을 위험에 빠뜨린다.
   (C) 기러기들은 기상 상태 때문에 낮은 고도에서 비행해야 할 때 훨씬 더 위험해진다.
   (D) 고층 건물에 충돌할 위험 때문에, 기러기들은 나쁜 날씨에 비행하지 않는 것이 더 좋다.

7 3단락에서, 글쓴이는 왜 "land development"를 언급하는가?

(A) 기러기들을 탈진하게 만드는 요인을 설명하기 위해
(B) 기러기들의 휴식을 위해 땅을 청소하는 것의 중요성을 강조하기 위해
(C) 현재의 이주 목적지와 예전의 것을 비교하기 위해
(D) 더 환경친화적인 건축의 필요성을 강조하기 위해

8 지문에 따르면, V자 모양으로 비행하는 것의 장점은 _____라는 것이다.

(A) 새들을 지상의 사람들에게 더 알아보기 쉽게 만든다
(B) 뒤쪽의 새들에게 가해지는 풍속 변화의 정도를 줄여준다
(C) 새들이 매년 올바른 장소에 반드시 돌아가게 해준다
(D) 과학자들이 새들의 연간 이주 패턴을 연구하는 것을 돕는다

9 네 개의 네모[■]는 다음 문장이 삽입될 수 있는 부분을 나타내고 있다.

캐나다 기러기는 비행 기술을 부모로부터 배우고, 따라서 상황에 따라 필요한 대로 비행 기술을 조정할 수 있기 때문에 휴식의 빈도는 무리에 따라 매우 다양하다.

이 문장은 어느 자리에 들어가는 것이 가장 적절한가?

10 **지시:** 지문 요약을 위한 도입 문장이 아래에 주어져 있다. 지문의 가장 중요한 내용을 나타내는 보기 3개를 골라 요약을 완성하시오. 어떤 문장은 지문에 언급되지 않은 내용이나 사소한 정보를 담고 있으므로 요약에 포함되지 않는다. **이 문제는 2점이다.**

> 캐나다 기러기들은 계절적 변화에 따라 북쪽에서 남쪽으로 그리고 그 반대로 이동한다.
>
> · (B) 뇌 내 화학적 변화와 먹이 섭취가 기러기의 여행의 주요 원인이다.
> · (D) 위험한 장애물들이 모든 여행에서 기러기들을 마주한다.
> · (E) V자 모양과 축적된 지방은 기러기들이 성공적으로 이동하는 것을 돕는다.

(A) 사람들은 새끼 기러기들에게 제대로 이동하는 방법을 가르쳐줄 수 있었다.
(C) 높은 고도에서 비행하는 것은 낮은 고도에서 하는 것보다 훨씬 더 춥다.
(F) 기러기 뇌에서의 화학적 변화는 날씨와 일조의 변화 때문이다.

02 Sound Film

p.266

1. (D)	2. (B)	3. (B)
4. 4th	5. (B)	6. 2nd
7. (A)	8. (A)	9. 3rd
10. (B)-3단락, (D)-4단락, (F)-2단락		

1 1900년대 초에 이르러, 무성영화는 성공적인 세계적 산업으로 성장했고 당시의 대중문화에서 확고한 위치를 점하게 되었다. 음성은 제공되지 않았지만, 관객들은 과장된 몸짓이나 적절한 때에 그림 콘티에 삽입된 중요 문구를 적은 큐카드를 보고 줄거리와 등장인물들을 이해했다. 때때로 영화 필름은 줄거리를 돋보이게 하기 위한 배경음악을 연주하는 라이브 음악가를 대동해서 전국을 순회하기도 했고, 실연 극단이 영화 공연을 따라다니면서 화면 속 배우들의 대사를 말해주어 영상을 보조하는 음성을 제공하기도 했다. 이러한 방법은 일부 관객을 만족시킬 수 있었지만, 사람들이 진정으로 갈망했던 것은 그들이 좋아하는 스타의 실제 육성을 듣는 것이었다.

2 대사를 재생하는 데 필요한 기술은 Thomas Edison에 의해 발명된 초기 음악 재생기인 축음기의 형식으로 이미 존재했는데, 이것은 상가에 판매되었고 이곳에서 고객들은 돈을 지불하고 각자의 청음기를 통해 한 곡의 음악이나 한 편의 연설을 들을 수 있었다. 이와 마찬가지로, 정교한 장치로 알려진 Kinetoscope(활동 사진 영사기)는 한 축에서 다른 축으로 감기면서 재생되는 원통이나 긴 띠의 영화 필름에 각인된 짧은 동영상을 재생하기 위해 회전하는 디스크를 이용하는데, 이것 역시 전용 영화관에서 엄청난 인기를 끌고 있었다. 그러나 이러한 영상은 작동하는 장치가 들어있는 박스에 난 작은 들여다보는 구멍을 통해서만 볼 수 있었는데, 이러한 디자인은 한 영화관에 여러 대의 기계를 팔 수 있게 하기 위해서 의도적으로 고안된 것이었다. Kinetoscope와 손님의 비율은 항상 1:1이었기 때문에, 극장주들은 증가하는 수요를 충족시키기 위해 될 수 있는 한 많은 기계를 구입하고자 하였다. **투자비용의 회수를 극대화하기 위해서, 극장주들은 더욱 많은 유료 관객의 만족을 위해 영화를 하얀 스크린에 영사해줄 Kinetoscope를 원했다.**

3 이로부터 이십 년 이상의 시간이 흐른 후, Edison에 의해 축음기와 Kinetoscope의 기능을 통합한 Kinetophone이 발명되었다. Kinetophone은 일종의 녹화 장비로서 영상이 촬영된 후에 립싱크 식으로 음성이 추가되거나, 전기자를 이용해서 영상과 음성이 동시에 녹화되는 방식으로 작동하였다. 극장에서 재생하기 위해서는 두 명의 기사가 함께 일해야 했는데, 한 명은 영사실에, 또 다른 한 명은 축음기와 함께 오케스트라 박스에 있어야 했다. **그들은 레코드에 레코드 바늘이 놓일 때 필름이 돌아가기 시작하도록 하기 위해 서로 움직임을 맞춰야 했다.** [5]하지만 Kinetophone은 눈부신 발명이라 부르기는 힘들었다. 영화가 완전히 별개의 기계에서 재생되기 때문에 둘 중 한쪽이 타이밍을 잘못 맞추거나 작동하지 않으면 영화 상영이 엉망이 되는 경우가 많았다. 극장주들은 영상과 음향을 일치시키는 작업이 제대로 되지 않는 것에 불만을 가졌는데, 이것은 Edison의 극장 환경에서의 실행에 대한 불충분한 개념화의 결과였다. 더욱이, 축음기가 넓은 공간을 모두 커버할 수 있을 만한 음량을 만들어낼 수 없다는 문제점도 있었다. 필름이 화면에 단순히 상영되기만 하는 동안 음성은 전기 확성기의 도움 없이 스피커만을 통해서 제공되어야만 했다.

4 [7]이러한 한계는 Lee De Forest에 의해 극복되었는데, 그는 음량을 증폭시키는 방법으로 특허를 얻어서 1925년에 단조 확성기가 도입될 수 있게 했다. 새로운 스피커는 극장에 꽉 들어찬 모든 관

객이 들을 수 있을 만큼 큰 소리로 음성을 재생할 수 있었고, ⁸새롭게 고안된 전기 콘덴서 마이크는 발성을 또렷하게 잡아내면서 잡음을 걸러 주어 더 나은 음질로 녹음할 수 있게 했다. Vitaphone 이라고 명명된 이 새로운 시스템은 1927년 가을, 최초의 'talkie', 즉 발성 영화인 'The Jazz Singer'의 개봉과 함께 대중의 이목을 끌었다. 이 소문은 입에서 입으로 전해졌고, 얼마 안 있어 관객들이 첨단 기술을 구경하기 위해, 또한 그것보다도 그 영화의 배우 Al Jolson의 목소리를 듣기 위해서 극장 앞에 줄지어 섰다.

5 많은 기술적 제약을 극복했음에도 불구하고, Vitaphone은 여전히 고작 몇 회만 상영될 수 있었던 레코드를 필름 전부와 함께 배송해야 하는 부담을 가지고 있었을 뿐 아니라, 영상과 음향의 일치 면에서도 여전히 문제를 나타내고 있었다. **이러한 이유로, Vitaphone은 영화산업에서 오랫동안 우위를 유지하지 못했고, 곧 필름에 소리를 추가하는 신기술에 지위를 빼앗겼다.** 필름에 소리를 추가하는 방식의 충실도가 높아지면서, 그것은 곧 발성 영화를 제작하는 최고의 방법으로 자리 잡았고, 영상오락에 대한 대중의 관심에 새 물결을 선도했을 뿐 아니라, 영화 산업이 새롭게 인정받는 계기가 되었다.

exaggerated [igzǽdʒərèitid] 과장된   cue card 큐카드(방송 중에 출연자에게 보여주는 대사·지시 따위를 써넣은 카드)
storyboard [stɔ́:ribɔ̀:rd] 그림 콘티   reel [ri:l] (릴에 감은) 필름
troupe [tru:p] 극단   complement [kámpləmènt] 보조하다
crave [kreiv] 갈망하다   phonograph [fóunəgrǽf] 축음기
arcade [ɑ:rkéid] 상가   elaborate [ilǽbərət] 정교한
cylinder [sílindər] 원통   celluloid [séljulɔ̀id] 영화 필름
spindle [spíndl] 축   movie parlor 영화관
peephole [pí:phòul] 들여다보는 구멍   apparatus [æ̀pərǽtəs] 장치
ratio [réiʃou] 비율   accommodate [əkámədèit] 충족시키다
incorporate [inkɔ́:rpərèit] 통합시키다
armature [á:rmətʃər] 전기자   playback [pléibæ̀k] 재생
projection booth 영사실   breakthrough [bréikθrù:] 눈부신 발명
synchronization [sìŋkrənizéiʃən] 영상과 음향의 일치
conceptualization [kənsèptʃuələzéiʃən] 개념화
implementation [ìmpləməntéiʃən] 실행
project [prədʒékt] 상영하다
amplification [æ̀mpləfikéiʃən] 증폭, 확장
patent [pǽtnt] 특허를 얻다   monotone [mánətòun] 단조의
conceive [kənsí:v] 고안하다   crisp [krisp] 또렷한
vocalization [vòukəlizéiʃən] 발성   talkie [tɔ́:ki] 발성 영화
fidelity [fidéləti] 충실도   usher [ʌ́ʃər] 선도하다

1 아래 문장 중 지문 속의 음영된 문장의 핵심 정보를 가장 잘 표현하고 있는 것은 무엇인가? 오답은 문장의 의미를 현저히 왜곡하거나 핵심 정보를 빠뜨리고 있다.

(A) 극장들은 관객의 관심을 줄거리에 끌어들이기 위해 관객에게 라이브 음악과 즉석 공연을 제공하곤 했다.
(B) 음악은 줄거리를 이해하는 데 매우 중요했기 때문에 영화 상연에 맞춰 연주할 라이브 음악가들이 필요했다.
(C) 1900년대 초반까지는 음성이 없었기 때문에, 관객들은 라이브 음악가들과 함께 배우들의 대사를 크게 소리 내어 읽곤 했다.

(D) 음악가들과 극단은 배경 음악을 제공하고 배우들의 대사를 말해주기 위해 때때로 영화 필름과 함께 가곤 했다.

2 지문의 단어 "elaborate"와 의미상 가장 유사한 것은?

(A) 산업의
(B) 복잡한
(C) 휴대용의
(D) 육중한

3 지문의 단어 "ratio"와 의미상 가장 유사한 것은?

(A) 불공정
(B) 비율
(C) 수량
(D) 교차점

4 네 개의 네모[■]는 다음 문장이 삽입될 수 있는 부분을 나타내고 있다.

투자비용의 회수를 극대화하기 위해서, 극장주들은 더욱 많은 유료 관객의 만족을 위해 영화를 하얀 스크린에 영사해줄 Kinetoscope를 원했다.

이 문장은 어느 자리에 들어가는 것이 가장 적절한가?

5 3단락에 따르면, Kinetophone이 눈부신 발명으로 여겨지지 않았던 이유는?

(A) 장치는 그것을 작동하는 데 많은 사람들을 필요로 했다.
(B) 오디오와 비디오가 종종 완벽하게 일치하지 않았다.
(C) 재생 장치가 고장 나는 경향이 있었다.
(D) 오디오 장비는 음악과 음성을 개별적으로 재생했다.

6 네 개의 네모[■]는 다음 문장이 삽입될 수 있는 부분을 나타내고 있다.

그들은 레코드에 레코드 바늘이 놓일 때 필름이 돌아가기 시작하도록 하기 위해 서로 움직임을 맞춰야 했다.

이 문장은 어느 자리에 들어가는 것이 가장 적절한가?

7 지문에 따르면, Vitaphone이 Kinetophone에 비해 개선된 주된 방법은 _____이었다.

(A) 소리를 증폭시키는 전자장치의 사용
(B) 영화가 대중에게 개봉되는 시점
(C) 한 번에 영화를 볼 수 있는 사람들의 수
(D) 재생에 필요한 기사의 수

8 지문에 따르면, 'The Jazz Singer'에 대해 추론할 수 있는 것은?

(A) 소리는 녹음을 재생함으로써 만들어졌다.
(B) Al Jolson이 처음으로 출연한 영화였다.
(C) 영화관에서의 초기 개봉은 연기되었다.
(D) 해외에서의 초연 때까지 알려지지 않았다.

9 네 개의 네모[■]는 다음 문장이 삽입될 수 있는 부분을 나타내고 있다.

이러한 이유로, Vitaphone은 영화산업에서 오랫동안 우위를 유지하지 못했고, 곧 필름에 소리를 추가하는 신기술에 지위를 빼앗겼다.

이 문장은 어느 자리에 들어가는 것이 가장 적절한가?

10 지시: 지문 요약을 위한 도입 문장이 아래에 주어져 있다. 지문의 가장 중요한 내용을 나타내는 보기 3개를 골라 요약을 완성하시오. 어떤 문장은 지문에 언급되지 않은 내용이나 사소한 정보를 담고 있으므로 요약에 포함되지 않는다. **이 문제는 2점이다.**

유성 영화의 발전은 일련의 단계를 거쳐 일어났다.
- (B) 소리와 영상을 일치시키려는 시도는 유성 영화 발전에 도움이 되었다.
- (D) 단조 확성기와 전기 콘덴서 마이크는 음성을 개선하기 위해 도입되었다.
- (F) 영화의 초기 음성 재생은 축음기와 Kinetoscope에 근거했다.

(A) 라이브 음악가들은 영화의 줄거리를 수백 명의 관객들에게 전달하는 것을 가능하게 했다.
(C) 'The Jazz Singer'는 배우들의 대화를 포함한 첫 번째 영화였다.
(E) Thomas Edison의 Kinetoscope 설계는 극장주들에게 좋은 평가를 받았다.

---

03 Airplanes

1. 2nd	2. (D)	3. (C)
4. (D)	5. (B)	6. 3rd
7. (B)	8. (B)	9. 3rd
10. (B) -4단락, (D) -3단락, (E) -5단락		

1 수천 년 동안, 사람들은 새가 나는 것을 관찰하고 이들이 하늘을 가르며 우아하게 나는 것을 흉내 내려고 해왔다. **어떤 이들은 깃털로 만든 인공날개를 이용해 보기도 했고, 다른 이들은 다빈치의 ornithopter 같은 복잡한 장치를 고안해내기도 했지만, 이런 모든 시도는 실패로 돌아갔다.** 공기보다 무거운 물체가 하늘을 날게 만드는 방법에 대한 의문은 이런 초기의 설계자들에게는 표면적으로 해결할 수 없는 문제였다.

2 놀랍게도, 19세기에 이르러서야 겉보기에는 무거워 보이는 물체인 연이 항공역학의 진보에 해답을 제시해 주었다. 연이 날 수 있는 비결은 바람이 연의 평평한 아랫면을 밀어 올려서 연이 올라갈 때, 그 공기의 흐름을 이용하여 중력을 거스를 수 있는 능력에 있다. 이러한 압력이 연의 몸체가 계속 공중에 떠 있게 해주는데, 이는 새가 날아오르거나 공중을 맴돌 때 그 비행고도를 유지하는 원리와 유사하다.

3 이러한 관찰결과에 힘입어, 1853년에 마침내 항공 역사상 획기적

인 사건이 일어났는데, 영국 요크셔 지방에서 유인비행이 처음으로 성공한 것이다. 그 비행체는 글라이더로, 기본적으로 연을 본떠 설계되었지만, 화물을 실을 수 있을 정도로 컸다. [4]영국인 발명가인 George Cayley가 디자인한 이 글라이더는 방향키가 없는 고정된 곡선형의 날개를 가졌고, 조종사를 위한 상반각의 공간이 갖추어져 있었는데, [5]이는 그가 여러 번의 사냥 원정에서 잡았던 왜가리의 골격구조에 기초해서 만들어진 것이었다. 최초의 비행에서는, 글라이더가 바람을 탈 때까지 여섯 명의 일꾼이 밧줄을 사용하여 내리막길을 따라 글라이더를 빠른 속도로 잡아당겼고, 글라이더는 약 100피트의 고도까지 올라가서 바닥에 추락하기 전까지 짧은 거리를 날았다. 이 간단한 실험은 방향 조절과 고도 유지 능력에 대한 다음 연구가 분수령을 이루도록 길을 닦아 주었다.

4 조종사가 기체를 더 잘 제어할 수 있게 해주는 방향제어기술의 진보는 효율적인 항공역학 원리에 대한 과학적 연구로부터 유래되었다. 비행을 위해 필요한 중요한 공학적 계산은 수학적인 작업을 통해서 얻어졌지만, 비행 선구자 Orville Wright와 Wilbur Wright 형제는 수차례에 걸친 비행 시도가 실망스러운 결과를 내자 이 자료의 정확성을 의심하게 되었고 이륙 후에 비행기를 제어할 필요성을 느끼게 되었다. 따라서 Wright 형제는 일련의 정밀한 실험을 시작했는데, 정확한 비행 공식을 세우기 위해 각종 표면에 가해지는 압력을 모의실험하기 위한 공기터널인, 한쪽 끝에 선풍기가 달린 막힌 사각 상자와 모형 비행기를 사용했다. **실험으로부터 새로운 자료를 얻은 후, 그들은 비행기의 날개를 구부리는 방식을 개발했다.** 이로 인해, 현대의 보조 날개와 유사하게 한쪽 날개는 높이고 다른 쪽 날개는 낮추게 되었고, 비행기의 횡전을 제어할 수 있게 되었다. 이후에 발명된 방향타는 조종사가 비행기의 측면 이동에 대한 추가적인 제어를 할 수 있게 해주었다.

5 최초의 이륙과 비행이 성공한 시점에서, 이제 남은 것은 최적 풍속 조건이 아닐 때에도 적당한 기압을 만들어내고 그 추진력을 지속시킬 수 있는 동력을 비행기에 공급하는 것이었다. 처음에는 증기 기관을 사용하여 이 문제를 해결하려 했으나, [7]여러 차례의 시도에도 불구하고 증기 기관의 엄청난 무게 때문에 이륙이 불가능했으므로 실제 크기의 증기 엔진을 이용할 수 없음을 알게 되었다. 이에 대한 해결책은 더욱 가벼운 새로운 내연엔진으로부터 얻을 수 있었는데, 이것은 신흥 자동차 산업이 널리 퍼지면서 개발된 새로운 엔진이었다. 1903년 12월 17일, 휘발유로 작동되는 이 동력기의 탑재는 최초로 자체 동력에 의해 가동되며 사람을 태우고 조종 가능한 비행을 성사시키는 데 이바지했는데, 이 비행기는 약 시속 30마일(시속 50킬로미터)의 속도로 12초 동안 비행했다.

6 내연엔진 비행기의 성능은 이후 50년간 기하급수적으로 발전했지만, 이 세대의 비행기의 성능은 현대의 제트기와는 비교조차 되지 않는다. [8]1939년에 제트기의 첫 비행이 있기 전에는, 비행기의 동력기는 비행기 전면에 장착된 프로펠러를 돌려서 비교적 느린 속도로 많은 공기를 밀고 나아갔다. 반면에, 제트기의 엔진은 비행기의 날개나 뒤쪽에 위치하며, 모터에 흡입된 공기를 점점 빨리 회전하는 일련의 원형 날에 통과시켜서 가속시킨다. **엔진을 빠져나가기 전에 공기는 놀라운 속도로 가속되고, 이 시점에서 연료가 공기에**

직접적으로 추가되어 점화되므로, 더 적은 양이지만 폭발적인 속도로 공기를 이동시킨다. 이러한 기술 혁신은 대기 속도를 2000퍼센트 이상 증가시켰고, 오늘날 언제나 이용 가능한 현대적이고 효율적인 교통수단의 등장을 가능하게 하였다.

mimic[mímik] 흉내내다 airborne[ɛ́ərbɔ̀ːrn] 하늘을 나는
ostensibly[ɑsténsəbli] 표면적으로
insurmountable[insərmáuntəbl] 해결할 수 없는
weighty[wéiti] 무거운 aerodynamics[ɛ̀əroudainǽmiks] 항공역학
counteract[kàuntərǽkt] 거스르다
undersurface[ʌ́ndərsə̀ːrfis] 아랫면 elevate[éləvèit] 올라가다
aloft[əlɔ́ːft] 공중에 soar[sɔːr] 날아오르다
hover[hʌ́vər] 공중을 맴돌다 milestone[máilstòun] 획기적인 사건
aviation[èiviéiʃən] 항공 glider[gláidər] 글라이더
cargo[káːrgou] 화물 rudderless[rʌ́dərlis] 방향키가 없는
dihedral[daihíːdrəl] (비행기 날개가) 상반각의
heron[hérən] 왜가리 expedition[èkspədíʃən] 원정
watershed[wɔ́ːtərʃèd] 분수령 subsequent[sʌ́bsikwənt] 다음의
bridle[bráidl] 제어하다 stem[stem] 유래하다
meticulous[mətíkjuləs] 정밀한
simulate[símjulèit] ~의 모의실험을 하다 an assortment of 각종
aileron[éilərɑ̀n] 보조 날개
roll[roul] (비행기·로켓 등의) 횡전(비행기의 앞부분과 뒷부분을 잇는 축을 중심으로, 좌우로 흔드는 것) lateral[lǽtərəl] 측면의
optimal[ɑ́ptəməl] 최적의 momentum[mouméntəm] 추진력
internal-combustion engine 내연엔진
exponentially[èkspounénʃəli] 기하급수적으로
accelerate[æksélərèit] 가속시키다 a series of 일련의
blade[bleid] 날 airspeed[ɛ́ərspìːd] 대기(對氣) 속도

1 네 개의 네모[■]는 다음 문장이 삽입될 수 있는 부분을 나타내고 있다.

어떤 이들은 깃털로 만든 인공날개를 이용해 보기도 했고, 다른 이들은 다빈치의 ornithopter 같은 복잡한 장치를 고안해내기도 했지만, 이런 모든 시도는 실패로 돌아갔다.

이 문장은 어느 자리에 들어가는 것이 가장 적절한가?

2 지문의 단어 "mimicking"과 의미상 가장 유사한 것은?

(A) 이용하는
(B) 기록하는
(C) 통합하는
(D) 모방하는

3 지문의 단어 "that"이 가리키는 것은?

(A) 바람
(B) 연
(C) 압력
(D) 몸체

4 3단락에 따르면, 다음 중 글라이더의 조종사에 대해 추론할 수 있는 것은?

(A) 글라이더가 신속하게 속도를 내는 것을 돕기 위해 비행기 바

끝쪽에서 시작해야 했다.
(B) Wright 형제가 비행기를 설계하는 것을 도왔다.
(C) 지면에 충돌할 수 있는 가능성 때문에 멀리 날기를 거부했다.
(D) 그가 날고 싶은 방향으로 조정할 수 없었다.

5 지문에서 글쓴이는 _____ 하기 위해 "the anatomy of herons"를 언급한다.

(A) 상반각이 어떻게 비행에 영향을 주는지 설명하기 위해
(B) Cayley가 어디에서 영감을 받았는지 보여주기 위해
(C) 동물의 비행과 글라이더의 비행을 대조하기 위해
(D) Cayley가 노련한 사냥꾼이었다는 것을 증명하기 위해

6 네 개의 네모[■]는 다음 문장이 삽입될 수 있는 부분을 나타내고 있다.

실험으로부터 새로운 자료를 얻은 후, 그들은 비행기의 날개를 구부리는 방식을 개발했다.

이 문장은 어느 자리에 들어가는 것이 가장 적절한가?

7 지문은 휘발유로 작동되는 동력기가 _____ 때문에 증기 기관보다 더 효과적이라고 진술한다.

(A) 더 작기 때문에
(B) 무게가 덜 나가기 때문에
(C) 물이 필요하지 않기 때문에
(D) 비용이 적게 들기 때문에

8 지문에 따르면, 제트기는 _____가 다른 비행기들과 다르다.

(A) 바람 저항 시기
(B) 추진 기관의 위치
(C) 성공적인 이륙을 하게 해주는 공기의 필요
(D) 비행 속도를 통제하는 능력

9 네 개의 네모[■]는 다음 문장이 삽입될 수 있는 부분을 나타내고 있다.

엔진을 빠져나가기 전에 공기는 놀라운 속도로 가속되고, 이 시점에서 연료가 공기에 직접적으로 추가되어 점화되므로, 더 적은 양이지만 폭발적인 속도로 공기를 이동시킨다.

이 문장은 어느 자리에 들어가는 것이 가장 적절한가?

10 지시: 지문 요약을 위한 도입 문장이 아래에 주어져 있다. 지문의 가장 중요한 내용을 나타내는 보기 3개를 골라 요약을 완성하시오. 어떤 문장은 지문에 언급되지 않은 내용이나 사소한 정보를 담고 있으므로 요약에 포함되지 않는다. 이 문제는 2점이다.

> 유인 비행의 발전은 항공역학의 기본 원리가 발견되자 빠르게 진행되었다.
>
> · (B) Wright 형제는 공중에서 비행기를 통제하는 기계 장치를 도입했다.
> · (D) 첫 번째 비행기는 추진기나 조종 장치가 전혀 없는 글라이더였다.

- (E) 비행기에는 바람이 매우 적거나 없는 환경에서 동력을 제공하는 엔진이 장착되었다.

(A) 현대 비행기의 보조 날개는 조종사들이 측면 횡전을 제어할 수 있게 한다.

(C) 연은 물체가 공기보다 가벼워지도록 무게를 줄임으로써 계속 떠 있을 수 있었다.

(F) 증기 기관은 무게 제약에도 불구하고 지속적으로 성공할 수 있다고 여겨졌다.

04 Solution Caves

p.274

1. (D)	2. 4th	3. (B)
4. 3rd	5. (A)	6. 3rd
7. (C)	8. (B)	9. 2nd
10. (B)-2단락, (C)-3단락, (E)-4~5단락		

1 동굴은 지구의 지형에 생기는 자연적인 구멍이며 다양한 지리적 형태를 드러낸다. Caverns라고도 불리는 동굴은 다양한 종류의 암석에서 발달하며, [1A]빙하의 침하, [1B]화산 활동, [1C]또는 물에 의한 침식을 포함한 여러 다양한 과정의 최종 결과물이다. 가장 흔한 형태는 가벼운 화학 반응의 산물인 종유굴로, 일반적으로 울퉁불퉁한 지형, 노출된 암붕, 불규칙하게 지표에 패여 있는 배수구와 지하로 특징지어지는 지질 현상의 결합물인 카르스트 지형 발달의 원인이 된다.

2 종유굴의 탄생은 대기 중으로 떨어지면서 이산화탄소를 흡수하여 더욱 산성을 띠게 되는 빗물과 함께 시작한다. 지면에 도달할 때, 빗물은 맨틀에 침투하면서 유기적 반응을 통해 더욱 산성화된다. 이 과정은 빗물이 닿는 곳이면 어디서든 석회석을 용해할 수 있는 약한 형태의 탄산(H_2CO_3)을 형성한다. 하지만 석회석은 불침투성이기 때문에, 물은 석회석 안에 자리 잡지 못하고, 작은 틈을 뚫고 지하수면으로 나아갈 수밖에 없게 된다. 빗물 속의 산성 화학물질이 석회석 내에 대개 방해석 광물의 형태로 존재하는 약염기성의 탄산칼슘과 반응할 때 침식이 발생한다. 이와 같은 침식은 '용해'라고 알려진 화학적 풍화작용의 한 형태이다. 결국, 틈은 점점 더 넓게 벌어져서, 더 많은 물이 들어오고 추가적인 용해를 발생시킨다. 작은 통로를 여는 이 초기 단계는 수천 년 또는 수백만 년이 걸릴지도 모르고, 대개 기후와 토양의 산성도에 좌우된다. 예를 들어, 산성인 토양이 있는 습한 기후는 알칼리성 토양이 있는 건조한 지역보다 더 빨리 도관을 생성한다.

3 알맞은 조건이 지속될 경우, 특정 수로는 팽창의 속도가 상당히 더 빠른 확장 단계에 들어선다. 과학자들은 결정적인 단계가 물의 수용량과 흐름이 합쳐져 침식의 속도를 급격히 증가시키는 대략적인 직경인 약 2분의 1센티미터 정도라고 생각한다. 가장 큰 도관은 이용 가능한 많은 물을 끌어들여 작은 도관을 기하급수적으로 앞지르기 시작한다. 결국, 지배적인 통로는 주변에 위치한 더 작은 통로를 모

두 집어삼킬 정도로 확장될 수도 있다. 종종 이 통로는 완전히 물로 채워지고, 지역 지리에 따라 바닥, 벽, 천장이 균일하게 침식되는 원형 또는 타원형 통로가 발달하게 된다.

4 [5]이 동굴의 뒤따른 발달은 지하수면에 의해 좌우된다. 지하수면이 동굴을 물로 완전히 채우고 오랜 기간 동안 많은 양이 흐르면, 지속적인 물의 흐름이 계속해서 동굴의 안쪽 면을 침식하기 때문에 광대한 동굴 망이 발달할 수 있다. 따라서 [5]가장 넓은 동굴은 지하수면을 따라 형성되고, 특별한 예는 길이가 500킬로미터가 넘는 것으로 조사된, 기록상 가장 긴 탐험 통로가 된 남부 켄터키의 Mammoth 동굴이다. 이 동굴의 인상적인 크기는 한 국립공원이 같은 이름을 사용하도록 했고 연간 2백만 명의 방문객을 끌어들인다. 그러나 Mammoth 동굴이 형성되었을 때와 같은 조건이 늘 안정적인 것은 아니다. 지하수면의 수위가 적당히 낮아지거나 지면이 하강하는 것은 동굴이 용해를 위한 최적 상태보다 떨어지게 만든다. 유입되는 수위가 낮아지면 천장이 대기에 노출되어 더는 침식이 일어나지 않지만, 벽과 바닥 부분은 용해 침식에 의해 동굴 바닥을 30에서 50미터까지 깊어지게 하고 협곡 모양을 만들어내는 변화를 계속 겪게 된다. 동굴 속 물의 느리거나 정지된 움직임은 전형적으로 작은 물줄기나 고인 웅덩이를 낳는다.

5 더욱이, 지하수면이 심각하게 낮아지거나 지각활동에 의해 급격히 융기되는 것은 동굴 속 지하수를 완전히 고갈시킨다. 이런 동굴은 지형 변화가 상당히 줄어드는 침체기로 접어들게 된다. 이 단계는 사실상 동굴이 확장의 측면에서 멈춘 것임을 보여준다. 그러나 빗물은 계속해서 떨어지고 아래로 흘러 들어 이동하면서 석회암과 반응한다. 물에 용해된 것은 분필과 유사한 결정화된 광물인 방해석으로, 석회석으로부터 추출된 것이다. 방해석의 침전과 퇴적은 동굴 천장과 바닥을 침식시키기보다는 더한다. 서서히, 동굴의 위쪽 면으로부터 물방울이 떨어지면서, 증발 작용이 일어나고 광물의 흔적이 남는다. 이 광물 퇴적물은 동굴의 천장에 달린 종유석이라고 불리는 원뿔처럼 생긴 구조를 형성한다. 동시에, 종유석 끝에서 바닥으로 미끄러져 떨어지는 물방울도 석순이라고 불리는 유사한 구조를 형성한다. 만약 종유석과 석순 짝이 충분히 커지면, 중간에서 합쳐져 기둥을 만들 수 있다. 대량의 종유석과 석순은 동굴 탐험가들을 위한 장관의 미적 볼거리를 만들어낸다.

cavity[kævəti] 구멍, 동공 topography[təpágrəfi] 지형
abrasion[əbréiʒən] 침식 karst[kɑːrst] 카르스트 지형
rugged[rʌ́gid] 울퉁불퉁한 acidic[əsídik] 산성인
organic[ɔːrgǽnik] 유기적인 percolate[pə́ːrkəlèit] 침투하다
impermeable[impə́ːrmiəbl] 불침투성의
calcium carbonate 탄산칼슘 weathering[wéðəriŋ] 풍화작용
enlargement[inlɑ́ːrdʒmənt] 확장
approximate[əprɑ́ksəmèit] 대략적인
drastically[drǽstikəli] 급격히 elliptical[ilíptikəl] 타원형의
uniformly[júːnəfɔ̀ːrmli] 균일하게
extraordinary[ikstrɔ́ːrdənèri] 특별한
spelunk[spilʌ́ŋk] (동굴을) 탐험하다
subsidence[səbsáidns] 하강, 침하 uplift[ʌ́plift] 융기
deplete[diplíːt] 고갈시키다 leach[liːtʃ] 침출되다
precipitation[prisipətéiʃən] 침전(물)

deposition [dèpəzíʃən] 퇴적(물)
evaporation [ivæpəréiʃən] 증발 작용
stalactite [stəlǽktait] 종유석　stalagmite [stəlǽgmait] 석순

1　1단락에 따르면, 다음 중 동굴 형성의 원인으로 언급되지 않은 것은?

(A) 빙하의 침하
(B) 화산 활동
(C) 물에 의한 침식
(D) 지각 융기

2　네 개의 네모[■]는 다음 문장이 삽입될 수 있는 부분을 나타내고 있다.

예를 들어, 산성인 토양이 있는 습한 기후는 알칼리성 토양이 있는 건조한 지역보다 더 빨리 도관을 생성한다.

이 문장은 어느 자리에 들어가는 것이 가장 적절한가?

3　지문의 단어 "uniformly"와 의미상 가장 유사한 것은?

(A) 급격하게
(B) 고르게
(C) 두드러지게
(D) 간헐적으로

4　네 개의 네모[■]는 다음 문장이 삽입될 수 있는 부분을 나타내고 있다.

결국, 지배적인 통로는 주변에 위치한 더 작은 통로를 모두 집어삼킬 정도로 확장될 수도 있다.

이 문장은 어느 자리에 들어가는 것이 가장 적절한가?

5　4단락에서 글쓴이는 왜 "Mammoth Cave"를 언급하는가?

(A) 동굴 형성 위치와 크기 사이의 연관성을 설명하기 위해
(B) 지하수면의 중요한 역할에 대한 주장에 반박하기 위해
(C) 빙하 침하 과정에 대한 추가 설명을 제공하기 위해
(D) 동굴 망 확장에 대한 가능한 이유를 반박하기 위해

6　네 개의 네모[■]는 다음 문장이 삽입될 수 있는 부분을 나타내고 있다.

이 동굴의 인상적인 크기는 한 국립공원이 같은 이름을 사용하도록 했고 연간 2백만 명의 방문객을 끌어들인다.

이 문장은 어느 자리에 들어가는 것이 가장 적절한가?

7　아래 문장 중 지문 속의 음영된 문장의 핵심 정보를 가장 잘 표현하고 있는 것은 무엇인가? 오답은 문장의 의미를 현저히 왜곡하거나 핵심 정보를 빠뜨리고 있다.

(A) 공기가 동굴 안으로 유입되면, 물을 밀어내어 공간의 크기를 크게 확장시킬 것이다.
(B) 용해 침식의 속도는 수면이 낮아지고 공기가 들어오면 더 빨라질 것이다.
(C) 수면이 낮아지면, 벽과 바닥 부분의 침식은 계속 진행되지만 천장은 그렇지 않다.

(D) 물이 줄어들면서, 바닥과 벽 부분의 지속적인 침식을 일으키는 공기가 들어온다.

8　지문의 단어 "deplete"과 의미상 가장 유사한 것은?

(A) 보충하다
(B) 고갈시키다
(C) 우회하다
(D) 줄어들다

9　네 개의 네모[■]는 다음 문장이 삽입될 수 있는 부분을 나타내고 있다.

이 단계는 사실상 동굴이 확장의 측면에서 멈춘 것임을 보여준다.

이 문장은 어느 자리에 들어가는 것이 가장 적절한가?

10　**지시:** 지문 요약을 위한 도입 문장이 아래에 주어져 있다. 지문의 가장 중요한 내용을 나타내는 보기 3개를 골라 요약을 완성하시오. 어떤 문장은 지문에 언급되지 않은 내용이나 사소한 정보를 담고 있으므로 요약에 포함되지 않는다. **이 문제는 2점이다.**

> **종유굴은 일련의 독특한 발달 단계를 나타낸다.**
> · (B) 종유굴의 형성은 물이 산성화되어 석회석과 반응하여, 그 암석을 용해시키고 작은 틈에 침투할 때 시작된다.
> · (C) 조건이 맞으면, 몇몇 통로들은 급속한 확장에 이르는 결정적인 단계를 거친다.
> · (E) 수위 또는 지반의 변동은 결국 동굴 발달의 정체기로 이어지고, 용해가 느려지거나 완전히 끝나는 것을 야기할 수 있다.

(A) 빗물은 지각 안에 고여 지하의 석회석과 기반암을 압축함으로써 동굴 형성을 촉진한다.
(D) 동굴 일생의 마지막 단계는 용해가 동굴 벽을 너무 광범위하게 침식시켜 동굴 천장이 그 무게에 눌려 무너질 때 일어난다.
(F) 남아 있는 어떤 물방울의 증발이라도 동굴 천장에 뿔 모양으로 만들어질 수 있는 광상을 만든다.

HACKERS **STRATEGY**

p.281

전략 1

Ex 식물은 광주성이 개화에 어떤 영향을 미치는가에 따라 세 종류로 크게 분류된다. 단일 식물은 밤의 길이가 임계일장과 같거나 더 길 때 개화한다. 이 임계일장은 식물종마다 상당히 다르지만, 대개 12시간에서 14시간 사이이다. 단일 식물의 개화의 시작은 짧은 일광 때문이 아니라, 길고 연속된 밤 때문이다. 단일 식물의 예로는 돼지풀과 꽃이 늦여름에서 가을에 피기 시작하는 포인세티아가 있다.

밤의 길이가 임계일장과 같거나 더 짧을 때 꽃을 피우는 식물은 장일 식물이라 불린다. 이 식물은 늦봄과 초여름에 밤이 짧아짐을 감지할 수 있으며, 이를 감지할 때 꽃을 피운다.

중일 식물이라 명명되는 일부 식물은 계절에 따른 낮과 밤의 길이의 변화가 아닌, 외부적인 혹은 내부적인 몇몇 다른 종류의 자극에 반응하여 개화를 시작한다. 이 식물의 다수는 연중 낮의 길이가 눈에 띄게 달라지지 않는 열대지방에서 유래했다.

photoperiodism [fòutəpíəriədìzm] 광주성(볕을 쬐는 시간의 변화에 따라 일어나는 생체의 반응성) **flower** [fláuər] 개화하다
short-day plant 단일 식물
critical day length 임계일장(식물의 개화에 영향을 줄 수 있는 낮 시간의 길이) **ragweed** [rǽgwìːd] 돼지풀
long-day plant 장일 식물 **day-neutral plant** 중일 식물
the tropics 열대 지방 **appreciably** [əprí:ʃiəbli] 눈에 띄게

HACKERS STRATEGY **APPLICATION**

p.284

1850년대에 노예제도 문제로 인해 기존의 휘그당과 민주당 사이에 분열이 일어났고, 이로 인해 제3당의 필요성이 대두하였다. 정치적 혼란 속에 등장한 이 새 정당은 북부와 노예제 폐지주의자들의 이익을 대변하기 위하여 창설되었다. 창설자 Alvan Bovay는 그 정당을 '공화당'이라고 부르기로 했는데, 그 이유는 그 명칭이 단순하기는 하지만 평등과 관련하여 역사적으로 중요했기 때문이었다.

공화당의 창립자들은 각 주의 권리 및 제한된 역할을 하는 국가 정부에 대한 입장을 표명했다. 공화당의 첫 출발은 1854년 2월 휘그당 탈당자들이 비밀리에 모여 새 정당의 창건을 논의하면서 시작되었다. 그러자 노예제도 반대세력들이 집결했고 위스콘신주에서 열린 첫 공청회에서 각 주의 노예제도 합법화 여부를 주민의 결정에 위임한, 논란이 많았던 캔자스네브래스카법안에 반대하는 결의안을 채택하였다. 두 번째 공청회에서 지역 주민의 작은 집단들은 정치 위원회를 해산하고 새 정당의 위원회 위원으로 다섯 명을 선출하였다. 이 소식이 전해지면서 공화당은 최초의 전당 대회를 개최하여 국가적

인 공약을 채택하는 동시에 의원 후보자를 지명함으로써 공식적으로 당을 구성했다. 미합중국에 편입되는 새로운 주들에 노예제도를 확장하겠다는 민주당원들의 계획을 무산시키기 위한 공동의 노력이 이루어짐에 따라 노예제를 둘러싼 긴장이 증가하였다. 선거에 출마하여 당선된 노예제도에 반대하는 공화당원들의 수가 증가하면서 양당을 더욱 자극하기에 이르렀다. 1856년 필라델피아에서 있었던 전국 대회에서 공화당은 John C. Freemont를 대통령 후보로 임명했고, '자유로운 땅, 자유로운 노동, 자유로운 언론, 자유인, Freemont!'가 공화당의 슬로건이 되었다. Freemont는 민주당에 패배하기는 했지만 제3당 후보로 출마했음에도 득표수의 3분의 1을 얻었고, 이를 통해 1860년 대선에 대한 낙관론을 신장시켰다.

존경받던 일리노이주 주의회 의원 Abraham Lincoln은 1860년에 공화당원으로는 최초로 대선에서 승리하였다. Lincoln은 남부 주에서는 한 표도 득표하지 못했음에도 불구하고 세 명의 경쟁 후보자를 제쳤다. Lincoln의 당선으로 60년에 걸친 민주당의 정치 집권은 종지부를 찍었고, 그의 당선 후 한 달도 안 되어서 남부는 미합중국에서 분리 독립하였다. 곧이어 남북전쟁이 발발했고 Lincoln은 미합중국을 유지하는 데 어려움을 겪었다. 남북전쟁 중 Lincoln은 당시 내각에 반대하여 노예를 해방시키는 노예 해방령에 서명했다. 그는 공화당 의회와 함께 노력하여, 노예제도를 금지하고 법 아래의 동등한 보호를 보장하는 미 헌법 제13조와 14조를 통과시켰다. 남북전쟁 후 재건 시대에 공화당은 민주당의 남부지역과의 연고로부터 도움을 받아 향후 몇 년간 사실상 누구의 반대도 받지 않고 집권했다.

turmoil [tə́ːrmɔil] 혼란 **abolitionist** [æbəlíʃənist] 폐지주의자
defector [diféktər] 탈당자 **rally** [rǽli] 집결하다
resolution [rèzəlúːʃən] 결의안
controversial [kàntrəvə́ːrʃəl] 논란이 많은
convention [kənvénʃən] 전당 대회 **platform** [plǽtfɔ:rm] 공약
mount [maunt] 증가하다 **concerted** [kənsə́:rtid] 공동의
galvanize [gǽlvənàiz] 자극하다 **secede** [sisíːd] 분리 독립하다
the Civil War (미국) 남북전쟁
cabinet [kǽbənit] 내각, (대통령의) 고문단
Emancipation Proclamation 노예 해방령 **outlaw** [áutlɔ̀:] 금지하다
reconstruction [rìːkənstrʌ́kʃən] (미국) 남북전쟁 후 재건 시대
unopposed [ʌ̀nəpóuzd] 누구의 반대도 받지 않고

공화당은 19세기 중반에 기존의 정당으로부터 발전했다.

(A) 공화당원들은 여성의 사회적 지위를 높이는 데 주된 역할을 했다.

(B) 공화당원들과 민주당원들은 새로운 지역에서의 노예 문제에 대해 뜻이 맞지 않았다.

(C) 이전의 패배 이후, 공화당은 Abraham Lincoln이 첫 번째 공화당 대통령으로 당선되면서 성공했다.

(D) Lincoln은 남북전쟁을 막고 그의 기득권을 지키기 위해 노력했다.

(E) 휘그당 탈당자들은 비밀 회합을 엶으로써 휘그당과 거리를 두

었다.

(F) 공화당은 주의 권리에 헌신했고 노예 제도 확산을 막는 데 있어 연합했다.

(C) 흑화식 도예는 그리스 도자기의 발달에 중대한 변천을 나타냈다.

(D) 흑화식 기법은 그리스 이외의 지역에 사는 예술가들에 의해 이용되었다.

HACKERS **PRACTICE**

p.286

1. (C)	2. (A)	3. (D)
4. (A)		5. (+), (−), (−), (−)
6. (+), (−), (+), (−)		7. (−), (−), (+), (−)
8. (+), (−), (+), (−)		9. (A), (E), (F)
10. (A), (C), (F)	11. (C), (D), (E)	12. (B), (D), (E)

VOCABULARY

1 (D)	2 (C)	3 (A)
4 (C), (D)	5 (C), (B), (D)	6 (D), (A), (B)
7 (A), (C), (B)	8 (D), (C), (A)	9 (D), (C), (A)
10 (B), (C), (A)	11 (D), (C), (A)	12 (D), (B), (B)

1 기원전 약 1050년부터 700년까지, 그리스 도자기는 장식 요소로서 기하학적인 형태와 고도로 양식화된 동식물 묘사를 사용하는 것으로 특징지어졌다. 하지만, 이것은 아테네의 예술가들이 흑화식 도예라고 알려진 새로운 기법을 도입하면서 달라졌다. 가마에 도자기 그릇이 넣어지기 전에, 탄산 칼륨과 철분이 풍부한 흙으로 구성된 검은 색소를 사용하여 사람 형태의 윤곽들이 그릇의 표면에 더해졌다. 그다음, 예술가는 날카로운 도구를 이용하여 색소에 섬세한 선들을 새기고는 했다. 이 기법의 장점은 사람의 생생한 모습이 창작될 수 있다는 것이었다. 사람 형체의 정확한 묘사는 그리스 도예에서 중요한 주제가 되었고, 이후의 양식들은 흑화식 도예에서 이용되었던 방법들을 통합하고 향상시켰다.

ceramics [sərǽmiks] 도자기
geometric [dʒìːəmétrik] 기하학적인
representation [rèprizintéiʃən] 묘사 **adopt** [ədɑ́ːpt] 도입하다
black-figure pottery 흑화식 도예(고대 그리스의 항아리 장식 기법)
vessel [vésl] 그릇 **kiln** [kiln] 가마 **pigment** [pígmənt] 색소, 안료
potash [pɑ́ːtæʃ] 탄산 칼륨
employ [implɔ́i] (기술·방법 등을) 이용하다
implement [ímpləmənt] 도구 **virtue** [vɔ́ːrtʃuː] 장점
accurate [ǽkjərət] 정확한 **portrayal** [pɔːrtréiəl] 묘사
incorporate [inkɔ́ːrpəreit] 통합하다, 포함하다

(A) 초기의 그리스 예술가들은 도자기 그릇을 다양한 종류의 디자인으로 장식했다.

(B) 사람 형체가 묘사되어 있는 그릇은 종교 의식에서 사용되

2 1997년에, 천문학자들은 별들을 발견하지 않았다면 우주의 빈 공간이었을 곳에 위치한 몇몇 은하계 사이의 별들을 발견했다. 이 발견 전까지는, 별들은 오직 은하계 내에서만 존재한다고 믿어져 왔었다. 모든 별들이 은하계 안에서 생기기 때문에, 무엇이 은하계 사이의 별들이 외딴 자리를 차지하게 했는지에 대한 많은 추측들이 있어 왔다. 하나의 학설은 두 은하계 사이의 충돌이 중력의 장애로 이어져 개개의 별을 방출했다는 것이다. 이 시나리오에서는, 은하계 사이의 별이 아주 작은 은하에 속해 있었을 가능성이 높은데, 이는 큰 은하의 중력은 별의 탈출을 막았을 것이기 때문이다. 다른 가설은 은하계 사이의 별들이 극도로 강력한 중력장이 있는 우주 공간인 거대한 블랙홀과의 상호작용으로부터 기인한다는 것이다. 이 학설의 지지자들은 은하계 사이의 별들이 한때 서로의 궤도를 도는 두 개의 별인 쌍성계의 구성 요소였다고 믿는다. 쌍성계의 별 하나가 블랙홀에 너무 가깝게 이동하면, 그것은 갇히게 되고, 이는 다른 하나의 별이 궤도를 벗어나 매우 빠른 속도로 멀어지기 시작하게 만든다. 만약 이 별이 충분한 속도에 이르면, 그것은 전체 은하계의 중력을 돌파하고 은하계 사이의 공간으로 이동해 나가게 된다.

astronomer [əstrɑ́ːnəmər] 천문학자
intergalactic [ìntərgəlǽktik] 은하계 사이의
otherwise [ʌ́ðərwaiz] 그렇지 않았다면
originate in 생기다, 비롯하다 **speculation** [spèkjuléiʃən] 추측
take up 차지하다 **solitary** [sɑ́ːləteri] 외딴
collision [kəlíʒən] 충돌 **gravitational** [grǽvitéiʃənl] 중력의
expel [ikspél] 방출하다 **hypothesis** [haipɑ́ːθəsis] 가설
proponent [prəpóunənt] 지지자
component [kəmpóunənt] 구성 요소 **binary star** 쌍성
orbit [ɔ́ːrbit] 궤도를 돌다; 궤도 **trap** [træp] 가두다
break out 벗어나다 **velocity** [vəlɑ́ːsəti] 속도
sufficient [səfíʃənt] 충분한

(A) 별이 어떻게 원래의 은하계 밖으로 이동하는지를 설명하기 위해 다양한 이론들이 제시되어 왔다.

(B) 은하계의 무리는 극도로 많은 수의 별을 포함한다.

(C) 희귀한 현상은 쌍성계의 파괴를 야기한다.

(D) 은하계 사이의 별은 블랙홀의 중력을 피한다.

3 1905년 피츠버그에서 처음으로 등장했던 nickelodeon은 입장료로 1니켈, 즉 5센트를 받던 동네의 작은 극장이었다. Nickelodeon은 온갖 잡다한 종류의 가게 앞에 딸린 개조된 공간에 위치하는 경우가 많았는데, 가격이 적당하고 재미있는 이 장소는 1908년까지 그 수가 대략 8,000개로 급격히 증가했을 정도로 인기가 좋았다. 빈약하게 장식되어 있었고 담배 연기로 가득 차 있었으며 우중충하고 어두웠던 nickelodeon은 다양한 주제에 대한 15분에서 20분 정도 길이의 '영화'를 보여주곤 했

다. Nickelodeon은 거의 200명의 관객을 수용할 수 있었으며, 관객들은 엉성한 의자에 앉아서 동네 소녀가 특정 장면의 분위기에 맞추려고 노력하며 연주하는 피아노 반주를 편하게 들을 수 있었다. 도시 인구가 늘어남에 따라, nickelodeon의 수는 점차 줄어들었는데, 이는 관객들이 점점 더 개봉영화가 상영되고 더 나은 음향시설과 단정한 안내원을 갖춘 대형 극장의 편안하고 잘 꾸며진 환경을 선호했기 때문이다.

neighborhood[néibərhùd] 동네 admission[ædmíʃən] 입장
converted[kənvə́:rtid] 개조된
storefront[stɔ́:rfrʌ̀nt] 가게 앞에 딸린 공간
affordable[əfɔ́:rdəbl] 가격이 적당한 venue[vénjuː] 장소
mushroom[mʌ́ʃruːm] 급격히 증가하다
sparsely[spáːrsli] 빈약하게 dingy[díndʒi] 우중충한
by degrees 점차 well-appointed[wèləpɔ́intid] 잘 꾸며진
first-run movie 개봉영화 usher[ʌ́ʃər] 안내원

(A) nickelodeon은 200명의 사람들까지 수용할 수 있었고 영화의 라이브 음악을 포함했다.
(B) nickelodeon이라는 명칭은 1니켈이었던 입장료로부터 비롯되었다.
(C) nickelodeon은 다양한 장르의 영화를 보여주는 것으로 유명했다.
(D) nickelodeon은 처음에는 인기 있었지만 결국 대형 극장으로 대체되었다.

4 1800년대 미국의 급격한 영토 확장은 무분별한 무상토지불하 정책이 수립되게 했고, 이는 1862년의 자영농지법의 수립으로 절정에 달했다. 토지를 점유하기 위해서는 충족시켜야 할 몇 가지 필요 조건들이 있었다. 첫째로, 자영 농민이 되고자 하는 21세의 가장은 국유지를 점유하는 목적을 서류로 작성해서 가장 가까운 곳의 토지 관공서에 제출해야 했다. 그러면 관공서는 공공문서를 검토해서 이전에 같은 지역에 대한 신고서가 들어온 적이 없는지 확인했다. 둘째로, 지원자에게는 자신이 불하받은 땅을 개발해야 했는데, 예를 들면 소유지 위에 가옥을 짓거나 토지를 개간하는 등의 일이었다. 5년 동안 계속 한 지역에서 거주하면, 따로 비용을 지불할 필요 없이 토지를 자기 것으로 만들 수 있었다. 이 법은 새로운 국가를 위한 새로운 농업적 기반을 형성하였고 이는 오늘날까지도 여전히 국가의 식량 공급을 지탱하고 있다. 더욱이, 공유지 불하는 백만 명이 넘는, 토지를 갖지 못한 농민들과 이주민들이 소유지와 독립적인 생계수단을 얻을 수 있도록 하여, 서구사회에서 지금까지 보지 못한 유례없는 새로운 중산층의 토대를 마련하였다. 1986년에 이 법안이 완전히 폐지되기 전까지, 미국 전체 토지의 약 10퍼센트에 달하는 2억 7천만 에이커가 연방정부에 의해 개인에게 수여되었다. 분명히, 이 법안은 미국의 경관 형성에 중요한 역할을 했다.

territorial[tèritɔ́:riəl] 영토의 expansion[ikspǽnʃən] 확장
land-grant[lǽndgrὲnt] 무상토지불하
culminate[kʌ́lmənèit] 절정에 달하다
Homestead Act (미국의) 자영농지법 fulfill[fulfíl] 충족시키다
claim[kleim] 토지를 점유하다 would-be[wúdbìː] ~이 되고자 하는

homesteader[hóumstèdər] 자영농민
file[fail] (증빙서류를) 제출하다 intention[inténʃən] 목적
tract[trækt] 구역 verify[vérəfài] 확인하다
previous[príːviəs] 이전의 applicant[ǽplikənt] 지원자
property[prápərti] 소유지 sustenance[sʌ́stənəns] 생계
unprecedented[ʌ̀nprésədèntid] 유례없는
hitherto[híðərtuː] 지금까지 repeal[ripíːl] 폐지하다
confer[kənfə́ːr] 수여하다 substantial[səbstǽnʃəl] 중요한

(A) 자영농지법은 많은 사람들이 토지를 소유할 수 있도록 허용한 뒤 미국에 극적인 영향을 미쳤다.
(B) 자영농지법에 관한 자격을 갖추기 위해서, 개인은 몇몇 필요 조건을 충족시켜야 했다.
(C) 자영농지법으로 개발된 농지의 수는 농업적 기반을 늘리는 결과로 이어졌다.
(D) 자영농지법은 미국이 너무 많은 땅을 획득했었기 때문에 발생하였다.

5 18세기 말에 영국에서 시작했던 산업 혁명은, 영국 사회에 중대한 영향을 미쳤다. 그것은 소비자들에게 더 많은 선택권을 제공했을 뿐 아니라 많은 사람들의 삶의 질 하락으로 이어지기도 했다.

산업 혁명의 이점들 중 하나는 그것이 많은 상품들의 가격을 크게 낮추었다는 것이었다. 이전에는, 옷, 요리 도구, 그리고 가구와 같은 상품들은 작은 작업장에서 장인들에 의해 만들어졌고, 이는 그것들을 상당히 값비싸게 만들었다. 하지만, 대량 생산법의 발달은 영국을 많은 양의 값싼 소비재로 넘치게 했다. 그 결과, 부유하지 않은 사람들조차 그들의 집 전체에 가구를 비치하고 상점에서 산 상품으로 가족들에게 옷을 입힐 형편이 될 수 있었다.

불행히도, 대량 생산을 가능하게 만들었던 공장 시스템은 노동자 계급의 구성원들에게 부정적인 결과를 가져왔다. 다수의 사람들이 산업 지역으로 이주하면서 발생했던 빠른 도시화는 혼잡하고 비위생적인 빈민가의 생성을 초래했다. 이러한 지역들에서는, 쥐와 같은 유해 동물들이 빠르게 번식했고 상수도가 오염되어, 질병의 확산을 야기했다. 게다가, 공장 소유주들은 직원들에게 아주 낮은 봉급으로 하루에 열두 시간을 일할 것을 흔히 요구했다. 고용주들은 특별한 기술이 필요 없는 광범위한 노동력을 이용할 수 있었기 때문에, 더 많은 보수를 제공하거나 노동 시간을 줄일 동기가 거의 없었다. 따라서, 많은 사람들에게, 산업 혁명은 벗어나는 것이 불가능했던 좋지 않은 건강 상태, 노역, 그리고 가난한 삶을 초래했다.

Industrial revolution 산업 혁명 decline[dikláin] 하락
craftspeople[krǽftspìːpl] 장인 mass production 대량 생산
flood[flʌd] 넘치게 하다 consumer goods 소비재
afford[əfɔ́ːrd] 형편이 되다 furnish[fə́ːrniʃ] (가구를) 비치하다
merchandise[mə́ːrtʃəndais] 상품
consequence[ká:nsəkwens] 결과 rapid[rǽpid] 빠른
urbanization[ə̀:rbənizéiʃən] 도시화
relocate[riːlóukeit] 이주하다
unsanitary[ʌ̀nsǽnətèri] 비위생적인 slum[slʌm] 빈민가

pest[pest] 유해 동물, 해충 breed[bri:d] 번식하다, 새끼를 낳다
water supply 상수도 contaminated[kəntǽminèitid] 오염된
access[ǽkses] 이용, 접근
compensation[kà:mpenséiʃən] 보수 toil[tɔil] 노역
poverty[pá:vərti] 가난 escape[iskéip] 벗어나다

주제 문장: 산업 혁명은 영국에 중대한 변화를 야기했다.

(A) 노동자들이 혹독한 생활 조건과 근로 조건에 대처해야 했다.
(B) 장인을 고용한 작업장들이 소비재를 생산했다.
(C) 대량 생산된 제품들은 수공품보다 품질이 더 낮은 경향이 있었다.
(D) 공장 소유주들은 특별한 기술이 필요 없는 많은 수의 노동자를 고용할 수 있었다.

6 수은은 실온에서 액체 형태를 취하는 유일한 금속 화학 원소이다. 그것은 한때 약효 성분이 있다고 믿어졌고 수명을 연장하기 위해 적은 양이 섭취되었다. 이제는 수은이 매우 유독해서 사람이 먹기에 위험하다고 알려져 있기는 하지만, 수은은 여전히 여러 실용적인 적용성을 가진다.

수은은 비금속 물질과 섞여 있는 금을 추출하는 데 사용될 수 있다. 이것은 수은의 원자 구조가 수은을 특정 금속들의 용제로 만들기 때문이다. 강바닥에서 금을 찾는 충적토 광부들은 모래나 토사에 수은을 더한다. 존재하는 모든 금은 수은에 용해되어, 아말감이라고 불리는 혼합물을 형성한다. 후에, 이 물질은 수은이 증발할 때까지 가열되어, 오로지 금만 남기게 된다.

수은은 관측소에서 사용되는 거대한 망원경을 만드는 데 이용되기도 한다. 이러한 기구들은 유입되는 빛의 방향을 어느 정도 바꾸어 멀리 있는 물체를 확대하는 유리로 된 큰 포물선 모양의 거울을 통상적으로 포함하고 있다. 문제는 이 유리 거울이 생산하기에 엄두를 못 낼 만큼 비싸다는 것이다. 하지만, 망원경 설계의 약간의 수정을 통해, 수은은 값싼 대안으로 쓰일 수 있는데 이는 그것이 액체 상태에서 고도로 빛을 반사하기 때문이다. 많은 양의 수은이 빠르게 회전되면, 그것은 유리 거울과 비슷한 방식으로 기능하는 부드럽고 굴곡진 표면을 형성한다.

mercury[má:rkjəri] 수은 medicinal[mədísinl] 약효가 있는
property[prá:pərti] 성분, 속성 longevity[la:ndʒévəti] 수명, 장수
toxic[tá:ksik] 유독한 application[æ̀plikéiʃən] 적용(성)
extract[ikstrǽkt] 추출하다 atomic[ətá:mik] 원자의
solvent[sá:lvənt] 용제(물질을 용해하는 데 쓰는 액체)
alluvial[əlú:viəl] 충적토의 riverbed[rívərbèd] 강바닥
silt[silt] 토사 dissolve[dizá:lv] 용해되다
evaporate[ivǽpəreit] 증발하다
observatory[əbzá:rvətɔ:ri] 관측소
instrument[ínstrəmənt] 기구
parabolic[pæ̀rəbá:lik] 포물선 모양의
magnify[mǽgnifai] 확대하다 distant[dístənt] 멀리 있는
prohibitively[prouhíbətivli] 엄두를 못 낼 만큼
modification[mà:difikéiʃən] 수정 alternative[ɔ:ltá:rnətiv] 대안
reflective[rifléktiv] (빛을) 반사하는 state[steit] 상태
curved[kə:rvd] 굴곡진

주제 문장: 수은의 특징들은 수은을 다양한 용도에 적합하게 만든다.

(A) 일부 금속은 수은과 섞이면 용해된다.
(B) 수은의 섭취는 인간에게 위험하다.
(C) 액체 수은은 매우 효과적으로 빛을 반사한다.
(D) 수은은 충분한 열에 노출되면 증발할 것이다.

7 1978년에, 미국 정부는 위성 위치 확인 시스템(GPS)이 된 최초의 위성 네트워크를 착수했는데, 이것은 수신기를 갖춘 장치에 시간과 장소 정보를 전송하는 항법 시스템이다. 그때 이래로, 미군은 이 기술에 점점 더 의존하게 되었고, 이는 만약 위기 중에 GPS를 이용할 수 없다면 어떤 일이 발생할지에 대한 우려로 이어졌다. 이 문제를 해결하기 위해, 국방부는 GPS의 대안으로 쓰일 것으로 의도된 시간 관성 측정 장치(TIMU)라고 불리는 새로운 항법 도구를 개발했다.

TIMU는 페니 동전의 3분의 1 크기의 매우 작은 장치로, 일곱 개의 필수 부품을 가지고 있다. 이것들 중 첫 번째는 원자시계인데, 이것은 원자 주위를 도는 양전하와 음전하 입자인 전자에 의해 방출되는 에너지의 빈도를 측정함으로써 매우 정확한 시간을 유지하는 기구이다. TIMU는 또한 장치의 방위와 움직임의 방향을 감지할 수 있는 세 개의 자이로스코프를 포함한다. 마지막으로, TIMU는 이동 속도를 계산하는 세 개의 가속도계를 가지고 있다. 시간, 방향, 그리고 속도를 측정함으로써, 이러한 기구들은 장치를 갖춘 사람의 움직임을 추적할 수 있고, 시작점이 확인되었다고 가정할 때, 위성으로부터의 정보에 의존하지 않고도 지속적으로 갱신된 위치 정보를 제공할 수 있다. 이것은 GPS가 일시적으로 장애가 있는 경우에 군 부대에 항법 지원이 가능할 것임을 의미한다. TIMU의 추가적인 장점은 해수면 아래 또는 동굴과 터널 안처럼, GPS 위성 신호가 도달할 수 없는 환경에서도 사용될 수 있다는 것이다.

satellite[sǽtəlait] 위성 navigation[næ̀vigéiʃən] 항법
equipped with ~을 갖춘 receiver[risí:vər] 수신기
dependent[dipéndənt] 의존하는 concern[kənsá:rn] 우려
unavailable[ʌ̀nəvéiləbl] 이용할 수 없는 crisis[kráisis] 위기
address[ədrés] 해결하다 serve[sə:rv] (특정한 용도로) 쓰이다
miniscule[mínəskjù:l] 매우 작은 frequency[frí:kwənsi] 빈도
emit[imít] 방출하다, 내보내다 electron[iléktra:n] 전자
particle[pá:rtikl] 입자 atom[ǽtəm] 원자
gyroscope[dʒáirəskoup] 자이로스코프(평형 상태를 측정하는 데
사용하는 기구) capable of ~을 할 수 있는
orientation[ɔ̀:riəntéiʃən] 방위
accelerometer[əksèlərá:mitər] 가속도계
calculate[kǽlkjuleit] 계산하다 rate[reit] 속도
track[træk] 추적하다 assume[əsú:m] 가정하다
identify[aidéntifai] 확인하다 rely on ~에 의존하다
temporarily[tèmpərérəli] 일시적으로
disabled[diséibld] 장애가 있는

주제 문장: TIMU는 미국 국방부에 의해 GPS의 대안으로 개발된 장치이다.

(A) GPS 정보를 받을 수 있는 민간 장치는 점점 더 보편화되었다.
(B) TIMU는 시간을 측정하는 아원자 입자에 의존하는 원자시계를 포함한다.
(C) 인식된 시작점으로부터의 이동은 위성의 도움 없이 측정된다.
(D) 해상과 지하 환경에서의 항법은 TIMU를 이용하면 가능하다.

8

낙타의 혹은 필요할 때 이용될 수 있는 물의 비축분을 저장하기 위해 사용된다는 널리 알려진 오해가 있다. 이 동물이 긴 시간 동안 물을 마시지 않고 갈 수 있게 해주는 많은 육체적 적응을 가지기는 하지만, 혹은 그 중 하나가 아니다. 하지만, 혹은 간과되어서는 안 될 두 가지 중요한 기능을 가지는데 이는 그 기능들이 낙타가 혹독한 사막 환경에서 생존하는 것에 필수적이기 때문이다.

우선, 낙타의 혹은 주로 지방 조직으로 구성된다. 다 자란 낙타는 혹에 최대 36킬로그램까지의 지방을 보유하고 낙타는 먹이를 찾아낼 수 없을 때와 같은 사막에서의 흔한 상황에서 대사 작용으로 이 물질을 에너지로 변화시킬 수 있다. 낙타가 아무것도 먹지 않고 다니는 것이 길어질수록, 그것의 혹은 더 작아질 것이다. 만약 혹이 완전히 없어진다면, 낙타는 굶주림 직전의 상태일 가능성이 높고 영양분을 받지 않는 한 곧 죽을 것이다. 다행히도, 낙타는 충분한 먹이를 섭취하고 쉴 기회를 가지기만 하면 혹을 매우 빠르게 보충할 수 있다.

또 다른 이점은 혹이 낙타가 사막의 극단적인 기온에 더 쉽게 대응할 수 있도록 해준다는 것이다. 혹은 낙타를 과열로부터 막아주는 한두 가지의 체온 조절 기능을 가지고 있다. 먼저, 지방은 열이 낭비되는 것을 어렵게 만드는 단열재이다. 낙타의 지방이 대량으로 등 위에 산더미로 저장되기 때문에, 낙타의 나머지 몸통은 단열이 거의 되지 않는데, 이는 열이 갇히지 않고 공기 중으로 지속해서 방출된다는 것을 의미한다. 혹이 체온에 영향을 주는 또 다른 방법은 혹의 존재가 낙타 몸통의 표면적을 늘려준다는 것이다. 표면적 용적비가 큰 동물들은 열 에너지를 더욱 효율적으로 내뿜을 수 있고, 따라서, 과열될 가능성이 적다.

misconception[mìskənsépʃən] 오해
hump[hʌmp] (낙타 등의) 혹 reserve[rizə́ːrv] 비축분
draw upon ~을 이용하다 adaptation[æ̀dæptéiʃən] 적응
overlook[òuvərlúk] 간과하다 harsh[haːrʃ] 혹독한
tissue[tíʃuː] (세포로 이루어진) 조직
metabolize[mətǽbəlaiz] 대사 작용으로 변화시키다
brink[briŋk] 직전 starvation[staːrvéiʃən] 굶주림
nourishment[nə́ːriʃmənt] 영양분 replenish[ripléniʃ] 보충하다
cope[koup] 대응하다
thermoregulatory[θə̀ːrmərégjulətɔ̀ːri] 체온 조절의
insulator[ínsəleitər] 단열재
dissipate[dísipeit] 낭비되다, 소멸되다
mound[maund] 더미, 언덕 insulation[ìnsəléiʃən] 단열
trap[træp] 가두다 surface area 표면적 volume ratio 용적비
radiate[réidieit] 내뿜다 thermal[θə́ːrml] 열의

주제 문장: 낙타의 혹은 낙타가 사막에서 생존할 수 있게 해주는 많은 중요한 역할을 한다.
(A) 낙타의 등에 저장된 지방은 먹이가 부족할 때 에너지로 사용될 수 있다.
(B) 낙타는 물 없이 장시간 동안 갈 수 있다.
(C) 낙타는 혹 때문에 체온을 더 잘 조절할 수 있다.
(D) 낙타의 혹에 포함된 조직은 효율적인 단열재이다.

9

전자 텔레비전이 실질적으로 미국 대중의 일상생활의 일부로 들어서게 된 것은 1930년대 후반과 1940년대 초기 무렵이었다. 1950년대에 이르자, 사람들 대부분은 텔레비전을 가지고 있었고 미국 문화의 원동력은 이미 철저하게 변해 있었다. 사람들은 운동, 독서 등의 활동을 하기보다 거실에서 더 많은 시간을 보내고 있었다. 사실, 1950년과 1955년 사이에 텔레비전의 평균 시청시간은 1440퍼센트나 상승했다. 이러한 현상은 사회적 일과뿐만 아니라 라디오, 신문 등 다른 대중 매체에도 커다란 영향을 미쳤는데 특히 영화에 가장 큰 영향을 미쳤다. 국내 영화산업은 집에서 즐길 수 있는 텔레비전 쇼의 인기에 가장 많은 영향을 받은 산업이었다.

TV의 편리함은 집에서 벗어나 오락을 즐기고 싶어하는 대중의 욕구에 의지했던 영화 산업과의 본격적인 경쟁을 유발했다. 하지만 텔레비전은 표를 사고 극장까지 갔다가 돌아와야 하는 번거로움 없이, 극장에서 누릴 수 있는 시각적인 즐거움을 그대로 제공해 주었다. 간단히 말해, 사람들은 점점 더 집에서 나가기를 원하지 않게 되었다. 이에 따라, 1950년대에는 TV가 미국 오락 문화에 준 충격의 여파로 영화산업이 '빈사' 상태에 이르게 되었다.

미국 전역의 영화 스튜디오들은 재빨리 영화 산업의 사그라지는 인기에 대응하기 위한 대책을 강구해 냈지만 별다른 효과는 없었다. 텔레비전은 여전히 흑백이었기 때문에, 영화 제작자들은 즉시 컬러 영화에 중점을 두었고 시네마스코프, 테크니컬러, 그리고 입체 영화 등의 영화기법을 시도하기도 했다. 이외에도 영화 화면을 넓히고, 안락의자를 설치하고, 무료 스낵을 제공하는 등 다른 시도들도 행해졌다. 이러한 유혹들이 처음에는 군중을 끌어들였지만, 관객들은 곧 흥미를 잃었고 끊임없이 진화하는 텔레비전의 세계로 돌아갔다.

이에 따라, 영화산업은 성인용 영화를 제공하는 방법으로 관객을 끌기 위한 또 다른 시도를 했다. 폭력, 비속어, 그리고 무엇보다도 선정적인 내용이 주류 영화의 일부분이 되었다. 이것은 영화의 큰 장점이었는데, 이는 그 당시 텔레비전은 수많은 어린이 시청자 때문에 그러한 내용을 내보낼 수 없었기 때문이다. 이즈음, 텔레비전 등장 이전에 한때 누렸던 1인당 점유비율에는 미치지 못했지만, 영화의 인기는 서서히 올라가기 시작했다. 불행히도, 텔레비전은 결국에는 영화를 따라잡았고 성인 대상의 쇼와 심야 특별프로그램을 제작하기 시작하여, 영화 관객은 다시 한번 감소했다. 영화의 인기를 재점화하려는 모든 시도에도 불구하고, 극장은 오늘날까지도 미국 오락 산업에서 자신의 지위를 지키는 데 있어서 고전을 면치 못하고 있다.

drastically[dræstikəli] 철저하게   routine[ruːtíːn] 일과
get away from ~에서 벗어나다   hassle[hǽsl] 번거로움
counteract[kàuntərǽkt] 대응하다   futilely[fjúːtli] 효과 없이
cinematic[sìnəmǽtik] 영화에 관한
Cinemascope[sínəməskòup] 시네마스코프(와이드스크린 방식의
영화; 상표명)
Technicolor[téknikÀlər] 테크니컬러(천연색 영화의 일종; 상표명)
reclining seat 안락의자   lure[luər] 유혹   vulgar[vʌ́lgər] 비속한
plethora[pléθərə] 과다   per capita 1인당
dwindle[dwíndl] 감소하다   reignite[rìːignáit] 재점화하다

지시: 지문 요약을 위한 도입 문장이 아래에 주어져 있다. 지문의 가장 중요한 내용을 나타내는 보기 3개를 골라 요약을 완성하시오. 어떤 문장은 지문에 언급되지 않은 내용이나 사소한 정보를 담고 있으므로 요약에 포함되지 않는다. **이 문제는 2점이다.**

> 텔레비전의 출현은 대중 오락의 더 전통적인 형태인 영화에 광범위한 영향을 미쳤다.
> - (A) 대부분의 사람들은 자신의 집에 남아 텔레비전을 보는 편안함을 극장에 가는 불편함보다 선호했다.
> - (E) 영화 산업 지도자들은 텔레비전을 제치고 영화의 인기를 회복하기 위해 새로운 창안을 내놓았다.
> - (F) 영화를 높은 연령의 관객들에게 맞춘 것은 영화에 대한 열광에 잠시 동안만 영향을 미쳤다.

(B) 극장에서 상영된 거의 모든 영화는 텔레비전에서도 방영되었다.
(C) 텔레비전이 나왔을 때, 그것은 사람들이 운동과 독서에 더 적은 시간을 투자하게 했다.
(D) 어린이 시청자들은 텔레비전에서 성인 대상의 쇼를 보는 것이 허용되지 않았다.

10 식물은 다른 종들과 마찬가지로 그들의 생명을 위협하는 포식에 민감하다. 초식동물의 지속적인 공격은 식물에 끊임없는 위협이 되고 있으며, 이는 식물의 자기방어 기제의 발달을 촉진했다. 식물의 자기방어 기제에 대한 연구에서 이런 방어 기제가 왜, 그리고 어떻게 발달했는지를 설명하려는 수많은 이론이 1950년대부터 수없이 제기되어 왔지만, 아직까지도 확실한 결론을 도출하지는 못하고 있다. 과학자들이 현시점에서 알고 있는 것은 이런 방어 수단들이 계속 발전하고 있다는 것과 식물과 초식동물은 화학적 방어기술을 앞다투어 발전시키는 일종의 무기 경쟁에 몰두하고 있다는 것이다. 식물들이 방어 수단을 마련하면, 곧이어 초식 포식자(주로 곤충)들도 식물에 접근할 수 있게 자신을 적응시켜서 이에 대응한다.

각각의 식물은 적의 접근이나 공격에 대응하기 위해 각기 다른 방법을 사용하거나, 그것들의 조합을 사용한다. 사시나무인 'Populus Tremuloides'는 좌우 폭이 좁은 잎꼭지를 가지고 있는데 이로 인해 어떤 작은 미풍에도 잎사귀가 흔들리는 결과를 초래한다. 이러한 떨림은 곤충이 잎의 표면에 붙어있는 것을 어렵게 만든다. 수많은 식물은 잎이 완전히 피면 이탈하는 두꺼운 모상체의 층을 발달시키는데, 이는 모든 종류의 곤충에 대해 물리적인 방어벽으로 기능한다. 이 두 가지의 방어 수단은 앞으로

다가올 수 있는 위험을 예방하기 위한 것이지만, 이미 와 있는 침략자에게 반격을 가하기 위한 방호 수단도 일부 존재한다. 이것의 한 예는 'Populus Deltoides'인데, 이 식물은 곤충이 줄기에 달라붙으면 턱잎의 아린을 통해서 송진을 분비한다. 이 송진은 대부분의 적에게 해로운 유독물질을 함유하고 있다. 또 다른 방법으로, 'Populus Grandidentata'는 포식자가 자신의 영양분을 모두 먹지 못하도록 하기 위해 외부에 꽃의 꿀샘을 만들어내는 방어수단을 가진다.

좀 더 최근의 연구는 병원균의 공격에 대한 식물의 일차적인 반응이 식물의 생존에 있어서 가장 중요하다는 것을 보여준다. 이 반응은 바로 식물의 방어 기제를 발동시키지만, 그것이 일어나는 경로에 대해서는 아직까지 밝혀지지 않고 있다. 현탁액 속에서 배양된 식물 세포를 이용한 최근의 연구는 병원균에의 노출이 시토졸 칼슘 농축액의 수위 변화, 반발성 산소류의 생성, 단백질 키나아제의 활성화, 그리고 새로운 지질 2차 전달자인 인지질산의 배출을 초래함을 밝혔다. 이러한 모든 반응은 식물이 외부 침입자를 인식한 후 1에서 4분 이내에 일어나서 거의 즉각적으로 방어 신호를 보내주고 식물을 보호해 준다.

susceptible[səséptəbl] 민감한   predation[pridéiʃən] 포식
herbivore[hə́ːrbəvɔ̀ːr] 초식동물   arms race 무기 경쟁
thereof[ðɛərʌ́v] 그것의   quaking aspen 사시나무
laterally[lǽtərəli] 좌우로   petiole[pétiòul] 잎꼭지
vibrate[váibreit] 흔들리다   breeze[briːz] 미풍
trichome[tríkoum] 모상체(식물체 표면의 돌기모양의 구조)
abscise[æbsáiz] (잎이) 이탈하다
secrete[sikríːt] 분비하다   resin[rézin] 송진
stipular[stípjulər] 턱잎의
bud scale 아린(식물에서 꽃이나 잎이 될 연한 부분을 보호하는 비늘
모양의 구조)   toxin[táksin] 유독물질
extraneous[ikstréiniəs] 외부에 발생한   floral[flɔ́ːrəl] 꽃의
nectary[néktəri] 꿀샘   pathogen[pǽθədʒən] 병원균
culture[kʌ́ltʃər] 배양하다   suspension[səspénʃən] 현탁액
cytosolic calcium 시토졸 칼슘   protein kinase 단백질 키나아제
lipid[lípid] 지질(脂質)   phosphatidic acid 인지질산

지시: 지문 요약을 위한 도입 문장이 아래에 주어져 있다. 지문의 가장 중요한 내용을 나타내는 보기 3개를 골라 요약을 완성하시오. 어떤 문장은 지문에 언급되지 않은 내용이나 사소한 정보를 담고 있으므로 요약에 포함되지 않는다. **이 문제는 2점이다.**

> 위험에 대응하여, 식물들은 파괴적인 침입자를 막는 방어 시스템을 이용한다.
> - (A) 식물들이 침입자에 대항해 스스로를 지키는 방법은 계속 발달하고 있다.
> - (C) 식물이 어떠한 박테리아의 신호나 바이러스의 원인 인자에 즉각 반응하는 것은 중요하다.
> - (F) 위협에 대한 식물의 반응은 숨은 적을 가까이 오지 못하게 하는 것에서부터 눈앞의 포식자에게 보복하는 것까지 매우 다양할 수 있다.

(B) 일부 포식자들은 식물의 꽃 속 꿀샘에서 영양분을 섭취한다.
(D) 많은 식물들은 침입자들이 가까이 왔을 때 펴지는 끝이 날카

로운 층을 가지고 있다.
(E) 연구원들은 식물이 방출하는 유독물질을 분리하는 방법을 알아냈다.

11 중세 유럽의 초기에는, 책은 존재하지 않았거나 최소한 현대에 널리 사용되고 있는 형태와 분량은 아니었다. 사람들의 대다수는 문맹이었고, 주로 영웅적 행위나 괴물과 관련된 문화적 이야기들은 이야기꾼, 음유시인, 시인 등에 의해서 구전되었다. 그러나 그 역사적인 시기를 거치면서, 인쇄된 책이 등장했고 이는 유럽 사회사에 있어 하나의 전환점이 되었다. 신화, 이야기, 역사적 서술을 보존하는 방법은 거의 전적으로 문서화되었다.

책을 만드는 전통적인 방법은 수년에 걸친 시간을 요하는 고된 작업으로 이루어졌다. 첫 번째 단계는 속로 쓸 동물 가죽을 보존 처리하는 것이었고, 그다음에는 잉크로 쓸 안료를 만들어 배합한 후 깃펜을 준비했으며, 마지막으로 실제로 글씨를 적기 위해서 각 페이지에 선을 그었다. 이러한 모든 준비 과정이 끝나면, 책의 모든 글씨는 서기에 의해 손으로 쓰여야 했고, 이 작업이 끝나면 책은 금이나 은, 또는 구리로 된 나뭇잎으로 화려하게 장식될 수 있었다. 따라서 단지 한 권의 책을 만드는 데도 노동의 집약과 비싼 생산 비용이 필요했는데, 이는 아주 적은 수의 책이 만들어졌고 엘리트계층만이 책을 소유할 수 있었으리라는 것을 의미한다.

의심할 여지 없이, 중세 시대에 대부분의 책에 대한 통제권을 가지고 책의 보관을 책임졌던 것은 가톨릭 교회였다. 그 당시의 교회는 사회의 중심이었고 귀족보다도 높은 지위에 있었으므로, 문학을 신의 영역으로 격상시킬 수 있는 지위에 있었다. 수도사들은 원본을 복사하는 임무를 맡았고, 모든 성직자는 글을 읽을 줄 알고 필사나 삽화에 재능이 있어야만 했다. 14세기에 이르러 책, 특히 성경에 대한 수요가 급격히 증가하면서, 수도원들은 오로지 이런 업무만을 전담하게 되었다. 흥미롭게도, 이 수도원들은 종교 서적뿐만 아니라 그리스, 로마 시대의 문학, 과학, 철학 등에 관한 서적들로 가득했던 도서관을 운영했는데, 수도원이 이런 역할을 수행하지 않았더라면 이러한 그리스, 로마 시대의 서적들이 오늘날까지 읽힐 수 있을 정도로 잘 보존되지 못했을지도 모른다.

1445년, Johann Gutenberg라는 이름을 가진 한 남자가 인쇄기를 발명해 유럽인의 삶을 완전히 바꿔버렸고, 궁극적으로는 전 세계인의 삶을 바꾸었다. Gutenberg의 인쇄기는 적은 비용의 원자재와 노동으로 빠르게 책을 생산할 수 있었다. 이는 그 당시 유럽 사회에 두 가지의 큰 영향을 미쳤다. 교황권의 약화와 일반 대중으로의 책의 보급이 그것이었다. 수도원 밖에서도 책을 인쇄할 수 있었을 뿐 아니라 저렴한 가격으로 책을 널리 이용할 수 있게 되어, 서민들도 성경이나 문학 작품을 구입할 수 있었다.

illiterate [ilítərət] 문맹의 **deed** [di:d] 행위
monstrosity [mɑnstrάsəti] 괴물 **orally** [ɔ́:rəli] 구전으로
minstrel [mínstrəl] 음유시인 **turning point** 전환점
narration [næréiʃən] 서술 **arduous** [ά:rdʒuəs] 고된
cure [kjuər] 보존 처리하다 **hide** [haid] 짐승의 가죽

pigment [pígmənt] 안료 **quill** [kwil] 깃펜 **rule** [ru:l] 선을 긋다
preparatory [pripǽrətɔ̀:ri] 준비의
long-hand [lɔ́:ŋhænd] 손으로 쓰기 **scribe** [skraib] 서기
illuminate [ilú:mənèit] 장식하다 **monastery** [mάnəstèri] 수도원
solely [sóulli] 오로지 **sacred** [séikrid] 종교의
papal [péipəl] 교황의 **dissemination** [disèmənéiʃən] 보급

지시: 지문 요약을 위한 도입 문장이 아래에 주어져 있다. 지문의 가장 중요한 내용을 나타내는 보기 3개를 골라 요약을 완성하시오. 어떤 문장은 지문에 언급되지 않은 내용이나 사소한 정보를 담고 있으므로 요약에 포함되지 않는다. **이 문제는 2점이다.**

> **중세 시대 동안, 책의 발전과 확산은 유럽 사회의 성장에 영향을 미쳤다.**
>
> · (C) 중세 시대의 문서는 종교 지배 당국에 의해 관리되고 만들어졌다.
> · (D) 손으로 만든 책은 많은 양의 노력과 시간을 필요로 했으며 일반인들의 사용을 위한 것이 아니었다.
> · (E) 대중 문화로의 책의 확산은 문서의 대량 생산 가능성의 결과였다.

(A) 중세 사회의 대부분의 사람들은 가톨릭 교회의 독실한 신자였다.

(B) 고대 서구 문명의 몇몇 중요한 문학 작품들은 열등한 인쇄 기술 때문에 유실되었다.

(F) 공공 도서관은 읽고 쓰기를 배우고 싶어한 사람들을 위해 교회에 의해 세워졌다.

12 종종 오해의 소지가 있는 Tin Pan Alley라는 명칭은 19세기 후반에서 20세기 초반까지 뉴욕 시에 모여서 대중 음악계를 이끌었던 음악 제작자와 작곡가들의 집단을 뜻한다. 원래 맨해튼의 Broadway와 Sixth Avenue 사이에 이러한 음악 산업의 선구자들이 거주하던 West 28th Street라는 특정 장소가 있었는데, 그게 이 집단이 'Alley(골목)'라고 불리게 된 이유이다. 수많은 피아니스트가 바로 이 거리에서 고객들을 끌기 위해 유행가를 연주했다. 비평가들은 그 소리를 양철 냄비의 소음에 비유했다. 비록 비난의 의미였지만, 그 지역의 상가 단지들은 Tin Pan Alley로 전 세계에 알려지게 되었다.

Tin Pan Alley의 시작은 일반적으로 많은 음악 제작자가 한 장소로 모여 들어온 시기인 1885년경으로 알려졌다. 원래 Tin Pan Alley의 상점들이 등장하게 된 이유는 낱장 악보 형태로 팔리는 많은 버전의 유행가를 인쇄하던 음악 제작자들 간의 경쟁 때문이었다. 멜로디에 대한 저작권 통제가 극도로 미미했기 때문에, 어떤 음악 제작자도 개별적으로는 유행을 따라갈 수 없었다. 이러한 이유로, 뉴욕 내 다른 지역의 개인 상인으로부터 사업의 주도권을 빼앗아 오기 위한 방편으로 일단의 제작 상점들은 서로 협력해서 Tin Pan Alley를 형성했다.

비록 이러한 작은 상점들은 미국에서 가장 큰 음악 상점들이 되었지만, 20세기 중반 즈음 음악 산업의 격동적인 변화에 따라 폐업하게 되었다. 정확히 무엇이 Tin Pan Alley의 몰락을 유발했고, 인식할 수 있는 독립체로서의 집단이 궁극적으로 언제 와해되었는지에 대해서는 논란이 있다. 어떤 전문들은 라디오와

축음기의 등장이 낱장 악보를 대체한 1930년대에 집단의 피할 수 없는 운명이 결정되었다고 생각한다. 할리우드의 주요 스튜디오가 Tin Pan Alley의 몇몇 가장 큰 제작사들을 사들인 것 또한 이 시기였다.

그러나 다른 전문가들은 1950년대에 로큰롤 음악이 등장하고 나서야 Tin Pan Alley가 마침내 운명을 결정지었다고 주장한다. 이 관점에 따르면, Tin Pan Alley의 제작자들은 이 새로운 형식의 음악의 지속력을 매우 과소평가했고, 소비자 취향의 변화에 적응하는 데 실패했다. Tin Pan Alley의 제작물들은 시대에 뒤떨어졌기 때문에, 인기가 없어졌고 제작해도 벌이가 되지 않았다.

이 지역의 상점들은 문을 닫았지만, Tin Pan Alley가 대중음악에 미쳤던 광범위한 영향은 음악 산업에 영원히 남았다. 유명한 연주자뿐만 아니라 아마추어 가수와 음악 팬들도 제작사를 이용하였다. 아마추어 가수와 음악 팬들에게 판매하기 위해서, 음악 상점들은 인기 있는 곡을 숙련되지 않은 음악가들도 읽고 연주할 수 있는 음악으로 고쳐야 했다. 이러한 상황 속에서 생겨난 음악의 다양성은 미국 대중음악에서 전례 없는 창작의 분출을 부추겼다.

misleading[mislíːdiŋ] 오해의 소지가 있는
assemblage[əsémblidʒ] 집단   congregate[káŋgrigèit] 모이다
dwell[dwel] 거주하다   alley[éli] 골목
clientele[klàiəntél] 고객들   tin pan 양철냄비
cluster[klʌ́stər] 단지, 무리   numerous[njúːmərəs] 많은
go out of business 폐업하다   shift[ʃift] 변화
demise[dimáiz] 몰락   entity[éntəti] 존재
phonograph[fóunəgræ̀f] 축음기   replace[ripléis] 대체하다
seal one's fate 운명을 결정짓다   plugger[plʌ́gər] 팬
tune[tjuːn] 곡   explosion[iksplóuʒən] 분출

지시: 지문 요약을 위한 도입 문장이 아래에 주어져 있다. 지문의 가장 중요한 내용을 나타내는 보기 3개를 골라 요약을 완성하시오. 어떤 문장은 지문에 언급되지 않은 내용이나 사소한 정보를 담고 있으므로 요약에 포함되지 않는다. 이 문제는 2점이다.

> 맨해튼의 특정 거리를 따라 있는 음악 상가의 유명한 단지인 Tin Pan Alley는 대중 음악 산업의 선두가 되었다.
>
> · (B) 음악 산업의 변화는 Tin Pan Alley의 몰락으로 이어졌지만, 정확히 왜 그리고 언제 그것이 무너졌는지는 논쟁되고 있다.
> · (D) 그러한 구역의 형성은 당시 통제가 없었던 악보 출판 체제가 원인이었다.
> · (E) 모든 사람이 일반적인 낱장 악보를 읽을 수 있던 게 아니었기 때문에, 고안된 대체 버전들은 독창성을 증가시켰다.

(A) 이 거리에서 음악가들이 만들어낸 소리는 Tin Pan Alley라는 명칭이 생기게 했다.
(C) 연극 방식보다 열등한 음악의 출현은 사람들이 Tin Pan Alley를 외면하게 했다.
(F) Tin Pan Alley의 거의 모든 고객들은 대형 극단의 감독과 제작자들이었다.

01 The Potlatch

p.300

1. (C)	2. (B)	3. (C)
4. (A)	5. (A)	6. (C)
7. (D)	8. (B)	9. 3rd

10. (A)-2단락, (C)-4단락, (E)-3단락

1 Potlatch는 미국의 태평양 북서부와 캐나다의 브리티시 컬럼비아 지역의 토착민 사회에서 행해지던 의례적인 재산의 분배이다. 이 관례는 주로 공동주택이나 넓은 야외에서 거행되어, [1B]새로운 아이의 탄생이나 젊은 부부의 결혼, 또는 성공적인 사냥 시즌 등의 특정한 사회적 사건의 기념 행사로서 기능했다. [1A]이 행사는 군사적 동맹이나 혈연적 결속을 공개적으로 알리는 것 외에도, [1D]상속을 기념하거나 기록 문서 대신 금액 지불 여부를 기록하는 데 이용될 수 있었다. 그러나 potlatch의 가장 주된 목적은 객관적이고 도덕적인 방법으로 부족 내의 부를 재분배하는 수단을 제공하여, 근본적으로 공동 환경에서 주최자가 물질적 재화의 독점자로서 느끼는 정신적인 부담감을 덜어 주는 것이었다.

2 Potlatch는 세 개의 주요 행사로 이루어져 있었는데, 모두 potlatch의 포괄적인 의미와 본질적으로 연관되어 있었다. [3]그중 첫째는 보통 언어나 물개 고기 등 수많은 종류의 음식을 먹으며 향연을 벌이는 것으로, 이것은 계절적으로 풍부한 생선, 성공적인 사냥으로부터 얻은 고래고기, 또는 기타 잉여 음식을 이웃과 나누던 전통을 반영한다. 예를 들어, 종족의 연장자나 참석을 위해 장거리를 여행해 온 사람들, 혹은 전통적인 의술사들과 같이 존경을 받는 손님들은 대단한 격식을 갖추어 자리가 배정되고 접대받았는데, 가장 많은 정성이 담긴 많은 양의 요리를 대접받았다. 식사의 호화로운 정도에 주최자의 관대함이 암묵적으로 나타났기 때문에, 식사는 일상적으로 사용하는 식기 대신 화려한 장식의 손으로 조각되거나 그림이 그려진 축제용 접시에 올려졌는데, 이러한 접시는 가보급 가치를 가진 경우가 많았고 어떤 때는 소형 카누만큼 거대한 경우도 있었다.

3 Potlatch의 또 다른 요소는 춤인데 노래와 함께 공연되는 경우가 많았고, 성공적인 추수를 기원하거나 죽은 친족을 기리기 위해, 또는 특별한 친족 관계의 결성을 축하하기 위해서 등 다양한 종교적 목적을 위해서 공연되었다. [5]각각의 가족마다 독자적인 민속춤을 추기 때문에, 이 모임은 주최자가 그가 이어받은 전통을 외부 부족의 구성원들을 포함한 다른 이들에게 과시할 비길 데 없는 기회를 제공해 주었다. 만약 초대받은 손님이 자신이 갈고닦은 전통 춤을 보여주고자 한다면, 먼저 허락을 구하거나 특정한 권유를 받아야 했다. 행사가 진행되는 동안, 일부 참가자들은 가족이나 조상 중 누군가에게 춤사위와 음악에 대한 지식을 물려주었던 영적 존재를 그려 넣은 가면을 쓰기도 했다. 주최자는 예복으로 단추가 달린 blanket

(인디언이 입었던 윗옷의 일종)을 입는 경우가 많았는데, 이것은 나중에 손님의 내방에 고마움을 표하고 다음 potlatch를 위해 춤을 기억해 줄 것을 당부하기 위한 선물로 주어졌다.

4 비록 선물을 주는 행위에 암시된 관대함이라는 개념이 이 관습을 행하는 주된 이유가 아니기는 하지만, 선물을 주는 관습이 세 번째이자 potlatch의 특성을 나타내는 가장 중요한 요소이다. 이는 빚을 갚고, 이웃에 의해서 제공된 노고에 대해 사례하며, 수립된 관계를 이어가기 위한 의식일 뿐만 아니라, 물질적인 소유로부터 속죄하고 공동의 가치를 다시금 분명히 하기 위한 기회였다. ⁷카누, 은대구 기름, 염소털 담요뿐 아니라 노래, 이름, 가문 문양까지도 선물로 내놓았는데, 이는 거의 파산에 이르도록 일족의 재산을 탕진시켰다. 때때로 재물이 고정되어 있거나 potlatch 장소로 가져오기 너무 번거로운 경우에는 영혼의 해방과 카타르시스의 분출이라는 사회의 지배적인 철학에 따라서 파괴해 버렸다. **구리는 그러한 물건 중 하나로 자주 부서진 상태로 운반되었는데, 이로써 금전적 가치는 낮추었지만 문화적인 의의는 강조했다.** 일단 조각을 받으면, potlatch를 기념하기 위해 그것을 색칠하거나 조각하는 것이 일반적이었다.

5 물질적 재산으로부터 속죄하는 사회의 관행이 근본적인 노동윤리와 어긋난다고 여겨지는 서구사회에 이러한 토착민들을 융화시키기 위해서, 미국과 캐나다 정부는 모두 1884년에 potlatch 관습을 금지하였다. 두 정부는 potlatch를 더 많은 재화에 노출된 해안가의 공동체에서 횡행하게 된 비이성적인 부의 파괴행위로 간주했다. 그 결과, potlatch를 행했던 사람들은 1951년 법이 폐지되기 전까지 박해를 피해 숨어서 비밀리에 의식을 행했다. 현대에 이르러, 이 관습은 졸업식, 태어날 아기를 위한 파티, 각종 기념일 등의 수많은 문화적 행사를 포함하도록 바뀌었다. 형식은 덜 엄격해졌지만, 이 관습의 지속적인 수행은 전통이 기억되고 다음 세대로 전승될 수 있게 해주고 있다.

indigenous[indídʒənəs] 토착의 longhouse[lɔ́:ŋhàus] 공동주택
marker[má:rkər] 기념행사 commemorate[kəmémərèit] 기념하다
in lieu of ~ 대신에 inherently[inhíərəntli] 본질적으로, 본래
comprehensive[kàmprihénsiv] 포괄적인 seal[si:l] 물개
tacit[tǽsit] 암묵적인 extravagance[ikstrǽvəgəns] 호화로움
ornate[ɔ:rnéit] 화려한 장식의 heirloom[ɛ́ərlù:m] 가보
devotional[divóuʃənl] 종교적인 robust[roubʌ́st] 양이 많은
kinship[kínʃip] 친족관계 unparalleled[ʌnpǽrəlèid] 비길 데 없는
bidding[bídiŋ] 권유 bequeath[bikwí:ð] 물려주다
purge[pə:rdʒ] 속죄하다 eulachon oil 은대구 기름
crest[krest] 가문 문양 anchored[ǽŋkərd] 고정된
cumbersome[kʌ́mbərsəm] 번거로운 comply with ~에 따르다
deliverance[dilívərəns] 해방 cathartic[kəθá:rtik] 카타르시스의
rampant[rǽmpənt] 횡행하는

1 1단락에 따르면, 다음 중 potlatch의 목적으로 언급되지 않은 것은?

(A) 서로 다른 사회 단위와의 관계를 기념했다.

(B) 인생의 주요한 행사를 기념하기 위해 행해졌다.

(C) 부자들이 그들의 귀중품을 나눠주는 것을 의무적이게 만들

었다.

(D) 소유권의 변화에 대한 공시의 역할을 했다.

2 지문의 단어 "objective"와 의미상 가장 유사한 것은?

(A) 느긋한

(B) 편견이 없는

(C) 약삭빠른

(D) 박식한

3 다음 중 potlatch를 소유한 사회에 대해 추론할 수 있는 것은?

(A) 장자 상속은 아주 흔한 관습이었다.

(B) 엄격하게 계급에 따른 구조를 가지고 있었다.

(C) 생계 수단으로 바다에 의존하고 있었다.

(D) 빈부 차이가 컸다.

4 지문의 단어 "tacit"과 의미상 가장 유사한 것은?

(A) 암시된

(B) 낡은

(C) 헛된

(D) 화려한

5 3단락에 따르면, 다음 중 춤 관습에 대해 사실인 것은?

(A) 각각의 가족은 특유의 춤 방식을 가지고 있었다.

(B) 손님들은 종종 춤을 추는 사람들에게 기념품을 선물했다.

(C) 각각의 손님들은 조상을 기리는 춤을 추도록 요청받았다.

(D) 주최자의 춤 의상을 받은 사람은 누구든 다음 potlatch를 주최하곤 했다.

6 지문의 단어 "their"가 가리키는 것은?

(A) 구성원

(B) 부족

(C) 손님

(D) 전통 춤

7 4단락에서, 글쓴이는 왜 "even songs, names, and crests"를 언급하는가?

(A) 빈곤한 가족들조차 potlatch에서 선물을 줄 수 있었음을 보여주기 위해

(B) potlatch 의식의 종교적인 요소를 강조하기 위해

(C) 가족의 재정에 있어서 이 개념의 중요성을 설명하기 위해

(D) 과도한 potlatch에 대한 비물질적인 소유물의 예를 제공하기 위해

8 아래 문장 중 지문 속의 음영된 문장의 핵심 정보를 가장 잘 표현하고 있는 것은 무엇인가? 오답은 문장의 의미를 현저히 왜곡하거나 핵심 정보를 빠뜨리고 있다.

(A) 캐나다와 미국 정부는 모두 토착민들을 완전히 파멸시키기 위해 potlatch를 금지했다.

(B) potlatch는 토착 공동체를 주류 사회에 통합시키기 위해 19세기에 미국과 캐나다에 의해 불법화되었다.

(C) 미국과 캐나다는 모두 potlatch를 낭비적이고 비합리적인 물건의 파괴라고 생각했기 때문에 potlatch를 막으려고 노력했다.

(D) potlatch를 금지하는 캐나다와 미국의 결정은 토착민들을 자본주의 사회에 통합시키려는 시도의 일부분이었다.

9 네 개의 네모[■]는 다음 문장이 삽입될 수 있는 부분을 나타내고 있다.

구리는 그러한 물건 중 하나로 자주 부서진 상태로 운반되었는데, 이로써 금전적 가치는 낮추었지만 문화적인 의의는 강조했다.

이 문장은 어느 자리에 들어가는 것이 가장 적절한가?

10 지시: 지문 요약을 위한 도입 문장이 아래에 주어져 있다. 지문의 가장 중요한 내용을 나타내는 보기 3개를 골라 요약을 완성하시오. 어떤 문장은 지문에 언급되지 않은 내용이나 사소한 정보를 담고 있으므로 요약에 포함되지 않는다. **이 문제는 2점이다.**

> 여러 가지 목적을 가진 potlatch는 다양한 활동들로 구성된다.
> · (A) 계절에 따른 음식의 잉여분이 연회 동안 공유되었다.
> · (C) 여러 가지 이유로 손님들에게 물건들이 제공되었다.
> · (E) 손님뿐 아니라 주최자에 의해서도 전통 춤이 추어졌다.

(B) 격식 있는 만찬 그릇이 주최자의 관대함을 보여주는 데 사용되었다.

(D) 관습의 금지에도 불구하고, 그것은 계속해서 비밀리에 행해졌다.

(F) 부족이 아닌 사람들이 potlatch에 초대되었지만, 보통 참석하지는 않았다.

02 Heat Islands

p.304

1. (A)	2. (B)	3. (B)
4. (C)	5. (D)	6. (A)
7. (B)	8. (C)	9. 2nd
10. (C)-4단락, (D)-2단락, (F)-3단락		

1 1880년에, 로스앤젤레스는 미국 서해안의 황량한 땅덩어리에 불과했다. 개척자들은 서쪽으로 이주하면서, 그곳에 정착해 드넓은 농토를 관개하고 과수원을 경작해서 미국에서 가장 부유한 농민층에 속하게 되었다. 그러나 시간이 지나면서 시원한 과일을 생산하던 과일나무는 뜨거운 포장도로와 고층빌딩으로 대체되었고, 이런 거대 도시화는 통상적인 도심지의 기온에 심각한 영향을 미쳤는데, 이에 따라서 도심지의 기온이 교외 지역보다 10도가량 더 높은 경우가 자주 있었고 10년에 1도 정도씩 계속해서 온도가 상승하고 있다. [2]등온선 지도는 어떤 한 지역의 월평균기온 또는 연평균기온의 지리적 분포를 보여주는데, 도시가 위치한 곳에서 온도의 급격한 상승이 나타나며 이것은 섬의 등고선에 비유되기 때문에 이 현상을 도시 열섬(Urban Heat Island), 즉 UHI라 부른다.

2 열섬현상은 대도시의 발달과 함께 생기는 경우가 많으며 이외의 인구 밀집 지역에서도 나타난다. 과학자들은 도시의 열섬들이 지구 표면온도의 점진적인 상승의 원인이라는 확신을 굳혀가고 있다. **열섬이 지구의 표면온도를 상승시키는 방식 중 하나는 더운 기후의 지역에서 냉장고와 에어컨 수요를 증가시키는 것이다.** 결국 이것은 더 높은 에너지 소비를 초래하며, 열을 가두는 온실가스를 배출하는 지역 발전소에 부담을 준다. 이외에도 열섬에서 나타나는 고온현상은 바람의 패턴, 강수량, 오존을 생성하는 스모그가 나타나는 빈도 등에 심각한 변화를 초래해서, 외곽 농업 지역의 기후에 해로운 영향을 끼친다.

3 이러한 환경 문제의 심각성 때문에 지리학자들은 근본적인 원인을 찾음으로써 이 현상을 해결하기 위한 연구를 해왔다. 고층 빌딩들과 도시 구조물 등의 도시의 기하학적 디자인은 자연환경보다 열을 잘 흡수하고 저장하는 표면을 가지고 있기 때문에 도시의 기온에 엄청난 영향을 미친다. 빛의 반사율을 의미하는 albedo는 아스팔트나 검정색 지붕 등 어두운 색의 건축 자재를 사용하면 감소하는데, [4]이런 어두운 색의 건축 자재는 광선 스펙트럼의 대부분의 영역을 흡수하지만, 많은 복사열을 주로 반사하지는 않는다. 이 현상은 일몰 후에도 열기를 오래 머무르게 하는데, 이로 인해 도시가 자체적으로 냉각될 수 없게 된다. [6/7]지중해 문화권에서는 열을 잘 흡수하지 않는 테라코타나 밝은 색조의 페인트를 사용해서 이러한 현상을 막고자 노력해왔고, 덕분에 많은 양의 태양광선이 대기 중으로 반사된다. 대조적으로, 미국인들은 건축의 미적 가치를 더 중시했기 때문에 비효율적이지만 시각적으로는 보기 좋은 자재들을 지속적으로 사용해왔다. 최근의 연구 결과에 따르면 색의 중요성은 실로 엄청나서 밝은 색의 지붕과 어두운 지붕 간의 온도 차가 70도를 넘을 수도 있다는 것이 밝혀졌다.

4 [7]열섬현상을 일으키는 주 원인 중 두 번째는 도시 환경의 초목 부족 현상이다. 많은 사람이 농촌을 떠나 도시로 이주해옴에 따라서 많은 초목이 새로운 도로나 기타 기반 구조물에 자리를 내주고 사라진다. 도시계획자들은 사라진 나무를 대체할 방법을 강구하기보다는 늘어나는 인구를 위해 충분한 주택과 빌딩을 건축하는 데 주의를 기울인다. 그들은 나무들이 풍속을 줄이거나, 건물에 그늘을 드리우고 잎으로 복사열을 흡수해서 햇빛을 차단함으로써 열을 감소시키는 명백한 수단을 제공해 준다는 것을 알아차리지 못한다. 예를 들어 덩굴식물로 에어컨 위를 덮으면 에어컨을 차게 유지시키고 더욱 효율적으로 작동하게끔 할 수 있다. 빌딩에서 가장 태양이 많이 내리쬐는 서쪽과 남쪽에 심어진 낙엽수들은 에너지 소비를 30퍼센트까지 줄이기에 충분한 그늘을 만들어 준다. 더욱이 관목과 덤불 등은 사람이 육체적인 활동을 할 때 땀을 흘리는 것처럼, 증발산을 통해서 수분을 방출해서 대기 중의 열을 상쇄한다. 식물은 뿌리를 통해 흡수한 지하수를 잎의 기공을 통해서 분비한다. 커다란 나무는 하루에 40갤런의 물을 방출하는 경우도 있는데, 이는 8시간 동안 켜놓은 100와트 전구에서 발생하는 정도의 열을 효과적으로 중화시

켜 준다. 이 과정의 열 상쇄 효과는 도시의 온도를 낮추는 데 큰 도움이 될 수 있다. 도시에 더욱 넓은 녹지를 창출하려는 집중적인 노력은 도시의 미관을 개선시켜 주기도 하지만, 무엇보다 가장 중요하게도 뜨거운 도시 환경을 완화시켜 준다.

irrigation [ìrəgéiʃən] 관개 orchard [ɔ́:rtʃərd] 과수
isothermic map 등온선 지도 spike [spaik] 급격한 상승
in tandem with ~와 함께 detrimental [dètrəméntl] 해로운
delve [delv] 연구하다 implementation [ìmpləməntéiʃən] 실행
linger [líŋgər] 오래 머물다
terracotta [térəkàtə] 테라코타 (붉은 갈색의 진흙)
striking [stráikiŋ] 두드러진 intercept [ìntərsépt] 차단하다
foliage [fóuliidʒ] 잎 vine [vain] 덩굴식물
deciduous [disídʒuəs] 낙엽과의 shrub [ʃrʌb] 관목
neutralize [njú:trəlàiz] 상쇄하다
atmospheric [æ̀tməsférik] 대기의
evapotranspiration [ivæ̀poutrænspəréiʃən] 증발산

1 지문의 구 "likened to"와 의미상 가장 유사한 것은?

(A) ~에 비유된
(B) ~에 부착된
(C) ~에 바쳐진
(D) ~으로 제한된

2 지문에 따르면, 열섬현상은 _____ 때문에 그렇게 불리게 되었다.

(A) 도시의 기온이 교외 지역보다 현저히 높기 때문에
(B) 도심 지역의 등온선이 섬의 등고선과 유사하기 때문에
(C) 대개 주요 섬의 상당히 산업화된 지역에서 일어나기 때문에
(D) 열섬현상이 발생하는 도시의 위치가 다른 지역으로부터 고립되어 있기 때문에

3 지문의 단어 "detrimental"과 의미상 가장 유사한 것은?

(A) 날카로운
(B) 유해한
(C) 증대하는
(D) 아첨하는

4 3단락에 따르면, 어두운 색의 건물은 _____으로써 기온 상승의 원인이 된다.

(A) 반사되는 복사 에너지의 양을 늘림으로써
(B) 근처 식물에 의한 에너지의 흡수를 억제함으로써
(C) 대기 중으로 많은 양의 열을 반사하지 않음으로써
(D) 거주자들이 에너지를 많이 사용하도록 요구함으로써

5 지문의 단어 "itself"가 가리키는 것은?

(A) 복사열
(B) 열기
(C) 일몰
(D) 도시

6 3단락에서, 글쓴이는 _____ 하기 위해 지중해 문화를 언급한다.

(A) 열섬현상에 대한 그들과 미국의 대응을 대조하기 위해
(B) 어두운 색으로 칠해진 건물의 부작용을 강조하기 위해
(C) 미국의 에너지 남용이 열섬현상을 야기한다고 주장하기 위해
(D) 아름다움과 기능이 모두 디자인으로 통합될 수 있음을 보여 주기 위해

7 지문에 따르면, 다음 중 열섬현상이 가장 일어나지 않을 것 같은 환경은?

(A) 초목이 빽빽한 어두운 색의 건물들
(B) 초목이 빽빽한 밝은 색의 건물들
(C) 초목이 거의 없는 어두운 색의 건물들
(D) 초목이 거의 없는 밝은 색의 건물들

8 아래 문장 중 지문 속의 음영된 문장의 핵심 정보를 가장 잘 표현하고 있는 것은 무엇인가? 오답은 문장의 의미를 현저히 왜곡하거나 핵심 정보를 빠뜨리고 있다.

(A) 도시가 자연에 좀 더 집중한다면, 훨씬 더 매력적으로 보일 것이다.
(B) 상승하는 기온으로 인해, 도시는 해결책으로 녹지에 의지하고 있다.
(C) 외관과 기온 모두를 위해, 도심 지역은 더 많은 녹지가 필요하다.
(D) 녹지의 조성은 도심 지역의 아름다움을 크게 더한다.

9 네 개의 네모[■]는 다음 문장이 삽입될 수 있는 부분을 나타내고 있다.

열섬이 지구의 표면온도를 상승시키는 방식 중 하나는 더운 기후의 지역에서 냉장고와 에어컨 수요를 증가시키는 것이다.

이 문장은 어느 자리에 들어가는 것이 가장 적절한가?

10 **지시:** 지문 요약을 위한 도입 문장이 아래에 주어져 있다. 지문의 가장 중요한 내용을 나타내는 보기 3개를 골라 요약을 완성하시오. 어떤 문장은 지문에 언급되지 않은 내용이나 사소한 정보를 담고 있으므로 요약에 포함되지 않는다. **이 문제는 2점이다.**

> **열섬현상은 주변의 온도를 높이는 수많은 요소들의 융합에 의해 발생한다.**
>
> · (C) 기온 상승은 냉각 효과를 지닌 식물의 부족 때문이다.
> · (D) 고온은 문제를 악화시키는 인간의 행동으로 이어진다.
> · (F) 빽빽하게 들어찬 건물은 많은 태양 복사열을 흡수하고 그것을 천천히 방출한다.

(A) 산업 도시의 스모그는 상승하는 기온 때문에 악화되고 있다.
(B) 로스앤젤레스는 열섬현상으로 가장 심하게 고통받아왔다.
(E) 식물은 뿌리를 통해 물을 흡수하고 그것을 대기 중으로 방출한다.

03 Symbiosis

p.308

1. (D)	2. (B)	3. (B)
4. (C)	5. (C)	6. (D)
7. (D)	8. (A)	9. 4th
10. (B)-4단락, (D)-3단락, (F)-5~6단락		

1 지구 상의 어떤 생명체도 혼자서 살아가지 않는다. 즉, 생존은 다른 종과의 상호작용에 달려 있다. 가장 흔한 상호관계는 동일한 먹이를 두고 경쟁하고, 먹이를 사냥하고, 먹히는 것을 피하는 것과 같이 먹이와 관련되어 있다. 다른 종에 대한 의존도가 생명체들이 상호의존적일 정도로 매우 높은 수준에까지 도달하면, ¹과학자들은 그러한 생명체들이 공생관계이며, 즉 한쪽 또는 쌍방의 지속적인 생존을 위해 필요한 장기간 유지되는 관계를 가지는 것으로 간주한다.

2 생물의 공생관계는 자연에서 흔히 찾아볼 수 있고 연구자들은 이러한 관계를 밝히는 데 깊은 관심을 가지고 있는데, 특히 그중 한 종의 생존이 인간에게 중요하게 쓰이는 경우 더욱 깊은 관심을 보인다. 예를 들면, 농업과 지속 가능한 생태계를 위해서는 생물에 대한 포괄적인 이해가 필요한데, 무지로 인해 종 간의 미묘한 관계가 단절된다면 그 종들은 멸종할 수도 있기 때문이다.

3 생물이 공생관계를 형성하는 한 가지 방법은 상대방의 존재로 인해서 양방 모두 상호적인 이득을 누리게 되는 경우이다. 이러한 종류의 관계는 상호공생관계라 불리며 대개 완전히 다른 식물이나 동물 사이에서 발생한다. 한쪽이 만들어내는 찌꺼기가 다른 한쪽의 먹이가 되거나, 한쪽이 상대방에게 그늘이나 보호, 은신처 등 생존에 필수적인 여건을 제공하기도 한다. 상호공생관계의 가장 흔한 형태는 한 생물이 자신보다 큰 동물의 입에 있는 음식 찌꺼기를 먹으며 구강을 깨끗하게 해주고 전반적인 청결을 유지할 수 있게 도와주는 형태이다. 상호공생관계의 다른 한 가지 종류로 질소 고정이 있는데, 이것은 대개 콩이나 클로버 등 뿌리에 박테리아의 거처를 제공해주는 콩과 식물에서 나타난다. ³이 박테리아는 대기 중의 질소를 식물이 사용할 수 있는 질소 화합물인 암모니아로 변환해주고, 콩과 식물은 대신 박테리아에게 산소와 양분을 공급해준다. 동물들은 필요로 하는 질소량 중 많은 부분을 콩과 식물을 섭취하여 얻기 때문에, 질소는 전체적인 생태계에도 매우 중요하다.

4 한편, 한쪽만이 이익을 얻고 상대방은 아무런 이익도 피해도 받지 않는다면, 이런 공생관계는 편리공생관계로 분류된다. 이것은 문자 그대로는 '테이블에 함께 있음'이라는 뜻인데, 이는 이 용어가 다른 집단이 먹지 않고 남긴 음식을 먹어 치우는 한 집단의 동물들을 지칭하기 위해 처음 쓰였기 때문이다. 상대방이 남긴 음식, 또는 상대방의 존재 자체로 인해 이익을 얻는 쪽을 뜻하는 commensal(공생 동물)은 몸집이 큰 육식동물을 따라다니는 작은 청소 동물인 경우가 많은데, 이런 관계에서 청소 동물은 그 육식동물이 버린 음식을 먹고 살아간다. 처음에는 편리공생의 정의를 음식에만 관련시켰지만, 지금은 의미가 확장되어 햇빛에 대한 접근 등의 다른 이익까지도 포

함한다. 우림지역에서는 빽빽한 수관이 지표면에 도달하는 빛의 양을 줄이므로, 키가 작은 식물들이 높은 수목의 그늘에 가려지게 되는 경우가 종종 생긴다. 착생식물은 더욱 많은 햇빛을 받기 위해 키가 큰 식물 위에 자리 잡는 작은 식물이지만, 기생식물처럼 영양분을 빨아들이지는 않는다.

5 공생관계의 마지막 형태인 기생은 가장 잘 알려졌을 뿐 아니라 가장 널리 연구되고 있다. 기생은 한 종이 다른 종에 의해 부정적인 영향을 받게 되는 경우로, 예를 들어 작은 기생충이 상대적으로 거대한 숙주에게 크게 두 가지 방법으로 해를 끼치는 경우가 있다. 첫째는 숙주 자체를 잡아먹어 숙주의 신체조직을 양분으로 사용하는 경우이다. 어떤 경우에는 사람의 피를 빨아먹는 십이지장충처럼 생물의 조직을 실제로 갉아 먹는 것을 수반하기도 하지만, 세포를 가로채서 그 세포가 만들어내는 자원을 전용하기도 한다. 예를 들어, 바이러스는 세포를 전용해서 자신을 복제하는 데 사용하고, 세포에 있는 자원이 전부 소진되면 세포는 폭발하여 다른 세포에 복제된 바이러스를 퍼뜨린다. **이러한 순환은 숙주가 더는 살 수 없거나 바이러스의 공격에 저항할 수 있게 될 때까지 계속된다.**

6 기생생물이 숙주에게 해를 끼치는 두 번째 경로는 독을 방출하는 것이다. ⁶이런 종류의 기생생물은 의도적으로 숙주에게 피해를 주려고 하는 것은 아니지만, 세포의 신진대사에서 생성된 부산물이 독소를 함유한다. 인류는 지속적으로 박테리아의 숙주가 되어왔고 일부 박테리아가 인간에게 독이 되는 부산물을 내보내는 것은 순전히 우연에 의한 것일 뿐이다. 예를 들어 외독소는 디프테리아(어린이가 많이 않는 급성 전염병)의 배설물인데, ⁷이는 인간에게 매우 유독한 물질이어서 신경계에 회복 불가능한 손상을 가져오는 한편, 생물조직에 염증을 일으키고 심장을 손상시킨다. 즉시 치료받지 않으면 감염된 사람 중 4분의 1이 사망한다. ⁸그러나 기생생물은 가능한 한 오랫동안 숙주를 살아남게 하는 편이 더 나은데, 이는 숙주가 기생생물의 번식을 위해 필요한 주된 자원이기 때문이다.

7 이러한 관계들은 고정되어 있는 것이 아니며, 공생관계의 한 형태가 다른 형태로 변하는 것도 드문 일이 아니다. 예를 들어 우리의 창자에 살고 있는 박테리아는 비타민K를 생성하는데, 이것은 이전의 편리공생관계에서 상호공생관계로 발전해 왔다는 것을 의미한다. 그러므로 모든 생명체가 상호의존적이라는 것과 다른 생물과의 상호관계를 인식하지 못한 채 어느 한 종을 없애는 것은 잠재적으로 생물권 전체에 심각한 반향을 야기할 수 있다는 것을 기억하는 것은 매우 중요하다.

symbiotic[sìmbiátik] 공생관계의
sustainable[səstéinəbl] 지속 가능한 sever[sévər] 단절하다
perish[périʃ] 멸종하다 divergent[divə́:rdʒənt] 다른
indispensable[ìndispénsəbl] 필수적인 leftover[léftòuvər] 찌꺼기
legume[légju:m] 콩과 식물 harbor[há:rbər] ~에게 거처를 제공하다
furnish[fə́:rniʃ] 공급하다 commensalism[kəménsəlìzm] 편리공생
scavenger[skǽvindʒər] 청소부 canopy[kǽnəpi] 수관
overshadow[òuvərʃǽdou] 가리다 epiphyte[épəfàit] 착생식물
perch[pə:rtʃ] 자리 잡다 parasitic[pæ̀rəsítik] 기생하는
diminutive[dimínjutiv] 작은 entail[intéil] 수반하다
hookworm[húkwə̀:rm] 십이지장충

hijack[háidʒæk] 가로채다, 납치하다   divert[divə́:rt] 전용하다
appropriate[əpróuprièit] 전용하다   explode[iksplóud] 폭발하다
liberate[líbərèit] 방출하다   metabolism[mətǽbəlìzm] 신진대사
exotoxin[èksoutáksin] 외독소   deterioration[ditìəriəréiʃən] 손상
inflame[infléim] 염증을 일으키다   intestine[intéstin] 창자
cardinal[káːrdənl] 중요한
interdependent[ìntərdipéndənt] 상호의존적인
repercussion[rìːpərkʌ́ʃən] 반향   biosphere[báiəsfìər] 생물권

1 1단락에 따르면, 다음 중 공생관계에 대해 사실인 것은?

(A) 이 관계는 먼 거리에 고립되어 있는 생명체에게만 나타난다.
(B) 이 관계는 한 종이 독립하면 깨진다.
(C) 이 관계는 자연 환경에서는 거의 발견되지 않는다.
(D) 이 관계는 최소한 한 종에게는 없어서는 안 된다.

2 지문의 단어 "perish"와 의미상 가장 유사한 것은?

(A) 밀착하다
(B) 사라지다
(C) 완화시키다
(D) 노력하다

3 지문에서 질소 고정에 대해 추론할 수 있는 것은?

(A) 콩과 식물은 질소 가스를 대기 중으로 다시 방출한다.
(B) 식물들은 대기 중의 질소를 직접 흡수할 수 없다.
(C) 암모니아가 만들어지고 식물들에 악영향을 미친다.
(D) 콩과 식물이 보통 박테리아보다 이익을 얻는다.

4 지문의 단어 "furnish"와 의미상 가장 유사한 것은?

(A) 끼었다
(B) 바르다
(C) 공급하다
(D) 숨막히게 하다

5 지문의 단어 "its"가 가리키는 것은?

(A) 존재
(B) 육식동물
(C) 청소 동물
(D) 음식

6 다음 중 6단락의 디프테리아에 대해 사실인 것은?

(A) 성장에 한계가 없다.
(B) 숙주가 번식하는 것을 방해한다.
(C) 대사 장애가 있다.
(D) 숙주를 직접적으로 공격하지 않는다.

7 글쓴이는 "causes irreparable deterioration"이라고 진술함으로써 그것이 _____을 의미한다.

(A) 탄력이 있음
(B) 치료할 수 있음
(C) 패배시킬 수 없음

(D) 치명적임

8 다음 중 6단락의 기생생물에 대해 추론할 수 있는 것은?

(A) 숙주가 오랫동안 살아남으면 득을 본다.
(B) 영양분이 있는 숙주의 피에 접근한다.
(C) 숙주가 다치지 않는 한에서 여러 가지 형태를 취한다.
(D) 숙주를 유독 물질로부터의 보호책으로 사용한다.

9 네 개의 네모[■]는 다음 문장이 삽입될 수 있는 부분을 나타내고 있다.

이러한 순환은 숙주가 더는 살 수 없거나 바이러스의 공격에 저항할 수 있게 될 때까지 계속된다.

이 문장은 어느 자리에 들어가는 것이 가장 적절한가?

10 지시: 지문 요약을 위한 도입 문장이 아래에 주어져 있다. 지문의 가장 중요한 내용을 나타내는 보기 3개를 골라 요약을 완성하시오. 어떤 문장은 지문에 언급되지 않은 내용이나 사소한 정보를 담고 있으므로 요약에 포함되지 않는다. 이 문제는 2점이다.

> **공생관계는 자연에서의 종간 관계의 중요성을 보여준다.**
> · (B) 관계는 때때로 한쪽은 이득을 얻고 다른 쪽은 영향을 받지 않게 편향된다.
> · (D) 서로 다른 두 개의 생물체가 서로에게 이롭다는 것은 사실이다.
> · (F) 관계는 숙주에게 해롭지만 상대에게는 도움을 준다.

(A) 두 생물체의 관계가 정해지면, 그것은 바꿀 수 없다.
(C) 한쪽이 다른 쪽을 위해 위생을 유지하는 것이 중요하다.
(E) 인간은 공생 생물 간의 균형을 깨뜨리는 원인이 된다.

04 History of the Clock Industry

p.312

1. (B)	2. (B)	3. (A)
4. (B)	5. (D)	6. (C)
7. (C)	8. (C)	9. 4th
10. (B)-2~3단락, (C)-4단락, (E)-5~6단락		

1 다양한 종류의 시계가 고대부터 사용되어 왔지만, 현대적 의미의 시계 산업의 역사는 18세기에 시작한다. 이전까지 시계와 손목시계는 주로 과학자나 부유한 애호가들의 영역에 국한되어 있었고, ¹대충 시간을 알려주는 데에만 사용되었다. 그러나 산업혁명으로 인해 야기된 교통의 변화는 시간 엄수를 필수로 만들었고 대중의 마음에 시간관념을 공고히 하는 것을 도왔다.

2 디자인, 생산, 그리고 무역 측면에서 영국은 현대 시계 산업의 선구자였다. 정확하고 휴대 가능한 시계를 만들려는 영국인의 경향은 증가하는 이동 인구의 요구에 완벽하게 들어맞았고, ²영국에서의 철도의 이른 발달은 19세기 초반 영국의 시장 패권 장악에 촉매제

를 제공했다. 철도의 안전하고 예측 가능한 운행은 시간을 엄수하는 것에 크게 좌우되었기 때문에, 기술자들이 초정밀 시계와 시간을 일치시킬 수 있도록 철도 시스템 전반에 걸쳐 시계들이 일정 간격마다 배치되었으며, 시계들이 계속해서 정확하게 맞춰질 수 있도록 철도 시스템 전반에 걸쳐 전보 서비스가 주기적으로 시간을 역으로 타전했다. 이는 사고를 예방하도록 도왔고 철도 회사들이 더 빡빡한 일정을 관리할 수 있게 한 한편, 여행자들이 도착, 출발 및 연결편을 더 정확히 예상할 수 있게 돕기도 했다. 이러한 발달은 충분한 재력을 가진 사람들이 회중시계를 구매하도록 유도하며 사회 전반적으로 급증한 시간의 중요성에 대한 인식을 지지했다. 따라서 철도 여행은 시계 수요를 증가시켰고 영국의 전반적인 시계 산업을 북돋았다.

3 하지만 영국 시스템에는 문제점이 있었는데, 그것은 경쟁자들에 의해 이용되었다. 즉, 영국 시장은 전적으로 수제 시계에만 집중되어 있었고, [4]소수만이 아는 기술로 이익을 얻은 탐욕스러운 시계공들이 기계화를 위협으로 보았으며, 적극적으로 '가짜 시계'를 만드는 기계의 사용에 반대하는 로비 활동을 벌였다. 그 결과, 영국 시계의 생산단가는 굉장히 높게 유지되었다. 하지만 영국인들이 기계화에 적대적이었던 것에 반해, 회사들이 금속판과 평형 바퀴와 같은 개별 부품의 생산 자동화를 실험하기 시작한 스위스는 그렇지 않았다. 몇몇 부품들을 만드는 데 기계를 사용함으로써 스위스 시계는 영국 시계보다 더 빠르고 낮은 가격에 제작될 수 있었다.

4 하지만 스위스는 완전히 기계화된 생산의 유혹에 항복하지 않았다. 대신 그들은 생산단계 초반에는 반제품을 만드는 데 기계를 사용하고, 마무리 작업은 고도로 숙련된 장인이 책임지는 유연한 시스템을 채택하였다. 이 방식은 양쪽 세계의 최고의 것을 제공했는데, [5A]이는 스위스 시계가 손재주의 다양성과 품질을 희생시키지 않으면서도 효율적으로 생산될 수 있었기 때문이다. [5B]최첨단 기계와 전문적이고 융통성 있는 노동 인력은 스위스 회사들이 변동하는 시장 수요와 소비자 선호에 빠르게 대응할 수 있게 하였으며, 스위스 시계, 특히 손목시계는 구매자들의 마음속에서 점차 '최고의 품질'과 동의어가 되었다. 그 결과, 많은 시계 제작자가 포괄적인 국가 상표 아래 그들의 손목시계를 성공적으로 내놓을 수 있었다. [5C]'스위스제'라는 이름으로 나온 손목시계는 본국과 해외의 보석방 및 다른 고급 상점에서 고가에 팔렸고, 궁극적으로 스위스는 인정받는 업계 선두주자로 영국을 앞질렀으며 20세기 중반까지 그 위치를 지켰다.

5 많은 스위스제 시계는 미국 시장으로 흘러들어 갔는데, 미국의 시계공들은 인지된 품질을 희생시킨 대신 양에 집중했다. 미국은 유럽에 비해 숙련된 시계공의 절대적인 수는 부족했지만, 미국의 장인들은 대량 생산 기술을 완성하면서 저렴한 시계를 위한 길을 마련했다. 1815년 무렵, 코네티컷의 기술자인 Eli Terry는 수력으로 가동되는 제조 공장을 사용하여 숙련된 노동자의 어떠한 조작이나 정교한 조정 없이도 조립 가능한, 완전히 동일하고 교체 가능한 부품들을 제작하고 있었다. 따라서 그의 시계는 장인이 필요 없이 견습생에 의해 빨리 생산될 수 있었다. Terry는 그의 사업의 상업적 가치를 이해하고 특허로 제작방식을 보호하려고 시도했지만, 그의 법적 조치는 밀려들어 오는 경쟁자들을 오랫동안 저지하지는 못했다. 다른 회사

들도 이를 따랐고, [7/8]1800년대 후반이 되자 미국은 시계를 빠르고 싸게 대량생산하고 있었다. 1899년 Ingersoll Watch Company의 'Yankee' 회중시계가 1달러에 판매되었고, 이러한 1달러 시계는 하루에 대략 8천 개씩 조립 라인에서 제작되었다.

6 [7]미국이 사실상 누구나 구매할 수 있는 시계를 생산할 수 있었다는 사실은 장점을 가지고 있었다. 미제 시계와 손목시계가 세계시장으로 밀려들었고, 결국 판매량뿐만 아니라 수익에서도 스위스 상표를 앞질렀다. 1945년과 1970년 사이에 스위스 손목시계의 세계시장 점유율은 80퍼센트에서 42퍼센트로 곤두박질쳤고, 1970년에는 두 곳의 미국 시계 회사 Timex와 Bulova가 전 세계 판매량과 총 수익에서 각각 1위를 차지했다.

hobbyist[hábiist] 애호가 cement[simént] 공고히 하다
frontrunner[frʌ́ntrʌ̀nər] 선구자 hegemony[hidʒéməni] 패권
chronometer[krənάmetər] 초정밀 시계
wire[waiər] 타전하다, 전보로 알리다 underpin[ʌ̀ndərpín] 지지하다
burgeon[bə́ːrdʒən] 급증하다 bolster[bóulstər] 북돋다
avaricious[æ̀vəríʃəs] 탐욕스러운 craftsman[krǽftsmən] 공예가
esoteric[èsətérik] 소수만 아는
antagonistic[æntǽgənístik] 적대적인
fabricate[fǽbrikèit] 제작하다
state-of-the-art[stéitəvðiàːrt] 최첨단의
fluctuation[flʌ̀ktʃuéiʃən] 변동 moniker[mάnəkər] 이름
fetch[fetʃ] 가격에 팔리다 high-end[hàiénd] 고급의
interchangeable[ìntərtʃéindʒəbl] 교체 가능한
manipulation[mənìpjuléiʃən] 조작 apprentice[əpréntis] 견습생
on the order of 대략

1 1단락에 따르면, 18세기 이전의 시계에 대해 추론할 수 있는 것은?

(A) 시간을 아는 것에 있어서 시계가 손목시계보다 선호되었다.
(B) 많은 시계와 손목시계들이 아주 정교하지는 않았다.
(C) 시계는 부자들에게 불필요한 것으로 여겨졌다.
(D) 시계는 주로 수송 회사들에 의해 사용되었다.

2 2단락에 따르면, 시계 산업에서의 영국의 선구성은 크게 _____ 때문이라고 할 수 있다.

(A) 알맞은 가격의 시계를 만드는 것에 대한 선호
(B) 철도 시스템의 이른 발달
(C) 시계를 더 정확하게 만드는 장치의 발명
(D) 안전 규정에 대한 철저한 엄수

3 지문의 단어 "sufficient"와 의미상 가장 유사한 것은?

(A) 충분한
(B) 달성할 수 있는
(C) 모호한
(D) 신중한

4 글쓴이는 왜 "fake clocks"를 언급하는가?

(A) 영국에서 만들어진 시계의 기능을 비판하기 위해
(B) 영국 장인들이 기계로 만든 시계를 조롱했던 것을 강조하기

위해

(C) 스위스가 영국제 시계에 대해 가졌던 오해를 지적하기 위해

(D) 영국에서 만들어진 시계와 스위스에서 만들어진 시계를 비교하기 위해

5 4단락에 따르면, 다음 중 대답할 수 없는 질문은?

(A) 스위스의 제작 방식의 이점은 무엇이었는가?

(B) 스위스는 어떻게 시장의 변화에 신속하게 반응했는가?

(C) 어떤 종류의 가게가 스위스 시계를 판매했는가?

(D) 영국은 스위스 세력의 위협에 어떻게 대응했는가?

6 아래 문장 중 지문 속의 음영된 문장의 핵심 정보를 가장 잘 표현하고 있는 것은 무엇인가? 오답은 문장의 의미를 현저히 왜곡하거나 핵심 정보를 빠뜨리고 있다.

(A) Terry는 그의 상품이 얼마나 금전적 가치가 있는지 알았지만, 그것을 보호하는 특허를 얻지 못했다.

(B) 경쟁자들이 그의 상품을 모방할 가능성이 높다는 것을 알고, Terry는 특허로 그의 방식을 보호하려고 했다.

(C) Terry는 특허로 그의 상업상의 이익을 보호하려고 했지만, 그의 노력은 장기적으로 소용이 없었다.

(D) Terry의 경쟁자 일부가 그의 방식을 사용하려고 했기 때문에, 그는 소송 절차를 밟기로 결심했다.

7 지문에 따르면, 5단락과 6단락의 관계는 무엇인가?

(A) 6단락은 5단락에서 서술된 상황이 어떻게 발생하게 되었는지 명백하게 설명한다.

(B) 6단락은 5단락에서 이야기된 문제가 어떻게 해결되었는지 설명한다.

(C) 6단락은 5단락에서 논의된 발전의 장기적인 영향을 자세하게 설명한다.

(D) 6단락은 5단락에서 제시된 정보를 새로운 방법으로 다시 설명한다.

8 다음 중 지문에서 결론 내릴 수 있는 것은?

(A) 19세기 동안 시계와 손목시계 제작 방법을 배우는 데 관심이 있는 장인들의 수가 감소했다.

(B) 18세기 동안 수제 시계의 일반적인 품질은 꾸준히 높아졌고 19세기 동안 떨어졌다.

(C) 시계를 살 형편이 되는 사람들의 비율이 18세기와 20세기 사이에 극적으로 증가했다.

(D) 기계화 방식으로 제작된 시계와 손목시계의 시간 정확도는 20세기에 빠르게 올라갔다.

9 네 개의 네모[■]는 다음 문장이 삽입될 수 있는 부분을 나타내고 있다.

그 결과, 많은 시계 제작자가 포괄적인 국가 상표 아래 그들의 손목시계를 성공적으로 내놓을 수 있었다.

이 문장은 어느 자리에 들어가는 것이 가장 적절한가?

10 지시: 지문 요약을 위한 도입 문장이 아래에 주어져 있다. 지문의 가장 중요한 내용을 나타내는 보기 3개를 골라 요약을 완성하시오. 어떤 문장은 지문에 언급되지 않은 내용이나 사소한 정보를 담

고 있으므로 요약에 포함되지 않는다. **이 문제는 2점이다.**

영국, 스위스, 그리고 미국이라는 세 개의 큰손들이 현대 시계 산업의 선두 주자로 부상했다.

- (B) 철도의 발전은 영국이 시계 제작과 판매에 우세를 점하는 것을 도왔지만, 영국 장인들은 혁신적인 제조 방식을 받아들이는 데 실패했다.

- (C) 스위스는 기술 혁신과 솜씨 좋은 장인을 통합했고 20세기까지 시계 산업을 장악하고 그 상태를 유지했다.

- (E) 대량 생산 기술의 숙달은 미국이 알맞은 가격의 시계를 제작할 수 있게 했고, 그들의 전 세계 판매 지분은 크게 증가했다.

(A) 18세기 이전에는, 영국의 시계와 손목시계에 대한 수요는 열광적인 과학자들과 부자들의 틈새 시장에 국한되었다.

(D) 미국은 20세기 후반까지 시계 산업에서의 스위스의 우위를 추월할 수 없었지만, 1800년대 후반에는 이미 고급 시장을 장악하고 있었다.

(F) 기계화된 생산에 대한 스위스의 열성적 추구는 그들의 일류 지위의 하락을 초래했고, 그 결과 영국의 시계공들이 이익을 얻었다.

HACKERS **STRATEGY**

p.319

전략1

Ex 나무는 두 가지 넓은 범주인 침엽수와 낙엽수로 분류될 수 있다. 침엽수는 좁거나 포개진 나뭇잎을 가지고 있으며, 원뿔형 열매 내부에 씨앗을 품고 있다. 거의 모든 침엽수는 상록수인데, 이는 이 나무들이 잎을 1년 내내 유지한다는 것을 의미한다. 침엽수는 가장 오래된 나뭇잎만 저절로 떨어지게 하는데, 그러한 나뭇잎은 대개 나무 하반부에 위치해 있으며 더 높은 곳에 새로 난 나뭇잎 만큼 많은 햇빛을 받지 않는다. 나뭇잎은 끝이 뾰족한 긴 바늘 모양이거나 작고 평평한 비늘 모양이다. 침엽수의 꽃으로 여겨지는 원뿔형 열매는 번식을 위한 씨앗을 방출하기 위해 해체될 것이다. 침엽수는 내구력과 크기로 유명하며, 현존하는 가장 크고 오래된 식물 중 일부이다.

반면 낙엽수는 원뿔형 열매에 씨앗을 품고 있지 않으며, 나뭇잎이 가을에 떨어진다. 그 전에, 나뭇잎은 주로 노란색, 주황색, 혹은 빨간색으로 변한다. 낙엽수는 또한 활엽수로도 알려졌는데, 이는 침엽수의 나뭇잎보다 넓은 잎을 가지고 있기 때문이다. 넓은 잎은 더 넓은 면적으로 광합성을 할 수 있게 하지만, 나뭇잎이 추운 날씨를 견디기에는 취약하다는 것을 의미하기도 한다. 새로운 나뭇잎은 매년 봄에 나온다. 낙엽수의 씨앗은 단단한 견과나 육과 내부에서 보호받으며 동물이 먹었을 때 분산된다. 참나무와 단풍나무는 낙엽수의 가장 일반적인 두 가지 예이다.

coniferous [kounífərəs] 침엽수의
deciduous [disídʒuəs] 낙엽수의 cone [koun] 원뿔형 열매
evergreen [évərgrìːn] 상록수
disintegrate [disíntəgrèit] 해체되다
durability [djùərəbíləti] 내구력, 튼튼함 foliage [fóuliidʒ] 나뭇잎
photosynthesis [fòutousínθəsis] 광합성 fleshy fruit 육과

HACKERS STRATEGY **APPLICATION** p.322

1861년부터 1865년까지 미국 전역에 휘몰아친 남북전쟁은 수십 년 간의 다각화의 끔찍한 결과였다. 19세기 초 내내, 북부와 남부는 서서히 서로 다른 길을 갔고 두 개의 특색 있고 매우 다른 지역으로 발전하였다.
북부의 토양과 기후는 대규모 농장보다는 소규모 농장에 유리했다. 남부보다 풍부한 천연자원에 힘입어 ᴱ산업이 번성하고 많은 대도시가 건설되었다(80만 명 이상의 주민이 거주했던 뉴욕이 가장 큰 도시였다). 1860년에 이르러 북부 주민의 4분의 1이 도시에 거주하였다. 1800년도와 1860년도 사이에는 농업에 종사하는 노동인구의 비율이 70퍼센트에서 40퍼센트로 대폭 하락하였다. 노예는 사라졌고 ᴳ유

럽에서 이주해온 도시와 공장의 이민노동자들로 대체되었다. 북부에서는 교통이 좀 더 용이하여, ᴮ국가 전체 철로의 3분의 2 이상이 이 지역에 있었고, 경제는 상승세를 타고 있었다. 북부 주민들은 휘그/공화당에 소속되어 있었으며 사업, 의료, 혹은 교육 종사자가 남부보다 훨씬 많았다. 북부의 아이들은 남부의 아이들보다 좀 더 학교에 다니기 쉬웠다.
남부의 비옥한 토양과 따뜻한 기후는 대규모 농장 및 담배와 목화 같은 작물에 이상적이었다. 농업의 수익성이 높아 산업발전에 대한 필요성을 느끼는 남부 주민은 거의 없었고, ᴰ노동력의 80퍼센트가 농업에 종사하였다. 뉴올리언스를 제외하면 대도시는 없었으며, 대부분의 도시는 유럽이나 북부의 목적지로 농산물을 보내는 선적항으로서 강가나 해안가에 위치했다. 남부 주민의 10분의 1만이 도심에 거주하였으며 도시 간 교통은 수로를 제외하고는 불편했다. 남부에는 국가 철로의 35퍼센트만이 위치해 있었다. 읽고 쓸 줄 아는 남부 백인 주민의 비율은 북부 백인 주민보다 약간 낮았고, 남부의 아이들은 학교에서 보내는 시간이 적었다. 성인으로서, ᶠ많은 남부 남성은 민주당에 가입하였고 농업뿐만 아니라 직업군인에 끌리는 경향이 있었다.

diversification [divə̀ːrsəfikéiʃən] 다각화
plantation [plæntéiʃən] 대규모 농장 pursuit [pərsúːt] 종사, 직업
large-scale [láːrdʒskèil] 대규모의 aside from ~을 제외하면
destination [dèstənéiʃən] 목적지
gravitate toward ~에 끌리는 경향이 있다

지시: 주어진 보기에서 적절한 구를 선택하여 관련 있는 지역에 연결시키시오. **이 문제는 3점이다.**

보기
(A) 유럽에서의 농산물 수입
(C) 농장에서의 노예 이용

북부
· (B) 철로의 대부분이 존재
· (E) 산업 기반 도시의 성장
· (G) 유럽 이민자에 의해 공급되는 노동력

남부
· (D) 농업에 기반을 둔 경제
· (F) 민주당과의 강한 제휴

HACKERS **PRACTICE**

p.324

1. (A)	2. (B)	3. (B), (C)
4. (C), (D)	5. (A), (C)	6. (B), (C)
7. (A), (B)	8. (B), (D)	

9. Painting – (C), (F)   Sculpture – (A), (D), (E)

10. Rogue Waves – (A), (D)

　　Tsunamis – (C), (F), (G)

11. Presidential – (C), (F), (G)

　　Parliamentary Cabinet – (B), (E)

12. Baroque – (C), (F), (G), (I)

　　Classical – (A), (B), (E)

VOCABULARY

1 (B), (D), (C)	2 (A), (B), (D)	3 (C), (A), (A)
4 (D), (C), (A)	5 (C), (D), (A)	6 (B), (C), (D)
7 (A), (B), (D)	8 (B), (C), (A)	9 (C), (D), (A)
10 (B), (A), (C)	11 (D), (A), (B)	12 (D), (B), (C)

1　균근은 유관 식물의 뿌리와 관련된 공생하는 균류이다. 균류가 유관 식물의 수분 흡수와 필수 영양소 흡수를 돕는 동안, 그 식물들은 균류에 영양이 풍부한 당을 제공한다. 균근 균류에는 두 가지 일반적인 유형이 있는데, 이는 내균근과 외균근이다.
[1]내균근은 현미경으로 봐야만 보이고, 균류의 더 미개한 선조 형태이다. [1]그들은 숙주 식물의 뿌리 세포에 침투하여 그 안에 산다. 이 균근은 상대적으로 종이 적지만 다양한 환경에 널리 퍼져 있고, 세상의 나무와 초본 식물군의 대다수에서 발견될 수 있다. 외균근은 더 최근에 진화하였고 맨눈에 보일 정도로 충분히 크다. [2]이 균근은 숙주 뿌리의 외부에 살고, 거기에서 뿌리 사이의 흙 속에 네트워크를 형성한다. 이 균근에는 많은 종이 있지만, 수천 종의 나무와만 관련이 있고 [2]온대 지방에 제한되어 있다.

mycorrhiza[máikəràizə] 균근　**symbiotic**[sìmbiátik] 공생하는
fungus[fʌ́ŋgəs] 균류　**vascular plant** 유관 식물
uptake[ʌ́ptèik] 흡수
endomycorrhizal[éndoumàikəráizəl] 내균근의
ectomycorrhizal[éktoumàikəráizəl] 외균근의
microscopic[màikrəskápik] 현미경으로 봐야만 보이는
primitive[prímətiv] 미개한　**flora**[flɔ́:rə] 식물군

지시: 표의 지정된 숫자 배열과 일치하는 올바른 보기를 선택하시오.

①	· 숙주 식물의 뿌리 안에 산다 · 너무 작아서 렌즈나 현미경 없이는 보이지 않는다

②	· 식물의 뿌리 외부 땅에서 산다 · 지구의 온화한 기후 지역에 제한된다

보기

(A)　① 내균근 ② 외균근

(B)　① 유관 식물 ② 숙주 식물

(C)　① 균근 ② 내균근

(D)　① 초본 식물군 ② 나무 식물군

2　합금은 새로운 물질을 형성하기 위해 금속과 적어도 하나의 다른 화학 원소가 결합한 것이다. 호박금과 청동은 인간에 의해 사용된 최초의 합금으로 기록된 사례의 두 가지이다.
　둘 다 주로 두 가지 금속으로 구성되는데, 호박금은 금과 은의 조합인 반면, 청동은 구리와 주석으로 구성된다. 하지만, 이러한 합금에도 극소량의 다른 금속 원소들이 들어 있기도 한데, 예를 들어 호박금 안에는 백금이 있고 청동 안에는 니켈이 있다. 호박금은 장인들에 의해 생산되었지만, [1]채굴될 수도 있었다. 그것의 주요 원천은 소아시아의 광상이었다. 고대에 사람들에 의해 활용된 청동은 인공 합금이었다.
　이러한 각각의 합금은 금속 성분 고유의 약점 때문에 사용되었다. [1]호박금은 금보다 견고했고 따라서 주화에 더 적합했다. 또한, 금과 은의 특정한 비율은 동전의 가치를 조정하기 위해 변경될 수도 있었다. [2]청동은 구리 대신 도구를 만들기 위해 사용되었는데 이는 그것이 더 단단하면서도 더 낮은 녹는 점을 가지고 있어서 주조하기 더 쉬웠기 때문이다. 게다가, 물에의 노출로 인해 침식될 가능성도 거의 없었다.

alloy[ǽlɔi] 합금　**electrum**[iléktrəm] 호박금
bronze[brɑːnz] 청동　**copper**[kɑ́:pər] 구리　**tin**[tin] 주석
trace[treis] 극소량　**platinum**[plǽtinəm] 백금
ore deposit 광상(유용한 광물이 땅속에 많이 묻혀 있는 부분)
artificial[ɑ̀ːrtifíʃəl] 인공의　**inherent**[inhírənt] 고유의
durable[dúrəbl] 견고한　**coinage**[kɔ́inidʒ] 주화
ratio[réiʃiou] 비율　**alter**[ɔ́:ltər] 변경하다, 다르게 하다
adjust[ədʒʌ́st] 조정하다　**in place of** ~을 대신하여
implement[ímpləmənt] 도구　**melting point** 녹는 점
cast[kæst] 주조하다　**erode**[iróud] 침식되다
exposure[ikspóuʒər] 노출

지시: 표의 지정된 숫자 배열과 일치하는 올바른 보기를 선택하시오.

①	· 일부 지역에서 자연적으로 형성된다 · 통화의 초기 형태를 만들기 위해 사용된다

②	· 개선된 도구의 생산에 참작된다 · 부식에 매우 강하다

보기

(A)　① 금 ② 은

(B)　① 호박금 ② 청동

(C)　① 구리 ② 주석

(D)　① 백금 ② 니켈

3 대부분의 사람이 옷감 짜는 일을 여성과 연관 지어 생각하지만, 베 짜기와 뜨개질은 원래 남성이 도맡았던 일이었다. 그러나 서구사회의 산업화로 인해서 대부분의 직물업이 공장의 기계 공정으로 바뀌면서, 베 짜기와 뜨개질 작업은 집에 남아있는 여성의 몫이 되었다. 베 짜기는 베틀을 이용해서 두 가닥의 실을 옷감으로 만드는 작업으로, 태피스트리나 양탄자를 만들 때 가장 흔히 사용되었다. ^B베 짜기는 씨실과 날실을 서로 직각으로 얽히게 짜는 작업을 포함한다. 재료로는 양모, 면화, 아마가 가장 흔하다. 또 다른 대중적인 방직기술인 뜨개질은 스웨터, 양말, 목도리 등의 의복처럼 실용적인 일상 용품을 만드는 데 사용된다. ^C뜨개질은 실로 만든 다양한 크기의 코를 서로 맞물리게 하여 수직이거나 평행인 실가닥의 연결에 의해 행해진다. 뜨개질은 기계를 이용하거나 손으로 직접 만들 수 있는데, 어떤 바느질 기법을 사용하는지에 따라 뜨개질 무늬를 매우 다양하게 만들 수 있다. 가장 기본적인 두 가지의 바느질 기법인 겉뜨기와 안뜨기를 조합하면 가장 복잡한 형태의 바느질 기법이 된다. 예를 들어, 가터뜨기는 단순히 겉뜨기와 안뜨기가 반복되게 하는 것이지만, 겉뜨기와 안뜨기의 변형은 메리야스뜨기가 된다.

weave[wi:v] 베를 짜다 knit[nit] 뜨개질하다, 겉뜨기
occupation[àkjupéiʃən] 일 textile trade 직물업
thread[θred] 가닥, 실 yarn[jɑːrn] 실 loom[lu:m] 베틀
tapestry[tǽpəstri] 태피스트리(다양한 색실로 그림을 짜 넣은 직물)
rug[rʌg] 양탄자 interlace[ìntərléis] 서로 얽히게 하다
weft[weft] 씨실 warp[wɔːrp] 날실 flax[flæks] 아마(亞麻)
horizontal[hɔ̀ːrəzántl] 수직의 parallel[pǽrəlèl] 평행의
loop[lu:p] (직물의) 코 purl[pəːrl] 안뜨기
garter stitch 가터뜨기(뜨개질의 한 기법)
alteration[ɔ̀ːltəréiʃən] 변형
stockinette stitch 메리야스뜨기(뜨개질의 한 기법)

지시: 주어진 보기에서 적절한 구를 선택하여 표를 완성하시오.

베 짜기	· 주로 태피스트리나 양탄자를 만들기 위해 사용된다 ·
뜨개질	· 손으로 또는 기계로 할 수 있다 ·

보기
(A) 산업화 이전에는 남자에 의해 거의 수행되지 않았다
(B) 정해진 각도로 두 가닥의 실을 꼬는 것으로 구성된다
(C) 여러 가닥을 합치기 위해 다양한 코를 맞물리게 하는 것을 포함한다
(D) 직물 생산의 가장 효과적인 방법으로 여겨진다

4 '종자식물'은 씨앗의 생산과 확산을 통해 번식하는 모든 종을 포함하는 식물의 분류이다. 그것은 '속씨식물'과 '겉씨식물'의 두 개 하위 분류로 나누어진다.
속씨식물은 흔히 꽃식물이라고 불리는데 이는 씨앗이 발달하는 씨방이 꽃의 일부이기 때문이다. 씨방은 씨앗이 적당히 일정한 온도를 유지하게 하고 탈수를 막음으로써 씨앗을 보호한다. 마

침내, 씨방은 여물고 열매가 될 것이다. 열매의 주된 기능은 씨앗의 확산을 용이하게 하는 것이다. 예를 들어, ^C그것은 동물에 의해 섭취될 수 있는데, 이후 그 동물은 어미그루로부터 떨어져 있는 지역에 소화되지 않은 씨앗을 배설한다. 이것이 열매가 맛있을 뿐만 아니라 영양분도 많은 이유로, 성공적인 번식은 먹이를 찾는 동물들에게 열매가 얼마나 매력적인지에 직접적으로 연관되어 있다.
그에 반해, 겉씨식물은 씨방으로 둘러싸이지 않은 씨앗을 생산한다. 대부분의 종에서, 미숙한 씨앗들은 대신 '구과' 안에 들어 있는데, 이는 씨방의 보호 기능과 관련있는 단단한 비늘 조각 다발이다. 소나무와 가문비나무에서 발견되는 방울열매들은 구과의 예시들이다. 종에 따라, ^D씨앗이 성숙하기까지 1년 또는 그 이상 걸릴 수 있고, 심지어 그다음에도 특정한 환경 조건이 충족되어야만 확산될 것이다. 많은 겉씨식물 종은 씨앗들을 이동시키기 위해 바람에 의존하는데, 씨앗들은 더욱 먼 거리를 이동하고자 고도를 유지할 수 있게 해주는 작은 날개 같이 생긴 부속물을 가지고 있다.

spermatophyte[spəːrmǽtəfàit] 종자식물
classification[klæ̀sifikéiʃən] 분류
reproduce[rìːprədúːs] 번식하다 dispersal[dispɔ́ːrsl] 확산
angiosperm[ǽndʒiəspə̀ːrm] 속씨식물
gymnosperm[dʒímnəspə̀ːrm] 겉씨식물 ovary[óuvəri] 씨방
dehydration[dìːhaidréiʃən] 탈수 ripen[ráipən] 여물다
facilitate[fəsíliteit] 용이하게 하다 excrete[ikskríːt] 배설하다
undigested[ʌ̀ndaidʒéstid] 소화되지 않은
enclosed[inklóuzd] 둘러싸인
strobilus[stroubáiləs] 구과(목질의 비늘 조각이 여러 겹으로 포개어져 둥글거나 원뿔형인 열매) cluster[klʌ́stər] 다발
cone[koun] (솔방울 같은) 방울열매 spruce tree 가문비나무
appendage[əpéndidʒ] 부속물

지시: 주어진 보기에서 적절한 구를 선택하여 표를 완성하시오.

속씨식물	· 씨방 안에서 성숙하는 씨앗을 가진다 ·
겉씨식물	· 단단하고, 비늘로 뒤덮인 구조로 씨앗을 보호한다 ·

보기
(A) 충분한 씨앗 확산을 위해 꽃을 생산한다
(B) 한 해 동안 수차례 씨앗을 내보낸다
(C) 씨앗을 새로운 지역으로 옮기기 위해 다른 생물을 이용한다
(D) 씨앗이 성숙하기 위해 상당한 시간을 필요로 한다

5 예술비평의 모든 분야에서 형식 대 내용에 대한 논쟁은 한 세기가 넘도록 학계를 지배해 왔다. 이 논쟁은 각각 형식주의 학파와 맥락주의 학파라는 두 개의 학파를 탄생시켰다. 이 두 개의 학파는 예술이 어떻게 감상되고 분석되고 해석되고 평가되어야 하는지에 관한 서로 다른 관점을 대표한다. 근본적으로, 두 개의 관점은 각기 예술 작품에서 무엇을 중점적인, 혹은 중요한 면으로 여기는지에 있어 달랐다. 형식주의적 접근은 순수한 예술적 가

치에 중점을 두는데, 구성, 색채, 형태, 그리고 특정한 기법들이 최우선으로 여겨진다. 형식주의자들은 예술 작품이 미적인 면에 있어서만 평가되어야 한다고 주장한다. 관람객의 반응이나 감상은 어떠한 작품 외적인 중요성으로부터가 아니라 미적인 가치에서 비롯된다. 어떤 이들은 이러한 관점에 한계가 있다고 보지만, 형식주의자들은 예술에 대한 깊은 이해는 역사적 혹은 사회적 맥락에 바탕을 둔 선입된 해석이나 분석으로부터의 분리를 필요로 한다고 본다.

이와는 상반되게, 맥락주의자들은 예술적 작품 생산의 원인이 된 환경의 본질적인 중요성을 옹호한다. [A]맥락주의는 예술의 의미가 그 작품이 제작되었을 당시의 사회역사학적 배경에서 찾을 수 있고, 주어진 작품이 역사적, 심리적 관점에서 가졌던 영향력에서도 찾을 수 있다고 주장한다. 맥락주의가 형식을 부정하는 것은 아니지만, 형식주의가 부인하고자 하는 [C]외적 요인들에 형식이 근거한다고 설명한다. 형식주의자들은 예술가의 이름을 흥미롭게 여기지만 중요하다고는 생각하지 않는 반면, 맥락주의자들은 그 예술가의 사회적 배경에 대한 이해가 특정 작품의 양식적 선택에 의미를 부여한다고 주장한다. 결국 두 학파 모두 서로의 관점을 인정하지 않았고, 이는 예술 비평 영역이 이분법적으로 뚜렷하게 갈리는 결과를 초래했다.

versus[vɔ́ːrsəs] ~ 대(對)　debate[dibéit] 논쟁
criticism[krítəsìzm] 비평　dominate[dάmənèit] 지배하다
school[skuːl] 학파　formalist[fɔ́ːrməlist] 형식주의자
contextualist[kəntékstʃuəlist] 맥락주의자
perspective[pərspéktiv] 관점　appreciate[əpríːʃièit] 평가하다
emphasis[émfəsis] 강조　priority[praió:rəti] 우선순위
aesthetic[esθétik] 미적인　external[ikstɔ́ːrnl] 외부적인
significance[signífikəns] 중요성
necessitate[nəsésətèit] 필요로 하다
separation[sèpəréiʃən] 분리
pre-designated[priːdézigneitid] 선입된
incompatibly[ìnkəmpǽtəbli] 상반되게
inherent[inhíərənt] 본질적인　contend[kənténd] 주장하다
socio-historic[sóusiouhistɔ̀:rik] 사회역사학적인
negate[nigéit] 부인하다
insignificant[ìnsignífikənt] 중요하지 않은
purport[pə́:rpɔ:rt] 주장하다　validate[vǽlədèit] 인정하다
dichotomy[daikάtəmi] 이분법　realm[relm] 영역

지시: 주어진 보기에서 적절한 구를 선택하여 맥락주의자들의 예술 분석 접근법을 완성하시오.

형식주의자	· 그림 자체의 눈에 보이는 특성에 두어진 신뢰 · 예술에 대한 날카로운 감상을 위한 이전 분류의 무시
맥락주의자	· ·

보기
(A) 주어진 환경에 의해 영향을 받은 것으로 예술 작품을 이해
(B) 예술 작품의 경제적 가치에 두어진 중요성

(C) 외부 요소에 근거한 예술 형태의 분석
(D) 예술가의 이름에 근거한 예술 작품에 대한 매료

6 혼동되거나 오인하기 쉬운 피아노와 하프시코드는 많은 특징을 공유하지만 근본적으로는 다른 악기이다. 중요한 차이점 중 하나는 건반의 구조이다. 피아노에는 88개의 건반이 있고, 7과 4분의 1의 옥타브 범위를 가진다. 반면, 하프시코드는 4에서 4와 2분의 1의 옥타브 범위만을 가진다. 이 두 악기 모두 건반은 목재로 되어 있지만 건반의 폭은 완전히 달라서, 피아노 건반은 하프시코드 건반 크기의 거의 두 배이다. 건반의 외형적인 구조 외에도, 악기의 내부적인 구조에 의해 음이 연주되는 방법은 매우 중요하다.

피아노는 건반을 누르면, 펠트로 덮인 작은 해머가 고정된 틀 위에 팽팽하게 달린 현을 두드리도록 디자인되었다. 현을 두드려서 생기는 진동은 소리를 유발하는 진동이 된다. 피아니스트는 원하는 소리를 낼 만큼의 적절한 압력을 가하기 위해서, 등, 어깨, 팔, 손 등을 이용하여 연주하는 데 체중과 근력을 충분히 실어야 한다. 따라서 피아니스트는 민감한 하프시코드에 적응하는 것을 어려워한다. [B]하프시코드의 건반은 직접적으로 현과 맞닿아 있기 때문에, 소리를 만들기 위해 어떤 수고나 근력도 필요로 하지 않는다. [C]하프시코드의 건반을 누르면 상단부에서 퀼을 붙들고 있는 얇은 나무 조각인 잭(jack)이 퀼이 현을 따라 움직이면서 다시 밑으로 돌아올 때까지 아래로부터 튀어나옴으로써 현을 당긴다. 잭은 건반이 어떠한 방법으로 눌리는지에 상관없이 퀼이 동일한 속도와 힘으로 현을 튕기도록 설계되었다. 이러한 하프시코드의 융통성 없는 특성은 역설적이게도 하프시코드를 가장 연주하기 쉬운 악기 중 하나이자 가장 정확한 소리를 내는 악기 중 하나로 만들었다.

misidentify[mìsaidéntəfai] 오인하다
harpsichord[hά:rpsikɔ̀:rd] 하프시코드(16~18세기의 건반 악기,
피아노의 전신)　quality[kwάləti] 특징
distinction[distíŋkʃən] 차이점　octave[άktiv] 옥타브(8도의 음정)
aside from ~ 외에도　rigid[rídʒid] 고정된
vibration[vaibréiʃən] 진동　adjust[ədʒʌ́st] 적응하다
sensitivity[sènsətívəti] 민감
quill[kwil] 퀼(하프시코드의 건반과 연결된 새 깃털로, 현을 뜯어 소리를
내는 역할을 함)　pluck[plʌk] 당기다
engineer[èndʒiníər] 설계하다　inflexible[infléksəbl] 융통성 없는

지시: 주어진 보기에서 적절한 구를 선택하여 하프시코드의 특징을 완성하시오.

피아노	· 연주자에 의한 가장 많은 통제를 허용한다 · 타격으로 유발되는 진동으로 소리를 만든다
하프시코드	· ·

보기
(A) 연주자의 등 힘을 이용한다
(B) 같은 선상의 축에 있는 현과 건반을 가지고 있다
(C) 현을 당기는 잭이 있다

(D) 금속으로 만든 건반이 있다

7 열전달은 물질을 통한 열 에너지의 이동이다. 대류와 전도가 이 현상의 두 가지 주된 방법이다.

대류는 열이 액체나 기체 상태의 물질인 유체 내에서 옮겨질 수 있게 한다. 공기나 물과 같은 유체의 온도가 상승하면, 분자들이 추가 에너지를 얻는데, 이는 분자들이 매우 빠르게 따로 떨어지기 시작하게 만든다. 가열된 유체가 확장되면서, 그것은 밀도가 낮아지고, 그 결과 상승하기 시작한다. 이 상향 이동은 더 차갑고 밀도 높은 유체를 대체하여, 그것을 아래쪽으로 밀어낸다. 열 자원이 남아 있다고 상정하면, 그 과정은 연이어 반복되고, 유체 곳곳에 열을 퍼뜨리는 대류 흐름을 만든다.

열이 고체를 통과하려면, 전도가 발생해야 한다. 고체의 분자들은 정밀한 배열로 서로 가깝게 가득 차 있는데, 이는 그것들이 열 에너지를 흡수할 때 서로로부터 떨어지는 것을 막는다. 대신에, ^A^열에 직접적으로 노출된 분자들은 빠르게 진동하기 시작할 것이고, 이는 온도의 상승을 야기한다. ^B^그런 다음 분자들은 인접한 분자들에 부딪힐 것이고, 그것들도 즉시 진동하게 만든다. 이 과정은 반복되며, 열 자원으로부터 더욱이 먼 분자들을 움직이게 만든다. 이러한 방식으로, 열은 더 높은 온도를 지닌 부분에서 더 낮은 온도를 지닌 부분으로 이동한다. 전도는 한 물체 내에서 에너지의 이동을 가능하게 할 뿐 아니라 서로 직접 접촉하고 있는 두 개의 독립된 물체들 사이에서도 가능하게 한다. 이것은 프라이팬에서 그 안에 있는 음식으로 열이 이동할 수 있는 방법을 설명하는데, 이는 프라이팬에서 빠르게 움직이는 분자들이 음식 분자에 충돌하고, 그것들을 진동하기 시작하게 만드는 것이다.

thermal [θɔ́ːrml] 열의 **convection** [kənvékʃən] 대류
conduction [kəndʌ́kʃən] 전도 **mechanism** [mékənizəm] 방법
fluid [flúːid] 유체 **molecule** [máːlikjuːl] 분자
dense [dens] 밀도가 높은 **displace** [displéis] 대체하다
assume [əsúːm] 상정하다 **consecutively** [kənsékjətivli] 연이어
pack [pæk] 가득 채우다 **rigid** [rídʒid] 정밀한
arrangement [əréindʒmənt] 배열 **absorb** [əbsɔ́ːrb] 흡수하다
expose [ikspóuz] 노출시키다 **vibrate** [váibreit] 진동하다
bump into ~에 부딪히다 **adjacent** [ədʒéisnt] 인접한
impact [impǽkt] 충돌하다, 영향을 미치다

지시: 주어진 보기에서 적절한 구를 선택하여 전도를 완성하시오.

대류	· 유체는 열을 흡수할수록 밀도가 낮아진다. · 에너지를 운반하는 흐름이 형성된다.
전도	· ·

보기
(A) 분자들은 가열되면 빠르게 진동한다.
(B) 분자들의 충돌은 에너지의 전달을 야기한다.
(C) 열 에너지는 열 자원과의 직접적인 접촉이 있을 때에만 분자들에 영향을 준다.
(D) 고체 물질은 온도가 상승함에 따라 약간 팽창한다.

8 미국 원주민들은 약 17,000년에서 11,000년 전 사이에 시베리아로부터 베링해협을 건너온 이래 북미대륙에 거주해오고 있다. 어떤 단일 사건도, 심지어 빙하기조차도 유럽에서 온 신대륙 정복자들의 등장만큼 그들에게 큰 영향을 끼치지는 못했다. 1492년 콜럼버스가 신대륙에 첫발을 내디뎠을 때부터 19세기까지, 원주민들에 대한 대량학살과 강제이주 정책은 부족들의 대규모 인구 감소와 멸종을 초래했다.

유럽인들의 등장 전에 인디언 원주민들은 사냥과 채집으로 생계를 꾸려가는 부족민이었다. 역사적으로 인디언들은 모두 자연환경과 연결된 영적인 믿음과 의술의 문화로서 기억된다. 각 부족은 기본적인 삶의 방식은 비슷했지만, 자신들만의 독특한 언어와 풍습을 가지고 있었다. 북미 토착 인디언들은 부족 간에 영토 분쟁이나 다른 소유물을 둘러싼 전쟁이 일상적인 관행처럼 자주 일어났음에도 불구하고, 대부분의 경우에 자연적이고 비교적 평화로운 삶을 영위했다.

유럽인의 이주는 토착 인디언들의 삶의 방식을 거의 모든 면에서 방해하였다. 무엇보다도 대다수의 인디언이 노예로 팔려갔는데, 그 예로 크리스토퍼 콜럼버스는 Haiti 섬의 Arawak족 25만 명을 노예로 데려갔다. 둘째로, 정복자들과 뒤이어 도착한 정착민들은 인디언들을 그들의 땅에서 내쫓고, ^D^그들을 가두기 위한 목적에서 마련된 멀고 척박한 거주지로 강제 이주시켰다. 이는 다양한 질병의 확산을 불러왔고, 이러한 환경에서는 지탱될 수 없었던 다수의 문화적 풍습이 사라지게 되었다. 사실, ^B^유럽인들은 미국 원주민들이 면역력을 가지고 있지 못했던 과다한 질병을 유입시켰다.

Bering Strait 베링해협
European Conquistadors 유럽에서 온 신대륙 정복자들
slaughter [slɔ́ːtər] 대량학살 **relocation** [rìloukéiʃən] 강제이주
massive [mǽsiv] 대규모의 **extinction** [ikstíŋkʃən] 멸종
entrance [éntrəns] 등장 **tribal** [tráibəl] 부족의
gatherer [gǽðərər] 채집자 **medicinal** [mədísənl] 의약의
interlink [ìntərlíŋk] 연결하다 **dispute** [dispjúːt] 분쟁
routine [ruːtíːn] 일상적인 **interrupt** [ìntərʌ́pt] 방해하다
first and foremost 무엇보다도
unfavorable [ʌ̀nféivərəbl] 좋지 않은 **upheld** [ʌ̀phéld] 지탱되는
a plethora of 과다한 **immune** [imjúːn] 면역의

지시: 주어진 보기에서 적절한 구를 선택하여 유럽인들의 등장 이후 미국 원주민들의 상황을 완성하시오.

유럽의 식민지화 이전의 미국 원주민	· 사냥과 채집으로 생계를 꾸려나 갔다 · 공통적인 생활방식을 가진 독립적인 부족으로 생활했다
유럽인들의 등장 이후의 미국 원주민	· ·

보기
(A) 사냥하기 위해 강과 호수를 따라 주로 카누를 타고 이동했다
(B) 많은 위험한 외래 질병에 의해 영향을 받았다
(C) 서구 유럽 정복자들의 기독교 신앙을 따랐다

(D) 그들을 수용하기 위해 설계된 거주지에 정착하도록 강요
되었다

9 회화와 조소는 오늘날 가장 인기 있는 예술적인 표현법의 두 가
지 형태이다. 조각보다 대략 2만 5천 년을 거슬러 올라가는 『회
화는 약 3만 2천 년 전에 인류가 행했던 최초의 예술적 활동이
었다. 최초의 회화는 프랑스의 Grotte Chauvet(쇼베 동굴)에
있는 동굴 벽에 새겨지고 색칠되었으며, 당시의 다양한 포유동
물을 묘사했다. 그러나 조각은 5천 년 전이 되어서야 이집트에
서 시작되었고, 그리스인들에 의해서만 계승되어 고급예술의 형
태로 승화될 수 있었다.

기본적으로 회화는 현탁된 안료와 접착제를 표면에 바르는 방법
이다. 회화는 항상 색, 그리고 색을 이용해서 2차원 또는 3차원
의 표면에 하나의 장면이나 사람, 혹은 사물을 표현하는 방법에
중점을 둔다. 반면에 『조각은 어떻게 공간을 차지하고, 공간과
어떤 관계를 맺으며, 우리의 공간에 대한 인식에 어떤 영향을 미
치는지와 같이 거의 공간적인 면에만 관심을 두는 표현 방법이
다. 조각은 항상 3차원적인 형태를 띠며, 일반적으로 인물, 신,
신화 속의 인물, 또는 상상 속의 생물을 표현한다.

사용되는 재료 면에서 볼 때, 회화와 조각은 극단적으로 다르다.
회화는 위에서 언급되었듯이, 그림을 그려 넣을 표면뿐 아니라,
안료와 『일종의 접착제를 칠할 도구를 필요로 한다. 표면의 예로
는 종이, 캔버스, 벽 등이 있다. 화가들은 오일, 구아슈, 고무 수
채화 물감, 잉크, 파스텔 등을 사용한다. 물론 물감을 칠할 도구
도 필요한데, 일반적으로 붓을 사용하지만 스펀지처럼 생긴 것
을 사용할 수도 있고, 물감을 흡수할 수 있는 도구라면 어떤 것
이든 사용 가능하다.

이와는 대조적으로 『조소에 사용되는 재료에는 제한이 없다. ^조
소는 어떤 물체가 가진 부피, 질감 등의 물리적, 의미적인 특성을
변화시키는 행위로 정의되므로, 사용 가능한 재료는 무한하다.
그럼에도 불구하고, 돌, 점토, 나무 등과 같이 전통적으로 사용
되어 온 몇 가지의 재료가 있다. 그러나 현대미술가들이 기체 등
이전에는 잘 사용되지 않던 재료를 사용하는 방법을 실험하기
시작하면서, 이 고전적인 표현법에 활기를 불어넣고 있다.

이 모든 차이점에도 불구하고, 회화와 조각은 같은 목적을 공유
하고 있다. 그것은 바로 인류의 경험을 기록하고, 설명하고, 전
달하는 것이다. 최초의 회화는 초기의 인간 문명이 접했던 포유
류나 기타 동물들에 대한 기록이었고, 이 기록으로 인해 이후의
세대가 그 지역에 어떤 동물들이 많이 살았는지 알 수 있게 되었
다. 고대 피라미드는 파라오와 신들의 조각상으로 장식되었는
데, 이는 그 신들과 귀족들의 삶이 기억될 수 있게 하기 위한 것
이었을 뿐 아니라, 그들의 생이 다음 세상으로 이어져 언젠가 되
살아날 수 있게 하기 위해서이기도 했다. 이 두 가지 경우 모두,
예술은 단지 미적인 즐거움을 주는 것 이상의 기능을 한다. 그것
은 바로 역사와 미래에 대한 희망을 한 세대로부터 다음 세대로
전한다는 점이다.

engrave[ingréiv] 새기다 **depict**[dipíkt] 묘사하다
mammal[mǽməl] 포유동물 **refine**[ri:fáin] 세련되게 하다
suspendid[səspéndid] 현탁(액체 속에 고체 미립자가 분산되는 것)된

pigment[pígmənt] 안료 **deity**[dí:əti] 신
mythological[mìθəlɑ́dʒikəl] 신화의 **medium**[mí:diəm] 도구
adhesive[ædhí:siv] 접착제 **mural**[mjúərəl] 벽의
gouache[gwɑːʃ] 구아슈(아라비아 고무로 만든 불투명한 수채화 물감)
absorption[əbsɔ́:rpʃən] 흡수
contextual[kəntékstʃuəl] 문맥상의 **attribute**[ǽtrəbjùːt] 특성
texture[tékstʃər] 질감 **contemporary**[kəntémpərèri] 현대의
revitalize[ri:váitəlàiz] 활기를 불어넣다 **bounty**[báunti] 많음
adorn[ədɔ́:rn] 장식하다

지시: 주어진 보기에서 적절한 구를 선택하여 관련 있는 예술적
인 표현법에 연결시키시오. 이 문제는 3점이다.

보기
(B) 보통 동물과 바다 생물을 표현한다
(G) 기껏해야 미적 즐거움의 역할을 한다
회화
· (C) 일종의 접착제를 사용한다
· (F) 예술적인 표현법의 가장 전통적인 형태이다
조소
· (A) 사물의 특성을 조작한다
· (D) 무제한적인 형태의 소재를 사용한다
· (E) 공간을 어떻게 다룰지에 집중한다

10 에너지가 대양을 통해 이동할 때, 그것은 물이 원형으로 움직이
게 만들어 파도의 생성을 야기한다. 이것들 중 대부분은 인간에
게 위협이 아니긴 하지만, 이상파랑과 쓰나미 같은 매우 파괴적
인 것들이 특정한 환경 하에서 형성될 수도 있다. 이상파랑은 주
위에 있는 파도보다 두 배 이상 높은 파도인데, 이 용어는 일반
적으로 극심한 폭풍 동안 가끔 발달하는 거대한 파도에만 사용
되기는 한다. 꽤 최근까지, 대부분의 과학자들은 이상파랑의 개
념을 일축했는데, 이러한 종류의 파도에 대한 보고들을 선원들
의 과장이라며 무가치한 것으로 보았다. 하지만, ^1995년에, 북
해의 석유 굴착 장치의 감지기가 그 지역의 다른 파도보다 상당
히 컸던 29.9미터의 파도에 부딪혔다고 기록했다. 이상파랑이
실제로 존재했다는 반박할 수 없는 증거로, 과학자들은 이상파
랑에 대한 추가 정보를 얻기 위해 합심하여 노력했다.

분명해진 한 가지는 이상파랑이 전에 가능하다고 생각되었던 것
보다 훨씬 더 크다는 것이었는데, 미국 해군연구소가 2004년에
허리케인 아이반 동안 40미터가 넘는 높이의 파도를 관측했다.
이 어마어마한 파도가 형성되는 정확한 과정은 알려지지 않았지
만, 연구원들은 바람과 해류 간의 상호 작용이 중요한 역할을 하
는 것이라고 추측한다. 모든 표면파들이 ᴮ바람으로부터 에너지
를 얻기는 하지만, 그것들의 모양과 속도는 해류에 의해 영향을
받는다. 바람이 다가오는 해류의 방향으로 바닷물을 불면, 파도
가 압축되어 위쪽으로 밀린다. 폭풍 동안 바람의 속도와 방향이
격렬하게 변동을 거듭한다는 점을 고려하면, 이 과정은 가끔 보
통보다 훨씬 큰 크기의 파도 하나를 만들어낼 수도 있다.

쓰나미의 경우, 근본적인 원인이 잘 입증되어 있는데, 가장 흔하게는 ^C지진에 의해 에너지가 물속에서 갑자기 방출된다는 것이다. 이것은 외부로 모든 방향에 일련의 쓰나미를 보낸다. 하지만, ^G쓰나미가 수면이 아닌 물속에서 이동한다는 점에 주목하는 것이 중요하다. 따라서, 많은 양의 에너지가 대양을 통해 움직이고 있음에도 불구하고, 심해 표면에는 그것의 조짐이 거의 없다. ^F쓰나미의 높이가 증가하는 때는 얕은 구역에 도달했을 때이다. 쓰나미는 30미터보다 높을 수 있고, 다수의 파도가 잇달아 같은 지역을 덮쳐 상당한 피해를 유발할 것이다. 예를 들어, 2004년에 인도양에서 발생했던 쓰나미는 약 23만 명의 사상자와 150억 달러의 재산상 피해를 야기했다. 이에 대응하여, 위험에 처한 지역의 국가들은 국제적인 쓰나미 경보 체계를 개발하기 위해 협력하기 시작했다.

destructive [distrʌ́ktiv] 파괴적인   rogue wave 이상파랑
occasionally [əkéiʒnəli] 가끔   severe [sivír] 극심한
dismiss [dismís] 일축하다   write off 무가치한 것으로 보다
exaggeration [igzæ̀dʒəréiʃən] 과장   oil platform 석유 굴착 장치
strike [straik] 부딪치다, 덮치다
irrefutable [irifjú:təbl] 반박할 수 없는
concerted [kənsə́:rtid] 합심한   apparent [əpǽrənt] 분명한
track [træk] 관측하다   exceed [iksí:d] 넘다
immense [iméns] 어마어마한
suspect [səspékt] 추측하다, 의심하다
oncoming [á:nkʌ̀miŋ] 다가오는   compress [kəmprés] 압축하다
velocity [vəlá:səti] 속도   fluctuate [flʌ́ktʃueit] 변동을 거듭하다
underlying [ʌ̀ndərláiiŋ] 근본적인   establish [istǽbliʃ] 입증하다
shallow [ʃǽlou] 얕은   multiple [mʌ́ltipl] 다수의
in succession 잇달아

지시: 주어진 선택지에서 적절한 구를 선택하여 관련 있는 파도의 유형에 연결시키시오. 이 문제는 3점이다.

보기
(B) 허리케인과 같은 열대 폭풍우 동안에만 형성된다
(E) 2004년 국제 경보 체계의 구축으로 이어졌다
이상파랑
· (A) 1995년에 처음으로 존재하는 것이 확인되었다
· (D) 움직이는 공기로부터 에너지를 받는다
쓰나미
· (C) 지진의 결과로 만들어진다
· (F) 해안선에 가까워지면서 높이가 증가한다
· (G) 수면 아래에서 이동한다

11 세계 정치사에서 미국이 차지하는 비중을 나타내는 한 가지 특성이 있다면, 그것은 대통령제일 것이다. 정치학자들은 미국을 '대통령제의 탄생지'라고 부른다. 이는 ^G미국이 인도네시아, 필리핀, 남미 대부분의 국가를 포함해 많은 국가가 채택한 대통령제를 처음으로 창시한 국가이기 때문이다. 초기의 대통령제는

영국 군주제에 대한 식민지 거주자들의 반감에 대한 반응으로 형성되었다. 아직까지도, 대통령제에 입각한 미국 정부는 영국이 채택하고 있는 의원내각제와 여러 가지 측면에서 대조를 이루고 있다.

두 제도는 각각의 제도에서 권력의 분립이 어떻게 이루어지는지에 관해서 결정적인 차이를 보인다. 대통령제는 행정부와 입법부라는 두 개의 대등한 부서로의 분립에 기반을 둔다. ^F행정부와 입법부는 서로 분리되어 있으며 어느 한쪽이 다른 한쪽에 권력을 행사할 수 없기 때문에 권력의 남용과 부패를 막아 안정을 유지할 수 있다. 행정부는 ^C국민의 직접 선거에 의해 선출되어 국민이 정부에 대한 강한 믿음을 가질 수 있게 해주는 대통령과 고문 혹은 참모라 불리는 내각으로 이루어진다. 하지만 어떠한 결정 사안에 대해서도 최종적인 결정은 대통령이 내린다. 입법부는 의회를 운영하며 여당에 의해 어떠한 방식으로도 통제되거나 영향받지 않는다.

그에 비해, 모든 종류의 의원내각제는 행정부가 입법부의 지지를 필요로 하는 것을 기반으로 하고 있다. 행정부와 입법부 사이에는 명확한 분립이 없고 분명한 지도자도 존재하지 않는다. 대통령제와 달리 의원내각제 정부의 행정부는 내각과 수상(혹은 다른 종류의 정부의 수장)으로 구성되는데, ^B이 둘은 의사결정 과정에서 동등한 영향력을 가진다. 정부의 수장은 위기 상황에서는 지정된 권한을 사용할 능력이 있지만, 평상시에는 내각의 한 구성원으로서의 역할을 수행할 뿐이다. 입법부는 의회로 구성되는데, 의회는 내각에 크게 영향을 받고, ^E법이나 정책안을 통과시키려면 내각의 승인을 필요로 한다. 따라서 대통령제에 비교할 때 의원내각제에서는 권력이 거의 분리되어 있지 않다.

presidential system 대통령제   birthplace [bə́:rθplèis] 탄생지
adopt [ədápt] 채택하다   reaction [riǽkʃən] 반응
repugnance [ripʌ́gnəns] 반감   monarchy [mánərki] 군주제
parliamentary cabinet system 의원내각제
overriding [òuvərráidiŋ] 결정적인   respective [rispéktiv] 각각의
division [divíʒən] 분립, 분리   executive [igzékjutiv] 행정부의
legislative [lédʒislèitiv] 입법부의   stability [stəbíləti] 안정
abuse [əbjú:s] 남용   corruption [kərʌ́pʃən] 부패
confidence [kánfədəns] 믿음   advisor [ædváizər] 고문
staff [stæf] 참모   in comparison 그에 비해   prime minister 수상
decision-making [disíʒənmèikiŋ] 의사결정
in the case of ~의 경우에는   crisis [kráisis] 위기
parliament [pá:rləmənt] 의회   approval [əprú:vəl] 승인
separation [sèpəréiʃən] 분리

지시: 주어진 보기에서 적절한 구를 선택하여 관련 있는 정치 제도의 종류에 연결시키시오. 이 문제는 3점이다.

보기
(A) 비상 사태에서 특권을 이용할 수 있는 내각
(D) 여당에 의해 관리되는 국가 재정
대통령제
· (C) 국민들에 의해 선출된 정부의 수장

- (F) 별개의 정부 단위 간에 분리된 권력
- (G) 이 유형의 제도를 채택한 첫 번째 국가인 미국

의원내각제
· (B) 모든 정부 당파에 의해 공유되는 의사 결정권
· (E) 내각의 승인에 의해 통과되는 법안

12 유럽 음악은 작곡된 시기에 따라서 크게 몇 개의 양식으로 분류될 수 있고, 각 시대에 널리 유행했던 다양한 양식을 포함하고 있다. 바로크 음악은 17세기에 서서히 발전되어 1700년과 1750년 사이에 결실을 맺었던 성악과 기악의 한 장르이다. 이후에 많은 곡에서 주요 악기로 쓰이게 된 기계식 오르간의 등장과 ^C교회 위상의 상승이 미친 큰 영향은 바로크 음악의 특징에 반영되어 있다. 작곡가들, 그중에서도 특히 J.S. 바흐, 헨델, 비발디는 『주 멜로디에서 거의 벗어나지 않는 장엄한 곡들을 작곡함으로써 자연과의 조화라는 종교적인 가치를 떠받들었다. 복잡하게 꾸며진 곡들은 첫 음부터 마지막 음까지 음의 세기를 일정하게 함으로써, ^G일관된 감정을 정성들여 유지할 수 있도록 작곡되었다. 이때 tremolo나 pizzicato 등의 더욱 다양한 연주법을 사용해서 동일한 청각적 표현의 묘사에 중점을 두는 것을 강조했다.

이와 동시에, 일부 작곡가들은 종교 합창의 형태를 변형시키고 온음계의 음조와 의성적인 대위법을 이용함으로써 성악의 쓰임을 증대하여, 종교적인 서술구조가 더욱 잘 전달될 수 있게 했다. 이를 통해 독창자가 배경 음악 위에 이해하기 쉬운 대사를 읊을 수 있게 되었고, 이러한 형태의 공연은 '머지않아 오페라로 발전하였으며, 아마도 이 시대에 등장했던 가장 눈에 띄는 유행이었을 것이다.

바로크 시대가 지나자 대위법과 장식적인 기교가 음악에서 차지하는 비중은 줄어들었고 그것들은 변조라 불리며 음조를 변화시키는 단선율 구조로 대체되었는데, 이에 따라 명확한 한 가지의 감정이 아닌 다양한 감정 요소를 전달하는 극적인 작품들이 많이 작곡되었다. 고전 음악이라는 용어는 이 직후의 시대를 지칭하는 것으로, 대략 1730년부터 1850년 사이에 나타났는데, 이 용어는 바흐와 후기 고전주의 시대의 저명한 작곡가인 베토벤 사이의 시대를 찬양하기 위해서 일반적으로 쓰이는 용어가 되었다. 이 장르의 특징은 ^E피아노를 선호하게 되어 오르간이 사라지게 되었다는 점이다. ^A많은 곡이 바이올린 등의 현악기에 더하여 이 새로운 건반악기에 중요한 역할을 부여했는데, 이 악기들은 타악기와 함께 클래식 오케스트라를 구성하고 있다. 기악편성법의 강화는 고전주의 장르의 음악적인 복잡성을 보충했는데, 고전주의 음악에서 ^B음악적 주제나 모티프가 다른 형식이나 변화된 형태로 반복되는 과정으로 정의되는 음악의 전개는 4개나 8개의 마디 길이를 한 단위로 하는 구절법을 이용해서 이루어졌다. 구조적인 측면에서, 고전주의 곡들은 계층으로 작은 악장들이 모여서 하나의 장대한 공연으로 완성되었고, 이러한 공연의 길이는 짧게는 30분에서 길게는 세 시간이었다.

encompass[inkʌ́mpəs] 포함하다   epoch[épək] 시대
genre[ʒɑ́:nrə] 장르   come to fruition 결실을 맺다
featured[fíːtʃərd] 주요의   sublime[səbláim] 장엄한
deviate from ~으로부터 벗어나다   intricately[íntrikətli] 복잡하게
emotive[imóutiv] 감정의   note[nout] 음
depiction[dipíkʃən] 묘사   augment[ɔːgmént] 증대시키다
mutate[mjúːteit] 변형시키다   sacred[séikrid] 종교의
choral[kɔ́ːrəl] 합창의   capitalize on ~을 이용하다
diatonic[dàiətánik] 온음계적인   tonality[tounǽləti] 음조
counterpoint[káuntərpɔ̀int] 대위법
storytelling[stɔ́:ritèliŋ] 서술구조
recognizable[rékəgnàizəbl] 인식할 수 있는
ornamentation[ɔ̀ːrnəməntéiʃən] 장식
homophonic[hàməfánik] 단선율의
modulation[màdʒuléiʃən] 변조(變調)
subsequent[sʌ́bsikwənt] 직후의
in common parlance 일반 용어로
canonize[kǽnənàiz] 찬양하다   stringed instrument 현악기
percussion[pərkʌ́ʃən] 타악기
aggrandizement[əgrǽndizmənt] 강화
instrumentation[ìnstrəməntéiʃən] 기악편성법
supplement[sʌ́pləmənt] 보충하다
phrasing technique 구절법(선율을 악상에 따라 적당하게 구분하는 방법)   hierarchically[hàiərɑ́:rkikəli] 계층적으로
movement[múːvmənt] 악장

지시: 주어진 보기에서 적절한 구를 선택하여 관련 있는 유럽 음악의 종류에 연결시키시오. **이 문제는 3점이다.**

보기
(D) 목소리의 응용을 자제했다
(H) 수많은 음악 용어를 만들었다
바로크
· (C) 종교의 높아진 중요성에 영향을 받았다
· (F) 주요 선율에서 거의 벗어나지 않는 곡을 작곡했다
· (G) 보통 한 번에 한 가지 감정에 집중했다
· (I) 오페라의 선행물이었다
고전
· (A) 여러 가지 많은 종류의 악기들을 포함했다
· (B) 변경된 양식에서 반복되는 음악적 주제를 가졌다
· (E) 피아노를 선호했다

HACKERS **TEST**

01 | Age Determination

p.340

1. (B)	2. (D)	3. (D)
4. (A)	5. (B)	6. (A)
7. (C)	8. (D)	9. 2nd

10. Absolute Dating – (D), (E), (G)

　　Relative Dating – (A), (C)

1 1940년대 이전의 고고학자와 지질학자들은 그들이 발견한 물체의 연대를 정확하게 추정할 수 있는 방법을 가지고 있지 못했다. 이후에 시카고 대학의 Manhattan Project를 통해 방사성 붕괴의 속도를 정확하게 측정하는 방법이 발견되었다. 10D이러한 새로운 절대연대 측정법이 표본 안의 특정 원소의 자연방사능을 측정해서 '지금으로부터 6천만 년 전'과 같은 식으로 정확한 연대를 확인하는 데 있어서 효과적임에도 불구하고, 위치나 상관관계를 통해 유물에 추정 연대를 부여하는 상대연대 측정법도 여전히 널리 사용되고 있다.

2 방사능 연대측정이라 불리는 가장 일반적인 절대연대 측정법은 방사성 원소의 붕괴를 통해 암석의 나이를 측정한다. **암석은 철, 마그네슘, 그리고 실리콘과 같은 다양한 안정적인 화학 원소를 포함하고 있는 결정들로 이루어져 있다.** 그러나 암석은 소량의 불안정한 원소들도 포함하고 있는데, 이들 '모' 동위원소들은 방사성 붕괴라고 알려진 현상에 의해 자연적으로 분해되어 '딸' 동위원소로 붕괴된다. 1붕괴되는 속도는 모원소의 반감기라는 개념, 즉 물질의 절반이 붕괴하는 데 소요되는 시간으로 표현된다. 예를 들어, 화성암이나 변성암은 결정화(結晶化)될 때, 그 내부에 우라늄-238의 일정량을 가두두는데, 이 우라늄-238은 45억 년의 반감기를 가진다. 그 기간 동안 이 물질의 절반은 납-206으로 붕괴되고, 45억 년이 더 지나면 나머지의 절반이 변질되어 원래의 4분의 1만 우라늄-238로 남게 되는 식이다. 만약 절반의 양이 남아있다면, 한 번의 반감기가 지났다는 것을 의미한다. 10G따라서 과학자들은 표본에서 한 동위원소에 대한 다른 동위원소의 비율을 측정함으로써 연대를 산정해낼 수 있다.

3 이 방법을 이용하면 암석 표본의 연대를 지구가 처음 생겨난 시기까지도 정확하게 예측할 수 있지만, 10E나무나 식물 섬유질과 같은 유기 물질의 연대를 추정하려면 탄소-14 연대측정이라는 약간 다른 접근방법을 사용해야 한다. 4이 방법의 기본적인 원리는 식물이 죽으면 더는 탄소를 얻지 못하게 되고, 이 시점부터 그것의 탄소-14 동위원소가 붕괴하기 시작한다는 사실이다. 탄소-14 동위원소는 Accelerated Mass Spectrometer를 사용하여 측정되는데, 이 기계는 다른 방사능 측정에서 사용되는 Geiger Muller 측정장치의 배율보다 1,000배 더 크게 확대하여 표본을 분석할 수 있다. 5이 기법의 유일한 단점은 유기 동위원소의 상대적으로 짧은 반감기 때문에, 50,000년보다 오래되지 않은 대상에만 적용이 가능하다는

점이다.

4 이러한 기법들이 등장하기 전에는, 고고학자와 지질학자들은 대개 상대연대 측정법의 사용에만 국한하였다. 이 측정법은 암석층, 지층에 대한 학문인 지층학으로 알려진 지질학의 한 갈래에 속한다. 10C퇴적암이 시간이 지남에 따라 축적되면서 퇴적암에 층이 생기는데, 이는 퇴적암이 과거에 지구에서 일어났던 역사적인 사건의 연속을 해독하는 단서를 지니고 있다는 것을 의미한다. 예를 들어, 지질학자들은 Grand Canyon에서 가장 오래된 암석은 협곡의 가장 아랫부분에 위치하고 있고 원생대 말기에 생성되었을 것이라고 추론했던 한편, 그 위에 덮여 있는 암석들은 더 나중의 고생대 시기에 생성되었을 것이라고 추론했다. 8이러한 추론은 '중첩의 법칙'이라고 불리는데, 이것은 외부 영향을 받지 않은 수평의 암석 배열의 경우 가장 오래된 암석층이 가장 밑부분에 놓이고, 그 위에는 덜 오래된 암석들이 생성된 순서대로 쌓이게 된다는 법칙이다. 이 법칙은 또한 지층의 가장 아랫부분에서 발견된 화석은 그 지역에서 가장 오래된 생명체의 흔적을 나타낸다는 것을 의미하기도 한다. 8드문 경우지만 퇴적되고 압축되어 암석으로 형성된 지층의 배열이 지각 대륙판의 충돌로 지각이 밀려들어 가는 것에 의해서 문자 그대로 뒤집어지기도 하는데, 이는 가장 최근의 암석이 가장 밑부분에 놓이게 된다는 것을 의미한다. 10A그러나 이것은 광범위한 단층과 파쇄된 암석에 의해 식별이 가능한데, 흩뜨려지지 않은 순서로 다른 지역에서 나타나는 같은 암석의 원래의 배열과 확연히 대조되기 때문이다.

archaeologist[àːrkiɑ́lədʒist] 고고학자
geologist[dʒiɑ́lədʒist] 지질학자
radioactive[rèidiouǽktiv] 방사능의　**gauge**[geidʒ] 측정하다
specimen[spésəmən] 표본　**ascertain**[æ̀sərtéin] 확인하다
chronological[krɑ̀nəládʒikəl] 연대순의
speculative[spékjulèitiv] 추리적인
radiometric[rèidioumétrik] 방사에너지 측정의
deterioration[ditìəriəréiʃən] 붕괴　**isotope**[áisətòup] 동위원소
spontaneously[spɑntéiniəsli] 자연적으로
degenerate[didʒénərèit] 붕괴하다　**half-life**[hǽflàif] 반감기
igneous[ígniəs] 화성의　**metamorphic**[mètəmɔ́ːrfik] 변성의
crystallize[krístəlàiz] 결정하다
chronicle[krɑ́nikl] 연대기 순으로 기록하다
magnification[mæ̀gnəfikéiʃən] 배율　**drawback**[drɔ́ːbæ̀k] 단점
advent[ǽdvent] 등장, 도래　**strata**[stréitə] (평행으로 쌓인) 층
sedimentary rock 퇴적암　**decipher**[disáifər] 해독하다
succession[səkséʃən] 연속　**deduce**[didjúːs] 추론하다
gorge[gɔːrdʒ] 협곡　**Proterozoic**[prɑ̀tərəzóuik] 원생대의
Paleozoic[pèiliəzóuik] 고생대의　**thrust**[θrʌst] 밀다
collide[kəláid] 충돌하다　**fault**[fɔːlt] 단층을 일으키다

1 지문에 따르면, 방사성 붕괴에 대해 추론할 수 있는 것은?

　(A) 모든 방사성 동위원소에 동일하다.

　(B) 방사성 붕괴가 일어나는 속도는 일정하다.

　(C) 딸 동위원소는 붕괴를 겪는다.

　(D) 현재 우라늄의 속도만 알려져 있다.

2 지문의 단어 "determine"과 의미상 가장 유사한 것은?

(A) 발달하다
(B) 끝내다
(C) 걱정하다
(D) 계산하다

3 지문의 단어 "its"가 가리키는 것은?

(A) 물질
(B) 표본
(C) 일생
(D) 식물

4 3단락에 따르면, Accelerated Mass Spectrometer는 _____ 하기 위해 사용된다.

(A) 동위원소의 수를 측정하기 위해
(B) 탄소의 종류를 식별하기 위해
(C) 방사능 농도를 측정하기 위해
(D) 암석의 표본을 분리하기 위해

5 3단락에서 글쓴이는 _____ 하기 위해 50,000년보다 오래되지 않은 대상을 언급한다.

(A) Accelerated Mass Spectrometer의 강점을 설명하기 위해
(B) 탄소-14 방법이 사용에 한계가 있다는 것을 보여주기 위해
(C) 유기체 동위원소의 중요성을 강조하기 위해
(D) Geiger Muller 분광계가 다룰 수 있는 범위를 제시하기 위해

6 지문의 단어 "succession"과 의미상 가장 유사한 것은?

(A) 연속
(B) 방해
(C) 중요성
(D) 손실

7 지문의 단어 "deduced"와 의미상 가장 유사한 것은?

(A) 암시했다
(B) 나타냈다
(C) 판단했다
(D) 주장했다

8 4단락에서, 글쓴이는 왜 지각 대륙판의 충돌을 언급하는가?

(A) 새로운 암석이 내륙에 만들어지는 구조를 명백하게 하기 위해
(B) 암석이 점점 층이 되는 과정을 설명하기 위해
(C) 상대연대 측정법은 더 이상 현대 과학에서 유용하지 않다는 것을 증명하기 위해
(D) 중첩의 법칙이 적용되지 않은 경우를 설명하기 위해

9 네 개의 네모[■]는 다음 문장이 삽입될 수 있는 부분을 나타내고 있다.

암석은 철, 마그네슘, 그리고 실리콘과 같은 다양한 안정적인 화학 원소를 포함하고 있는 결정들로 이루어져 있다.

이 문장은 어느 자리에 들어가는 것이 가장 적절한가?

10 지시: 주어진 보기에서 적절한 구를 선택하여 그들이 나타내는 연대 측정법의 종류에 연결시키시오. **이 문제는 3점이다.**

보기
(B) 인력을 요하는 표본 굴착의 필요성을 없앤다
(F) 표본의 주 원료를 알아내기 위해 표본에 화학 물질을 바른다
절대연대 측정법
· (D) 인공 유물의 정확한 연대를 파악할 수 있다
· (E) 탄소-14 동위원소를 사용해서 식물의 연대를 추정한다
· (G) 암석의 모체와 딸의 성분 비율을 측정한다
상대연대 측정법
· (A) 지질 변화의 경우 다른 지역을 고려한다
· (C) 역사적 사건의 순서를 확인하기 위해 층 내 암석을 관찰한다

02 Mesopotamian and Egyptian Civilizations

1. (C)	2. (B)	3. (B)
4. (D)	5. (C)	6. (C)
7. (B)	8. (C)	9. 4th
10. Mesopotamia – (B), (E) Egypt – (C), (D), (G)		

1 기원전 4000년경, 비옥한 초승달 지대로 알려진 티그리스강과 유프라테스강 사이의 범람원 지역에 살던 수렵 채집인들은 방랑적인 삶의 방식을 중단하고 정착 농경지에 자리를 잡았다. [1]안정적인 식량 수급은 구성원 간의 협동을 필요로 하는 인구 증가의 시대를 열었고, 이는 메소포타미아 제국이라는 거대한 규모의 정치적 조직의 탄생으로 이어졌다. 400년 후, 이집트가 복잡한 부족적 특성을 띠었던 신석기 문화에서 잘 정비된 군주제로 빠르게 변화함에 따라 비슷한 변화가 나일강 기슭을 따라 나타났다.

2 함께 문명의 발상지로 알려진 이 두 문화는 거의 동시에 등장했지만, 두 문화 간에는 주로 독특한 지리적 구성에서 기인한 근본적인 차이점이 존재하였다. 이집트는 나일강으로부터 양분을 공급받는, 중심지를 관통하는 비옥한 지역을 제외하면 완전히 메말랐다. 세 면은 사막에 의해서, 나머지 한 면은 지중해에 의해 가로막혀 있기 때문에, 외부의 영향을 받지 않고 나일강의 생명력을 부여하는 속성을

506 | 토플 인강·단어암기 MP3 HackersIngang.com

숭배하는 단일적인 문화적 정체성을 띠게 되었고, 이는 정치 체제의 상징적 근간을 형성하였다. [10E]반면, 메소포타미아 문명은 넓은 지역에 흩어져 있었고 이로 인해서 독립적인 도시들이 여러 지역에 뿌리내리게 되었다. 이들 도시에서의 생활은 끊임없이 예측할 수 없는 극심한 홍수의 괴롭힘을 받았기 때문에, 대도시들은 어려움에 처하게 되면 서로를 침략해야 할 상황에 몰리게 되는 경우가 많았다. [10E]그 결과는 격렬한 격변의 연속이었고, 이 때문에 화합과 결합이 희박했다.

3 수 세기에 걸친 시간 동안 수많은 집단이 번갈아가면서 비옥한 초승달 지역을 장악했다. 제국들의 발전과 쇠퇴가 반복되었는데도 불구하고, 이 지역의 문화는 기본적으로 변하지 않았다. 처음으로 등장한 대제국은 수메르인의 제국으로, 대략 기원전 3000년 전부터 이 지역을 통치하기 시작했다. 왕은 중요하기는 했지만 신성시되지는 않았고 대신 인간과 신을 이어주는 소통자로서의 역할을 수행했다. [6]그들의 주요 업무 중 하나는 씨앗을 심기 가장 좋은 시기를 결정하는 것이었다. 이러한 필요가 예측하기 힘든 범람원의 변화를 기록하고 자원을 관리하기 위한 세계 최초의 문자인 설형문자의 발전을 촉진했다. [10C]메소포타미아인들에게 종교가 중요하긴 했지만, 이집트에서처럼 삶의 모든 면에 스며들 정도는 아니었다. [7]이 때문에, 사회구성원의 규칙과 책임을 명확히 서술한 엄격한 법이 존재했고, 그중 가장 유명한 것은 함무라비 법전이다. 이 법전과 다른 유물들을 통해 고고학자들은 메소포타미아 사회가 엄격한 계급들로 이루어진 고도로 조직화된 사회라는 것을 발견했다. [10B]개개인이 땅을 소유할 수 있었으며, 이는 왕의 권력을 견제하는 역할을 수행했던 더욱 강력한 상인 계층의 등장으로 이어졌다.

4 메소포타미아의 불안정한 발달과는 완전히 대조적으로, 고대 이집트는 그 제국기의 대부분에 걸쳐 안정을 유지했다. 이집트는 기원전 3100년에 처음으로 통일되었고 기원전 525년 페르시아에 정복될 때까지 안정된 상태로 유지되었다. [10G]이러한 환경적, 정치적인 안정기는 나일 강이 정기적인 범람을 보여주듯이 우주는 규칙과 예측성에 따라 움직인다는 중심사상으로 이어졌다. 윤리적인 면에서는, 법과 질서가 유지되고 인류가 자신의 욕망과 행동을 자제할 의무를 짐으로써 사회가 지속적으로 번영할 수 있었다. 통치자 파라오는 저승신의 아들인 호루스의 화신으로 여겨졌고, 따라서 그의 권력은 절대적이었다. [10D]사회의 정점에서, 파라오가 모든 토지, 산업, 상업을 독점했으므로 경제는 파라오에 의해 좌우되었고, 이집트의 생활의 모든 일면에 대한 압도적인 국가의 통제가 존재하였다. 그는 재정에 대한 의무 외에도, 신을 숭배하기 위해 의식을 행하고 신전을 건설하였다.

floodplain[flʌ́dplèin] (수위가 높을 때 물에 잠기는) 범람원(原)
Fertile Crescent 비옥한 초승달 지대(나일강과 티그리스강과 페르시아만을 연결하는 고대 농업 지대)
sedentary agrarian settlement 정착 농경지
coordination[kouɔ̀ːrdənéiʃən] 협동
Neolithic[nìːəlíθik] 신석기 시대의
Cradle of Civilization 문명의 발상지
simultaneously[sàiməltéiniəsli] 동시에
fundamental[fʌ̀ndəméntl] 근본적인

composition[kàmpəzíʃən] 구성 arid[ǽrid] 메마른
save for ~을 제외하고는 swath[swɑθ] 지역
nourish[nə́ːriʃ] 자양분을 주다 insulate[ínsəlèit] 가로막다
unanimous[juːnǽnəməs] 단일적인
unadulterated[ʌ̀nədʌ́ltərèitid] 다른 요소가 섞이지 않고 순수한
subservient[səbsə́ːrviənt] 숭배하는
scatter[skǽtər] 뿔뿔이 흩어지게 하다 take root 뿌리 내리다
plague[pleig] 괴롭히다 metropolis[mitrápəlis] 대도시
tempestuous[tempéstʃuəs] 격렬한 sequence[síːkwəns] 연속
upheaval[ʌphíːvəl] 격변 cohesion[kouhíːʒən] 결합
tenuous[ténjuəs] 희박한 divine[diváin] 신성한
liaison[lìːeizɔ́ːŋ] 소통자 infiltrate[ínfiltreit] 스며들게 하다
delineate[dilínièit] 서술하다 Code of Hammurabi 함무라비 법전
obligate[ábləgèit] 의무를 지우다 subdue[səbdjúː] 자제하다
incarnation[ìnkɑːrnéiʃən] 화신 apex[éipeks] 정점
monopolize[mənápəlàiz] 독점하다
overwhelming[ðuvərhwélmiŋ] 압도적인

1 1단락에 따르면, 글쓴이가 떠돌아다니며 살던 사람들이 한곳에 정착하기 시작한 결과로 암시하는 것은?

(A) 그들은 풍부한 식량 비축 덕분에 더 이상 사냥할 필요가 없었다.
(B) 자연에 대한 경외에 근거한 종교가 즉시 탄생하였다.
(C) 늘어나는 인구를 관리하기 위한 정치 체제에 대한 필요성이 생겼다.
(D) 강의 범람을 처리할 방법을 개발해야 했다.

2 지문의 단어 "emerged"와 의미상 가장 유사한 것은?

(A) 회합했다
(B) 나타났다
(C) 작동되었다
(D) 발달했다

3 아래 문장 중 지문 속의 음영된 문장의 핵심 정보를 가장 잘 표현하고 있는 것은 무엇인가? 오답은 문장의 의미를 현저히 왜곡하거나 핵심 정보를 빠뜨리고 있다.

(A) 나일강의 삶을 중심으로 한 문화적 정체성은 외부 문화의 영향에 매우 저항적인 정치 체제를 낳았다.
(B) 정치 체제의 기반은 지리적 고립으로 인해 외부의 영향을 받지 않고 나일강에 의존하는 동질적인 문화였다.
(C) 사막과 지중해 사이에 위치한 나일강에서 발달한 문화는 복잡한 정치 체제 때문에 영향력이 있었다.
(D) 정치 체제의 상징적인 특성은 나일강에 형성된 문화가 외부 세력의 영향에 저항하기 위한 조치를 취하도록 했다.

4 지문의 단어 "sequence"와 의미상 가장 유사한 것은?

(A) 선택
(B) 집중
(C) 분배
(D) 연속

5 지문의 단어 "Their"가 가리키는 것은?

(A) 집단

(B) 제국

(C) 수메리아인

(D) 신

6 3단락에 따르면, 설형문자의 발전은 _____에 대한 필요에 의해 촉진되었다.

(A) 나라의 영토를 통치하기 위해

(B) 왕의 권위를 높이기 위해

(C) 농업 활동을 다스리기 위해

(D) 종교 의식을 기록하기 위해

7 3단락에서, 글쓴이는 왜 "the Code of Hammurabi"를 언급하는가?

(A) 왕의 권력이 어떻게 상인 계층의 견제를 받았는지 보여주기 위해

(B) 메소포타미아인들이 따랐던 법의 예를 제시하기 위해

(C) 초기 메소포타미아인들이 가졌던 개인의 권리를 정의하기 위해

(D) 메소포타미아의 법과 고대 이집트의 법을 대조하기 위해

8 지문의 단어 "apex"와 의미상 가장 유사한 것은?

(A) 근원

(B) 핵심

(C) 절정

(D) 상징

9 네 개의 네모[■]는 다음 문장이 삽입될 수 있는 부분을 나타내고 있다.

그는 재정에 대한 의무 외에도, 신을 숭배하기 위해 의식을 행하고 신전을 건설하였다.

이 문장은 어느 자리에 들어가는 것이 가장 적절한가?

10 지시: 주어진 보기에서 적절한 구를 선택하여 관련 있는 문명의 종류에 연결시키시오. 이 문제는 3점이다.

보기
(A) 왕의 권력은 국가가 더 세속화될수록 약해졌다.
(F) 신과 소통할 수 있는 사람은 가장 신성한 존재로 여겨졌다.

메소포타미아
· (B) 토지 소유권과 강한 경제력이 있었던 계층이 나타났다.
· (E) 다양한 지역에 있던 각각의 도시들은 끊임없는 혼란을 겪었다.

이집트
· (C) 종교는 개인의 삶의 모든 부분에 영향을 미쳤다.
· (D) 전능한 왕이 사회의 모든 영역을 통치했다.
· (G) 우주는 안정적이고 일관된다는 믿음이 퍼졌다.

---

03 Parasitic Plants

p.348

1. (A)	2. (C)	3. (A)
4. (B)	5. (C)	6. (D)
7. (B)	8. (B)	9. 2nd
10. Hemiparasites – (B), (E), (G)		
Holoparasites – (C), (D)		

1 모든 생물은 성장하고 번식하며 생명에 필요한 일상적 기능을 수행하기 위해 에너지원을 필요로 한다. 먹이사슬에 대한 통념에 따르면, 태양이 먹이 사슬의 최상층에서 식물에 에너지를 제공해주고, 식물은 다른 생물에게 먹히고, 이 생물도 또 다른 생물에게 잡아먹히고, 이러한 과정이 계속해서 이어진다. 이는 대부분의 종에서 확실한 사실이지만, 태양을 효율적으로 이용할 수 없어 뿌리조직을 이용해 먹이를 '물고' 그 먹이의 생명 유지에 필요한 영양분을 '빨아들인다'는 점에서 흡혈귀와 유사하게 다른 식물들에게 달라붙어서 살아가야만 하는 식물도 있다.

2 [2]모든 기생식물은 독특한 적응조직, 즉 기생근이라고 불리는 변형된 뿌리를 가지고 있는데, 이는 기생식물들이 영양분이나 수분을 뽑아내기 위해서 다른 식물에 고정될 수 있게 해준다. 이는 중요한 특징인데, 숙주식물에 붙어살지만 기생근이 없어 숙주의 수분이나 영양분을 빨아들이지 못하므로 기생식물은 아닌, 착생식물이라 불리는 식물도 있기 때문이다. [3]그러한 진짜 기생식물은 기생근이 숙주식물의 어느 부위를 뚫고 자라는지에 따라서 두 부류로 구분할 수 있다. 첫째는 반기생식물로, 뿌리에서 줄기로 수분이 이동하는 목질부에 달라붙어 살고, [10D]두 번째 종류는 전기생식물로, 숙주식물의 영양분이 분배되는 체관부에 붙어서 살아간다.

3 [10G]반기생식물은 희생양으로부터 물과 용해된 무기물만을 빼앗기 때문에, [10E]스스로 광합성을 통해 탄수화물을 생산해야만 한다. [4]이 과정은 엽록소를 필요로 하므로 이 도둑들은 초록 빛깔을 띠게 되는데, 이는 보통 식물의 잎과 이들을 시각적으로 구분할 수 없게 한다. 그러므로 식물학자들은 반기생식물을 구별하기 위해서는 뿌리를 자세히 관찰하여야 하는데, 반기생식물의 뿌리는 종류에 따라서 숙주의 줄기나 뿌리 부위로 뻗는 자그마한 털 같은 돌기를 특징으로 한다. [10B]이들은 실제로 숙주의 조직을 관통하지는 않으나 대신에 숙주의 세포막에 달라붙는데, 이는 세포막의 넓은 표면적으로 인해 더욱 효과적인 액체 운송이 가능하기 때문이다.

4 겨우살이는 이러한 생존전략의 적절한 예시인데, 겨우살이의 붉은 색과 하얀색 열매들은 새들에게 먹힌 다음 소화기관을 통과해서 나뭇가지 위에 배설된다. 이러한 끈적끈적한 씨가 안착하면, 씨에서 기생근이 자라기 시작하고, 이 기생근은 나무껍질을 관통하여 나무의 목질부에 달라붙는다. 그리고 나무로부터 필요한 수분을 흡수하여 성장을 시작한다. 이런 방식으로 겨우살이는 다양한 종류의 나무에 얹혀 자랄 수 있게 되고, 숙주에 대한 침입이 심할 경우에는 치명적인 결과가 나타나기도 하지만, 일반적으로 이러한 피해는 숙주

의 성장을 둔화시키는 정도에 그친다.

5 하지만 더욱 유해한 전기생식물의 경우에는 그렇지 않은데, 전기생식물은 기생근을 숙주의 체관부 전체에 뻗치게 해놓고 자신에게 필요한 탄수화물의 대부분을 숙주식물로부터 탈취하는데, 이는 숙주식물이 시들어서 말라 죽을 위기에 놓이게 하는 경우가 많다. 전기생식물은 에너지 생산을 위한 광합성을 필요로 하지 않으므로 엽록소를 만들지 않으며, [10]따라서 다양한 색깔의 잎과 줄기 조직을 그 특징으로 하고, 다른 모든 기생식물과 마찬가지로 다양한 종류의 꽃을 피우는데 세계에서 가장 큰 꽃인 화려한 Rafflesia도 그중 하나다.

6 이 거대한 식물은 모든 필요 영양분을 Tetrastigma 덩굴이라는 숙주식물로부터 빨아들인다. 드물지만 지나친 탐닉에 의해 숙주가 죽음에 이를 정도의 손실로 약화되지 않는다면, Rafflesia가 흡수하는 영양분의 양에는 제한이 없는 듯 보이며, 따라서 Rafflesia가 최종적으로 피우게 될 꽃의 크기에도 제한이 없게 되는 것이다. 이것이 황폐화된 숙주식물의 껍질을 뚫고 피면, 종종 직경 1미터가 넘는, 실로 엄청난 크기의 화려함을 과시한다. 썩은 시체 냄새와 비슷한 이 꽃의 냄새는 파리와 딱정벌레를 수 마일 밖으로부터 유인하는데, 이들은 떼를 지어 몰려와 꽃을 수분하여 4백만여 개의 씨를 만드는 데 도움을 준다. Rafflesia의 씨앗은 동물들에 의해 다른 덩굴에 퍼지는데, 새로운 Rafflesia는 더욱 거대한 꽃을 피울 준비를 갖출 때까지 덩굴에 붙어서 숨어 자라다가 결국에는 자신들이 있던 자리에 진이 다 빠진 Tetrastigma의 말라 죽은 껍질만을 남기면서 이러한 생명의 주기가 계속된다.

7 기생식물이 끼치는 피해의 정도는, 겨우살이처럼 상대적으로 양호한 것에서부터, Rafflesia처럼 더욱 심각한 것에 이르기까지 기생식물의 종류에 따라 매우 다르게 나타난다. 그러나 반기생식물과 전기생식물 모두, 성공적인 기생식물은 적어도 성공적으로 번식을 마치기 전까지는 숙주를 죽이지 않는다는 생태의 일반법칙을 따른다.

devour[diváuər] 먹다 leech[liːtʃ] ~에 달라붙다
life-sustaining[làifsəstéiniŋ] 생명을 유지하는
parasitic[pærəsítik] 기생하는 haustorium[hɔːstɔ́ːriəm] 기생근
flora[flɔ́ːrə] 식물 extract[ikstrǽkt] 뽑아내다
epiphyte[épəfàit] 착생(着生)식물 derive[diráiv] 끌어내다
hemiparasite[hèmipǽrəsàit] 반(半)기생생물
xylem[záiləm] 목질부(木質部)
holoparasite[hàləpǽrəsait] 전(全)기생생물
phloem[flóuem] 체관부 extort[ikstɔ́ːrt] 빼앗다
carbohydrate[kàːrbəháidreit] 탄수화물
photosynthesis[fòutousínθəsis] 광합성
chlorophyll[klɔ́ːrəfìl] 엽록소 bandit[bǽndit] 도둑
indistinguishable[ìndistíŋgwiʃəbl] 구분할 수 없는
foliage[fóuliidʒ] 잎 botanist[bátənist] 식물학자
projection[prədʒékʃən] 돌기 genus[dʒíːnəs] 종류
latch[lætʃ] 달라붙다 membrane[mémbrein] (식물의) 세포막
stratagem[strǽtədʒəm] 전략 exemplify[igzémpləfài] 예증하다
mistletoe[mísltòu] 겨우살이 excrete[ikskríːt] 배설하다
infestation[infestéiʃən] (체내) 침입
malevolent[məlévələnt] 악의적인 wrest[rest] 탈취하다

behemoth[bihíːməθ] 거대 조직체
overindulgence[òuvərindʌ́ldʒəns] 지나침
ravage[rǽvidʒ] 황폐화하다 extravagance[ikstrǽvəgəns] 화려함
monumental[mànjuméntl] 엄청난 odor[óudər] 냄새, 향기
corpse[kɔːrps] 시체 beetle[bíːtl] 딱정벌레
swarm[swɔːrm] 떼지어 모이다 pollinate[pálənèit] 수분시키다
stealth[stelθ] 은밀 mammoth[mǽməθ] 거대한
husk[hʌsk] 껍질 exhausted[igzɔ́ːstid] 진이 다 빠진
pathogenicity[pæθoudʒənísəti] 병원성(病原性)
benign[bináin] 양호한, 온화한

1 지문의 단어 "devoured"와 의미상 가장 유사한 것은?
(A) 먹힌
(B) 배가 튀어나온
(C) 높아진
(D) 축적된

2 지문에 따르면, 글쓴이는 왜 "epiphytes"를 언급하는가?
(A) 기생식물의 다른 종류를 설명하기 위해
(B) 식물이 영양분을 얻는 다양한 방법을 제시하기 위해
(C) 기생식물의 정의를 명확하게 하기 위해
(D) 기생근의 역할을 강조하기 위해

3 지문에 따르면, 기생식물의 반기생식물 또는 전기생식물로의 분류는 _____에 의해 결정된다.
(A) 변형된 뿌리가 숙주에 붙어 있는 위치
(B) 숙주로부터 영양분을 흡수하는 속도
(C) 잡아먹는 종의 종류
(D) 기생하는 기생균의 유무

4 3단락에 따르면, 반기생식물은 _____ 때문에 일반 식물과 시각적으로 구별되지 않는다.
(A) 같은 모양의 뿌리를 가지고 있기 때문에
(B) 엽록소 때문에 같은 색조를 갖기 때문에
(C) 줄기에 작은 돌기가 있기 때문에
(D) 같은 향을 내뿜기 때문에

5 지문의 단어 "lethal"과 의미상 가장 유사한 것은?
(A) 뜻밖의
(B) 잔인한
(C) 치명적인
(D) 수명이 짧은

6 지문의 단어 "that"이 가리키는 것은?
(A) 화려함
(B) 직경
(C) 꽃
(D) 냄새

7 아래 문장 중 지문 속의 음영된 문장의 핵심 정보를 가장 잘 표현하고 있는 것은 무엇인가? 오답은 문장의 의미를 현저히 왜곡하

거나 핵심 정보를 빠뜨리고 있다.

(A) Tetrastigma 덩굴에 동물이 찾아오면, 이들은 Rafflesia가 새로운 꽃을 성장시킬 기회를 빼앗는다.

(B) Rafflesia의 새로운 생장물은 동물들이 씨앗을 가져와 다른 Tetrastigma 덩굴에 침투시키면 생긴다.

(C) Rafflesia는 동물들이 다른 Tetrastigma에 씨앗을 퍼뜨리게 하는 주기로 성장한다.

(D) Tetrastigma는 씨앗이 퍼지지 않기 때문에 많은 동물들을 끌어들일 꽃을 아직 피우지 않았다.

8 지문의 단어 "severe"와 의미상 가장 유사한 것은?

(A) 부정적인
(B) 극도의
(C) 분열시키는
(D) 누적하는

9 네 개의 네모[■]는 다음 문장이 삽입될 수 있는 부분을 나타내고 있다.

이것이 황폐화된 숙주식물의 껍질을 뚫고 피면, 종종 직경 1미터가 넘는, 실로 엄청난 크기의 화려함을 과시한다.

이 문장은 어느 자리에 들어가는 것이 가장 적절한가?

10 **지시:** 주어진 보기에서 적절한 구를 선택하여 관련 있는 식물의 종류에 연결시키시오. **이 문제는 3점이다.**

보기
(A) 번식의 목적으로 꽃을 피울 수 없다
(F) 영양분 공급을 차단하여 항상 숙주를 죽게 한다

반기생생물
· (B) 숙주식물의 세포막에 넓은 표면적으로 달라붙는다
· (E) 스스로 탄수화물을 만들기 위해 광합성을 한다
· (G) 숙주식물로부터 물과 용해된 무기물만을 뽑아낸다

전기생생물
· (C) 다양한 색깔의 잎과 줄기를 나타낸다
· (D) 숙주의 영양분 이동 세포에 달라붙는다

04 Sources of Modern African History

p.352

1. (B)	2. (B)	3. (D)
4. (A)	5. (C)	6. (C)
7. (D)	8. (A)	9. 1st

10. Written Resources – (C), (E)
Oral Resources – (A), (B), (F)

1 무수한 현인은 아프리카 역사에 대해 학자들에게 접근 가능한 자원이 부족하다고 간주하는 것이 아프리카 과거의 세부적 이해를 방해한다고 주장해왔다. **일부는 심지어 아프리카에 확인할 수 있는 역사 자체가 있기는 한 건지 과감히 질문하기까지 했다.** 그러나 역사 기록이 유럽이나 동아시아처럼 문서화가 잘 된 지역들만큼 완전하지는 않지만, 그럼에도 불구하고 아프리카 역사는 통찰력이 있는 자료들로 가득하다. 이로부터 역사가들은 아프리카의 지나간 나날에 대해 최소한 부분적이라도 의미 있는 묘사를 할 수 있는 유용한 정보를 추출할 수 있다. 이러한 자원은 문서든지 구술이든지 간에, 세계의 가장 매혹적인 대륙 중 하나의 잘 알려지지 않은 먼 옛날에 대해 빛을 비춰줄 필수적인 도구이다.

2 비록 흩어져 있고 대륙의 특정 지역에 크게 한정되어 있지만 많은 양의 문서가 실제로 존재한다. ^{10E}이 문서의 대부분은 아라비아어나 유럽어로 보존되어 있다. ²전자는 이슬람교도의 침입의 결과로서 생겼고 12세기 동안 널리 퍼졌다. ^{3C}문서에는 고위 인사의 부고, ^{3B}정치 선전, ^{3A}여행기가 포함된다. 아라비아의 문서 중 다수는 현저히 논쟁적인 어투를 쓰며 종교적인 목적으로 가득 차 있지만, 일부는 여행 경로, 천연자원, 농업에 관한 풍부한 세속적인 정보를 포함한다. 상대적으로 부족한 것은 공문서인데, 구할 수 있는 공문서는 비교적 객관적인 자료를 제공하며, 아라비아어는 확실히 북아프리카의 넓은 지역을 통틀어 외교 담화에 사용되었다. ^{10C}공문서는 종종 재판 결과, 조약, 금융 거래 등 상상력이 부족하고 지루한 문서에 지나지 않기 때문에 첫눈에는 영감을 주지 않는 것으로 보일 수도 있지만, 이야기와 달리 공문서는 극도로 객관적인 어조로 쓰였기 때문에 이러한 공식 기록은 높은 수준의 신빙성이 있다.

3 유럽어로 쓰인 자료에 대해 말하자면, 이 기록들은 주로 식민지 종주국의 관점에서 쓰였다. ^{10E}가장 초기의 자료 중에는 기독교 선교사가 작성한 자료들이 있는데, ⁴선교사들은 아프리카의 외딴 지역으로 가서 고립된 부족의 묘사를 처음으로 기록하였다. 선교사들은 토착민들과 함께 살고 그들의 언어를 배우면서 사회적이고 문화적인 정보를 서부 세계로 전달하는 유일한 위치에 있었다. 그들은 현지의 풍습, 의식, 옷, 그리고 행동을 깜짝 놀랄 정도로 자세하게 묘사하였다. 그러나 그들의 이야기에는 현저한 편견이 있었는데, 그것은 비신자들의 소위 미개하고 원시적인 사회를 향한 종종 경멸적인 태도였다. 유사하게 유럽인 탐험가들과 식민지 통치자들이 쓴 문서의 내용과 어조는 식민지의 목적에 매우 찬성하는 경향이 있었다.

4 토착 부족의 관점에서 쓰인 문서의 부재는 아프리카 언어가 언어의 다양성에 대한 세계에서 가장 주요한 예 중 하나임에도 불구하고, 아프리카 언어의 대부분이 문자가 없다는 사실에 의해 대부분 설명될 수 있다. 문자로 표기할 수 있는 스와힐리어와 하우사어조차도 시와 신화에 제한되어 있었다. <mark>이처럼 사하라 사막 이남의 아프리카에서 현존하는 토착 자료의 다수가 구술 자료에 매우 의존하고 있기 때문에, 그것은 구술 역사에 접근할 때와 동일한 주의를 기울이면서 보아야 한다.</mark> 사실상, 이 지역의 사회는 기록을 보존하는 전문 학자들이나 애호를 발달시킨 적이 없다. ^{10A}그리고 대개 빠르게 진화하는 구술 문서는 동시대의 추세와 사람들이 의식적으로든 무의식적으로든 어떻게 주관적으로 그들만의 역사를 건설하는지를 더 잘

보여준다. 이 한계는 일부 역사가들이 구술 역사를 공상적인 것으로 생각하도록 하였고, 실제로 구술과 공문서나 고고학적 증거 사이에는 불일치가 있었다.

5 ⁶하지만 이러한 위험에도 불구하고 구술 문서는 고유의 가치를 확실히 가지고 있는데, ¹⁰ᶜ이는 토착민들의 관점을 보여주기 때문이다. ¹⁰ᴮ그들은 살아있는 박물관으로 기능하면서 아프리카의 문화를 설명하고, 역사가가 역사를 새로운 관점에서 보도록 유도한다. 공문서와 달리 구전은 역사를 그저 보존하거나 보여주는 것이 아니라, 역사를 창조하고 예술적이거나 재미있는 방식으로 나타낸다. 그리고 이러한 꾸밈이 항상 허구인 것은 아니다. 일부 서사시는 역사적 일상생활을 정확히 보여주는 정보나 비유적인 표현으로 가득 차 있고, 이러한 이야기는 세대에서 세대로 구두로 전달된다. 예를 들어, '실라마카의 서사시'에서 우리는 왕의 양 떼를 돌보도록 선택된 양치기들의 목축 사회와 하나의 가죽끈은 엄지발가락 위에 있고 다른 하나는 발뒤꿈치에 있는, 무두질한 황소 가죽으로 만든 신발을 사람들이 어떻게 신었는지에 대해 알 수 있다. ⁸역사가들은 구술의 가치를 깨닫고 열광적으로 인터뷰에 눈길을 돌렸고, 이는 생활사라는 구술의 완전히 새로운 장르가 생겨나게 했다. 사람들은 식민지와 식민지 이후의 경험에 대한 기억을 공유하고, 개인적인 삶에 대해 말하고, 가족에서 가족으로 오래 전해져 내려온 이야기를 상술하도록 요청받는다. 문서 및 고고학적 증거와 비교하기 위해 나란히 놓였을 때, 구술은 아프리카의 문화와 역사에 대해 잠깐 들여다보는 것 이상을 전달한다. 오히려 아프리카의 살아있는 영혼의 스냅 사진을 찍어준다.

innumerable [injú:mərəbl] 무수한 pundit [pʌ́ndit] 현인
allege [əlédʒ] ~을 주장하다 dearth [də:rθ] 부족
preclude [priklú:d] 방해하다 antiquity [æntíkwəti] 먼 옛날
obituary [oubítʃuèri] 부고 dignitary [dígnətèri] 고위 인사
polemical [pəlémikəl] 논쟁하는 secular [sékjulər] 세속적인
discourse [dískɔːrs] 담화 little more than ~에 지나지 않는
judicial [dʒuːdíʃəl] 재판에 의한
matter-of-fact [mǽtərəvfǽkt] 객관적인 style [stail] 어조
authenticity [ɔ̀ːθentísəti] 신빙성 missionary [míʃənèri] 선교사
alongside [əlɔ́ːŋsàid] ~와 함께 pejorative [pidʒɔ́ːrətiv] 경멸하는
slant [slænt] 경향이 있다 in favor of ~에 찬성하여
foremost [fɔ́ːrmòust] 가장 주요한
transcribe [trænskráib] 문자로 표기하다 extant [ékstənt] 현존하는
sub-Saharan 사하라 사막 이남의 literati [lìtərá:ti] 학자들
penchant [péntʃənt] 애호, 취미 fanciful [fǽnsifəl] 공상적인
discrepancy [diskrépənsi] 불일치 pitfall [pítfɔ̀ːl] 위험
intrinsic [intrínsik] 고유의 illuminate [ilúːmənèit] ~을 설명하다
induce [indjúːs] 유도하다 oral tradition 구전
embellishment [imbéliʃmənt] 꾸밈 fiction [fíkʃən] 허구
epic [épik] 서사시 imagery [ímidʒəri] 비유적인 표현
flock [flɑk] 양떼 tan [tæn] (가죽을) 무두질하다 ox [ɑks] 황소
hide [haid] 가죽 big toe 엄지발가락 heel [hi:l] 발뒤꿈치
recount [rikáunt] 상술하다
juxtapose [dʒʌ́kstəpòuz] (비교, 대조를 위해) ~을 나란히 놓다

1 지문의 단어 "precludes"와 의미상 가장 유사한 것은?

(A) 허락하다

(B) 방해하다

(C) 유발하다

(D) 설립하다

2 다음 중 이슬람교도에 대해 2단락으로부터 추론할 수 있는 것은?

(A) 아프리카의 천연자원을 이용하는 데 관심이 있었다.

(B) 아프리카 문화에 미친 전면적인 영향은 즉각적인 것이 아니었다.

(C) 지역 부족들로부터의 강한 저항에 부딪혔다.

(D) 그들의 법률 체제는 아프리카의 토속적인 가치와 충돌했다.

3 다음 중 아라비아의 문서로 언급되지 않은 것은?

(A) 여행기

(B) 정치 선전 글

(C) 고위 인사의 부고

(D) 주석이 달린 전기

4 3단락에 따르면, 다음 중 기독교 선교사들의 설명에 대해 사실인 것은?

(A) 이전에는 서구에서 이용할 수 없었던 정보를 가지고 있었다.

(B) 식민지 통치자들이 원주민들을 대했던 방식에 대해 비판적이었다.

(C) 토착민 지도자들의 인용구를 포함했다.

(D) 발행 전에 종교 지도자들의 검열을 받았다.

5 아래 문장 중 지문 속의 음영된 문장의 핵심 정보를 가장 잘 표현하고 있는 것은 무엇인가? 오답은 문장의 의미를 현저히 왜곡하거나 핵심 정보를 빠뜨리고 있다.

(A) 분명하게도, 사하라 사막 이남 아프리카의 토착 구술 역사에 대해 지나치게 많은 관심이 부활한 것은 경고의 시선으로 바라봐야 한다.

(B) 결과적으로, 현재 이용할 수 있는 사하라 사막 이남 아프리카의 토착 자료는 역사학자들의 주의 깊은 정밀 조사의 결과이다.

(C) 본질적으로, 구술 역사에 부여된 것과 동일한 신중함이 현존하는 사하라 사막 이남 아프리카의 많은 토착 자료들에도 확대되어야 한다.

(D) 필연적으로, 사하라 사막 이남 아프리카의 정말 많은 토착 구술 자료가 존재한다는 사실은 학자들에게 조용한 열광을 받으며 환영받을 것이다.

6 아프리카 역사의 자료에 대한 전반적인 논의에서 5단락의 목적은?

(A) 다른 단락들에서 논의된 주제들에 대한 간결한 결론을 제공한다.

(B) 학자들이 토론하고 탐구해야 할 새로운 질문들을 소개한다.

(C) 이용 가능한 자료들의 전반적인 문맥에서 구술 자료의 잠재적인 가치를 논의한다.

(D) 구술 자료와 기록 문서를 비교할 때의 상대적인 결함을 탐구한다.

7 지문의 단어 "convey"와 의미상 가장 유사한 것은?

(A) 설명하다

(B) 자극하다

(C) 포용하다

(D) 제공하다

8 지문에서 결론 내려질 수 있는 것은?

(A) 아프리카의 역사학자들이 연구할 가치가 있다고 여기는 자료의 범위가 확대되었다.

(B) 아프리카인들이 과거에 어떻게 생활했는지 보여주는 초상화는 절대 알려지지 않을 것이다.

(C) 아프리카는 구술 자료가 기록 자료보다 얼마나 더 가치 있는지를 보여주는 예이다.

(D) 아프리카 역사에 대한 설명은 너무 편파적이어서 근본적으로 믿을 수 없다.

9 네 개의 네모[■]는 다음 문장이 삽입될 수 있는 부분을 나타내고 있다.

일부는 심지어 아프리카에 확인할 수 있는 역사 자체가 있기는 한 건지 과감히 질문하기까지 했다.

이 문장은 어느 자리에 들어가는 것이 가장 적절한가?

10 **지시:** 주어진 보기에서 적절한 구를 선택하여 적절한 자료에 연결시키시오. **이 문제는 3점이다.**

보기
(D) 사하라 사막 이남의 아프리카의 제한된 지역에 국한되어 있다
(G) 입증이 불가능한 정보에 의존한다
기록 자료
· (C) 행정 사무에 대한 귀한 정보를 포함한다
· (E) 아라비아와 기독교 전도사들에 의해 만들어졌다
구술 자료
· (A) 상응하는 추세에 따라 변동하는 경향이 있다
· (B) 학자들이 새로운 관점에서 역사를 조사하도록 한다
· (F) 토착민들의 관점을 대표한다

ACTUAL TEST 1

01 Earth's Energy Balance

p.360

1. (B)	2. (B)	3. (C)
4. (B)	5. (B)	6. (D)
7. (A)	8. (C)	9. 2nd
10. (A)-4단락, (C)-2단락, (F)-3단락		

1 열역학 제1 법칙에 따르면, 에너지와 물질 모두가 투과할 수 있는 경계를 가진 개방계에 들어가는 에너지의 양은 최종적으로 나가는 양과 같다. 이 기본 법칙은 지구의 평균 온도가 매년 비교적 변함이 없는 이유가 된다. 태양에 의해 발산되는 전자기 방사선은 지구의 대기와 표면에서 사용 가능한 에너지의 99.97퍼센트를 차지하는데, 흡수되면서 공기, 물, 그리고 대지의 온도를 상승시킨다. 그러나 이것은 지구가 우주로 다시 반사하는 열에 의해 상쇄되고, 이는 지구의 에너지 균형이라고 일컬어지게 된 균형 상태를 만들어낸다.

2 대기의 외층을 관통하는 모든 태양 에너지가 지구의 에너지 비축량의 일부로 여겨질 수 있는 것은 아니다. 이 에너지의 일부는 주로 가시광선과 자외선 같은 단파 복사 형태로서, ²기체 분자 혹은 공기 중에 떠 있는 먼지나 재의 아주 작은 조각에 부딪치는 방사선이 무작위 방향으로 굴절되는 확산의 과정을 거쳐 대기 입자에 의해 흩어진다. 그 결과, 태양으로부터 오는 총 방사선의 약 7퍼센트가 즉시 우주로 돌아간다. 옅은 색의 물질이 반사율이 높다는 사실은 사용 가능한 태양 에너지의 양을 제한하는 또 다른 요소이며, 이는 알베도 효과로 알려진 현상이다. 들어오는 방사선의 대략 24퍼센트가 구름층에 의해 반사되고, ³또 다른 4퍼센트가 높은 알베도율을 지닌 대지 지역, 즉 극지방과 같이 많은 양의 얼음과 눈, 혹은 사막의 모래와 같이 빛을 반사하는 다른 물질들로 덮여 있는 지역에 의해 반사된다.

3 나머지 방사선의 가장 많은 부분은 지구 표면의 대륙과 대양에 의해 흡수되는 한편, 적은 부분은 대기의 입자에 의해 흡수된다. ⁵물질이 태양 방사선을 흡수하면서, 그 구성 원자들의 운동 에너지는 증가한다. 원자들은 더욱 빨리 진동하기 시작하고, 이는 물질의 온도를 높인다. 이는 태양 에너지의 흡수가 지구를 뜨겁게 만든다는 뜻이다. 그러나 뜨거워지는 정도는 한정적인데, 이는 지구의 온도가 높아지면서 물질이 열의 형태로 장파 복사를 발산하기 시작하기 때문이다. 방출되는 열에너지의 양은 온도의 상승에 비례한다. 온도가 2배가 되면, 방사되는 에너지는 16배만큼 증가한다. 특정 지점에서는 들어오고 나가는 에너지의 양이 같아져서 물질의 온도가 더 높아지는 것을 방지할 것이다.

4 ⁶비록 지표면에 의해 발산되는 열 중 적은 양은 곧장 대기를 지나

우주로 흩어지지만, 대부분은 대기의 물질에 의해 흡수된다. 이러한 입자들의 온도는 그것들이 에너지를 모든 방향으로 똑같이 내뿜기 시작할 때까지 상승한다. 대략 반 정도가 지표면으로 다시 내려와 대지와 물에 의해 재흡수된다. 나머지는 반대 방향으로 이동하여 우주로 빠져나가거나 더 높은 고도에 있는 물질에 의해 흡수된다. 온실효과로 알려진 이 순환은 에너지가 우주로 방출되는 지점인 대기 외층에 미칠 때까지 반복된다.

5 ⁷열이 지표면과 대기 사이에서 왔다 갔다 하는 이 이동은 지구를 거주 가능하게 만드는 데 핵심적인 역할을 한다. 에너지의 재순환 및 우주로의 이동의 지연은 평균 표면 온도를 대략 섭씨 15도로 만든다. 만약 지구에 대기가 없다면 평균 표면 온도는 200퍼센트 이상 내려갈 것이다.

6 지구의 에너지 균형은 지구의 기후 변화를 유발하는 많은 요소에 의해 영향을 받을 수 있다. 기후 강제력이라 불리는 이 요소들 중 태양 광도의 변화나 지구 궤도의 주기적인 이탈 같은 것들은 대기로 들어오는 에너지의 양을 변화시킨다. 이외의 요소들은 다른 측면의 변화를 가져온다. 예를 들어, 화석연료를 태우는 것은 열에너지의 효과적인 흡수체인 이산화탄소와 메탄의 대기 중 농도를 증가시킨다. 이는 온실효과를 심화하므로, 열이 우주로 다시 이동하는 비율을 감소시켜 점차 표면 온도를 증가시킨다. 물론 지구가 더 따뜻해지면서, 그것은 궁극적으로 들어오고 나가는 에너지 간에 새로운 균형이 달성될 때까지 더 많은 양의 열을 발산한다.

thermodynamic [θə̀ːrmədainǽmik] 열역학의
open system 개방계(외계와 에너지나 물질을 교환하는 계)
permeable [pə́ːrmiəbl] 침투할 수 있는
fundamental [fʌ̀ndəméntl] 기본의
explain [ikspléin] ~의 이유가 되다
electromagnetic radiation 전자기 방사선 emit [imít] 발산하다
compensate for 상쇄하다 equilibrium [ìːkwəlíbriəm] 균형
penetrate [pénətrèit] 관통하다 shortwave [ʃɔ́ːrtwèiv] 단파
ultraviolet [ʌ̀ltrəváiəlit] 자외선의 diffusion [difjúːʒən] 확산
miniscule [mínəskjùːl] 아주 작은, 극소의
suspend [səspénd] (공중에) 뜨다 deflect [diflékt] 굴절하다
reflective [rifléktiv] 반사하는 landmass [lǽndmæ̀s] 대륙
take in 흡수하다 kinetic energy 운동 에너지 atom [ǽtəm] 원자
proportional [prəpɔ́ːrʃənl] 비례하는 by a factor of ~배만큼
dissipate [dísəpèit] 흩어지다 altitude [ǽltətjùːd] 고도
back and forth 왔다 갔다 habitable [hǽbitəbl] 거주 가능한
climate forcing 기후 강제력 fluctuation [flʌ̀ktʃuéiʃən] 변화
luminosity [lùːmənásəti] 광도 deviation [dìːviéiʃən] 일탈
orbit [ɔ́ːrbit] 궤도 intensify [inténsəfài] 심화하다

1 지문의 단어 "fundamental"과 의미상 가장 유사한 것은?
   (A) 간단한

(B) 본질적인

(C) 주요한

(D) 강제적인

2 2단락에 따르면, 확산은 _____ 때 일어난다.

(A) 빛의 파장이 변할 때

(B) 에너지가 물질에 의해 방향이 바뀔 때

(C) 방사선이 분자에 의해 흡수될 때

(D) 공기 중의 입자들이 흩어져 있을 때

3 2단락에 따르면, 지표면의 알베도율에 대해 추론할 수 있는 것은?

(A) 들어오는 태양 방사선의 양에 따라 변한다.

(B) 대기와 땅의 온도가 내려감에 따라 증가한다.

(C) 지역의 환경 조건에 따라 다르다.

(D) 넓은 범위에 구름이 덮인 지역에서는 일정하게 유지된다.

4 지문의 단어 "constituent"와 의미상 가장 유사한 것은?

(A) 첫째의

(B) 구성하는

(C) 이질적인

(D) 다음의

5 3단락에 따르면, 원자들이 더 빠르게 진동하도록 만드는 것은?

(A) 물질에 의해 발산되는 열의 강도가 증가한다.

(B) 물질이 가지고 있는 에너지의 양이 변한다.

(C) 물질의 구조가 운동 에너지에 의해 변한다.

(D) 물질에 의한 열 에너지의 방사가 빨라진다.

6 4단락에 따르면, 지구에 의해 발산하는 대부분의 열에 일어나는 일은?

(A) 대기권의 더 높은 고도에 들어가기 전에 흩어진다.

(B) 공기 중으로 방사된 직후 우주로 배출된다.

(C) 대기의 분자들에 의해 다시 표면으로 반사된다.

(D) 방출되기 전에 공기 중의 분자들에 흡수된다.

7 지문에서 4단락과 5단락의 관계는 무엇인가?

(A) 4단락은 기상 작용을 설명하고 5단락은 그것의 중요한 영향들 중 한 가지를 서술한다.

(B) 4단락은 기상 변화에 대한 이론을 제시하고 5단락은 뒷받침하는 증거를 제공한다.

(C) 4단락은 에너지 현상을 논의하고 5단락은 그것의 근본적인 원인들을 약술한다.

(D) 4단락은 대기의 열 전달에 대해 서술하고 5단락은 예를 제시한다.

8 지문의 단어 "this"가 가리키는 것은?

(A) 에너지

(B) 우주

(C) 온도

(D) 대기

9 네 개의 네모[■]는 다음 문장이 삽입될 수 있는 부분을 나타내고 있다.

그 결과, 태양으로부터 오는 총 방사선의 약 7퍼센트가 즉시 우주로 돌아간다.

이 문장은 어느 자리에 들어가는 것이 가장 적절한가?

10 지시: 지문 요약을 위한 도입 문장이 아래에 주어져 있다. 지문의 가장 중요한 내용을 나타내는 보기 3개를 골라 요약을 완성하시오. 어떤 문장은 지문에 언급되지 않은 내용이나 사소한 정보를 담고 있으므로 요약에 포함되지 않는다. **이 문제는 2점이다.**

> 지구에 흡수된 에너지는 지구가 결국 방출하는 양과 일치한다.
> · (A) 지구에 의해 방사된 열은 우주에 들어가기 전에 지표면과 대기 사이를 왔다 갔다 한다.
> · (C) 일부 태양 방사선은 대기의 분자에 의해 분산되거나 구름과 행성 표면의 특성들에 의해 반사된다.
> · (F) 태양 에너지의 대부분은 지표면의 물질에 의해 흡수되어, 열을 발산하게 만든다.

(B) 기후 변화는 지표면에 들어오고 나가는 에너지 간의 균형을 어지럽힌다.

(D) 지구의 온도는 온실효과가 아니었으면 위험한 수준으로 떨어질 것이다.

(E) 대기 중의 분자들은 태양에 의해 발산된 장파 에너지를 오랜 시간 동안 유지한다.

02 Triggers of City Planning in America

p.364

11. (D)	12. (A)	13. (C)
14. (B)	15. (C)	16. (B)
17. (D)	18. (C)	19. 4th
20. (B)-3단락, (D)-2단락, (E)-4단락		

1 19세기에 미국의 산업화는 전례 없는 성장을 이룩했고, 그 결과 더 높은 비율의 사람들이 도시 환경에 거주하게 되었다. 12B철로는 도시와 농촌 지역의 차이를 메웠고, 12D도시의 공장들은 노동자들이 더 나은 수입을 찾아 농촌 생활을 떠나도록 했으며, 12C이민자들의 물결은 해외로부터 미국의 도시로 몰려들었다. 13도시화의 종합적인 결과는 도시가 규모 면에서 너무 급속하게 폭발적으로 증가했기 때문에, 누구도 어떠한 종합적이고 전략적인 도시개발계획을 실행할 선견지명이나 기회를 가지지 못했다는 것이다. 대신, 도시의 조직은 시장의 힘과 급변하는 환경에 대처할 의지와 지식이 부족한 분리된 정부 단체들에 맡겨졌다. 진정 정식으로 조직된 형태의 도시 계획이 미국의 의제에서 주목을 받은 것은 제1차 세계대전 직전인 20세기 초였으며, 몇 가지 주요 발달이 도시 계획의 최종적인 수립을 유발하도록 도왔다.

2 점점 더 많은 사람이 한정된 지역에 잔뜩 밀려 들어오면서 인구 과잉은 도시 거주자들의 걱정거리가 되었다. 공장 근로자들은 일반적으로 빈민가에 있는 쓰러져가는 건물의 저렴한 주택을 제공받았으며, 이윤을 추구하는 집주인들은 보통 주택에 최대한 많은 사람을 집어넣기 위해 주택을 다수의 구역으로 나누었다. 15이민자들은 종종 아무 공터에나 모여서 간이 주택을 지었고, 이는 '판자촌'으로 불리는 거대한 집단 공동체를 형성하였다. 이러한 곳들은 열악한 편의 시설을 제공했고 사람들을 서로 불편할 정도로 가깝게 살게 했다. 보통 바깥의 길거리도 편한 것은 아니었다. 수많은 보행자는 사람들이 가득 찬 거리를 철로 및 상인들과 공유했고, 혼란스러운 북새통은 마을을 돌아다니는 것을 짜증 나게 만들었다. 인구 과잉과 관련된 불편함의 결과로, 사람들은 덜 밀집하여 거주하도록 도시 지역을 조직하는 방법들을 생각하기 시작했다. 그것을 달성하는 방법에 관한 제안은 도로를 넓히고 보도를 추가하는 것은 물론이고, 사용되지 않는 건물을 적당한 값의 주택으로 전환시키는 것을 포함하였다.

3 도시 설계의 조직적인 개혁을 향한 최초로 확실하게 인식되는 자극은 1800년대 중후반에 매우 필요했던 위생 개혁의 형태로 나타났는데, 이는 도시 지역의 불결함에 대해 커져가는 불쾌감에서 발달하였다. 비록 미국의 도시들은 유럽의 도시들만큼 많이 불결하지는 않았지만, 그럼에도 불구하고 오늘날의 기준으로는 극도로 더러운 곳이었다. 공장에서는 유독 가스가 쉴 새 없이 뿜어져 나왔고, 공장은 처리되지 않은 화학물질들을 냇가로 바로 흘려 보냈다. 대부분의 도시에는 하수 시설이 없었고, 사람들은 쓰레기를 골목길 또는 아무 데나 편한 곳에 내다버렸다. 16심지어 미국의 수도에서도 돼지들이 자유롭게 돌아다녔고 말들이 길거리에 대변을 보았으며, 백악관에조

차도 해충이 들끓었다고 한다. 고약한 악취 외에도, 제대로 된 위생 시설의 부족으로 인해 세균이 급증했고 폐결핵과 콜레라의 치명적인 발생을 포함하여 수많은 전염병이 돌게 되었다. 이렇게 무시무시한 사건들의 여파로, 사회운동가들과 정부 관료들이 지방자치단체들을 정화하기 위한 계획을 논의하기 위해 모였다.

4 도시 계획의 탄생을 촉진한 또 다른 전개는 도시 미화 운동이었는데, 이 운동은 도시들을 심미적으로 더욱 쾌적하게 만들기 위한 것이었다. 이 취지가 나타난 한 방식은 더 많고 더 넓은 녹지공간의 설계와 건설에서였다. 1850년에 대다수의 도시공원은 몇 에이커밖에 되지 않았다. 그러나 공원을 위해 843에이커를 따로 떼어둔 New York 시의 과감한 조치는 전국의 도시들의 선망과 영감이 되는 선례가 되었다. Central Park의 건설은 1858년에 시작되었고, 이 '도시의 심신을 되살리는 초록빛 오아시스'의 창조는 Baltimore, St. Louis, San Francisco와 같은 도시들도 곧 그들만의 자랑할만한 대규모 공공녹지를 가지게 되는 분기점이 되었다. 공원을 육성하는 것 외에도, 환경 미화의 지지자들은 공공 기념물을 설치하고, 정부 청사를 고전 양식으로 설계하고, 정형 정원을 만드는 것을 옹호했다.

5 1910년 즈음에는, '도시 계획'이라는 용어가 공무원들과 지역사회의 기타 주요 구성원들이 쓰는 용어가 되었다. 비록 최선의 진행 방식에 대해서는 의견이 갈렸으나, 18대부분의 사람은 도시 성장의 모든 양상을 관리할 일종의 중앙집권화된 단체가 필요하다는 것에는 동의했다. 이 책무는 1930년대경 나타나기 시작한 도시 계획 위원회에 위임되었다. 계획 위원회에는 미래를 위한 안전하고, 책임감 있고, 지속 가능한 건설을 할 수 있도록 하는 전반적인 이상과 규제 도구들의 밑그림을 그리는 업무가 주어졌다. 위원회들은 시장 및 시 의회와 긴밀히 협력하면서 곧 미국 도시의 생활 여건을 개선하는 데 진전을 보이기 시작했다.

come to the forefront 주목을 받다 run-down[rʌ́ndàun] 쓰러져가는
congregate[kɑ́ŋgrigèit] 모이다
makeshift[méikʃìft] 간이의, 임시변통의 shanty town 판자촌
substandard[səbstǽndərd] 열악한, 수준 이하의
proliferation[prəlìfəréiʃən] 급증
proximity[prɑksíməti] 가까움, 근접 hustle and bustle 북새통
impetus[ímpətəs] 자극 uneasiness[ʌníːzinis] 불쾌감
filthiness[fílθinis] 불결함 noxious[nɑ́kʃəs] 유독한
defecate[défikèit] 대변을 보다 vermin[və́ːrmin] 해충
unsavory[ʌnséivəri] 고약한 stench[stentʃ] 악취
proliferation[prəlìfəréiʃən] 급증
tuberculosis[tjubə̀ːrkjulóusis] 폐결핵
aftermath[ǽftərmæ̀θ] 여파 watershed[wɔ́ːtərʃèd] 분기점, 분수령
beautification[bjùːtəfikéiʃən] 미화 facet[fǽsit] 양상

11 지문의 단어 "unprecedented"와 의미상 가장 유사한 것은?

(A) 절제된
(B) 자유로운
(C) 원인 불명의
(D) 전례 없는

12 도시 지역에 거주하는 사람들의 증가하는 비율의 요인으로 나열된 것이 아닌 것은?

(A) 신도시의 건설
(B) 철로
(C) 이민자들의 유입
(D) 공장 일자리

13 1단락에 따르면, 도시화의 전반적인 결과는 무엇이었는가?

(A) 도시들은 새로운 정부 단체를 만들어야만 했다.
(B) 도시들은 시장의 힘을 잘 이해하는 지도자들을 찾기 시작했다.
(C) 도시들은 너무 빠르게 성장하여 도시 개발을 위한 철저한 계획이 실현되지 않았다.
(D) 도시들은 농촌 지역의 주변 공동체 대부분을 집어삼켰다.

14 아래 문장 중 지문 속의 음영된 문장의 핵심 정보를 가장 잘 표현하고 있는 것은 무엇인가? 오답은 문장의 의미를 현저히 왜곡하거나 핵심 정보를 빠뜨리고 있다.

(A) 제1차 세계대전 이전에, 미국의 도시 계획은 많이 조직화되어 있지 않았지만, 몇 개의 결정적인 상황들이 전쟁 이후에 결국 그것이 일정한 형태를 갖추게 하는 데 도움을 주었다.
(B) 1900년대 초반에서야 정돈된 도시 계획이 미국에서 우선순위가 되었고, 몇 개의 중요한 사건들은 이후 그것의 이행에 기여했다.
(C) 20세기 초반에, 많은 핵심 개발들은 도시 계획이 미국의 다른 더 긴급한 문제들에 자리를 양보하게 만들었다.
(D) 일정한 형태를 갖춘 도시 계획이 마침내 미국에서 시작되었을 때, 제1차 세계대전이 막 시작되려는 참이었다.

15 다음 중 2단락의 인구 과잉 주택에 대한 논의로부터 추론할 수 있는 것은?

(A) 공장들은 보통 노동자들에게 주택을 제공하지 않았다.
(B) 공장 노동자들은 일반적으로 집과 직장 사이의 먼 거리를 통근했다.
(C) 판자촌의 주택들은 별로 오래 견디도록 지어지지 않았다.
(D) 집주인들은 보통 그들의 황폐한 건물에 세를 들 사람들을 찾기 어려웠다.

16 지문에서 글쓴이는 왜 "the White House"를 언급하는가?

(A) 미국의 얼마 없는 위생적인 장소의 예를 제시하기 위해
(B) 위생 문제에서 제외된 곳은 없었다는 것을 강조하기 위해
(C) 위생 개선의 주요 원인을 강조하기 위해
(D) 특별한 건물과 평범한 주택의 청결도를 대조하기 위해

17 지문의 단어 "manifested"와 의미상 가장 유사한 것은?

(A) 주장했다
(B) 정의했다
(C) 변형했다
(D) 드러났다

18 5단락에 따르면, 다음 중 사람들이 도시 계획을 어떻게 생각했는지에 대해 사실인 것은?

(A) 대부분의 인구가 공식적인 도시 계획은 불필요하다고 생각했다.
(B) 지역 사회의 지도자들은 누가 도시 계획을 실행해야 하는지에 대해 합의할 수 없었다.
(C) 대다수의 시민들이 하나의 단체가 도시 계획을 책임져야 한다는 것을 받아들였다.
(D) 진정한 도시 계획이 그들의 일생 동안 가능할 것이라고 생각한 사람은 거의 없었다.

19 네 개의 네모[■]는 다음 문장이 삽입될 수 있는 부분을 나타내고 있다.

그것을 달성하는 방법에 관한 제안은 도로를 넓히고 보도를 추가하는 것은 물론이고, 사용되지 않는 건물을 적당한 값의 주택으로 전환시키는 것을 포함하였다.

이 문장은 어느 자리에 들어가는 것이 가장 적절한가?

20 지시: 지문 요약을 위한 도입 문장이 아래에 주어져 있다. 지문의 가장 중요한 내용을 나타내는 보기 3개를 골라 요약을 완성하시오. 어떤 문장은 지문에 언급되지 않은 내용이나 사소한 정보를 담고 있으므로 요약에 포함되지 않는다. 이 문제는 2점이다.

> 산업화는 19세기 미국에 빠른 도시화를 불러왔고, 도시 계획의 형식 체계의 필요성을 불러일으켰다.
>
> · (B) 도시 계획의 초기 전조는 위생 개선의 형태로 나타났는데, 미국 도시들의 더러운 환경에 반응한 것이었다.
> · (D) 인구 과잉 주거지와 거리에 대한 대중의 우려는 사람들이 인구 밀도가 희박한 도시를 설계할 수 있는 방법에 대해 생각하도록 했다.
> · (E) 도시 계획을 일으켰던 발전 중에 도시를 더 아름답게 만들기 위해 계획된 활동들을 장려하는 사회 운동이 있었다.

(A) 잇따른 치명적인 전염병의 발생 이후, 시 정부는 그들의 도시를 청소할 방법을 찾아야 했다.

(C) 도시 미화 운동이 New York 시의 강력한 지지를 얻었지만, 그것의 활동들은 미국의 다른 지역에 거의 영향을 주지 않았다.

(F) 생활 여건이 너무 끔찍했기 때문에, 도시 계획 위원회는 단기 비용에도 불구하고 지속 가능한 개발을 촉진시키는 권한을 부여받았다.

ACTUAL TEST 2

01 Marine Bioluminescence

p.368

1. (C)	2. (D)	3. (A)
4. (C)	5. (B)	6. (A)
7. (A)	8. (D)	9. 3rd

10. (C)−2~3단락, (D)−5단락, (F)−4단락

1 Pliny the Elder(AD 23-79)는 그의 저서 '박물지'에서 어둠 속에서 빛을 내는 썩은 나무를 묘사했는데, 이는 도깨비불로 알려지게 된 현상이다. 현대에 와서, 도깨비불이 사실은 생체 발광하는, 즉 화학 반응을 통해 자체적인 빛을 내는 나무에 서식하는 곰팡이에 의해 야기된 효과라는 것이 밝혀졌다. 생체 발광이 곰팡이 특유의 것은 아니고, 곤충, 거미류, 그리고 지렁이의 다양한 종에서도 나타난다. 예를 들어, 반딧불이는 짝을 유인하기 위해서는 물론이고, 포식자들에게 자신들이 맛이 없음을 경고하기 위해 번쩍이는 빛을 낸다. 그런데 대다수의 생체 발광 생물이 발견되는 곳은 육지가 아니라 세계의 바닷속이고, 해양 생물의 거의 모든 주요 군에 빛을 내는 구성 생물이 적어도 몇몇 있다. 연구자들은 바다의 비교적 길고 안정된 진화사와 특히 깊은 깊이에서의 상대적인 빛의 부족이 바다를 생체 발광의 출현을 위한 이상적인 환경으로 만들었다고 믿는다.

2 생체 발광을 일으키는 반응은 많은 화학적 전제 조건을 가진다. 관련된 주요 물질은 빛을 생성하는 색소인 발광소이다. 어떤 종들은 자체적인 발광소를 합성하는 생물학적 과정을 발달시킨 한편, 다른 종들은 다른 생체 발광 생물을 잡아먹거나 그들과의 공생 관계를 통해 발광소를 얻는다. ²발광 효소라고 불리는 효소가 있는 곳에서 발광소가 산소 분자에 의해 산화될 때 빛이 생성되는데, 발광 효소는 반응의 촉매 역할을 하며, 이때 빛, 산화 발광소, 그리고 물이 부산물로 방출된다. 어떤 경우에는, 생체 발광이 일어나기 위해 보통 칼슘이나 마그네슘의 전하를 띠는 이온도 필요하다.

3 생체 발광이 처음 나타났을 때, 생물학자들은 생체 발광에 의해 주어지는 정확한 진화적 이점을 확실하게 밝히지는 못했지만, 한 가지 단서는 관련된 화학 반응이 산소의 분해를 가져온다는 사실에서 발견된다. 많은 생체 발광 생물이 처음에는 산소가 없는 환경에서 진화했기 때문에, 나중에 진화한 식물의 광합성을 통해 생성된 산소 분자는 그들에게 유독했을 것이다. 이는 단세포 해양 생물에서의 생체 발광의 발생과 일관된다. 해양 식물의 진화 이전에 먼저 존재했던 다수의 그러한 생물이 이후에 생체 발광을 발달시켰고, 이는 산소를 제거할 방법이었을 가능성이 있다. ⁴반면, 식물 이후에 나타난 돌말과 같은 대부분의 단세포 생물은 빛을 생성하는 반응을 수행할 필요가 없었는데, 이는 아마 그들이 종으로서 존재하기 시작했을 때부터 산소가 그들의 환경의 일부였기 때문이다.

4 산소 제거 가설의 타당성은 여전히 논란의 여지가 있지만, 생체 발광의 원래 목표가 어떤 것이든 생체 발광은 그 이후 다른 많은 기능을 수행했고, 그중 더욱 일반적인 것 중 하나는 다른 생물로부터의 보호이다. 예를 들어, 많은 바다 생물은 포식자를 피하기 위해 빛을 발산하고, 흡혈 오징어는 그러한 종의 하나이다. 포식자가 있는 곳에서, 흡혈 오징어는 예비 공격자를 놀라고 혼란스럽게 하는 빛나는 점액을 뿜어내는데, 이는 흡혈 오징어의 탈출을 용이하게 한다. 아톨라 해파리는 '도난 경보기'로 유명한데, 이는 빛을 일종의 신호 기제로 사용하는 것이다. 포식자에 의해 위협을 받았을 때, ⁶아톨라 해파리는 그 공격자를 잡아먹는 더 큰 물고기를 유인하는 일련의 밝은 섬광을 내뿜는다. 다른 생체 발광 생물은 적발을 피하기 위해 빛을 내는데, 이는 역발광이라고 일컬어지는 전략이다. 상어와 같은 많은 포식자는 아래로부터 사냥을 하며, 햇빛을 배경으로 그들 위에 있는 목표물의 윤곽을 감지한다. 이에 대항하려고, 어떤 피식자 종은 배경에 섞여 들어가기 위해 자체적인 빛을 생성한다. 빛의 상황이 달라짐에 따라 생체 발광의 정도를 조정함으로써, 이러한 종들은 사실상 발견이 불가능한 상태로 남을 수 있다.

5 ⁸역발광은 효과적인 사냥 기제로서의 역할도 하는데, 이는 쿠키커터상어의 사례에서 명백히 목격된다. 역발광을 하는 피식자처럼, 쿠키커터상어도 위로부터 오는 빛에 자신을 일치시키기 위해 자신을 빛내지만, 동시에 목표물을 속이기 위해 가슴지느러미 부근의 작은 살점만 빛나지 않는 상태로 남겨 둔다. 고등어와 참치 같은 작은 포식자들은 그 어두운 형체를 작은 물고기로 착각하여 가까이 헤엄쳐 가는데, 이는 상어에게 그들을 먹어 치울 충분한 기회를 제공한다. 마찬가지로, 일부 생물들은 빛의 원천 그 자체를 피식자를 유인하는 데 효과적인 미끼의 일종으로 사용한다. 아귀라고 알려진 심해 생물군은 이 행동으로 유명하다. 아귀의 이마에서부터 뻗어 나온 얇은 조직에는 발광하는 살덩어리가 붙어 있는데, 이는 낚시꾼에 의해 사용되는 미끼 및 낚시 도구와 흡사하다. 아귀는 정지한 채로 밝게 빛나는 미끼를 머리 앞에서 앞뒤로 흔들고, 생물이 빛에 유인되자마자 날카로운 이빨로 그것을 베어 문다.

bioluminescence[báiouluːmənésns] 생체 발광   rot[rɑt] 썩다
glow[glou] 빛나다   foxfire[fάksfàiər] 도깨비불
fungi[fʌ́ndʒai] 곰팡이   arachnid[ərǽknid] 거미류
worm[wəːrm] 지렁이   evolutionary[èvəlúːʃənèri] 진화적인
emergence[imə́ːrdʒəns] 출현
prerequisite[priːrékwəzit] 전제 조건   luciferin[luːsífərin] 발광소
pigment[pígmənt] 색소   synthesize[sínθəsàiz] 합성하다
symbiotic[sìmbiάtik] 공생의   oxidize[άksədàiz] 산화하다
in the presence of ~가 있는 곳에서
luciferase[luːsífərèis] 발광 효소   catalyst[kǽtəlist] 촉매
emit[imít] 내뿜다   byproduct[báiprὰdʌkt] 부산물

charged[tʃɑ́ːrdʒd] 전하를 띠는 determine[ditə́ːrmin] 밝히다
bestow[bistóu] 주다 degradation[dègrədéiʃən] 분해
consistent[kənsístənt] 일관된 incidence[ínsədəns] 발생
diatom[dáiətɑm] 돌말 validity[vəlídəti] 타당성
open to debate 논란의 여지가 있는 evade[ivéid] 피하다
eject[idʒékt] 뿜어 내다 mucus[mjúːkəs] 점액
startle[stɑ́ːrtl] 놀라게 하다 would-be[wúdbiː] 예비의
facilitate[fəsílətèit] 용이하게 하다 burglar alarm 도난 경보기
detection[ditékʃən] 적발, 감지 illumination[ilùːmənéiʃən] 발광
silhouette[sìluét] 윤곽 against the backdrop of ~을 배경으로
counter[káuntər] 대항하다 pectoral fin 가슴지느러미
mackerel[mǽkərəl] 고등어 tuna[tjúːnə] 참치
mistake[mistéik] 착각하다 devour[diváuər] 먹어 치우다
anglerfish[ǽŋglərfiʃ] 아귀 filament[fíləmənt] 조직
bait[beit] 미끼 tackle[tǽkl] 낚시 도구
stationary[stéiʃənèri] 정지한

1 아래 문장 중 지문 속의 음영된 문장의 핵심 정보를 가장 잘 표현하고 있는 것은 무엇인가? 오답은 문장의 의미를 현저히 왜곡하거나 핵심 정보를 빠뜨리고 있다.

  (A) 과학자들은 전 세계 바다의 안정성뿐 아니라 지속적인 빛의 부족이 바다를 생체 발광 능력을 지닌 생물들의 이상적인 서식지로 만든다고 주장한다.
  (B) 생물학자들은 충분한 양의 빛이 없고 일관된 환경이 수년 동안 지속되는 환경에서 생체 발광이 더욱 일반적이라고 생각한다.
  (C) 바다는 비교적 어둡고 오랜 시간 동안 큰 변화 없이 지속되었기 때문에 생체 발광의 발달에 매우 적합했다고 생각된다.
  (D) 해양 환경은 다른 생물군계보다 더 어두운데, 이는 왜 생체 발광이 전 세계 바다에서 계속 진화하고 있는지를 설명한다.

2 다음 중 생체 발광에 필요한 화학 물질이 아닌 것은?

  (A) 발광소
  (B) 발광 효소
  (C) 산소
  (D) 산화 발광소

3 지문의 단어 "them"이 가리키는 것은?

  (A) 생물
  (B) 환경
  (C) 분자
  (D) 식물

4 돌말에 대해 지문으로부터 추론할 수 있는 것은?

  (A) 현재 생체 발광을 발달시키고 있다.
  (B) 광합성을 할 수 없다.
  (C) 산소에 의해 불리한 영향을 받지 않는다.
  (D) 해양 식물에 유독하다.

5 지문의 단어 "facilitates"와 의미상 가장 유사한 것은?

  (A) 승인하다
  (B) 용이하게 하다

  (C) 격려하다
  (D) 방해하다

6 4단락에 따르면, 아톨라 해파리는 _____하기 위해 빛을 생산한다.

  (A) 자신의 위치로 큰 포식자를 유인하기 위해
  (B) 위협이 될 수 있는 잠재적인 공격자를 확인하기 위해
  (C) 달아나기 전에 더 큰 생물의 주의를 딴 데로 돌리기 위해
  (D) 먹힐 수 있는 물고기가 더 가까이 헤엄쳐 오도록 유도하기 위해

7 지문의 단어 "stationary"와 의미상 가장 유사한 것은?

  (A) 움직이지 않는
  (B) 기다리는
  (C) 수색하는
  (D) 지켜보는

8 5단락에서 글쓴이의 주요 목적은 _____하는 것이다.

  (A) 역발광의 유용성을 강조하는 것
  (B) 생체 발광하는 피식자의 두 가지 유형을 대조하는 것
  (C) 수생 사냥꾼들이 어떻게 빛을 만들어낼 수 있는지 설명하는 것
  (D) 포식자의 생체 발광의 용도를 설명하는 것

9 네 개의 네모[■]는 다음 문장이 삽입될 수 있는 부분을 나타내고 있다.

  예를 들어, 반딧불이는 짝을 유인하기 위해서는 물론이고, 포식자들에게 자신들이 맛이 없음을 경고하기 위해 번쩍이는 빛을 낸다.

  이 문장은 어느 자리에 들어가는 것이 가장 적절한가?

10 지시: 지문 요약을 위한 도입 문장이 아래에 주어져 있다. 지문의 가장 중요한 내용을 나타내는 보기 3개를 골라 요약을 완성하시오. 어떤 문장은 지문에 언급되지 않은 내용이나 사소한 정보를 담고 있으므로 요약에 포함되지 않는다. **이 문제는 2점이다.**

  > **생체 발광은 생물체에 의한 빛의 생성과 발산이며, 해양 환경에서 특히 일반적이다.**
  >
  > · (C) 화학적 반응은 빛을 발생시키고, 이것은 유해한 물질을 제거하는 하나의 방법으로 처음 발달했을 것이다.
  > · (D) 생체 발광은 포식자가 피식자를 더 가까이 헤엄쳐 오도록 유도할 수 있게 해주어, 공격자가 그들을 먹을 수 있게 해준다.
  > · (F) 해양 생물은 스스로를 눈에 덜 띄게 만들거나, 공격자로부터 도망가거나, 포식 동물을 먹는 생물을 유인하기 위해 빛을 내뿜는다.

  (A) 포식 동물은 먹이의 위치를 파악하고 확인하기 위해 생체 발광을 사용한다.
  (B) 생체 발광의 최초의 목적에 대해 논의가 진행 중인데, 생물학자들은 공격 기능 이론과 방어 기능 이론을 지지하는 사람들로 나뉜다.

(E) 많은 화학물질이 결합하여, 생물들이 발광하고 여러 가지 독소를 제거하게 해준다.

02 Expansion of the Universe

p.372

11. (A)	12. (B)	13. (B)
14. (D)	15. (C)	16. (B)
17. (C)	18. (C)	19. 2nd
20. (B)-5단락, (C)-2~3단락, (F)-4단락		

1 20세기 초 Edwin Hubble의 연구는 우주의 규모와 범위에 초점이 맞춰져 있었다. 당시에는, 여전히 일반적으로 우리 은하가 우주에 있는 모든 것을 포함한다고 여겨졌지만, Hubble은 우주가 사실은 훨씬 더 클 가능성이 있다고 믿었다. 캘리포니아의 Wilson 산에 구축된 강력한 새 망원경을 활용하여, 그는 안드로메다라는 이름의 천체에 시선을 고정했고, 다수의 개별적인 별들이 모인 하나의 집합처럼 보이는 것을 관측했다. 11Hubble은 안드로메다 자체가 은하라고 추측했다. 즉, 그는 안드로메다가 우리 은하의 외부에 있다고 생각했다. 그러나 이를 증명하기 위해서 그는 안드로메다의 지구로부터의 거리를 측정할 필요가 있었다.

2 지금처럼, 당시에도 천문학적 거리를 측정하는 것은 표준 촉광이라고 불리는 것을 요구하는 굉장히 힘든 과제였다. 표준 촉광은 무리에 있는 모든 천체들의 고유한 특성 때문에, 알려진 절대 광도를 가지는 한 무리의 천체들이다. 그러한 무리에 속하는 존재가 밝혀진다면, 그것의 절대 밝기를 지구에서 보이는 겉보기 밝기와 비교하여 거리가 측정될 수 있다. **이 방법은 빛이 먼 거리를 이동하면서 일관된 비율로 약해지기 때문에 가능하다.** 12Hubble은 케페우스형 변광성의 형태로 안드로메다의 표준 촉광을 찾았는데, 케페우스형 변광성은 일이나 주 단위의 정해진 주기 동안 광도가 변화하고, 빛 변동 주기의 길이에 일치하는 절대 광도를 가지는 별의 일종이다. 그 주기에 기반하여 별의 광도를 계산한 다음 그것을 망원경을 통해 관찰된 광도에 비교함으로써, Hubble은 안드로메다가 우리 은하의 외부에 멀리 있음을 밝혔고, 결정적으로 그것이 하나의 은하임을 증명했다.

3 그 후, Hubble은 관측을 다른 은하들로 확장했고, 그 은하들의 지구로부터의 거리를 측정하는 것에 더해 그것들에 의해 방사되는 빛의 스펙트럼도 분석했다. 그는 은하로부터의 빛이 항상 파장이 긴, 빛 스펙트럼의 빨간색 쪽을 향해 이동한다는 것을 발견했다. 적색 편이로 알려진 이 현상은 은하가 그것이 발산하는 광파를 효과적으로 펼치면서 지구로부터 멀어지고 있다는 것을 보여주는데, 더 심한 적색 편이는 더 높은 상대 속도를 나타낸다. 13중요하게도, Hubble은 지구로부터 더 멀리 있는 은하들이 가까이 있는 은하들보다 더 빠른 속도로 지구에서 멀어지고 있다는 것을 발견했다. 이 관측에 대한 유일한 설명은 우주가 팽창하고 있다는 것이다.

4 Hubble의 공적은 우주론에 즉각적이고 깊은 영향을 미쳤다. 팽창하는 우주는 우주가 먼 과거에는 사실 더 작았다는 것을 암시하는데, 이는 우주의 기원에 관한 새로운 모델인 빅뱅이론을 낳았고, 이 이론은 우주가 한때는 매우 뜨겁고 밀도가 높은 상태에서 시작하여, 그 이래로 커져 왔다고 말한다. 15첫 팽창 이후, 우주는 물질이 형성되기에 충분할 정도로 식었다. 연구자들은 이 물질의 끌어당기는 중력이 팽창을 더디게 하고 있다고 가정하며, 두 가지 가능한 미래를 암시했다. 그 두 가지는 팽창이 최종적으로 역전되어 우주가 수축하는 '닫힌' 우주와, 팽창이 무한하게 계속되는 '열린' 우주이다. 이러한 가능성들 중 어떤 것이 가장 가망이 있는지를 알아내는 것은 우주가 그 안에 있는 물질의 밀도에 비해 얼마나 빠르게 팽창하고 있는지의 관점에서 복잡한 계산을 필요로 했고, 수십 년 동안 우주론자들은 합의에 도달하는 데 실패했다.

5 20세기 후반은 모든 것을 바꿔 놓은 극적인 발견을 가져왔다. 관측 기술의 발달은 천문학자들이 그 어느 때보다도 우주를 더 면밀하게 들여다보도록 해주었고, 17B그들은 우주 팽창에 대해 더 알기 위해 100억 광년 이상 떨어진 가장 멀리 있는 가시적인 은하들로 눈을 돌렸다. 이러한 별들의 집합에서, 연구자들은 많은 Ia형 초신성을 수색하여 찾았다. 17DIa형 초신성은 각기 같은 밝기를 가지는 거대한 별의 폭발로, 17A천문학자들이 그것을 표준 촉광으로 활용하여 거리를 측정하는 것을 가능하게 했다. 거리를 계산하고 적색 편이까지 측정한 후, 연구자들은 놀라운 발견을 했다. 그 초신성은 기존에 존재하던 우주 팽창 모델 하에서 예상되었던 것보다 지구로부터 약 15퍼센트나 더 멀리 있었고, 이 불일치는 우주의 팽창이 사실상 더뎌지지 않고 빨라지고 있음을 암시했다. 어떤 과학자들은 계속 증가하는 속도로 은하들을 떠미는 암흑 에너지라고 불리는 불가사의한 힘을 상정했지만, 가속화의 정확한 이유는 불확실하여 현대 과학의 가장 큰 미스터리 중 하나로 남아 있다.

expansion[ikspǽnʃən] 팽창 investigation[invèstəgéiʃən] 연구
the Milky Way 은하 galaxy[gǽləksi] 은하
comprise[kəmpráiz] 포함하다 telescope[téləskòup] 망원경
set one's sight on ~에 시선을 고정시키다, ~을 목표로 삼다
astronomical object 천체 standard candle 표준 촉광
luminosity[lùːmənásəti] 광도 inherent[inhíərənt] 고유한
apparent[əpǽrənt] 겉보기의 Cepheid variable 케페우스형 변광성
fluctuate[flʌ́ktʃuèit] 변화하다 correspond[kɔ̀ːrəspánd] 일치하다
wavelength[wéivleŋθ] 파장 redshift[rédʃift] 적색 편이
velocity[vəlásəti] 속도 profound[prəfáund] 깊은
cosmology[kɑzmálədʒi] 우주론 dense[dens] 밀도가 높은
contract[kántrækt] 수축하다 infinitely[ínfənitli] 무한하게
consensus[kənsénsəs] 합의 light year 광년
explosion[iksplóuʒən] 폭발 discrepancy[diskrépənsi] 불일치
posit[pázit] 상정하다 enigmatic[ènigmǽtik] 불가사의의

11 1단락에 따르면, Edwin Hubble은 _____하기 위해 안드로메다와 지구 사이의 거리를 측정하려고 했다.

(A) 안드로메다가 별들의 독립계라는 것을 보여주기 위해
(B) 은하 내에서 안드로메다의 위치를 측정하기 위해
(C) 안드로메다가 은하만큼 많은 별을 가지고 있다는 것을 증명하기 위해

(D) 우주의 정확한 크기에 대한 논쟁을 해결하기 위해

12 글쓴이는 _____ 하기 위해 "Cepheid variable"을 언급한다.

(A) 안드로메다의 별들이 강한 광도를 나타낸다는 것을 암시하기 위해
(B) 거리 측정이 어떻게 가능했는지를 설명하기 위해
(C) Hubble에 의한 천문학적인 발견의 예를 제시하기 위해
(D) Hubble이 어떻게 안드로메다의 밝기를 측정했는지 설명하기 위해

13 지문에 따르면, 왜 우주는 팽창하고 있다고 결론 내려졌는가?

(A) 은하들에 의해 발산되는 빛의 스펙트럼이 속도에 영향을 받지 않는다.
(B) 더 멀리 떨어진 별의 집단들은 더 높은 상대 속도와 관련된다.
(C) 지구에서 더 가까운 은하들에 의해 발산되는 광파가 더 길다.
(D) 빠르게 움직이는 은하들은 더 큰 적색 편이를 만드는 것으로 관찰되었다.

14 지문의 단어 "profound"와 의미상 가장 유사한 것은?

(A) 하찮은
(B) 직접적인
(C) 긍정적인
(D) 강렬한

15 물질에 대해 4단락으로부터 추론할 수 있는 것은?

(A) 원래 매우 뜨겁고 밀도가 높은 상태에서 존재했다.
(B) 빅뱅의 원인이 되는 에너지를 만들어냈다.
(C) 우주의 태초에는 존재하지 않았다.
(D) 우주의 팽창을 역전시키고 있는 힘을 발휘한다.

16 아래 문장 중 지문 속의 음영된 문장의 핵심 정보를 가장 잘 표현하고 있는 것은 무엇인가? 오답은 문장의 의미를 현저히 왜곡하거나 핵심 정보를 빠뜨리고 있다.

(A) 미래의 열리거나 닫힌 우주의 가능성에 대한 연구는 물질의 중력 인력에 대한 새로운 발견으로 이어졌다.
(B) 우주가 점점 줄어드는 속도로 커지고 있다는 가설에 근거하여, 전문가들은 그것이 영원히 더 작아지거나 팽창할 것이라고 생각했다.
(C) 천문학자들은 물질에 의해 발휘되는 중력이 우주가 축소하는 원인이 되고 있으며, 이것이 계속해서 줄어들지 않거나 멈출 것이라고 생각한다.
(D) 우주 내 물질의 팽창은 우주의 팽창을 역전시키거나 그것이 영원히 지속되도록 할 추가적인 중력을 발생시키고 있다.

17 지문에 따르면, 다음 중 Ia형 초신성에 대해 사실이 아닌 것은?

(A) 천문학자들이 측정 수단으로 활용한다.
(B) 지구에서 멀리 떨어진 먼 은하에 위치한다.
(C) 은하의 팽창을 일으키는 거대한 폭발을 발생시킨다.
(D) 각각 정확히 같은 수준의 광도를 나타낸다.

18 지문의 단어 "discrepancy"와 의미상 가장 유사한 것은?

(A) 우연
(B) 허위
(C) 불일치
(D) 부족

19 네 개의 네모[■]는 다음 문장이 삽입될 수 있는 부분을 나타내고 있다.

이 방법은 빛이 먼 거리를 이동하면서 일관된 비율로 약해지기 때문에 가능하다.

이 문장은 어느 자리에 들어가는 것이 가장 적절한가?

20 지시: 지문 요약을 위한 도입 문장이 아래에 주어져 있다. 지문의 가장 중요한 내용을 나타내는 보기 3개를 골라 요약을 완성하시오. 어떤 문장은 지문에 언급되지 않은 내용이나 사소한 정보를 담고 있으므로 요약에 포함되지 않는다. 이 문제는 2점이다.

> 많은 20세기의 발견들이 팽창하는 우주에 대한 현대 과학의 이해에 기여했다.
>
> · (B) 먼 은하에 대한 관측은 우주의 팽창 속도가 가속화되어 왔다는 것을 보여주었고, 이는 알기 어려운 힘에 의해 설명될 수 있는 현상이다.
> · (C) Edwin Hubble의 1900년대 초기 연구는 은하들이 점점 더 멀리 떨어지고 있음을 증명하였다.
> · (F) 우주 기원에 대한 이론이 고안되었고, 과학자들은 장차 우주에 무슨 일이 일어날지 예측하려고 시도했다.

(A) 우주의 본질에 대한 연구는 우주가 단일점에서 시작했다는 것을 밝혀냈고, 전문가들은 우주가 계속해서 무한하게 팽창할 것이라고 예상한다.
(D) 20세기 초반의 천문학자들은 먼 은하의 적색 편이를 확인하기 위해 특정한 종류의 표준 촉광을 활용했다.
(E) 천문학자들은 왜 우주의 팽창 속도가 증가하고 있는지에 대한 많은 이론을 가지고 있다.

|H|A|C|K|E|R|S|

해커스인강 HackersIngang.com
본 교재 인강 · 빈출어휘 암기&지문녹음 MP3 · iBT 리딩 실전모의고사

고우해커스 goHackers.com
토플 보카 외우기 · 토플 스피킹/라이팅 첨삭 게시판 · 토플 공부전략 강의 · 토플 자료 및 유학 정보